Purchasing and Supply Management

The McGraw-Hill Series in Operations and Decision Sciences

Purchasing and Supply Management

Fifteenth Edition

P. Fraser Johnson, PhD
*Leenders Supply Chain Management
Association Chair
Professor, Operations Management
Ivey Business School
Western University*

Anna E. Flynn, PhD
*Formerly Clinical Associate Professor
Supply Chain Management
Thunderbird School of Global
Management*

*Formerly Associate Professor
Institute for Supply Management*

Mc
Graw
Hill
Education

PURCHASING AND SUPPLY MANAGEMENT, FIFTEENTH EDITION
International Edition 2015

10 09 08 07 06 05 04 03 02 01
20 16 15 14
CTP SLP

When ordering this title, use ISBN 978-981-4577-22-9 or MHID 981-4577-22-7.

www.mhhe.com

About the Authors

P. Fraser Johnson is the Leenders Supply Chain Management Association Chair at the Ivey Business School, Western University. Dr. Johnson received his Ph.D. in Operations Management from Ivey in 1995 and, following graduation, joined the Faculty of Commerce and Business Administration at the University of British Columbia. He returned to Ivey as a faculty member in 1998, where he teaches courses in supply chain management and operations. Prior to joining Ivey, Professor Johnson worked in the automotive parts industry where he held a number of senior management positions in finance and operations. His experience includes managing automotive parts facilities in both Canada and the United States and overseeing a joint venture partnership in Mexico. Professor Johnson is an active researcher in the area of supply chain management, and he has authored articles that have been published in a wide variety of magazines and journals. Fraser has also authored a number of teaching cases. He is an associate editor for *The Journal of Supply Chain Management* and sits on the editorial review board for the *Journal of Purchasing and Supply Management*. Professor Johnson has worked with a number of private- and public-sector organizations in both consulting and corporate education assignments in the United States, Canada, and Europe.

Anna E. Flynn is a former faculty member at Thunderbird School of Global Management and Arizona State University, where she was also director of the undergraduate program in supply chain management. She also served as vice president and associate professor at the Institute for Supply Management (ISM), where she developed and taught two- to five-day seminars in the United States, Canada, Mexico, the Caribbean, Hong Kong, and Lisbon. She has worked as a research associate for CAPS Research, a global network of executives and academics focused on strategic supply management knowledge and practice. Anna is author of *Leadership of Supply Management* (2008); co-editor (with Cavinato and Kauffman) of *The Supply Management Handbook* and author of Chapter 7, "Knowledge-Based Supply Management" (McGraw-Hill, 2006); co-author (with Farney, 2000) of the *NAPM Supply Management Knowledge Series,* Volume IV: *The Supply Management Leadership Process;* and co-author (with Leenders, 1994) of *Value-Driven Purchasing: Managing the Key Steps in the Acquisition Process.* She earned a bachelor's degree in international studies from the University of Notre Dame, an MBA from Arizona State University, and a Ph.D from Arizona State University.

Preface

Purchasing and supply management has become increasingly visible in a world where supply is a major determinant of corporate survival and success. Supply chain performance influences not only operational and financial risks but also reputational risk. Extending the supply chain globally into developing countries places new responsibilities on the supplier and supply, not only to monitor environmental, social, political, and security concerns but also to influence them. Thus, the job of the supply manager of today goes way beyond the scope of supply chain efficiency and value for money spent to search for competitive advantage in the supply chain. Cost containment and improvement represent one challenge; the other is revenue enhancement. Not only must the supply group contribute directly to both the balance sheet and the income statement; it must also enhance the performance of other members of the corporate team. Superior internal relationship and knowledge management need to be matched on the exterior in the supply network to assure that the future operational and strategic needs of the organization will be met by future markets. The joy of purchasing and supply management lives in the magnitude of its challenges and the opportunities to achieve magnificent contributions.

For more than 80 years this text and its predecessors have championed the purchasing and supply management cause. Based on the conviction that supply and suppliers have to contribute effectively to organizational goals and strategies, this and previous editions have focused on how to make that mission a reality.

A great deal has happened in the supply field since the 14th edition was published. Continuing advances in MIS and technology provide new ways to improve supply efficiency and effectiveness. New security, environmental, and transparency requirements and the search for meaningful supply metrics have further complicated the challenges faced by supply managers all over the world. As a consequence, several changes and updates have been made to the 15th edition. First, the new edition provides an opportunity to incorporate the latest theory and best practice in supply chain management into the text. Wherever appropriate, real-world examples and current research are used to illustrate key points. Second, the application of information technology to supply chain processes continues to change rapidly, including the evolution of cloud-based computing. The text has been updated accordingly, including a major revision to Chapter 4. Third, there are also several important emerging issues—including sustainability, challenges of managing risk in a global supply chain, and collaboration—that are addressed in this text. Lastly, nearly one-third of the cases have been replaced with new cases that cover topics such as negotiation, outsourcing, risk management, and sustainability. Thus, the examples in the text and more than 45 real-life supply chain cases afford the chance to apply the latest research and theoretical developments in the field to real-life issues, opportunities, decisions, and problems faced by practitioners.

In this edition the focus on decision making in the supply chain has also been strengthened considerably. The chapter sequence reflects the chronological order of the acquisition process. Criteria for supply decisions have been identified in three categories: (1) strategic, (2) operational, and (3) additional. It is the third category with balance sheet and income statement considerations, all dimensions of risk, environmental, and social considerations that is growing in relevance, making sound supply decisions an even more complex challenge.

Since the sixth edition nearly 40 years ago, Michiel R. Leenders has been an author of this text. As Professor of Operations at the Ivey Business School, Mike has been one of the great leaders in the supply field for more than half a century. His accomplishments include authorship of three other procurement books, founding director of the Ivey Purchasing Managers Index, and a long list of articles and presentations at international conferences. In 2003, Mike received the International Federation of Purchasing and Materials Management's highest research honor in the form of the Hans Ovelgonne Award. Mike did not participate in this edition, although his past contributions are still evident throughout this text.

A book with text and cases depends on many to contribute through their research and writing to expand the body of knowledge of the field. Thus, to our academic colleagues our thanks for pushing out the theoretical boundaries of supply management. To many practitioners, we wish to extend our gratitude for proving what works and what does not and providing their stories in the cases in this text. Also many case writers contributed their efforts so that approximately one-third of all the cases in this edition are new.

Case contributors in alphabetical order included: Carolynn Cameron, Garland Chow, Jorge Colazo, Jenni Denniston, Dominque Fortier, Manish Kumar, Glen Luinenberg, Eric Silverberg, Dave Vannette, and Marsha Watson.

Instructor and student supplements are available on this book's website at **www.mhhe.com/johnson15e.** Instructor ancillaries are password-protected for security.

The production side of any text is more complicated than most authors care to admit. At McGraw-Hill Education Christina Kouvelis, Kaylee Putbrese, Michelle Valenti, Jane Mohr, Dheeraj Chahal and many others contributed to turn our efforts into a presentable text.

The support of Dean Bob Kennedy and our colleagues at the Ivey Business School has been most welcome.

The assistance of the Institute for Supply Management in supporting the continuous improvement of supply education is also very much appreciated.

P. Fraser Johnson

Anna E. Flynn

Brief Contents

Table of Contents

ix

Portfolio

Chapter 13
Supplier Evaluation and Supplier Relationships 365

Chapter 14
Global Supply Management 395

Chapter 15
Legal and Ethics 432

Chapter One

Purchasing and Supply Management

Chapter Outline

Purchasing and Supply Management
Supply Management Terminology
Supply and Logistics

The Size of the Organization's Spend and Financial Significance

Supply Contribution
The Operational versus Strategic Contribution of Supply
The Direct and Indirect Contribution of Supply

The Nature of the Organization

Supply Qualifications and Associations

Challenges Ahead
Supply Chain Management

Measurement
Risk Management
Sustainability
Growth and Influence
Effective Contribution to Organizational Success

The Organization of This Text

Conclusion

Questions for Review and Discussion

References

Cases

Key Questions for the Supply Decision Maker

Should we

- Rethink how supply can contribute more effectively to organizational goals and strategies?
- Try to find out what the organization's total spend with suppliers really is?
- Identify opportunities for meaningful involvement in major corporate activities?

How can we

- Align our supply strategy with the organization's strategy?
- Get others to recognize the profit-leverage effect of purchasing/supply management?
- Show how supply can affect our firm's competitive position?

Every organization needs suppliers. No organization can exist without suppliers. Therefore, the organization's approach to suppliers, its acquisition processes and policies, and its relationships with suppliers will impact not only the performance of the suppliers, but also the organization's own performance. No organization can be successful without the support of its supplier base, operationally and strategically, short- and long-term.

Supply management is focused on the acquisition process recognizing the supply chain and organizational contexts. Special emphasis is on decision making that aligns the supplier network and the acquisition process with organizational goals and strategies and ensures short- and long-term value for funds spent.

There is no one best way of organizing the supply function, conducting its activities, and integrating suppliers effectively. This is both interesting and challenging. It is interesting because the acquisition of organizational requirements covers a very wide and complex set of approaches with different needs and different suppliers. It is challenging because of the complexity and because the process is dynamic, not static. Moreover, some of the brightest minds in this world have been hired as marketing and sales experts to persuade supply managers to choose their companies as suppliers. It is also challenging because every supply decision depends on a large variety of factors, the combination of which may well be unique to a particular organization.

For more than 80 years, this text and its predecessors have presented the supply function and suppliers as critical to an organization's success, competitive advantage, and customer satisfaction. Whereas in the 1930s this was a novel idea, over the past few decades there has been growing interest at the executive level in the supply chain management and its impact on strategic goals and objectives.

To increase long-term shareholder value, the company must increase revenue, decrease costs, or both. Supply's contribution should not be perceived as only focused on cost. Supply can and should also be concerned with revenue enhancement. What can supply and suppliers do to help the organization increase revenues or decrease costs? should be a standard question for any supply manager.

The supply function continues to evolve as technology and the worldwide competitive environment require innovative approaches. The traditionally held view that multiple sourcing increases supply security has been challenged by a trend toward single sourcing. Results from closer supplier relations and cooperation with suppliers question the wisdom of the traditional arm's-length dealings between purchaser and supplier. Negotiation is receiving increasing emphasis as opposed to competitive bidding, and longer-term contracts are replacing short-term buying techniques. E-commerce tools permit faster and lower-cost solutions, not only on the transaction side of supply but also in management decision support. Organizations are continually evaluating the risks and opportunities of global sourcing. All of these trends are a logical outcome of increased managerial concern with value and increasing procurement aggressiveness in developing suppliers to meet specific supply objectives of quality, quantity, delivery, price, service, and continuous improvement.

Effective purchasing and supply management contributes significantly to organizational success. This text explores the nature of this contribution and the management requirements for effective and efficient performance. The acquisition of materials, services, and equipment—of the right qualities, in the right quantities, at the right prices, at the right time, with the right quality, and on a continuing basis—long has occupied the attention of managers in both the public and private sectors.

Today, the emphasis is on the total supply management process in the context of organizational goals and management of supply chains. The rapidly changing supply scene, with cycles of abundance and shortages, varying prices, lead times, and availability, provides a continuing challenge to those organizations wishing to obtain a maximum contribution from this area. Furthermore, environmental, security, and financial regulatory requirements have added considerable complexity to the task of ensuring that supply and suppliers provide competitive advantage.

PURCHASING AND SUPPLY MANAGEMENT

Although some people may view interest in the performance of the supply function as a recent phenomenon, it was recognized as an independent and important function by many of the nation's railroad organizations well before 1900.

Yet, traditionally, most firms regarded the supply function primarily as a clerical activity. However, during World War I and World War II, the success of a firm was not dependent on what it could sell, since the market was almost unlimited. Instead, the ability to obtain from suppliers the raw materials, supplies, and services needed to keep the factories and mines operating was the key determinant of organizational success. Consequently, attention was given to the organization, policies, and procedures of the supply function, and it emerged as a recognized managerial activity.

During the 1950s and 1960s, supply management continued to gain stature as the number of people trained and competent to make sound supply decisions increased. Many companies elevated the chief purchasing officer to top management status, with titles such as vice president of purchasing, director of materials, or vice president of purchasing and supply.

As the decade of the 1970s opened, organizations faced two vexing problems: an international shortage of almost all the basic raw materials needed to support operations and a rate of price increase far above the norm since the end of World War II. The Middle East oil embargo during the summer of 1973 intensified both the shortages and the price escalation. These developments put the spotlight directly on supply, for their performance in obtaining needed items from suppliers at realistic prices spelled the difference between success and failure. This emphasized again the crucial role played by supply and suppliers.

As the decade of the 1990s unfolded, it became clear that organizations must have an efficient and effective supply function if they were to compete successfully in the global marketplace. The early 21st century has brought new challenges in the areas of sustainability, supply chain security, and risk management.

In large supply organizations, supply professionals often are divided into two categories: the tacticians who handle day-to-day requirements and the strategic thinkers who possess strong analytical and planning skills and are involved in activities such as strategic sourcing. The extent to which the structure, processes, and people in a specific organization will match these trends varies from organization to organization, and from industry to industry.

The future will see a gradual shift from predominantly defensive strategies, resulting from the need to change in order to remain competitive, to aggressive strategies, in which firms take an imaginative approach to achieving supply objectives to satisfy short-term and long-term organizational goals. The focus on strategy now includes an emphasis on process and knowledge management. This text discusses what organizations should do today to remain competitive as well as what strategic purchasing and supply management will focus on tomorrow.

Growing management interest through necessity and improved insight into the opportunities in the supply area has resulted in a variety of organizational concepts. Terms such as *purchasing, procurement, materiel, materials management, logistics, sourcing, supply management,* and *supply chain management* are used almost interchangeably. No agreement exists on the definition of each of these terms, and managers in public and private institutions may have identical responsibilities but substantially different titles. The following definitions may be helpful in sorting out the more common understanding of the various terms.

Supply Management Terminology

Some academics and practitioners limit the term *purchasing* to the process of buying: learning of the need, locating and selecting a supplier, negotiating price and other pertinent terms, and following up to ensure delivery and payment. This is not the perspective taken in this text. *Purchasing, supply management,* and *procurement* are used interchangeably to refer to the integration of related functions to provide effective and efficient materials and services to the organization. Thus, purchasing or supply management is not only concerned with the standard steps in the procurement process: (1) the recognition of need, (2) the translation of that need into a commercially equivalent description, (3) the search for potential suppliers, (4) the selection of a suitable source, (5) the agreement on order or contract details, (6) the delivery of the products or services, and (7) the payment of suppliers.

Further responsibilities of supply may include receiving, inspection, warehousing, inventory control, materials handling, packaging scheduling, in- and outbound transportation/traffic, and disposal. Supply also may have responsibility for other components of the supply chain, such as the organization's customers and their customers and their suppliers' suppliers. This extension represents the term *supply chain management,* where the focus is on minimizing costs and lead times across tiers in the supply chain to the benefit of the final customer. The idea that competition may change from the firm level to the supply chain level has been advanced as the next stage of competitive evolution.

In addition to the *operational responsibilities* that are part of the day-to-day activities of the supply organization, there are *strategic responsibilities*. *Strategic sourcing* focuses on long-term supplier relationships and commodity plans with the objectives of identifying opportunities in areas such as cost reductions, new technology advancements, and supply market trends. The Sabor case in Chapter 2 provides an excellent example of the need to take a strategic perspective when planning long-term supply needs.

Lean purchasing or *lean supply management* refers primarily to a manufacturing context and the implementation of just-in-time (JIT) tools and techniques to ensure every step in the supply process adds value, that inventories are kept at a minimum level, and that distances and delays between process steps are kept as short as possible. Instant communication of job status is essential and shared.

Supply and Logistics

The large number of physical moves associated with any purchasing or supply chain activity has focused attention on the role of logistics. According to the Council of Supply Chain Management Professionals, "Logistics management is that part of supply chain management that plans, implements, and controls the efficient, effective forward and reverse flow and storage of goods, services, and related information between the point of origin and the point of consumption in order to meet customers' requirements."[1] This definition includes inbound, outbound, internal, and external movements. Logistics is not confined to manufacturing organizations. It is relevant to service organizations and to both private- and public-sector firms.

The attraction of the logistics concept is that it looks at the material flow process as a complete system, from initial need for materials to delivery of finished product or service to the customer. It attempts to provide the communication, coordination, and control needed to avoid the potential conflicts between the physical distribution and the materials management functions.

Supply influences a number of logistics-related activities, such as how much to buy and inbound transportation. With an increased emphasis on controlling material flow, the supply function must be concerned with decisions beyond supplier selection and price. The Qmont Mining case in Chapter 4 illustrates the logistics considerations of supplying multiple locations.

Organizations are examining business processes and exploring opportunities to integrate boundary-spanning activities in order to reduce costs and improve lead times. For example, Renault-Nissan announced in 2014 that it would integrate supply chain management activities, including purchasing and logistics, with manufacturing and R&D. The company had targeted €4.3 billion in annual savings from this initiative.[2]

[1] Council of Supply Chain Management Professionals, http://cscmp.org/about-us/supply-chain
-management-definitions, accessed February 15, 2014.

[2] M. Williams, "Renault-Nissan Could integrate SCM Functions," *Automotive Logistics*, February 5, 2014,
www.automotivelogisticsmagazine.com/news/renault-nissan-could-integrate-scm-functions,
accessed February 15, 2014.

Supply chain management is a systems approach to managing the entire flow of information, materials, and services from raw materials suppliers through factories and warehouses to the end customer. The Institute for Supply Management (ISM) glossary defines *supply chain management* as "the design and management of seamless, value-added processes across organizational boundaries to meet the real needs of the end customer. The development and integration of people and technological resources are critical to successful supply chain integration."[3]

The term *value chain,* a term commonly used in the strategy literature, has been used to trace a product or service through its various moves and transformations, identifying the costs added at each successive stage.

Some academics and practitioners believe the term *chain* does not properly convey what really happens in a supply or value chain, and they prefer to use the term *supply network* or *supply web.*

The use of the concepts of purchasing, procurement, supply, and supply chain management will vary from organization to organization. It will depend on (1) their stage of development and/or sophistication, (2) the industry in which they operate, and (3) their competitive position.

The relative importance of the supply area compared to the other prime functions of the organization will be a major determinant of the management attention it will receive. How to assess the materials and services needs of a particular organization in context is one of the purposes of this book. More than 45 cases are provided to provide insight into a variety of situations and to give practice in resolving managerial problems.

THE SIZE OF THE ORGANIZATION'S SPEND AND FINANCIAL SIGNIFICANCE

The amount of money organizations spend with suppliers is staggering. Collectively, private and public organizations in North America spend about 1.5 times the GDPs of the United States, Canada, and Mexico combined, totaling at least $29 trillion U.S. dollars spent with suppliers.

Dollars spent with suppliers as a percentage of total revenues is a good indicator of supply's financial impact. Obviously, the percentage of revenue that is paid out to suppliers varies from industry to industry and organization to organization, and increased outsourcing over the last decade has increased the percentage of spend significantly. In almost all manufacturing organizations, the supply area represents by far the largest single category of spend, ranging from 50 to 80 percent of revenue. Wages, by comparison, typically amount to about 10 to 20 percent. In comparison, the total dollars spent on outside suppliers typically ranges from 25 to 35 percent of revenues. The Delphi Corporation case in Chapter 13 is a good illustration of the significance of spend in a manufacturing organization. Total purchases were $17 billion compared to revenues of $28 billion.

The financial impact of the corporate spend is often illustrated by the profit-leverage effect and the return-on-assets effect.

---

[3] Institute for Supply Management, "Glossary of Key Supply Management Terms," www.ism.ws.

Profit-Leverage Effect

The profit-leverage effect of supply savings is measured by the increase in profit obtained by a decrease in purchase spend. For example, for an organization with revenue of $100 million, purchases of $60 million, and profit of $8 million before tax, a 10 percent reduction in purchase spend would result in an increase in profit of 75 percent. To achieve a $6,000,000 increase in profit by increasing sales, assuming the same percentage hold, might well require an increase of $75 million in sales, or 75 percent! Which of these two options—an increase in sales of 75 percent or a decrease in purchase spend of 10 percent—is more likely to be achieved?

This is not to suggest that it would be easy to reduce overall purchase costs by 10 percent. In a firm that has given major attention to the supply function over the years, it would be difficult, and perhaps impossible, to do. But, in a firm that has neglected supply, it would be a realistic objective. Because of the profit-leverage effect of supply, large savings are possible relative to the effort that would be needed to increase sales by the much-larger percentage necessary to generate the same effect on the profit and loss (P&L) statement. Since, in many firms, sales already has received much more attention, supply may be the last untapped "profit producer."

Return-on-Assets Effect

Financial experts are increasingly interested in return on assets (ROA) as a measure of corporate performance. Figure 1–1 shows the standard ROA model, using the same ratio of figures as in the previous example, and assuming that inventory accounts for 30 percent of total assets. If purchase costs were reduced by 10 percent, that would cause an extra benefit of a 10 percent reduction in the inventory asset base. The numbers in the boxes show the initial figures used in arriving at the 10 percent ROA performance.

FIGURE 1–1
Return-on-Assets Factors

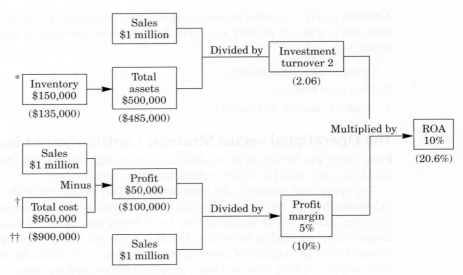

*Inventory is approximately 30 percent of total assets.
†Purchases account for half of total sales, or $500,000.
††Figures in parentheses assume a 10 percent reduction in purchase costs.

The numbers below each box are the figures resulting from a 10 percent overall purchase price reduction, and the end product is a new ROA of 20.6 percent or about an 100 percent increase in return on assets.

Reduction in Inventory Investment

Charles Dehelly, senior executive vice president at Thomson Multimedia, headquartered in Paris, France, said: "It came as quite a surprise to some supply people that I expected them to worry about the balance sheet by insisting on measuring their return on capital employed performance."[4] Mr. Dehelly was pushing for reductions in inventory investment, not only by lowering purchase price, as shown in the example in Figure 1–1, but also by getting suppliers to take over inventory responsibility and ownership, thereby removing asset dollars in the ROA calculations, but also taking on the risk of obsolescence, inventory carrying, and disposal costs. Since accountants value inventory items at the purchaser at purchased cost, including transportation, but inventory at the supplier at manufacturing cost, the same items stored at the supplier typically have a lower inventory investment and carrying cost.

Thus, it is a prime responsibility of supply to manage the supply process with the lowest reasonable levels of inventory attainable. Inventory turnover and level are two major measures of supply chain performance.

Evidently, the financial impact of supply is on the balance sheet and the income statement, the two key indicators of corporate financial health used by managers, analysts, financial institutions, and investors. While the financial impact of the supply spend is obviously significant, it is by no means the only impact of supply on an organization's ability to compete and be successful.

SUPPLY CONTRIBUTION

Although supply's financial impact is major, supply contributes to organizational goals and strategies in a variety of other ways. The three major perspectives on supply are shown in Figure 1–2:

1. Operational versus strategic.
2. Direct and indirect.
3. Negative, neutral, and positive.

The Operational versus Strategic Contribution of Supply

First, supply can be viewed in two contexts: operational, which is characterized as *trouble avoidance,* and strategic, which is characterized as *opportunistic*.

The operational context is the most familiar. Many people inside the organization are inconvenienced to varying degrees when supply does not meet minimum expectations. Improper quality, wrong quantities, and late delivery may make life miserable for the ultimate user of the product or service. This is so basic and apparent that "no complaints" is assumed to be an indicator of good supply performance. The difficulty is that many users never expect anything more and hence may not receive anything more.

[4] M. R. Leenders and P. F. Johnson, *Major Changes in Supply Chain Responsibilities* (Tempe, AZ: CAPS Research, March 2002), p. 104.

FIGURE 1–2
Purchasing's Operational and Strategic Contributions

Source: Michiel R. Leenders and Anna E. Flynn, *Value-Driven Purchasing: Managing the Key Steps in the Acquisition Process* (Burr Ridge, IL: Richard D. Irwin, 1995), p. 7.

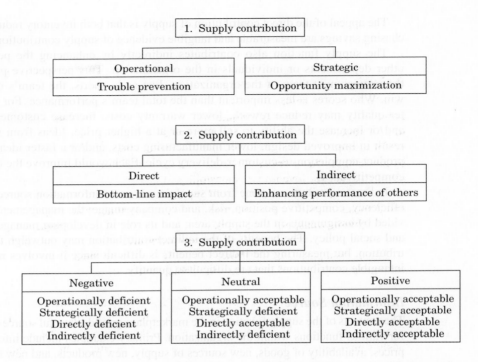

The operational side of supply concerns itself with the transactional, day-to-day operations traditionally associated with purchasing. The operational side can be streamlined and organized in ways designed to routinize and automate many of the transactions, thus freeing up time for the supply manager to focus on the strategic contribution.

The strategic side of supply is future oriented and searches for opportunities to provide competitive advantage. Whereas on the operational side the focus is on executing current tasks as designed, the strategic side focuses on new and better solutions to organizational and supply challenges. (Chapter 2 discusses the strategic side in detail.)

The Direct and Indirect Contribution of Supply

The second perspective is that of supply's potential direct or indirect contribution to organizational objectives.

Supply savings, the profit-leverage effect, and the return-on-assets effect demonstrate the direct contribution supply can make to the company's financial statements. Although the argument that supply savings flow directly to the bottom line appears self-evident, experience shows that savings do not always get that far. Budget heads, when presented with savings, may choose to spend this unexpected windfall on other requirements.

To combat this phenomenon, some supply organizations have hired financial controllers to assure that supply savings do reach the bottom line. Such was the case at Praxair, a global supplier of specialty gases and technologies. The chief supply officer and the CFO agreed that a financial controller position was needed in the supply organization to support financial analysis and budgeting. Validating cost savings and linking cost savings to the business unit operating budgets were an important part of this person's responsibilities.[5]

[5] Leenders and Johnson, *Major Changes in Supply Chain Responsibilities*, p. 89.

The appeal of the direct contribution of supply is that both inventory reduction and purchasing savings are measurable and tangible evidence of supply contribution.

The supply function also contributes indirectly by enhancing the performance of other departments or individuals in the organization. This perspective puts supply on the management team of the organization. Just as in sports, the team's objective is to win. Who scores is less important than the total team's performance. For example, better quality may reduce rework, lower warranty costs, increase customer satisfaction, and/or increase the ability to sell more or at a higher price. Ideas from suppliers may result in improved design, lower manufacturing costs, and/or a faster idea-to-design-to-product-completion-to-customer-delivery cycle. Each would improve the organization's competitiveness.

Indirect contributions come from supply's role as an information source; its effect on efficiency, competitive position, risk, and company image; the management training provided by assignments in the supply area; and its role in developing management strategy and social policy. The benefits of the indirect contribution may outweigh the direct contribution, but measuring the indirect benefits is difficult since it involves many "soft" or intangible contributions that are difficult to quantify.

Information Source

The contacts of the supply function in the marketplace provide a useful source of information for various functions within the organization. Primary examples include information about prices, availability of goods, new sources of supply, new products, and new technology, all of interest to many other parts of the organization. New marketing techniques and distribution systems used by suppliers may be of interest to the marketing group. News about major investments, mergers, acquisition candidates, international political and economic developments, pending bankruptcies, major promotions and appointments, and current and potential customers may be relevant to marketing, finance, research, and top management. Supply's unique position vis-à-vis the marketplace should provide a comprehensive listening post.

Effect on Efficiency

The efficiency with which supply processes are performed will show up in other operating results. While the firm's accounting system may not be sophisticated enough to identify poor efficiency as having been caused by poor purchase decisions, that could be the case. If supply selects a supplier who fails to deliver raw materials or parts that measure up to the agreed-on quality standards, this may result in a higher scrap rate or costly rework, requiring excessive direct labor expenditures. If the supplier does not meet the agreed-on delivery schedule, this may require a costly rescheduling of production, decreasing overall production efficiency, or, in the worst case, a shutdown of the production line—and fixed costs continue even though there is no output. Many supply managers refer to user departments as internal customers or clients and focus on improving the efficiency and effectiveness of the function with a goal of providing outstanding internal customer service.

Effect on Competitive Position/Customer Satisfaction

A firm cannot be competitive unless it can deliver end products or services to its customers when they are wanted, of the quality desired, and at a price the customer feels is fair.

If supply doesn't do its job, the firm will not have the required materials or services when needed, of desired quality, and at a price that will keep end-product costs competitive and under control.

The ability of the supply organization to secure requirements of better quality, faster, at a better price than competitors, will not only improve the organization's competitive position, but also improve customer satisfaction. The same can be said for greater flexibility to adjust to customers' changing needs. Thus, a demonstrably better-performing supply organization is a major asset on any corporate team.

A major chemical producer was able to develop a significantly lower-cost option for a key raw material that proved to be environmentally superior as well as better quality. By selling its better end product at somewhat lower prices, the chemical producer was able to double its market share, significantly improving its financial health and competitive position as well as the satisfaction of its customers.

Effect on Organizational Risk

Risk management is becoming an ever-increasing concern. The supply function clearly impacts the organization in terms of operational, financial, and reputation risk. Supply disruptions in terms of energy, service, or direct or indirect requirements can impact the ability of the organization to operate as planned and as expected by its customers, creating operational risks.

Given that commodity and financial markets establish prices that may go up or down beyond the control of the individual purchaser, and that long-term supply agreements require price provisions, the supply area may represent a significant level of financial risk. Furthermore, unethical or questionable supply practices and suppliers may expose the organization to significant reputation risk.

Effect on Image

The actions of supply personnel influence directly the public relations and image of a company. If actual and potential suppliers are not treated in a businesslike manner, they will form a poor opinion of the entire organization and will communicate this to other firms. This poor image will adversely affect the purchaser's ability to get new business and to find new and better suppliers. Public confidence can be boosted by evidence of sound and ethical policies and fair implementation of them.

The large spend of any organization draws attention in terms of supplier chosen, the process used to choose suppliers, the ethics surrounding the supply process, and conformance to regulatory requirements. Are the suppliers chosen "clean" in terms of child labor, environmental behavior, and reputation? Is the acquisition process transparent and legally, ethically, strategically, and operationally defensible as sound practice? Do supply's actions take fully into account environmental, financial, and other regulatory requirements, such as national security?

Global brands have come under increased scrutiny for their sourcing policies, accused of turning a blind eye to the labor practices of their suppliers. The collapse of a Bangladeshi factory in April 2013, killing more than 1,100 people, focused worldwide attention on poor working conditions and low pay for workers manufacturing garments for companies that included Walmart, Benetton, and Loblaws. The disaster spurred a debate about the responsibility of large retailers to ensure that their supplier factories met acceptable safety standards and paid their workers a living wage. There are an estimated 5,000 garment factories in Bangladesh, employing approximately 3.6 million workers, many of whom are paid the minimum wage of $38 a month.

Maintaining a proper corporate image is the responsibility of every team member and supply is no exception.

Training Ground

The supply area also is an excellent training ground for new managers. The needs of the organization may be quickly grasped. Exposure to the pressure of decision making under uncertainty with potentially serious consequences allows for evaluation of the individual's ability and willingness to make sound decisions and assume responsibility. Contacts with many people at various levels and a variety of functions may assist the individual in learning about how the organization works. Many organizations find it useful to include the supply area as part of a formal job rotation system for high-potential employees.

Examples of senior corporate executives with significant supply experience include Mary Barra, CEO of General Motors; Willie A. Deese, executive vice president, Merck & Co.; and Richard B. Jacobs, president of Eaton Corporation's Filtration Division.

Management Strategy

Supply also can be used as a tool of management strategy and social policy. Does management wish to introduce and stimulate competition? Does it favor geographical representation, minority interest, and environmental and social concerns? For example, are domestic sources preferred? Will resources be spent on assisting minority suppliers? As part of an overall organization strategy, the supply function can contribute a great deal. Assurance of supply of vital materials or services in a time of general shortages can be a major competitive advantage. Similarly, access to a better-quality or a lower-priced product or service may represent a substantial gain. These strategic positions in the marketplace may be gained through active exploration of international and domestic markets, technology, innovative management systems, and the imaginative use of corporate resources. Vertical integration and its companion decisions of make or buy (insource or outsource) are ever-present considerations in the management of supply.

The potential contribution of supply to strategy is obvious. Achievement depends on both top executive awareness of this potential and the ability to marshal corporate resources to this end. At the same time, it is the responsibility of those charged with the management of the supply function to seek strategic opportunities in the environment and to draw top executive attention to them. This requires a thorough familiarity with organizational objectives, strategy, and long-term plans and the ability to influence these in the light of new information. Chapter 2 discusses both potential supply contributions to business strategy *and* the major strategy areas within the supply function.

Progressive managers have recognized the potential contributions of the supply management area and have taken the necessary steps to ensure results. One important step in successful organizations has been the elevation to top executive status of the supply manager. Although titles are not always consistent with status and value in an organization, they still make a statement within and outside of most organizations. Currently, the most common title of the chief supply officer is vice president, followed by director and manager.

The elevation of the chief supply officer to executive status, coupled with high-caliber staff and the appropriate authority and responsibility, has resulted in an exciting and fruitful realization of the potential of the supply function in many companies. Chapter 3 discusses supply organizations issues in greater detail.

THE NATURE OF THE ORGANIZATION

The nature of the organization will determine how it will structure and manage its supply function. Whether the organization is public or private and produces goods or services or both, its mission, vision, and strategies, its size, number of sites, location, financial strength, and reputation will all be factors influencing its supply options and decisions. These will be addressed broadly in this first chapter and will be added to subsequently in this text.

Public or Private Organization

Public institutions, including all levels of government from municipal to state or provincial to federal, tend to be service providers but are not exclusively so and are subject to strict regulatory requirements regarding acquisition processes and policies. The public sector in many countries also includes education, health, utilities, and a host of agencies, boards, institutes, and so forth. The Wentworth Hospital case in Chapter 7 provides an example of supply in a public-sector context. This case illustrates how many purchases in the public sector can be for capital and indirect supplies, which creates challenges for supply to influence purchasing decisions that ensure best value.

A large segment of the acquisition needs of public institutions is concerned with the support of the organization's mission and maintenance of facilities and offices. Concerns over public spending deal with transparency and fairness of access to all eligible suppliers, social aims such as support of minority and disadvantaged groups, and national security. Need definition and specification are often part of the supply manager's responsibilities and are often geared to allow for multiple bidders.

That not all public organizations are alike is evident from Figure 1–3, which shows just some of the differences among public bodies.

Nongovernmental organizations (NGOs) and other nonprofit organizations would have a breakdown similar to those listed for public organizations, but might also operate internationally.

Private Organizations

Private organizations, which include companies with publicly traded stocks, tend to have fewer constraints on need definition, specification, and supplier selection. The laws of the

FIGURE 1–3
Differentiations for Supply Management in Public Organizations

Level:	Municipal	⟷	State or Provincial	⟷	Federal
Mission:	Social Aims	⟷	Other or Combination	⟷	Economic
Revenue Generation:	Limited	⟷	Combination	⟷	Substantial
Size:	Small	⟷	Medium	⟷	Large
Number of Sites:	Single	⟷	Few	⟷	Many

FIGURE 1–4 **Differentiations for Supply Management in Private Organizations**

Goods or Services:	Manufacturer ◄────►	Combination	◄────►	Services
Strategy:	Low cost ◄────►	Combination	◄────►	Differentiation
Size:	Small ◄────►	Medium	◄────►	Large
Number of Sites:	Single ◄────►	Few	◄────►	Many
Location:	Domestic ◄────►	Few International ◄────►		Many International
Financial Strength:	Weak ◄────►	Medium	◄────►	Strong
Reputation:	Poor ◄────►	Medium	◄────►	Outstanding

land (covered in Chapter 5) will establish the main ground rules for commerce. Transparency of commitments with suppliers has recently become more relevant to ensure that long-term commitments are properly disclosed in the company's financial statements. Whereas in public institutions standardization is seen as a means of fairness to suppliers, in private companies, custom specifications are seen as a means of securing competitive advantage.

Figure 1–4 shows some of the influencers that will affect supply management in private organizations. It is clear that for both public and private organizations these differences will affect supply significantly and some generalizations on supply impact follow.

Goods or Service Producers

Another major supply influence is whether the organization produces goods or services or both. Goods producers, often called manufacturers, may produce a wide range of products, both in the industrial goods category and in consumer goods. For goods producers, normally the largest percentage of total spend of the organization is on materials, purchased parts, packaging, and transportation for the goods produced. For service providers (and the range of possible services is huge), normally the largest percent of spend is focused on services and the process enabling the delivery of the services. The Erica Carson case in this chapter describes a supply decision in a large services organization, a financial institution. This case illustrates the opportunities for supply to contribute to the customer value proposition.

The following table identifies what the impact on organizational requirements is likely to be depending on whether the organization is primarily focused on manufacturing or providing a service:

Manufacturer	Service Provider
• The largest portion of needs is generated by customer needs. • The largest portion of spend with suppliers will be on direct requirements which comprise products sold to customers.	• The largest portion of needs is generated by capital, services, and other requirements enabling employees to provide the service. • In retailing the largest spend is focused on resale requirements.

Very few organizations are pure manufacturers or service providers. Most represent a mixture of both. A restaurant provides meals and drinks as well as service and a place to eat.

An insurance company provides insurance policies and claim service as well as peace of mind. An R&D organization performs research, as well as research reports, models, and prototypes. A manufacturer may supply capital goods as well as repair service and availability of replacement parts.

Wholesalers, distributors, and retailers provide resale products in smaller quantities and in more convenient locations at more convenient times than the manufacturers can provide. For these resellers the ability to buy well is critical for success.

Resource and mining organizations explore for natural resources and find ways and means of bringing these to commodity markets. Educational institutions attempt to transform students into educated persons, frequently providing them with meals, residences, classrooms, parking facilities, and, hopefully, diplomas or degrees. Health organizations provide diagnostic and repair services using a very large variety of professionals, equipment, facilities, medicines, and parts to keep their clients healthy and functioning.

It is no surprise that the nature of the organization in terms of the goods and services it provides will significantly affect the requirements of its supply chain.

The Mission, Vision, and Strategy of the Organization

Supply strategy has to be congruent with organizational strategy. Therefore, the mission, vision, and strategy of the organization are the key drivers for how the supply function will be managed and how supply decisions are made and executed. A nonprofit organization with social aims may acquire its office needs totally differently from one that competes on cost in a tough commercial or consumer marketplace. An innovation-focused organization may define flexibility quite differently from one that depends largely on the acquisition and transformation or distribution of commodities.

In the past, the supply manager was largely focused on the traditional value determinants of quality, quantity, delivery, price, and service as the five key drivers of sound supply decisions. Today's supply managers face a host of additional concerns, as corporate mission, vision, and strategies require concerns over risk, the environment, social responsibility, transparency, regulation, and innovation as well. Thus, the old adage of value for money, a guiding principle for supply managers for centuries, has become a lot tougher over the last few decades and continues to evolve. The text and cases in this book are focused on major supply decisions appropriate for the unique organization in which the supply professional is employed.

The Size of the Organization

The larger the organization, the greater the absolute amount of spend with suppliers. And the amount of the spend will be a major determinant of how many resources can be allocated to the acquisition process. Given a cost of acquisition of 1 to 2 percent of what is acquired, for a $100,000 purchase, up to $2,000 can be spent on acquisition. However, a $100 million acquisition can afford up to $2 million and a $1 billion spend up to $20 million.

Therefore, the larger the amount of spend, the greater the time and care that can and should be allocated to acquisition. Therefore, in very small organizations, the responsibility for acquisition may be a part-time allocation to one or more individuals who probably wear multiple hats. In very large organizations, supply professionals may be completely dedicated to one category of requirements on a full-time basis. And a supply group may count hundreds of professionals.

Single or Multiple Sites

An additional influence is whether the organization operates out of a single or multiple sites. The simplest situation is the single site. The supply situation becomes more complex as the number of sites increases. Transportation and storage issues multiply with multiple sites along with communication and control challenges. This is especially true for multinationals supplying multiple sites in different countries.

Financial Strength

Supply management stripped to its bare essentials deals with the exchange of money for goods and services. With the acquiring company responsible for the money and the supplier for the goods and services, the ability of the buying organization to pay will be a very important issue in the supplier's eyes. And the ability to pay and flexibility on when to pay depend on the financial strength of the organization. The stronger the buying organization is financially, the more attractive it becomes as a potential customer. A supplier will be more anxious to offer an exceptionally good value proposition to an attractive customer. And the ability and willingness to pay quickly after receipt of goods or services add valuable bargaining chips to any purchaser.

Reputation

Corporate reputation in the trade is another important factor in building a positive corporate image both for suppliers and purchasers. If supply management is defined as the fight for superior suppliers, then a strong corporate image and reputation are valuable contributors. Superior suppliers can pick and choose their customers. Superior suppliers prefer to deal with superior customers. Superior customers enhance a superior supplier's reputation. "You are known by the company you keep" applies in the corporate world just like it does in personal life. And supply managers can significantly affect their company's image by their actions and relations with suppliers.

For a long time the reputation of Fisher & Paykel (F&P) in New Zealand and Australia was such that any F&P supplier could use this as a persuasive argument for gaining additional customers in that area of the world. "If you are good enough to supply F&P, you are good enough for us" was the implication. A good buyer–supplier relationship is built on the rock of impeccable performance to contract agreements. Pay the right amount on time without hassle and deliver the right quality and quantity of goods or services on time and charge the correct price without hassle. These commitments are not as simple as they sound. Moreover, superior customers and superior suppliers add ethical treatment; advance communications on future developments in technology, markets, and opportunities for improvements as additional expectations; and are continually striving to do better.

Corporate reputations are built on actions and results, not on noble intentions. It takes time to build a superior reputation, but not much time to harm a reputation.

SUPPLY QUALIFICATIONS AND ASSOCIATIONS

In recognition that the talent in supply has to match the challenges of the profession, public and private organizations as well as supply associations have taken the initiative to ensure well-qualified supply professionals are available to staff the function.

Education

Although there are no universal educational requirements for entry-level supply jobs, most large organizations require a college degree in business administration or management. Several major educational institutions, such as Arizona State University, Bowling Green State University, George Washington University, Miami University, Michigan State University, and Western Michigan University, now offer an undergraduate degree major in Purchasing/Supply/Supply Chain/Logistics Management as part of the bachelor in business administration degree. In addition, many schools offer certificate programs or some courses in supply, for either full- or part-time students. A number of schools, including Arizona State, Michigan State, NYU Stern, and Howard University, also offer a specialization in supply chain management as part of a master of business administration degree program.

In Canada, the Ivey Business School has offered for over 60 years a purchasing and supply course as part of its undergraduate and graduate degree offerings. Other universities such as HEC, Laval, York, Queens, University of British Columbia, and Victoria have followed suit; academic interest in supply chain management is at an all-time high.

While, obviously, a university degree is not a guarantee of individual performance and success, the supply professional with one or more degrees is perceived on an educational par with professionals in other disciplines such as engineering, accounting, marketing, information technology (IT), human resources (HR), or finance. That perception is important in the role that supply professionals are invited to play on the organizational team.

Professional Associations

As any profession matures, its professional associations emerge as focal points for efforts to advance professional practice and conduct. In the United States, the major professional association is the Institute for Supply Management (ISM), founded in 1915 as the National Association of Purchasing Agents. The ISM is an educational and research association with over 40,000 members who belong to ISM through its network of domestic and international affiliated associations.

In addition to regional and national conferences, ISM sponsors seminars for supply people. It publishes a variety of books and monographs and the leading scholarly journal in the field, *The Journal of Supply Chain Management,* which it began in 1965. Additionally, ISM and its Canadian counterpart, the Supply Chain Management Association (SCMA), formally the Purchasing Management Association of Canada, work with colleges and universities to encourage and support the teaching of purchasing and supply management and related subjects and provide financial grants to support doctoral student research.

ISM launched the Certified Professional in Supply Management (CPSM) program in May 2008. The CPSM program focuses skill development in areas such as supplier relationship management, commodity management, risk and compliance issues, and social responsibility.

Since the early 1930s, ISM has conducted the monthly "ISM Report on Business," which is one of the best-recognized current barometers of business activity in the manufacturing sector. In 1998, the association initiated the Nonmanufacturing ISM Report on Business. The survey results are normally released on the second business day of each month. The Ivey Purchasing Managers Index (Ivey PMI), conducted by the Ivey Business School, is the Canadian equivalent of ISM's Report on Business, but covers the complete Canadian economy, including the manufacturing services and government sectors.

In 1986, CAPS Research (formally the Center for Advanced Purchasing Studies) was established as a national affiliation agreement between ISM and the College of Business at Arizona State University. CAPS is dedicated to the discovery and dissemination of strategic supply management knowledge and best practices. It conducts benchmarking studies, runs executive round tables and best practices workshops, and publishes research reports in a wide range of areas.

In Canada, the professional association is the Supply Chain Management Association (SCMA), formally the PMAC, formed in 1919. Its membership of approximately 8,000 is organized in 10 provincial and territorial institutes from coast to coast. Its primary objective is education, and in addition to sponsoring a national conference, it offers an accreditation program leading to the Supply Chain Management Professional (SCMP) designation.

In addition to ISM and SCMA, there are other professional purchasing associations, such as the National Institute of Governmental Purchasing (NIGP), the National Association of State Purchasing Officials (NASPO), the National Association of Educational Procurement (NAEP), and the Association for Healthcare Resource and Materials Management (AHPMM).

Several of these associations offer their own certification programs. Most industrialized countries have their own professional purchasing associations. CIPS (Chartered Institute of Purchasing and Supply) has affiliates in the United Kingdom, Australia, New Zealand, Africa and China, and Hong Kong. Other examples include the Indian Institute of Materials Management and the Japan Materials Management Association. These national associations are loosely organized into the International Federation of Purchasing and Supply Management (IFPSM), which has as its objective the fostering of cooperation, education, and research in purchasing on a worldwide basis among the 48 national and regional purchasing associations worldwide, representing approximately 250,000 supply professionals.

CHALLENGES AHEAD

There are at least six major challenges facing the supply profession over the next decade: supply chain management, measurement, risk management, sustainability, growth and influence, and effective contribution to corporate success.

Supply Chain Management

The success of firms like Walmart and Zara in exploiting supply chain opportunities has helped popularize the whole field of supply chain management. Nevertheless, significant challenges remain: While the giant firms in automotive, electronics, and retailing can force the various members of the supply chain to do their bidding, smaller companies do not have that luxury. Thus, each organization has to determine for itself how far it can extend its sphere of influence within the supply chain and how to respond to supply chain initiatives by others. Clearly, opportunities to reduce inventories, shorten lead times and distances, plan operations better, remove uncertainties, and squeeze waste out of the supply chain are still abundant. Thus, the search for extra value in the supply chain will continue for a considerable period of time.

Measurement

There is significant interest in better measurement of supply not only to provide senior management with better information regarding supply's contribution, but also to be able to assess the benefits of various supply experiments. No one set of measurements is likely to suffice for all supply organizations. Therefore, finding the set of measures most appropriate for a particular organization's circumstances is part of the measurement challenge.

Risk Management

A study at Michigan State University found that supply chain disruptions and supply chain risk are among the most critical issues facing supply chain managers.[6] Supply chains have become increasingly global and, therefore, face risks of supply interruptions, financial and exchange rate fluctuations, lead time variability, and security and protection of intellectual property rights, to name only a few. The trend to single sourcing and lean global supply chains has also created the increased risks for supply disruptions.

Supply managers need to continually assess risks in the supply chain and balance risk/reward opportunities when making supply decisions. For example, the attraction of lower prices from an offshore supplier may create longer-term high costs as a result of the need to carry additional safety stock inventories or lost sales from stock-outs. The Russel Wisselink case in Chapter 9 describes how one organization ran into problems in a low cost country sourcing program. Risk management will be covered in more detail in Chapter 2.

Sustainability

Responsibility for reverse logistics and disposal has traditionally fallen under the supply organization umbrella (see Chapters 16 and 17). These activities include the effective and efficient capture and disposition of downstream products from customers. More recently, however, pressures from government and consumer groups are motivating organizations to reduce the impact of their supply chains on the natural environment. For example, the European Union (EU) has set aggressive targets for greenhouse gas reductions and cuts to overall energy consumption, and has implemented new legislation as a result. Supply will be at the forefront of sustainability initiatives. Senior management will expect supply to work with suppliers to identify solutions for the environmental and sustainability challenges they face.

Growth and Influence

Growth and influence in terms of the role of supply and its responsibilities inside an organization can be represented in four areas as identified in a CAPS Research focus study.[7] In the first place, supply can grow in the percentage of the organization's total spend for which it is meaningfully involved. Thus, categories of spend traditionally not involving purchasing, such as real estate, insurance, energy, benefit programs, part-time help, relocation services, consulting, marketing spend with advertising and media agencies, travel and facilities management, IT, and telecommunications and logistics, have become part of procurement's responsibility in more progressive corporations.

[6] S. A. Melnyk et al., *Supply Chain Management 2010 and Beyond: Mapping the Future of the Strategic Supply Chain* (The Eli Broad College of Business at Michigan State University, 2006).

[7] Leenders and Johnson, *Major Changes in Supply Chain Responsibilities*.

Second, the growth of supply responsibilities can be seen in the span of supply chain activities under purchasing or supply leadership. Recent additions include accounts payable, legal, training and recruiting, programs and customer bid support, and involvement with new business development.

Third, growth can occur in the type of involvement of supply in what is acquired and supply chain responsibilities. Clearly, on the lowest level, there is no supply involvement at all. The next step up is a transactionary or documentary role. Next, professional involvement implies that supply personnel have the opportunity to exercise their expertise in important acquisition process stages. At the highest level, meaningful involvement, a term first coined by Dr. Ian Stuart, represents true team member status for supply at the executive table. Thus, in any major decision taken in the organization, the question *What are the supply implications of this decision?* is as natural and standard as *What are the financial implications of this decision?*

Fourth, supply can grow by its involvement in corporate activities from which it might have been previously excluded. While involvement in make-or-buy decisions, economic forecasts, countertrade, in- and outsourcing, and supplier conferences might be expected, other activities such as strategic planning, mergers and acquisitions, visionary task forces, and initial project planning might be good examples of broader corporate strategic integration.

Each of these four areas of opportunity for growth allows for supply to spread its wings and increase the value of its contributions.

Effective Contribution to Organizational Success

Ultimately, supply's measure of its contribution needs to be seen in the success of the organization as a whole. Contributing operationally and strategically, directly and indirectly, and in a positive mode, the challenge for supply is to be an effective team member. Meaningful involvement of supply can be demonstrated by the recognition accorded supply by all members of the organization.

How happy are other corporate team members to have supply on their team? Do they see supply's role as critical to the team's success? Thus, to gain not only senior management recognition but also the proper appreciation of peer managers in other functions is a continuing challenge for both supply professionals and academics.

THE ORGANIZATION OF THIS TEXT

In this first chapter are listed the more common influences for all organizations. In subsequent chapters, we will cover various decisions regarding organizational and supply strategies, organization supply processes, make or buy, the variety of organizational needs, and how to translate these into commercial equivalents. These will be followed by decisions on quality, quantity, delivery, price, and service—the traditional five value criteria—culminating in supplier selection. Suppliers are located domestically and internationally and their location will affect how supply should be managed. The legal and ethical framework for supply establishes the framework for the contract between these two parties. How to evaluate supplier performance and how to relate to suppliers is followed by a section on supply chain associated responsibilities which may or may not be part of the supply manager's assignment. This text concludes with the evaluation of the supply function, its performance reporting, and current trends in the field.

Conclusion

If the chief executive officer and all members of the management team can say, "Because of the kinds of suppliers we have and the way we relate to them, we can outperform our competition and provide greater customer satisfaction," then the supply function is contributing to its full potential.

This is the ambitious goal of this text: to provide insights for those who wish to understand the supply function better, whether or not they are or will be employed in supply directly.

Questions for Review and Discussion

1. What is the profit-leverage effect of supply? Is it the same in all organizations?
2. "Supply is not profit making; instead, it is profit taking since it spends organizational resources." Do you agree?
3. What kinds of decisions does a typical supply manager make?
4. "In the long term, the success of any organization depends on its ability to create and maintain a customer." Do you agree? What does this have to do with purchasing and supply management?
5. Is purchasing a profession? If not, why not? If yes, how will the profession, and the people practicing it, change over the next decade?
6. Differentiate between purchasing, procurement, materials management, logistics, supply management, and supply chain management.
7. In what ways might e-commerce influence the role of supply managers in their own organizations? In managing supply chains or networks?
8. In the petroleum and coal products industry, the total purchase/sales ratio is 80 percent, while in the food industry it is about 60 percent. Explain what these numbers mean. Of what significance is this number for a supply manager in a company in each of these industries?
9. How does supply management affect return on assets (ROA)? In what specific ways could you improve ROA through supply management?
10. How can the expectations of supply differ for private versus public organizations? Services versus goods producers?

References

Carter C. R.; L. M. Ellram, L. Kaufmann; C. W. Autry; X. Zhao; and T. E. Callarman, "Looking Back and Moving Forward: 50 years of the *Journal of Supply Chain Management*," *Journal of Supply Chain Management* 50, no. 1, 2014, pp. 1–7.

Cavinato, J. L.; A. E. Flynn; and R. G. Kauffman. *The Supply Management Handbook.* 7th ed. Burr Ridge, IL: McGraw-Hill/Irwin, 2007.

Johnson, P. F., and M. R. Leenders, *Supply's Organizational Roles and Responsibilities,* Tempe, AZ: CAPS Research, May 2012, 118 pages.

Lambert, D. M. *Supply Chain Management: Processes, Partnerships and Performance,* Sarasota, Florida: Supply Chain Management Institute, 2004.

Leenders, M. R., and H. E. Fearon. "Developing Purchasing's Foundation," *The Journal of Supply Chain Management* 44, no. 2 (2008), pp. 17–27.

Leenders, M. R., and A. E. Flynn. *Value-Driven Purchasing: Managing the Key Steps in the Acquisition Process.* Burr Ridge, IL: Irwin Professional Publishing, 1995.

Villena, V. H., E. Revilla, and T. Choi, "The Dark Side of Buyer-Supplier Relationships: A Social Capital Perspective," *Journal of Operations Management* 29, no. 6 (2011), pp. 561–576.

Case 1–1

Denniston Spices

Amy Lin, materials planner at Denniston Spices, in Phoenix, Arizona, was faced with an important problem caused by a supplier who was implementing a new enterprise resource planning (ERP) system. It was Tuesday, April 9, 2014, and during a call the previous day from Juan Aranda, sales manager at Whittingham Foods, Amy learned that potential supply problems might occur starting in September as the new system was implemented at the Whittingham's Indianapolis plant. In order to avoid stockouts, Juan asked Amy to provide a forecast of her plant's needs for September to November by April 30th, so he could make arrangements to have product shipped to Denniston in late August.

DENNISTON SPICES

Founded in 1903 by Walter J. Denniston, Denniston Spices was a global leader in the food industry—manufacturing, marketing, and distributing a wide variety of spices, mixes, condiments, and other seasoning products to the retail, commercial, and industrial markets. Headquartered in Chicago, the company had sales revenues of $5.5 billion and sold its products in more than 100 countries worldwide. Its customers included retail outlets, food manufacturers, restaurant chains, food distributors, and food service businesses. Denniston Spices was also a leading supplier of private label items.

The Phoenix plant manufactured and distributed spices, herbs, extracts, and seasoning blends to retail and industrial customers in the southwest United States. Amy Lin was responsible for managing approximately 300 stock-keeping units (SKUs) consisting of spices and compounds, purchased from Whittingham Foods, which was the sole supplier for these products. All SKUs supplied to the Phoenix plant by Whittingham came from their Indianapolis facility.

INVENTORY CONTROL

It was company policy that each SKU had minimum safety stock inventory to protect against stockouts. Safety stock levels were set by the materials planners and typically ranged from two to four weeks. Reorder points were set at the safety stock level for each SKU plus four weeks, which reflected the lead time from Whittingham Foods for most products. Orders were constrained by minimum order quantities set by the supplier.

Forecasting and setting reasonable safety stock levels were made difficult because of variability in demand, particularly from industrial customers. Many of the Phoenix plant's industrial customers were small- and medium-sized manufacturers that ordered sporadically.

Prices for products supplied by Whittingham Foods ranged from $50 to $250 per pound, and had shelf-lives of either 90, 180, or 270 days. The major challenge in Amy's role was to balance high inventory costs and short shelf lives with the risks of stockout costs and inventory spoilage. Denniston Spices offered 10-day delivery lead times to its customers and it typically took 2 to 7 days for an order to be processed and shipped. The Phoenix plant had a customer service level target of 98 percent.

INVENTORY BUILD FOR AUGUST

The call from Juan Aranda did not come as a surprise to Amy, who had known for several weeks that Whittingham Foods was implementing a new ERP system and at some point she would need to purchase additional safety stock inventory. Whittingham Foods was as key supplier to several Denniston plants, and switching suppliers was not feasible for such a short period of time due to the costs and administrative issues related to government regulations regarding the certification of suppliers. While there was a possibility they would not experience any problems and supply would not be interrupted, Amy did not want to take any chances and had the full support of her boss, Kevin Sherman, the director of purchasing.

As a starting point, Amy collected demand data for eight SKUs during July to November period in 2012 and 2013 (see Exhibit 1). For each of the eight SKUs, she also collected information related to safety stock levels,

minimum order quantities (MOQ), shelf life, and cost per pound. She purposely selected SKUs from different final products that included a range of costs and annual demand, with the objective of developing an inventory build policy for the SKUs ordered from Whittingham Foods. Amy knew that certain events in 2012 and 2013 distorted the data. For example, the company had expanded in 2013 through an acquisition and the plant increased production in order to build additional finished goods inventories as a result of a facility consolidation project in the fall of 2013.

As Amy looked at the data on her spreadsheet, she wondered if it would be possible to balance stockout risks with inventory holding and inventory spoilage costs. It was important that she develop a preliminary plan within the next week so she could get it approved by the director of purchasing and the general manager. Margins were tight and Amy knew that she had to do her best to develop a plan that controlled costs without jeopardizing customer service levels.

EXHIBIT 1   **Historical Usage for Whittingham Products**

SKU #	Year	July	Aug.	Sept.	Oct.	Nov.	Safety Stock (lb.)	MOQ (lb.)	Shelf Life (Days)	Cost ($/lb.)
		Monthly Demand (lb.)								
W9450	2012	51	208	80	75	103	1,000	200	90	$ 90
	2013	0	325	3,060	4,770	7,024				
W9451	2012	3,251	5,794	2,492	1,830	3,052	3,600	200	90	$ 195
	2013	956	2,854	2,730	2,621	3,786				
W9452	2012	979	680	460	894	778	600	200	180	$ 65
	2013	360	336	282	325	550				
W9453	2012	189	229	271	397	420	650	200	180	$ 110
	2013	549	642	1,019	1,655	2,588				
W9454	2012	52	56	54	45	50	100	200	270	$ 235
	2013	16	76	18	0	20				
W9455	2012	7	2	0	20	0	400	200	270	$ 65
	2013	724	304	304	376	424				
W9456	2012	120	4	55	1	60	15	80	270	$ 120
	2013	16	1	43	17	15				
W9457	2012	41	157	54	117	0	320	80	270	$ 120
	2013	0	131	82	69	0				

Case 1–2

Erica Carson

"We will do it for 10 percent less than what you are paying right now." Erica Carson, purchasing manager at Wesbank, a large western financial institution, had agreed to meet with Art Evans, a sales representative from D.Killoran Inc., a printing supplier from which Wesbank currently was not buying anything. Art Evans's impromptu and unsolicited price quote concerned the printing and mailing of checks from Wesbank.

Wesbank, well known for its active promotional efforts to attract consumer deposits, provided standard personalized consumer checks free of charge. Despite the increasing popularity of Internet banking, the printing of free checks and mailing to customers cost Wesbank $8 million in the past year.

Erica Carson was purchasing manager in charge of all printing for Wesbank and reported directly to the vice president of supply.

It had been Erica's decision to split the printing and mailing of checks equally between two suppliers. During the last five years, both suppliers had provided quick and quality service, a vital concern of the bank. Almost all checks were mailed directly to the consumer's home or business address by the suppliers. Because of the importance of check printing, Erica had requested a special cost analysis study a year ago, with the cooperation of both suppliers. The conclusion of this study had been that both suppliers were receiving an adequate profit margin and were efficient and cost-conscious and that the price structure was fair. Each supplier was on a two-year contract. One supplier's contract had been renewed eight months ago; the other's expired in another four months.

Erica believed that Killoran was underbidding to gain part of the check-printing business. This in turn would give Killoran access to Wesbank's customers' names. Erica suspected that Killoran might then try to pursue these customers more actively than the current two suppliers to sell special "scenic checks" that customers paid for themselves.

Chapter Two

Supply Strategy

Chapter Outline

Levels of Strategic Planning

Major Challenges in Setting Supply Objectives and Strategies

Strategic Planning in Supply Management

Risk Management
Operational Risk
Financial Risk
Reputational Risk
Managing Supply Risk
The Corporate Context

Strategic Components
What?
Quality?

How Much?
Who?
When?
What Price?
Where?
How?
Why?

Conclusion

Questions for Review and Discussion

References

Cases

Key Questions for the Supply Decision Maker

Should we

- Become more concerned about the balance sheet?
- Develop a strategic plan for purchasing and supply management?
- Spend a major part of our time on strategic, rather than operational, issues?

How can we

- Anticipate the professional changes we will face in the next 10 years?
- Ensure supply is included as part of the organization's overall strategy?
- Generate the information needed to do strategic planning?

In strategic supply, the key question is: How can supply and the supply chain contribute *effectively* to organizational objectives and strategy? The accompanying question is: How can the organizational objectives and strategy properly reflect the contribution and opportunities offered in the supply chain?

A *strategy* is an *action plan* designed to achieve specific *long-term goals and objectives*. The strategy should concentrate on the *key factors necessary* for success and the *major actions* that should be taken now *to ensure the future*. It is the process of determining the relationship of the organization to its *environment*, establishing long-term *objectives*, and achieving the desired relationship(s) through efficient and effective *allocation of resources*.

LEVELS OF STRATEGIC PLANNING

To be successful, an organization must approach strategic planning on three levels:

1. *Corporate*. These are the decisions and plans that answer the questions of What business are we in? and How will we allocate our resources among these businesses? For example, is a railroad in the business of running trains? Or is its business the movement (creating time and space utility) of things and people?
2. *Business Unit*. These decisions mold the plans of a particular business unit, as necessary, to contribute to the corporate strategy.
3. *Function*. These plans concern the how of each functional area's contribution to the business strategy and involve the allocation of internal resources.

Several studies have reinforced the notion that linking supply strategy to corporate strategy is essential, but many firms do not yet have mechanisms in place to link the two.[1]

---

[1] R. M. Monczka and K. J. Petersen, *Supply Strategy Implementation: Current State and Future Opportunities* (Tempe, AZ: CAPS Research, 2008). S. D. Hunt and D. Davis, "Grounding Supply Chain Management in Resource-Advantage Theory: In Defense of a Resource-Based View of the Firm," *Journal of Supply Chain Management* 48, no. 2 (2012), pp. 14–20.

FIGURE 2–1
**Supply
Strategy
Congruent with
Organizational
Strategy**

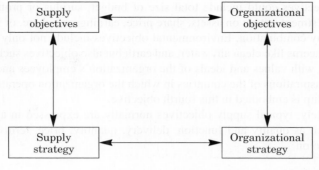

FIGURE 2–2
**Supply
Strategy
Links Current
and Future
Markets to
Current and
Future Needs**

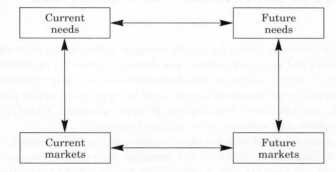

Effective contribution connotes more than just a response to a directive from top management. It also implies inputs to the strategic planning process so that organizational objectives and strategies include supply opportunities and problems.

This is graphically shown in Figure 2–1 by the use of double arrows between supply objectives and strategy and organizational objectives and strategy.

A different look at supply strategy is given in Figure 2–2. This shows an effective supply strategy linking both current needs and current markets to future needs and future markets.

One of the significant obstacles to the development of an effective supply strategy lies in the difficulties inherent in translating organizational objectives into supply objectives. For example, Tony Brown, senior vice president of global sourcing at Ford Motor Company, was implementing a new supply strategy that he believed would improve performance in the areas of quality, technology, delivery, cost, and speed to market. However, the company chairman and CEO William Clay Ford Jr. will be interested in issues such as how the new supply strategy will improve earnings per share and create shareholder value. (See the Ford Motor Company case at the end of the chapter.)

Normally, most organizational objectives can be summarized under four categories: survival, growth, financial, and environmental. Survival is the most basic need of any organization. Growth can be expressed in a variety of ways. For example, growth could be in size of the organization in terms of number of employees or assets or number of operating units, or number of countries in which the organization operates, or in market share.

Financial objectives could include total size of budget, surplus or profit, total revenue, return on investment, return on assets, share price, earnings per share, or increases in each of these or any combination. Environmental objectives include not only traditional environmental concerns like clean air, water, and earth but also objectives such as the contribution to and fit with values and ideals of the organization's employees and customers, and the laws and aspirations of the countries in which the organization operates. The notion of good citizenship is embodied in this fourth objective.

Unfortunately, typical supply objectives normally are expressed in a totally different language, such as quality and function, delivery, quantity, price, terms and conditions, service, and so on.

MAJOR CHALLENGES IN SETTING SUPPLY OBJECTIVES AND STRATEGIES

The first major challenge facing the supply manager is the effective interpretation of corporate objectives and supply objectives. For example, given the organization's desire to expand rapidly, is supply assurance more important than obtaining "rock bottom" prices?

The second challenge deals with the choice of the appropriate action plan or strategy to achieve the desired objectives. For example, if supply assurance is vital, is it best accomplished by single or dual sourcing, or by making in-house?

The third challenge deals with the identification and feedback of supply issues to be integrated into organizational objectives and strategies. For example, because a new technology can be accessed early through supply efforts, how can this be exploited? The Spartan Heat Exchangers case at the end of this chapter provides an illustration of how supply should be integrated to corporate strategy. The changes in corporate strategy and objectives at Spartan necessitate changes in supply strategy.

The development of a supply strategy requires that the supply manager be in tune with the organization's key objectives and strategies and also be capable of recognizing and grasping opportunities. All three challenges require managerial and strategic skills of the highest order, and the difficulties in meeting these challenges should not be minimized.

STRATEGIC PLANNING IN SUPPLY MANAGEMENT

Today, firms face the challenge of prospering in the face of highly competitive world markets. The ability to relate effectively to outside environments—social, economic, political, legal, and technological—to anticipate changes, to adjust to changes, and to capitalize on opportunities by formulating and executing strategic plans is a major factor in generating future earnings and is critical to survival. Supply must be forward looking.

A supply strategy is a supply action plan designed to permit the achievement of selected goals and objectives. If well developed, the strategy will link the firm to the environment as part of the long-term planning process. An overall supply strategy is made up of substrategies that can be grouped together into six major categories:

1. *Assurance-of-supply strategies.* Designed to ensure that future supply needs are met with emphasis on quality and quantity. Assurance-of-supply strategies must consider

changes in both demand and supply. (Much of the work in purchasing research [see Chapter 17] is focused on providing the relevant information.)

2. *Cost-reduction strategies.* Designed to reduce the laid-down cost of what is acquired or the total cost of acquisition and use—life-cycle cost. With changes in the environment and technology, alternatives may be available to reduce an organization's overall operating costs through changes in materials, sources, methods, and buyer–supplier relationships.

3. *Supply chain support strategies.* Designed to maximize the likelihood that the considerable knowledge and capabilities of supply chain members are available to the buying organization. For example, better communication systems are needed between buyers and sellers to facilitate the timely notification of changes and to ensure that supply inventories and production goals are consistent with the needs. Supply chain members also need better relations for the communication needed to ensure higher quality and better design.

4. *Environmental-change strategies.* Designed to anticipate and recognize shifts in the total environment (economic, organizational, people, legal, governmental regulations and controls, and systems availability) so that it can turn them to the long-term advantage of the buying organization.

5. *Competitive-edge strategies.* Designed to exploit market opportunities and organizational strengths to give the buying organization a significant competitive edge. In the public sector, the term *competitive edge* usually may be interpreted to mean strong performance in achieving program objectives.

6. *Risk-management strategies.* Whereas the various aspects of the previous five types of strategies have been covered earlier in this text, the issue of risk management has not yet been discussed. Therefore, this section will be expanded here, not to imply greater importance, but to assure adequate coverage.

RISK MANAGEMENT

Every business decision involves risk, and supply is no exception. In financial investments a higher rate of return is supposed to compensate the investor or lender for the higher risk exposure. Risks in the supply chain can be classified into three main categories: (1) operational: the risk of interruption of the flow of goods or services, (2) financial: the risk that the price of the goods or services acquired will change significantly, and (3) reputational risk.

All three risks affect the survival, competitiveness, and bottom line of the organization and may occur simultaneously.

Operational Risk

Every business continuity plan recognizes that supply interruptions and delays may occur. Catastrophic events such as earthquakes, tornadoes, hurricanes, war, floods, or fire may totally disable a vital supplier. Strikes may vary in length, and even short-term interruptions related to weather, accidents on key roads, or any other short-term factor affecting the supply and/or transport of requirements may affect a buying organization's capability to provide good customer service.

A distinction can be drawn between factors beyond the purchaser's or supplier's control, such as weather, and those that deal directly with the supplier's capability of selecting its own suppliers, *managing internally, and its distribution* so as to prevent the potential of physical supply interruption. Careful supplier evaluation before committing to purchase can mitigate against the latter type of supply interruption. In situations of ongoing supply relationships, communication with key suppliers is essential. Such is the situation in the Sabor case at the end of the chapter. Ray Soles is concerned about the potential shortage of a key raw material and must come to an agreement with his suppliers to avoid possible supply disruptions.

Unfortunately, supply interruptions increase costs. If last-minute substitutions need to be made, these are likely to be expensive. Idle labor and equipment, missed customer delivery promises, and scrambling—all have increased costs associated with them.

Financial Risk

Quite different from supply interruptions are those risks directly associated with changes in the price of the good or service purchased. A simple example comes from the commodity markets. Increases in the price of oil affect prices paid for fuel, energy, and those products or services that require oil as a key ingredient or raw material.

A purchaser who has committed to a fixed-price contract may find a competitor able to compete because commodity prices have dropped. Currency exchange rate changes and the threat of shortages or supply interruption also will affect prices, as will arbitrary supplier pricing decisions. Changes in taxation, tolls, fees, duties, and tariffs also will affect cost of ownership.

Given that both supply interruption and price/cost risks directly impact any organization's ability to meet its own goals and execute its strategies, supply chain risks—whether they are on the supply side, internal to the organization, or on the customer side—need to be managed properly.

Reputational Risk

Reputational risk may be even more serious than operational or financial risks, because the loss of reputation may be catastrophic for a company. Both legal and ethical supply issues may affect the company's reputation. "You are known by the company you keep" applies not only to one's personal life, but also to corporate life. Thus, the reputation of a company's supply chain members will affect its own image. The internal and external communications decisions and behavior of supply personnel can have both negative and positive impacts. Therefore, the content of the legal issues and ethics (Chapter 15) is highly relevant to reputational risk. Adverse publicity with respect to bribery, kickbacks, improper quality, improper disposal and environmental practices, dealings with unethical suppliers, and so on, can be extremely damaging.

Managing Supply Risk

Managing supply risks require: (1) identification and classification of the risks, (2) impact assessment, and (3) a risk strategy.

Given that supply is becoming more and more global and supply networks more complex, risk identification is also becoming more difficult. The preceding discussion identifying supply interruption and price/cost changes as two categories has been highly simplified. Technology, social, political, and environmental factors have not even been mentioned yet. Technology has the potential of interrupting supply through the failure of systems and through obsoleting existing equipment, products, or services, or drastically changing the existing cost/price realities. A purchaser committed to a long-term, fixed-price contract for a particular requirement may find a competitor can gain a significant advantage through a technology-driven, lower-cost substitute. Environmental regulation changes can drastically offset a supplier's capability to deliver at the expected price or to deliver at all.

Because the well-informed supply manager is probably in the best position to identify the various supply risks his or her organization faces, such risk identification should be a standard requirement of the job, including the estimation of the probability of event occurrence.

Impact assessment requires the ability to assess the consequences of supply interruption and/or price/cost exposure. Correct impact assessment is likely to require the input of others in the organization, such as operations, marketing, accounting, and finance, to name just a few. Assessed potential impact from identified risk may be low, medium, or high.

Combining potential impact assessment with the probability of event exposure creates a table of risks with low probability and low impact on one extreme and high probability with high impact on the other.

Obviously, high-impact, high-probability risks need to be addressed or, better yet, avoided, if at all possible.

Managing supply risks should be started at the supply level, but may escalate to the overall corporate level. Relatively simple actions such as avoiding high-risk suppliers or high-risk geographical locations, dual or triple sourcing, carrying safety stock, hedging, and using longer-term and/or fixed- or declining-price contracts and protective contract clauses have been a standard part of the procurement arsenal for a long time. If most purchasers had their way, they would like to transfer all risk to their suppliers! However, the assumption of risk carries a price tag, and a supplier should be asked to shoulder the risk if it is advantageous to both the supplier and purchaser to do so.

The Corporate Context

Supply risk is only one of the various risks to which any organization is exposed. Traditionally, financial risks have been the responsibility of finance, property insurance part of real estate, and so on. The emergence of a corporate risk management group headed by a risk manager or chief risk officer (CRO) allows companies as a whole to assess their total risk exposure and seek the best ways of managing all risks.

A supply manager's decision not to source in a politically unstable country because of his or her fear of supply interruption may also miss an opportunity to source at a highly advantageous price. A corporate perspective might show that the trade-off between a higher price elsewhere and the risk of nonsupply favors the apparently riskier option. Mergers and acquisitions as well as insourcing and outsourcing represent phenomena full of opportunities and risks in which supply input is vital to effective corporate risk resolution. The decision about how much risk any organization should be willing to bear and whether it should self-insure or seek third-party protection is well beyond the scope of this text. Nevertheless, it is clear that risk management is going to be an area of growing concern for supply managers.

FIGURE 2–3
Strategic
Supply
Planning
Process

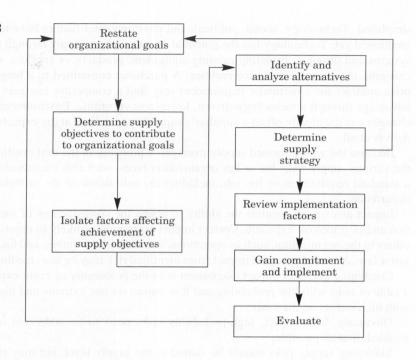

Figure 2–3 is a conceptual flow diagram of the strategic supply planning process. It is important to recognize that the planning process normally focuses on *long-run opportunities* and not primarily on immediate problems.

STRATEGIC COMPONENTS

The number of specific strategic opportunities that might be addressed in formulating an overall supply strategy is limited only by the imagination of the supply manager. Any strategy chosen should include a determination of what, quality, how much, who, when, what price, where, how, and why. Each of these will be discussed further. (See Figure 2–4.)

What?

Probably the most fundamental question facing an organization under the "what" category is the issue of make or buy, insourcing, and outsourcing. Presumably, strong acquisition strengths would favor a buy strategy. (See Chapter 5: Make or Buy, Insourcing, and Outsourcing.)

Also included under the heading of what is to be acquired is the issue of whether the organization will acquire standard items and materials readily available in the market, as opposed to special, custom-specified requirements. Standard items may be readily acquired in the marketplace, but they may not afford the organization the competitive edge that special requirements might provide.

Who?

The whole question of who should do the buying and how to organize the supply function has been addressed in Chapter 3. The key decisions are whether the supply function should be centralized or not, where staff should be located geographically, and to what extent top management and other functions will be involved in the total acquisition process. To what extent will teams be used to arrive at supply strategies?

When?

The question of when to buy is tied very closely to the one of how much. The obvious choices are now versus later. The key strategy issue really lies with the question of forward buying and inventory policy. In the area of commodities, the opportunity exists to go into the futures market and use hedging. The organized commodity exchanges present an opportunity to offset transactions in the spot and future markets to avoid some of the risk of substantial price fluctuation as discussed in Chapter 10.

What Price?

It is possible for any organization to follow some specific price strategies. This topic already has been extensively discussed in Chapter 11. Key trade-offs may be whether the organization intends to pursue paying a premium price in return for exceptional service and other commitments from the supplier, a standard price target in line with the rest of the market, or a low price intended to give a cost advantage. Furthermore, the pursuit of a cost-based strategy as opposed to a market-based strategy may require extensive use of tools such as value analysis, cost analysis, and negotiation. For capital assets, the choice of lease or own presents strategic alternatives, as discussed in Chapter 16.

Where?

Several possibilities present themselves under the question of where to buy. Many of these are discussed in Chapter 12 under "Source Selection." Obvious trade-offs include local, regional, domestic, or international sourcing; buying from small versus large suppliers; single versus multiple sourcing; and low versus high supplier turnover, as well as supplier certification and supplier ownership. Lastly, through reverse marketing or supplier development, the purchaser may create rather than select suppliers.

How?

A large array of options exists under the heading of "how to buy." These include, but certainly are not limited to, supply chain management integration systems and procedures; choice of technology; e-commerce applications; use of various types of teams; use of negotiations, auctions, competitive bids, blanket orders, and open order systems; systems contracting; group buying; long-term contracts; the ethics of acquisition; aggressive or passive buying; the use of purchasing research and value analysis; quality assurance programs; and reduction of the supply base. Most of these will be discussed in Chapters 3 through 12 in this text.

Why?

Every strategy needs to be examined not only for its various optional components, but also for the reason why it should be pursued. The normal reason for a strategy in supply is to make supply objectives congruent with overall organizational objectives and strategies at both an operational and strategic level. Other reasons may include market conditions, both current and future. Furthermore, there may be reasons internal to the organization, both outside of supply and inside supply, to pursue certain strategies. For example, a strong engineering department may afford an opportunity to pursue a strategy based on specially engineered requirements. The availability of excess funds may afford an opportunity to acquire a supplier through backward/vertical integration. The reasons inside supply may be related to the capability and availability of supply personnel. A highly trained and effective supply group can pursue much more aggressive strategies than one less qualified. Other reasons may include the environment. For example, government regulations and controls in product liability and environmental protection may require the pursuit of certain strategies.

What makes supply strategy such an exciting area for exploration is the combination of the multitude of strategic options coupled with the size of potential impact on corporate success. The combination of sound supply expertise with creative thinking and full understanding of corporate objectives and strategies can uncover strategic opportunities of a size and impact not available elsewhere in the organization.

Conclusion

The increasing interest in supply strategies and their potential contribution to organizational objectives and strategies is one of the exciting developments in the whole field of supply. Fortunately, as this chapter indicates, the number of strategic options open to any supply manager is almost endless. A significant difficulty may exist in making these strategies congruent with those of the organization as a whole. The long-term perspective required for effective supply strategy development will force supply managers to concentrate more on the future. The coming decade should be a highly rewarding one for those supply managers willing to accept the challenge of realizing the full potential of supply's contribution to organizational success.

Questions for Review and Discussion

1. What role can (should) supply play in determining a firm's strategy in the area of social and environmental issues and trends?
2. How can the supply manager determine which cost-reduction strategies to pursue?
3. Can you have a supply strategy in public procurement? Why or why not?
4. Why should a supply manager consider hiring (or obtaining internally) an employee without any supply background?
5. What can supply do to assist in minimizing a firm's risk of product liability lawsuits?
6. What factors have caused the current interest in, and attention to, strategic purchasing and supply planning?

7. What type of data would supply need to contribute to an organization's strategic growth? How might supply obtain such data?

8. How can supply sell itself more effectively internally?

9. What do you believe to be the most difficult obstacles to making a supply function strategic?

10. Why should supply be concerned about the balance sheet?

References

Carter, P. L.; R. M. Monczka; G. L. Ragatz; and P. L. Jennings. *Supply Chain Integration: Challenges and Good Practices*. Tempe, AZ: CAPS Research, 2009.

Cox, A. *Strategic Sourcing*. Warwickshire, UK: Earlsgate Press, 2008.

Hallikas, J.; A. K. Kähkönen; K. Lintukangas; and V. M. Virolainen, "Supply Management—Missing Link in Strategic Management?" *Journal of Purchasing and Supply Management* 17, no. 3 (2011), pp. 145–147.

Hitt, M. A., "The Relevance of Strategic Management Theory and Research for Supply Chain Management," *Journal of Supply Chain Management* 47, no. 1 (2011), pp. 9–13.

Johnson, P. F., and M. R. Leenders. "Minding the Supply Savings Gaps." *MIT Sloan Management Review* 51, no. 2 (2010), pp. 25–31.

Johnson, P. F., and M. R. Leenders. *Supply Leadership Changes*. Tempe, AZ: CAPS Research, March 2007, 106 pages.

Monczka, R. M.; P. L. Carter; and W. J. Markham. *Risk Management Across the Extended Value Chain*. Tempe, AZ: CAPS Research, June 2012.

Monczka, R. M. and K. J. Petersen. *Supply Strategy Implementation: Current State and Future Opportunities*. Tempe, AZ: CAPS Research, 2008.

Zsidisin, G. A.; G. L. Ragatz; and S. A. Melnyk. "The Dark Side of Supply Chain Management." *Supply Chain Management Review* 9, no. 2 (2005), pp. 46–52.

Case 2–1

Spartan Heat Exchangers Inc.

On June 10, Rick Coyne, materials manager at Spartan Heat Exchangers Inc. (Spartan), in Springfield, Missouri, received a call from Max Brisco, vice president of manufacturing: "What can the materials department do to facilitate Spartan's new business strategy? I'll need your plan next week."

SPARTAN HEAT EXCHANGERS

Spartan was a leading designer and manufacturer of specialized industrial heat transfer equipment. Its customers operated in a number of industries, such as steel, aluminum smelting, hydro electricity generation, pulp and paper, refining, and petrochemical. The company's primary products included transformer coolers, motor and generator coolers, hydro generator coolers, air cooled heat exchangers, and transformer oil coolers. Spartan's combination of fin-tube and time-proven heat exchanger designs had gained wide recognition both in North America and internationally.

Sales revenues were $25 million and Spartan operated in a 125,000-square-foot plant. Spartan was owned by Krimmer Industries, a large privately held corporation with more than 10,000 employees worldwide, headquartered in Denver.

Rick Coyne summarized the business strategy of Spartan during the past 10 years: "We were willing to do anything for every customer with respect to their heat transfer requirements. We were willing to do trial and error on the shop floor and provide a customer with his or her own unique heat transfer products." He added, "Our design and manufacturing people derived greatest satisfaction making new customized heat transfer products. Designing and research capabilities gave us the edge in developing and manufacturing any kind of heat transfer product required by the customer. Ten years ago, we were one of the very few companies in our industry offering customized services in design and manufacturing and this strategy made business sense, as the customers were willing to pay a premium for customized products."

MANUFACTURING PROCESS

The customized nature of Spartan's product line was supported by a job shop manufacturing operation with several departments, each of which produced particular component parts, feeding a final assembly area. Each job moved from work center to work center, accompanied by a bill of material and engineering drawing. The first process involved fitting a liner tube (in which the fluid to be cooled passed) into a base tube. This base tube, made of aluminum, was then pressure bonded to the inner liner tube through a rotary extrusion process that formed spiral fins on the base tube. The depth of the fins and the distance between them determined the amount of airflow across the tubes, and thus the cooling efficiency and power of the unit.

After the tubes were formed, cabinet and end plate fabrication began. The tubes were welded to the cabinet and the end plates. Flanges were then welded to pairs of tubes on the other side of the end plates to create a looped system. The unit was then painted and fans and motors were installed. Finally, the unit was tested for leaks and performance, crated, and shipped to the job site for installation.

MATERIALS DEPARTMENT

Spartan's buyers sourced all raw material and components required by manufacturing and were responsible for planning, procurement, and management of inventories.

Rick managed an in-house warehouse used for housing the raw material inventories, maintained adequate buffer inventories, and executed purchase contracts with vendors, ensuring specifications were met while achieving the best possible price. Rick's department included two buyers, a material control clerk, an expediter, and two shippers-receivers.

It was common for Spartan to have multiple vendors for raw material supply, and the materials group used more than 350 vendors for its raw materials, with current lead times ranging from a few days to six weeks. This wide supplier base was necessitated by the customization strategy adopted by the company. Rick noted that approximately 35 percent of Spartan's purchases were for aluminum products, mainly tubes and sheets. On average the plant had $3.5 million worth of inventory, in the form of both raw and work in process. Raw material inventory constituted approximately 40 percent of the total. Rick estimated that Spartan had inventory turns of four times per year, which he believed was comparable to the competition.

Manufacturing operations regularly complained about material shortages and stockouts, and regular inventory audits indicated significant discrepancies with inventory records on the company's computer system. Furthermore, a significant amount of stock was written off each year due to obsolescence. Rick suspected that production staff regularly removed stock without proper documentation and that workers frequently deviated from established bills of material.

NEW BUSINESS STRATEGY

Competition in the heat exchanger industry had increased dramatically over the past decade, with much of the new competition coming from Korea and Europe. Korean firms, with their low cost base, competed primarily on price, while European firms focused on standardizing their product lines to a few high-volume products and competed on delivery lead time and price. Spartan's competitors in Europe used assembly-line manufacturing processes, rather than batch or job shop operations.

Senior management viewed the competition from Europe and Korea as an imminent threat. Many of Spartan's customers had recently developed aggressive expectations regarding pricing and delivery lead times, and some key customers had decided to opt for standard product design, sacrificing custom design for lower cost and faster delivery.

The changing nature of the industry forced senior management to reexamine their business strategy. As a result, in January, a multidiscipline task force representing engineering, manufacturing, and sales was formed with the mandate to formulate a new five-year business strategy.

The new corporate strategy was finalized in May and reviewed with the management group on June 1 in an all-day staff meeting. The central theme of the new strategy was standardization of all product lines, in terms of both design and manufacturing, reducing variety to three or four basic lines for each product category. The sales department would no longer accept orders for specialized designs. The aim of the new strategy was to reduce the delivery lead time from 14 weeks to 6 weeks and to lower production costs dramatically.

NEW CHALLENGES FOR THE MATERIALS DEPARTMENT

Max Brisco indicated that he expected the materials group to play a major role in support of the new corporate strategy and needed to know by next week the specifics of Rick's plan. The task force had set a number of ambitious targets. First, customer lead times for finished products were to be reduced to six weeks from the current average of 14 weeks. Second, the new objective for inventory turns was 20 times. Meanwhile, raw material stockouts were to be eliminated. Third, Max believed that product standardization also would provide opportunities to reduce costs for purchased goods. He expected that costs for raw materials and components could be cut by 10 percent over the next 12 months.

Rick fully supported the new direction that the company was taking and saw this as an opportunity to make major changes. He knew that Max would want the specifics of his plan during the meeting in a week's time.

Case 2–2

Sabor Inc.

In mid-April, Ray Soles, vice president of supply chain management at Sabor Inc., had become increasingly concerned about the potential shortage of supply of marconil, a new high-tech raw material for air filtration. Sabor Inc.'s three suppliers, during the last two weeks, had advised Ray Soles to sign long-term contracts and he was trying to assess the advisability of such commitments.

SABOR INC.

Sabor Inc. of Cleveland, Ohio, produced high-quality consumer and industrial air conditioning and heating units. An extensive network of independent and company-owned installation and sales centers serviced customers throughout the North American market. Total company sales last year totaled $800 million.

AIR FILTRATION AND MARCONIL

Sabor Inc. for decades had sold air humidification and air filtration units along with its prime units in air heating and cooling. Until three years ago, air filtration had accounted for about 7 percent of total corporate sales and had been sold primarily as add-ons to a new air cooling/heating system. However, with the advent of marconil, air filtration had started to increase significantly as a percentage of total sales. Marconil, a new high-tech product developed as part of the U.S. space effort, had a range of unique properties of high interest to a variety of industries. In the case of air filtration, when processed by a Sabor Inc. developed and patented process, marconil could be transformed into a thin, very light, and extremely fine meshlike sponge material capable of filtering extremely small particles.

Given the population's sensitivity to air quality and the increasing number of people with asthma and allergies, the new Sabor filters became popular, not only with new Sabor air system installations but also as retrofits in older air conditioning and heating systems. Moreover, compared to electronic air cleaners that cost about three times as much to install and required monthly cleaning, marconil filters had to be replaced every six months, guaranteeing a continued sales volume of filters for years to come. When combined with an ultraviolet light unit, which killed airborne bacteria, a marconil air cleaning system was considered a huge leap forward in air treatment.

The manufacturing cost of a marconil filter accounted for about 28 percent of its selling price.

AIR FILTRATION SALES

Along with the marconil filtration system introduction three years ago, Sabor's marketing department had initiated a significant promotional campaign directed at both the industrial and consumer sectors. Marketing's ability to forecast sales accurately had not been impressive, according to Ray Soles. For the first year, marketing had forecast marconil filter sales at $1 million, when in reality they sold $11 million. In the second year, the forecast was for $15 million and actual sales were $29 million, and, in the third year, a forecast of $40 million turned into actual sales of $72 million. The marketing department expected sales growth to level off over the next three years to a rate of 20 percent per year.

MARCONIL SUPPLY

Sabor's first marconil supplier was Bilt Chemical, a longtime supplier of paints and adhesives to Sabor and a large, diversified, innovative chemical producer that held the patent on marconil. Ray Soles did not like the idea of single sourcing and, therefore, when marconil requirements rose significantly in the second year, he brought in a second supplier, Warton Inc., which not only produced the marconil raw materials (under license from Bilt Chemical), but also manufactured a variety of marconil products in the textile and automotive fields. In the third year, Ray had secured a third supplier, G. K. Specialties, a much smaller company than Bilt Chemical and Warton Inc., which also produced marconil under license for its own applications in aerospace and the military, but which had some excess capacity that it sold on the open market.

All three suppliers sold marconil at identical prices, which had increased over the past three years. Actual volumes purchased by Sabor Inc. from each of the three suppliers were as shown in Exhibit 1. The current price of marconil from all three suppliers was $50.00.

SUPPLIER PROPOSALS FOR LONG-TERM CONTRACTS

During the first two weeks of April, Ray Soles was visited by each of his current three marconil suppliers with Bilt Chemical first. Each warned that a shortage of marconil supply was looming and that unless Ray was willing to sign a long-term contract, they would not be in a position to guarantee supply. However, each proposal was different.

Bilt Chemical proposed a five-year contract with take-or-pay commitments of 25,000 pounds for the current year and 20 percent annual increases in volume for each of the following years. Prices were subject to escalation

EXHIBIT 1

Sabor Marconil Purchases and Prices

Company	Capacity (in pounds)	Purchases (in pounds)		
		Year 1	Year 2	Year 3
Bilt Chemical	80,000	5,000	10,000	20,000
Warton Inc.	40,000	0	3,000	8,000
G. K. Specialties	20,000	0		4,000
Prices		$39.00	$42.00	$44.00

for energy, raw material, and labor every quarter based on the current $50.00 price per pound.

Warton Inc. proposed a two-year contract for 10,000 pounds each year with similar price provisions to those of Bilt Chemical.

G. K. Specialties suggested an agreement for 12.5 percent of Sabor's annual requirements, which could be dropped at any time by either party, but which proposed a price of $56.00 for the current year, to be adjusted semiannually, thereafter based on inflation, energy, labor, and material.

Although Ray Soles did not know much about the actual manufacturing process for marconil, he had heard that increases in capacity were expensive. He also understood that two of the three component raw materials for marconil were by-products from industrial processes that were reasonably stable.

Since Ray Soles had been able to buy almost all of Sabor's needs on quarterly, semiannual, or annual contracts, he was not particularly keen on departing from his current supply practice. He had heard some rumors that in a few years a much lower-cost substitute for marconil might be developed. He suspected that, therefore, his current suppliers were anxious to tie Sabor to a long-term commitment.

APRIL 15

On April 15, the Bilt Chemical sales representative sent an e-mail to Ray Soles requesting a meeting on April 22. The e-mail concluded, "I would like to bring my sales manager so that we may discuss our proposal for the marconil with you. We will not be able to guarantee you supply after August 1, if you are unable to commit."

Case 2–3
Ford Motor Company: Aligned Business Framework[2]

Tony Brown, senior vice president of global sourcing at Ford Motor Company (Ford), was putting the finishing touches on his plan for the company's new supply chain strategy—"Aligned Business Framework" (ABF). ABF was a bold step that would significantly change the relationships between Ford and its suppliers. Tony described his motivation: "We want to operate a supply chain management system that delivers on the dimensions of quality, technology, delivery and cost, while executing programs in a disciplined fashion with faster time-to-market."[3]

It was August 10, 2005, and Tony was expected to review the final details of his proposal with company chairman and CEO William Clay (Bill) Ford Jr. before making a formal public announcement the following month. ABF would substantially reduce the number of suppliers and give those that remained long-term contracts and early involvement in new product development programs. Tony expected that the strategy would provide benefits to Ford through overall lower costs, while suppliers would benefit from

long-term financial stability and profitability. The question remained, however, how he would convince Ford's supplier community to commit to the principles of ABF.

FORD MOTOR COMPANY

Founded in 1903, Ford was the no. 2 U.S. automaker with global sales of approximately $177 billion. In 2005, its global brands included Ford, Lincoln, Mercury, Jaguar, Land Rover, Aston Martin, and Volvo.[4] In recent years all of the "Detroit 3" (General Motors, Ford, and Chrysler) automakers were struggling under intense global competition, rising fuel prices, and steep product discounts and rebates. In the most recent quarter, Ford reported a $1.1 billion operating loss and the company's debt had recently been downgraded to junk-bond status. To turn around company performance, Ford had announced plans to cut its salaried workforce, reduce capacity by closing plants and selling the Hertz rental car division, and ramp up production of hybrid vehicles.[5]

---

[2] This case has been written on the basis of published sources only. Consequently, the interpretation and perspectives presented in this case are not necessarily those of Ford Motor Company or any of its employees.

[3] Tom Stundza, "Ford Has a Better Idea," *Purchasing* 135, no. 12 (2006), p. 49.

[4] Ford Motor Company 2005 annual report.

[5] Jeffrey McCracken, "Ford Retools: Seeks Big Savings by Shaking Up Parts Supply System," *The Globe & Mail,* September 29, 2005, p. B19.

ALIGNED BUSINESS FRAMEWORK (ABF)

The Ford global supply chain included approximately 2,500 production and 9,000 nonproduction suppliers, with operations in more than 60 countries, supporting 107 Ford manufacturing sites. Total purchases in 2005 were more than $90 billion for roughly 250 production commodities (e.g., seats, heating and cooling systems, advanced electronics, and steering systems) and 500 nonproduction commodities (e.g., health care, software, logistics, and marketing and advertising services). The more than 130,000 active production parts accounted for approximately $70 billion of total annual purchases.[6]

Historically Ford leaned heavily on suppliers for annual across-the-board price reductions that averaged approximately 3 percent, although requests for more substantial reductions were commonplace. This environment had created contemptuous relationships between Ford and its suppliers, which were reinforced through annual performance evaluations and bonuses for buyers based on achieving year-over-year price reduction objectives. The foundation of the new ABF strategy was a cultural shift from confrontational to collaborative supplier relationships. Tony commented on his assessment of Ford's current supply chain strategy: "We have a problem with the business model in this industry. It is not working effectively for our suppliers. It is not working effectively for us. When my day is dominated by issues related to financially distressed suppliers, commodity price shocks, quality problems and costs issues, it's clear to me that there must be a better approach."[7]

ABF targeted companywide cost reductions of 10 percent of Ford's annual spend of production parts by 2010—$7 billion per year—by adopting what Tony considered best practices approach to supply chain management and supplier partnerships: "It's an environment between Ford and a select family of suppliers where innovative ideas can emerge, and then be incubated, evaluated and incorporated into our products."[8] Under the new system, preferred suppliers would be matched with Ford purchasing and engineering managers to work on projects to achieve quality, cost, and delivery goals. The 20 key elements of the ABF that Tony planned to propose are provided in Exhibit 1, which Brown described as "a kinder, gentler era of cooperation from global suppliers that can be implemented beyond North America."[9]

EXHIBIT 1   Key Elements of ABF[10]

Ford Commitments	Bilateral Commitments	Supplier Commitments
• Up-front reimbursement of supplier engineering, design, and testing • Long-term sourcing • Improved commonality and reuse • Improved product, cycle plan, and forecast volume stability • Sharing of forecast volumes and product plans (beyond 3 years) • More disciplined program execution through Ford Global Product Development system	• Achieve best-in-class quality • Data transparency • Agree on detailed cost models • Focus on total costs, included elimination of emphasis on bins • Competitive cost at Job no. 1, with less emphasis on year-over-year price reductions • Open collaboration on global manufacturing, engineering footprint • Ongoing senior leadership communication • Data exchange remains confidential	• Share current financial data to demonstrate health • Backstop other commodity suppliers • Manage and assure proper working conditions in their facilities and in the facilities of sub-tiers • Sourcing of minority- and women-owned suppliers • Use mutually agreeable multi-party agreement in directed tier 2 sourcing scenarios • Technological innovations will be provided to Ford

[6] www.ford.com/aboutford/microsites/sustainability-report-2006-07.

[7] Stundza, "Ford Has a Better Idea, p. 49.

[8] Ibid.

[9] Ibid.

[10] Presentation by Tony Brown, October 7, 2005, www.oesa.org/cmspages/getAttch.php?id=180.

Tony was proposing that in the first phase of the ABF implementation, his supply organization would focus on 20 high-impact commodity groups, such as seats, tires, and bumpers, where the automaker spent approximately $35 billion per year with 200 suppliers. The plan was to reduce the number of suppliers for these commodities to 100 by the 2009 model year. In the long term, Tony's objective was to shrink the production supply base from 2,500 to 1,000.[11]

FINALIZING THE PLAN

Tony recognized that there would be a great many questions from other Ford executives, members of his purchasing organization and suppliers regarding how ABF would be implemented. There were obviously going to be winners and losers from the existing Ford supplier community under ABF and many of Ford's existing suppliers would have to be told that they would not be participating in future programs. The preferred suppliers would have many questions regarding how their relationships would function with Ford in the future. For example, it was expected that suppliers would benefit from higher capacity utilization as a result of the increased production volumes. Furthermore, additional benefits were anticipated from greater collaboration, early supplier involvement in new product development, and supplier innovation. How would the associated costs and benefits be measured and shared among Ford and its suppliers?

Ford had a decades-long tradition of confrontational relationships with its supplier community. A recent survey of North American automotive tier 1 suppliers ranked Ford second to last with a score of 157 versus top-ranked Toyota at 415 and Honda at 375 (scale: 500 = very good, 0 = very poor).[12] Turning around relationships with suppliers could take years. Given the difficult times in the industry and at Ford, Tony knew that Bill Ford would have questions about supplier skepticism regarding the company's motivations behind ABF and how quickly the plan would start to show results.

Tony Brown believed that it was necessary to make major changes to Ford's supply chain if the company was going to survive. As he got ready for his meeting with Mr. Ford, Tony pondered how he should proceed with implementation, and specifically how suppliers could be convinced to buy into the principles of ABF. Tony commented on the challenges that ABF presented: "This is not business as usual. We're not only asking our suppliers to step up. We're also asking ourselves to step up."[13]

---

[11] Jeffrey McCracken, "Ford Retools: Seeks Big Savings by Shaking Up Parts Supply System," p. B19.

[12] John Henke, *Planning Perspectives,* Birmingham, Michigan, 2008.

[13] "Ford Key Suppliers Roll Out Innovative Business Model," Ford Motor Company press release, September 29, 2005, http://media.ford.com.newsroom/release.

Chapter Three

Supply Organization

Chapter Outline

Key Questions for the Supply Decision Maker

Should we

- Separate sourcing and commodity management responsibilities?
- Use cross-functional sourcing teams to make better supply decisions?
- Move towards greater centralization?

How can we

- Fit supply's organizational structure better with the structure of the corporate organizational structure?
- Gain the maximum benefits from our organizational structure?
- Structure and manage teams for effectiveness and efficiency?

Every organization in both the public and private sector is in varying degrees dependent on materials and services supplied by other organizations. No organization is self-sufficient. Even the smallest office needs space, heat, light, power, communication and office equipment, furniture, stationery, and miscellaneous supplies to carry on its activities. Purchasing and supply management is, therefore, one of the key business processes in every organization. Almost every company has a separate supply function as part of its organizational structure. One important management challenge is ensuring effective use of the resources and capabilities of the supply organization and the supply chain or network to maximize supply's contribution to organizational objectives.

Managing the balance between the competitive environment, corporate strategy, and organizational structure is an ongoing process for every company. Senior management selects strategies designed to address competitive challenges and adopts an appropriate corporate organizational structure to complement the company's strategy. The structure of supply has to be congruent with this organizationwide structure. The challenge for the chief purchasing officer (CPO) is to manage the supply organization to deliver the maximum benefits within the predefined structure. For example, a chief executive might decide that a decentralized organizational structure is appropriate in order to allow flexibility in responding to customer requirements. The supply organization also would be decentralized to the various business units to fit the corporate organizational model.

The organizational structure of the supply function influences how supply executes its responsibilities, how it works with other areas of the firm, and the skills and capabilities needed by supply personnel. Regardless of the structure adopted, work must be assigned to ensure the efficient and effective delivery of goods and services to the organization. This requires managing personnel and delegating responsibilities. Managing the people in the supply organization to their full potential is a significant challenge.

In this chapter, three questions are addressed: (1) What are the objectives of supply? (2) How might supply be organized to achieve these objectives effectively and efficiently? (3) What are the activities and responsibilities of supply management?

OBJECTIVES OF SUPPLY MANAGEMENT

The standard statement of the objectives of the supply function is that it should obtain the *right materials* (meeting quality requirements), in the *right quantity,* for delivery at the *right time* and *right place,* from the *right source* (a supplier who is reliable and will meet its commitments in a timely fashion), with the *right service* (both before and after the sale), and at the *right price* in the short and long term. The supply decision maker might be likened to a juggler, attempting to keep several balls in the air at the same time, for he or she must achieve these seven *rights* simultaneously.

It is not acceptable to buy at the lowest price if the goods delivered are unsatisfactory from a quality/performance standpoint, or if they arrive two weeks behind schedule. On the other hand, the *right* price may be higher than normal if the item in question is an emergency requirement where adherence to normal lead time would result in a higher total cost of ownership. The *right price* is one aspect of lowest total cost of ownership. The supply decision maker attempts to balance the often conflicting objectives and makes trade-offs to obtain the optimum mix of these seven rights. Obtaining this balance with an eye to both the short term and the long term requires supply managers to have both a tactical and strategic perspective.

A more encompassing statement of the overall goals of supply would include the following nine goals:

1. *Improve the organization's competitive position.* As a strategic player, the activities of supply management must be focused on contributing to overall organizational strategy, goals, and objectives. Supply managers must identify and exploit opportunities in the supply chain to contribute to revenue enhancement, asset management, and cost reduction. Supply can secure the lowest total cost source of supply, provide access to new technologies, and design flexible delivery arrangements, fast response times, access to high-quality products or services, and product design and engineering assistance.

Companies that are successful in the long run must constantly look for opportunities in the supply chain to provide a superior value proposition for their customers, and supply represents a key area for such opportunities. Strategic supply is concerned with the long-term survival and prosperity of the organization. It focuses on bottom-line impact, the income statement, and the balance sheet. Chapter 2 discusses the potential contributions of purchasing and supply management to the overall strategy of the organization and specific internal supply strategies for strengthening the organization's competitive position.

2. *Provide an uninterrupted flow of materials, supplies, and services required to operate the organization.* Stockouts or late deliveries of materials, components, and services can be extremely costly in terms of lost production, lower revenues and profits, and diminished customer goodwill. For example: (1) an automobile producer cannot complete the car without the purchased tires, (2) an airline cannot keep its planes flying on schedule without purchased fuel, (3) a hospital cannot perform surgery without purchased surgical tools, and (4) an office cannot be used without purchased maintenance services.

3. *Keep inventory investment and loss at a minimum.* One way to ensure an uninterrupted material flow is to hold large inventories. But inventory assets require use of capital that cannot be invested elsewhere, and the cost of carrying inventory may be

20 to 50 percent of its value per year. For example, if supply can support operations with an inventory investment of $10 million instead of $20 million, at an annual inventory carrying cost of 30 percent, the $10 million reduction in inventory represents a savings of $3 million in addition to freeing $10 million in working capital.

4. *Maintain and improve quality.* A certain quality level is required for each material or service input; otherwise the end product or service will not meet expectations or will result in higher-than-acceptable costs. The cost to correct a substandard quality input could be huge. For example, a spring assembled into the braking system of a diesel locomotive can cost less than $5.00. However, if the spring turns out to be defective when the locomotive is in service, the replacement cost is in thousands of dollars, caused by the teardown required to replace the spring, the lost revenue to the railroad because the locomotive is not in service, and the possible loss of locomotive reorders. Continuous improvement in supplier quality is directly linked to an organization's ability to compete effectively on a worldwide basis.

5. *Find or develop best-in-class suppliers.* The success of supply depends on its ability to link supply base decisions to organization strategy and its skill in locating or developing suppliers, analyzing supplier capabilities, selecting the appropriate supplier, and then working with that supplier to obtain continuous improvements. Only if the final selection results in suppliers who are both responsive and responsible will the firm obtain the items and services it needs.

6. *Standardize, where possible, the items bought and the processes used to procure them.* Standardization refers to the process of agreeing on a common specification or process. Specifications and processes may be standardized across an organization, an industry, a nation, or the world. Supply should constantly strive to standardize its capital equipment, materials, maintenance, repair, and operating (MRO) supplies, and services purchases wherever and whenever possible. For materials, standardization often leads to lower risk in the marketplace, lower prices through volume purchase agreements, and lower inventory and tracking costs while maintaining service levels. In the case of capital equipment, standardization results in reduction in MRO inventories and reduced costs for training staff on equipment operation and maintenance. In the case of services, standardization leads to supply base reduction, lower operating costs, more consistent service levels, and lower prices. Supply management process standardization also can result in shortened cycle time, lower transaction costs, and greater opportunities to share knowledge across functional and organizational boundaries. Because standardization touches on multiple stakeholders, it usually requires cross-functional and sometimes cross-organizational teamwork.

7. *Purchase required items and services at lowest total cost of ownership.* Purchased goods and services in the typical organization represent the largest share of that organization's total costs. Consequently, the profit-leverage effect discussed in Chapter 1 can be significant. Price is the most convenient method to compare competing proposals from suppliers. However, supply's responsibility is to obtain the needed goods and services at the lowest total cost of ownership, which necessitates consideration of other factors—such as quality levels, after-sales service, warranty costs, inventory and spare parts requirements, downtime, and so forth—that in the long term might have a greater cost impact on the organization than the original purchase price.

8. *Achieve harmonious, productive internal relationships.* Supply managers cannot effectively accomplish their goals and objectives without effective cooperation with the appropriate individuals in other functions. Therefore, it is useful to examine relationships between supply and key internal business partners:

Supply and design engineering. Close to 70 percent of the value of any given requirement is established during the first few phases of the standard acquisition process: recognition and description of need. Therefore, close cooperation between design engineering and supply to assure proper specifications is essential. The design must be driven by final customer requirements for value and satisfaction, and be designed for manufacturability and procurability. It is obvious that such close liaison also needs proper involvement of marketing, operations, and finance/accounting to recognize these opportunities and constraints. It is during the design phase that all of these varied interests need to be appropriately incorporated, something that is unlikely to happen unless the various functional experts can represent their points of view well and are able to work effectively as a team. Too frequently, the failure to include supply considerations properly at the design stages results in inadequate product or service performance, costly delays, rework, and end user dissatisfaction.

Supply and operations. In most organizations, close supply–operations coordination is essential to operational excellence. In manufacturing companies especially, the total task of integrated logistics, meeting end-customer demands on the one side and using the supply networks on the other, while managing material and information flow, equipment, people, and space effectively, represents an incredible challenge. Meeting quality, delivery, quantity, cost, flexibility, and continuity objectives profitably and competitively requires strategic as well as tactical skills of both operations and supply managers.

Supply and marketing/sales. Since supply and marketing are mirror images of each other, with negotiation and customer service in common, there are benefits from greater integration of the two functions. Although research indicates that supply is not typically included in marketing planning, supply and marketing often serve on new product development teams in organizations. Supply can offer information on current and future market conditions and negotiation expertise; and marketing can keep supply up to date on marketing campaigns, special promotions, and sales forecasts and involve supply in meetings with end customers to help supply better understand customer needs. In many organizations, there is an effort to use a strategic sourcing process for spend categories such as advertising and media. This effort requires close cooperation of supply and marketing.

Supply and accounting/finance. Supply and accounting/finance interact in the areas of accounts payable, planning, and budgeting. Lack of horizontal goal alignment often leads to behavior in one area that conflicts with behavior in the other area. For example, finance/accounting may adopt a payment policy that is at odds with the payment terms of the contract. From the finance perspective, holding onto cash as long as possible is a good way to contribute to the organization's financial goals. From the supply perspective, building sound, mutually beneficial relationships with key suppliers contributes to financial performance. Supply managers often argue that accounting focuses too much on short-term gains from holding cash rather than the longer-term benefits of a strong buyer–supplier relationship that is influenced by paying according to contractual payment terms. Improved communication between supply and accounting/finance and greater goal congruence can help to alleviate some of the problems. Supply can help finance by providing funds flow forecasts, focusing on inventory minimization, and providing market information.

9. *Accomplish supply objectives at the lowest possible operating costs.* It takes resources to operate supply: salaries, communications expense, supplies, travel costs, computer costs, and accompanying overhead. The objectives of supply should be achieved as efficiently and economically as possible. Process inefficiencies represent waste and lead to excessive operating costs and unnecessarily high total cost of ownership. Supply managers should be continually alert to improvements possible in purchasing and supply processes, methods, procedures, and techniques. For example, opportunities to reduce transaction costs include e-procurement systems that automate the process from requisition to payment and purchasing cards and e-catalogs for small-value purchases. Companies with efficient supply processes can create competitive advantage through reduced costs, improved flexibility, faster time to market, and greater compliance, while allowing supply personnel to concentrate on value-added activities.

The objectives of supply must ultimately contribute to the attainment of short- and long-term organizational strategy, goals, and objectives. The process and function can be organized in a number of different ways to maximize supply's contribution effectively and efficiently.

ORGANIZATIONAL STRUCTURES FOR SUPPLY MANAGEMENT

Ultimately the supply organization structure must be aligned with the corporate structure and strategy. In addition, organizational size and the need for specialization with supply also need to be taken into account.

Small and Medium-Sized Organizations

In practice it has been proven that assigning the supply function to supply professionals, properly trained and charged with the appropriate responsibilities and authorities, contributes more efficiently and effectively to organizational goals and strategies than assigning supply responsibilities to those for whom supply is a secondary responsibility. Nevertheless, in single business unit organizations, particularly small enterprises, it is not unusual to see supply responsibilities shared by a variety of individuals who have no supply expertise and purchase their own requirements from local retailers or wholesalers. As the size of the business unit increases, the idea of assigning a professional the responsibility of supply emerges and a separate function is created.

The size and activities of the supply function in a single business unit organization will depend on a number of factors, such as the size of the company and the nature of its business. Figure 3–1 provides an example of a supply organization in a typical medium-sized,

FIGURE 3–1

Example of a Typical Supply Organization in a Single-Location, Medium-Sized Company

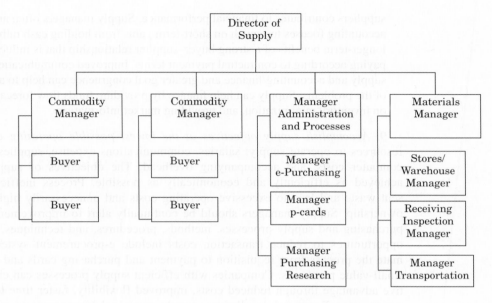

single business unit enterprise. Obviously in small companies where the supply staff consists of only one or two individuals, the staff is expected to be flexible in terms of their capabilities and skills. Specialization will occur as the organization gets larger and the company can afford to hire additional supply personnel.

Large Organizations

In large companies the centralization–decentralization issue is of key importance for the supply structure. The overall corporate structure sets the framework for the supply structure. Structural options can be viewed as a continuum ranging from centralized at one extreme to decentralized at the other. Centralization refers to where spending decisions are made, not where the purchasing and supply staff are located geographically. Therefore, the degree of centralization is reflected by the amount of spend managed or controlled by corporate supply. Three common organizational models are:

1. Centralized, where the authority and responsibility for most supply-related functions are assigned to a central organization.
2. Hybrid, where authority and responsibility are shared between a central supply organization and business units, divisions, or operating plants. Hybrid structures may lean more heavily toward centralized or decentralized depending on how decision-making authority is divided. One type of hybrid supply structure is a "center-led" organization in which strategic direction is centralized and execution is decentralized.
3. Decentralized, where the authority and responsibility for supply-related functions are dispersed throughout the organization.

CAPS Research conducts a wide range of benchmarking reports that can be accessed through their website. The benchmark reports include a breakdown of supply staff at the operational and strategic levels in the participating organizations.

Centralized and Decentralized Supply Structures

There are advantages and disadvantages to centralization and to decentralization. Table 3–1 summarizes the advantages and disadvantages of a centralized supply structure and Table 3–2 summarizes the advantages and disadvantages of a decentralized supply structure.[1]

Hybrid Supply Structure

In an organization with multiple business units, divisions or business units often sell different products or services requiring a different mix of purchased items. Often the division or business unit is operated as a profit center where the division manager is given total responsibility for running the division, acts as president of an independent firm, and is judged by profits made by the division. Since purchases are frequently the largest single controllable cost of running most businesses and have a direct effect on its efficiency and competitive position, the profit-center manager may insist on having direct authority over supply. This has led firms to adopt decentralized–centralized supply, or a hybrid organizational structure, in which the supply function is partially centralized at the corporate or head office and partially decentralized to the business units.

Often the corporate supply organization works with the business unit supply departments in those tasks that are more effectively handled on a corporate basis: (1) establishment

TABLE 3–1 Potential Advantages and Disadvantages of Centralization	Advantages	Disadvantages
	• Strategic focus	• Lack of business unit focus
	• Greater buying specialization	• Narrow specialization and job boredom
		• Cost of central unit highly visible
	• Ability to pay for talent	• Corporate staff appears excessive
	• Consolidation of requirements—*clout*	• Tendency to minimize legitimate differences in requirements
	• Coordination and control of policies and procedures	• Lack of recognition of unique business unit needs
	• Effective planning and research	• Focus on corporate requirements, not on business unit strategic requirements
		• Most knowledge sharing one-way
	• Common suppliers	• Even common suppliers behave differently in geographic and market segments
	• Proximity to major organizational decision makers	• Distance from users
	• Critical mass	• Tendency to create organizational silos
	• Firm brand recognition and stature	• Customer segments require adaptability to unique situations
	• Reporting line—*power*	• Top management not able to spend time on suppliers
	• Cost of purchasing low	• High visibility of purchasing operating costs

[1] M. R. Leenders and P. F. Johnson, *Major Structural Changes in Supply Organizations* (Tempe, AZ: CAPS Research, 2000).

TABLE 3–2

Potential Advantages and Disadvantages of Decentralization

Advantages	Disadvantages
• Easier coordination/communication with operating department • Speed of response • Effective use of local sources	• More difficult to communicate among business units • Encourages users not to plan ahead • Operational versus strategic focus • Too much focus on local sources—ignores better supply opportunities • No critical mass in organization for visibility/effectiveness—"whole person syndrome" • Lacks clout
• Business unit autonomy	• Suboptimization • Business unit preferences not congruent with corporate preferences • Small differences get magnified
• Reporting line simplicity • Undivided authority and responsibility	• Reporting at low level in organization • Limits functional advancement opportunities
• Suits purchasing personnel preference • Broad job definition • Geographical, cultural, political, environmental, social, language, currency appropriateness • Hide the cost of supply	• Ignores larger organization considerations • Limited expertise for requirements • Lack of standardization • Cost of supply relatively high

of policies, procedures, controls, and systems; (2) recruiting and training of personnel; (3) coordination of the purchase of common-use items in which more "clout" is needed; (4) auditing of supply performance; and (5) development of corporatewide supply strategies. Therefore, hybrid organizational structures attempt to capture the benefits of both centralized and decentralized structures by creating an organizational structure that is neither completely centralized nor decentralized. (See Figure 3–2.)

Structure affects processes, procedures, systems, and relationships. Whether supply is centralized, decentralized, or a hybrid, supply personnel must focus on maximizing the advantages of the structure and minimizing the disadvantages. Supply managers can develop and implement strategies to overcome the obstacles and fully exploit the opportunities of organizational and supply structure.

Specialization within the Supply Function

If the supply organization is to contribute well to organizational goals and objectives, it needs to be staffed by professionals with clearly defined responsibilities. Specialization within the supply department allows staff to develop expertise in particular areas and may require the creation of specialized groups within the supply organizational structure. Most large supply organizations consist of four general areas of specialization: sourcing and commodity management, materials management, administration, and supply research.

FIGURE 3–2
Potential
Advantages
of the Hybrid
Structure

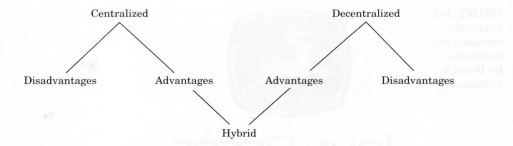

Sourcing and Commodity Management

These personnel develop commodity strategies, identify potential suppliers, analyze supplier capabilities, select suppliers, and determine prices, terms, and conditions of supplier agreements; they create contracts and purchase orders. This activity is normally further specialized by type of commodity to be purchased, such as raw materials (which may be further specialized); fuels; capital equipment; office equipment and supplies; and MRO. Figure 3–3 presents a job description for a commodity specialist at Deere & Company.

A variation of commodity management is project buying, in which the specialization of buying and negotiation is based on specific end products or projects, requiring the buyer to be intimately familiar with all aspects of the project from beginning to end. Project buying might be used in the supply organization of a large general contractor, where the purchasing for each job is part of a self-contained, temporary organization. At the completion of the project, the buyer then would be reassigned to another project. The United States Defense Acquisition University trains special project managers who are responsible for the proper acquisition and development of new military equipment initiatives. Such projects may last as long as 20 years.

Materials Management

This group manages the contract after it is signed, directs the flow of materials and services from the supplier, and keeps track of the supplier's delivery and quality commitments to avoid any disruptive surprises. If problems develop, the materials management group pressures and assists the supplier to resolve them. Materials management activities are frequently handled at the local plant or office level and involve regular communication with suppliers concerning requirements, such as order quantities and delivery dates. Figure 3–4 presents a job description for a supply management planner.

Administration

This group handles the physical preparation and routing of the formal purchase documents, manages the department budget, keeps the necessary data required to operate the department, and prepares reports needed by top management and supply. These personnel will likely manage operation of information systems, including e-procurement systems, B2B e-commerce, and electronic data interchange (EDI).

FIGURE 3–3
Commodity
Specialist Job
Description
for Deere &
Company

JOHN DEERE

Job Title:	Commodity Specialist
Department:	Supply Management
Job Function:	Locate sources for and procure materials, products, supplies or services to support the assigned commodity requirements of the enterprise. Manage the relationships with suppliers.

Primary Duties:

1. Manage source selection and development through a team process including the evaluation of cost, quality, and manufacturing systems.
2. Develop and manage internal and external supplier/customer relationships, including strategic alliances where appropriate.
3. Lead and/or participate on simultaneous engineering teams; facilitate the integration of suppliers into the product delivery process (PDP).
4. Evaluate the cost-effectiveness of designs, procure tooling, and qualify processes to assure the product meets specifications.
5. Make recommendations for design change and/or influence design through personal or supplier involvement.
6. Develop and execute supply management strategies to manage cost, quality, and continuous improvement.
7. Develop material control and logistics objectives.
8. Act as a primary communications link between tactical and strategic purchasing functions and business units; participate in team activities.

Supply Research

Supply researchers work on special projects relating to the collection, classification, and analysis of data needed to make better purchasing decisions. Activities include studies on use of alternate materials, long-range demand, price and supply forecasts, and analysis of what it should cost an efficient supplier to produce and deliver a product or service.

This group is also responsible for performing benchmarking studies. Johnson Controls, a global automotive supplier, uses its "materials best business practice" process to benchmark purchases at the commodity level. Cross-functional teams, made up of staff from supply, engineering, and finance, evaluate commodities and work with suppliers to eliminate or reduce gaps in performance requirements.[2]

[2] M. Siegfried, "Fundamental Best-In-Class Values," *Inside Supply Management* 19, no. 7, (2008) p. 30.

FIGURE 3–4
Supply
Management
Planner Job
Description
for Deere &
Company

JOHN DEERE

Job Title: Supply Management Planner
Department: Supply Management
Job Function: To expedite, schedule, and/or analyze requirements for purchased
                    materials in accordance with established requirements and inventory
                    control criteria. May interact with suppliers to establish procedural
                    agreements, obtain delivery commitments, and resolve quality problems.

Primary Duties:

1. Manages specific supplier performance and feedback along with managing day-to-day
   business plan and relationships with supplier.
2. Plans and/or executes inventory goals by product/supplier and plans/develops delivery
   system to meet material control objectives (i.e., JIT delivery, P.O.U.D., EDI).
3. Schedules material based on requirements and expedites deliveries that are delinquent
   or expected to be delinquent. Tracks and resolves problems with inbound shipments.
4. Interprets systems output to determine items requiring follow-up to suppliers on
   materials ordered to assure on-time delivery.
5. Is involved with the day-to-day problem resolution/corrective action with suppliers: to
   scrap, return, reclaim, or replace rejected material. Is responsible for bringing products
   within specifications.
6. Acts as the primary communications link between tactical and strategic purchasing
   functions and business unit; participates in supply management team activities.
7. Costs and implements current part revisions, including tooling, as part of the decision
   processing activity. Also reads and reacts to engineering decisions.
8. Conducts price/economic order quantity analysis and compares multiple quotes,
   including piece price, freight, duty, performance systems, and supplier rating. Also
   investigates invoice price errors.

Structure for Direct and Indirect Spend

Direct spend includes any goods that go into the end product or service; indirect spend is
comprised of the goods and services that are needed to run the organization. Indirect spend
includes purchases such as professional services, utilities, travel, employee benefits, and
office supplies. In many organizations, the locus of control over direct spend is in a highly
centralized supply group. This makes sense because anything that ultimately touches the
final customer is worthy of expertise.

Indirect spend, on the other hand, is often outside the loop of a structured sourcing process and supply authority and responsibility is often left in the hands of the internal user. For

example, a marketing manager needing to hire temporary labor would conduct the purchasing process in his or her own way. This highly decentralized approach leads to a fragmented spend for temporary labor, including multiple suppliers, multiple rates, and varying contract terms and conditions. This is partly due to the belief that these types of purchases require a level of knowledge and expertise not found in a typical supply department.

The increasing focus on strategic cost management has led many senior managers to turn their attention to indirect spend to realize cost savings, reductions, or avoidances. To better manage indirect spend, some organizations will pull indirect spend categories into the purchasing process. Others expect supply managers to convince internal users that there is value in following a structured sourcing process. In some cases, supply provides analysis and recommendations, but the budget owner makes the purchasing decision. Cross-functional teams consisting of internal users (often across business units) and buyers or commodity managers may be given responsibility for the category. Sourcing, evaluating, and selecting suppliers for indirect spend will be discussed in greater detail in Chapter 12. Any purchase dollars that are not managed through a structured sourcing process may represent a target for cost savings, reduction, or avoidance.

Managing Organizational Change in Supply

Firms frequently make major changes to their supply organizational structure. A CAPS Research focus study was conducted, in part, to answer two questions: (1) Why are there so many structural changes in supply organizations at large companies? (2) If the hybrid organizational structure is theoretically so attractive, then why do so many large firms not use this structure and/or move out of it?[3] First, the researchers found that organizational structure change was the result of a change in the overall corporate organizational structure. In none of the situations did the chief purchasing officer (CPO) have free choice to select the supply organizational structure that he or she deemed appropriate for the circumstances. Rather, the supply organizational structure was forced to be congruent with the overall corporate structure. The challenge for supply executives, therefore, was to maximize the benefits of the organizational structure while minimizing the disadvantages.

Secondly, there are a number of implementation issues to consider when making a major organizational structure change in supply. Major changes affect the lives of many people and create an atmosphere of apprehension among the staff. Implementing change places significant pressures on the CPO, who not only has to worry about managing the day-to-day affairs of the supply department, but also has to successfully implement the organizational change. The challenges associated with these issues frequently contribute to the need to seek assistance from consultants when implementing a major structural change.

The Lambert-Martin Automotive Systems Inc. case at the end of this chapter describes a large automotive parts company with a decentralized supply function. The recent appointment of a new CEO has resulted in questions being asked about whether the company should rethink its organizational structure and centralize some supply activities.

Changes toward Centralization

Two major concerns facing organizations when they move the supply function towards greater centralization are sources of supply talent and the availability of information related to the total corporate spend. During the transition, the source of supply talent at all levels

---

[3] Leenders and Johnson, *Major Structural Changes in Supply Organizations.*

of the supply function is a significant challenge. Experienced senior corporate-level supply personnel may not exist in-house. How and where to develop such organizational talent represented an important implementation issue. Some firms place a greater priority on CPO credibility within the organization, as opposed to previous supply experience. Others identify new CPOs with previous supply experience to handle the change process. At the middle and junior levels, additional staff with specialized skills in areas such as contracting is required. Quite often, the existing supply talent in the decentralized organization is perceived to lack the required training or experience needed in the new centralized environment.

Changes toward Decentralization

The CAPS Research focus study identified one implementation issue unique to the sites in the study moving toward decentralization: how to dismantle the centralized supply unit effectively. For example, Ontario Hydro created a shared services function that was responsible for negotiating corporatewide agreements and establishing and maintaining corporate purchasing policies, while the business units were responsible for materials management activities. The approach taken by Hoechst was to create a separate legal entity, Hoechst Procurement International, which would also offer purchasing services to other companies on a fee-for-service basis. The key objective in both situations was to preserve at least some of the organization's core supply capabilities and talent, while adapting to the new structural requirements of the company.

ORGANIZING THE SUPPLY GROUP

Once the corporate organizational structure is set, no matter what organizational design is chosen, delegation takes place within it. Whether the organization structure is based on functions, products, or business processes is immaterial; what really matters is that work must be assigned and executed in accordance with strategic plans and organizational goals. It follows logically that organizational planning and delegation are important segments of the integration of strategic goals and organizational designs.

The following sections describe the key aspects of supply organizational design, including the role of the chief purchasing officer, supply's status in the organization, and its reporting relationship and internal relationships. Even though the focus is on large supply organizations, many of the comments are also relevant for smaller supply organizations.

The Chief Purchasing Officer (CPO)

The chief purchasing officer (CPO) or chief supply officer (CSO) is defined as the "most senior" or "top level" executive in a "firm's corporate (executive level) office *or* major division, such as a strategic business unit (SBU), who has formal authority and responsibility to manage his or her firm's (or SBU's) purchasing, buying or sourcing functions for the procurement of goods and services from external suppliers."[4] The CPO's responsibilities may be divided and apportioned among managers and departments, but the functional responsibility and authority of the CPO should be definitely recognized. Moreover, functionalization implies that all the responsibilities reasonably involved in the supply function

[4] T. E. Hendrick and J. Ni, *Chief Purchasing Officers' Mobility, Compensation Benchmarks, and Demographics: A Study of Fortune 500 Firms* (Tempe, AZ: CAPS Research, 2007).

must be given to the CPO, covering the relevant supply network links as well as the full range of organizational needs. The essential principle is that there are certain universally recognized duties pertinent to this function and that these duties should be placed in a separate group equal in status with the other major functions of the organization.

Changes in the supply management field have affected everything from what the function is called to the titles of the people performing the tasks to the tasks that are performed. There is no common title for the individual who holds the top supply position in a large organization in North America. Depending on the role of supply in the organization, the reporting line, and where it is placed on the organization chart, the title may be chief purchasing officer, vice president, director, or manager. Attached to that may be purchasing, procurement, supply management, sourcing, strategic sourcing, logistics, or supply chain management. It is quite common to see CPO titles such as vice president, strategic sourcing and supply; vice president, purchasing; vice president, supply chain management; or director, global procurement. The titles in the cases used in this text provide a good range of titles in current use.

Profile of the CPO

The following profile of the average CPO emerged from a recent CAPS Research focus study.[5] The average CPO is a well-educated 51-year-old who has been at his or her organization for 14 years and CPO for 4.6 years, compared to 5.9 years in 1995. While most CPOs have previous experience in supply, approximately 80 percent of the CPOs in the study had worked in at least one other function. Approximately 70 percent of CPOs had the title of vice president and the title most likely included the word *procurement, purchasing, supply chain,* or *supply management* in it, such as vice president, global procurement or vice president of supply chain management.

Typically there are one to two levels between the CPO and the CEO. The most common CPO reporting lines were senior vice president/group VP (22 percent), executive vice president (17 percent), vice president of finance/CFO (17 percent), and president/CEO (13 percent). Seventy-seven percent of the CPOs in the CAPS study reported to one of the top five executive position categories (president/CEO, COO, executive vice president, senior vice president/group vice president, and CFO/vice president of finance).

The CPO may have overall management responsibility for nontraditional purchases such as corporate travel, food services, real estate, IT hardware and software, printing, and benefits. Additionally, the CPO might have responsibility for logistics (which includes inbound and outbound transportation, fleet management, warehousing, materials handling, order fulfillment, inventory management, supply/demand planning, and management of third-party logistics providers), quality, accounts payable, document/contract management, leadership of the supply process, materials, distribution, and facility management.

CPO Trends

Several trends have emerged in the past decade regarding the profile and role of the CPO:[6]

- Education levels are increasing. Almost all CPOs hold a bachelor's degree; about half, a graduate degree, typically an MBA.

[5] P. F. Johnson and M. R. Leenders, *Supply's Organizational Roles and Responsibilities* (Tempe, AZ: CAPS Research, May 2012).

[6] P. F. Johnson, and M. R. Leenders, *Supply Leadership Changes* (Tempe, AZ: CAPS Research, 2007).

- Reporting lines are changing. CPOs tend to report higher in the organization than they did in the 1980s and 1990s.
- CPOs are increasingly being hired from outside the organization rather than promoted from within. CPO tenure with their organization declined to 14 years in 2011, from 18 years in 1995, and more than one-third of CPOs are hired into the position from another firm.
- CPOs are increasingly being hired from functional areas other than supply. This was the case in approximately 40 percent of the CPOs in the CAPS Research study.
- When a new CPO replaces a current CPO, the current CPO is promoted or leaves the company for a similar position in another firm.
- CPO reporting lines change every 2.5 years on average, which means that the typical CPO will have at least two different bosses during his or her tenure in the role.
- The CPO role is still new in many organizations.

Reporting Relationship

The executive to whom the CPO reports gives a good indication of the status of supply and the degree to which it is emphasized within the organization. If the chief purchasing officer has the title of vice president and reports to the CEO, this indicates that supply has been recognized as a top management function. Reporting to the CEO, however, is not essential. CEOs in large organizations have a broad portfolio of responsibilities, ranging from shareholder relations to corporate strategy. Reporting to one of the other top five senior executives (executive vice president, senior vice president/group vice president, and CFO/vice president of finance) in the firm can provide supply the organizational clout and exposure needed to play a significant role. These individuals may have more time and interest in the supply chain issues facing the organization. If supply reports to an executive too low in the organization, the less influence supply is likely to have on corporate strategy.

When supply is not given the same status as other functions, it must be placed under another senior functional executive. In many cases, supply reports to the chief financial officer because of the immediate impact of supply decisions on cash flows, the size of the annual spend, and the amount of money tied up in inventory. Organizational focus on strategic cost management also supports the decision to place supply under finance. In organizations where a high percentage of annual spend is for production requirements, supply often reports to the top manufacturing executive. In a shared services model, supply along with legal, accounting, human resources, and other functions might report to an administrative vice president. In a heavily engineering-oriented firm, the reporting relationship might be to the chief of engineering to get closer communication and coordination on product specification and quality control.

Factors that influence the level at which the supply function is placed in the organizational structure cover a broad spectrum. Among the major ones are:

1. The amount of purchased material and outside services costs as a percentage of either total costs or total income of the organization. A high ratio emphasizes the importance of effective performance of the supply function.
2. The nature of the products or services acquired. The acquisition of complex components or extensive use of subcontracting represents a difficult supply problem.
3. The extent to which supply and suppliers can provide competitive advantage.

The important consideration in determining to whom supply should report relates to where it will be most effective in realizing its contribution to the organization's objectives. Supply should report at a level high enough in the organization so that the key supply aspects of strategic managerial decisions will receive proper consideration.

SUPPLY ACTIVITIES AND RESPONSIBILITIES

Supply management can be described as a series of activities that must be managed effectively for the organization to deliver best value to the final customer. Roles and responsibilities of supply fall into four general categories: (1) what is acquired, (2) supply chain activities, (3) type of involvement in categories 1 and 2, and (4) involvement in corporate activities.[7]

What Is Acquired

The items acquired by the supply group vary from organization to organization and items are added or deleted depending on circumstances in the buying organization. The acquisition segments include raw materials, standard and special direct purchases, MRO, capital, services, and resale. Nontraditional purchases are spend categories that have typically been managed outside of the purchasing and supply management process. In some organizations, purchasing activities are limited to production-related materials and services, leaving responsibility for nonproduction or indirect materials and services in the hands of users.

The amount of annual spend that falls outside the management or control of supply ranges from a low of about 2 percent to a high of about 40 percent. This often includes large amounts for capital equipment, utilities, insurance, computers and software, travel, real estate, and construction services. Senior management in many organizations has recognized the significant opportunities from applying the skills of their supply group and the benefits of a structured sourcing process in the acquisition of nontraditional materials and services.

The Iowa Elevators case demonstrates the opportunities for supply to capture cost reductions in a large service organization. Exhibit 2 in the case provides a list of spend categories that include direct (e.g., farm supplies) and indirect (e.g., travel) purchases.

Supply Chain Activities

Supply has assumed greater responsibilities in a wide range of areas, including those not seen as traditional, as companies strive to leverage profit opportunities and create competitive advantage through their supply practices. Today's supply management organization has more responsibilities than the traditional "buying" activities once associated with the function. The activities handled by the supply function vary from firm to firm, even within the same industry. However, regardless of company size, there are a number of activities common to most supply organizations (see Table 3–3).

The addition or deletion of activities in any organization can be categorized as internally or externally focused. Internally focused activities include accounts payable, centralized coordination of purchasing, cost management, legal, materials management and logistics,

---

[7] M. R. Leenders and P. F. Johnson, *Major Changes in Supply Chain Responsibilities* (Tempe, AZ: CAPS Research, 2002).

TABLE 3–3
Supply
Activities

Area of Responsibility	Activities
Purchasing/buying	• Creating contracts and supply agreements for materials, services, and capital items • Managing key purchasing processes related to supplier selection, supplier evaluation, negotiation, and contract management
Purchasing research	• Identifying better techniques and approaches to supply management, including benchmarking processes and systems • Identifying medium- and long-term changes in markets and developing appropriate commodity strategies to meet future needs • Identifying supply chain trends and opportunities for better materials and services
Inventory control	• Managing inventories and expediting material delivery • Establishing and monitoring vendor-managed inventory systems
Transportation	• Managing inbound and outbound transportation services, including carrier selection
Environmental and investment recovery/disposal	• Managing supply chain–related activities to assure compliance with legal and regulatory requirements and with company environmental policies • Managing disposal of surplus materials and equipment
Forecasting and planning	• Planning production and forecasting short-, medium-, and long-term requirements
Outsourcing and subcontracting	• Evaluating potential suppliers and negotiating contracts • Supporting the transition from internal production to external supply and vice versa
Nonproduction/nontraditional purchases	• Managing cost-effective delivery of nonproduction and nontraditional purchases, such as office supplies, security services, janitorial services, advertising, and insurance
Supply chain management	• Implementing and managing key supplier relationships and supplier partnerships, including supplier development and participation on cross-functional and cross-organizational teams • Developing strategies that use the supply network to provide value to end customers and contribute to organizational goals

production planning, quality, and supply budget and financial management. Externally focused activities may have either a supplier focus or a customer focus. Supplier-focused activities include inbound logistics, supplier development, raw material procurement for suppliers, supplier evaluation and communication, e-procurement, and outsourcing or subcontracting. Customer-focused activities include outbound logistics, involvement with new business development and new product development, and programs and customer bid support.

Type of Involvement

Supply can have no involvement, documentary, professional, or meaningful involvement in what is acquired and in supply chain activities. No involvement means supply is excluded completely. Documentary involvement requires the supply function to act as a recorder, a sender of purchase orders, or a receiver of bids, but important supply decisions are made outside supply. Professional involvement implies that supply professionals have the opportunity to exercise their expertise in important acquisition process stages. Meaningful involvement means that parties outside the supply group are willing and able to take supply considerations into account in managing their own areas of responsibility. They routinely and actively request input and assistance from supply personnel and, in turn, also are involved in supply decisions traditionally considered the prerogative of supply. One measure of meaningful involvement is the extent to which supply is expected to take part in major corporate activities.

Involvement in Corporate Activities

Major strategic corporate initiatives include mergers and acquisitions, new facility planning, new product development, outsourcing, revenue enhancement, technology planning, corporate e-commerce initiative, and corporate cost reduction initiative.

Influence of the Industry Sector on Supply Activities

The industry sector influences supply responsibilities. Firms that manufacture discrete goods such as cars, consumer electronics, apparel, and furniture face a significant number of dynamic, product-related pressures that affect the supply function and that are less likely to occur in commodity-oriented process industries. These pressures include changing consumer preferences, product innovation, and relatively short product life cycles.

Purchased materials and services also represent a high percentage of the cost of sales for firms in discrete goods industries. For example, purchased materials and services can represent 60 to 80 percent of the average cost of an automobile. Consequently, firms in discrete goods industries are likely to have supply departments that play a key role in each step in the materials cycle, from product design to production.

The role of supply in process industry firms, such as oil and gas, chemicals, glass, and steel industries, is typically different compared to firms in discrete goods industries. Many process industry firms have two supply organizations: a specialized supply group, such as a commodity trading department, that frequently handles purchasing for important raw materials and a purchasing group responsible for the acquisition of materials, supplies, and services that support the operation of facilities. For example, it is common practice for crude oil acquisition in most large integrated oil companies to be handled by a commodity trading group, while other purchases are handled by the supply organization. As a result, although the cost of purchased materials and services might represent a substantial portion of the total cost of sales, the supply function for firms within processing industries is frequently excluded from the acquisition of the single most important raw material.

In the public not-for-profit sector and service sectors, most purchases are for end use within the organization itself, with the exception of purchases for resale, such as in distribution and retail. In fast-growing organizations, capital purchases may represent a large percentage of total acquisition expenditures.

SUPPLY TEAMS

Corporate organization structures are leaner, flatter, more adaptive, and more flexible than in the past. Rigid functional structures have been replaced by a greater dependence on cross-functional teams that overlay the functional organization to push decisions lower in the organizational hierarchy. Teams bring together a number of people, often from different functional areas, to work on a common task. It is believed that teams provide superior results compared to individual efforts as a result of the range of skills, knowledge, and capabilities of team members. They also promote cross-functional cooperation and communication and may facilitate consensus building in the organization.

Teams are used by a number of functions for a variety of purposes, such as improvements in quality, cost, or delivery; product development; process engineering; and technology management. They can be project oriented or ongoing. Project teams are brought together for a limited time to achieve a specific goal or outcome, such as completion of a capital project or an e-commerce initiative. Ongoing teams continue indefinitely, such as a commodity-sourcing team that manages the purchasing process and supplier relationships.

Leading and Managing Teams

Changing to a team-based workplace requires a significant level of commitment and training of management and individual team members. Critical success factors include:

- Supportive organizational culture, structure, and systems.
- A common compelling purpose, measurable goals, and feedback for individuals and the team.
- Organized for customer satisfaction rather than individual functional success.
- All functional areas involved in up-front planning, shared leadership roles, and role flexibility.
- The right people (right qualifications), in the right place (on a team that needed their skills), at the right time (when those skills were needed).
- A common, agreed-upon work approach and investment in a high level of communication.
- Dedication to performance and implementation with decisions delegated to the appropriate level.
- Integration of all relevant functional areas and various teams throughout the project life cycle.

Senior management often tries to combine the flexibility of decentralized supply management and the buying power and information sharing of centralized supply through the use of teams. Various types of purchasing and supply management teams may be used, including cross-functional teams, teams with suppliers, teams with customers, teams with both suppliers and customers, supplier councils (key suppliers), purchasing councils (purchasing personnel only), commodity management teams (purchasing personnel only), and consortia (pool buying with other firms).

Cross-Functional Supply Teams

Cross-functional teams consist of personnel from multiple functions focused on a supply-related task. It is generally believed that high-performing, cross-functional teams will get better results on the task, with greater benefit to the organization as a whole, at lower costs, in less time, with greater stakeholder buy-in. Effective cross-functional teams save time by allowing a simultaneous, rather than a sequential, approach. For example, if key stakeholder groups are involved in the development of a new process from concept through design, development, and rollout, the process may be better to start with, more widely accepted, and adopted quickly. The cycle time may be less than the nonteam approach but more of the work is concentrated at the beginning of the process.

Three important cross-functional supply teams are sourcing, new product development, and commodity management.

Sourcing Teams

A cross-functional sourcing team includes supply and representatives from other relevant functional areas. The team can focus on a wide range of projects including developing cost-reduction strategies; developing local, business unit, or organizationwide sourcing strategies; evaluating and selecting suppliers; performing value analysis; analyzing spend; and identifying consolidation opportunities.

For example, to foster internal strategic business alignment, the CPO at General Mills created a position called director of sourcing operations (DSO). The prime focus of the DSO was to work with cross-functional business unit teams comprised of marketing, R&D, manufacturing, distribution, and accounting on important strategic initiatives. The DSO brought a sourcing perspective and provided a leadership role and alignment between sourcing strategies and business unit strategies. Specific initiatives were proposed as part of the annual business plan and DSO performance was evaluated considering team results.[8]

New Product/Service Development Teams

Effective new product or service development processes can improve an organization's competitive position. Cross-functional teams can shorten development cycle times, improve quality, and reduce development costs by operating concurrently rather than sequentially. Rather than each functional area performing its task and passing the project off to the next functional area, the key functional groups—usually design, engineering, manufacturing, quality assurance, purchasing, and marketing—work on the new product development simultaneously. Because a large percentage of a product's cost is purchased materials, early supplier involvement is often needed. When surveyed, many supply managers report greater involvement in new product/service design and development.

Commodity Management Teams

Commodity management teams are formed when expenditures are high and the commodity is complex and important to success. These are generally permanent teams that provide increased expertise, more cross-functional coordination and communication, better control over standardization programs, and increased communication with suppliers. They develop and implement commodity strategies aimed at achieving the lowest total cost of ownership. They engage in a number of activities, including supply base reduction, consolidation of requirements, supplier quality certification, management of deliveries and lead times, cost savings projects, and management of supplier relationships.

The Delphi Corporation case in Chapter 13 describes how the company used approximately 30 commodity teams, across four categories—chemical, electrical, metallic, and technological—to manage approximately 80 percent of its spend.

---

[8] Johnson and Leenders, *Supply Leadership Changes*, p. 59.

Other Types of Supply Teams

In addition to the three common forms of cross-functional teams, there are at least six additional approaches to supply teams: supplier participation, customer participation, co-location of supply, co-location of suppliers, supplier councils, and supply councils.

Teams with Supplier Participation

Supplier participation in cross-functional sourcing teams depends on the nature of the assignment. For example, it makes sense to include suppliers in teams assigned to develop supplier capabilities or improve supplier responsiveness, but not on teams assigned to evaluate and select new suppliers.

Involving suppliers at the product design stage can produce substantial benefits and is common in discrete goods manufacturing industries, such as automotive and consumer electronics. The development of the Boeing 777 commercial aircraft made extensive use of supplier participation on cross-functional teams, enabling successful design and production in record time. Automotive manufacturers periodically give suppliers primary responsibility for designing major components, such as seating systems. The Ford Motor Company case in Chapter 2 provides an example of a company that engages suppliers early in the product-development process to identify opportunities for cost and quality improvements and supplier innovation.

Intellectual property issues and confidentiality are perhaps the biggest obstacles to supplier participation, particularly when new product design is involved. Some firms ask suppliers to sign confidentiality agreements to minimize the potential effect of this obstacle on the team's effectiveness.

Teams with Customer Participation

In an effort to be truly customer driven, some organizations include end customers on their teams. For example, when a commercial airframe maker designs a new passenger aircraft, it makes sense to have potential airline customers participate in the design team. They know best the characteristics a new aircraft must have from the airline perspective, given its anticipated passenger loads, route structures, maintenance plans, and passenger service strategies. If supply is also included in teams with end customers, there is a greater opportunity to deliver the greatest value in the shortest cycle time.

Co-location of Supply with Internal Customers

Locating buyers with internal customers (e.g., engineering or operations) can help to break down barriers between functions as individuals get to know, and learn to work with, each other. Close proximity fosters greater awareness that leads to better understanding of the goals, strategies, and challenges of each group. Also, internal customers are more likely to involve supply in decisions if the buyer is readily accessible when questions arise. Buyers can "sell" other departments on their worth by providing market intelligence including information on availability, suppliers, and specific commodities. The best selling point is a measurable outcome such as cost reduction, improved quality, or a better specification.

Co-location of Suppliers in the Buying Organization

As organizations look for ways to do more work with fewer people and achieve the productivity and competitiveness goals of the firm, they are increasingly looking to suppliers for expertise and assistance. Having key supplier personnel located in the buying organization who can function as buyers, planners, and salespeople can improve buyer–seller communications and processes, absorb work typically done by the firm's employees, and reduce administrative and sales costs.

Supplier Councils

A number of large firms, such as General Motors and Boeing, use supplier councils to manage supplier relationships. Supplier councils usually consist of 10 to 15 senior executives from the company's preferred supplier base, along with six to eight of the buying firm's top management. For example, General Motors has two primary forums for formal discussions with suppliers. The GM Supplier Business Council consists of 10 global suppliers who meet with the vice president of global purchasing and supply chain on a monthly basis to address broad, industrywide topics. The second forum is a global GM Supplier Business Meeting that is webcasted to GM's suppliers each month to gain input on GM-specific topics. Suppliers who participate in this webcast represent approximately 80 percent of the value of GM vehicles.

Supplier councils usually meet two to four times per year and deal with supply policy issues at the buying firm with the objectives of developing relationships and improving communication with the supply base. Supplier councils allow suppliers to be proactive participants in the supply management activities at the buying firm and can be useful forums to communicate strategies to key suppliers, identify problems with the supply base early on, and agree upon competitive targets in areas such as cost, quality, and delivery.

Supply Councils

Supply councils, also referred to as purchasing councils, are generally comprised of senior supply staff and are established to facilitate coordination among the business units, divisions, or plants. Many firms use supply councils as a means of sharing information among decentralized units, or coordinating activities focused on a specific problem that might involve several supply groups. The goals of the council are to manage buyer–supplier relationships properly and to encourage continuous improvement.

For example, Wellman, a manufacturer and distributor of polyester fibers and PET resins, had a decentralized supply organization, where plant purchasing reported to the local manager at each site. The corporate purchasing council consisted of site purchasing leadership. It concentrated on standardizing purchasing processes, standardizing goods and services across sites, aggregating requirements and leveraging volume for lower prices, and simplifying and streamlining the materials process. The council also formulated annual business plans and objectives for purchasing.[9]

CONSORTIA

Purchasing consortia are a form of collaborative purchasing that is used by both public and private-sector organizations as a means of delivering a wider range of services at a lower total cost. Purchasing consortia can take one of several forms, ranging from informal groups that meet regularly to discuss purchasing issues, to the creation of formal centralized consortia for the purpose of managing members' supply activities. Consortia are quite

[9] Leenders and Johnson, *Major Changes in Supply Chain Responsibilities*.

common in not-for-profit organizations, particularly educational institutions and health care organizations. Interest in the concept in the for-profit sector was sparked by the ability to run Internet-based consortiums, also called electronic exchanges or marketplaces, and the lack of antitrust obstacles (see Chapters 4 and 15).

Savings through price reductions are a primary motivation for the creation and participation in purchasing consortia. Other benefits are opportunities for staff reductions, product and service standardization, improved supplier management capabilities, specialization of staff, and better customer service.

Despite the benefits, hesitation to participate in consortia may be due to concerns about:[10]

- *Antitrust issues.* Collaboration might be viewed as anticompetitive by the U.S. Department of Justice's Antitrust Division and/or the Federal Trade Commission.
- *Bureaucracy.* The consortium may become bureaucratic, difficult to manage, and costly to coordinate.
- *Complexity.* Fear that "open enrollment" will bring together buyers with widely diverse needs and philosophies toward buyer–seller relations, resulting in untenable complexity and dysfunction.
- *Competitors.* Fear that the competition might be allowed to join.
- *Confidentiality.* Disclosure of sensitive information. Therefore, most items purchased through consortia are nonstrategic, such as MRO components and routine services.
- *Supplier resistance.* Strong suppliers may resist participating in consortium arrangements.
- *Distribution channels.* Some believe existing distributors provide adequate pricing and services.
- *Equality.* A firm currently has preferred relationships with suppliers/free riding. The unequal size of member organizations can create difficulties with respect to the allocation of benefits.
- *Uncertainty.* Some were concerned costs would not decline and service levels would.
- *Standardization and compliance.* The degree of uniqueness of requirements and the costs of standardizing products and services.
- *Governance.* Loss of control and reporting relationships were concerns.

Successful consortia are able to address these hurdles by achieving the following six objectives:[11]

1. Reducing total costs for the members through lower prices, higher quality, and better services.
2. Eliminating and avoiding all real and perceived violations of antitrust regulations.
3. Installing sufficient safeguards to avoid real and perceived threats concerning disclosure of confidential and proprietary information.

---

[10] T. E. Hendrick, *Purchasing Consortiums: Horizontal Alliances among Buying Firms Buying Common Goods and Services* (Tempe, AZ: Center for Advanced Purchasing Studies, 1997); P. F. Johnson, "The Pattern of Evolution in Public Sector Purchasing Consortia," *International Journal of Logistics: Research & Applications* 2, no. 1 (1999), pp. 57–73.

[11] Hendrick, *Purchasing Consortiums: Horizontal Alliances among Buying Firms Buying Common Goods and Services.*

4. Mutual and equitable sharing of risks, costs, and benefits to all stakeholders, including buying firms/members, suppliers, and customers.

5. Maintaining a high degree of trust and professionalism of the consortium stakeholders.

6. Maintaining a strong similarity among consortium members and compatibility of needs, capabilities, philosophies, and corporate cultures.

Conclusion

There is no one perfect organizational structure for supply. Its organizational structure will mirror the overall corporate structure. The challenge for supply executives is to maximize the benefits of their organizational structure, whether it is centralized, decentralized, or hybrid. Major research into organizational issues over the last decade has provided useful insights into innovative attempts to integrate the supply function and suppliers more effectively into organizational goals and strategies. No matter where the supply function is situated on the organization chart, each individual member of the supply organization has the opportunity to improve relations with internal customers and suppliers in an effort to make a greater contribution to organizational objectives.

Questions for Review and Discussion

1. Relate the objectives of supply to (1) a company producing automobiles, (2) a large fast-food restaurant chain, (3) a financial institution, and (4) an integrated oil company.

2. What are the challenges faced by a supply manager working in a highly centralized structure? In a highly decentralized structure?

3. How does specialization within supply differ in small and large organizations?

4. What are the reasons for giving the CPO a title and reporting line equal to marketing, engineering, or other key business functions?

5. What are indicators that supply is "meaningfully involved"?

6. What are the challenges in expanding the role of the CPO?

7. What implementation factors would you consider when asked to change the supply organization from a centralized to a hybrid structure? What factors would you consider if moving from decentralized to centralized?

8. How is team buying likely to affect the purchasing/supply function over the next decade?

9. Why and how would you go about setting up a consortium for the purchase of fuel, oil, furniture, corrugated cartons, or office supplies?

References

Driedonks, B. A.; J. M. P. Gevers; A. J. van Weele. "Managing Sourcing Team Effectiveness: The Need for a Team Perspective in Purchasing Organizations." *Journal of Purchasing and Supply Management* 16, no. 2 (2010), pp. 109–117.

Feisel, E.; E. Hartmann; L. C. Giunipero. "The Importance of the Human Aspect in the Supply Function: Strategies for Developing PSM Proficiency." *Journal of Purchasing and Supply Management* 17, no. 1 (2011), pp. 54–67.

Hendrick, Thomas E. *Purchasing Consortiums: Horizontal Alliances among Firms Buying Common Goods and Services.* Tempe, AZ: Center for Advanced Purchasing Studies, 1997.

Hendrick, Thomas E., and Jeffrey Ogden. *Chief Purchasing Officers' Compensation Benchmarks and Demographics: A 2001 Study of Fortune 500 Firms.* Tempe, AZ: Center for Advanced Purchasing Studies, 2002.

Johnson, P. Fraser. "Supply Organizational Structures." Critical Issues Report, CAPS Research, August 2003.

Johnson, P. Fraser. "The Pattern of Evolution in Public Sector Purchasing Consortia." *International Journal of Logistics: Research and Applications* 2, no. 1 (1999), pp. 57–73.

Johnson, P. F., and M. R. Leenders. *Supply's Organizational Roles and Responsibilities.* Tempe, AZ: CAPS Research, May 2012, 118 pages.

Johnson, P. F., and M. R. Leenders, *Supply Leadership Changes.* Tempe, AZ: CAPS Research, 2007.

Leenders, Michiel R., and P. Fraser Johnson. *Major Structural Changes in Supply Organizations.* Tempe, AZ: Center for Advanced Purchasing Studies, 2000.

Leenders, Michiel R., and P. Fraser Johnson. *Major Changes in Supply Chain Responsibilities.* Tempe AZ: Center for Advanced Purchasing Studies, 2002.

McCue, Cliff, and Eric Prier. "Using Agency Theory to Model Cooperative Public Purchasing." *Journal of Public Procurement* 8, no. 1, 2008, pp. 1–35.

Nollet, Jean, and Martin Beaulieu, "Should an Organization Join a Purchasing Group?" *Supply Chain Management* 10, no. 1 (2005), pp. 11–17.

Schneider, L., and C. M. Wallenburg. "50 Years of Research on Organizing the Purchasing Function: Do We Need Any More?" *Journal of Purchasing and Supply Management* 19, no. 3 (2013), pp. 144–164.

General Motors 2013 Sustainability Report, www.gmsustainability.com/report.html#/issues/supply, accessed February 17, 2014.

Case 3–1

Iowa Elevators

Scott McBride, director of purchasing at Iowa Elevators, was reviewing information collected by his analyst, Cathy Ritchie, as he prepared for a meeting with the executive management team scheduled for Wednesday, June 11. Scott had been asked by Walter Lettridge, Iowa Elevator's CEO, to present a five-year plan for the purchasing department at the meeting. In preparation for the meeting, Scott asked Cathy to prepare a report analyzing all expenditures made by the company with outside suppliers over the previous year. It was now June 3, and Scott knew there was still a lot of work that had to be completed to get ready for the meeting the following week.

IOWA ELEVATORS

Iowa Elevators was one of the largest grain-handling companies in the United States. Headquartered in Des Moines, Iowa, the company had annual revenues of $2.3 billion and employed more than 2,500 people. Its two business units were the grain-handling and marketing division and the farm supplies division.

The grain-handling and marketing division operated approximately 300 grain elevators in the Midwest. This division represented approximately 75 percent of total company revenues, although total revenues had declined by 20 percent from the previous year due to drought conditions that had affected farm crop production. Over the previous five years, the company had invested heavily in upgrading its elevator system to improve throughput and increase capacity in key regions.

The farm supplies division sold crop-protection products, equipment and supplies, fertilizer, and seed through its network of country elevators and approximately 30 marketing centers. Revenues for this division had doubled over the previous five years as part of a strategy to tap the company's country elevator network to diversify its revenue base.

Iowa Elevators had a past reputation for steady financial performance and profitability. However, the company had seen a steady decline in profitability over the previous three years. In the most recent fiscal year, it experienced a loss of $11 million after taxes and a sharp decline in working capital. Management attributed its disappointing results to lower volumes in its grain-handling and marketing division and increased competition. Despite its rising market share, operating margins at the farm supplies division had remained flat.

Concern over the financial performance of the company led to a decision by the board of directors to make changes to the executive team. In February, Walter Lettridge, a veteran of the grain-handling industry, was brought in as the new president and CEO. Shortly afterward, Jose Sousa joined Iowa Elevators as the new chief financial officer. Both Walter and Jose had worked together at a competitor of Iowa Elevators.

Immediately after joining the company, Walter went to work creating a major cost-cutting initiative, which would include reductions in headcounts, capital expenditure budgets, and overhead expenses. As part of this process, Scott McBride was asked to present a five-year plan to the executive management team, including annual cost reduction targets.

PURCHASING AND SUPPLY MANAGEMENT

Scott supervised a group of 11 people (see Exhibit 1) who were responsible for the acquisition of requirements for head office and some regional sales and administrative offices. Its major purchases were information technology (hardware and software); printing for forms, brochures, and advertising; office supplies; and company automobile leases. The only change in the purchasing organization within the last year had been the addition of a travel coordinator as a result of a contract for air travel and car rentals. The purchasing organization was part of the corporate services organization, which also included the human resources and information technology groups, and reported to the CFO.

Iowa Elevators had a history of decentralized management, with individual divisions held accountable for their own operations and bottom-line performance. As a result, local elevator managers acted autonomously but were responsible for local market share and profitability. In addition, the elevator managers also made decisions concerning the amount and variety of crop-protection products, fertilizer, and seed stock to handle in their retail

EXHIBIT 1   Iowa Elevators Purchasing Department

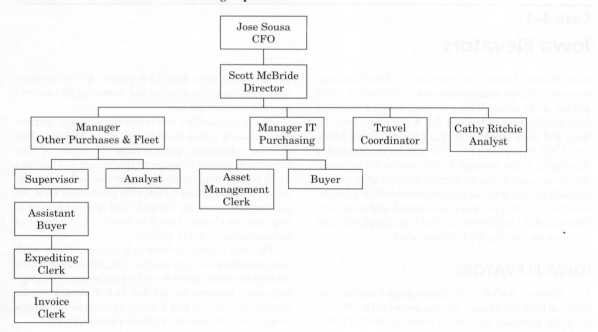

operation. Purchases for elevator operations were handled locally and monitored based on spending limits set in annual operating budgets.

The farm supplies division had a group of four product managers who were responsible for the three main product segments (crop-protection products, equipment and supplies, and fertilizer and seed). These individuals were responsible for supplier selection, product mix, branding, and promotion and assisted elevator and marketing center managers in the areas of promotion, new product development, and inventory planning.

ANALYSIS OF CORPORATE SPEND

In a meeting in early May, Scott was asked by Walter Lettridge and Jose Sousa to present his five-year plan for the purchasing department at an executive management team meeting on June 11. Walter had scheduled time for a number of senior managers to present their plans and ideas aimed at returning the company to profitability. During the meeting, Walter commented to Scott: "I expect purchasing to deliver cost savings and your group needs to play a more significant role in the company. You need to explain what you can deliver and explain how you intend to accomplish your objectives. As far as I am concerned,

everything is on the table right now. We need to return the company to profitability and I am not afraid to make some major changes in terms of how we run this business."

Recognizing the need to present a thorough plan, Scott enlisted the support of his analyst, Cathy Ritchie, to help him collect and organize data. The data collection focused on two questions: (1) How much money did Iowa Elevators spend with its outside suppliers? and (2) How much inventory did the company carry? The data collection process had been complicated by the variety of management systems at different levels and at different locations. Scott believed that if more time had been available, Cathy might have been able to capture more spend and inventory data.

Cathy's analysis identified a total corporate spend of $728 million. Although the company dealt with more than 1,500 suppliers, 20 suppliers accounted for approximately 45 percent of the total spend and the top five represented 35 percent. (The top five suppliers consisted of two railway companies and three suppliers to the farm supplies division for crop protection and fertilizer.) She estimated that average annual inventories in the farm supplies division were nearly $120 million with annual purchases of $310 million. A summary of Cathy's key findings is reported in Exhibits 2 and 3.

EXHIBIT 2
Total Purchases by Category ($000)

Spend Category	Annual Spend*
Farm supplies	$ 254,406
Information technology and telecommunications	17,187
Fees, levies, memberships	26,301
Energy	8,602
Financial services and interest expense	24,461
Fleet	4,229
Insurance	5,239
Packaging	10,551
Professional services	7,708
MRO & construction	127,829
Transportation services	208,927
Travel and entertainment	3,557
Other	17,350
Miscellaneous and unclassified	11,926
Total	$ 728,273

* Data for the most recent fiscal year.

EXHIBIT 3
Farm Supplies
Division
Inventory
($000)

Category	Average Inventory	Annual Purchases
Crop protection products	$ 65,098	$ 124,696
Equipment and supplies	22,388	13,743
Fertilizer	20,938	130,557
Seed	10,389	41,787
Total	$ 118,813	$ 310,783

THE MIS PROPOSAL

Scott was aware that the MIS Group had been asked to make a similar presentation to the executive management team. The chief information officer (CIO) had informed Scott that he would be requesting $10 million in additional spending beyond standard upgrades over the next five years with anticipated cost savings of about $500,000 per year.

PREPARATION FOR THE MEETING

Scott viewed the upcoming meeting as an opportunity to redefine the role of purchasing at Iowa Elevators. His session with executive management was expected to last approximately 90 minutes, and he wanted to prepare a five-year plan with specific objectives for each year, including cost reduction targets. In particular, his plan for the coming year had to be very specific and include identifiable projects and initiatives, schedules, project plans, and expected costs and benefits.

As part of his proposal, Scott also wanted to establish a budget and human resource requirements that would be needed to support his recommendations. While he regarded his staff as competent, Scott recognized that he would require new managerial resources if the role of corporate purchasing was to be expanded. Consequently, he also planned on proposing a new organization structure and establishing a headcount plan and budget for the purchasing department.

As Scott reviewed Cathy's report, he began considering where he was going to start and what could be accomplished. His major concern would be resistance from the divisions and field elevator managers, and he wondered what, if anything, could be done to address any organizational resistance to his recommendations.

Case 3–2

Lambert-Martin Automotive Systems Inc.

Arthur Thomas, vice president of global purchasing, Engine Systems Group at Lambert-Martin Automotive Systems Inc. (Lambert-Martin), was preparing for the biggest challenge of his career. Bill McLaren, president and CEO, had asked Arthur the previous day to take over as the company's new chief purchasing officer (CPO), replacing Jeff Trudell, who was retiring in two months, after eight years in the role. As a first step, Bill asked Arthur to put together some ideas regarding potential changes to the purchasing organization at Lambert-Martin. During their meeting, Bill commented, "Our business plan calls for the company to grow from $10 billion in sales this year to $15 billion in five years. It is essential that we take advantage of opportunities in our supply chain to support our growth objectives and to keep costs in line."

Bill suggested that Arthur review the current organization structure, develop alternatives, and meet with the group vice presidents to solicit their input. It was Tuesday November 6, and Arthur was scheduled to meet with Bill at the end of the month to review his preliminary ideas and recommendations.

LAMBERT-MARTIN AUTOMOTIVE SYSTEMS INC.

Lambert-Martin was a U.S.-based supplier to the global automotive industry, with headquarters in Troy, Michigan. Its origins dated back to the early days of the automotive industry, when the company was formed in 1924 with the merger of Lambert Clutch and Gear Company and Martin

Engine Systems. It was a recognized leader in drivetrain technology, providing innovative products that improved fuel economy, emissions, and performance. Its main product lines were drivetrain components, including transmission control units, engine valve components, friction materials, and turbochargers. With 70 manufacturing facilities across 22 countries, it provided components to most major original equipment manufacturers.

The company invested heavily in product engineering and new product development. Its engineers worked closely with customers on new vehicle programs, and the Lambert-Martin Technology Center, also located in Troy, was a source of new product innovation.

Lambert-Martin operated under a decentralized model with five business groups: Engine Systems, Emission Products, Ignition Technology, Engine Cooling Systems and Transmission Technology. Corporate office functions included accounting and finance, human resources, engineering, information technology, legal, and a small purchasing staff. Group vice presidents operated autonomously with control over sales and manufacturing operations, including purchasing.

The largest group by sales was Transmission Technology, with annual revenues of approximately $3 billion, while annual revenues at the other four groups ranged from $1.5 to $2.0 billion. For the most recent fiscal year, cost of sales represented 80 percent of revenues, while purchases were 50 percent; and selling, general, and administrative expenses were 9 percent. Net earnings after tax were $690 million.

The Purchasing Organization

Most purchasing staff were located in the five business groups, each with a vice president of purchasing that reported directly to their respective group vice president. The group purchasing functions were responsible for commodity strategies, sourcing, quality control, cost reductions, and supplier development. The corporate purchasing group managed the supplier technology portal, supplier scorecards, risk management reporting, and the supplier manual. Historically, the CPO had a dual role as vice president of purchasing for one of the groups as well as responsibility for the corporate purchasing organization. For example, Jeff Trudell had the title of vice president global supply for the Transmission Technology Group as well as being the company's CPO. Similarly, in his new role, Arthur would maintain his current position as vice president of global purchasing, Engine Systems Group, and add the corporate CPO title.

PREPARING FOR THE MEETINGS

Arthur Thomas was a mechanical engineer with 20 years of experience in the automotive parts industry. He joined Lambert-Martin 15 years prior, originally working in engineering and product management in the Emission Products Group. After five years in engineering, Arthur was asked to join the purchasing organization in Engine Systems, where he held positions as strategic sourcing manager, director of supplier development, and director of commodity management before being promoted to his current role, which he had held for the last three years.

As vice president of global purchasing for the Engine Systems Group, Arthur reported to Bill McLaren, who, until his recent promotion, had been group vice president of Engine Systems. During his tenure as head of purchasing for the group, Arthur could see where Lambert-Martin's decentralized purchasing organizational structure constrained the company from capturing important opportunities in its supply chain. Specifically, the lack of communication among the purchasing organizations in the business groups meant that spend information for common suppliers was not shared, thereby potentially missing opportunities for price reductions through consolidation of purchases. Secondly, Arthur felt that because purchasing in each of the groups had separate organizations for sourcing, quality control, and supplier development, it would be possible to reduce overhead costs and improve the effectiveness of these activities through increased centralization.

Arthur had recently read a focus study report prepared by CAPS Research, *Supply's Organizational Roles and Responsibilities,* which indicated that approximately 10 percent of the large companies in the survey had decentralized purchasing organizational structures, and the majority—approximately two-thirds—used the hybrid structure. With a new CEO who was looking for opportunities to make positive changes at the company, Arthur thought this would be a good time to take a fresh look at Lambert-Martin's purchasing organizational structure and the roles and responsibilities of the groups and head office functions. His meetings with the five group vice presidents were scheduled for mid-November. As he sat at his desk, Arthur wondered what questions he should ask during these meetings. Buy-in from the group vice presidents would be essential if any major changes were to occur. Furthermore, Bill McLaren was expecting some alternatives from Arthur regarding where he saw opportunities and how the purchasing function would be able to make a greater contribution to the strategic and financial goals of Lambert-Martin.

Chapter **Four**

Supply Processes and Technology

Chapter Outline

The Supply Management Process
Strategy and Goal Alignment
Ensuring Process Compliance
Information Flows
Steps in the Supply Process

1. Recognition of Need
2. Description of Need
   Purposes and Flow of a Requisition
   Types of Requisitions
   Early Supply and Supplier Involvement
3. Identification of Potential Sources
   Issue an RFx
4. Supplier Selection and Determination of Terms
5. Preparation and Placement of the Purchase Order
6. Follow-Up and Expediting
   Assess Costs and Benefits
7. Receipt and Inspection
   Eliminate or Reduce Inspection
8. Invoice Clearing and Payment
   Aligning Supply and Accounts Payable
   Cash Discounts and Late Invoices
9. Maintenance of Records and Relationships
   Linking Data to Decisions
   Manage Supplier Relationships

Improving Process Efficiency and Effectiveness
A Supply Process Flowchart
Strategic Spend
Nonstrategic Spend

Information Systems and the Supply Process
Benefits of Information Systems Technology
ERP Systems
Cloud Computing and the Supply Chain
Electronic Procurement Systems
Electronic or Online Catalogs
EDI
Marketplaces
Online Reverse Auctions
Radio Frequency Identification (RFID)

Implications for Supply

Policy and Procedure Manual

Conclusion

Questions for Review and Discussion

References

Cases

Key Questions for the Supply Decision Maker

Should we

- Use an e-procurement system to improve the efficiency of the supply process?
- Use online reverse auctions to buy goods and services?
- Consider establishing a supplier-managed inventory program for MRO requirements?

How can we

- Handle lower-value purchases more efficiently?
- Streamline the process so that supply managers are more involved in the earlier stages?
- Communicate more effectively with our internal business partners?

Identifying and streamlining key business processes to reduce costs, grow revenues, and manage assets represents an opportunity in most organizations. Critical processes are embedded in all areas of the organization, including new product development, supply, operations, marketing, sales, and accounts payable. Managing these processes, understanding what makes each process efficient and effective, and clarifying how each process interacts with other processes and activities are critical to the success of the organization as a whole. Understanding how and when to apply information technology solutions to business processes is also an ongoing challenge.

Purchases can represent 50–70 percent of costs for manufacturing organizations and 30–40 percent for service firms. While this indicates the importance of supply in procuring a significant portion of organizational resources, it also suggests the challenges of designing an efficient and effective process for a diverse spend. Ultimately, however, the simplest definition of supply is the exchange of money (the buyer's responsibility) for goods and services (the supplier's responsibility).

The first key decision is: Which process or processes will be most effective and efficient to support this exchange? The options for managing the information flows of a supply process have expanded along with supply management's range of responsibilities. The nature of the requirement will dictate the information exchanges between the purchaser and supplier. Is the purchase one-time or repetitive? How are volumes, specifications, and shipping schedules communicated? Are the purchases part of a short-term or long-term contract? How will prices be established and how will payment be made?

The acquisition process is closely tied to almost all other business processes and also to the external environment, creating a need for complete information systems and cross-functional cooperation. For example, supply must work with engineering to determine specifications, operations to determine production schedules, and finance to arrange payment. In the past 30 years, there have been remarkable advancements in information technology used in the recording, transmission, analysis, and reporting of information within organizations and their supply chain networks.

Most people recognize the strategic importance of information and knowledge management. They also recognize that technology provides tools that can improve efficiency and effectiveness when applied appropriately to a business process. The Internet and availability of integrated systems, such as enterprise resource planning (ERP) software, have had a substantial impact on the acquisition process and its management. Supply managers need to stay abreast of technological developments and be able to assess the fit of each new tool with the organization's goals and strategy. Thus, the second key decision is: What information systems might be used to support or enable efficient and effective processes?

This chapter focuses, first, on the critical steps of a robust supply management process, one with structure and discipline. Once the basic supply process is understood, tools and techniques are addressed that might improve the efficiency and effectiveness of the entire process or specific categories of spend. If the process itself is flawed, then a process improvement program must be undertaken before the process is automated. Remember, process first and technology last.

THE SUPPLY MANAGEMENT PROCESS

A process is a set of activities that has a beginning and an end, occurs in a specific sequence, and has inputs and outputs. The supply management process starts with need recognition and ends with monitoring suppliers and relationships. The steps include: recognize and describe need, identify potential sources, select source(s), determine price and terms, follow up and expedite, receive, pay invoice, and monitor.

A process-oriented person considers the flow of information, materials, services, and capital throughout the process no matter how many functions or departments touch it. A functionally oriented person only considers the steps for which his or her department is responsible. If supply personnel are not involved until potential sources are identified, they and the internal business partner may miss the opportunity for supply and suppliers to add value in the need recognition and description stages. Waste is driven into the process in the forms of unnecessary costs, long cycle times, and missed opportunities because the buying organization, operating out of *functional silos,* manages the process sequentially rather than simultaneously.

Five major reasons for developing a robust supply process are as follows:

1. Large number of items.
2. Large dollar volume involved.
3. Need for an audit trail.
4. Severe consequences of poor performance.
5. Potential contribution to effective organizational operations inherent in the function.

Strategy and Goal Alignment

The first step in optimizing the supply process is building internal consensus around the opportunities to add value to the organization. The focus is: Where, when, and how can supply contribute to short- and long-term goals and strategies of the organization?

Vertical and horizontal alignment of strategy and goals is required for supply to fully contribute to the organization. Vertically, if the supply strategy at the functional or business unit level is out of sync with organizational strategy, then supply decisions will hinder rather than assist with the achievement of organizational goals (see Chapter 2).

Horizontal alignment between and among functional areas is also required. For example, to attain profitability targets, the finance group's cash flow goals may lead to a payment policy that conflicts with the supply group's goal to contribute to profitability through long-term partnerships with key suppliers in which payment terms were a key negotiating point. Personnel at all levels must work to align strategies and goals vertically and horizontally to maximize organizational opportunities.

Individuals from many functions play valuable roles in a successful acquisition process. The users and specifiers of the good or service (supply's internal customers or internal business partners) play a role in recognizing and describing the need. They are usually the budget owners and the primary information sources for technical descriptions; volume requirements; and quality, delivery, and service targets.

How and when internal users communicate with supply varies. Sometimes internal customers hand off information to supply once they have clearly defined the requirement. Other times, supply personnel bring market intelligence such as supply availability, price trends, or new technology to the need recognition and description stages. When value can be created in the early stages of the process, the internal business partners and supply should interact early and often in cross-functional sourcing teams, new product or service design teams, and commodity management teams (see Chapter 3).

Often, however, supply takes the lead role in analyzing and selecting the supplier(s) and determining price and other terms and conditions such as payment, delivery, quality and service. Other functional areas may step in as well. For example, operations, logistics, warehousing, shipping and receiving, legal, marketing, information systems, engineering, and accounts payable all play a role in the process, but are typically part of different functional areas with a different reporting line than supply.

Each stakeholder has goals and objectives relative to the purchase. When these conflict, the total cost of owning, consuming, and disposing of a purchase may increase unnecessarily. Because of this risk, many senior managers foster a process orientation through cross-functional teams, and by creating shared or common goals, objectives, and metrics.

Ensuring Process Compliance

Increasing the rate of internal compliance with the supply process can be challenging. Often nonsupply staff make unauthorized buying decisions (sometimes referred to as "maverick buying") that lead to higher total cost of ownership and undermine supply's credibility internally and externally. The root causes of noncompliance must be identified and eliminated.

Organizational structure affects process compliance. In a highly decentralized organization where supply decisions are made at the business unit, plant, or division level, supply councils composed of site leaders may be beneficial. The council works to standardize goods, services, and processes across sites; aggregate requirements and leverage volume for lower prices; simplify and streamline the materials management process; formulate annual business plans; and establish objectives for supply. Without a supply council and willing participation by site supply leaders, the organization may have multiple suppliers of the same goods and services with disparate prices, terms and conditions and varying levels of quality and service. Even in a highly centralized organization there may be high levels of noncompliance. Process improvements and consistent delivery of results to internal business partners may increase compliance.

Organizational culture also influences process compliance. A mandate from top management to use the supply process can stop or reduce maverick buying in some organizational cultures. In others, mandates mean little and supply personnel must persuade and convince users to comply.

Information systems may compel compliance by eliminating alternative purchasing paths, reducing process cycle time, and instilling confidence in users that delays will be minimal.

Information Flows

There are four basic information flows involving supply.

Inward Flows (1) Information from within the organization is sent to supply, including statements of need for materials and services. (2) Information from external sources is sent to supply. This may come from suppliers (e.g., prices, and deliveries) or from other sources (e.g., general market conditions and import duties).

Outward Flows (1) Information from within supply is sent to others within the organization. This includes supplier pricing, market conditions, and supply forecasts for cash flow budgeting. (2) Information, such as requests for quotes or proposals, is sent from supply to external sources (e.g., suppliers).

Supply must be able to manage effectively information flows involving both internal and external partners in the supply chain. Information systems enable the efficient flow of information and support effective decision making. These tools are discussed later in this chapter.

Steps in the Supply Process

The supply process is basically a communications process. Determining what needs to be communicated, to whom, and in what format and time frame is at the heart of an efficient and effective supply management process. It is essential for supply professionals to determine when, where, and how they can add value and when, where, and how they can extricate themselves from steps that are best left to other people or to technology.

The essential steps in the supply process are:

1. Recognition of need.
2. Description of need.
3. Identification and analysis of possible sources of supply.
4. Supplier selection and determination of terms.
5. Preparation and placement of purchase order.
6. Follow-up and/or expediting the order.
7. Receipt and inspection.
8. Invoice clearing and payment.
9. Maintenance of records and relationships.

1. RECOGNITION OF NEED

A purchase originates when a person or a system identifies a definite need in the organization—what, how much, and when it is needed.

The supply department helps anticipate the needs of using departments. Supply policy and practice may encourage or require the use of standardized items, provide procedures for special or unusual orders, and limit the use of rush orders. Also, since the supply department tracks price trends and general market conditions, placing forward orders may be essential to protect against shortage of supply or increased prices. Supply should inform users of the normal lead time and any major changes for all standard purchased items.

Since the greatest opportunity to affect value is when needs are recognized and described (product or service conception and design), the supply manager and supplier can contribute more in these steps than later in the acquisition process. (See Chapter 6 for additional information on value creation.) Early supply and supplier involvement, often as members of new product development teams, provides information that may lead to cost avoidance or reduction, faster time to market, and greater competitiveness. As discussed in Chapter 3, many organizations are turning to cross-functional teams to bring different functional areas, and suppliers, into the process as early as possible.

2. DESCRIPTION OF NEED

The purchaser must know exactly what the internal customers want. And internal requirements should be driven by a clear understanding of the external customer's needs. It is essential to have an accurate description of the need, whether it is a tangible good, a service, or goods and services bundled together. Unclear or ambiguous descriptions, or overspecified materials, services, or quality levels will lead to unnecessary costs. Supply management and the user, or the cross-functional sourcing team, share responsibility for accurately describing the item or service needed.

Purposes and Flow of a Requisition

A requisition is the document used to communicate needs internally between users/specifiers and supply management according to established internal controls. The flow of the requisition is determined by who needs access to the information to perform their duties, the need for an audit trail, and evidence of proper authorization.

A requisition is a gatekeeping tool to manage the flow of information through three gates: (1) authority, (2) internal clarity, and (3) internal clearance.

Gate 1: Authority   Does the requisitioner have the authority to make the specified request—goods or services—and at the specified budget level? The supply department establishes who has the power to requisition, prevents unauthorized requisitions, and communicates to suppliers that a requisition is not an order.

Gate 2: Internal Clarity   Is the need described in a clear and unambiguous way? Uniform terms or standardized commodity or service codes should be used to describe required articles or services. The importance of proper nomenclature or commodity coding cannot be overemphasized. The most effective way to secure this uniformity is to maintain a database of common purchased items. A coding structure that standardizes purchases brings order and consistency and supports an efficient and effective process. A general catalog lists all the items used, and a stores catalog lists all items carried in stock. Depending on the technological sophistication of the organization, catalogs may be in an electronic file, on e-catalogs, or hard copy. Difficulties arise when supplier codes (manufacturers or service providers), industry codes, and company codes are different. While software is available to cleanse data and apply standard coding schemas, these tools are not perfect.

If adequately planned and properly maintained, coding schemas promote uniformity in description, reduce the number of odd sizes or grades of articles requisitioned, and facilitate accounting and inventory procedures. If poorly planned, maintained, or used, they may be confusing and expensive beyond their projected benefits. Convincing internal users that a standard item will suffice is an ongoing challenge for supply personnel.

Typically only one item is included on a purchase requisition, particularly for standard items. For special items not regularly stocked, several items may be covered by one requisition if for the same delivery date. This simplifies recordkeeping, since specific items are secured from different suppliers, call for different delivery dates, and require separate purchase orders and treatment.

Gate 3: Internal Clearance   Descriptions should be reviewed before preparing documentation to communicate externally with potential suppliers. Quantity, based on anticipated needs, should be compared to economical quantities. The delivery date should allow time to secure quotations and samples, if necessary, and to execute the purchase order and obtain delivery. The requisitioner should be notified if there is a time or delivery constraint that drives in additional expense. Consistent lack of adequate lead time is an indicator of a process problem that must be analyzed and resolved.

This review may be performed by a buyer or a team or it may be system generated. In an ERP or e-procurement system, preloaded data establish decision rules for requisitioning, order points, and suppliers and include triggers to send red flags for buyer review. It is management by exception. Humans are flagged when the system detects a problem based on thresholds set by decision makers.

For lower-value and lower-risk purchases, the buyer should question a specification if a modification would deliver more value. For example, the buyer might recommend a substitute if there are market shortages or lower-priced or better alternatives. A high degree of interaction between the buyer and the user is required in the early stages of need definition because of the impact of future market conditions. At best, an inaccurate description may result in loss of time; at worst it may have serious financial consequences and cause disruption of supply, hard feelings internally, lost opportunity for a product or service improvement, and loss of supplier respect and trust.

Types of Requisitions

There are several types of purchase requisitions, including standard requisitions, traveling requisitions, a bill of materials, and stores/inventory requisition.

Standard Requisition   The following information should be included on a standard requisition:

1. Date.
2. Number (identification).
3. Originating department.
4. Account to be charged.

5. Complete description of material or service desired and quantity.
6. Date material or service needed.
7. Any special shipping or service-delivery instructions.
8. Signature of authorized requisitioner.

Electronic requisitions typically have prefilled fields for standard or recurring information. Some organizations include fields for "suggested supplier" and "suggested price."

Traveling Requisition   People have always adopted and adapted new technology to business processes. The traveling requisition was an innovation used for recurring requirements and standard parts to reduce operating expenses. In a manual system, the traveling requisition is a form on cardstock that contains a complete description of the item. The requisitioner sends the card to supply, indicating quantity and date needed. Supply enters the supplier, price, and purchase order (PO) number on the traveler and sends it back to the requisitioner, who files the card until the next reorder.

The process of determining which items are appropriate for use on a traveling requisition and the flow of the information are useful when transitioning to an electronic system.

Bill of Materials   A bill of materials (BOM) simplifies the requisitioning process for frequently needed line items in organizations that make a standard item over a relatively long period of time.

A BOM includes all materials and parts, including allowance for scrap, to make one end unit: for example, a two-slice toaster. Production scheduling notifies supply of the quantity (e.g., 18,000) scheduled for production next month. Supply "explodes" the BOM by multiplying through by 18,000 to determine the total quantity of material needed for next month's production. Comparison of these numbers with inventory yields the open-to-buy figures. A materials requirement planning (MRP) or enterprise resource planning (ERP) system is preloaded with pricing information on suppliers with long-term agreements, and order releases are generated to cover the open-to-buy amounts. (Chapter 8 provides more detail on MRP.)

Stores/Inventory Requisition   Needs may be met by a material requisition from inventory or the transfer of surplus stock from another department or division.

Early Supply and Supplier Involvement

For purchases that are of strategic or critical value to the buying organization, it is usually advisable to manage the process through a cross-functional sourcing team (see Chapter 3). For lower-value purchases, the buyer should question a specification if it appears that the organization might be served better through a modification. For example, the buyer might recommend a substitute if there are market shortages of the desired commodity or lower-priced or better alternatives are available. Since future market conditions play such a vital role, it makes sense to have a high degree of interaction between the supply and specifying groups in the early stages of need definition. At best, an inaccurate description may result in some loss of time; at worst it may have serious financial consequences and cause disruption of supply, hard feelings internally, lost opportunity for a product or service improvement, and loss of supplier respect and trust.

3. IDENTIFICATION OF POTENTIAL SOURCES

Supplier selection constitutes an important part of the supply function. It involves (1) identifying potential qualified sources and (2) assessing the probability that a purchase agreement would result in on-time delivery of satisfactory product/service with appropriate before and after sale service at lowest total cost of ownership. Supplier selection is discussed in detail in Chapter 12, "Supplier Selection." This section addresses the tools available to communicate with potential suppliers.

Issue an RFx

When items are not covered by a contract, the buyer has four options for communicating with potential suppliers: (1) Issue a request for information (RFI)—an optional step that is *not* a solicitation for business. The three options for soliciting business are: (1) request for quotation (RFQ), (2) request for proposal (RFP), or (3) request or invitation for bid (RFB or IFB).

There are no commonly accepted definitions of these terms, so it is important for buyers to communicate clearly to potential suppliers the analysis and selection process. Often each solicitation tool signifies a level of complexity of the purchase, dollar value, and degree of risk the supplier bears.

Request for Information (RFI)

An RFI is issued to gather information about potential suppliers' products and services. Even though the Internet enables fairly quick and easy searches, many supply organizations still prepare and send (electronically or by mail) RFIs to suppliers. An RFI is *not* a solicitation for business or an offer to do business. As the name suggests, an RFI is for information-gathering purposes only.

Request for Quotation (RFQ)

Typically, an RFQ is issued when there is a clear and unambiguous description of the need: for example, a grade of material, a stock-keeping unit (SKU), or other commonly accepted terminology. An RFQ is basically a price comparison tool for commonly used commodities sold in an open and free market where quotations can be easily obtained.

The RFQ is a standard requisition form that includes a list of potential suppliers. It is prepared, checked, signed, and transmitted electronically (e-procurement system, e-mail, or fax) or mailed to potential suppliers. Quotations are recorded, the buyer selects a supplier(s), typically on the basis of price, and a purchase order is prepared and placed with the chosen supplier.

Request for Proposal (RFP)

An RFP is used for more complex requirements in which price is only one of several key decision factors. Typically the buyer is planning to negotiate price and terms. An RFP includes a detailed description of the requirement and invites bidders to use their expertise to develop and propose one or more solutions. The Northeastern Hospital case in Chapter 13 provides an example of an organization using an RFP and the process used to evaluate proposals.

Request for Bid

A request or invitation for bid is used in a competitive bid process with or without the opportunity to negotiate after bid receipt. A detailed bid specification package, similar to an RFP, is developed. It is important to communicate to suppliers how the final selection will take place. Will this be a sealed competitive bid in which the contract will be awarded based on the lowest bid? Will the bids be the starting point from which negotiations will take place?

4. SUPPLIER SELECTION AND DETERMINATION OF TERMS

Analysis and selection of the supplier lead to order placement. Applicable tools range from a simple bid analysis form to complex negotiations. Supplier selection methods are discussed in Chapter 12; issues related to quality are covered in Chapter 7, quantity and inventory in Chapter 8, delivery in Chapter 9, and pricing in Chapter 10.

5. PREPARATION AND PLACEMENT OF THE PURCHASE ORDER

A purchase order is used unless the supplier's sales agreement or a release against a blanket order is used instead. Failure to use the proper contract form may result in serious legal complications or improper documentation. Even where an order is placed by telephone, a confirming written order should follow. In no instance—unless it is for minor purchases from petty cash—should materials be bought without proper documentation.

All companies have purchase order forms. In practice, however, all purchases are not governed by the conditions stipulated on the purchase order. Many are governed by the sales agreement submitted by the seller. Every company seeks to protect itself as completely as possible. Responsibilities that the purchase order form assigns to the supplier are often transferred to the buyer in the sales agreement. Therefore, management is anxious to use its own sales agreement when selling its products and services, and its own purchase order form when buying. Chapter 15 discusses the legal implications.

Format

Purchase order format and routing varies. The essential requirements are the serial number, date of issue, name and address of the supplier, the quantity and description, date of delivery, shipping directions, price, terms of payment, and conditions governing the order.

The conditions might include:

1. Indemnification clause—to guard the buyer from damage suits caused by patent infringement.
2. Price provisions, such as "If the price is not stated on this order, material must not be billed at a price higher than last paid without notice to us and our acceptance thereof."
3. A clause stating that no charges will be allowed for boxing, crating, or drayage.
4. Stipulation that the acceptance of the materials is contingent on inspection and quality.
5. A requirement, in case of rejection, that the seller receive a new order before replacement is made.

6. A precise description of quality requirements and the method of quality assurance/control.

7. Provision for cancellation of the order if deliveries are not received on the date specified in the order.

8. A statement that the buyer refuses to accept drafts drawn against the buyer.

9. Quantity provisions for overshipments or undershipments.

10. Special interest provisions—for example, arbitration or the disposition of tooling.

Routing

While a discussion about routing may seem unnecessary in the age of electronic processes, it is important to understand the flow of information. Who needs access to purchase order information, and why? How information is made available, on paper documentation or electronically, is a matter of process design and organizational capability.

Externally, the supplier needs the information on a PO. Giving or sending a purchase order does not constitute a contract until it has been accepted. Typically, the supplier sends an acknowledgment to confirm acceptance of the order and to complete the contract. What constitutes mutual consent and the acceptance of an offer is primarily a legal question (See Chapter 15). Without an acknowledgement, the buyer can only assume that delivery will be made by the requested date. When delivery dates are uncertain, the buyer needs definite information in advance to plan operations effectively.

Internally, the supply department requires access (electronically or hard copy), accounts payable for the payment process, and receiving and/or stores to plan for and confirm receipt and incoming inspection if required.

Blanket and Open-End Purchase Orders

Blanket or open-end purchase orders reduce costs by reducing the number of purchase orders issued. A blanket order usually covers a variety of items. An open-end order allows for addition of items and/or extension of time. Blanket orders are used to buy maintenance, repair, and operations (MRO) items and production-line requirements used in volume and purchased repetitively over a period of months.

The original purchase order contains all negotiated terms and conditions for estimated quantities over a period of time. Subsequently, releases of specific quantities are made against the order. Releases may be executed by supply or, more efficiently, by production scheduling directly to the supplier. An open-end order may remain in effect for a year, or until changes in design, material specification, or conditions affecting price or delivery necessitate renegotiations.

Master Service Agreement (MSA)

A master service agreement is an agreement wherein the supplier(s) provides predetermined services over a specified period of time with total costs not to exceed an amount previously agreed upon. The scope of work for each function or level of service is fully defined and agreed upon before the period of performance starts. Costs are generally fixed for the period of performance and usually have a "not to exceed" value. MSAs are usually awarded for periods of one year or longer.

6. FOLLOW-UP AND EXPEDITING

After issuing a PO, the buyer may follow up and/or expedite the order.

Follow-up is routine order tracking to ensure the supplier can meet delivery promises. An appropriate follow-up date is indicated with the order. Progress inquiries may be made by phone, e-mail, fax, or in-person. Early notification of problems such as production scheduling, quality, or delivery enables appropriate action. Follow-up on strategic or critical spend, especially large-dollar and/or long lead-time buys, may be about advance shipping notices (ASNs) or percentage of the production process completed as of a certain date. Follow-up may not occur on lower-value purchases or it may be built into the electronic supply system whereby buyers are only notified of exceptions.

Responsibility for follow-up with a services supplier may be placed in the user department to help ensure user compliance with prior commitments and deadlines. Follow-up on internal commitments may become a joint responsibility for the supply manager as well as the supplier. Extensive user interface with supplier personnel before and during service delivery also affects other aspects of services contract administration. For example, if a service is performed on-site after hours, security check-in sheets and access systems may be used to verify work patterns or area activity. Periodic site visits and a walk-through of the facility with the supplier's representative may lead to a better understanding of user needs. Some form of benchmarking against other providers may also be useful.

Figure 4–1 shows an example of a follow-up form.

Expediting is the application of pressure on a supplier to meet the original delivery promise, to deliver ahead of schedule, or to speed up delivery of a delayed order. Threats of order cancellation or loss of future business may be used. Expediting should be necessary on only a small percentage of the POs issued. If the buyer has done a good job of analyzing supplier capabilities, only reliable suppliers—ones who will perform according to the purchase agreement—will be selected.

Frequently, expediting is caused by poor planning inside the buying organization and may indicate the need for internal process improvements. If material requirements planning is adequate, the buyer should not need to ask a supplier to move up the delivery date except in unusual situations. Of course, in times of severe scarcity, the expediting activity assumes greater importance.

Assess Costs and Benefits

One of the costs of doing business with a supplier (and vice versa) is the cost associated with follow-up and expediting. One form of risk assessment and mitigation is matching the degree and type of follow-up with the spend category strategy (typically based on the importance of the purchase to the organization).

Follow-up and expediting that cost more than the value added is a form of process waste. It should be captured and included in the total cost of ownership assessment. Expediting may be a prime target for root cause analysis and a reduction or elimination plan. Often, the analysis reveals that the need for expediting is driven by decisions made in the buying organization, not by the supplier, and internal change is needed.

FIGURE 4–1
Follow-Up
Form

Source: Arizona
Public Service
Company.

aps.

PURCHASE ORDER FOLLOW-UP
(Please Rush Reply)
PURCHASING DEPARTMENT • P.O. BOX 21666 • PHOENIX, ARIZONA 85036

Date _____
This is our _____ Request
Please Answer Immediately

REPLY TO ITEMS CHECKED BELOW BY
☐ This Form   ☐ Wire   ☐ Phone

Our Purchase Order No.	Request for Quotation No.	Your Invoice No.	Date	Amount	Your Reference

☐ 1. RUSH SHIPMENT. ADVISE EARLIEST DATE.
☐ 2. WHEN WILL SHIPMENT BE MADE? IF SHIPPED, ADVISE METHOD.
☐ 3. PLEASE TRACE SHIPMENT.
☐ 4. IF SHIPMENT HAS BEEN MADE, MAIL INVOICE, TODAY.
☐ 5. PLEASE MAIL RECEIPTED FREIGHT BILL.
☐ 6. WHY DID YOU NOT SHIP AS PROMISED? ADVISE WHEN YOU WILL SHIP.
☐ 7. WILL YOU SHIP ON DATE SHOWN ON PURCHASE ORDER?
☐ 8. RELEASE SHIPMENTS AS SHOWN UNDER REMARKS.
☐ 9. PLEASE MAIL US ACCEPTANCE COPY OR OUR PURCHASE ORDER.
☐ 10. PLEASE ACKNOWLEDGE OUR ORDER.
☐ 11. PLEASE MAKE YOUR SHIPPING DATE MORE SPECIFIC.
☐ 12. WHEN WILL BALANCE OF ORDER BE SHIPPED.
☐ 13. WHEN WILL PRICES BE SUBMITTED? PLEASE RUSH.
☐ 14. PLEASE MAIL SHIPPING NOTICE.
☐ 15. PLEASE INDICATE OUR PURCHASE ORDER NUMBER ON PAPERS REFERRED TO OR ATTACHED.

☐ 16. WE HAVE NO RECORD OF TRANSACTION COVERED BY INVOICE. ADVISE DATE OF SHIPMENT, NAME OF PERSON PLACING ORDER AND FURNISH SIGNED DELIVERY RECEIPT COPY.
☐ 17. INVOICE RETURNED HEREWITH.
☐ 18. INVOICE IS REQUIRED IN _____ COPIES.
☐ 19. PRICE OR DISCOUNT IS NOT IN ACCORDANCE WITH QUOTATION.
☐ 20. TERMS ON INVOICE ARE NOT IN ACCORDANCE WITH THE PURCHASE ORDER.
☐ 21. ENCLOSED INVOICE SENT TO US IN ERROR.
☐ 22. DIFFERENCE IN QUANTITY.
☐ 23. UNIT PRICE INCORRECT.
☐ 24. EXTENSION INCORRECT.
☐ 25. PURCHASE ORDER NO. LACKING OR INCORRECT.
☐ 26. SALES TAX DOES NOT APPLY – See reverse side of Purchase Order.
☐ 27. SHOULD BE BILLED F.O.B. DESTINATION.
☐ 28. HAVE YOU CONSIDERED THIS ORDER COMPLETE?
☐ 29. _____

Reply: _____

Vendor By _____
Purchasing By _____
510-00J

SEND WHITE AND PINK COPIES WITH CARBON INTACT.   WHITE COPY IS RETURNED WITH REPLY.

7. RECEIPT AND INSPECTION

The proper receipt of goods and services is of vital importance. Many smaller and single-site organizations have centralized receiving in one department. Often receiving reports to supply management (see Chapter 16). If just-in-time inventory management systems have been implemented, materials from certified suppliers or supplier partners bypass receiving and inspection and are delivered directly to the point of use. (See Chapter 8.) Receiving also may be bypassed for small-value purchases.

The prime purposes of receiving are to:

1. Confirm that the order placed has actually arrived.
2. Check that the shipment arrived in good condition.
3. Ensure the quantity ordered has been received.
4. Forward the shipment to its proper destination (storage, inspection, or use).
5. Ensure that proper documentation of the receipt is registered and accessible to appropriate parties.

Shortages may occur because material has been lost in transit, short-shipped, tampered with, or damaged in transit. Physical counts can be forced by blocking receiving from access to the quantity ordered. If accurate amounts are entered into the system, the order is closed out, inventory records updated, and the invoice cleared for accounts payable to authorize payment.

Eliminate or Reduce Inspection

One goal of supply management is to ensure that quality is built in internally during the design stage and externally in the suppliers' processes. This reduces or eliminates incoming inspection. (See Chapter 7, "Quality"; Chapter 9, "Delivery"; and Chapter 13, "Supplier Evaluation and Relations.")

In a just-in-time (JIT) environment, production parts go right from the receiving dock to production. This is only possible when the supplier is capable of achieving the right level of quality consistently and the carrier is capable of meeting the delivery windows consistently. When quality is not assured, incoming inspection is required. Damage may also occur during transit, which has implications for carrier inspection and logistics processes. Decisions must be made about the need for inspection, the appropriate type of inspection, and the most cost-efficient and effective method of inspection.

8. INVOICE CLEARING AND PAYMENT

An invoice is a claim against the buying organization. Typically it shows order number and itemized price. Invoice clearance procedures are not uniform. Checks and audits of invoices are established based on cost-benefit analysis. The cost of a person's time to resolve minor variances may exceed the value of the variance. A decision rule may be used that stipulates payment of the invoice as submitted, as long as the difference is within prescribed limits: for example, plus or minus 5 percent or $25, whichever is smaller. Accounts payable tracks variances to identify suppliers that are intentionally short-shipping.

Payment for services may vary somewhat from payment for goods. Some services require prepayment, such as an eminent speaker; some, immediately upon delivery, such as hospitality services, whereas others can be delayed, such as telephone services. It may be difficult for small suppliers to offer extended payment terms, and early payment may generate price or other concessions. Progress payments are usual for large contracts spread over time, whereas regular payments are appropriate for ongoing services such as building maintenance or food service.

Supply or accounting may be responsible for clearing invoices (see Chapter 16). If assigned to accounting, supply is relieved of a nonvalue-adding task, accounting tasks are concentrated in a single function, and a check and balance is established between the commitment to buy and payment. If assigned to supply, immediate action can be taken because supply placed the original order.

When the invoice is handled by accounting in a paper-based process, the following procedure is typical:

1. Duplicate invoices are mailed directly to the accounts payable (AP) department. AP time-stamps, checks for accuracy, and certifies for payment except where the purchase order and the invoice differ. AP files one copy; one is returned with payment.

2. Invoices at variance with the purchase order on price, terms, or other features are referred to supply for approval.

If information is missing or does not agree with the purchase order, the invoice is returned to the supplier for correction. Ordinarily, the buyer insists that discounts (see Chapter 10) be computed from the receipt of the corrected invoice, not from the date originally received.

If a purchase order is canceled and cancellation charges are paid, supply provides accounting with a "change notice" that defines the payment before approval.

If supply clears invoices, the procedure is:

1. After review and adjustments for corrections, the original invoice is forwarded to accounting to be held until supply authorizes payment. The duplicate invoice is retained by supply.
2. When the receiving report is sent to supply, it is checked against the invoice. If the two agree, supply keeps both documents until it receives assurance from inspection that the goods are acceptable.
3. Supply then forwards its duplicate copy of the invoice and the receiving report to accounting, where the original copy of the invoice is already on file. Accounting issues payment.

The three-way match of data from the purchase order, the invoice, and receiving also occurs in an electronic procurement system.

Aligning Supply and Accounts Payable

Often, payment terms are not met. The root causes of late payment are typically either slow cycle time in the accounts payable process or conflict between finance and supply policy. Slow cycle time can occur because of errors on the invoice, paper-based processes, inefficient mailroom processes at the buying organization, and limited human resources in the mailroom, accounting, and/or supply. Information systems and electronic fund transfers may help address these problems by shortening the cycle time.

Lack of alignment causes conflict between supply and accounting. Supply views suppliers as valuable contributors to the organization's success. Living up to the terms and conditions of the contract is one indicator of the commitment to performance of both parties. When buyers negotiate payment terms and their organization fails to live up to those terms, this should be seen as a serious breach by all functional representatives.

Accounting views cash management as a primary contributor to the organization's success. Paying accounts as late as possible allows the buying organization the use of its money for a longer period of time. The perspective on suppliers may be that they are expendable and easily replaceable.

Management may put accounts payable and supply into one department to force goal alignment through structure and reporting relationship. Or accounts payable and supply may serve on a joint team to resolve inconsistencies and align processes. The Ross Wood case in Chapter 16 illustrates how changing the accounts payable process and combining accounts payable and supply can improve process efficiency and effectiveness.

Cash Discounts and Late Invoices

Sometimes suppliers are slow to invoice, and supply must request the invoice. Or suppliers request payment prior to the receipt of material or services. When invoices provide for cash discounts, should you pay the invoice within the discount period, even though the material may not actually have been received, or do you withhold payment until the material arrives, even at the risk of losing cash discounts?

The arguments for withholding payment of the invoice until after the goods have arrived are:

1. Frequently the invoice does not reach the buyer until late in the discount period or after it, if the supplier fails to invoice promptly.
2. It is poor practice to pay without an opportunity for inspection. Legally, the title to the goods may not pass to the buyer until acceptance of them.
3. Commonly, invoices are dated on the shipment date. The buyer should state that the discount period runs from the later of either the date of goods receipt or invoice date.

The arguments for clearing the invoice for payment without awaiting the arrival, inspection, and acceptance of the material are:

1. The financial consideration from discounts may be substantial.
2. Failure to take the cash discounts reflects unfavorably on the credit standing of the buyer.
3. With reputable suppliers, mutually satisfactory adjustments will be made easily.

9. MAINTENANCE OF RECORDS AND RELATIONSHIPS

The final step is to update records, including supplier performance scorecards. Electronic files or hard copies of the order-related documents are stored or filed. Law, accounting standards, company policy, and judgment determine which records are to be kept and for how long. For example, a purchase order is evidence of a contract. It may be retained much longer (normally seven years) than the requisition, which is an internal memorandum.

The basic records to be maintained, either manually or electronically, are:

1. PO log, which identifies all POs by number and indicates the open or closed status of each.
2. PO file, containing a copy of all POs, filed numerically.
3. Commodity file, showing all purchases of each major commodity or item (date, supplier, quantity, price, PO number).
4. Supplier history file, showing all purchases placed with major suppliers.
5. Outstanding contracts against which orders are placed as required.
6. A commodity classification of items purchased.
7. A database of suppliers.

Additional record files may include:

1. Labor contracts, giving the status of union contracts (expiration dates) for all major suppliers.
2. Tool and die record showing tooling purchased, useful life (or production quantity), usage history, price, ownership, and location. This may prevent paying more than once for the same tooling.

established and efficiency tools, especially electronic ones, are used. Second, suppliers are prequalified and tools for efficient order placement are used.

Efficiency relates to the number of tasks performed in a set amount of time. For nonstrategic spend, efficiencies are gained by reducing the number of requisitions coming into the supply department, the number of purchase orders issued to suppliers, and the number of invoices and payments processed. Two continual problem areas for supply managers, small value purchases and rush orders, are largely resolved through the use of efficiency tools.

Small Value Orders

A Pareto analysis of annual spend usually reveals that roughly 70 to 80 percent of transactions account for only 10 to 15 percent of spend. These are C items, typically, maintenance, repair, and operating supplies (MRO), with low average transaction amounts. For some goods and services that fall into this category it might be possible that the costs of processing the order and delivering the goods or services may be greater than the value of the purchase. The process cost to transact a $50 purchase may be as much as a $5,000 one. The goal is to minimize the acquisition costs (the process costs not the price) of nonstrategic spend while assuring availability.

The problem of small monetary value orders is resolved by simplifying or automating the process or consolidating purchases to reduce the acquisition cycle time (time from need recognition to payment), reduce administrative cost, and free up the buyer's time for higher-value or more critical purchases. A few examples follow:

1. Vendor/supplier-managed inventory (VMI/SMI), stockless buying, or systems contracting can be used. This is typical for MRO items. (See explanation earlier in this chapter.)

2. A procurement card (also called a purchasing card or a P-card) is a credit card that is provided to internal customers to purchase directly from established suppliers. (See discussion in next section.)

3. Supply sets up blanket orders against which internal customers issue release orders; suppliers provide summary billing.

4. An electronic procurement or an electronic data interchange (EDI) system is used. Ordering and reordering occur automatically based on preestablished reorder points.

5. In reverse auctions, the buyer prequalifies suppliers and invites them to an online auction during which bidders submit bids and the buyer awards a contract for the predefined items for a set period of time.

6. Authority levels and bidding practices are adjusted, and an e-procurement system, telephone, or e-mail is used for ordering.

7. Integrated suppliers are used to provide a variety of supplies.

8. Low-value order placement is outsourced to third parties.

9. Persuasion may be employed to increase the number of standardized items requested.

10. Small requisitions are held until a reasonable total, in dollars, has been accumulated.

11. Specific supplies or type of supplier is assigned to a requisition calendar so that all requests are received on the same day.

12. Invoice-less payments (self-billing) are arranged.

13. Users place orders directly with suppliers.
14. A blank check purchase order is issued in which a signed, blank check is sent along with the PO. The supplier ships the full order, completes the check, and deposits it. This reduces paperwork (receiving reports, inventory entries, and payments), saves postage, often enables a larger cash discount, and saves time in accounts payable.
15. Outsource responsibility for small-value purchases to a third-party purchasing services provider. For example, some firms prefer to use third-party firms to handle their plant stores' operations for MRO components.

Reducing the Number of Requisitions Marked Rush or Emergency

Frequently, an excessive number of requisitions are marked "rush." Emergencies, such as style or design changes, equipment breakdowns, and unexpected changes in market conditions, may justify a rush order.

However, some "rush" orders cannot be justified. These include requisitions caused by: (1) faulty inventory control, (2) poor production planning or budgeting, (3) lack of confidence in the ability of the supply department to get material to the user by the proper time, and (4) the sheer habit of marking requests "rush." Unnecessary costs occur because of errors from working under pressure and the impact on price to compensate the supplier for the added burden (real or perceived) of a rush order.

Education and process improvements may reduce the problem. Supply must educate users about the proper supply procedure and enlist the support of other functions to gain compliance. For example, the requisitioner has to secure approval from the general manager and any extra costs that can be calculated are charged back.

Improvements in process efficiency increase the credibility of the process and the supply group. These include preapproved suppliers, purchasing cards, electronic catalogs, and e-procurement systems that reduce lead and cycle time and allow users to issue requests directly to a supplier against an existing contract.

Corporate Purchasing Cards

Corporate purchasing cards (also called procurement cards or P-cards) are credit cards issued to internal customers (users) in the buying organization to purchase low-dollar-value, high-volume goods and services. P-cards reduce administrative costs (for people, system use and third-party providers) by reducing the number of purchase orders generated and processed and by shortening the process cycle time for authorizing, tracking, purchasing, reconciling, and reporting purchases. P-card use supports other process initiatives such as consolidating spend and suppliers. They can be merged with technology to be electronic commerce compatible and data sensitive to capture information that is integrated into an ERP system.

Holders of the card are given dollar limits and lists of preferred suppliers with whom supply has already negotiated prices and terms. P-cards automate many aspects of the system, thereby eliminating purchase orders and individual invoices and ensuring suppliers of fast payment, two or three days versus 30+ in a typical system. By moving the transaction activities to the user department, the supply cycle time and transaction costs are reduced. Also, buyers (and accounts payable) are freed from the day-to-day transactions for small-value purchases and can focus on higher-value purchases and issues.

The General Services Administration (GSA) found that purchases under $2,500 accounted for approximately 2 percent of total federal government spending, but represented

85 percent of total procurement transaction volume. Implementation of purchasing cards to handle low-value purchases generated estimated savings of $54 to $92 per transaction while simultaneously reducing the time required to process paperwork transactions by two to six weeks.[1]

The primary perceived risk of P-cards is loss of control. Card issuers have instituted controls that (1) determine, at the point of sale, if the purchase meets preset dollar limits per card; (2) limit the number of transactions per day; (3) limit the value of a single transaction; (4) determine if it is an approved supplier; and (5) limit purchases to specific commodities. By establishing daily and monthly querying and reporting, the administrator manages by exception rather than focusing on monthly statement details.

The most sophisticated card programs are able to (1) track and report sales tax information for audit purposes, (2) track and prepare 1099 forms for unincorporated service providers, (3) identify whether the supplier is a minority business owner, (4) capture specific product information, (5) identify which cost center should be charged for the purchase, and (6) include different types of purchases, including travel and entertainment expenses and fleet expenses.

Supplier- or Vendor-Managed Inventory (SMI/VMI), Stockless Buying, or Systems Contracting

Supplier- or vendor-managed inventory (SMI/VMI), systems contracting, or stockless buying are a more sophisticated merging of the ordering and inventory functions than blanket contracts.

Systems Contracting

Systems contracts rely on periodic billing procedures, allow nonsupply personnel to issue order releases, employ special catalogs, and require suppliers to maintain minimum inventory levels. Normally, the volume of contract items is not specified. These systems improve inventory turnover rates.

This technique is used most frequently in buying repetitive items such as office supplies and maintenance, repair, and operating supplies (MRO). MRO supplies are many types of items, all of comparatively low value and needed immediately when any kind of a plant or equipment failure occurs. The technique is built around a blanket-type contract that is developed in great detail regarding approximate quantities to be used in specified time periods, prices, provisions for adjusting prices, procedures to be followed for daily requisitioning and delivery within a short time (normally 24 hours), simplified billing procedures, and a complete catalog (often online) of all items covered by the contract.

In an electronic procurement system, the buyer or requisitioner communicates electronically each item and quantity required. If there are large-volume requirements from a specific supplier, the supplier stores items in the customer's plant as though it were the supplier's warehouse. The buyer's contact with the supplier is electronic. The system works as follows:

1. The buyer places the blanket order for a family of items, such as fasteners, at firm prices.
2. The supplier delivers predetermined quantities to the inventory area set aside in the buyer's plant. The items are still owned by the supplier.
3. The buyer sometimes inspects the items when they are delivered.
4. The computer directs storage to the appropriate bin or shelf.

[1] R. J. Palmer, M. Gupta, and R. Dawson, "U.S. Government Use of Card Technology," Defense Acquisition University (July 2010), www.dau.mil.

5. The buyer places POs electronically, thus relieving the supplier's inventory records.
6. Pick sheets are prepared and the items are picked from the supplier's inventory.
7. The supplier submits a single invoice monthly for all items picked.
8. The buyer's accounting department makes a single monthly payment.
9. A summary report is electronically generated, at predetermined intervals, showing the items and quantity used for the buyer's and supplier's analysis, planning, and restocking.

Systems contracting is used in service organizations as well as manufacturing and for high-dollar-volume commodities as well as MRO supplies. The shorter cycle time from requisition to delivery leads to substantial inventory reductions and greater compliance with the supply process. The amount of red tape or bureaucracy is minimal. Since the user normally provides a good estimate of requirements and compensates the supplier in case the forecast is not good, the supplier risks little in inventory investment. The degree of cooperation and information exchange required between buyer and supplier often results in stronger relationships than normally exhibited in a traditional arm's-length trading situation.

Vendor- or Supplier-Managed Inventory (VMI or SMI)

In VMI systems, the supplier is responsible for maintaining the buying organization's inventory levels. The supplier has access to inventory levels (often electronically) and generates purchase orders. Typically, the supplier manages the buyer's inventory at the buyer's location.

The supplier pulls stock, packs, ships, and invoices. This procedure reduces process cycle time by reducing the number of people/functions touching the process. These systems are tools for managing small orders. VMI may also be used for consignment inventory wherein payment is made after inventory is used.

Large retailers, such as Walmart, use VMI systems with their key suppliers such as Procter & Gamble. In these arrangements, stock at Walmart's distribution centers is owned by the supplier and invoices are issued when the goods are shipped to a store. EDI is used to handle inventory reconciliation and invoicing.

INFORMATION SYSTEMS AND THE SUPPLY PROCESS

Information systems include interconnected components that collect, process, and store raw data and distribute information to support decision making, control, and coordination within the organization. While information systems can be manual (paper based), most information systems rely on information technology infrastructure, consisting of hardware and software, to operate.

Information system technology allows organizations to be connected with important partners in their supply chain networks. Capabilities to exchange reliable information with these partners quickly and cost effectively is essential for the improvement of supply chain performance.

There are a number of technology tools available to improve process efficiency and effectiveness. These tools enable process effectiveness in two ways: (1) They make data more transparent, accurate, and accessible to decision makers, and (2) they relieve supply decision makers of lower-value-adding tasks, allowing them to focus on higher-value-adding tasks, spend categories, and internal (other functional areas, top management) and external (suppliers) relationships. Also, the development of decision support and knowledge management systems enables more sophisticated modeling and facilitates more complex decisions involving multiple variables.

To determine which information systems might be used to support or enable efficient and effective processes, it is important to understand (1) the benefits of the technology, (2) the technology options that provide these benefits, and (3) the trade-offs in costs and benefits when choosing technology.

This section covers information systems in a supply context, and addresses the following: ERP systems, cloud computing, e-procurement, online catalogs, electronic data interchange (EDI), marketplaces, online reverse auctions, and radio frequency identification (RFID).

Benefits of Information Systems Technology

Information system technology can provide seven important benefits to the organization:

Cost reduction and efficiency gains. These can be achieved by streamlining the supply processes and freeing up supply staff to do more value-adding work.

Data accessibility. Quick and easy access to critical data in real time aids sound decision making, makes it easier to identify supply problems earlier, and provides useful information for negotiations.

Speedier communication. Faster communication improves supply chain effectiveness and efficiency, especially with global suppliers. Faster turnaround may increase market share and lower inventories.

Dedicate resources to strategic issues. More resources (e.g., staff and budgets) can be spent on strategic supply initiatives, and strategic and critical suppliers and projects because less time is spent on administrative and tactical supply activities.

Data accuracy. Automation decreases errors, especially data entry errors. Benefits include lower inventories (safety stock) and stockouts, lower expediting costs, and improved customer satisfaction.

Systems integration. Integration across departments, suppliers, and customers can provide accurate information on a timely basis to assist with production and materials planning and decision making.

Monetary control. Enterprise systems can provide control over how and where money is spent.

ERP Systems

Enterprise resource planning (ERP) systems refer to a type of computer software that contains a suite of applications that integrate various functions within the organization (e.g., operations, supply, marketing, and accounting/finance) and facilitates the connection to supply chain stakeholders, such as suppliers and customers. Using a common data management system, ERP systems allow users to share information across departments, and in some cases across the supply chain, in real time. An additional advantage of ERP is that it eliminates dispersed organizational information systems, thereby reducing opportunities for errors in transaction processes.

ERP represents an extension of standalone MRP (materials requirements planning and later materials resource planning) systems that became popular in the late 1980s and 1990s and focused originally on manufacturing firms (see Chapter 8 for a detailed coverage of MRP). Today, ERP systems are used by firms in the manufacturing, services, governmental, and nonprofit sectors. While SAP AG and Oracle are the largest providers of ERP software, there are a large number of small ERP solutions suppliers, typically targeting specific industry sectors.

Most organizations have supply chain management modules as part of their ERP systems. These can include purchasing, forecasting and planning, order tracking, shipping and receiving, scheduling, and inventory management.

The cost of ERP systems and implementation can be expensive and disruptive to the organization. For large organizations, total costs can run in the tens of millions of dollars, take several years, and involve hundreds of consultants and project managers. Many small and medium-sized enterprises (SMEs) cannot afford the capital outlay of ERP software and may instead adopt cloud-based systems that offer the cost advantage of pay-as-you-go fees as opposed to up-front capital costs (see the following section on cloud computing).

Business processes used to support company legacy systems can evolve over time and become inefficient. Implementation of ERP systems requires evaluation of and changes to business processes. As with most projects, poor preparation is a leading cause of failure, so proper understanding of how processes are currently used and the changes required is the essential starting point for ERP system implementation. This can be particularly challenging in a decentralized organization that may have very different processes and policies. Reviewing business processes as part of an ERP implementation project represents an opportunity to improve process efficiency and standardize and align processes across the organization.

The significant costs and effort required to implement ERP systems are justified on the basis of eliminating the costs of maintaining legacy systems; operating efficiencies in areas such as inventory control and customer service levels as a result of systems integration; improved visibility, and the ability to make decisions quickly using real-time information; standardization of processes and policies (e.g., product coding); improved order tracking; and access to a common database that can be used for analytics.

Adopting ERP systems also comes with potential disadvantages beyond cost and organizational effort to implement and train employees on the new system. It is difficult to customize ERP systems, and companies may have to change or forego unique processes. Once firms commit to an ERP system, switching costs are high. Fees to support the system and upgrade costs can be expensive and, where possible, should be negotiated at the outset. Lastly, the anticipated benefits can be overestimated, extending the payback on the investment.

Cloud Computing and the Supply Chain

It is common for organizations to install new software applications layered over existing legacy systems. For supply, examples include procurement, inventory management, transportation, and forecasting systems provided by companies such as Descartes, JDA, and Manhattan Associates. Cloud solutions provide access to software applications, in some cases working on top of legacy systems, which provides the advantages of cost-effectiveness and flexibility.

The National Institute of Standards and Technology (NIST) defines cloud computing as "a model for enabling ubiquitous, convenient, on-demand network access to a shared pool of configurable computing resources (e.g., networks, servers, storage, applications, and services) that can be rapidly provisioned and released with minimal management effort or service provider interaction."[2] Cloud computing can be private (operated for a single organization, managed internally or by a third party), public (operated over a network for general public use), community (operated for specific organizations, managed internally or by a third party), or hybrid (some combination of private, community, and/or public). Individuals are exposed to cloud applications in their personal lives in a variety of common technologies, such as accessing e-mail through Gmail, managing their music library on iTunes, or using some operating systems, such as Microsoft Office 365, on their computers.

There are three main elements of cloud computing important to supply:[3]

Software as a Service (SaaS): Applications that reside in the cloud, which users are able to rent on a pay-for-use basis. SaaS is the largest and most mature part of cloud computing.

Platform as a Service (PaaS): Software development technologies that allow users to create customized processes or tools specific for their needs.

Infrastructure as a Service (IaaS): Shared server capacity that permits the sharing of computing power and storage and that can be accessed as needed on a pay-for-use basis.

Advocates of cloud solutions claim that it provides the advantages of lower costs and increased flexibility. First, IaaS means that the costs of cloud computing are variable, based on a pay-as-you-go model, so organizations are able to avoid expensive capital investments in new systems. Second, PaaS permits implementation of cloud-based systems easier and faster. Proponents of cloud systems claim that new applications can be set up faster, with less ongoing maintenance, permitting allocation of information technology resources to other areas. Third, the interconnectedness of cloud computing provided by SaaS improves transparency and visibility across the end-to-end supply chain. Communication and workflows are more reliable and robust, compared to traditional methods such as e-mail and EDI.

Adaption of cloud-based systems is expected to continue to grow rapidly. Estimates for the market size of cloud technology are $150 to $200 billion by 2020.[4] However, skeptics of cloud computing have raised concerns in the areas of cost, reliability, security, and regulation. Despite claims of the cost advantages of cloud computing, careful analysis is required to understand the fee structure and compare it to the costs of acquiring the application and hosting it internally. Similarly, there are concerns that some cloud applications are not as reliable and managed as well as on-premises infrastructure, resulting in service interruptions. Security is a major issue with most information systems, and the concept of third-party managed infrastructure can be unsettling. Concerns include hackers that can compromise data security, service providers using data without permission, and vulnerability to viruses, worms, and malware. There are a number of regulatory issues, mainly related to data transport and access, especially in cases where data storage and infrastructure are hosted in a foreign country. Government regulations are vague in some areas and are expected to change and evolve. For now, users should get as much clarity as possible about the legal and regulatory issues for their organization before adopting cloud computing.[5]

[2] Reference: http://csrc.nist.gov/publications/nistpubs/800-145/SP800-145.pdf, accessed February 27, 2014.

[3] G. Courtin, *Supply Chain and the Future of Applications* (London, U.K.: SCM World, October, 2013).

[4] http://csrc.nist.gov/publications/nistpubs/800-145/SP800-145.

[5] A. McAfee, "What Every CEO Needs to Know About the Cloud," *Harvard Business Review* 89, no. 11 (November 2011), pp. 124–132.

Electronic Procurement Systems

E-procurement is an applications software package that allows the requisitioning, authorizing, ordering, receiving, invoicing, and paying for goods and services through the Internet and is frequently a module in the company's ERP system. Firms such as Oracle and SAP dominate the e-procurement market because their software can provide real-time integration with their ERP systems. Because of the costs of acquiring ERP and e-procurement systems, many small and medium-sized enterprises (SMEs) use cloud computing services, enabled by SaaS, to acquire e-procurement capabilities.

Some organizations use e-procurement to automate from requisition-to-order and others from requisition-to-pay. An end-to-end e-procurement system that includes contracts and e-payables in the cycle is referred to as procure-to-pay.

The adoption of an e-procurement system is often driven by existing process inefficiency, low internal compliance, high transaction costs, low spend visibility, and low control over organizational spend. Performance metrics for an e-procurement system often include: (1) the percent of organizational spend under supply's control, (2) requisition-to-order costs, (3) requisition-to-order cycles, and (4) percent of off-contract (maverick) spend. A survey of chief purchasing officers about their use of e-procurement technology found the benefits were: (1) better visibility of what they are spending globally by supplier, region, and commodity, (2) faster, better product development by tapping suppliers as an innovation source, and (3) tighter risk reduction and mitigation.[6]

From the internal user/customer perspective, a successful e-procurement system is one that makes life easier—faster ordering, faster fulfillment, and a broader range of choices. Depending on the policies and procedures implemented, it may be possible to satisfy internal users as well as meet the requirements for internal control, cost savings, and supply base management.

Streamlining the Receiving, Invoicing, and Payment Process

Should the e-procurement system include receiving, invoicing, and payment? A valid question is: Does the organization need to receive an invoice? The invoice provides no new information, yet it costs money to handle.

In an invoiceless system, suppliers are notified that payment, based on the agreed-upon cash discount schedule, will be made in a set number of days from receipt of satisfactory merchandise (and they may specify that payment will be made only after the complete shipment has been received). A system match between the PO, receiving report, and inspection report (if conducted) is made, and a check is generated or funds are electronically transmitted on the receipt date at the agreed-upon payment term. The receiving report must be accurate; the PO fully priced, including taxes and cash discount terms; and purchases must be made FOB destination, since there is no way to enter in freight charges. The PO then is the controlling document.

Commodity Coding Schema

Commodity managers need commodity codes to effectively source, track, and manage spend by category. Users, who want to get to the product quickly and easily, need robust

---

[6] D. Jones, "Best Practices: Selecting and Implementing ePurchasing Products," Forrester Research (May 22, 2013).

item descriptions that are easily searched. The procurement team must respond to the needs of both stakeholders.

The value of a hierarchical commodity coding schema is the ability to evaluate expenditures according to any level of the hierarchy. If a company, such as an architectural, graphic arts, or printing firm, spends a significant amount on writing utensils and supplies, spend analysis may be at the **class** (ink and lead refills) or **commodity** (pen refills) levels. This reveals opportunities to consolidate suppliers, find better sources, negotiate volume discounts, or optimize the supply chain in some other way. If this spend is insignificant, analysis may be on the higher **family** (office supplies) or **segment** (office equipment, accessories, and supplies) categories only.

The U.N. Standard Products and Services Code (UNSPSC) provides an open, global, multisector standard for efficient, accurate classification of products and services. Some supply managers are dissatisfied because the UNSPSC often does not address specific industries or products at a level of detail required for meaningful commodity spend analysis. Also, it is difficult to make updates in an automated environment. Different divisions of the same organization often assign different UNSPSC codes to the same commodity. To effectively use UNSPSC, all databases within an organization and its supply chain need to use the same version of UNSPSC, support backward compatibility for earlier versions, and keep it updated. Costs can be prohibitive.

Many procurement departments use government-issued, industry-specific, or proprietary code systems that do not directly integrate or embed UNSPSC. Proprietary codes are developed by, and useful to, a single company. Often they are not hierarchical, meaning they lack roll-up and drill-down capabilities for spend analysis. Such coding schemas can be expensive to develop and maintain, and it can be expensive to require trading partners to use the same code.[7]

Electronic or Online Catalogs

An e-catalog or online catalog is a digitized version of a supplier's catalog. It allows buyers to use a web browser to view detailed buying and specifying information about the supplier's products and/or services. Product catalogs include (1) product specification data, and (2) transaction data. Product specification data describe the products and are the same for all buyers. Transaction data (price, shipping and billing addresses, and quantity discounts) are customized to each buyer.

Suppliers have a number of options to digitize their catalogs. The buyer's solutions provider can typically convert the supplier's catalog to a suitable format. Alternatively, the supplier can purchase an out-of-the box software package and make the conversion or purchase the services of the software provider. Or a data aggregator can develop a library of product specifications from a variety of suppliers and license organizations to use the product specifications and assist in developing the transaction data. In a catalog network, a host company collects the catalogs and customizes the transaction data for each buyer. The buyer can either pull the catalogs onto the company server or access them from the host company. Or the supplier may allow the buyer to "punch out" or access a supplier-hosted catalog.

---

[7] A. E. Flynn, *Catalog Management: Implementation Strategies* (Tempe, AZ: CAPS Research, October 2004).

Supply can create buyer-controlled catalogs that combine information, such as pricing and specifications, from one or multiple suppliers. Simple database software packages permit the creation of such catalogs, and most enterprise resource planning (ERP) systems have features that permit the creation of customized catalogs. The supplier is responsible for updating and maintaining the catalogs.

In-house catalogs permit the user to customize content in terms of supply options and pricing, or to restrict supply options. These catalogs support item standardization and volume purchasing from approved suppliers. The catalog can be integrated into the company's system to streamline the process and track spending patterns.

EDI

EDI has been in existence since the 1960s, but it did not receive widespread attention and adoption until the 1990s. EDI allows computer-to-computer exchange of business documents between two organizations using agreed standards to structure the message data. The sender converts documents from their application format to a standard EDI message format and transmits the message either directly or through a third party. EDI involves B2B transactions only—individual consumers do not use EDI to purchase goods or services. Documents commonly exchanged via EDI include purchase orders, shipping schedules and notifications, and invoices. EDI has been widely adopted in the manufacturing, transportation, and retailing sectors. Companies such as Walmart, General Motors, Home Depot, and Target require supplier compliance with EDI.

EDI provides secure transmission and fast turnaround of large amounts of data; greater accuracy internally and with trading partners; shorter process cycle time that may help to lower inventory, provide electronic logs or audit trails, and reduce administrative costs.

EDI requires the use of standard message formats, which vary depending on industry and method of transmission. The most popular are ANSI X12, which is commonly used in North America, and UN/EDIFACT, which is widely used outside of North America. Certain variations of formats are used in specific industries, such as the Uniform Commercial Standard (UCS) in grocery and retail, and the Voluntary Inter-Industry Commerce Standards (VICS) in consumer packaged goods.

Value-added networks (VANS) are third-party organizations that provide EDI services for a fee. The primary services provided by VANS are transmitting information and providing data storage, similar to e-mail boxes. VANS are frequently used by small and medium-sized organizations that do not have EDI software capability in-house. Companies may also join VANS because of a requirement by one or more trading partners.

Increasingly, EDI transmissions are sent via the Internet, sometimes allowing organizations to bypass VANS, but some organizations still use data transmission lines. Using EDI over the Internet has meant that some firms have adopted AS1 and AS2 protocols that rely on XML, SMTP, and HTTP/HTTPS to send documents as S/MINE attachments, allowing them to bypass VANS.

The established B2B networks and systems provided by EDI, which has become the standard in many industries, means that EDI will continue to play an important role in the foreseeable future. The volume of EDI transactions continues to grow annually and the volume of global EDI transactions is estimated at 20 billion per year. However, firms are expanding the number of B2B communication methods and message formats. B2B marketplaces, described in the following section, provide an alternative to EDI.

Marketplaces

An *extranet* is a private intranet that is extended to authorized users outside the company, such as suppliers, also referred to as *private marketplaces*. Private marketplaces improve supply chain coordination and information sharing with key business partners. Through a web-based interface, suppliers can link into a customer's systems, and vice versa, to perform any number of activities, such as checking inventory levels, tracking the status of invoices, or submitting quotes. Because the information exchange is electronic, supply professionals are freed to spend time on value-added activities rather than entering data or checking the status of shipments or payments. The largest and perhaps most successful example of a private marketplace is Walmart's RetailLink.

Unlike B2C marketplaces such as eBay, Amazon, and Alibaba, public B2B marketplaces that developed in the early 2000s have, for the most part, disappeared or changed their business model. These marketplaces were in two groups: independent and consortia. Examples include FreeMarkets (independent marketplace providing reverse auction services) and Quadrem (consortia marketplace in the mining industry). A handful of public marketplaces have survived, such as the health care marketplace Global Health Exchange (GHX).

In contrast to a private marketplace, an *intranet* is a single and widely accessible (for authorized users only) network set up to share information and communicate with company employees. It is a private, secure internal Internet. Intranets communicate information and facilitate collaboration among employees and are sometimes linked to the company's ERP system. They can be used to display supplier catalogs, provide lists of approved suppliers, and post company supply policies. Supply processes can be enhanced by allowing employees to place orders via web browsers, approve and confirm purchases electronically, and generate POs electronically. The main advantages of supply-based intranets are low transaction costs and reduced lead times.

Online Reverse Auctions

Auctions have been used for commercial transactions for centuries. Generally, auctions are classified on the basis of competition, between sellers or buyers, and forward or descending prices. For example, the Dutch flower auctions are declining-price auctions with competition between buyers, while a traditional English-style auction, involving the sale of equipment or furniture, is a rising-price auction with multiple buyers. These models and the Internet provide new techniques for determining price, quality, volume allocations, and delivery schedules with suppliers.

Internet auction events can be open offer, private offer, posted prices, and reverse auctions.

Open Offer Auctions   Suppliers select items, see the most competitive offers from other suppliers, and enter as many offers as they want up until a specified closing time.

Private Offer Auctions   The buyer offers a target price and quantity. Suppliers enter offer(s) on select item(s) by a specific time. The buyer evaluates and posts a "status." The status levels are:

Accepted: The supplier is awarded the contract, contingent on final qualification.

Closed: The supplier may no longer submit offers on the item.

BAFO (best and final offer): The supplier may submit one more offer for the item.

Open: Bidding may be continued for as many rounds as necessary to accept or close all items.

Posted Price Auctions   The buyer posts the acceptable price; the first supplier to meet it gets the award.

Reverse Auctions

A reverse auction is an online, real-time, dynamic, declining-price auction for goods or services between one buying organization and a group of prequalified suppliers. Suppliers compete by bidding against each other online using specialized software. Suppliers see the status of their bids in real time. The supplier with the lowest bid or lowest total cost bid is usually awarded the business.

When to Use Reverse Auctions

A reverse auction is an alternative sourcing method to RFPs/RFQs, sealed bids, face-to-face negotiations, and spot buys from the commodity markets. At a minimum, the following conditions are required:

1. Clearly defined specifications, including technological, logistical, and commercial requirements.
2. A competitive market with qualified suppliers willing to participate. Typically, at least three suppliers are required. More than six suppliers may add unnecessary costs and complexity.
3. An understanding of the market conditions in order to set appropriate expectations for a reserve price.
4. Buyer and seller familiarity and competency using the auction technology.
5. Clear rules of conduct: for example, conditions for extending auction length and award criteria.
6. The buyer is prepared to switch suppliers if necessary.
7. The buyer believes that the projected savings justify a reverse auction.

Conducting Reverse Auction Events

There are three stages: preparation, the auction event, and implementation and follow-up.

Preparation   The purchaser identifies or certifies appropriate suppliers; sets the quality, quantity, delivery, and service requirements and length of contract; trains internal team members and supplier representatives on the auction technology; tests the technology and communicates the process and award criteria.

Event   Price visibility can be handled by showing rank order, percentage, or proportional differences. Bid ranks can be adjusted for nonprice factors, such as differences in transportation costs or quality.

Auction rules should be known up-front and strictly followed to foster credibility and encourage future participation. Suppliers must know the length of the auction and the rules for extending the time period. Suppliers and the buyer can typically communicate during the auction. Messages may or may not be visible to other participants. Technical assistance should also be available.

Implementation and Follow-Up   The purchaser announces the results to participants and responds to questions. Negotiation or clarification may occur before the final contract is signed.

The auction leader communicates the outcome internally. For example, accounting needs to know if there is a change of suppliers and/or pricing. Anything that might improve auctions should be documented.

Issues with Reverse Auctions

Potential ethical transgressions on behalf of buyers are:

1. Buyer knowingly accepts bids from suppliers with unreasonably low prices.
2. Buying firm submits phantom bids during the event to increase the competition artificially.
3. Buyer includes unqualified suppliers to increase price competition.

Potential ethical issues involving suppliers are:

1. Supplier collusion.
2. Suppliers bid unrealistically low prices and attempt to renegotiate afterwards.
3. Suppliers "bird watch" or participate in the event but do not bid to collect market intelligence. A rule requiring bids before entering the auction may preclude this behavior.
4. Suppliers submit bids after the auction event in an attempt to secure the business.

Potential Problems with Using Online Auctions[8]

There are a number of problems that might arise. These include:

- The risk of interrupting good supplier relationships.
- The risk of developing a reputation for aggressive price-buying over other considerations.
- The costs of running the auction versus expected savings.
- The cost savings potential of auctions versus sourcing processes such as RFP/RFQ and negotiation.
- Significant up-front preparation and cost required compared to determining price through an RFP/RFQ.
- Actual price when unforeseen costs are factored in versus bid price.

The Portland Bus Company at the end of this chapter provides an example of a company that uses electronic reverse auctions and the implications for making sourcing decisions.

Radio Frequency Identification (RFID)

RFID tags contain a chip and antenna that emit a signal, using energy from a radio frequency reader, which contains information about the container or its individual contents. RFID tags can be passive, active, or battery-assisted passive and vary widely in memory, frequency, power source, and cost. The most common are passive, read-only tags.

RFID technology has many applications in everyday life, such as employee identification badges and highway toll payment devices. Three primary applications of RFID in

---

[8] P. F. Johnson, "Supply Organizational Structures," CAPS Research, June 2003.

the supply chain are real-time tracking of inventory, product tracking, and transportation. RFID can track the movement of inventory through the supply chain. For example, it can show inventory levels in the warehouse. Several industries use RFID to track product through the manufacturing process. Automotive manufacturers use RFID tags to manage the assembly of cars, coordinating the delivery of the proper components, such as seats and engines, to the assembly line. Transportation service providers use RFID technology to track rolling stock and coordinate maintenance schedules. The potential benefits of RFID in the supply chain include lower costs by the elimination of manual counting and bar coding of incoming and outgoing material; automatic tracking of inventory levels; faster, easier, and more accurate inventory identification and picking; and reduced spoilage through improved stock rotation.

RFID is not without drawbacks. First, it adds another level of information and the firm's information systems must have the capability to capture, process, and analyze the data as they are collected. Problems persist with the ability to capture reliable data collected by the readers. Second, implementation requires investments in information technology and equipment, and support is required from consultants and systems engineers. Although the costs of RFID tags have decreased, they still remain relatively expensive compared to other technology alternatives (e.g., bar codes). As a result, many firms do not feel that adopting the technology provides a reasonable return on investment. Third, concerns have been raised about security during data transmission and privacy issues for consumers.

IMPLICATIONS FOR SUPPLY

When applying technology to the acquisition process, supply professionals still play a critical decision-making role. They provide the investigative and analytical skills to source, evaluate, and select suppliers; the influencing and persuading skills to negotiate the best deal for the organization; and a strategic and long-term planning approach to anticipate and prevent problems down the road. The transactional side is streamlined and responsibility for actually placing orders delegated to the user whenever possible.

With rapidly changing technology, it is difficult to predict what the future will look like. It is, therefore, important to identify the key questions that decision makers in supply management must answer before embarking on an e-commerce path. These include:

1. Should we be a leader or a follower?
2. What should be acquired through e-commerce?
3. What tools should we use to acquire those items?
4. Who should we use as a service provider?

1. *Should we be a leader or a follower?* Management must decide to be an early adopter of new technology or wait to see what emerges as the norm or standard. Early adopters often report that, despite the difficulties encountered, there are advantages to being further along than later adopters. Those who choose to wait tend to believe that the high risks and costs associated with adopting new technology in its infancy far outweighs whatever competitive advantages might be gained. Relevant factors are the organization's risk aversion and success with past technology implementation.

2. *What should be acquired through e-commerce?* Should the organization purchase indirect goods and services, direct requirements, or both through e-commerce tools, strategic or nonstrategic goods and services? Supply managers must consider the characteristics of each category of purchase (see Chapter 6 for a discussion of purchases categories) to determine what might be successfully procured online. This analysis includes consideration of the existing and desired buyer–supplier relationship to ensure that the method of procurement does not adversely harm the relationship.

3. *What tools should we use?* Streamlining tools range from lower technology tools, such as procurement cards, to high-technology tools, such as online reverse auctions, e-catalogs, and integrated e-RFx systems. A decision to adopt e-commerce does not necessarily mean that all the available tools will be adopted. The decision maker must determine the appropriateness of the tool to the type of material or service under consideration, the nature of the buyer-supplier relationship, and the comfort level of the internal stakeholders and the suppliers. Decisions related to the adoption of enterprise systems (e.g., ERP systems) are made by the CEO, usually with input from executive leaders such as the CFO and CIO. Supply operates under the umbrella of the company's management information systems, which can affect the range of e-commerce applications available.

4. *Who should we use as a service provider(s)?* If a third-party service provider is used, such as cloud computing, a careful assessment must be made of the available providers. Several critical technical issues are compatibility with, or ease of migration from, existing software; scalability (can it grow with your needs?); the supplier's technical reputation and experience with supply chain management; and expertise of the staff. Some of the key considerations beyond the technical issues are the long-term viability of the provider, user-friendliness of the software, fee structure, and service and support—offline and online.

POLICY AND PROCEDURE MANUAL

A policy and procedure manual may also contribute to the development of an efficient and effective process. It is a carefully prepared, detailed statement of organization, duties of the various personnel, and procedures and data systems (including illustrative forms used, fully explained). A manual is essential for a well-conceived training program, internal transfers, and communication about the process with nonsupply colleagues. The requirements of the Sarbanes-Oxley Act add greater importance to internal controls, standardized processes, and consistent use.

The preparation process may reveal inconsistencies and discrepancies that lead to process improvements. Careful advance planning of the coverage, emphasis, and arrangement is essential. It should include a clear definition of the purposes of the manual and its uses. Both purpose and use influence length, form, and content. A manual may cover only policy or it may include a description of the organization and some level of description of procedures. Current manuals and sample manuals from other organizations can serve as guides.

Department personnel and internal stakeholders such as design, engineering, marketing, operations, and production should discuss and check the contents for errors and modifications. The manual should reflect the actual policy and procedures, or drive process changes. The manual may be posted on the organization's intranet and/or in loose-leaf form. The chief executive officer may enhance credibility by writing a foreword defining the supply department's authority and endorsing its policy and procedures.

Common topics are authority to requisition; competitive bidding; approved suppliers; supplier contracts and commitments; authority to question specifications; purchases for employees; gifts, blanket purchase orders; confidential data; rush orders; supplier relations; lead times; determination of quantity to buy; over and short allowance procedure; local purchases; capital equipment; personal service purchases; repair service purchases; authority to select suppliers; confirming orders; unpriced purchase orders; documentation for purchase decisions; invoice clearance and payment, invoice discrepancies; freight bills; change orders; samples; returned materials; disposal of scrap and surplus; determination of price paid; small-order procedures; salesperson interviews; and reporting of data.

Conclusion

The supply management process has come under increasing scrutiny because of (1) the unrelenting focus on cost management, and (2) the realization that standardized processes and internal and external integration can lead to competitive advantage. Robust processes are the foundation of a successful supply organization.

As supply managers continue to transition to a more strategic role in many organizations they also will continue to test and apply new technologies to the supply process. The future holds much promise for technology-enabled process improvements. The challenges are great, but those who see the opportunity for cost reductions, faster cycle times, better integration with key supply chain stakeholders, and improved communication flows will continue to seek ways to use these new tools to their best advantage. Information systems and information technology enable a supply organization to contribute efficiently and effectively to organizational goals and strategies. Without structured and disciplined supply processes, technology expenditures may leave the organization with too many tools and not enough integration or utilization.

Questions for Review and Discussion

1. Where in the supply process is there the greatest opportunity to add value and why?
2. What are the steps in a robust supply management process?
3. What contribution to supply efficiency might be effected through the use of (a) an e-procurement system, (b) online catalogs, and (c) online reverse auctions?
4. What approaches, other than the standard supply procedure, might be used to minimize the small-value-order problem?
5. When would you issue an RFQ rather than an RFP and why?
6. What records are needed for efficient operation of the supply function? How can data collection throughout the process help or hurt buyer–supplier relationships?
7. What are the costs and benefits of follow-up and expediting? Are there opportunities to reduce total cost of ownership at this stage of the process?
8. How can an e-procurement system reduce the problem of small orders? Rush orders?
9. When should you use reverse auctions to select a supplier?
10. What arguments would you use to convince a supplier to participate in a reverse auction?
11. How does the use of an e-procurement system change the nature of the skills and knowledge required of supply management personnel?
12. What possible improvements in supply processes could technology offer in the future?

References   Beall, S. et al. *The Role of Reverse Auctions in Strategic Sourcing.* Tempe, AZ: CAPS Research, 2003.

Cegielski, C. G.; L. A. Jones-Farmer; Y. Wu; and B. T. Hazen. "Adoption of Cloud Computing Technologies in Supply Chains: An Organizational Information Processing Theory Approach." *International Journal of Logistics Management* 23, no. 2 (2012), pp. 184–211.

Digitally Integrating the Supply Base, CAPS Research Benchmarking Report, February 2014, www.capsresearch.org.

Flynn, A. E. "Raytheon's Buyerless Tools." Practix 6. Tempe, AZ: CAPS Research, March 2003.

Giunipero, L.; E. Ramirez; and E. Swilley, "The Antecedents and Consequences of E-Purchasing Tools in Supply Management." *Journal of Marketing Theory and Practice* 20, no. 3 (2012), pp. 279–292.

Johnson, P. F. "Supply Organizational Structures." *Critical Issues Report.* Tempe, AZ: CAPS Research, June 2003.

Johnson, P. F., and R. D. Klassen. "e-Procurement," *MIT Sloan Management Review* 46, no. 2 (2005), pp. 7–10.

Johnson, P. F.; R. D. Klassen; M. R. Leenders; and A. Awaysheh. "Utilizing E-Business Technologies in Supply Chains: The Impact of Firm Characteristics and Teams." *Journal of Operations Management* 25, no. 6 (2007), pp. 1255–1274.

McAfee, A., "What Every CEO Needs to Know About the Cloud." *Harvard Business Review* 89, no. 11 (November 2011), pp. 124–132.

Yeniyurt, S.; S. Watson; C. R. Carter; and C. K. Stevens. "To Bid or Not to Bid: Drivers of Bidding Behavior in Electronic Reverse Auctions." *Journal of Supply Chain Management* 47, no. 1 (2011), pp. 60–72.

Case 4–1

Qmont Mining

Alice Winter, working on a summer internship at Qmont Mining, was trying to determine how the supply systems for remote locations could be improved.

QMONT MINING

Qmont Mining, a major metals producer with headquarters in Vancouver, British Columbia, had extensive holdings all over the Canadian North. Supply management had been completely decentralized until very recently. A consulting study had recommended a move to more centralized supply management, including purchasing and logistics. The purchasing and stores manager at Qmont's largest mine in British Columbia, Harry Davidson, had been asked to pursue this idea and to make recommendations on potential improvements. Harry had hired Alice Winter, a college

student in logistics, to work as a summer intern to assist him. Harry had said to Alice: "A good project for you to work on is the way we handle supply for remote locations. I suspect that we could do substantially better, but I really don't have any hard data."

REMOTE LOCATIONS

Alice found out that Qmont had 17 remote locations, ranging from three small mines that had a buyer/storekeeper on site to two mine start-ups, nine exploration sites, and three development projects with a distance of 5,000 kilometers (km)[9] between the farthest ones and 300 km between the closest ones. Qmont made a distinction between exploration sites where

[9] 1 km = 0.60 miles.

the potential for ore was totally unproven to development sites where the possibility of mineralization had been proved, but where the extent of mineralization had to be determined. Qmont used its own drilling crews at these two types of sites, although most mining companies preferred to use contract drillers. Qmont managers believed that for security, availability, and cost reasons they needed full control and in-house crews. Typically, at both exploration and development sites an engineer or geologist would be in charge. All supplies for these sites would be flown in by bush planes on floats or by helicopters.

ACCOUNTING INFORMATION

Alice Winter decided to visit the accounting department at Vancouver headquarters first to see what she could learn about supply in remote locations. She found out that accounting paid all invoices from suppliers who claimed to have supplied a remote location even when no confirmation of orders, deliveries, or receipts was available. This occurred in about one-third of all invoices. The accountant explained: "Getting suppliers to provide odd requirements in a hurry and to get bush pilots to fly them in is a constant hassle. The last thing we want to do is lose the goodwill of these suppliers because we don't have our records straight and delay payments."

DEVELOPMENT AND EXPLORATION SITE DATA

Alice did get the chance to review the previous year's actual supplier invoices for three different sites (one development and two exploration) over a four-month summer period. Communication between actual sites and suppliers occurred in two main ways. Since site leaders were in regular contact via satellite with head office personnel in exploration or engineering, they frequently asked the head office contacts to place specific orders for them. In

addition, it was common for remote site personnel to contact suppliers directly and place orders. Moreover, when a drill needed a quick replacement part, apparently it was not unusual to place orders with several suppliers at the same time in the hope that at least one would deliver quickly. Drill and crew downtime was seen as very expensive.

The site accounting records showed that the total supply spend for these three sites totaled about $1,850,000. Of this total, approximately:

- $220,000 was for drilling equipment including drill bits and rods.
- $120,000 for MRO suppliers.
- $420,000 for air transport covering seven different suppliers, of which air transport of personnel in and out of sites cost about $170,000.
- $180,000 for fuel.
- $80,000 for food.

Alice uncovered 22 instances of multiple deliveries of the same item within days to the same site from different suppliers and 12 instances of multiple deliveries of the same item from the same supplier within a few days. There were 14 instances where the airfreight bill was at least 10 times higher than the value of the item transported.

NEXT STEPS

After several weeks of gathering this information, Alice wondered what her next steps should be. One option would be to gather similar information for all remote sites to get a more complete picture and to extend the time period. Another would be to get more specific about the details of each order and each supplier. She knew that she would be meeting with Harry Davidson in a few days to discuss her progress and findings to date. She also expected Harry to ask her what she believed she should do next.

Case 4–2

Eastern Pharmaceuticals Ltd.

In the afternoon of September 12, Andrew Baines, assistant purchasing manager at Eastern Pharmaceuticals Ltd. (Eastern), was discussing the purchase of packaging materials and contract filling of tablet samples with a supplier's representative. When the details of the packaging purchase order were finalized, Andrew told the sales representative,

John Cao, of Lucas Paper & Box Company (Lucas), that he would send him the purchase order for the packaging components and 25 percent of the contract filling. John replied that Shannon Baily, of the marketing department, had promised him 100 percent of the contract filling. "This is the first I've heard of that," snapped Andrew. "It's not marketing's responsibility," he continued, controlling his temper, "to decide what percentages of contract filling a particular supplier will get. Purchasing arranges the contract filling with the suppliers that can give the best quality, delivery, and price."

John Cao, an experienced sales representative, remained unperturbed. He replied that he had always dealt with both marketing and purchasing and that sometimes purchasing was not involved at all in the projects. He said that in this case where both marketing and purchasing were involved, he was just keeping purchasing informed of what marketing wanted. Andrew closed the meeting by politely telling John that he would have to clear up the situation between the two departments. He told John that he would let him know how much of the contract packaging Lucas would be getting.

Andrew Baines, his boss Matt Roberts, and a senior buyer made up the total purchasing staff at Eastern. One of Andrew's responsibilities was to handle the purchase of the marketing department's requirements. He also acted as liaison between the department and the production planning, manufacturing, and packaging departments. In recent weeks Andrew was finding the job more and more frustrating.

EASTERN PHARMACEUTICALS

Located in Seattle, Washington, Eastern carried an extensive line of prescription and nonprescription items that were mostly manufactured in its own plant. The company had approximately 15,000 drugstore customers plus hospital and government accounts. Annual sales of close to $150 million were handled by 50 sales representatives from coast to coast. Although the nonprescription items, known as over-the-counter (OTC) products, were promoted directly to the drug stores, most business was generated by convincing the doctors to prescribe Eastern's products for their patients. No selling or advertising was directed at the consumer.

The company's sales strategy was that Eastern sales representatives would give samples to a doctor after getting a verbal promise to prescribe. These samples would be used to start the patient on an Eastern product, and the doctor would write a prescription for the patient to pick up at the drugstore. With a large number of similar products on the market, it was a difficult marketing problem to keep Eastern's brand name in the doctor's mind days or weeks after the sales representative's visit. To help solve this problem, sales representatives asked the doctors to sign forms requesting additional samples at specific intervals.

The sales and marketing department had been recently reorganized, and the two new people, Shannon Bailey, sales promotion manager, and John Slaughter, advertising manager, were understandably anxious to do a good job. Both had made a lot of progress in working with John Cao, standardizing the samples to be used for sales promotions and advertising mailings. Essentially, both samples were now the same; the only difference was that the advertising sample was enclosed in an outer mailer to be sent to the doctor.

THE FILLING CONTRACT

The packaging contract under discussion totaled $88,000. In the past year, Lucas had sold $80,000 worth of materials annually to Eastern. Lucas's annual sales were $32 million.

John Cao had designed an attractive new style of sample. Basically, it was a folded card holding strips of tablets that could be pushed through one at a time, as required by the patient. This one idea was to be used in the near future to sample several other tablet products. John had developed the idea for marketing, expecting that he would get both the printing and contract filling.

Although Eastern did 90 percent of their manufacturing and packaging, they did not have the equipment to heat seal the strip into the folded cards. When goods came in from a contract packager such as Lucas, they were held in inventory until required by marketing.

THE RELATIONSHIP BETWEEN MARKETING AND PURCHASING

While Shannon and John had been able to work well together, they were having their difficulties in getting the cooperation of other departments involved. Frequent instances of sample mailings being late or sales representatives being out of stock continued to plague the success of their program. Delays had been caused by late ordering of components from outside suppliers, shortages of tablets, and mailing lists being incorrectly printed. In their attempts to remedy the situation, Shannon and John had trampled on a few toes. During attempts to investigate the causes for these delays, the vice president of operations discovered that there were usually good reasons offered by the departments involved.

Purchasing, manufacturing, and information systems pointed out that they could not drop their usual work "every time marketing wanted something in a rush." The feeling expressed by the production planner was typical of most department managers: "It is fine to get out the samples but rather pointless if we are running out of finished product in the meantime. Some of those unusual sample cartons slow down production up to 50 percent."

While it was part of Andrew's job to coordinate marketing's sample requirements, he was not making much progress. His attempts to get each department to cooperate met with the usual arguments that marketing was only one department and had to wait its turn. Shannon and John at times grew impatient with Andrew's efforts, and they started to go directly to each department manager.

Andrew felt that the action taken by Shannon telling the supplier how much contract filling business he would get was the last straw. With this in mind, he went to see Matt Roberts to try to get a policy statement on the matter. Andrew wanted to know where the line was drawn between purchasing's and marketing's responsibility in matters dealing with company suppliers.

Matt explained that, because the marketing promotion expenditure totaled $34 million or 22 percent of sales, Eastern, like most other companies in the industry, faced similar purchasing–marketing problems. If marketing managers were responsible for their budgets, they had the right to spend $1 each for 10,000 items, or if they wanted, they could buy 5,000 items for $2 each and still stay within their budget. It was a marketing decision whether they were getting better results from the $1 or $2 item. For these items, purchasing merely produced a purchase order to confirm the deal already made by marketing with the supplier. The policy applied to nonproduction items, such as calendars, letter openers, diet sheets, patient history cards for doctors, or displays and posters for drugstores. In contrast, production and inventory purchases had last year reached 20 percent of sales revenues.

However, Matt pointed out that final selection of sources for any purchased items that had to be packaged by the plant had always been the responsibility of the purchasing department. In this particular case, there was still a significant inventory of old style samples in the building, which marketing had not considered when they promised John Cao 100 percent of the contract filling. Andrew felt that placing all the contract filling right away would build up the stock of samples unnecessarily. Besides this, he had negotiated a better price from another reliable supplier, Sheppard Packaging, and felt that he would give the balance of 75 percent to them.

Marketing, Matt Roberts explained, was only charged for samples as they were shipped to sales representatives or sent out to doctors. Therefore, marketing was not too concerned about inventory levels as long as there were no shortages. Packaging components and bulk products held in inventory were not segregated from trade sizes in the warehouse or in financial reports. Only the finished samples were given a special account number so that the marketing budget could be debited as the samples were sent out.

NEXT STEPS

Matt Roberts suggested that Andrew set up a meeting the following week with Shannon and John so that each department could state its case and settle on a process for managing marketing-related purchases. Andrew agreed and replied: "I understand that marketing wants things to happen quickly, but we need to follow sound purchasing practices. We should listen to their suggestions regarding supplier selection—after all it is their budget—but the final decision should rest with purchasing. We have the responsibility to see that the greatest possible value is received for every dollar spent. How do we know prices are reasonable without getting other quotations?"

Case 4–3

Portland Bus Company

Richard Kaplan, buyer at Portland Bus Company ("PBC"), in Portland, Oregon, was preparing for his meeting with Laura Henning, business consultant for Bothe US operations, on October 14. Laura would be assisting Richard in managing a series of reverse auctions for approximately 290 components involving seven suppliers. This would be

PBC's first use of reverse auctions, and several important decisions had to be made before finalizing arrangements for the online bidding event. Before his meeting with Laura, Richard was to review alternatives for the auction process, including the type of auction to be used and the policy for selecting suppliers.

EXHIBIT 1   Supplier Profiles

Supplier	Profile	Current Spend
Dawson Manufacturing	Sheet metal and aluminum fabrication, using laser, CNC machining and plasma cutting technologies. Facility size: 110,000 sq. ft. Subsidiary of a North American-based automotive parts manufacturer with annual revenues of $2 billion.	$575,000
Imperial Fabrication	Sheet metal fabrication using laser and computer integrated systems for the design, engineering and manufacturing of quality custom and standard products. Process capabilities: laser cutting, welding, punching, and bending. Facility size: 100,000 sq. ft. Privately held.	$650,000
Neelin Mfg. Inc.	Contract manufacturing, machining, stamping, and assembly operations. Facility size: 80,000 sq. ft. Privately held.	Being considered for future business
C.R.N. Products Inc.	Sheet metal fabrication, assembly, and painting for small- and high-volume production. Facility size: 60,000 sq. ft.	$210,000
Benson Sheet Metal	Stamping and punching presses, riveting, steel shearing, tube forming, spot welding, and coating services. Facility size: 50,000 sq. ft. Privately held.	$460,000
Beranger Enterprises Ltd.	Light sheet metal processing and welding (1/2″ and thinner) as well as CNC machining and turning of carbon steel, stainless steel, and aluminum. Facility size: 100,000 sq. ft. Privately held.	$40,000
Camber Machining Ltd.	Machining, metal punching, and fabrication, using CNC equipment and on-site engineering capabilities. Facility size: 50,000 sq. ft. Privately held.	$40,000

PORTLAND BUS

PBC was owned by Dawe Motors, a leading global producer of passenger cars and commercial vehicles, headquartered in the United Kingdom. The Portland plant assembled body shells for the Dawe Bus Division. The shells were shipped from Portland to a facility in Medford, Oregon, approximately 275 miles away, for final assembly and painting.

Approximately 550 people worked at the PBC plant. David McGregor, director of materials, headed a staff of 12 people, who were responsible for materials planning, inventory control, and purchasing. Total annual purchases were approximately $250 million across five main commodity groups: fabricated metal, systems, fiber glass, electrical, and power train. However, approximately 75 percent of purchases were set up through corporate purchasing with strategic suppliers, leaving about $60 million to be sourced through David's organization. Richard reported directly to David and was responsible for sourcing fabricated metal components.

METAL COMPONENTS

During the last three months, Richard had analyzed the company's spend in three fabricated metal parts categories: hinges, brackets, and ducts. Ten suppliers were currently responsible for 290 different part numbers, representing an annual spend of approximately $2 million. It had been more than two years since a thorough review of these commodity categories had been conducted, and Richard felt that under current market conditions, significant opportunities existed for cost savings.

Four of the PBC's current suppliers were not in Richard's future plans because of concerns regarding past performance. Furthermore, Richard intended to include a new supplier, Neelin Mfg. Inc., in the online bidding event. Exhibit 1 provides profiles of the seven suppliers

EXHIBIT 2
Reverse Auction Packages

Package	# Part Numbers	Annual Spend ($)
Hinges	7	32,551
Ducts 1	10	208,838
Ducts 2	13	106,236
Brackets 1	12	53,773
Brackets 2	12	119,912
Brackets 3	3	65,389
Brackets 4	9	111,500
Brackets 5	16	54,901
Brackets 6	13	65,997
Brackets 7	12	78,950
Brackets 8	21	48,108
Brackets 9	39	83,557
Brackets 10	15	84,630
Brackets 11	14	55,673
Brackets 12	16	64,734
Brackets 13	7	137,624
Brackets 14	2	71,675
Brackets 15	21	219,922
Brackets 16	18	133,896
Brackets 17	20	166,114
Brackets 18	10	49,771
Total	*290*	*2,013,751*

that Richard was considering for participation in the reverse auction.

THE REVERSE AUCTION

Richard decided to group components into packages as opposed to running 290 separate online bidding events. Eventually, he settled on 21 packages of complementary components, which were similar in terms of manufacturing processes, quality requirements, and production volumes (see Exhibit 2).

PBC's parent company had a contract with Bothe AG, an online bidding event solutions provider, to provide assistance and technical support to all of its divisions for reverse auctions. Located in Europe, North America, and Asia, Bothe provided a range of consulting and technology platforms, working with approximately 200 companies in the automotive, construction, machinery manufacturing, and office sup-

plies industries. Its services included online auctions, supply contract negotiations, supplier management, and a range of web-based technology solutions. The Dawe passenger car division in Europe had recently completed a reverse auction project with Bothe and was very satisfied with the results.

Laura Henning, business consultant for Bothe US operations, had been assigned to work with Richard to manage the reverse auction project. Laura and her team would be responsible for:

1. Working suppliers to set up the Bothe technology platform and providing training to their employees.
2. Communicating relevant documentation to suppliers regarding details of the auction packages, such as part specifications, quality requirements, and volumes.
3. Conducting a test auction with suppliers, and subsequently addressing any technical issues or questions that arise.

4. On the day of the auction, Bothe would monitor the online bidding event and provide helpdesk support to all parties involved. The Bothe platform allows the buyer to watch the reverse auction live.

5. After the auction, Bothe would provide a detailed auction report to the buyer, including the results, which would be available approximately two hours after the auction event.

Laura had indicated that once arrangements were finalized it would take a maximum of two weeks to install the Bothe platform at the suppliers and to train their staff. Testing the platform would take an additional one or two days. Richard expected that suppliers would need at least two weeks to review the packages and prepare for the auctions. Consequently, Richard was planning to run the auctions starting the middle of November, and he hoped to have everything completed by the Christmas holiday.

PREPARING FOR THE REVERSE AUCTION

The meeting on October 14 was to finalize the schedule for the reverse auction events, review alternatives for the auction process, including the type of auction to be used, and set policies for selecting suppliers. Since this was PBC's first reverse auction, David McGregor was sensitive that any decisions might have implications for similar projects in the future. Consequently, he expected to review Richard's plan before proceeding.

Laura explained to Richard that there were a variety of methods for conducting a reverse auction, and the primary decisions included visibility (e.g., what the bidders would see during the auction), length of the auction, policies for extending the length of the auction, and target pricing. For example, the Bothe system could be configured such that every bidder could see the current best price only, a ranking of all bid prices (displayed by color codes), or the bidder's rank only (e.g., best, second, third, etc.). Laura also indicated that while most auctions ran 15 or 30 minutes, it was not uncommon to have policies that extended the event provided there was still bidding activity at the end of the designated time. Furthermore, buyers in some reverse auctions set target prices to provide a pricing benchmark for bidders.

Lastly, Richard needed to decide on what basis the packages should be awarded and to what extent prices could be negotiated following the auction. David had indicated to Richard that he expected a 25 percent reduction in costs as an outcome of the reverse auction project. Richard felt that other factors needed to be considered beyond price. For example, he recognized that there would be costs of switching suppliers, and he wondered how this should be taken into account when awarding business. For example, should the lowest bidder be awarded the package if the price savings was less than the costs of switching? Furthermore, to what extent should PBC take into consideration long-term supply relationships when making the final sourcing decision from the reverse auctions? Richard wanted to be clear and up-front as possible with the suppliers, some of whom he expected may be reluctant to participate.

Chapter **Five**

Make or Buy, Insourcing, and Outsourcing

Key Questions for the Supply Decision Maker

Should we

- Change the way we currently take make or buy decisions?
- Consider insourcing more?
- Outsource more?

How can we

- Improve our ability to find insourcing opportunities?
- Ensure that supply considerations receive full attention in make or buy decisions?
- Better develop our outsourcing expertise?

MAKE OR BUY

One of the most critical decisions in any organization is make or buy. When any organization is formed, a series of make or buy decisions need to be made. As the organization grows and adds or drops products and/or services, make or buy decisions continue to be made. In this text, make, buy, insource, and outsource are defined as follows. For any new product or service, make or buy decisions need to be made. A make decision means the organization will produce the good or provide the service internally. A buy decision means the good or service will be procured from a supplier. Later, when internal and/or external circumstances change, make or buy decisions are reviewed and some or all may be reversed. Insourcing refers to reversing a previous buy decision. An organization chooses to bring in-house an activity, product, or service previously purchased. Outsourcing reverses a previous make decision. Thus an activity, product, or service previously done in-house will be purchased. See Figure 5–1. Supply managers can play a major role in make or buy as well as insourcing and outsourcing decisions.

The character of the organization is colored by the organization's stance on the make or buy decision. It is one of vital importance to an organization's productivity and competitiveness. Historically, the make option tended to be favored by many large organizations, resulting in backward integration and ownership of a large range of manufacturing and subassembly facilities. Major purchases were largely confined to raw materials, which were then processed in-house.

Managerial thinking on this issue changed dramatically in the 1990s with increased global competition, pressures to reduce costs, downsizing, and focus on the firm's core competencies. The trend changed to buying services or goods that might historically have been provided or manufactured internally. Management trends favoring flexibility and focus on corporate strengths, closeness to the customer, and increased emphasis on productivity and competitiveness reinforce the idea of buying. It would be unusual if any one organization were superior to competition in all aspects of manufacturing or creating services. By buying from capable suppliers those requirements for which the buying organization has no special manufacturing or service advantage, the management of the buying organization can concentrate better on its main mission. With the world as a marketplace, it is the purchaser's responsibility to search for or develop world-class suppliers suitable for the strategic needs of the buying organization.

FIGURE 5–1   **Make or Buy and Insourcing and Outsourcing Decisions**

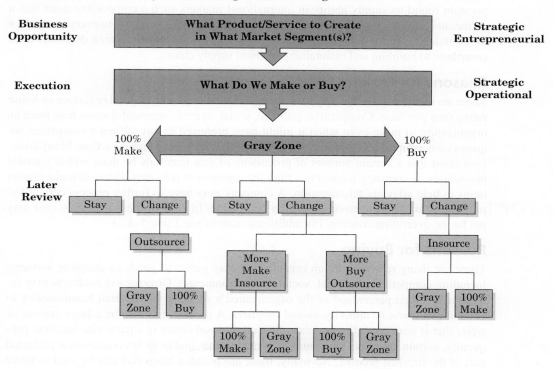

A recent North American phenomenon has been the tendency to purchase services that were traditionally performed in-house. These include security, food services, and maintenance, but also programming, training, engineering, accounting, accounts payable, legal, research, personnel, information systems, and even contract logistics and supply. Thus, a new class of purchases involving services has evolved.

The make or buy decision is an interesting one because of its many dimensions. Almost every organization is faced with it continually. For manufacturing companies, the make alternative may be a natural extension of activities already present or an opportunity for diversification. For nonmanufacturing concerns, it is normally a question of services rather than products. Should a hospital have its own laundry, operate its own dietary, security, and maintenance services, or should it purchase these from suppliers? Becoming one's own supplier is an alternative that has not received much attention in this text so far, and yet it is a vital option in every organization's supply strategy.

What should be the attitude of an organization's management toward this make or buy issue? Many organizations do not have a consciously expressed policy but prefer to decide each issue as it arises. Moreover, it can be difficult to gather meaningful accounting data for economic analysis to support such decisions.

In the aggregate for the individual firm, the question is: What should our organization's objective be in terms of how much value should be added in-house as a percentage of final product or service cost and in what form? A strong supply group would favor a buy tendency when other factors are not of overriding importance. For example, one corporation found its supply ability in international markets such a competitive asset that it deliberately divested itself of certain manufacturing facilities common to every competitor in the industry. In the long term, make or buy and insource or outsource decisions must contribute to building and maintaining resilient supply chains.

Reasons for Making

There are many reasons that may lead an organization to produce a good or service in-house rather than purchase. Competitive, political, social, or environmental reasons may force an organization to make even when it might have preferred to buy. When a competitor acquires ownership of a key source of raw material, it may force similar action. Many countries insist that a certain amount of processing of raw materials be done within national boundaries. A company located in a high-unemployment area may decide to make certain items to help alleviate this situation. A company may have to further process certain by-products to make them environmentally acceptable. In each of these instances, cost may not be the overriding concern. For additional reasons see Table 5–1.

Reasons for Buying

There are many reasons why an organization may prefer to purchase goods or services, including competitive, political, social, or environmental. Government contracts may require a specified percentage of the organization's spend to go to small businesses or to veteran-, woman-, or minority-owned suppliers. A process may require a large amount of water that is scarce locally, or create difficult disposal issues in a particular location. Frequently, certain suppliers have built a reputation that makes their component a preferred part of the finished product. Normally, these are branded items that can be used to make the total piece of equipment more acceptable to the final user. The manufacturers of transportation, construction, or mining equipment frequently let the customer specify the power

TABLE 5–1
Why Make?

1. The quantities are too small and/or no supplier is interested or available.
2. Quality requirements may be so exacting or so unusual as to require special processing methods that suppliers cannot be expected to provide.
3. Greater assurance of supply or a closer coordination of supply with the demand.
4. To preserve technological secrets.
5. To obtain a lower cost.
6. To take advantage of or avoid idle equipment and/or labor.
7. To ensure steady running of the corporation's own facilities, leaving suppliers to bear the burden of fluctuations in demand.
8. To avoid sole-source dependency.
9. To reduce risk.
10. The purchase option is too expensive.
11. The distance from the closest available supplier is too great.
12. A significant customer required it.
13. Future market potential for the product or service is expanding rapidly.
14. Forecasts of future shortages in the market or rising prices.
15. Management takes pride in size.

TABLE 5–2
Why Buy?

1. The organization may lack managerial or technical expertise in the production of the items or services in question.
2. Lack of production capacity. This may affect relationships with other suppliers or customers as well.
3. To reduce risk.
4. The challenges of maintaining long-term technological and economic viability for a noncore activity.
5. A decision to make, once made, is often difficult to reverse. Union pressures and management inertia combine to preserve the status quo. Thus, buying outside is seen as providing greater flexibility.
6. To assure cost accuracy.
7. There are more options in potential sources and substitute items.
8. There may not be sufficient volume to justify in-house production.
9. Future forecasts show great demand or technological uncertainty, and the firm is unable or unwilling to undertake the risk of manufacture.
10. The availability of a highly capable supplier nearby.
11. The desire to stay lean.
12. Buying may open up markets for the firm's products or services.
13. The ability to bring a product or service to market faster.
14. A significant customer may demand it.
15. Superior supply management expertise.

plant brand and see this option as advantageous in selling their equipment. For additional reasons see Table 5–2.

The arguments advanced for either side of the make or buy question sound similar: better quality, quantity, delivery, price/cost, service, lower risk, greater opportunity to contribute to the firm's competitive position, and ability to provide greater customer satisfaction. Therefore, each individual make or buy decision requires careful analysis of both options. Even in the make decision, there will likely be a significant supply input requirement and there is even a greater one for the buy option. Thus, supply managers are constantly required to provide information, judgments, and expertise to assist the organization in resolving make or buy decisions wisely.

The Gray Zone in Make or Buy

Research by Leenders and Nollet suggests that a "gray zone" may exist in make or buy situations. There may be a range of options between 100 percent make or 100 percent buy. (See Figure 5–1.) This middle ground may be particularly useful for testing and learning without having to make the full commitment to make or buy. Particularly in the purchase of services, where no equipment investment is involved, it may be that substantial economies accrue to the organization that can substitute low-cost internal labor for expensive outside staff or low-cost external labor for expensive internal staff.

A good example of a gray zone trade-off in the automotive industry is the supplier who takes over design responsibility for a component from the car manufacturer. In maintenance, some types of servicing can be done by the purchaser of the equipment, other types by the equipment manufacturer.

The gray zone in make or buy may offer valuable opportunities or superior options for both purchaser and supplier.

SUBCONTRACTING

A special class of the make or buy spectrum is the area of subcontracting. Common in military and construction procurement, subcontracts can exist only when there are prime contractors who bid out part of the work to other contractors: hence the term *subcontractor*. In its simplest form, a subcontract is a purchase order written with more explicit terms and conditions. Its complexity and management vary in direct proportion to the value and size of the program to be managed. The management of a subcontract may require unique skills and abilities because of the amount and type of correspondence, charts, program reviews, and management reporting that are necessary. Additionally, payment may be handled differently and is usually negotiated along with the actual pricing and terms and conditions of the subcontract.

The use of a subcontract is appropriate when placing orders for work that is difficult to define, will take a long period of time, and will be extremely costly. For example, aerospace companies subcontract many of the larger structural components and avionics. Wings, landing gears, and radar systems are examples of high-cost items that might be purchased on a subcontract. The subcontract is normally administered by a team that might include a subcontract administrator (SCA), an equipment engineer, a quality assurance representative, a reliability engineer, a material price/cost analyst, a program office representative, and/or an on-site representative.

Managing the subcontract is a complex activity that requires knowledge about performance to date as well as the ability to anticipate actions needed to ensure the desired end results. The SCA must maintain cost, schedule, technical, and configuration control from the beginning to the completion of the task.

Cost control of the subcontract begins with the negotiation of a fair and reasonable cost, proper choice of the contract type, and thoughtfully imposed incentives. Schedule control requires the development of a good master schedule that covers all necessary contract activities realistically. Well-designed written reports and recovery programs, where necessary, are essential. Technical control must ensure that the end product conforms to all the performance parameters of the specifications that were established when the contract was awarded. Configuration control ensures that all changes are documented. Good configuration control is essential to "aftermarket" and spares considerations for the product.

Unlike a normal purchase order of minimal complexity, where final closeout may be accomplished by delivery and payment, a major subcontract involves more definite actions to close. These actions vary with the contract type and difficulty of the item/task being procured. Quite often large and complex procurements require a number of changes during the period of performance. These changes result in cost claims that must be settled prior to contract closure. Additionally, any tooling or data supplied to the contractor to support the effort must be returned. All deliverable material, data, and reports must be received and inspected. Each subcontract's requirements will vary in the complexity of the closure requirements; however, in all cases a subcontract performance summary should be written to provide a basis for evaluation of the supplier for future bidder or supplier selection. Such a report also is necessary in providing information for subsequent claims or renegotiation.

Subcontracts may also apply to services. For example, the "primary supplier" of an item of Durable Medical Equipment, Prosthetics, Orthotics, and Supplies (DMEPOS) is the enrolled supplier that bills Medicare for reimbursement. The primary supplier is responsible for the overall service of furnishing the item and coordinating the care in compliance with the physician's order and Medicare rules and guidelines. The primary supplier may subcontract certain services such as purchase of inventory, delivery, and instruction on use of the item, and repair of rented equipment.

INSOURCING AND OUTSOURCING

Insourcing and outsourcing occur when the decisions are made to reverse past make or buy decisions. Just because the decision to make or buy was properly made originally, this does not mean it cannot be changed. New circumstances inside the organization, in the market, or in the environment may require the organization to reverse its stance on a previous make or buy decision.

If the previous decision to make or buy was improperly made and can be corrected subsequently, this should be done. However, the arguments for constantly reassessing past make or buy decisions are particularly strong. Perceived risks may have been minimized or eliminated. New technology may permit processes previously considered impossible. New suppliers may have entered the market or old suppliers may have left. New trade-offs between raw materials and components, such as substitution of steel by plastic, may result in new options. It is this constant change in volumes, prices, capabilities, specifications, suppliers, capacities, regulations, competitors, technology, and managers that requires supply managers to review their current make and buy profile continuously in identifying new strengths and weaknesses, opportunities, and threats.

The two questions that need to be addressed on an ongoing basis by a cross-functional team including supply, operations, accounting and marketing are: (1) Which products or services are we currently buying that we should be doing in-house? (2) Which products and services that we are currently doing in-house should we be buying from suppliers?

Insourcing

Insourcing, the often forgotten twin of outsourcing, deals with past buy decisions that are reversed. Given the demands on procurement managers' time, the likelihood that supply managers will initiate an insourcing initiative is relatively small. Continuing to buy is likely to be standard practice. From a supply perspective there are, however, several reasons why supply might have to trigger an insourcing initiative. The most obvious reason is when an existing source of supply goes out of business or drops a product or service line and no other supplier is available. Assuming the requirement for product or service continues, the supply manager needs to find an alternate source. Supplier development or the creation of a new supplier who was previously not selling the product or service is one option. The other is to insource. Similarly, a sudden massive increase in price, the purchase of a sole source by a competitor, political events and regulatory changes, or a lack of supply of a key raw material or component required for the manufacture of the purchased product might force supply to consider insourcing. Thus, anything that threatens assurance of supply may provide supply a reason for insourcing. This might be called the necessity argument: "We would prefer not to produce this product or service in-house, but we really don't have any other options."

There are other organizational factors that may make insourcing an attractive option. The reasons would be similar to the "make" arguments provided earlier in this chapter in the make or buy discussion. We may have developed a unique process for this product or service. Our quality, delivery, total cost of ownership, or flexibility would be vastly improved.

We could provide superior customer service and satisfaction. Insourcing would greatly enhance our competitive ability. This might be called the opportunity argument: "We would prefer to do this in-house because it would give us a strategic competitive advantage."

After the decision to insource has been taken, the smooth transition from suppliers to internal manufacture or service delivery will require supply's special attention. In the first place, how do we discontinue our dealings with our existing supplier(s)? Can the change-over occur simultaneously with current contract expiries or may penalties have to be paid to terminate existing commitments?

With any insourcing initiatives, there is also a new supply issue in terms of raw materials, components, equipment, energy, and services required to produce the particular requirement just insourced. Therefore, supply's capability to provide the required inputs competently is one of the factors to be considered in any insourcing decision.

The Alicia Wong case at the end of this chapter is an interesting example of an insourcing decision. This case describes the opportunity to produce mustard in-house, rather than purchasing it from an outside supplier. Because mustard is used in many products, the decision focuses not only on whether this insourcing is an attractive proposition, but also, if the decision is to go ahead, how to ensure it will be successful. The Wentworth Hospital case in Chapter 7 illustrates a situation where insourcing contract repair services is being considered as a result of a combination of cost and supplier performance issues.

Outsourcing

Organizations outsource when they decide to buy something they had been making in-house previously. For example, a company whose employees clean the buildings may decide to hire a janitorial firm to provide this service. Depending on the good or service, suppliers may be domestic (onshore) or international (offshore). Offshoring is discussed in Chapter 14, "Global Supply Management." A huge wave of outsourcing and privatization (in the public sector) has hit almost all organizations since the late 1980s. Public and private organizations have outsourced a broad range of functions and activities formerly performed in-house as they downsize, "right-size," and eliminate headquarters staff to focus on value-added activities and core competencies to survive and prosper.

Almost no function is immune to outsourcing. Some activities, such as janitorial, food, and security services, have been outsourced for many years. Information Technology (IT), legal, and health care services such as radiology have received much attention recently as targets for outsourcing. Other popular outsourcing targets are mail rooms, copy centers, and corporate travel departments. Accounts payable, human resources, marketing/sales, finance, administration, logistics, engineering, and even supply are examples of functions now outsourced.

An entire function may be outsourced, or some elements of an activity may be outsourced and some kept in-house. For example, some of the elements of information technology may be strategic, some may be critical, and some may lend themselves to lower cost purchase and management by a third party. Identifying a function as a potential outsourcing target, and then breaking that function into its components, allows the decision makers to determine which activities are strategic or critical and should remain in-house, and which can be outsourced.

The growth in outsourcing in the logistics area is attributed to transportation deregulation, the focus on core competencies, reductions in inventories, and enhanced logistics management computer programs. Lean inventories mean there is less room for error in deliveries, especially if the organization is operating in a just-in-time mode. Trucking companies have added logistics to their businesses—changing from merely moving goods from point A to point B, to managing all or a part of all shipments over a longer period of time, typically three years, and replacing the shipper's employees with their own. Logistics companies have computer tracking technology that reduces the risk in transportation and allows the logistics company to add more value to the firm than it could if the function were performed in-house. Third-party logistics (3PL) providers offer integrated operations, warehousing, and transportation services. The ability to track freight using electronic data interchange technology and a satellite system to tell customers exactly where its drivers are and when the delivery will be made is critical in a just-in-time environment, where the delivery window may be only 30 minutes.

For example, Hewlett-Packard turned over its inbound raw materials warehousing in Vancouver, Washington, to Roadway Logistics. Roadway's 140 employees operate the warehouse 24 hours a day, seven days a week, coordinating the delivery of parts to the warehouse and managing storage. Hewlett-Packard's 250 employees were transferred to other company activities. Hewlett-Packard reports savings of 10 percent in warehousing operating costs.

The reasons for outsourcing are similar to those advanced for the buy option in make or buy decisions earlier in this chapter. There is a key difference, however. Because the organization was previously involved in producing the product or service itself, the question arises: What happens to the employees and space and equipment previously dedicated to this product or service now outsourced?

Layoffs often result, and even in cases where the service provider (third party) hires former employees, they are often hired back at lower wages with fewer benefits. Outsourcing is perceived by many unions as efforts to circumvent union contracts. The United Auto Workers union has been particularly active in trying to prevent auto manufacturers from outsourcing parts of their operations. Additional concerns over outsourcing include:

- Loss of control.
- Exposure to supplier risks: financial weakness, loss of supplier commitment, slow implementation, promised features or services not available, lack of responsiveness, poor daily quality.
- Unexpected fees or "extra use" charges.
- Difficulty in quantifying economics; conversion costs.
- Supply restraints.
- Attention required by senior management.
- Possibility of being tied to obsolete technology, and
- Concerns with long-term flexibility and meeting changing business requirements.

As organizations have gained more experience in making outsourcing decisions and crafting outsourcing contracts, they have become better at applying sourcing and contracting expertise to these decisions. From writing the statement of work (SOW) or request for proposal (RFP) to defining the terms and conditions, the success of an outsourcing agreement lies in the details.

There are two cases on outsourcing at the end of this chapter that are illustrative of outsourcing decisions in different contexts. Garland Chocolates is considering outsourcing packaging for Edgeworth Toffee rather than investing in expensive capital equipment. The Marshall Insurance Company case deals with a proposal by a supplier to handle forms and printed materials inventory management. The Garland Chocolates case presents outsourcing in a traditional manufacturing context, while the Marshall case illustrates outsourcing a service in an administrative setting.

IMPLICATIONS FOR SUPPLY

Supply and logistics management may be involved in make or buy and insource or out-source decisions in two ways: (1) Some or all of the activities of the supply and logistics functions may be a target for outsourcing. (2) Supply and logistics may be part of an internal team conducting analysis for a make or buy, or insource or outsource decision.

Outsourcing Supply and Logistics

While the supply function may be outsourced completely, the procurement of indirect or noncore spend is more likely to be outsourced than procurement of direct or core spend. Benefits from outsourcing procurement may include improved process compliance and control, optimized working capital, and improved process efficiency.

There are three types of procurement outsourcing contracts: procure-to-pay (P2P), source-to-contract (S2C), and source-to-pay (S2P). P2P contracts cover the procurement activities of day-to-day purchasing (approval workflow, material acquisition, purchase order, expediting, material and invoice receipt, and invoice payment), performance management (financial performance, compliance management, policies and procedures, and performance and results reporting), and accounts payable (master data maintenance, process payment request, travel and expense (T&E) claims processing, EDI/P-card administration, month-end closing, supplier inquiries, and reporting). Source-to-contract (S2C) procurement outsourcing includes spend data management, strategic sourcing, supplier management, and demand management. Source-to-pay (S2P) procurement outsourcing is an end-to-end suite that includes all the processes in procure-to-pay and source-to-pay.

For example, in 2007, Microsoft selected Accenture as its procurement process outsourcing provider. Accenture rolled out common processes across 95 countries in 36 languages from four service centers. Operational costs were reduced by 35 percent, plus negotiated savings were up 35 percent from the prior year. Standardized global processes and increased transparency enabled early payment discount savings of over $10 million.[1]

Many tasks associated with the logistics function as well as the entire function itself have been heavily outsourced. According to Capgemini's 17th Annual Third Party Logistics study (2012), transactional, operational, and repetitive activities such as transportation, warehousing and freight forwarding tend to be the most frequently outsourced. Shippers outsourced 54 percent of their transportation spend and 39 percent of their warehouse operations. The three primary reasons for outsourcing logistics activities are improved services, reduced costs, and increased ability to focus on core competencies.

Deciding what represents a core competency to an organization is not always an easy task, nor is the decision always the same for a specific function. For example, ownership and management of an in-house fleet of vehicles may be subject to the decision to outsource or maintain in-house. In an organization where the sales force is large, the cars for sales representatives may be seen as an extension of the sales force, and part of the company's ability to outperform the competition in personal sales. Many of the functions of fleet may be outsourced—leasing rather than owning vehicles, maintenance, resale

---

[1] www.accenture.com/SiteCollectionDocuments/PDF/Accenture-Procurement-BPO-Infographic-final.pdf.

of vehicles—but the contact with the drivers may be retained as an in-house function because keeping the drivers (sales force) happy is critical to the success of the organization. In a utility company, the mechanical expertise needed to maintain specialty vehicles may be seen as part of the company's core competency, whereas the maintenance of the automobile fleet may not. The outsourcing decision is a function of many factors, and each organization must assess these factors based on the goals and objectives and long-term strategy of the organization.

Supply's Role in Insourcing and Outsourcing

Research indicates that supply has had relatively moderate involvement in the outsourcing decisions made in many organizations. However, given the nature of these insourcing and outsourcing decisions, supply managers should be heavily involved to add in the following ways:

- Providing a comprehensive, competitive process.
- Identifying opportunities for insourcing or outsourcing.
- Aiding in selection of sources.
- Identifying potential relationship issues.
- Developing and negotiating the contract.
- Ongoing monitoring and management of the relationship.

The strategic importance of make or buy and insourcing and outsourcing decisions is high, so management must ensure these decisions are right. Appropriate supply input is critical when making these decisions and in managing the outcomes.

Conclusion Make or buy, insourcing and outsourcing are key strategic decisions for any organization. That each of these decisions can be reviewed and reversed at a later date, as conditions warrant, adds to the challenge of maintaining an appropriate mix of in-house activities and purchased goods and services. Effective supply management requires an ongoing active contribution from supply into this continuing assessment process. The more skilled the supply group at exploiting market opportunities and developing competitive sources, the more ready the organization should be to buy and outsource.

Questions for Review and Discussion

1. Why should an organization switch from buying to making?
2. What is insourcing? How might one make the decision to insource an activity or not?
3. Why is the make or buy decision considered strategic?
4. What is the gray zone in make or buy? What are its implications?
5. Why might an organization decide to outsource? Can you give an example?
6. What is subcontracting? How does subcontracting differ from a typical purchase order (PO)?
7. Why would an organization outsource its logistics? Engineering? Marketing?

8. In the public sector what name is frequently used for outsourcing? What are some major advantages to outsourcing in the public sector?

9. What role is expected of supply once an outsourcing decision has been made?

10. If you were the sole owner of your own company, would you favor making or buying? Why?

References
Brewer, B.; B. Ashenbaum; and J. R. Carter. "Understanding the Supply Chain Outsourcing Cascade: When Does Procurement Follow Manufacturing Out the Door?" *Journal of Supply Chain Management* 49, no. 3 (July 2013), pp. 90–110.

Dabhilkar, M. "Trade-Offs in Make-Buy Decisions." *Journal of Purchasing and Supply Management* 17, no. 3 (2011), pp. 158–166.

Halvey, J. K., and B. M. Melby. *Business Process Outsourcing: Process, Strategies and Contracts.* 2nd. ed. Hoboken, NJ: John Wiley & Sons, 2007.

Kroes, J. R., and S. Ghosh. "Outsourcing Congruence with Competitive Priorities: Impact on Supply Chain and Firm Performance." *Journal of Operations Management* 28, no. 2 (2010) pp. 124–143.

Langley, C. J. *2013 Third-Party Logistics Study: The State of Logistics Outsourcing.* Phoenix, AZ: Capgemini Consulting.

Leuschner, R.; C. R. Carter; T. J. Goldsby; and Z. S. Rogers. "Third-Party Logistics: A Meta-Analytic Review and Investigation of its Impact on Performance." *Journal of Supply Chain Management* 50, no. 1 (2014) pp. 21–43.

Li, M., and T. Y. Choi. "Triads in Services Outsourcing: Bridge, Bridge Decay and Bridge Transfer." *Journal of Supply Chain Management* 45, no. 3 (2009), pp. 27–39.

Park, J. K., and Y. K. Ro. "The Impact of a Firm's Make, Pseudo-make, or Buy Strategy on Product Performance." *Journal of Operations Management* 29, no. 4 (2011), pp. 289–304.

Van der Valk, W., and J. van Iwaarden. "Monitoring in Service Triads Consisting of Buyers, Subcontractors and End Customers." *Journal of Purchasing and Supply Management* 17, no. 3 (2011) pp. 198–206.

Vitasek, K.; K. Manrodt; and M. Ledyard. *Vested Outsourcing: Five Rules That Will Transform Outsourcing*, 2nd ed. New York: Palgrave Macmillan, 2013.

Case 5–1

Garland Chocolates

Shanti Suppiah, director of operations at the Garland Chocolates plant in Durham, North Carolina, was preparing for a team meeting scheduled for Monday, March 18, to decide what to do about declining margins for the Edgeworth Toffee brand. Options were to invest in new equipment or outsource manufacturing and packing. It was Wednesday, March 12, and Shanti needed to prepare her analysis and develop a recommendation prior to the meeting.

GARLAND CHOCOLATES

Headquartered in London, UK, Garland Chocolates (Garland) was a leading global food manufacturer with annual revenues of $3 billion. The company produced a wide range of chocolate and confectionary products, under more than 65 brands. It operated more than 50 plants globally, including eight plants in the United States. Garland's products were among the leading brands in the industry, and the Durham plant manufactured 20 product lines that were distributed to retail customers in North America, including grocery store chains, boutique candy shops, and convenience stores.

Garland's brands were managed by cross-functional teams with representatives from sales and marketing, operations, finance, engineering, purchasing, and distribution. Each team was governed by corporate goals for growth, profitability, and brand management, but was given significant autonomy to make strategic and tactical decisions in order to achieve their business performance objectives (BPOs).

The competitive nature of the industry placed an upper limit on prices, so margins were determined by production and supply chain efficiencies. Consequently, cost control and continuous improvement were high priorities. The company's enterprise resource planning (ERP) system generated weekly BPO reports for team members.

THE EDGEWORTH TOFFEE BRAND

Production of Edgeworth Toffee was a two-step process: manufacturing and packing. The product was manufactured in two formats. The first format was a fixed-size, retail-ready pack, which contained a half-pound of toffee. The second format was a 10-pound bulk package that was placed in stores so that customers could select the amount of toffee they wanted and self-pack the product. Production of the fixed-size format was approximately 2,500 cases a year, compared to approximately 3,000 cases a year of the bulk format. Both formats sold for $145 per case.

There were two dedicated packing lines for Edgeworth Toffee, one for each format. However, the packing lines had long outlived their useful lives, and efficiencies had declined in recent years (see Exhibit 1). Furthermore, sales of Edgeworth Toffee had been flat for the past couple of years, and

in an effort to spur consumer interest in the brand, marketing was proposing a new marketing strategy that included a facelift for the packaging. However, the new packaging would require a different type of packing technology. John Slaughter, the representative from marketing on the Edgeworth Toffee team, felt that the introduction of new packaging combined with a new marketing campaign could deliver as much as a 20 percent increase in sales. It was unclear to Shanti whether the new marketing strategy would be enough to stimulate increased sales, or if the product was mature and a decline in demand was inevitable.

THE MANUFACTURING AND PACKING LINE REPLACEMENT OPTIONS

The accounting department set standard costs for each product line annually. Exhibit 1 provides the standard costs for Edgeworth Toffee, and Exhibit 2 shows actual operating performance data for the manufacturing and packing lines. As shown in Exhibit 2, the packing line was operating at 48 percent efficiency, and the scrap rate was nearly 10 percent. Annual maintenance costs on the packing line were approximately $18,000 per year and expected to increase by at least 25 percent in the next 12 months.

Working with Ian Haase, purchasing manager at the Durham plant and a member of the Edgeworth Toffee team, Shanti obtained an estimate of $140,000 for the cost of replacing the two packing lines for Edgeworth Toffee, including installation. It was expected that the new equipment would be able to achieve the BPO efficiency and scrap rate targets and be able to accommodate the new packaging that marketing was recommending.

Shanti also felt that it was time to examine replacement of the manufacturing line. The manufacturing and packing lines had originally been installed together more than 20 years earlier. Although efficiency of the

EXHIBIT 1   **Operating Standard Costs for Edgeworth Toffee**

	$ per case	%
Selling price	$145.00	100
Raw material	24.65	17
Packaging material	29.00	20
Labor—manufacturing	13.05	9
Labor—packing	7.25	5
Overhead & depreciation	21.75	15
Total cost	95.70	66
Margin	49.30	34

EXHIBIT 2   **Manufacturing and Packing Line Performance Statistics**

Measure	Standard (%)	Actual (%)
Manufacturing efficiency	80	76
Manufacturing scrap rate	1.2	1.5
Packing efficiency	80	48
Packing scrap rate	1.2	9.6

manufacturing line was close to the target of 80 percent, it was also showing signs of deterioration. The efficiency rate had declined to 76 percent, compared to more than 90 percent five years prior, and it had become increasingly more difficult to find replacement parts. A new manufacturing line would cost approximately $600,000 installed.

OUTSOURCING

In addition to investigating options to replace the existing manufacturing and packing lines, Shanti had also looked into outsourcing. A preliminary review indicated that there would be substantial coordination costs if only packing was outsourced; therefore, outsourcing manufacturing and packing was investigated. Ian and Shanti selected two contract manufacturers to submit proposals, Martin Contract Manufacturing (Martin) and Dasari Inc. Bids were requested from both for the existing packaging and the new packaging proposed by marketing. In order to make sure the suppliers were well informed about the manufacturing and packing processes, both were invited to tour the Durham plant, and they were provided with detailed information and related data regarding the operation of the lines.

Following a review of the proposals submitted by the suppliers, Ian and Shanti decided that Martin had the best bid. Martin quoted a cost of $68.00 for manufacturing and packing for both the current packaging and marketing's new packaging. The supplier would be responsible for raw material and packaging material costs. In addition, Garland would pay $35,000 in tooling costs up front. Martin indicated

that it would need six months to ramp up production of Edgeworth Toffee.

THE TEAM MEETING

As Shanti looked at the information on her laptop that had been collected regarding manufacturing and packing of Edgeworth Toffee, she knew that something had to be done to address the declining margins of the brand as a result of increased production costs. Investing in new equipment seemed like an obvious solution; however, the capital investment would be significant and her proposal would need to exceed the company's 10 percent cost of capital rate to get approval by finance.

While reviewing the proposal by Martin, Shanti felt that some of the overhead costs at the Durham plant could be eliminated if production of Edgeworth Toffee was outsourced. The estimate provided by the accounting department was that overhead costs allocated to the brand could be reduced by approximately 30 percent if production was outsourced.

Historically, the company's strategy had been to control production of its products to ensure quality and delivery performance. Garland had an excellent reputation with it customers and the customer service level for Edgeworth Toffee was a line fill rate of 98 percent. However, if the case to outsource could be made successfully to the team on Monday, Shanti felt that senior management would approve the proposal. This was an important decision and she wanted to make a clear recommendation at the meeting on Monday, supported by a thorough analysis of both options.

Case 5–2

Marshall Insurance Company

Kara Murphy, purchasing manager with Marshal Insurance Company (Marshall), in Spokane, Washington, was evaluating a proposal submitted from David Callum, from Gilmore Printing (Gilmore). David was proposing that Gilmore take responsibility for managing all forms and printed materials inventory for the Marshall Automobile Club. Kara could see the advantages of outsourcing management of printed materials, but she remained concerned that this arrangement would not provide the service that clients and employees had come to expect. It was Thursday, June 12, and David was expecting a response from Kara on Tuesday, June 17, during a meeting scheduled for that afternoon.

MARSHALL INSURANCE COMPANY

The Marshall Insurance Company was a large, publicly held, personal lines property and casualty insurer. Founded in 1948, it had $73.5 billion in total assets. The Marshall Automobile Club (MAC) was a division of Marshall that provided roadside assistance services to its clients 24 hours a day, 365 days a year. Its more than 750,000 clients included both individuals and corporations.

MAC provided services to two customer groups, corporate clients, such as original equipment automotive manufacturers (OEMs) who provide free roadside assistance plans with new vehicle purchases, and individuals (or retail clients). Individual members could choose from a variety of plans for families that provided coverage for cars, trucks, motorcycles, and recreational vehicles. In addition to traditional roadside services, MAC offered features such as a trip planning, a travel reservation service, and trip interruption insurance.

Individual clients would join MAC through an online registration tool or by completing a form at a local Marshall office. Payment was typically made using a credit card. OEM clients sent their membership information to MAC daily in encrypted data files. Both individual and corporate client membership information was processed at the Spokane office, where membership cards were prepared and sent out along with an information kit that included a welcome letter, handbook, various promotional materials, and a keychain. Kits were customized for each client, in some cases using OEM letterhead if the member was joining as part as a new vehicle purchase plan. Anywhere from 2,000 to 3,000 kits were assembled each week, which took the time of two full-time staff. It was common to have more staff work on kit assembly in periods of strong demand. Storeroom staff were paid $900 per week plus benefits.

Kara's responsibilities included managing the 3,000 square foot storeroom, where printed materials were stored and kits were assembled. In addition to materials for distribution to new clients, other printed materials included MAC marketing brochures and promotional materials. In total, more than 250 different printed products were held in inventory. In order to take advantage of discounts from printing suppliers, MAC had four to six months of inventory for many products.

THE GILMORE PROPOSAL

During a meeting the previous week, David Callum proposed to Kara that his company take responsibility for managing forms and printed materials for MAC. The proposal indicated that Gilmore would manage relationships with printing suppliers, including inventory management, kit fulfillment, and distribution to clients. David described how they were providing this service to other large corporate clients, in a range of industries, that were interested in eliminating manual

back-office operations. He indicated that the typical fee was approximately $3.00 per kit, including mailing costs. The purpose of the meeting on Tuesday was to see if there was interest from Kara in pursuing the proposal; at that time Kara would need to provide David with details regarding annual volumes and materials involved.

Kara could see the advantages of outsourcing management of the storeroom operations and kit assembly. Office space was at a premium at Marshal, and the storeroom could easily be converted to other uses. The headaches associated with ordering materials and maintaining inventory records could be eliminated.

However, Kara did have concerns. First, she was suspicious that Gilmore was looking to take over all the printing business for MAC. Although an important supplier, Gilmore was currently responsible for approximately 30 percent of the printing purchases for MAC. Under the outsourcing arrangement proposed by David, Gilmore would take over existing contracts with Marshall suppliers, but as these contracts expired, it would be up to Gilmore to decide who would do the printing.

Secondly, timely processing of client membership cards and kits was critical. The expectation was that these materials would be processed within 24 hours. Kara was worried about maintaining service levels under an outsourcing arrangement with Gilmore. Furthermore, client information was confidential, and Kara had concerns about security and ensuring that Gilmore did not use the MAC client database for other purposes, such as advertising and promoting products and services for other customers.

PREPARING FOR THE MEETING

Kara felt that the proposal from David had merit and she wanted to give it careful consideration. As she examined the information he had left with her, Kara wondered how to proceed. Were the risks worth the potential problems? What questions should she ask at the meeting on Tuesday? And were there any conditions she should place on the arrangement with Gilmore if they were to proceed?

Case 5–3

Alicia Wong

Alicia Wong, Corporate Supply Manager, Thain Foods Limited, wanted to prepare a proposal to manufacture mustard in-house. Mustard, an important ingredient in many of the

company's products, was currently purchased from an outside supplier. She hoped a comprehensive proposal could be prepared in one-month's time for the CEO's approval.

GENERAL COMPANY BACKGROUND

Thain Foods Limited (TFL) had been in business for more than 30 years. Its products included a wide range of syrups, fudges, cone dips, sauces, mayonnaise, and salad dressings. Its customers were major food chains, hotels, and restaurants in North America and Europe.

TFL believed in continuous improvement to its operations. Over the last two years, it invested more than $2 million in plant facilities, the bulk of it new, state-of-the-art process equipment and process control. All production and process control functions were computerized for maximum efficiency.

TFL employed about 120 people. It had a corporate structure of CEO; president; executive vice president, domestic sales; and national account manager and used a network of food brokers who sold and promoted its products.

THE SUPPLY AREA

Alicia was responsible for supply and reported directly to the CEO. She had an inventory control officer, a buyer, and a receiver under her supervision. Purchases could be classified into five different types: labels, packaging, raw materials, commodities, and MRO supplies. Mustard was an important raw material used in many of TFL's products.

CURRENT PRACTICE: PURCHASING MUSTARD EXTERNALLY

Whenever mustard was required, the buyer e-mailed the supplier and requested that it prepare the appropriate amount to be picked up by a truck from TFL. The purchase order would be prepared before the truck left for the supplier, normally the next day. The mustard supplier used mustard seed as its raw material and blended in the other ingredients after the seed had been reduced to mustard flour. Every month TFL purchased 500 drums, or 100,000 liters, of mustard. The cost of the mustard itself was $64 per drum. Freight costs were borne by TFL and amounted to about $8 per drum. TFL operated three eight-hour shifts, five days a week. Each worker was paid about $20 per hour. It took about 10 minutes of a worker's time to handle each drum. This included pouring the mustard into the processing kettle, making sure other added ingredients mixed well, and rinsing the drums. The drums were bulky and, because they could not be used in the plant for other purposes, had to be

rinsed for a contractor who took them away. The costs of disposing of the drums in this manner were negligible. Other costs and overhead of purchasing were $0.02 per liter.

SUGGESTED CHANGE: MANUFACTURING MUSTARD IN-HOUSE

The mustard to be produced at TFL would be composed of roughly 60 percent solid, 20 percent water, and 20 percent vinegar. The solid portion was a spice blend, consisting essentially of mustard flour, salt, and other spices that could be readily bought. Water was not a problem because the city provided a reliable supply. Vinegar was already a raw material that TFL ordered in bulk regularly from suppliers. Alicia therefore believed that it was a simple matter for TFL to make the mustard for its own use. TFL only needed to buy the spice blend and add water and vinegar in the right proportions. She approached a supplier who indicated that it could make the spice blend at a delivered price of $0.15 per liter for TFL, including freight. However, it needed time for tests to ensure that the blend would be of the right quality for TFL's use. Vinegar cost TFL $0.1875 per liter delivered in 15,000 liter lots. And TFL was paying $0.025 per liter for water. Alicia also checked whether production had the time and equipment to make the mustard. Production felt that the change would not be too drastic and no additional workers would be necessary. However, it would use up more of the existing workers' time. Production calculated that the change would entail a total labor and overhead cost of about $0.105 per liter of mustard using standard cost accounting for labor time and overhead charges.

Alicia organized an information gathering and discussion session involving supply, production, quality assurance, and distribution to discuss the proposed change. The workers were keen on the idea because this meant that they would no longer have to haul and rinse the bulky drums (water and vinegar could be easily channeled to the mixing containers using existing pipes). However, quality assurance expressed concern about the quality of mustard if produced in-house. Because the mustard was an ingredient in many of TLF's products, such a change might adversely affect the quality and taste of these products.

Alicia wanted her proposal for in-house manufacture of mustard to be in the company's best interest and wondered how to proceed next.

Need Identification and Specification

Key Questions for the Supply Decision Maker

Should we

- Rethink our approach to strategic requirements?
- Initiate a simplification and standardization program?
- Change our specification method?

How can we

- Define our internal needs better to suppliers?
- Improve our acquisition of services?
- Leverage our environmental successes in the supply chain?

Need identification and specification are major value influencers. Therefore, two key decisions are addressed in this chapter: (1) How do we determine organizational needs? and (2) How do we translate and communicate these needs to (potential) suppliers?

Organizational needs that must be met by outside suppliers arise in every part of the organization and with every employee. Furthermore, if the organization serves a customer base with goods and/or services, these customer needs could well be the main drivers of the acquisition system of the organization. Therefore, for an automobile manufacturer, by far the largest portion of its spend with suppliers (for Toyota close to 80 percent of its total costs) is spent on materials and parts that will comprise the vehicle sold to customers. A good place to start addressing the need questions is to identify the major influencers of those needs. Need identification depends on the nature, size, and location of the organization as described in the first chapter. In this chapter the category of need will be addressed as well as description of needs.

NEED CRITERIA IN THE VALUE PROPOSITION

The management of supply is keenly concerned about the value proposition for specific needs acquired from suppliers. The criteria for deciding what, in a particular instance, represents good value fall into three levels: (1) strategic, (2) traditional, and (3) additional current.

The Moren Corporation (A) case at the end of this chapter is a good example of the application of the three levels of criteria to the service acquisition on a major capital project. What criteria should apply to the design of a project, and what are the implications of purchasing the design from an outside firm?

1. Strategic Criteria

The overarching question about any organizational requirement is the strategic impact. Is this a strategic requirement or not?

One potential and frequently used attribute is the financial implication or impact of the requirement. Major spend areas can be identified by a breakdown of any organization's acquisition needs according to an ABC or Pareto analysis in which "A" items or about 10 percent of the number of separate needs account for 70 percent to 80 percent of the dollar value of the total corporate spend. Focusing significant management attention on these "A" items or high spend needs makes a lot of sense. Strategic sourcing is often used for this category to align supply strategy with corporate strategy.

Other criteria for making a requirement strategic include risk reduction, access to new technology or new markets, assurance of supply in tight markets, revenue enhancement, potential competitive benefits, and corporate image or reputation improvement. These other criteria may be less obvious and require the supply manager to think strategically at a corporate level rather than on an operational and process-focused level. Creativity and a focus on the future are also required to identify which needs are strategic and which ones are not. Corporate requirements do not always reach the supply manager with labels attached: strategic or nonstrategic. Thus, a major contribution opportunity for the supply manager is to bring to light strategic implications of certain requirements, given specific market conditions and corporate strategic aspirations.

The identification of a requirement as strategic demands a very high degree of subsequent supply attention.

2. Traditional Criteria

Traditional criteria for supply management comprise the traditional value proposition of (1) quality, (2) quantity, (3) delivery, (4) price and (5) service. These five criteria have been labeled traditional because they have been identified in supply literature for more than 100 years. They make common sense, are largely quantifiable, and make up a large percentage of most existing supplier evaluation systems.

1. **Quality:** Quality covers both functionality: "Does it do the job we want done?" and conformance to specification: "Does it fit the specification agreed to?" Failure to meet quality criteria makes the product or service unacceptable, with potentially serious consequences for the supply organization and its customers. Therefore, meeting quality standards is a first and minimum demand on suppliers.

2. **Quantity:** The quantity supplied has to be sufficient to meet demand.

3. **Delivery:** The timing of the delivery has to meet the purchasing company's needs. This can be fast or slow, but must be as promised.

4. **Price:** On the assumption that the previous three criteria of quality, quantity, and delivery are up-front requirements that must be met, or order qualifiers, then price can be used as the "order getter." The distinguishing difference may be the price and terms offered by different suppliers. The four criteria of quality, quantity, delivery, and price are covered in significant detail in the following four chapters. Therefore, their treatment in this chapter is short.

5. **Service:** Although in practice many purchasers refer to a supplier as providing good service when the supplier delivers regularly on time, that is not the only definition of service. Service may include design, recordkeeping, transportation, storage, disposal, installation, training, inspection, repair, and advice, as well as a willingness to make satisfactory adjustments for misunderstandings or clerical errors. Some supply managers include the supplier's willingness to change orders on short notice and be particularly responsive to

unusual requests as part of their evaluation of the service provided. To cover some types of service, suppliers issue guarantees, covering periods of varying length. Some service factors may only come to light after a trade relationship has been established.

If the service is vital to the success of the purchase, such as installation for equipment, or training of operators, then it needs to be specified as part of the requirement. Service components like a helpful and pleasant attitude, though real, may be more difficult to quantify, yet distinguish one supplier from another.

Many suppliers specifically include the cost of service in the selling price. Others absorb it themselves, charging no more than competitors and relying on the superior service for the sale. One of the difficult tasks of a purchaser is to get only as much of this service factor as is really needed without paying for the excessive service the supplier may be obliged to render to some other purchaser. In many instances the service department of a manufacturing concern is maintained as a separate organization and profit center. The availability of service is an important consideration for the buyer in securing the "best buy" at the outset.

The Moren Corporation (B) case at the end of this chapter requires special consideration of the traditional five criteria as they apply on a major construction project.

3. Additional Current Criteria

Supply management has become more complicated over the past decades. Additional criteria have been added beyond strategic and traditional, thereby increasing the difficulty of assuring a sound value proposition.

These additional current criteria include: financial, risk, environmental impact, innovation, regulatory compliance, and social and political factors.

1. Financial

Financial criteria beyond price include improvement of the corporate financial statements, both balance sheet and income statement, to raise the company's attractiveness in the eyes of the investment community. They include revenue enhancement, working capital and accounts receivable reduction, cash flow improvement, inventory reduction, and any other initiative that improves return on assets or investment, raises the share price, or lifts the company's financial ratings.

2. Risk

Every business decision involves risk, and supply is no exception. Supply chain risk can be classified into three main categories: (1) operational risk: in supply terms, the risk of interruption of the flow of goods or services, (2) financial risk: in supply terms, the risk that the price or total cost of the goods or services acquired will change significantly, and (3) reputational risk: in supply terms, risk that the reputation of the enterprise is adversely affected by the method of acquisition or the behavior of the supplier. All three risks affect the survival, competitiveness, and bottom line of the organization and may occur simultaneously. Chapter 2 provides more detail on managing supply risks.

3. Environmental

Climate change and water, earth, and air pollution have raised environmental concerns that must be addressed in all areas of the supply chain. While disposal of hazardous goods has been a responsibility of supply managers for several decades, environmental issues have grown considerably. Reexamining the total supply chain from an environment perspective raises questions way beyond hazardous goods disposal. The amount of energy and water and scarce resources used, the transportation and handling systems and distances traveled, the discharge of undesirable gases into the air or substances into the earth—all influence the design, movement, creation, and disposal phases in the supply chain to minimize the "footprint." Thus, the "best buy" has to include environmental impact as a standard consideration.

4. Innovation

Innovation as a criterion for determining best value refers to the pursuit of continuing improvement. Current suppliers are expected to provide suggestions for value improvement and total cost of ownership reduction on an ongoing basis. Such suggestions may require the supply organization to make changes in design, communication, handling, advance notice, scheduling, or any other supply chain practice that can be improved. Innovation suggestions may also involve supplier changes and any other suggestions that may improve the purchaser's revenues or costs. The reason for including innovation as an additional value criterion is that the supplier is forced to ask, How can we do better? and What can make my customer more successful?

5. Regulatory Compliance and Transparency

All agreements reached between buyers and sellers have to comply with the relevant laws and regulations.

Failure to comply can damage the reputation of the parties and result in fines or citations. The legal framework for trade is covered in Chapter 15, "Legal and Ethics." An extensive and growing legal and regulatory structure affects trade in most developed countries, and compliance is not a minor matter. Moreover, financial scandals and new accounting standards have increased demands for greater transparency on all financial dealings of a company. Therefore, long-term contracts, lease obligations, and hedge positions have to be reported properly. Failure to do so may mislead investors and incur the wrath and penalties of a range of industry watchdogs and regulators.

6. Social and Political Factors

Corporate social responsibility (CSR) has become prominent in the last decade. Companies are supposed to behave like good corporate citizens and recognize that they have social responsibilities in the countries in which they operate. Therefore, dealing with socially responsible suppliers is a plus for the supply organization's image and reputation as well as its ability to develop resilient and sustainable supply chains. Promoting opportunities for disadvantaged, minority, and small business suppliers to quote and receive corporate orders is seen as a socially desirable action. MRO and small value purchases are typical categories of needs wherein socially disadvantaged and small suppliers can make a reasonable value proposition. Activists often link environmental and social sensitivity together as one area where organizations must demonstrate a willingness to search for better solutions. Building an environmentally advanced facility in a high unemployment area of the country would be seen as a concrete example.

Political concerns do not refer to paying politicians under the table. They include a willingness to support the government in its priorities, rather than opposing them. If it is possible to support "Buy Local" government initiatives, then a company is expected to do so, even if it is not a hard regulatory requirement. Assisting government training initiatives and working on government-sponsored industry panels would be additional examples.

The collective set of strategic, traditional, and additional current criteria for need identification and subsequent supply chain decisions makes for a complex analysis in which judgment also plays an important part. Not every acquisition will require an exhaustive analytical review, but the supply professional through experience and judgment learns which criteria are likely to be relevant for any particular acquisition.

The Carson Manor case at the end of this chapter deals with the challenge of evaluating service supplier bids in response to a request for proposals based on a fairly broad definition of needs. How do you know that one consultant fits your needs better than another?

CATEGORIES OF NEEDS

Organizational needs can be classified broadly into seven categories. These are (1) resale, (2) raw or semiprocessed materials, (3) parts, components, and packaging, (4) maintenance, repair, and operating supplies (MRO), (5) capital assets, (6) services, and (7) other. Each of these categories covers a wide range of requirements (see Table 6–1).

TABLE 6–1
Categories of Needs

Categories of Needs	
1. Resale	Resellers comprise retailers, wholesalers, distributors, agents, brokers, and traders. What they can resell covers the full range of the remaining five categories below.
2. Raw and Semiprocessed Materials	Most users of materials are converters, such as factories, and this category includes commodities, agricultural, and industrial.
3. Parts, Components, and Packaging	Assemblers use parts and components produced by their suppliers to create a finished product. Parts and components may be standard or special depending on the decision of the designer of the finished product.
4. Maintenance, Repair, and Operating Supplies (MRO) and Small Value Purchases (SVP)	Every organization has MRO requirements and SVPs. The availability of MRO suppliers is critical to maintain continued uninterrupted operation of the office, factory, facility, etc. Because many MRO requirements are relatively small in dollar value, SVPs are also included in this category. For SVPs, assuring availability at minimum acquisition cost is a challenge.
5. Capital Assets	Any requirement that accountants classify as capital, and, therefore, an investment, becomes a capital item. Equipment, IT, real estate, and construction are included in this category. Capital items can be depreciated, are often bought under a separate budgetary allocation, and may require special financing arrangements.
6. Services	Services are intangible and nonmanufactured. Every organization acquires a variety of services.
7. Other	Anything not covered by the above categories falls into this last one. Major requirements could be energy and water. This category would also include unusual and infrequent requirements, probably better dealt with on an ad hoc or project basis.

In large organizations it is usual to assign supply professionals all or part of a category of requirements. In small organizations one person may have to cover the full range. The supply execution required for each category may be different, as discussed below.

1. Resale

Since resellers represent a distribution channel between buyers and sellers, the abilities to buy well and sell profitably are critical to success. Resellers who do not take possession of goods or supply additional services may charge a small margin. The potential for a reseller's customer to bypass the reseller and deal directly with the reseller's supplier is an ever-present threat, as is the possibility that the reseller's supplier will bypass the reseller and deal directly with the reseller's customers. For example, Honda recently decided to discontinue selling its nonautomotive products such as ATVs and motorbikes through separate dealers and to consolidate all Honda brand products with automotive dealerships. Insurance companies often sell their products and services through brokers as well as their own sales force. Airlines sell direct to customers as well as through online and brick and mortar travel agencies.

For resellers who take ownership of the goods they resell, the largest single cost is the price they pay for the goods. Therefore, financial management of receivables and payables and cash flow is a major skill required most along with logistics management. Walmart is reputed to be able to sell a very large portion of its store merchandise before it has to pay its suppliers. In effect, its suppliers are financing Walmart's operations and inventories.

Manufacturers may choose to resell some products to complete a full line and may offer maintenance, lubricants, or parts to improve the attractiveness of their products in use.

In the fashion industry, the ability of the retail buyer to spot trends and assess the likelihood that a given style or color of garment will sell well is a critical attribute.

2. Raw and Semiprocessed Materials

Raw materials are basic substances in their natural, modified, or semiprocessed state that are used as inputs to a production process. For example, a steelmaker needs iron ore or scrap steel, coke, and a range of additives to create finished steel with particular properties. Commodities in the agricultural world are subject to availability and price fluctuations. Industrial commodities also experience supply and demand effects on price. Commodities that are traded on exchanges show daily price variations, and buyers need to decide whether to buy forward or hand to mouth as well as decide on hedging strategies.

The purchases of large commodity buyers, such as Nestle for coffee and cocoa and Coca Cola for sugar, will affect market prices. Commodity supply managers need to be fully aware of market conditions. Supply and demand, price movements, and proper timing of acquisition commitments are critical. Semiprocessed materials—steel sheets instead of ingots, frozen pork bellies instead of hogs, cocoa butter instead of beans—tend to move in price as the basic raw material moves with a producer's margin added.

Frequently labeled converters, suppliers of semiprocessed materials often are much smaller companies than the providers of their raw materials. Converters may find themselves squeezed between their suppliers and customers, each of which is trying to off-load the risk of unfavorable price movement.

3. Parts, Components, and Packaging

It is unusual for an assembler to make all of its products' parts and components itself. Therefore, it is common to depend on suppliers to provide the necessary parts, components, and packaging. Design engineers and design experts determine what parts and components to buy and which to make in-house. They also decide whether to design standard parts and components into the product or to specify custom design. The advantage of standard parts and components is their ready availability. The disadvantage is the ease of copying. Motorola for many years had a very high percentage of custom-designed electrical and electronic components in their product line. While affording duplication protection, this practice also delayed new product introduction and increased component costs. Therefore, a major initiative was undertaken to get engineers to design out of suppliers' catalogs. Failure to capture market share led Google to acquire the company to take advantage of Motorola's patents and expertise. The company was renamed Motorola Mobility–A Google Company, but was sold to Lenovo in 2014, thereby providing Lenovo a global supply chain and access to the smartphone market.

Since product design is a major influencer of product cost and speed to market, early supplier involvement (ESI) is a fruitful concern for this category.

Packaging is another specialized requirement, with major disposal, environmental, and transportation implications. Since packaging is discarded by the purchaser, it has potential environmental impact. Yet the package has to protect its contents as it finds its way from product manufacturer to final user. Damage during transport is a cost few parties are willing to assume. For some consumer items, such as cosmetics, the package can be a significant sales influencer. For a number of items, the packaging may be worth more than its contents: for example, beverage containers, including beer. For consumer items, marketers, packaging designers, and packaging engineers are concerned with the aesthetic, sales appeal, labeling, regulatory, and safety aspects. Specialty packaging suppliers may for a fee or as a free service offer advice on various packaging options. For nonconsumer goods, the primary packaging concerns are likely to be cost, environmental impact, and adequate contents protection given the types of handling and transportation modes the packaged goods will experience.

4. Maintenance, Repair, and Operating Supplies

Every organization has MRO requirements. Even the one-person office needs paper, IT, janitorial supplies, and so forth. For some companies MRO requirements are huge. Syncrude, the world's largest oil sands operator, has over 150,000 stock keeping units (SKUs) in its MRO category. For many organizations, because of the diversity of the MRO category and the large number of relatively small requirements (C items), the challenge is keeping acquisition costs down relative to the value of what is purchased. It doesn't make sense to spend $500 acquiring one $3 item. Therefore, MRO acquisition deals with many small value purchases (SVPs) and SVPs are linked with the MRO category. Typical supply solutions include systems contracting wherein one supplier is chosen to provide a large variety of products—for example, all office, plumbing, or electrical supplies on a daily or twice weekly delivery schedule. Designated employees will order their department's needs electronically from a catalog, and the supplier provides accounting with a biweekly detailed invoice providing specific account totals by department. Letting users order their own needs directly saves time and acquisition cost. Acquisition expertise is required to identify the needs, to select a supplier, to develop a contract, and to monitor performance.

5. Capital Assets

Capital assets are long-term assets that are not bought or sold in the regular course of business, have an ongoing effect on the organization's operations, have an expected use of more than one year, involve large sums of money, and generally are depreciated. Assets may be tangible or intangible. Historically, tangible assets (land, buildings, and equipment) have been the primary focus of managerial attention because they were the key drivers of wealth. Today, intangible assets (patents, copyrights, ideas, and knowledge) are important generators of wealth. Intangible assets are especially challenging because traditional accounting procedures do not include valuation methods for intangibles.

Capital expenditures are the result of investment and strategic decisions as opposed to expenses and are shown on the balance sheet as assets. Accountants create separate capital budgets, calculate depreciation, and advise on tax implications of capital purchases. Financing capital purchases requires special attention. Capital equipment can be acquired new or used and may be purchased outright or leased.

According to the U.S. Census Bureau, U.S. businesses typically invest between $1 and $1.5 trillion annually in new and used capital goods. In a weak economy, businesses tend to cut back on capital investments and in a strong economy capital expenditures flow again. The impact of such behavior on the sustainability of the supplier is one area of concern for supply managers when they evaluate suppliers. Too little investment or inconsistent investment in capital assets may signify serious organizational problems that will affect the supplier's ability to deliver quality goods or services in the long term.

The Challenge of Procuring Capital Assets The acquisition of capital goods may represent a key strategic move for an organization that could affect its competitive advantage for years to come. Or it could be a routine matter of no great consequence. In capital intensive industries such as mining or airlines, the acquisition of capital goods represents one of the single largest purchase categories and one of the greatest opportunities for supply to affect top-line (revenue) and bottom-line growth. A major nuclear power plant may take a decade to plan and build and may cost billions. Capital purchases are routine for a rapidly growing fast-food chain that may start up and equip hundreds of store locations per year. Companies with large fleets of cars may turn over one-third of the fleet each year and have a fleet manager assigned to decide which vehicles to acquire, how to dispose of vehicles, and select insurance and maintenance providers.

The risks associated with the acquisition of capital assets can be high. From the budgeting process to the design of equipment or buildings, determination of location for real estate purchases, and decisions about enterprisewide hardware and software, many factors play into the ultimate success or failure of a capital project. Clearly defined supply objectives that are linked to, and aligned with, organizational strategy and supported by robust supply processes are as important to successful capital acquisition and management as they are to noncapital purchases. Because of the high dollar amount and the long-term consequences of many capital projects, the application of tools and techniques such as enterprisewide spend analysis; standardization of equipment, including hardware and software; globalization of processes; and cost visibility are important.

The strategy for a specific capital acquisition depends on a number of factors, including the frequency of the purchase, the projected total cost of ownership, the amount and timing of cash flows, and the potential impact of the purchase on business operations.

For example, if assets are replaced at regular intervals, it makes sense to form a close working relationship with the supplier and focus on continuous improvement. At the U.S. Postal Service, for example, the mission of the organization is universal service at a reasonable cost in a timely manner. To achieve this mission consistently, large volumes of letters and packages must be sorted accurately and quickly. Therefore, sorting equipment is a strategic capital acquisition for the Postal Service. Because of design requirements and the desire for standardized equipment across the national organization, only a few suppliers are available. The category management team works closely with these suppliers to develop the specification, manage the cost structure, and deliver equipment in a shortened cycle time that delivers consistent quality, operating speed, and lowest total cost of ownership.

For one-time or infrequent high-value purchases, total cost of ownership analysis of the purchase and of the total supply chain costs is appropriate. There are many costs beyond purchase price that affect the true "cost to the organization" of any particular buy and especially for capital assets. A generally accepted figure is that the purchase price makes up from 30 percent to 50 percent of the total cost of ownership (TCO) of a capital purchase. Other factors, such as maintenance and repair costs, operating costs, downtime, and yield play key roles. Supply personnel must acquire the skills and knowledge necessary to develop total cost of ownership models that estimate and capture costs throughout the supply chain. Nonroutine capital asset acquisition may require a cross-functional project team representing users, marketers, designers, financial experts, and supply experts. If appropriate expertise is lacking internally, outside consultants may be brought in.

New Technology—New Equipment Competitive advantage stems from product or service differentiation or low-cost production. New technology frequently permits an organization to gain competitive advantage on both grounds—different products and services at significantly lower cost. New technology is, therefore, of significant strategic interest to most organizations. And new technology almost always implies new equipment and new processes. It is this strategic dimension of new equipment acquisition that has traditionally been overlooked by supply. Intellectual property rights, speed of acquisition, installation and debugging, continuing supplier support for operational performance and upgrades, and development of the next generation of technological advances become prime matters of corporate concern.

For example, in the semiconductor industry, capital equipment purchases normally represent the largest single percentage category of all purchase dollars. At Intel, the goal is to tie capital equipment purchasing and equipment service to performance-based contracting. Thus, the supplier gets paid for uptime and quality output. The more the running time exceeds agreed-to output goals, the greater the rewards for the supplier. Future plans are driven by the need for continuous improvement in cost per wafer and number of wafers per year per machine. Only a few key supplier partners are included in Intel's longer-range technology road maps planning process—looking five years out. Total cost of ownership, not just the cost of the equipment itself, drives future technology decisions. The corporate team approach is required to manage this process and exceptionally capable individuals need to represent supply on the corporate team.

Equipment purchases involve, in part, engineering and production considerations and, in part, factors largely outside the scope of these functions. From the former standpoint, there are eight commonly recognized reasons for purchase: (1) capacity, (2) economy in operation and maintenance, (3) increased productivity, (4) better quality, (5) dependability in use, (6) savings in time or labor costs, (7) durability, and (8) safety, pollution, and emergency protection. Beyond these engineering questions are those that only the marketing, supply, or financial departments, or general management itself, can answer. Is this a key strategic commitment? Are style changes or other modifications in the present product essential or even desirable? Is the market static, contracting, or expanding? Does the company have the funds with which to buy the machine that theoretically is most desirable, or is it necessary, for financial reasons, to be satisfied with something that is perhaps less efficient but of a lower initial cost? What should be done in a case in which the particular equipment most desirable from an engineering standpoint is obtainable only from a manufacturer that is not thoroughly trustworthy or perhaps is on the verge of bankruptcy? Should we be the first or the last purchaser of this equipment? Such questions are quite as important in the final decision as are the more purely engineering ones. For this reason it is sound practice to form a cross-functional sourcing team including representatives from engineering, using departments, finance, marketing, and supply to work jointly on major equipment acquisitions.

6. Services

Services are intangible and nonmanufactured. They may be closely associated with a good: for example, IT services that come with hardware. Table 6–2 lists a variety of common services.

TABLE 6–2
Services

Advertising	Household/office moves	Research & development
Architectural	Information systems	Sales promotion
Auditing	Inspections	Security
Banking	Insurance	Signage
Cafeteria/catering	Interior decorating/space planning	Snow removal
Computer programming	Janitorial	Space/storage rental
Construction	Landscaping/lawn service	Telephone
Consulting	Legal service	Temporary help
Contract packaging	Mail services	Training
Courier services	Maintenance	Transport of goods
Customs brokerage	Medical	Trash removal/disposal
Data processing	Payroll	Travel (air, hotel, auto rental)
Demolition	Photography	Utilities (electric, gas, water)
Engineering design	Property management	Vending service
Environmental cleanup	Records management	Workers' compensation insurance
Hazardous waste disposal	Recruiting/outplacement	
Health benefit plans	Reproduction/copying	

Every organization, whether in the manufacturing, public/governmental, or service sector, requires services in the course of its operations. The service sector is growing as a portion of GDP and so is the percent of spend for services. It is not only the sheer dollar volume spent to acquire services but also the impact of these services on organizational success that makes the effective acquisition of services a significant and important challenge.

According to the 2013–2014 World Factbook, the U.S. GDP is composed of 79.7 percent services, 19.2 percent industry (manufacturing), and 1.1 percent agriculture. If the economy were broken into three segments: manufacturing, service, and public, then manufacturing organizations have a higher percent of spend allocated to the purchase of goods than services, and public/governmental and service organizations have a much higher percent allocated to services than goods. Service organizations have the highest percent of spend for services.

The magnitude of the dollars spent to acquire services indicates that a professional supply department that attained a reduction of even 5 percent in overall prices paid would have a major impact on an organization's profitability. If the focus were placed on lowering total cost of ownership, the contribution from a structured sourcing process and knowledgeable supply managers would be even greater.

What Makes Services Different? A commonly mentioned attribute is the inability to store services because many are processes (which may or may not be associated with a product). This implies that timing of the delivery has to coincide with the purchaser's specific delivery needs, and the consequences of improper timing may be serious and costly. To accommodate a variety of customers, service providers need to ensure that sufficient capacity is available. The inability to store services also creates quality assurance difficulties. It may not be possible to inspect a service before its delivery. And, by the time of delivery, it may be too late to do anything about it. Anyone who has ever suffered through a boring speaker or a bad airline flight will attest to that.

The specification and measurement of quality in a service may present significant difficulties. Frequently, services have both tangible and intangible components. In the hospitality industry, the tangible side deals with how well customers' food and drink needs are met. The intangible side deals with the customer's need to be liked, respected, pampered, and treated as a valued client. Such needs are met when service personnel are friendly, courteous, and enthusiastic; when they show they appreciate their customers' patronage; when they are knowledgeable about the products they are selling; when they use sales techniques tactfully and effectively; and when they strive to meet each customer's unique expectations for quality service.

Service can be classified by type as well as characteristics. Service management texts provide a framework for identifying key service aspects for better analysis. These aspects include value, degree of repetitiveness, tangibility, standardization, the nature of demand (continuous, periodic, or discrete) and service delivery, the direction and production of the service, and the skills required for it. These nine factors create hundreds of combinations, a significant specification and acquisition challenge.

Many services have traditionally been acquired directly by users outside the supply area. However, concern over transparency, conflicts of interest, and value for money have resulted in a continuing shift of responsibility for service acquisition to supply professionals. This has resulted in substantial organizational benefits and growth in supply's involvement in an increasing percentage of the organization's total spend.

7. Other

The other category covers anything not included in the previous six categories and forms a convenient catch-all.

Energy, water, and air are sometimes included in the MRO category. However, for some organizations, energy and water, in particular, may be major expenditures and should be managed quite differently from the MRO category.

Unusual and infrequent requirements by definition fall outside of the "normal" range and have to be dealt with on an ad hoc or project basis. The purchase of a bronze statue of the founder of the company for display in the corporate office lobby might qualify as an example.

For all seven categories of needs the common acquisition challenge involves the determination of best buy under the circumstances. This requires recognizing not only the traditional criteria of quality, quantity, delivery, and price, but also the risk and strategic, environmental, technological, and social and political implications. Considerable judgment may be required of the supply professional. Consultation with users, specifiers, customers, regulators, financial, and other experts may have to precede the decision about what constitutes the best buy and what processes should be used to assure effective acquisition.

REPETITIVE OR NONREPETITIVE REQUIREMENTS?

For all categories of spend, the next question is, repetitive or not? For repetitive requirements a system or process of acquisition can be designed. A purchase order or contract may be placed without going through the usual acquisition process once a supplier is established for a particular repetitive order. In these cases, the process consists of order, receive, and pay according to contract terms and conditions.

Contract length is also a consideration for repetitive purchases. Product or service life cycle and design stability influence contract length. For a concrete block manufacturer, the requirement for cement is likely to be very long term. Aside from the forecastability of demand for a requirement, the supply manager may wish to consider for how long he or she is willing to commit to a particular supplier. Generally, shorter contracts, mean greater flexibility to switch suppliers, while longer contracts typically mean the price should be lower. Considerable judgment is required to deal effectively with this trade-off.

For nonrepetitive requirements, depending on the category and the need criteria, an ad hoc decision needs to be made regarding the process of acquisition. If the nonrepetitive requirement is small and insignificant, treating it as a small value purchase order (SVPO) and having the user order it directly on a purchase card may be adequate. On the other extreme, the acquisition of a multimillion-dollar piece of equipment may require the efforts of a project team to finance, specify, and acquire the equipment.

COMMERCIAL EQUIVALENTS

Every acquisition is intended to fulfill a need. Therefore, the first step in the acquisition process is to determine what is needed and why. The next step is to translate these needs into commercial equivalents so that suppliers can understand what is needed. The temptation is to collapse these two steps into one. In consumer terms we say, "I need an aspirin,"

FIGURE 6–1
Opportunity to Affect Value during the Six Steps of the Acquisition Process

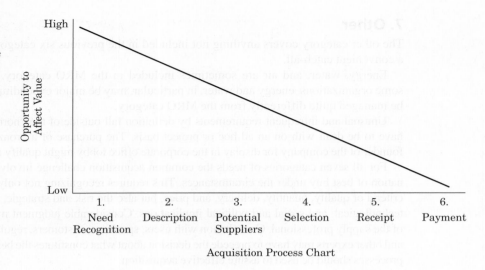

Acquisition Process Chart

rather than "I need to cure my headache." We say, "I need a nail to nail two pieces of wood to each other," rather than "I need to fasten these two pieces of wood together." This is an important distinction.

It is generally recognized that about 70 percent of the opportunity for value improvement lies in the first two phases of the acquisition process: (1) need identification and (2) specification. Therefore, each step should be analyzed separately to ensure that value opportunities are not overlooked (see Figure 6–1).

For example, many options exist for fastening two pieces of wood together, including a nail, staple, bolt, screw, or glue. Specifying the need first based on the functionality required and then identifying the variety of options to meet the need create the opportunity for lower cost and better, or more innovative, solutions. The supply professional has the responsibility to suggest potential value improvements on the commercial equivalent presented by a designer or specifier. Early supply and supplier involvement prevents the hassles associated with trying to reverse a design decision after it has been made and approved technically.

EARLY SUPPLY AND SUPPLIER INVOLVEMENT

Given the opportunity to greatly affect value during the need identification and specification stages, it is essential that supply considerations are brought to bear on decisions during these two stages. This is fundamental in value analysis/value engineering. Early supply involvement and early supplier involvement (ESI) help assure that what is specified is also procurable and represents good value. Various organizational approaches, such as staffing the supply area with engineers, co-locating supply people in the engineering or design areas, and using cross-functional teams on new product or service development or reviews, have been used to address effective early supply involvement.

The second step in the acquisition process involves translating the organization's needs into commercial language so that suppliers can understand what is required. This requires not only an understanding of what the market can supply, but also which type of description might be preferable under the circumstances.

METHODS OF DESCRIPTION

The using, requesting, or specifying department must be capable of reasonably describing what is required to be sure of getting exactly what is wanted. Description also begins the process of allocating risk and reward between the buyer and seller by divvying up responsibility for performance or functionality.

Although the prime responsibility for determining what is needed usually rests with the using or specifying department, the supply department has the direct responsibility of checking the description given. Supply professionals should not be allowed to alter arbitrarily the description or the quality. They should, however, have the authority to insist that the description be accurate and detailed enough to be perfectly clear to every potential supplier. The supply professional also must call to the attention of the requisitioner the availability of other options that might represent better value.

The description of an item may take any one of a variety of forms or may be a combination of several different forms. For our discussion, *description* will mean any one of the various methods by which a buyer conveys to a seller a clear, accurate picture of the required item or service. The term *specification* will be used in the narrower and commonly accepted sense referring to one particular form of description.

The methods of description will be discussed in order:

1. By brand.
2. "Or Equal."
3. By specification.
   a. Physical or chemical characteristics.
   b. Material and method of manufacture.
   c. Performance.
4. By engineering drawing.
5. By miscellaneous methods.
   a. Market grades.
   b. Sample.
6. By a combination of two or more methods.

Brand

Two questions about using branded items are: One, is brand a desirable description? Two, how should a particular brand be selected?

Description by brand or trade name indicates a reliance on the integrity and the reputation of the supplier. It assumes that the supplier is anxious to preserve the goodwill attached to a trade name and is capable of doing so. Furthermore, when a given requirement is purchased by brand and is satisfactory in the use for which it was intended, the purchaser has every right to expect that any additional purchases bearing the same brand name will correspond exactly to the quality first obtained. The buyer is, in effect, transferring responsibility and risk for performance onto the supplier of the branded item and may pay a premium.

There are certain circumstances under which description by brand is desirable and necessary:

1. When, either because the manufacturing process is secret or because the item is covered by a patent, specifications cannot be developed.
2. When specifications cannot be developed with sufficient accuracy by the buyer because the supplier's manufacturing process calls for a high degree of that intangible labor quality sometimes called *expertise* or *skill,* which cannot be defined exactly.
3. When the quantity bought is so small that the cost of developing specifications is too high.
4. When end customers or users have real, even if unfounded, preferences in favor of certain branded items, a bias the supply professional may find almost impossible to overcome.

Objections to purchasing branded items mostly relate to cost. Although the price may be in line with the prices charged by other suppliers for similarly branded items, the whole price level may be so high as to cause the buyer to seek unbranded substitutes. For example, the purchaser may prefer using trisodium phosphate over a branded cleaning compound costing 50 percent to 100 percent more. Also, undue dependence on brands tends to restrict the number of potential suppliers and deprives the buyer of the possible advantage of a lower price or even of improvements brought out by competitors.

"Or Equal"

It is not unusual, particularly in the public sector, to see requests for quotations or bids that will specify a brand or a manufacturer's model number followed by the words "or equal." In these circumstances, the buyer tries to shift the responsibility for establishing equality or superiority to the bidder without going to the expense of having to develop detailed specifications.

Specification

Specification constitutes one of the best known of all methods employed. A specification is a detailed, exact statement prescribing materials, dimensions, and quality of work for something to be built, installed, or manufactured. It is common practice to specify the test procedure and results necessary to meet quality standards as part of the specification as well as instructions for handling, labeling, transportation, and disposal to meet environmental regulations. A lot of time and effort has been expended in making it possible to buy on a specification basis, to standardize product specifications, and to reduce the number of types, sizes, and designs of the products accepted as standard.

Advantages of buying with specifications include:

1. Evidence exists that thought and careful study have been given to the need and the ways in which it may be satisfied.
2. A standard is established for measuring and checking materials as supplied, preventing delay and waste that would occur with improper materials.

3. An opportunity exists to purchase identical requirements from a number of different sources of supply.

4. The potential exists for equitable competition. This is why public agencies place such a premium on specification writing. In securing bids from various suppliers, a buyer must be sure that the suppliers are quoting for exactly the same material or service.

5. The seller will be responsible for performance when the buyer specifies performance.

Seven limitations in using specifications, assuming the buying organization is capable of specifying, are:

1. There are requirements for which it is practically impossible to draw adequate specifications.

2. The use of specifications adds to the immediate cost.

3. The specification may not be better than a standard product, readily available.

4. The cost is increased by testing to ensure that the specifications have been met.

5. Unduly elaborate specifications sometimes result in discouraging potential suppliers from placing bids in response to inquiries.

6. Unless the specifications are of the performance type, the risk and responsibility for the adaptability of the item to the use intended rests wholly with the buying organization.

7. The minimum specifications set up by the buying organization are likely to be the maximum furnished by the supplier.

Specification by Physical or Chemical Characteristics

Specification by physical or chemical characteristics provides definitions of the properties of the materials the purchaser desires. They represent an effort to state in measurable terms those properties deemed necessary for satisfactory use at the least cost consistent with quality.

Specification by Material and Method of Manufacture

The second type of specification prescribes both the material and method of manufacture. Outside of some governmental purchases, such as those of the armed forces, this method is used when special requirements exist and when the buying organization is willing to assume the risk and responsibility for results. Many organizations are not in this position, and as a result, comparatively little use is made of this form of specification.

Specification by Performance or Function

The heart of performance specification is the understanding of the required functions. It is not easy to think of the basic function the item must perform. We tend to speak of a box instead of something to package in, a bolt instead of something that fastens. We think of a steak, instead of something to eat, and a bed, instead of something to sleep on.

Performance or function specification in combination with a request for proposal (RFP) is employed to a considerable extent, partly because it puts the responsibility for a satisfactory product or service back on the seller. Performance specification is results and use oriented, leaving the supplier with the decisions on how to provide the most suitable product or service. This enables the supplier to take advantage of the latest technological developments and to substitute anything that exceeds the minimum performance required.

The satisfactory use of a performance specification is absolutely dependent on securing the right kind of supplier. It should be noted that it may be difficult to compare quotations and the supplier may include a risk allowance in the price.

Description by Engineering Drawing

Description by a design or dimension sheet is common and may be used in connection with some form of descriptive text. It is particularly applicable to the purchase of construction, electronic and electrical assemblies, machined parts, forgings, castings, and stampings. It is an expensive method of description not only because of the cost of preparing the print or computer program itself but also because it is likely to be used to describe an item that is quite special as far as the supplier is concerned and, hence, expensive to manufacture. However, it is probably the most accurate of all forms of description and is particularly adapted to acquiring those items requiring a high degree of manufacturing perfection and close tolerances.

Miscellaneous Methods of Description

There are two additional methods of description: description by market grades and description by sample.

Description by Market Grades

Purchases on the basis of market grades are confined to certain primary materials. Wheat and cotton,[1] lumber, steel, and copper are commodities. For some purposes, purchase by grade is entirely satisfactory. Its value depends on the accuracy with which grading is done and the ability to ascertain the grade of the material by inspection.

Furthermore, the grading must be done by those in whose ability and honesty the purchaser has confidence. It may be noted that even for wheat and cotton, grading may be entirely satisfactory to one class of buyer and not satisfactory to another class.

Description by Sample

Still another method of description is by submission of a sample of the item desired. Almost all purchasers use this method from time to time but ordinarily (there are some exceptions) for a minor percentage of their purchases and then more or less because no other method is possible.

Good examples are items requiring visual acceptance such as wood grain, color, appearance, smell, and so on.

Combination of Descriptive Methods

An organization frequently uses a combination of two or more of the methods of description already discussed. The exact combination found most satisfactory for an individual organization will depend on the type of good or service needed by the organization.

Sources of Specification Data

There are three major sources from which specifications may be derived: (1) individual standards set up by the buying organization; (2) standards established by certain private agencies, either other users, suppliers, or technical societies; and (3) governmental standards.

[1] For agricultural raw materials, such as wheat and cotton, the grades are established by the U.S. Department of Agriculture. They include all food and feed products, the standards and grades for which have been established in accordance with the Federal Food and Drug Act, the Grain Standards Act, and other laws enacted by Congress. Establishing grades acceptable to the trade is essential to the successful operation of a commodity exchange.

Individual Standards

Individual standards require extensive consultation among users, engineering, supply, quality control, suppliers, marketing, and, possibly, ultimate consumers. This means the task is likely to be arduous and expensive.

A common procedure is for the buying organization to formulate its own specifications on the basis of the foundation laid down by the governmental or technical societies. To avoid errors, some organizations send out tentative specifications, even in cases where changes are mere revisions of old forms, to several outstanding suppliers in the industry to get the advantage of their comments and suggestions before final adoption.

Standard Specifications

If an organization wishes to buy on a specification basis, yet hesitates to develop its own, it may use one of the so-called standard specifications. These have been developed as a result of a great deal of experience and study by both governmental and nongovernmental agencies, and substantial effort has been expended in promoting them. They may be applied to raw or semimanufactured products, to component parts, or to the composition of material. The well-known SAE steels, for instance, are a series of alloy steels of specified composition and known properties, carefully defined, and identified by individual numbers.

When they can be used, standard specifications have major advantages. They are widely known, commonly recognized, and readily available to every supply professional. Furthermore, the standard should have somewhat lower costs of manufacture. They have grown out of the wide experience of producers and users, and, therefore, should be adaptable to the requirements of many users.

Standard specifications have been developed by a number of nongovernmental engineering and technical groups. Among them may be mentioned the American Standards Association, the American Society for Testing Materials, the American Society of Mechanical Engineers, the American Institute of Electrical Engineers, the Society of Automotive Engineers, the American Institute of Mining and Metallurgical Engineers, the Underwriters Laboratories, the National Safety Council, the Canadian Engineering Standards Association, the Institute of Scrap Recycling Industries, the National Electrical Manufacturers Association, and many others.

While governmental agencies have cooperated closely with these organizations, they have also developed their own standards. The National Institute of Standards and Technology (nist.gov) in the U.S. Department of Commerce compiles commercial standards. The General Services Administration coordinates standards and federal specifications for the nonmilitary type of items used by two or more services. The Defense Department issues military (MIL) specifications.

The American National Standards Institute (ANSI) is a private, nonprofit organization that administers and coordinates the U.S. voluntary standards and conformity assessment system. Its mission is to enhance the global competitiveness of U.S. business and the U.S. quality of life by promoting and facilitating voluntary consensus standards and conformity assessment systems and safeguarding their integrity.[2]

Administered by ANSI, the National Resource for Global Standards (NSSN) is a search engine that provides users with standards-related information from developers, including

---

[2] American National Standards Institute, February 2014. www.ansi.org.

organizations accredited by the American National Standards Institute (ANSI), other U.S. private-sector standards bodies, government agencies, and international organizations. The NSSN can be a valuable resource for purchasers who need access to various standards.[3]

Government, Legal, and Environmental Requirements

Federal legislation concerning environmental factors, employee health and safety, security, and consumer product safety requires vigilance on the part of supply professionals to be sure that products purchased meet government requirements. The Occupational Safety and Health Administration (known as OSHA) of the U.S. Department of Labor has broad powers to investigate and control everything from noise levels to sanitary facilities in places of employment. The Environmental Protection Agency (EPA) develops and enforces regulations related to environmental laws. The Consumer Product Safety Act gives broad regulatory power to a commission to safeguard consumers against unsafe products. Supply professionals have the responsibility to make sure that the products they buy meet the requirements of the legislation. Severe penalties, both criminal and civil, can be placed on violators of the regulations.

STANDARDIZATION AND SIMPLIFICATION

The terms *standardization* and *simplification* are often used to mean the same thing. Strictly speaking, they refer to two different ideas. *Standardization* means agreement on definite sizes, design, quality, and the like. It is essentially a technical and engineering concept. *Simplification* refers to a reduction in the number of sizes, designs, and so forth. It is a selective and commercial problem, an attempt to determine the most important sizes (for instance, of a product) and to concentrate production or use on these wherever possible. Simplification may be applied to articles already standardized as to design or size or as a step preliminary to standardization.

The challenge in an organization is where to draw the line between standardization and simplification, on the one hand, and suitability and uniqueness, on the other. Clearly, as economic and technological factors change, old standards may no longer represent the best buy. Frequently, by stressing standardization and simplification of the component parts, rather than the completed end product, production economies may be gained, combined with individuality of end product. Simultaneously, procurement advantages are gained in terms of low initial cost, lower inventories, and diversity in selection of sources. The automotive industry, for example, has used this approach extensively to cut costs, improve quality, and still give the appearance of extensive consumer options.

Sasib, a manufacturer of equipment for the food and beverage industry, headquartered in Italy, found that product standardization was an important issue for its large global customers, such as Coca Cola and Heineken. The chief purchasing officer described the importance of standardization and the role of supply: "Standardization is important to us, not just for leveraging purchases across the group, but also in terms of our ability to design and build a product for our customer that is consistent, regardless of where it is manufactured. We also want to be able to exchange and optimize manufacturing capacity. For example,

---

[3] See www.nssn.org or www.ansi.org.

we need to develop the flexibility to build machines in the United States that are designed in Europe and vice versa. More importantly, our customers are expecting standardization across our product lines. This can only be done if we use the same suppliers that can provide support everywhere in the world. Consequently, we use top-quality suppliers with global supply and service networks. Previously, the companies were dealing with local suppliers. Even in situations where divisions used common suppliers, prices and specifications differed substantially."[4]

Service categories may also be simplified and standardized, although the personal and intangible nature of services may complicate the effort. For example, organizations with a high annual spend on travel may centralize travel to capture cost savings by simplifying or reducing the number of hotel chains travelers may stay in or standardize to one chain. An individual traveler may be dissatisfied with the corporate travel policy because she does not see the organizationwide benefits.

Conclusion

Need definition and translation of needs into commercial equivalents are the first two steps in the acquisition process. Needs are qualified at three levels. At level 1, needs are defined as strategic or nonstrategic. At level 2, quality, quantity, delivery, price, and service form the traditional value criteria for any acquisition. Level 3 criteria include additional financial considerations beyond price, risk, the environment, innovation, and social and political concerns. Considerable judgment is required of the supply professional to include the relevant criteria for specific needs. Needs or requirements cover seven major categories: (1) resale, (2) raw and semiprocessed materials, (3) parts, components, and packaging, (4) maintenance, repair, and operating supplies, (5) capital assets, (6) services, and (7) other.

Supply professionals may specialize in one or several of these categories to become fully acquainted with specific markets and suppliers. Translating organizational needs into commercial equivalents is the second step of the acquisition process and affords many opportunities for value improvements. Early supply and supplier involvement in the first two steps in the acquisition process is essential for effective value improvements. There are many methods of description of organizational needs, each with its own advantages and disadvantages. Lastly, standardization and simplification are used to improve value by reducing the number and variety of requirements.

[4] Michiel R. Leenders and P. Fraser Johnson, *Major Structural Changes in Supply Organizations* (Tempe AZ: Center for Advanced Purchasing Studies, 2000).

Questions for Review and Discussion

1. Why is it preferable to separate need identification and specification or defining commercial equivalents into two separate stages?
2. Why is early supply/supplier involvement (ESI) important?
3. Why is capital goods acquisition different from the purchase of raw materials?
4. What are some major challenges in the acquisition of services? Please use examples.

5. What are some effective supply methods for dealing with maintenance, repair, and operating (MRO) requirements?

6. Compare the acquisition of resale requirements to the acquisition of parts, components, or packaging.

7. Why should a supply professional not acquire by "brand"?

8. What are the disadvantages of specifying by performance? What are the advantages?

9. What is the difference between standardization and simplification?

10. How does a supply professional know that a certain requirement is strategic?

11. How would you determine the environmental impact of a particular acquisition?

References

American National Standards Institute, www.ansi.org.

Askin, R. G., and J. B. Goldberg. *Design and Analysis of Lean Production Systems*, New York: Wiley, 2001.

Axelsson, B., and F. Wynstra. *Buying Business Services*. West Sussex, U.K.: John Wiley & Sons, 2002.

Contino, R. *The Complete Equipment-Leasing Handbook*. New York: AMACOM, 2006.

Ellram, L. M.; W. L. Tate, and C. Billington. "Services Supply Management: The Next Frontier for Improved Organizational Performance. *California Management Review* 49, no. 4 (2007), pp. 44–66.

Pullman, M., and M. Sauter. *Sustainability Delivered: Designing Socially and Environmentally Responsible Supply Chains*. New York: Business Expert Press, 2012.

Case 6–1

Moren Corporation (A)

Moren Corporation was building three additional generation stations to serve its rapidly expanding energy market. To link these stations with a total area grid, a new method of carrying the power lines using ornamental tubular poles instead of towers had been adopted. Moren had had no previous operating experience with poles and decided to subcontract the design engineering, fabrication, and erection of the new line.

For the first phase of engineering design, Mr. John Carter, the vice president of supply, faced the responsibility of deciding with which supplier the business was to be placed after his staff had developed the information needed. He was aware that Moren had only three years in which to complete the entire project, and yet he had to ensure high-quality work.

COMPANY BACKGROUND

Moren Corporation, established in 1895, was one of the largest power utilities in the eastern United States. It serviced a highly industrialized area of 10 fossil-fueled plants. With assets of over $19 billion and demand doubling every decade, it had already earmarked funds to increase its kilowatt capacity from 8.4 million to 13 million over a four-year period.

The company was well known for its advanced technology and its good public relations. Both purchasing and engineering departments were centralized and located in the head office in the area's largest city. The new construction program was a heavy strain on both the professional and financial resources of the company, placing increased emphasis on the use of qualified people and suppliers outside the corporation.

TRANSMISSION LINE BACKGROUND

Although Moren was stepping up its older lines to 230 kV, by management decision and in accordance with the technological trend, 345 kV was adopted for the new line. It was to link the new generating stations in Addison, Smithfield, and Mesa Valley with the area grid, some 140 miles in total.

Until now, Moren had used structural steel towers exclusively for carrying its power line. These were strong but visually prominent and attracted adverse comments from a public daily growing more aesthetically sophisticated. A relatively new development in the transmission field was the introduction of the ornamental tubular power pole. Approximately 2,000 miles of line using these poles had been installed with good success in various parts of the country. Most installations were relatively short sections in densely populated areas. A line using poles costs twice as much as the conventional towers but is still substantially cheaper than underground installation. Conscious of the great strides made in power pole design and use, Moren management decided to specify poles for the new lines.

Because of the volume of conversion and projected expansion work, Mr. Carter and the project engineers knew that the tower manufacturers and erection companies with whom they had dealt in the past would not have the capacity to handle all the elements of the new pole concept. Furthermore, with no experience in 345 kV or pole suspension, Moren had to rely on the know-how of others for the new line and needed the services and guidance of competent subcontractors.

The total job involved three major phases.

1. Engineering design called for layout as well as a functional pole specification and project guidance.
2. Pole manufacture involved a manufacturing proposal consisting of a specific design to meet the functional specifications as well as manufacturing volume and schedule deadline capabilities.
3. Pole installation involved excavation, foundation setting, pole erection, and line stringing. Preliminary cost estimates for the total project were as follows:
   a. Phase 1—Engineering: $1,500,000–$1,800,000
   b. Phase 2—Pole manufacture: $90 million
   c. Phase 3—Installation: $78 million

Mr. Carter and the chief engineer were not satisfied that any individual supplier could handle the total contract well. They decided, therefore, to subcontract each phase to a reliable source of high expertise within that phase, so that optimum overall benefits would accrue to Moren. The first sourcing decision dealt with the engineering phase.

DESIGN ENGINEERING SELECTION

All through the spring and half of the summer, Oliver Dunn, the buyer, worked with the transmission engineering section of the system engineering department of the company to establish parameters and locate a suitable design source. By late July he was able to make his recommendation to the director of purchases (see Exhibit 1).

It was normal practice at Moren to provide a very brief summary for the director of purchases on all major contracts. A large file containing detailed information was built up by the buyers and purchasing agents involved. Normally, some preliminary discussions were held as the project progressed, so that Mr. Carter was reasonably informed by the time the official recommendation was prepared. Should he wish to see more information he could request the file at any time.

All three of the engineering firms considered were large and engaged in a wide variety of engineering consulting services. Travers & Bolton (T&B) and Crown Engineering (CE) had both done considerable work for Moren in the past and had performed satisfactorily. Pettigrew Associates had its head office in New York and maintained branches in 10 American cities. Pettigrew employed over 3,800 people, had a good credit rating, and had annual sales in excess of $480 million per year.

EXHIBIT 1 **Quotation** **Summary**	Description	Design 140 miles 345 kV transmission line for Addison-Smithfield-Mesa Valley
	Recommended vendor:	Pettigrew Associates, New York, N.Y.
	Location: Their premises	Using department: General engineering
	Buyer: O. Dunn	Total value: Established $1,740,000 salaries + burden
	P.O. No.: Date	Approval:

Moren had never used Pettigrew in any of its projects. All three engineering firms had some tubular pole experience with short-line sections in other parts of the country. Aside from the design requirements, the consulting engineering firm was also expected to evaluate the bids from pole manufacturing and erection subcontractors.

Additional Information

1. The transmission section of our general engineering department is unable to perform the design work of all the planned transmission work for the next three years, and it is necessary to contract some portion of this work. Travers & Bolton is already assigned the conversion of the 120kV to 230, and it is recommended that this 140-mile Addison-Smithfield-Mesa

Valley 345 kV be contracted to some competent engineering firm.
2. We had sessions with each of the three below mentioned engineering firms to acquaint them with our needs and learn of their capabilities. The work they will perform is as follows: Make routine sections; make subsurface investigations; make electrical hardware and general project designs; and furnish miscellaneous specifications, drawings, and technical data required to procure the right of way, hardware, structural steel, and the awarding of contracts for construction. It is estimated this work will total 12,300 labor-hours. There will also be approximately $144,000 worth of computer services and general out-of-pocket expenses in addition to the labor-hours.
3. Bid comparison is:

Supplier	Estimated Labor-Hours	Basic Average Cost per Labor-Hour (w/o fringes)	Approximately Fringes (assumed same for all)	Overhead and Profit	Estimated $/hour
Travers & Bolton	14,350	$60.00	20%	65.5%	$120.00
Crown Engineering	–	$60.00	20	80.0	$129.60
Pettigrew Associates	12,190	$60.00	20	85.0	$133.20

It is recommended that this contract be awarded to Pettigrew even though their cost per hour is higher than the others. Total cost will be influenced by the capabilities and productivity of the company chosen, and, therefore,

Pettigrew may not cost us any more; it is the desire of Moren management to have Pettigrew perform such a job with Moren as our first experience with them. Both T&B and CE have done considerable work for Moren.

Case 6–2

Moren Corporation (B)

Moren Corporation was building three additional generating stations to serve the rapidly expanding energy market. To link these stations with the total area grid, a new method of carrying the power lines using ornamental tubular poles instead of towers had been adopted. Moren lacked experience with poles and decided to subcontract the design engineering, fabrication, and erection of the new line. [For company background and line projection information and the selection of engineering consultants see Moren (A) case.]

Having selected its consultants for its first 345 kV transmission line and placed its order for the fabrication of the poles and hardware, Moren was ready to locate a

suitable contractor to do the foundation work, erect the poles, and string the lines.

Purchasing and engineering had been pursuing this concurrently with the search for a fabricator, because Moren wanted to get started on the line by the fall. Gordon Yarrow, supervisor of materials purchasing, was responsible to the vice president of supply, John Carter, for this contract.

CONSTRUCTION SELECTION

One company, T.D. Rapier, had done almost all Moren's transmission work for over the last five years, but, with

EXHIBIT 1
Moren
Corporation—
345 kV
Transmission
Line Addison-
Smithfield-
Mesa Valley

Bidder	Line Construction	Foundation Installation	Total
		Comparison of Bids	
Line contractors			
(D)	$47,103,840	$53,079,648	$100,183,488
(E)	38,117,804	44,617,110	82,734,914
(F)	41,390,640	37,778,478	79,169,118
(G) T.D. Rapier	37,485,360	37,993,872	75,479,232
(H) McTaggart Construction	43,433,700	27,672,804	71,106,504
(I)	36,192,072	No bid	
Consulting engineer's prior estimate	47,750,400	30,612,400	78,362,800
Foundation contractors:			
(J)		73,775,574	
(K)		38,966,364	
(L)		35,201,376	

the consultant's help, a good cross section of qualified line builders had been invited to bid. In addition, several foundation companies were asked to quote on the subgrade work. This helped to test the market to determine whether foundation contractors could build foundations cheaper than line builders. Mr. Carter reserved the right to award separate contracts for above- and below-grade work.

Two meetings were held with the bidders, one for the line builders and another for the foundation contractors, at which all aspects of the job were fully discussed. The unit prices were based on current wage rates and working conditions and were subject to adjustment by a percentage equal to 0.80 times the percentage change in the average wage rates.

By September the consulting engineers were able to provide purchasing with an evaluation of the bidding and computation, enabling the attached summary to be compiled (see Exhibit 1).

Notes

1. Two line contractors and one foundation contractor declined to bid.
2. The two lowest line constructors, Rapier and McTaggart, were evaluated, plus the possibility of a split award to (*L*) for foundations and (*I*) for above-grade work. However, McTaggart is recommended for the following reason:
   a. Offers lowest bid.
   b. Highly experienced. Built thousands of miles of line in mountain, desert, and swamp. Experience included 230, 345, 500, and 750 kV construction.
   c. Presently working for several other power companies.
   d. Recommended by our design engineers and consultants.
   e. Has done considerable work in this state through a subsidiary, although not for Moren.

Case 6–3

Carson Manor

In late November, Ms. Elaine Taylor, director of supply for the city of Winston, was reviewing proposals for the Carson Manor study. Three consulting groups had responded to a request for proposal (RFP) to study the operation of the city-owned old-age home. Ms. Taylor knew that her recommendations for selection of a consultant would have to be completed by mid-December.

CARSON MANOR

Carson Manor was opened about 30 years ago for persons requiring nursing care. Carson had a bed capacity of 470. Staff totaled 235 with nonmanagement personnel unionized under the District Service Workers Union Local 325.

Day-to-day operations of the Carson Manor were the responsibility of the Carson Manor administrator, who reported to Mr. Henry Davis, the city's director of social services. Policy and budget plans were developed by Mr. Davis and his staff in conjunction with Carson administrative staff and the Carson Manor Committee of Management (CMCM). The CMCM consisted of five aldermen who were appointed or volunteered to fill these positions. The CMCM reported to another aldermanic committee, with broader community service concerns, called the Committee for Community Services. This committee reviewed major expenditures and decisions impacting community service policy. All major expenditures were then reviewed by the Board of Control, consisting of the mayor and four elected controllers, prior to being sent to city council for final approval.

As director of social services, Mr. Davis reported to the city administrator, Mr. J. Peterson, who in turn reported to the mayor. The combined elected and appointed reporting structure is shown in Exhibit 1.

PURCHASING AND SUPPLY DIVISION (PSD)

The PSD had purchasing and disposal authority for the city's engineering, fire, landfill/sanitation departments, and social services division, and for city hall building support. The city operated separate purchasing departments in the public utilities commission, the libraries, and the police department. Purchasing authority was granted to the PSD director and her buyers by municipal bylaw. This bylaw outlined the limits of purchasing authority and formed the basis of the PSD's Policy Manual for Purchasing, Tendering, and Disposal.

The main objective of the PSD was to respond to the needs of other departments and divisions for goods and services at minimum cost, consistent with desired quality, delivery timing, and reliability. The PSD had expertise in the purchasing and tendering of goods and certain services, such as equipment rental, maintenance contracts, and engineering/architectural consulting. However, it had not dealt extensively with management consulting service procurement at that time.

Elaine Taylor became director of PSD two years ago at the age of 35. Prior to this, she was chief buyer and assistant director of purchasing for the city of Forestview, similar in size to Winston. Elaine reported to the city treasurer, Mr. R. Holbright, and dealt directly with other department and

EXHIBIT 1
Reporting
Structure

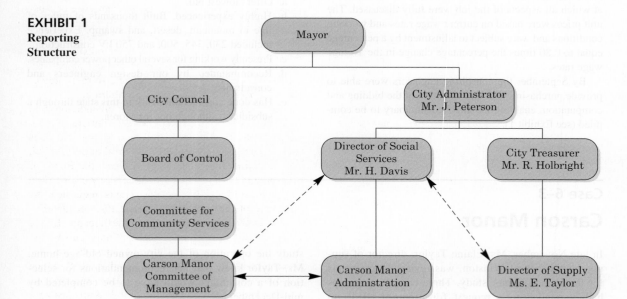

EXHIBIT 2   Carson Manor

Excerpts from "The Municipal Home for the Aged, a Review and Alternatives." A report to the Carson Manor Committee of Management by J. Peterson, City Administrator, and H. Davis, Director of Social Services.

Page 29

Increasing levels of care required by Carson Manor residents have a major influence on costs, since care essentially is translated into staff to provide the necessary services. No objective classification of resident care requirements has ever been carried out at the Carson Manor although there is no question that current residents and even new applicants require much more nursing care than was formerly the case.

Page 33

An operational review could be carried out by an independent consulting firm of the State's Department of Community and Social Services and would provide a thorough analysis of options and possible areas for improvement at the Carson Manor.

Such an approach would provide a firm basis for the development of strategies for operational change but would not guarantee implementation of the necessary changes.

Page 34

The overall advantage of an operational review would be the ability to identify, in depth, problem areas at the Carson Manor for which change strategies could be developed by the city. Such strategies might include contract management of a specific service, for example. This type of analysis would provide solid ground for future planning. On the negative side of the balance are the costs of such a study and the necessity to subsequently develop and implement changes for the identified problem areas.

division heads on purchasing matters, as shown in Exhibit 1. She managed a staff of 15, including three buyers.

THE CARSON MANOR STUDY

The Carson Manor had a history of problems related to budgeting and cost control. City council felt that the cost per bed was unnecessarily high, when compared to privately run institutions. Eight months ago the council directed the city administrator, Mr. Peterson, and the director of social services, Mr. Davis, to prepare a report for submission to the Carson Manor Committee of Management in early June. The report was to contain:

1. An analysis of the comparative costs at Carson Manor and other state facilities.
2. A review of the feasibility of increasing cost efficiency.
3. A review of the implications of possible alternatives such as:
   a. Contract management.
   b. An in-depth operational review and cost efficiency study carried out by an external agency.

The requested internal report, titled "The Carson Manor for the Aged, a Review and Alternatives," was tabled

on June 9. It revealed that Carson Manor costs were approximately 14 percent higher than state averages on a per-bed basis. The report highlighted the difficulties of measuring and controlling costs in the absence of a patient classification system that would enable standard levels of nursing care to be developed. The report recommended an operational review by an outside agency and outlined some general guidelines and objectives. Sections of the internal report, related to these guidelines and objectives, are shown in Exhibit 2.

Council accepted the report's recommendations and directed Messrs. Peterson and Davis to initiate an independent consultant's study of Carson Manor. This was not a budgeted expense and the approval of the CMCM, the Committee of Community Services, the Board of Control, and City Council were necessary prior to letting a consulting contract. Mr. Davis requested the assistance of Elaine Taylor and the PSD in identifying and evaluating potential study participants. Elaine Taylor handled the Carson Manor Study personally, since it was beyond the scope of responsibilities and experience of her buyers. She drafted an RFP, which is shown in Exhibit 3. In-state consulting organizations were contacted and a list of consulting companies with

EXHIBIT 3   Request for Proposal

You are invited to submit a proposal for the purpose of conducting an administrative and operational review of the Carson Manor for elder citizens. The review is to include all aspects of operation at the home, including, but not restricted to, assessment of resident care requirements, review of administration, organizational design, and staffing. The main sections of the home include laundry and housekeeping, nursing and physiotherapy, dietary, special services, property, building maintenance, and administration. The review is to be conducted by examination and administration.

On the basis of the review, you are to develop comprehensive recommendations for introducing improved operating and cost efficiencies for the future operation of the home. All recommendations should offer alternatives, identify savings to be achieved and the related cost in order to implement the recommendations, projected impact on staff and administration, and strategies for implementation that are consistent with the city's role as operators of the home, as well as provisions for ensuring the maintenance of the current quality of care.

It is our intent that the cost of the review and subsequent implementation of the recommendations is to be recovered from savings achieved in the operations of the home.

Your Proposal Is to Include the Following Information

a. Proposed methodology for undertaking the review.
b. Names and qualifications of persons to be involved in the review and development of subsequent recommendations.
c. An estimate of the time required to undertake the review and develop the recommendations.
d. Documentation and references demonstrating your ability to successfully implement recommendations in similar circumstances.
e. Potential cost savings that may be achieved as a result of the review.
f. A copy of any contracts or agreements that are to be entered into as a result of being retained to conduct the review.

It is to be noted that your fee structure including upset limits is to be identified separately; however, included in the operating cost, calculations with the savings are to be shown as a net amount.

relevant experience was developed. Five consulting companies were invited to submit proposals.

Prebid conferences were held in September. The consulting companies sent representatives for preliminary inspections of Carson Manor and for informal discussions of the scope, terms of reference, and evaluation criteria to be used in the proposal evaluation. Three proposals were submitted by closing, on November 17, with the following cost breakdown.

Proposal	Bid
Patientcare Ltd.	$35,000
Clarke-Hamilton Ltd.	47,000
Standardcare Ltd.	77,000

Patientcare and Standardcare were both large operators of nursing homes; Clarke-Hamilton was a management consulting firm located 100 miles away.

Prior to evaluating the bids, Elaine summarized the proposals as shown in Exhibit 4. As she sat preparing to evaluate the proposals, she wondered what evaluation criteria and weightings she should use, keeping in mind the needs of the social services division and the content of the RFP.

In addition, she knew that her recommendations and justifications had to be forwarded to the city administrator by December 19, prior to seeking approval of the various committees of elected officials.

EXHIBIT 4   **Proposals for Carson Manor Review**

	Patientcare	Clarke-Hamilton	Standardcare

1. Methodology	Require liaison person from city administration to assist team.
	1. Collect data.
	2. Review program.
	3. Conduct interviews.
	4. Determine and evaluate operational policies.
	5. Analyze staff and cost.
	6. Evaluate financial situation.
	7. Prepare report of funds and recommendations.
	8. Administration and project control.
	9. Provide assistance with implementation if required.
	  – Intend to utilize Department of Health general guidelines for work standards/patient classifications with judgment applied.
	  – May not leave Home with a system to use in the future.
		Suggest a steering committee be formed from city management and Carson Manor administration.
		1. Discuss terms of review with steering committee.
		2. Examine pertinent documentation.
		3. Review all sections.
		4. Conduct interviews and physical tour.
		5. Identify opportunities for improvement in all sections.
		6. Develop detailed recommendations.
		7. Review recommendations with Management.
		8. Prepare and present final report.
		9. Implement recommendations if required.
		  – Work standard/patient classification to remain in place to be utilized by Home staff to maintain standards at minimal ongoing cost.
			Maintain contact with Carson Manor management staff.
			1. Review operational statistics.
			2. Analyze organizational and operating procedures.
			3. Review and assess level of service in each section.
			4. Identify problems and potential improvements.
			5. Develop staffing schedules for comparison against existing and cost effectiveness.
			6. Identify problems in respect to physical environment.
			7. Provide draft report.
			8. Assess availability of skills required to implement.
			9. Prepare final report and recommendation.
			10. Assist with implementation if required.

2. Anticipated Reduction and Implementation Costs	"Patientcare is prepared to estimate the sum of all proposed operating deficiencies; if implemented, cost would far exceed the cost of the study and would be at least $700,000."	"The benefits received by our client in terms of reduced operating costs, improved cost effectiveness, and operations improvement have invariably outweighed the costs for our services. The benefit to cost ratio from our assignments has varied from 3 to 1 to as much as 30 to 1 or higher."	"With respect to savings, it is difficult to make a definitive statement without having actually completed the study. However, based on previous experience, it is expected that savings should be in the order of 8 to10 percent of total expenses, which would be approximately $1.1 million in the case of Carson Manor.

(Continued)

EXHIBIT 4 **Proposals for Carson Manor Review** *(Continued)*

	Patientcare	Clarke-Hamilton	Standardcare
3. Experience	– Functional programming and operations at 11 institutions. – List of five (5) other consulting projects. – All appear large in scope. – Manage nursing homes and chronic hospitals. – Own or lease many other facilities.	– Operational reviews in 11 institutions—mainly hospitals with three regional centers. – Extensive experience in specific areas again, mainly in hospitals. – Experience in implementing two different types of work standard/patient classification systems and MIS systems. – Extensive management consulting experience.	– Appear to have extensive background in similar situations. – Extensive list of 15 facilities either completed or in process. – Manage Henford Lodge—150-bed restorative care program. – Operational review of Martin Nursing Home. – Owns or manages 2,400 nursing home bed and units in this state and Florida.
4. References	*Church Nursing Home, Dexter* – Could not locate in Dexter or surrounding area. *Littlefield Municipal Hospital, Marsland, Saskatchewan* – Spoke to administration who advised they consulted on construction of an addition to the hospital. Review only of size, layout, and facilities required. No operational or management review undertaken. *Judd Park Nursing Home Expansion, Detroit* – Could find no home operating under the name in Detroit or surrounding area. *All other references were either impractical to contact or were areas currently owned.	*Department of Community and Social Services* – Firm conducted operational review at Webster Regional Centre and they were satisfied with their performance. Although not totally implemented, it appeared that they would meet or surpass their estimated savings. *Webster Regional Center Mgt.* – Talked to administrator who was satisfied with the manner in which they conducted their review. Very professional approach with minimum of disruptions. *Regional Municipality of Gast City, Greenfield Home for the Aged* – Firm performed salary review.	*Ward Home for the Aged* – Firm completed operational review and currently involved in implementation. Particular emphasis on restorative care techniques in nursing dept. Certain operations being contracted out. Project uncompleted; however, appears they will meet their projected savings of $280,000. *Due to high cost of service, no further references were checked.

Quality

Key Questions for the Supply Decision Maker

Should we

- Initiate a total quality management program?
- Initiate a Six-Sigma program?
- Certify suppliers?

How can we

- Improve customer satisfaction with quality?
- Reduce the costs of quality?
- Improve the measurement of quality of services?

Quality, quantity, delivery, price, and service are the five most common supply requirements. In this chapter on quality, two key questions are addressed: (1) How do we assure quality? and (2) How do we know that what we ordered meets expectations?

Quality is an area where corporate strategy and our supply network become key influencers. When it comes to quality of output, there are three choices: (1) better than our competitors, (2) the same quality as our competitors, and (3) lower quality than our competitors (see Figure 7–1). All three are legitimate market niches for goods or services, but they are different and require different approaches to quality in acquisition.

If an organization competes on quality in its marketplaces, then the supply network or external supply chain and the internal supply chain have to be able to provide competitive advantage and differentiation.

This chapter deals with the tools and techniques used to decide what constitutes good value given the customers' needs and what the market can supply.

ROLE OF QUALITY IN SUPPLY MANAGEMENT

Quality has always been a major concern in supply management. The traditional definition of quality meant conformance to specifications. In the total quality management context, the definition was enlarged to represent a combination of corporate philosophy and quality tools directed toward satisfying customer needs. Even in its simplest definition, quality

FIGURE 7–1
**Market Niches
for Quality**

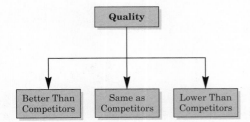

continues to represent significant challenges; in its broader context, it may well determine an organization's ability to survive and prosper in the years ahead.

While material requirements planning (MRP), manufacturing resource planning (MRP II), and just-in-time (JIT) and lean production have revolutionized the quantity, delivery, and inventory aspects of materials management, they have also required a new attitude toward quality. When no safety stock is available and required items arrive just before use, their quality must be fully acceptable. This extra pressure, along with all other good reasons for insisting on good quality, has sparked major efforts by purchasers to seek supplier quality assurance. In many cases these efforts have involved supplier certification programs or partnerships, including the establishment of satisfactory quality control programs at the premises of those who supply the suppliers.

As the service sector grows in size and importance in many economies, the special challenges of defining, measuring, and assuring quality of services are an even bigger concern to supply managers. The challenges include adapting and applying quality tools such as lean thinking to service operations; certifying or partnering with service providers such as marketing and media companies, law firms, and consultancies; and managing supplier relationships as more and different services are outsourced and moved offshore. The inclusion of services spend under the umbrella of the purchasing and supply management organization puts additional pressure on these groups to develop the knowledge and skill sets of people, and adopt processes and technology appropriate to services.

The interest in quality has reinforced the need for a team buying approach, the trend to supplier rationalization, data transparency and accessibility, cooperative buyer–supplier relations, longer-term contracts, contingency planning, and a reevaluation of the role of the price–quality trade-off in purchase decisions. To understand the role of quality in procurement, it is necessary to determine what constitutes a "best buy," and what actions purchasers might take to ensure that the right quality is supplied.

The quality concept argues that an organization's products or services are inseparable from the processes used to produce them. Just focusing on the product or service without examining the process that produces it is likely to miss the key to continuous improvement. If the process is not in statistical control and targeted for continuous improvement, the quality of the products produced is likely to suffer. Likewise, if the process for service delivery is not efficient and effective and targeted for continuous improvement, the quality of the delivered services is likely to suffer.

Every organization can be seen as part of a chain of organizations that has suppliers to one side and customers to the other. Every organization performs three roles: customer, converter, and supplier (see Figure 7–2). As a converter, every organization needs to add value as its part of the chain or network.

FIGURE 7–2
The Transformation and Value-Added Chain

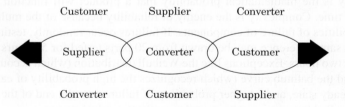

Customer	Supplier	Converter
Supplier	Converter	Customer
Converter	Customer	Supplier

The same idea can be applied on a micro level inside every organization. Each department or function itself is part of an internal chain performing the same three roles: customer, converter, and supplier to other internal functions, and, in some cases, to external customers and suppliers. Here also, the value-added concept is important. Each department or function must add value and strive to minimize the cost of doing so by process control and continuous improvement in congruence with organizational goals and strategies. If a focus on key business processes has blurred the lines among traditional functions such as supply, production, and sales, then the cross-functional team must assume responsibility for quality.

DEFINING QUALITY

Practitioners often use the term *quality* to describe the notions of function, suitability, reliability and conformance with specifications, satisfaction with actual performance, and best buy. This is highly confusing. The definitions of these terms are discussed below.

Quality

Quality, in the simplest sense, refers to the ability of the supplier to provide goods and services in conformance with specifications. Quality also may refer to whether the item performs in actual use to the expectations of the original requisitioner, regardless of conformance with specifications. Thus, it is often said an item is "no good" or of "bad quality" when it fails in use, even though the original requisition or specification may be at fault. The ideal, of course, is achieved when all inputs acquired pass this use test satisfactorily.

Function

Function refers to the action(s) that an item or service is designed to perform. For example, the function "something that fastens" might be performed by a number of items including a nail, a screw, a button, and a zipper.

Suitability

Suitability refers to the ability of a material, good, or service to meet the intended functional use. In a pure sense, suitability ignores the commercial considerations and refers to fitness for use. In reality, that is hardly practiced. Gold may be a better electrical conductor than silver or copper but is far too expensive to use in all but special applications. That is why chips are wired with gold and houses with copper. The notion of "best buy" puts quality, reliability, and suitability into a sound procurement perspective.

Reliability

Reliability is the mathematical probability that a product will function for a stipulated period of time. Complexity is the enemy of reliability because of the multiplicative effect of probabilities of failure of components. If failures occur randomly, testing is flexible because the same inference may be drawn from 20 parts tested for 50 hours as for 500 parts tested for two hours. Exceptions like the Weibull distribution (which accounts for the aging effect) and the bathtub curve (which recognizes the high probability of early failure, a period of steady state, and a higher probability of failure near the end of the useful life) also can be handled but require more complex mathematical treatment.

From a procurement standpoint, it is useful to recognize the varying reliabilities of components and products acquired. Penalties or premiums may be assessed for variation from design standard depending on the expected reliability impact.

Quality Dimensions

Considerable interest in the use of quality as a competitive tool has reawakened management appreciation of the contribution that quality can make in an organization. On the supply side, how well suppliers perform may be crucial to the buying organization's own success in providing quality goods and services. A variety of surveys show that, in many organizations, at least 50 percent of the quality problems stem from goods and services supplied by suppliers. Moreover, management tools and techniques such as lean production, MRP, JIT, and stockless purchasing all require that what is delivered by a supplier conform to specifications. Furthermore, it is not realistic to insist that suppliers supply quality goods without ensuring that the buying organization's own quality performance is beyond reproach. This applies to the procurement organization, its people, policies, systems, and procedures as well. Quality improvement is a continuing challenge for both buyer and seller. Moreover, close cooperation between buying and selling organizations is necessary to achieve significant improvement over time.

Quality is a complex term, which, according to Professor David Garvin of the Harvard Business School, has at least eight dimensions:

1. *Performance.* The primary function of the product or service.
2. *Features.* The bells and whistles.
3. *Reliability.* The probability of failure within a specified time period.
4. *Durability.* The life expectancy.
5. *Conformance.* The meeting of specifications.
6. *Serviceability.* The maintainability and ease of fixing.
7. *Aesthetics.* The look, smell, feel, and sound.
8. *Perceived quality.* The image in the eyes of the customer.

From a procurement point of view, the ninth dimension should be "procurability"—the short- and long-term availability on the market at reasonable prices and subject to continuing improvement.

"Best Buy"

The decision on what to buy involves more than balancing various technical considerations. The most desirable technical feature or suitability for a given use, once determined, is not necessarily the desirable buy. The distinction is between technical considerations that are matters of dimension, design, chemical or physical properties, and the like, and the more inclusive concept of the "best buy." The "best buy" assumes, of necessity, a certain minimum measure of suitability but considers ultimate customer needs, cost and procurability, transportation, and disposal as well.

If the cost is prohibitive, a somewhat less suitable item may have to suffice. Or if, at whatever cost or however procurable, the only available suppliers of the technically perfect item lack adequate productive capacity or financial strength, then, too, something else must be used. Also, frequent reappraisals are necessary. If the price of copper increases from $0.70 a pound to $1.50 or more, its relationship to aluminum or other substitutes may change.

The "best buy" is a combination of characteristics, not merely one. The specific combination finally decided on is almost always a compromise, since the particular aspect of quality to be stressed in any individual case depends largely on circumstances. In some instances, the primary consideration is reliability; questions of immediate cost or facility of installation or the ease of making repairs are all secondary. In other instances, the lifetime of the item is not so important; efficiency in operation becomes more significant.

The decision on what constitutes the "best buy" for any particular need is as much conditioned by marketing as by procurement and technical considerations. To reach a sound decision on the "best buy" requires all relevant stakeholders—marketing, engineering, operations, and supply—to work closely together. The ability and willingness of all stakeholders to view the trade-offs in perspective will significantly influence the final decisions reached.

Determining the "Best Buy"

It is generally accepted that the final verdict on technical suitability for a particular use should rest with those involved in using, engineering, specifying, or resale. Supply's right to audit, question, and suggest must be recognized along with the need for early involvement of procurement during the design phase.

To meet its responsibility, supply must insist that economic and procurement factors be considered and share its suggestions with those immediately responsible for specification. The purchaser is in a key position to present the latest information from the marketplace that may permit modifications in design, more flexibility in specifications, or changes in manufacturing methods that will improve value for the ultimate customer. Cross-functional teams are preferable to an adversarial approach to "best buy" determinations.

THE COST OF QUALITY

Prior to the 1950s, the quality–cost curve was thought to be similar to the economic order quantity curve, or broadly U-shaped (see Figure 7–3). Under this notion, it was considered acceptable to live with a significant defect level, because it was assumed that fewer defects would increase costs.

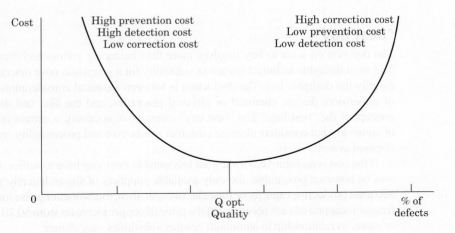

FIGURE 7–3
The Traditional View of the Quality–Cost Trade-off

Cost

High prevention cost
High detection cost
Low correction cost

High correction cost
Low prevention cost
Low detection cost

0

Q opt.
Quality

% of defects

FIGURE 7–4
**The Current
View of the
Quality–Cost
Trade-off**

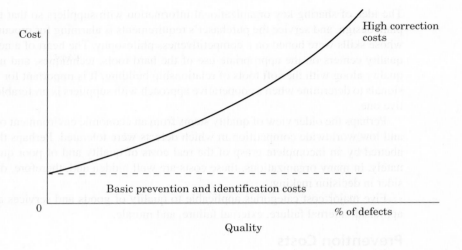

Thanks to the contribution of leaders like Deming, Juran, Shingo, and Crosby, a new perspective on quality and its achievability emerged. According to this view of quality, every defect is expensive, and prevention or avoidance of defects lowers costs (see Figure 7–4). The cost of quality, then, is the cost of *not* producing a good or providing a service right the first time. Rework drives up the cost of quality.

Interestingly enough, it used to be that purchasers were willing to pay more for higher-quality products or services, recognizing the benefits to the purchaser's organization, but also assuming that the supplier might have to incur higher costs to achieve better quality. If quality were "inspected in," this would indeed be a higher-cost solution. Deming argued that the stress in quality should be in making it right the first time, rather than inspecting quality in. Making it right the first time should be a lower-cost solution. Therefore, it is reasonable for a purchaser and seller to work together on achieving both improved quality and lower costs!

Many supply policies and procedures have been designed on the principle that competition is at the heart of the buyer–seller relationship. What keeps the seller focused is the fear that another supplier might take away sales by offering better quality, better price, better delivery, or better service. The assumption was that a supplier switch was inexpensive for the purchaser and that multiple sourcing gave the purchaser both supply security and control over suppliers.

The emergence of quality as a prime supply criterion challenged this competitive view. Current thinking is that it is very difficult to find a high-quality supplier and even more difficult to create a supplier who will continually improve quality. In fact, it may require extensive work of various experts in the supply organization, along with the appropriate counterparts in the selling organization, to achieve continuing improvement in quality. Under these circumstances, it is not realistic to use multiple sources for the same end item, to switch suppliers frequently, and to go out for quotes regularly.

Single sourcing often causes considerable purchaser nervousness especially in today's environment with a slow growing global economy, the uncertainty of the impact of climate change and volatile weather patterns, and political upheaval in many regions of the world.

The idea of sharing key organizational information with suppliers so that they can better plan, design, and service the purchaser's requirements is alarming for procurement experts whose skills were honed on a competitiveness philosophy. The heart of a new approach to quality centers on the appropriate use of the hard tools, techniques, and mathematics of quality along with the soft tools of relationship building. It is important for supply professionals to determine when a cooperative approach with suppliers is preferable to a competitive one.

Perhaps the older view of quality stems from an economic environment of high demand and low worldwide competition in which defects were tolerated. Perhaps this was further abetted by an incomplete grasp of the real costs of quality and of poor quality. Unfortunately, in many organizations, these costs are well hidden and, therefore, difficult to consider in decision making.

Five major cost categories applicable to quality of goods and services are prevention, appraisal, internal failure, external failure, and morale.

Prevention Costs

Prevention costs relate to all activities that eliminate the occurrence of future defects or nonconformance to requirements. These include such diverse costs as various quality assurance programs; precertifying and qualifying suppliers and processes; employee training and awareness programs; machine, tool, material, and labor checkouts; preventive maintenance; and single sourcing with quality suppliers, as well as the associated personnel, travel, equipment, and space costs.

Appraisal Costs

Appraisal costs represent the costs of inspection, testing, measuring, and other activities designed to ensure conformance of the product or service to quality standards and performance requirements. Appraisal costs might occur at both the seller's and buyer's organizations as each uses a variety of inspection systems to ensure quality conformance. If appraisal requires setting aside batches, or sending product to a separate inspection department, detection costs should include, aside from the inspection cost itself, extra handling and inventory tie-up costs in terms of space, people, equipment, materials, and associated reporting systems. The advantages of using the supplier's quality control (QC) reports and making it right the first time are evident. For services, appraisal costs might include process or service audits.

Internal Failure Costs

Internal failure costs are the costs incurred within the operating system as a result of poor quality. Included in internal failure costs are returns to suppliers, scrap and rework, reinspection and retesting, lost labor, order delay costs including penalties, machine and time management, and all costs associated with expediting replacement materials or parts or the carrying of extra safety stock.

External Failure Costs

External failure costs are incurred when poor-quality goods or services are passed on to the customer and include costs of returns, replacement of services, warranty costs, and management time handling customer complaints. Unfortunately, when poor-quality parts are incorporated in assemblies, disassembly and reassembly costs may far outweigh the cost of the original part itself. When a defective product gets into the hands of customers or their customers, the possibility of consequential damages arises because a paper roll did not meet specifications, the printer missed an important deadline, a magazine did not reach advertisers and subscribers on time, and so on. There may be health or safety consequences from defective products. External failure costs for services occur during or after the delivery of the service. Examples include the cost of correcting a bank statement, reprocessing an application, or reteaching a seminar that failed to meet agreed-upon outcomes. These costs are the most expensive because of the possible effects on individual customer goodwill and lost sales and profits. The loss of customers, the inability to secure new customers, and the penalties paid to keep existing customers are also part of external failure costs.

Morale Costs

One cost seldom recognized in an accounting sense is the morale cost of producing (or having to use) defective products or services. Aside from the obvious productivity impact, it may remove pride in one's work or the incentive to keep searching for continuing improvement. The motivation to work hard and well may be replaced by a "don't care" attitude.

An Overall Quality–Cost Perspective

It is so unpleasant to detail the costs of defective quality that the temptation is strong to ignore them. And that is exactly what many organizations have done for many years. They also have built these costs into internally accepted standards. As a consequence, the opportunity to improve quality is great in most organizations.

Some organizations have attempted to quantify the total cost of quality, and the outcome of such studies suggests that 30 to 40 percent of final product cost may be attributable to quality. There is a huge incentive to tackle quality as a major organizational challenge. For example, Kodak's Supplier Quality Process expects suppliers to meet or exceed world-class standards of performance in quality and the reliability, cost, and delivery of the products and services provided. One element is the cost of quality model used to quantify, in dollars, quality performance of suppliers by looking at defects per part per million (DPPM), delivery, lead times, administrative costs of corrective actions, and potential line down situations. The model may also be used in benchmarking suppliers in e-auctions and on sourcing activities.[1]

QUALITY MANAGEMENT TOOLS AND TECHNIQUES

The question of how to assure quality is important for all three roles played by an organization: customer, converter, or supplier of goods or services. This section addresses tools and techniques for assuring quality, including lean thinking; total quality management (TQM); continuous improvement or kaizen; quality function deployment (QFD); Six Sigma; statistical process control (SPC); sampling; inspection and testing; and supplier certification.

[1] Source: www.kodak.com/ek/uploadedFiles/Content/About_Kodak/Our_Company/Doing_Business_with_Kodak/Purchasing/SupplierQualityProcess.pdf, February 2014.

Lean Enterprise

Lean thinking is a management philosophy focused on maximizing customer value while minimizing waste, typically in the form of overproduction, waiting, transportation, nonvalue-adding processes, inventory, motion, and costs of quality (scrap, rework, and inspection). Lean was first used to describe Toyota's Production System in the late 1980s and has also been called just-in-time (JIT) manufacturing. Today, lean principles and practices are applied in all industries and services, including health care and government.

The goal is to optimize the flow of products and services through value streams that flow internally across technologies, assets, and departments to customers and externally with supply chain partners. The product or service flows when pulled by the next downstream step. A value stream is a series of steps executed in the right way and at the right time to create value for the customer. Each step in a value stream must be valuable to the customer, capable, available, adequate, and flexible. A step is capable if it gets the exact same result every time, available if it can be performed whenever it is needed, adequate if there is capacity to perform it exactly when it is needed, and flexible if it can respond rapidly to changing customer desires without creating inefficiencies.

Lean supply networks require advanced modeling tools that consider all costs and provide optimized strategies across a network of distribution centers, plants, contract manufacturers, sourcing options, and logistical lanes. Demand variability drives waste into the network. Therefore, lean enterprises use tools such as IT solutions that solve complex optimization problems yet are easy to use and deploy, capable of responding to real-time information, and integrate and align internal and external supply chain partners globally.

Honda's strategy is to move production as close to customers as possible to minimize lead times and inventories and to move design close to production to maximize information flow while minimizing response time. Honda's lean enterprise includes designing and making high-volume products for each world region entirely within the region and cross-trading niche products between regions to capture scale economies.

Total Quality Management (TQM)

Total quality management (TQM) is a philosophy and system of management focused on long-term success through customer satisfaction. It was developed in Japan after W. Edwards Deming taught statistical quality control to the Union of Japanese Scientists and Engineers (JUSE) in 1950. Total quality control (TQC) was reimported to the United States in the 1980s and contributed to the revitalization of U.S. industries. It is known internationally as total quality management (TQM).

In a TQM effort, all members of an organization participate in improving processes, products, services, and the culture in which they work. Top management develops the vision for total quality and provides the commitment and support, including progress reviews, to realize this vision. The customer can be internal or external and is anyone in the supply chain who receives materials from a previous step in the chain. The methods for implementing this approach come from the teachings of such quality leaders as Philip B. Crosby, W. Edwards Deming, Armand V. Feigenbaum, Kaoru Ishikawa, and Joseph M. Juran.

Deming's 14 Points

A core concept in implementing TQM is Deming's 14 points, a set of management practices to help companies increase their quality and productivity. These are:[2]

1. Create constancy of purpose for improving products and services.
2. Adopt the new philosophy.
3. Cease dependence on inspection to achieve quality.
4. End the practice of awarding business on price alone; instead, minimize total cost by working with a single supplier.
5. Improve constantly and forever every process for planning, production, and service.
6. Institute training on the job.
7. Adopt and institute leadership.
8. Drive out fear.
9. Break down barriers between staff areas.
10. Eliminate slogans, exhortations, and targets for the workforce.
11. Eliminate numerical quotas for the workforce and numerical goals for management.
12. Remove barriers that rob people of pride of workmanship, and eliminate the annual rating or merit system.
13. Institute a vigorous program of education and self-improvement for everyone.
14. Put everybody in the company to work accomplishing the transformation.

From this list, four important features of TQM emerge:

1. Quality must be integrated throughout the organization's activities.
2. There must be employee commitment to continuous improvement.
3. The goal of customer satisfaction and the systematic and continuous research process related to customer satisfaction drive TQM systems.
4. Suppliers are partners in the TQM process.

TQM stresses quality as the integrating force in the organization. For TQM to work, all stages in the production process must conform to specifications that are driven by the needs and wants of the end customer. All processes, those of the buyer and the suppliers, must be in control and possess minimal variation to reduce time and expense of inspection. This in turn reduces scrap and rework, increases productivity, and reduces total cost. TQM is more than a philosophy. It involves the use of several tools, such as continuous improvement or *kaizen*, quality function deployment (QFD), and statistical process control to achieve performance improvements.

The following sections describe how quality management techniques are used and how they apply to the supply function.

Continuous Improvement

Continuous improvement, sometimes called by its Japanese name, kaizen, refers to the relentless pursuit of product and process improvement through a series of small, progressive steps. It is an integral part of both just-in-time (JIT) and TQM. Continuous improvement

---

[2]www.asq.org/learn-about-quality/total-quality-management/overview/overview.html.

should follow a well-defined and structured approach and incorporate problem-solving tools such as Pareto analysis, histograms, scatter diagrams, check sheets, fishbone diagrams, control charts, run charts, and process flow diagrams.

The plan–do–check–act cycle, sometimes called the Deming Wheel, provides a good model for conducting continuous improvement activities.

Plan: Collect data and set performance target.

Do: Implement countermeasures.

Check: Measure and evaluate the results of countermeasures.

Act: Standardize and apply improvement to other parts of the organization.

For example, at Thomas Jefferson University Hospitals in Philadelphia, operating room patient flow from preadmissions testing to the post-anesthesia unit was marked by inefficiencies, including delays and bottlenecks. By forming kaizen teams and executing events to identify and eliminate root causes, the hospital realized significant efficiencies.[3]

At Honda, the purchasing policy is "Best possible quality, cost, delivery, development, and environment (QCDDE): sensing worldwide, acting worldwide, creating worldwide." The goal is to help achieve the company's 2020 Vision of providing "good products that maximize the joy of customers with speed, affordability and low CO2 emissions."[4]

Quality Function Deployment (QFD)

Quality function deployment (QFD) is an important aspect of TQM. It is a comprehensive quality system aimed specifically at satisfying the customer throughout the development and business process—end to end. It is a method for listening and effectively responding to the voice of the customer to develop higher-quality new products at less cost and in less time. The QFD method can be used for both tangible products and nontangible services across business sectors.[5] It has been used successfully by companies, including Accenture, Boeing, Continental Rehabilitation Hospital, Ford, and the U.S. Department of Defense. Modern QFD addresses the four Ss of today's lean business environment: speed, smart, slim and sustainable.

QFD is a comprehensive quality system that:

- Seeks both spoken and unspoken customer needs.
- Maximizes "positive" quality (such as ease of use, fun, luxury) that creates value.
- Translates these into actions and designs by using transparent analytic and prioritization methods.
- Empowers organizations to exceed normal expectations.
- Provides a level of unanticipated excitement that generates value.

QFD is based on teamwork and customer involvement. It integrates marketing, design, engineering development, manufacturing, production, and supply in new product development from the conception stage through final delivery. Through coordination and integration, rather than the traditional sequential development approach, QFD allows the end customer's needs and wants to be communicated at the product development stage and then drive the

[3] http://rube.asq.org/2013/10/lean/operating-room-patient-flow.pdf?WT.ac=CAR-35766

[4] http://world.honda.com/CSR/report/pdf/2013/report_2013.pdf, p. 81.

[5] Source: QFD Institute, www.qfdi.org/what_is_qfd/what_is_qfd.htm.

design and production stages. More time is spent up front in product development, but by accurately defining customer needs and wants, the total time spent on the design cycle is reduced because fewer design changes are made in later stages of the process.

The four integrated stages of the QFD process are:

1. *Product or service planning,* to determine design requirements.
2. *Parts deployment,* to determine parts characteristics for manufactured goods.
3. *Process planning,* to determine manufacturing requirements or service process elements.
4. *Production or action planning,* to determine production requirements or service action plans.

Buyer and supplier integration into the process can benefit the organization by:

1. Reducing or eliminating engineering or service design changes during product or service development.
2. Reducing product or process development cycle time.
3. Reducing start-up cycle time.
4. Minimizing product or service failures and repair or service replacement costs over the product or service life.
5. Creating product or service uniformity and reliability during production or service delivery.

From the perspective of supply management, well-functioning buyer–supplier relationships are a key contribution that purchasers and supply managers can make to the organizations' TQM and QFD efforts. Supply-base rationalization (determining the optimum number of suppliers to meet business needs) and closer relationships with key suppliers through partnering arrangements or strategic alliances go hand in hand with quality initiatives (see Chapter 13). The importance of matching supply performance measures to the strategic initiatives of the organization is also important if TQM and QFD are to be successful. For example, if supply's performance is measured by a reduction in the prices of materials and improved operating efficiency rather than the quality of supplier relationships, then purchasers may buy on the basis of price alone. This will undermine the quality initiatives of the firm. Integration of functions and processes throughout the firm, and with key suppliers, is a critical component of global competitiveness.

Six Sigma

A Six Sigma (6σ) approach to quality focuses on preventing defects by using data to reduce variation and waste. This quality initiative was developed by GE and Motorola and has been adopted by many organizations. Six Sigma quality means there are no more than 3.4 defects per million opportunities. Technically, 6σ or six standard deviations are very close to zero defects and correspond to a Cpk value (discussed later in this chapter) of 2.0. Six Sigma initiatives have measurable goals such as cost reduction or profit increase through improvements in cycle time, delivery, safety, and so on.

Six Sigma methods may also be adapted to service processes. First, categorize service processes as highly customized, mass customized, or standard. While opportunities may exist in any category, the greatest occur in standardized services such as credit card account services, fast-food, benefits processing, and payroll or accounts payable. The next step is defining a service defect. A service defect is a flaw in a process that results in a lower level of customer satisfaction or a lost customer. Easily quantified measures are lost customers, customer satisfaction ratings, and service turnaround times. After identifying a service defect, conduct root cause analysis, then develop and implement improvement action plans.

According to Kubiak and Benbow, writing for the ASQ, Six Sigma is defined in several ways:

1. It is a philosophy based on the view that all work is processes that can be defined, measured, analyzed, improved, and controlled. Processes require inputs (x) and produce outputs (y). If you control the inputs, you will control the outputs.

2. It is a set of tools, including statistical process control (SPC), control charts, failure mode and effects analysis, and flowcharting. These are qualitative and quantitative techniques to drive process improvement.

3. It is a methodology with five steps: define, measure, analyze, improve, and control (DMAIC). This is the most widely adopted and recognized Six Sigma methodology.[6]

The common elements of Six Sigma initiatives are:

- A management environment that supports the initiatives as business strategy. Organizational support is provided by designated executives and champions who set the direction for project selection and deployment.
- Well-defined projects with bottom-line impact.
- Teams whose members have statistical training. Levels include black belt, master black, green, yellow, and white belts. Each level has specific roles and project responsibilities.
- Emphasis on the DMAIC approach.

Statistical Process Control (SPC)

Dr. W. Edwards Deming, the well-known American quality control specialist, assisted Japanese manufacturers in instituting statistical quality control (SQC) beginning in the 1950s. Dr. Deming showed that most processes tend to behave in a statistical manner and that understanding how the process behaves without operator interference is necessary before controls can be instituted. Managing quality using SQC techniques involves sampling processes and using the data and statistical analysis to establish performance criteria and monitor processes. Statistical process control (SPC) is a technique that involves testing a random sample of output from a process in order to detect if nonrandom, assignable changes in the process are occurring. Because almost all output results from a manufacturing or transformation process of some sort, process control is the preferred approach to controlling product quality.

The first step in quality assurance is making sure that the supplier's process capability and the buyer's acceptable quality range mesh. If the natural range of the supplier's process is wider than the range of the buyer's quality requirements, then the buyer

[6] Thomas M. Kubiak and D. W. Benbow, *The Certified Six Sigma Black Belt Handbook, 2nd ed.* (ASQ Quality Press, 2009, pp. 1–2).

must negotiate with the supplier to have the supplier narrow the natural range through process improvements such as operator training or machine improvements. If it is not economically feasible or the supplier is unable or unwilling to make improvements for some reason, then the buyer may seek another supplier rather than incur the extra cost of inspection, rework, and scrap.

From the buyer's perspective, the basic steps in assuring quality through statistical process control are:

1. Buyer establishes required quality specifications.
2. Supplier determines process capability.
   a. Identify common or chance causes of variation.
   b. Identify special or assignable causes of variation.
   c. Eliminate special causes.
3. Compare buyer's quality requirements to supplier's process capability.
4. Make adjustments, if necessary.
   a. Negotiate with supplier for process improvements.
   b. Seek an alternate supplier.

Causes of Variation

Since no process can produce the same exact results each time the activity is performed, it is important to establish what kind of variation is occurring and eliminate as much as possible. A process capability study identifies two types of variation: (1) common causes or random variation and (2) special or assignable causes of variation.

Common or chance causes of variation. These causes are intrinsic to the process and will always be there unless the process is changed. They may be related to machine, people, material, method, environment, or measurement. For instance, machine lubrication, tool wear, or operator technique would be common causes that result in inconsistent output. If too many defects occur because of common causes, then the process must be changed.

Special or assignable causes of variation. These causes are outside, nonrandom problems such as breakdown of machinery, material variation, or human error. These must be identified and eliminated. Otherwise, the output will fall outside the acceptable quality range. Statistical process control procedures are primarily concerned with detecting and eliminating assignable or special causes.

Process capability

A process is capable when there are no special or assignable causes of variation, only common or chance causes. It is capable of meeting specifications consistently. The process is said to be *in statistical control* or *stable and predictable*. If a process is capable, then the probability of a process meeting customer specifications can be predicted. The process averages a set number of standard deviations within the specifications.

In determining whether or not a process is stable, the supplier must determine what the natural capability of the process is and whether or not the upper and lower capability limits meet the specifications of the buyer. When a process is "in control," the supplier can predict the future distributions about the mean. For a process to be capable and in control, all the special causes of variation in output have been eliminated, and the variation from common causes has been reduced to a level that falls within the acceptable quality range specified by the buyer.

Design engineers establish the upper and lower specification limits based on a specific design function.

Upper specification limit (USL). The USL is the maximum acceptable level of output.

Lower specification limit (LSL). The LSL is the minimum acceptable level of output. The USL and the LSL are related to a specific product specification; they are independent of any process. The allowable difference between a physical feature and its intended design is the *tolerance*. For example, design engineering writes a specification for a rod to have a diameter of 2 inches with a tolerance of $\pm$ .005 inches. The LSL is 1.995 inches, and the USL is 2.005 inches. Any rods produced within this range are within tolerance.

Process Capability Index (Cp). This index combines process spread and tolerance into one index and indicates whether process variation is satisfactory. The higher the Cp, the more capable the process is of producing parts that are consistently within specification. This index assumes the process is centered between the USL and the LSL and that processes are 6 sigma wide, representing 99.7 percent of the output of a normal process.

A process with a Cp of less than 1.0 is generally considered not capable. If the capability index is greater than 1.0 the process is capable of producing 99.7 percent of parts within tolerance. The Cp is calculated as:

$$Cp = \frac{USL - LSL}{6\sigma}$$

For example, if the tolerance is 2.000 inches $\pm$ .0005 inches and the standard deviation of the process (σ) was .0016 inch.

$$Cp = \frac{2.005 - 1.995}{6 \times .0016} = 1.04$$

A Cp of 1.33 has become a standard of process capability. Purchasers can specify process capability expectations. Some organizations require a higher value of 2.0. A higher value means fewer defects and greater quality.

Cpk Index. This index adjusts the Cp for the effect of noncentered distribution. Cpk is defined as the lower of either of the following:

$$\frac{\text{Upper tolerance limit} - \overline{X}}{\text{Process spread}} \quad \text{or} \quad \frac{\overline{X} - \text{Lower tolerance limit}}{\text{Process spread}}$$

$\overline{X}$ is the process mean, and the process spread is equal to three standard deviations of the output values, or the spread on one side of the process average. A process with a Cpk of

1. Less than 1.0—unacceptable because part of the process distribution is out of specification.
2. Between 1 and 1.33—marginal because the process distribution is barely within specification.
3. Greater than 1.33—acceptable because the process distribution is well within the specification.

Process Control

Process control is a key aspect of TQM. It is a method of monitoring a process to prevent defects. Both the center and the variation around the center are measured. Quality control charts are the primary tool.

Quality control charts.   In processes using repetitive operations, the quality control chart is invaluable. The output can be measured by tracking a mean and dispersion. The X-bar chart is useful for charting the population means and the R chart the dispersion.

Upper and lower control limits.   Upper (UCL) and lower (LCL) control limits can be set so that operator action is required only when the process or machine starts to fall outside of its normal desirable operating range. The UCL represents an upward shift of $3 \times \sigma$ from the mean value of a variable. The LCL represents a similar downward shift. For a normally distributed output, 99.7 percent should fall between the UCL and the LCL. The process is stable as long as output falls within the established limits.

Figure 7–5 illustrates this "wandering" type of behavior at a steel mill. The rolling operation controls the thickness of the steel. Each hour the operator collects thickness data and enters on the chart the means of samples taken from the process. An R chart is the plot of the range within each of the samples. If the mean or range falls outside its acceptable limits, the process is stopped. Action is then taken to determine the cause for the shift so that corrections can be made.

FIGURE 7–5
Control Chart

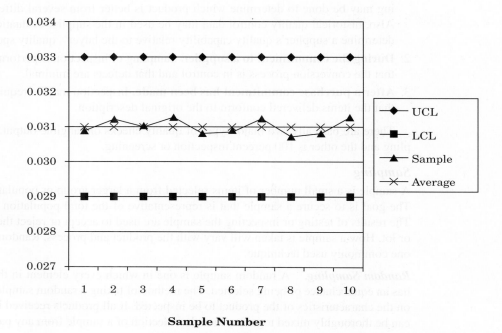

Control Chart

Sample Number

The control chart uses random sampling techniques (discussed in the next section). It is well suited to most manufacturing and service operations producing large output where it is not necessary to screen every item produced: for example, stamping steel parts or processing applications in an insurance office.

Sampling, Inspection, and Testing

As discussed earlier in this chapter, each organization is a customer, a converter, and a supplier. Therefore, there are three opportunities for each organization to experience poor quality: as a supplier whose goods or services fail to meet customers' quality specifications, as a converter whose process fails to produce to customers' quality specifications, and as a customer who receives goods or services that fail to meet its quality specifications.

The high cost of correcting poor-quality products and services drives the focus on building in quality rather than inspecting it after production or delivery. Building it right the first time is the primary goal of the quality management programs discussed in this chapter. Managing the costs of quality is also an important part of the quality management process. Decisions about sampling, testing, and inspection drive costs into the process and ultimately into the final product or service. These decisions are cost-benefit decisions wherein the goal is to balance the cost of sampling, testing, and inspection against the risk of either accepting a lot with more than an acceptable level of defects or of rejecting a good lot. Lowering either risk requires a larger sample size, and this leads to higher costs.

Sampling, testing, and inspection are quality management tools that may be used at three different stages in the acquisition process.

1. **Before a purchase commitment is made to a supplier.** It may be necessary to test samples to see if they are adequate for the intended purpose. Similarly, comparison testing may be done to determine which product is better from several different sources. Also, historical quality control data may be used in the supplier evaluation process to determine a supplier's quality capability relative to the buyer's quality specifications.

2. **During the commitment to a supplier.** Sampling or inspection is performed to ensure that the conversion process is in control and that defects are minimal.

3. **After a purchase commitment has been made.** Inspection may be required to ensure that the items delivered conform to the original description.

There are basically two major types of quality checks on tangible output. One is sampling and the other is 100 percent inspection or screening.

Sampling

A sample is a small number of items selected from a larger group or population of items. The goal is to secure a sample that is representative of the total population being tested. The results of testing or inspecting the sample are used to accept or reject the entire batch or lot. How a sample is taken will vary with the product and process. Random sampling is one commonly used technique.

Random Sampling. A random sample is one in which every element in the population has an equal chance of being selected. The method of taking a random sample will depend on the characteristics of the product to be inspected. If all products received in a shipment can be thoroughly mixed together, then the selection of a sample from any part of the total of the mixed products will represent a valid random sample. For example, if a shipment of 1,000 balls of supposedly identical characteristics is thoroughly mixed together and a random sample of 50 balls is picked from the lot and inspected and five are found to be defective, it is probable that 10 percent of the shipment is defective.

If the product has characteristics that make it difficult or impractical to mix together thoroughly, then consecutive numbers can be assigned to each product, and tables or computer programs of random numbers can be used to draw a sample for detailed inspection. The general rule of statisticians when drawing a random sample is: Adopt a method of selection that will give every unit of the product to be inspected an equal chance of being drawn.

Sequential Sampling.   Sequential sampling may be used to reduce the number of items inspected in accept–reject decisions without loss of accuracy. It is based on the cumulative effect of information that every additional item in the sample adds as it is inspected. After each individual item's inspection, three decisions are possible: accept, reject, or sample another item. A. Wald, one of the pioneers of sequential sampling development, estimated that, using his plan, the average sample size could be reduced to one-half, as compared to a single sampling plan.

In a simple version of sequential sampling, 10 percent of the lot is inspected, and the whole lot is accepted if the sample is acceptable. If the sample is not acceptable, an additional 10 percent may be inspected if the decision to reject cannot be made on the basis of the first sample. These methods reduce the cost of quality.

100 Percent Inspection or Screening

It is often held that 100 percent inspection, or screening, is the most desirable inspection method available. This is not true. Experience shows that 100 percent inspection seldom accomplishes a completely satisfactory job of separating the acceptable from the nonacceptable or measuring the variables properly. Actually, 200 or 300 percent inspection or even higher may have to be done to accomplish this objective.

Depending on the severity of a mistake, an error of discarding a perfectly good part may be more acceptable than passing a faulty part. In some applications, the use of such extreme testing may increase the cost of a part enormously. For example, in certain high-technology applications, individual parts must be accompanied by their own individual test "pedigrees." Thus, a part that for a commercial application might cost $0.75 may well end up costing $50.00 or more and perform the identical function.

One of the many contributions of Shigeo Shingo in Japan was the development of foolproof, simple "poka yoke" devices that permit inexpensive, rapid 100 percent inspection to ensure zero defects. A simple example is the three-prong power cable connector that can only be inserted in the proper manner.

Testing

Testing products may be necessary before a commitment is made to purchase. The original selection of a given item may be based on either a specific test or a preliminary trial.

When suppliers offer samples for testing, the general rule followed by purchasers is to accept only samples that have some reasonable chance of being used. Buyers are more likely to accept samples than to reject them, since they are always on the lookout for items that may prove superior to those in current use. For various reasons, however, care has to be exercised. The samples cost the seller something and the buyer will not wish to raise false hopes on the part of the salesperson. Sometimes, too, the buyer lacks adequate facilities for testing or testing may be costly to the buyer. To meet these objections, some organizations insist on paying for all samples accepted for testing, partly because they believe that a more representative sample is obtained when it is purchased through the ordinary trade channels and partly because the buyer is less likely to feel under any obligation to the seller. Some organizations pay for the sample only when the value is substantial; some follow the rule of allowing whoever initiates the test to pay for the item tested; some pay for it only when the outcome of the test is satisfactory. The general rule, however, is for sellers to pay for samples on the theory that, if sellers really want the business and have confidence in their products, they will be willing to bear the expense of providing free samples.

Use and Laboratory Tests. The type of test varies, depending on such factors as the attitude of the buyer toward the value of specific types of tests, the type of item in question, its comparative importance, and the buyer's facilities for testing.

A use test alone may be considered sufficient, as with paint and floor wax. One advantage of a use test is that the item can be tested for the particular purpose for which it is intended and under the particular conditions in which it will be used. However, there is a risk that failure may be costly or interrupt performance.

A laboratory test alone may be adequate and may be conducted by a commercial testing laboratory or in the organization's own quality control facility. For retailers, a test may be given in one or more stores to establish whether consumer demand is sufficient to carry the product.

Commercial Testing Labs and Services. The type of inspection required may be so complicated or expensive that it cannot be performed satisfactorily in the buyer's or seller's own organization. The services of commercial testing laboratories may be used, particularly for new processes or materials or for aid in setting specifications. Also, the use of an unbiased testing organization may lend credibility to the results. For example, air, water, and soil samples are often sent to commercial labs to test for compliance with EPA standards.

Furthermore, standard testing reports of commonly used items are available from several commercial testing laboratories. They are the commercial equivalent of consumer's reports and can be a valuable aid.

The actual procedure for handling samples need not be outlined here. It is important to make and keep complete records concerning each individual sample accepted. These records should describe the type of test, the conditions under which it was given, the results, and any representations made about it by the seller. It is sound practice to discuss the results of such tests with supplier representatives so that they know their samples have received a fair evaluation.

Inspection upon Receipt

The ideal situation is one in which no receiving inspection is necessary because the joint buyer–supplier quality assurance effort has resulted in outstanding quality performance with reliable supplier-generated records. However, not all organizations have reached this enviable goal. The type of inspection, its frequency, and its thoroughness vary with circumstances. In the final analysis, this is a matter of comparative costs. How much must be spent to ensure compliance with specifications?

The purpose of inspection upon receipt is to assure the buyer that the supplier has delivered an item that corresponds to the description furnished. Receiving inspection may be used initially for products or services of new suppliers. If quality is consistently within specification, then the level of inspection may decrease. Unfortunately, production or service delivery methods and skills, even of established suppliers, change from time to time; operators or service providers become careless; errors are made; and occasionally a seller may try to reduce production costs to the point where quality suffers. Good supply policy may lead to an increase in inspection while cause and remedy are determined. While the goal is to eliminate the need for inspection by building in quality, inspection is used in some situations.

In setting specifications, it is desirable to include the procedure for inspection and testing as protection for both buyer and seller. The supplier cannot refuse to accept rejected goods on the ground that the type of inspection to which the goods would be subjected was not known or that the inspection was unduly rigid. Supplier and purchaser need to work out both the procedure for sampling and the nature of the test to be conducted. This way both supplier and purchaser should achieve identical test results, no matter which party conducts the test. Whereas in some situations purchasers may be more sophisticated in quality control and, in others, the suppliers are more sophisticated, it is sensible for both sides to cooperate on this issue.

Adjustments and Returns

The supply department, aided by the using, inspection, or legal department, is responsible for prompt action on adjustments and returns. Any nonconforming product, material, or equipment must be secured to avoid the possibility of inadvertent processing, pilferage, or additional damage while its disposition is being deliberated. Some organizations use a material review board to decide how to deal with specific nonconforming materials.

The actual decision about what can or should be done with material that does not meet specifications is both an engineering and a procurement question. Nonconforming material can be rejected and returned at the supplier's expense or held for disposition instructions. In either case, the buyer must inform the supplier if the shipment is to be replaced with acceptable material or if other alternatives are being considered. Frequently, a material may be used for another purpose or substituted for some other grade. One alternative is to rework the material and deduct the additional processing cost from the purchase price. Also, the supplier may send a technical representative to the buyer's organization to provide complete satisfaction, particularly in the case of new types of equipment or new material.

The costs incurred when materials are rejected may be divided into three major classes: (1) transportation costs, (2) testing cost, and (3) contingent expense. The buyer and seller must decide how to allocate these costs between them. This is partially affected by the kind of material rejected, trade customs, the essential economies of the situation, the buyer's cost accounting procedure, and the positions of strength of each organization. Typically, transportation costs both to and from the rejection point are charged back to the supplier. Inspection or testing costs are ordinarily borne by the buyer and are considered a part of purchasing or inspection costs.

Contracts or trade customs often provide that the supplier will not be responsible for contingent expense. This is, however, perhaps the greatest risk and the most costly item of all from the buyer's standpoint. Incoming materials that are not of proper quality may seriously interrupt production; their rejection may cause a shortage of supply that may result in customer penalties, delay or actual stoppage of production, extra handling, and other expense. Labor and/or equipment time may be expended in good faith on material later found to be unusable. It is, in general, however, not the practice of buyers to allocate such contingent costs to the supplier. Some buyers, however, insist on agreements with their suppliers to recover labor, equipment, or other costs expended on the material before discovery of its defective character.

The frequency of defective materials or services decreases drastically when there is a buyer–supplier partnership or a joint quality program. The resolution of difficulties from defective or late deliveries is usually handled in a highly professional and efficient manner, avoiding the nastiness of blame, avoidance, and litigation threats.

The Quality Assurance and Quality Control Group

The primary responsibilities of a quality assurance and quality control department or function are to establish and maintain effective controls for monitoring processes and equipment and supporting efforts to help suppliers and their suppliers to design, implement, and monitor continuous quality improvement programs. Additionally, their responsibilities include the technical task of inspecting incoming material or monitoring in-house production. The group also plays a key role in supplier certification; initiates materials studies; and inspects samples provided by suppliers. Frequently it must investigate claims and errors, related both to incoming items and to outgoing or finished products. It may examine material returned to stores to determine its suitability for reissue. Similarly, it may be called on to examine salvage material and to make a recommendation about its disposition.

The structure and location of the quality assurance function constitute a relevant problem of administration. In most cases, the work of inspection is performed by a separate department whose work may be divided into three main parts: the inspection of incoming materials, the inspection of materials in the process of manufacture, and the inspection of the finished product. The assignment of this work to a separate department is supported partly on the ground that if the inspectors of materials in process and of the finished product report to the executive in charge of operations, there may be occasions when inspection standards are relaxed in order to cover up defects in production. In some organizations, the quality assurance function reports to the supply manager.

Many quality control software programs are available. They have resolved the tedium of extensive calculations and charts and provide a range of applications. Standard programs, for example, select sampling plans, calculate sample statistics and plot histograms, produce random selection of parts, plot operating characteristics (OC) curves, and determine confidence limits.

Assuring the Quality of Purchased Services

As addressed in Chapter 6, "Need Identification," services fall along a continuum of highly tangible to highly intangible, and intangibles cannot be inventoried. These two aspects of service can create special quality measurement difficulties.

Parasuraman, Zeithaml, and Berry defined service quality as "the degree of discrepancy between customers' normative expectations for the service and their perceptions of the service performance." They defined "desired service" as the level of service representing a blend of what customers believe "can be" and "should be" provided and "adequate service" as the minimum level of service customers are willing to accept.

According to the 2013 *ASQ Global State of Quality Research: Analysis, Trends, and Opportunities,* manufacturing-based organizations are nearly twice as likely as service-focused organizations to use quality measures to drive higher performance by promoting challenging goals as part of variable performance compensation, and to support predictive analytics.[7]

In highly tangible services such as construction, quality control can be geared heavily toward the measurement of the tangible, in ways similar to standard quality assurance and control. However, all aspects of the ability of the actual service provider(s) (people) to consistently perform the service at the desired quality level are vital to the performance evaluation process. This means the quality of the intangibles must also be assessed. Intangibles such as "Were the supplier's personnel sufficiently courteous when dealing with the purchaser's employees?" may be measured by a survey or by the number of complaints received. But it is important to recognize that any standard, at best, will be imprecise.

Because the nature of many services prevents storage, delivery tends to be instantaneous. In other words, quality control will have to be performed while the service delivery is in progress, or afterward. And it may be difficult to interrupt the process, even if simultaneous quality control is possible. Therefore, the quality risk in services may be relatively high compared to the purchase of products. In cases of quality failure, it may not be possible to return the services for a full refund.

Postservice evaluation is an essential component in effective service acquisition. The same checklist that was used in sourcing may also be used for postservice evaluation.

Informal Evaluation

At the very least, an informal evaluation might suffice. In the case of consulting services, this might include two questions:

1. Did your problem or issue get resolved to your satisfaction?
2. Would you rehire this consultant in the future for another problem or issue?

Additional questions regarding conformance to expectations of quality, timeliness, and cost are appropriate, as well as feedback on the professionalism and service orientation of the consultant personnel.

Quality risk avoidance may be achieved by certifying service providers, doing business with service suppliers found to be satisfactory in the past, avoiding repeat business with suppliers who did not do a good job, carefully checking suppliers beforehand with other users with similar needs, and using carefully worded preservice delivery communications with the supplier and service users to ensure common understanding of requirements and expectations.

Formal Evaluation

A formal service quality evaluation process developed by Parasuraman, Zeithaml, and Berry identifies five quality dimensions:

Reliability: ability to perform the promised service dependably and accurately.

Responsiveness: willingness to help customers and provide prompt service.

---

[7] ASQ, *Global State of Quality Research: Analysis, Trends, and Opportunities 2013,* p. 5, http://rube.asq .org/2013/04/global-quality/the-asq-global-state-of-quality-discoveries-2013.pdf

Assurance: knowledge and courtesy of employees and their ability to inspire trust and confidence.

Empathy: caring, individualized attention the firm provides its customers.

Tangibles: physical facilities, equipment, and appearance of personnel.[8]

The survey process measures the gap between service expectations along each dimension and the perceptions of actual service performance. In a refinement of SERVQUAL, the authors added three questions to strengthen the validity of the assessment: (1) Have you experienced a recent service problem with the company? (2) If so, was it resolved to your satisfaction? (3) Would you recommend the service firm to a friend?[9]

Ultimately, the goal of effective acquisition of services is to obtain best value. In this sense there is no difference between the acquisition of services and goods. And the best buy in services represents the appropriate trade-off between quality, quantity, delivery, price/cost, and other relevant factors. In the assessment of quality of purchased services, the following characteristics might be considered: value, repetitiveness, tangibility, direction, production, nature of demand, nature of delivery, degree of customization, and the skills required for producing the service. Each of these will be discussed in turn.

Value of the Service

One broad cut at services would be to classify services as high, medium, or low value. This could be done in the typical ABC/Pareto analysis or portfolio analysis that looks at both value and risk to acquire. ABC classification would focus quality attention on high-spend services. Portfolio analysis would focus more quality attention on services with potential high impact on the organization. For example, the improper removal of asbestos from a building may make the whole building unusable. A consultant to assist in the long-term strategic planning of the organization may have a very significant, long-term impact. Quality assurance and quality control efforts might be organized according to classification.

Degree of Repetitiveness

For the acquisition of repetitive services, it may be possible to develop a standard quality assessment tool and gather quality information on a regular basis. The quality of unique service requirements may be more difficult because the quality is assessed as the service is delivered. Electronic sourcing tools that are used to acquire repetitive services that are easily standardized and low risk to acquire may also be used to collect quality feedback from users.

Degree of Tangibility

By definition, every service tends to have an intangible dimension, such as the conviviality dimension in the hospitality industry. Even so, some services can be seen as more tangible than others. For example, an architect will produce a drawing or a design that can be examined by others and that ultimately will result in a physical structure. Although the structural features of the physical representation of the design can be examined for quality purposes,

---

[8] A. Parasuraman, V. A. Zeithaml, and L. L. Berry, "A Conceptual Model of Service Quality and Its Implications for the Future," *Journal of Marketing*, Fall 1985, pp. 41–50; and "SERVQUAL: A Multiple-Item Scale for Measuring Consumer Perceptions of Service Quality," *Journal of Retailing*, Spring 1988, pp. 12–40. These two references likely were the first presentations of this approach.

[9] Parasuraman, et al., "Refinement and Reassessment of the Scale," *Journal of Retailing*, Winter 1991, pp. 433.

the aesthetic features of the design are much more difficult to evaluate and subject to a wide variety of responses.

On the other hand, the advice from a consultant on a new marketing strategy may be almost totally intangible. The development of quality standards in any contract for services is difficult. For services where there is no accompanying good, qualifications for the people or equipment providing the service may be used as quality markers. For example, the number of personnel in the organization who have appropriate training in the particular discipline, and the capability of the various pieces of equipment, can be specified ahead of time and measured against in the quality assessment. Unfortunately, many segments of the service sector are plagued by high personnel turnover, and the addition or loss of a few key people can make a significant difference in the quality provided.

Expressions of levels of satisfaction or dissatisfaction by various users or experts may be used. For example, how many complaints are received about the cleanliness of the building? Or how many experts believe the software program to be acceptable? It should be recognized that the selection of experts or evaluators represents a statistical quality problem. Some people may be more eager than others to express their opinions, and their views may not be representative of the whole group. Relying solely on complaints may give a biased response.

Direction of the Service
Another aspect of service deals with whether or not it is directed at people. For example, food services are for people; maintenance services may be for buildings or equipment. When services are directed at people, it is important to recognize the special needs of the persons who will be most affected by the service. The ultimate user likely will play a major role in both the specification of the service and the assessment of quality received. If services directed at people have an important intangible component, assessment may require a period of exposure of both supplier and purchaser personnel to each other to determine compatibility.

Production of the Service
Services can be produced by people or equipment, or a combination of both. Services of low labor intensity may have a high capital or asset component. Typical examples would include real estate and equipment rentals, computer processing, transportation, and communication services, as well as custom processing of a machine-intensive nature. In the specification stage, understanding the underlying technology or asset base is important partly because it drives the quality delivered. During the acquisition stage, potential suppliers can be assessed on the basis of their asset capacity and availability as well as the state of their technology. These factors then become part of the quality assessment. The delivery of this kind of service is more likely at the location of the supplier's premises or of its equipment, although hookup may be directly to the purchaser's site. Quality monitoring and evaluation may be process oriented, with emphasis on the performance of the underlying capital asset.

Services with high labor intensity include activities like hand harvesting, installation and maintenance, education, health support, and security, as well as the full range of professional activities like consulting, engineering, accounting, medical, and architectural services. Here the quality of the "people component" is the primary concern.

Services involving largely lower- to medium-skilled people may focus more on cost minimization and efficiency. Services requiring highly skilled individuals may require the purchaser to distinguish between levels of professional skill and may require extensive ongoing communication between requisitioner and supply manager through all phases of the acquisition process to accurately assess quality delivered.

Nature of the Demand

The demand for a particular service may be continuous, periodic, or discrete.

The typical example of a continuous service may be insurance or a 24-hour, around-the-clock security service. Periodic service may be regular, such as once a week or once a month, as with regular inspections, or it may vary with need, as in repair services. It may be possible to monitor the quality of a continuous or periodic service and make alterations as information about the quality of service becomes evident. However, this may be more difficult if the person(s) actually providing the service is (are) different each time the service is provided. Some of this type of variation may be reduced by specifying the actual people who will perform a service and requiring that no personnel changes can be made without prior approval.

A discrete or one-shot service may be the acquisition of an interior decorator to suggest a new color scheme for an office complex. The quality monitoring capability may have to be shifted to the various stages in the delivery process, if this is possible. The problem may be that by the time the service is delivered, it is too late to make significant quality improvements.

Nature of Service Delivery

The nature and place of service delivery may have significant acquisition repercussions. For example, if the delivery of the service occurs on the premises of the purchaser, the contract agreement may have to address a number of provisions. For example, in construction or installation services, questions of security; access; nature of dress; hours of work; applicability of various codes for health, security, and safety; what working days and hours are applicable; and what equipment and materials are to be provided by whom are all issues that need to be addressed as part of the contract. It is vital to determine which issues are related to the quality of the service and how to write these terms clearly.

On the other hand, when the service is provided on the supplier's premises or elsewhere, many of these concerns may not arise, provided the service is not directed at personnel of the purchaser.

Degree of Standardization

It makes a substantial difference whether a service is standard or customized specifically for the purchaser. Generally speaking, the less the consumer contact, the more standard the service becomes, and, probably, the less the importance of intangibles. Quality assessments may be easier because suppliers can be prequalified or certified and a standard type of supplier evaluation exists.

With highly customized services, the specification process may become more difficult and the options more difficult to understand. The involvement of the end consumers in this specification process then becomes more important. The acquisition process itself may be less definite, since various suppliers may offer substantially different options. Evaluation of supplier performance may have to recognize the purchaser's share of responsibility for quality at the point of delivery.

Skills Required for the Service

The production of a service may require a full range of skills, from unskilled on the one extreme to highly skilled on the other. In services requiring relatively unskilled labor, such as grass cutting and other simple maintenance tasks, price emphasis is likely to be high and ease of entry into (and exit from) the service also may be high. Quality may be monitored primarily through user feedback.

As discussed earlier, the acquisition of highly skilled services may focus far more on qualifications of the skilled persons, concern over the specific persons who will be performing the service, and recommendations from other skilled persons and users. Frequently, in highly professional services, the cost of the professional service may be relatively low compared to the benefit expected. For example, a good design may increase sales substantially; a good architect may be able to design a low-cost, but effective structure; and a good consulting recommendation may turn around a whole organization. It often is difficult to deal with this trade-off between the estimated costs for the job and the estimated benefits. If the buyer wants to link outcome to quality, then there must be some means of assessing cause and effect to determine if high (or low) quality was due to the services provided by the service provider or actions within the buying organization.

Supplier Certification

Supplier certification is a process of evaluating and recognizing the quality performance of an organization's suppliers. Standards are established for quality, and often delivery and productivity performance as well. Suppliers that consistently meet these standards are certified. Suppliers benefit from systematic improvements that may increase their profitability; they typically are considered first for new business; and they are often publically recognized by the buying organization. Buying organizations benefit by consistently receiving required quality and delivery levels and enjoying systematic improvements over time. Continuing involvement with suppliers may lead to common quality standards and agreement on inspection methods and ways of improving quality while decreasing inspection and overall cost.

Purchasers often conduct a quality capability or quality assurance survey on the supplier's premises either before a new supplier is given an order or before a supplier is allowed to quote. This is to ensure that the supplier is capable of meeting the specifications and quality standards required. The practice is common in many types of organizations including high-technology areas and most larger organizations.

The survey is normally conducted by relevant departments such as engineering, manufacturing, supply, and quality control personnel for goods or user group, purchasing, and quality control for services. It examines the supplier's equipment, facilities, and personnel as well as quality control systems and processes. The supplier's supply chain management initiatives are also examined. These include the supplier's efforts to seek cooperation and compliance in quality standards from its suppliers and its suppliers' suppliers and the supplier's commitment to ongoing quality improvement. Managing quality through tiers of suppliers is an ongoing challenge, especially with global supply networks.

The decision to purchase only from certified suppliers extends beyond quality considerations. In organizations pursuing partnerships with suppliers, quality certification is usually the first category of interorganizational alignment. In many industries, a minimum level of quality capability is a standard requirement for any supplier and corporate survival may depend on it.

The quality target is to have the right quality by making it right the first time, rather than inspecting in quality. It is this pressure to create quality at its source that is behind all quality improvement programs. The same philosophy also should apply to the supply department itself and the purchaser's own organization. It is very difficult for a purchaser to insist that suppliers meet stringent quality requirements when it is obvious to the suppliers that the supply organization itself shows no sign of a similar commitment. Any supply department wishing to start a quality drive may want to apply quality standards to its own performance on all of the phases in the acquisition cycle. Not only will this create familiarity with statistical quality control and quality standards in the supply department itself, but it also gives supply the right to ask for similar commitment by others.

QUALITY STANDARDS AND AWARDS PROGRAMS

At the international level, the International Organization for Standardization (ISO) runs several quality-related programs. Organizations in various countries also offer quality awards. The following are discussed in this section: ISO 9000 Quality Standards, ISO 14000 Environmental Standards, The U.S. Malcolm Baldrige Award, and the Japanese Deming Award.

ISO 9000 Quality Standards[10]

The International Organization for Standardization (ISO) in Geneva, Switzerland, provides common standards across the world. The American National Standards Institute (ANSI) and the Canadian Standards Association (CSA) are North American members. The ISO 9000 quality standards, which were first adopted in 1987 and revised in 1994, 2000, 2008, and are now being reviewed for a 2015 update.

According to the ISO, the ISO 9000 family of standards represents an international consensus on good quality management practices. It consists of standards and guidelines relating to quality management systems and related supporting standards. According to the 2013 *ASQ Global State of Quality Research: Analysis, Trends and Opportunities,* manufacturing organizations are 1.5 times more likely than service-focused organizations to use ISO as a quality framework.

ISO 9001:2008 is the standard that provides a set of standardized requirements for a quality management system, regardless of what the user organization does, its size, or whether it is in the private or public sector. It is the only standard in the family against which organizations can be certified—although certification is not a compulsory requirement of the standard. It provides a tested framework for a systematic approach to managing organizational processes to consistently deliver product that satisfies customers' expectations. It defines the requirements a quality system must meet, but does not dictate how they should be met in any specific organization. This leaves scope and flexibility for implementation in different business sectors and business cultures, as well as in different national cultures.

[10] Source: *Information about the International Standards Organization can be found on their website at* *www.iso.org*

The other standards in the family cover specific aspects such as fundamentals and vocabulary, performance improvements, documentation, training, and financial and economic aspects.

Checking That It Works

1. The standard requires the organization itself to audit its ISO 9001:2008–based quality system to verify that it is managing its processes effectively, or, to put it another way, to check that it is fully in control of its activities.

2. In addition, the organization may invite its clients to audit the quality system in order to give them confidence that the organization is capable of delivering products or services that will meet their requirements.

3. Lastly, the organization may engage the services of an independent quality system certification body to obtain an ISO 9001:2008 certificate of conformity. This last option has proved extremely popular in the marketplace because of the perceived credibility of an independent assessment.

The organization may thus avoid multiple audits by its clients or reduce the frequency or duration of client audits. The certificate can also serve as a business reference between the organization and potential clients, especially when supplier and client are new to each other, or far removed geographically, as in an export context.

ISO 14000 Environmental Standards[11]

ISO 14000, similar to ISO 9000 in management principles, focuses on environmental issues. ISO 14000 standards describe the basic elements of an effective environmental management system (EMS) and do not replace federal, state, and provincial environmental laws and regulations.

The ISO 14000 series consists of two standards related to EMS. ISO 14004:2004 provides guidelines on the elements of an environmental management system and its implementation and discusses principal issues involved. ISO 14001:2004 specifies the requirements for such an environmental management system. Fulfilling these requirements demands objective evidence that can be audited to demonstrate that the environmental management system is operating effectively in conformity to the standard. For example, with Honda's encouragement and assistance, nearly 90 percent of Honda's U.S. original equipment suppliers have achieved third-party ISO 14001 certification for environmentally sound production processes.

ISO 14006:2011 focuses on guidelines for incorporating ecodesign. ISO 14064-1:2006 Greenhouse gases—Part 1 is a specification with guidance at the organization level for quantification and reporting of greenhouse gas emissions and removals.

The Malcolm Baldrige National (U.S.) Quality Award

The annual Malcolm Baldrige National Quality Award is intended to recognize U.S. organizations in manufacturing, service, small business, health care, education, and nonprofit. The award recognizes excellence in quality achievement and quality management. The criteria are organized into seven categories: leadership; strategic planning; customer focus;

[11] ISO 9000 Essentials, www.iso.org/iso/iso_9000_essentials

measurement, analysis, and knowledge management; workforce focus; operations focus; and results. The criteria are designed to help organizations enhance their competitiveness by focusing on two goals: delivering ever-improving value to customers and improving overall organizational performance. It is also designed to motivate U.S. companies to improve quality and productivity, provide standardized quality guidelines and criteria for evaluating quality improvement efforts, and provide guidance to U.S. organizations striving to make improvements by describing how winning organizations were able to achieve their successes. The diffusion of TQM practices is one of the most important aspects of the Baldrige Award.

The Baldrige Award evaluates both quality management programs and achievement of results, with heavy emphasis on organizationwide financial performance. In its 2012 survey of the 100 top hospitals, Truven Analytics found that nearly 70 percent of teaching hospitals reported formal use of the Baldrige criteria to develop organizational goals and/or to process improvement initiatives.

Changes to the award criteria relative to suppliers and services contributed to the decline of applications from for-profit organizations and finally no applications from for-profits in 2013. A revision process may reinstate the relevance of the award in the perception of executives in for-profit organizations.

The Deming Prize

To commemorate Dr. Deming's contribution and friendship and to promote the continued development of quality control in Japan, the Union of Japanese Scientists and Engineers (JUSE) created the Deming Prize. Established in 1950, it is given annually to domestic or overseas organizations that have implemented TQM suitable for their management philosophy, scope/type/scale of business, and management environment. The Deming Grand Prize is given to previous winners of the Deming Prize that have maintained and further enhanced the level of TQM for more than three years after winning the Deming Prize. The Deming Prize for Individuals is open only to Japanese candidates. In 2013, Komatsu Shantui Construction Machinery Co., Ltd (China) and SCG Logistics Management Company Limited (Thailand]) won the Deming Prize and Meidoh Co., Ltd (Japan) and Rane Brake Lining Limited (India) won the Deming Grand Prize. The Deming Prizes carry a tremendous amount of international prestige.

Similar prizes are awarded in Canada and other countries.

Conclusion Quality is one of the essential requirements for supply along with quantity, delivery, price, and service. The continuous pursuit of zero defects over many decades has evolved an impressive array of quality diagnostic and improvement tools. Making it right the first time rather than inspecting quality in is the prevailing wisdom.

Service goes beyond the essential tangible support a supplier is expected to provide such as installation of a new piece of equipment. Services are intangible—reflecting responsiveness, flexibility, willingness to provide assistance in case of emergency, evidence of concern for continuous improvement, and friendliness. Thus, service is more difficult to specify, but very real in actual supplier–purchaser dealings. It is easy to promise and difficult to obtain. Both high quality and service form the basis for a longer-term successful relationship between a buyer and a seller and for supply chain cooperation and effectiveness.

Questions for Review and Discussion

1. Why should a purchaser be familiar with the mathematics of quality control and inspection?
2. How might you establish a supplier certification program?
3. How does the degree of tangibility of a service influence quality assessment?
4. How could a quality philosophy be applied to a supply department?
5. What are the various costs associated with quality, and why is it difficult to determine the magnitude of some of these costs?
6. Why was Deming so insistent on single sourcing? What are the risks associated with single sourcing and how might they be mitigated?
7. What does it mean if a supplier is ISO 9000 certified? ISO 14000 certified?
8. What are the trade-offs between 100 percent inspection and sampling?
9. What constitutes a "best buy"?
10. What are some of the aspects of quality assurance when buying services?

References

American National Standards Institute, www.ansi.org

ASQ, *Global State of Quality Research: Analysis, Trends, and Opportunities 2013*, asq.org.

Besterfield, D. H. *Quality Improvement*. 9th ed. Upper Saddle River, NJ: Prentice-Hall, 2012.

Bozdogan, K., *Towards an Integration of the Lean Enterprise System, Total Quality Management, Six Sigma and Related Enterprise Process Improvement Methods*, MIT Engineering Systems Division, August 2010, http://esd.mit.edu/WPS/2010/esd-wp-2010-05.pdf.

Coimba, E. *Kaizen in Logistics and Supply Chains*. New York: McGraw-Hill Professional, 2013.

International Standards Organization, www.iso.org

Juran, J. M., and J. A. De Feo. *Juran's Quality Handbook: The Complete Guide to Performance Excellence*. 6th ed. New York: McGraw Hill, 2010.

Kubiak, T. M., and D. W. Benbow, *The Certified Six Sigma Black Belt Handbook*. 2nd ed. ASQ Quality Press, 2009.

Leenders, M. R., and P. F. Johnson. *Major Structural Changes in Supply Organizations*. Tempe, AZ: Center for Advanced Purchasing Studies, 2000.

Ptacek, R., and J. Motwani. *Pursuing Perfect Service: Using a Practical Approach to Lean Six Sigma to Improve the Customer Experience and Reduce Costs in Service Industries*. Chelsea, MI: MCS Media, Inc., 2011.

Ritzman, L. P.; L. J. Krajewski; and M. K. Malhotra. *Operations Management*. 10th ed. Toronto: Pearson Prentice Hall, 2013.

Sasser, Jr., W. E., and F. F. Reichheld. "Zero-Defections: Quality Comes to Services." *Harvard Business Review*, September–October 1990, pp. 105–111.

Case 7–1

The Power Line Poles

Moren Corporation was building three additional power-generating stations to serve the rapidly expanding energy market. To link these stations to the existing area grid, a new method of carrying the power lines using ornamental tubular poles, instead of towers, had been adopted. The second phase of the project involved pole manufacture to a functional engineering design with parameters. Mr. Gordon Yarrow, supervisor of materials purchasing, wondered how to deal with the exceptions to the contract terms quoted by Henry Nelson Company, the preferred pole supplier.

BIDDING PROCEDURES—PRESELECTION

Gordon Yarrow had the responsibility to recommend a pole manufacturer. Gordon had the consulting engineers' services and the experience of his own engineering department to assist him. The consulting engineering firm on the project had been selected in August, and by early spring of the following year it had furnished Moren with functional specifications for the poles, cross arms, and hardware. Moren engineers recommended that the quotations should first be obtained on the most pressing portion of the line linking Addison to Smithfield. This amounted to about half of the total project distance. The expectation was that the experience gained on this first section would guide the contracts on the remaining half. Mr. Yarrow

had to ensure a start on the 345 kV line by the fall. This left not much time in which to develop pole prototypes and to perform the engineering tests in advance of erection. The number of potential suppliers was limited by two major requirements. Each supplier had to have a design computer program and a large press-brake for heavy metal.

FIRST PROGRESS REPORT

In May, having received bids from eight potential suppliers, Gordon Yarrow was able to give his superior a brief rundown on his progress. He told Mr. Carter he had encountered quite a spread in prices and that there were disturbing gaps in engineering information in some cases, but he believed the timetable could be met.

Mr. Yarrow went over all detailed information and prices in the following weeks with Mr. Northrup, Moren's senior transmission project engineer, and together they rejected four bidders. (See Exhibit 1 for the remaining quotes).

At the request of Mr. Northrup, Gordon next sent engineering information only (no prices) on the four remaining bidders to Moren's engineering consultants for a complete analysis of the bids on the basis of the requested design, a comparison of designs furnished, and exceptions to specifications. Mr. Northrup agreed to meet with bidders *M, N,* and *P* to resolve the engineering and

EXHIBIT 1 Quotation Summary—Poles and Arms 345 kV Line Addison-Smithfield Section

	Bidders			
	M	**N**	**O**	**P**
	Norris Steel Co.	Structures Cdn., Ltd.	Henry Nelson Co.	Jordan Pole Co.
Bid (in $000)	$22,400	$24,160	$24,640	$27,896
Extra for base	1,400	—	—	—
Escalation	252	Firm	Firm	500
Total	$24,052	$24,160	$24,640	$28,396

Quantity: 390 type 3A, 61 type 3B, 24 type 3C, 7 type 3D, 8 type 3E. Total 490

EXHIBIT 2   Comments on the Exceptions to Specifications in Nelson Company's Bid

Exception 1
The exception to the method of shipping would relieve Nelson of the responsibility for poles during shipment from the southern factory to your storage yards.

Exception 2
In Nelson's bid, no material could be rejected on the basis of low Charpy values shown on the mill test reports or by sampling on anything but the thickest plate of the heat. Similarly, welding materials or techniques would not be subject to rejection because of low Charpy results, which is inconsistent with the intent of the specifications.

Exception 3
Excessive bolt projections represent a hazard to installation and maintenance personnel and would also increase construction costs.

Exceptions 4 and 5
Under Nelson Company's proposed Welding and Inspection Specifications, the purchaser would be prohibited from using radiography to determine weld quality, even for the purpose of clarifying the interpretations of ultrasonic indications or for use where ultrasonic inspection cannot be made. Only visual or magnetic particle inspection would be permissible for any welds except the pole shaft to base plate weld and the longitudinal welds at the lap joints. Some welds, such as the arm to butt plate welds, are virtually impossible to adequately inspect after they are completed and require inspection while the work is being performed; most inspection techniques except radiography are of questionable value following galvanizing; all inspection would have to be made in the fabricator's plant. Henry Nelson Company's proposed inspection procedures are less stringent than AWS-D1.0.69 in allowing 3/16" or smaller defects regardless of spacing.

Exception 6
Nelson's Conditions of Sale give the purchaser only five days from unloading to make claims for damaged or defective material. The warranty clause is unclear in that it can be interpreted to mean that Nelson has one year in which to make corrections but no provision for correcting defective material unless found in the five-day inspection period. It is our understanding that the intent is to provide a one-year warranty but the words do not so state.

Escalation Clause
Delays in delivery that are not caused by the purchaser should not be charged to the purchaser.

fabricating capabilities of each. This was not necessary for bidder *O* (Henry Nelson Company) because the company was already working for Moren.

In mid-June Mr. Northrup called Gordon Yarrow to share his findings. He said, "I have serious reservations about three bidders, *M, N,* and *P,* based on equipment, plant capacity, and ability to meet our deadlines. Our consultants agree."

"Based on engineering and fabricating experience, our first recommendation is Nelson. I will confirm this in writing. However, these exceptions to our specifications would still have to be resolved. I will leave these

to you to work out." Mr. Northrup handed a sheet of comments to Gordon Yarrow (See Exhibit 2).

NELSON'S EXCEPTIONS

After his visit with Mr. Northrup, Gordon Yarrow returned to his office and examined Nelson's quotation. Not knowing whether Nelson would be recommended by the engineers, he had not paid much attention to Nelson's exceptions to Moren's bid requirements. There were six exceptions noted on Mr. Northrup's summary. Gordon wondered how he should tackle them.

Case 7–2

Caledon Concrete Mixers

As Sarah Jenkins, materials manager at Caledon Concrete Mixers, ended her conference call with Jon Del Rosario from corporate purchasing, she wondered what recommendations she should make regarding the selection of a gearbox supplier. The corporate purchasing group in Chicago was advocating switching to a new supplier, but Sarah remained concerned about the risks of ending a long-term supply arrangement with a key supplier. It was now December the 3rd and she wanted to make a final recommendation before the plant shut down for the annual Christmas holiday break.

CALEDON CONCRETE MIXERS

Located north of Toronto, Canada, in Caledon, Ontario, Caledon Concrete Mixers (CCM) was a manufacturer of truck-mounted concrete mixers. Founded in 1910, the company employed 140 people in its 150,000 square foot plant, including 100 unionized hourly workers, and had annual sales of approximately $25 million. Nearly 40 percent of company sales were exported, mainly to the United States.

CCM had a strong reputation for quality and service in the industry. It operated as a private business until 2003, when it was purchased by Illinois Machinery Corporation (IMC). IMC was a global manufacturer and marketer of access equipment, specialty vehicles, and truck bodies for the defense, concrete placement, refuse hauling, and fire and emergency markets. Annual revenues in the most current fiscal year were $9 billion and IMC had approximately 18,000 employees.

Concrete mixer transport trucks were designed to mix concrete and haul it to the construction site. Customers typically specified the truck model, which was ordered from the original equipment manufacturer. CCM fitted the vehicle with the concrete mixing equipment, which included a large drum and discharge system. Systems were customized based on vehicle size (e.g., 2–6 axles), discharge system (front or rear), and capacity (maximum capacity to carry 14 cubic yards of payload).

IMC had an operation in St. Louis that manufactured a similar product line to CCM under a different brand name, with annual revenues approximately double the Canadian plant. Although IMC operated under a decentralized model, CCM and the St. Louis operation cooperated in areas of engineering, purchasing, and sales, while operating autonomously with separate leadership teams. One key area for synergies

was in supply, where combining purchases between the two operations for some products had yielded significant savings. Jon Del Rosario, purchasing manager in the corporate purchasing group in Chicago, was responsible for coordinating purchasing between the Caledon and St. Louis plants.

Sarah Jenkins was responsible for materials management at CCM. An MBA graduate from the Ivey Business School, Sarah had worked at CCM for more than 20 years. Reporting to the general manager, her responsibilities included logistics and transportation, purchasing, inventory control, and production planning. Her counterparts in finance and accounting, quality, operations, sales, HR, and engineering rounded out the senior management team.

THE GEARBOX

While the concrete mixer truck was in operation, it was necessary to continuously rotate the load to prepare the concrete and avoid consolidation. The gearbox was located at the bottom of the large mixing drum and was used to transmit torque from the hydraulic motor drive shaft, which rotated the drum. The gearbox also permitted the operator to adjust the speed and direction of the rotation.

The gearbox was one of approximately 150 components that CCM used for the assembly of their concrete mixers. The gearbox used by CCM came in two variations, depending on the model of the concrete mixer. Each gearbox cost approximately $3,600 and volumes at CCM ranged from 950 to 1,100 units per year.

CURRENT SUPPLY ARRANGEMENT

CCM and the St. Louis operation both used BGK GmbH as the single source for gearboxes. BGK was a large diversified German manufacturing company with annual revenues of 12 billion euros. The division that supplied CCM produced gearboxes for industrial applications in a wide range of industries, such as material handling equipment, energy, and mining. The company had a reputation for high quality and reliability, although its products were typically more expensive than those of their competitors.

The relationship with CCM and BGK dated back more than 30 years. BGK offered a standard one-year warranty on its gearboxes, but Sarah was not aware that CCM had ever experienced any notable quality problems and customers were generally satisfied with performance of the product.

IMC had also used BGK as their single supplier for many years. At the time of the acquisition of CCM, the IMC purchasing group was surprised to learn that CCM had a better price for its gearboxes. Prices for both CCM and IMC were aligned following the completion of the acquisition in 2003.

Despite the long history with BGK, both CCM and IMC had become increasingly unhappy with the service and responsiveness of the supplier and its apparent unwillingness to react to their concerns. Strong economic expansion in Asia created increased demand for BGK gearboxes and the company was unable to expand capacity to keep pace with increasing sales. It had been hampered by a combination of restrictive labor rules in Germany regarding overtime and a steel shortage two years prior.

Second, BGK did not have distribution operations in North America. Gearboxes were shipped via ocean freight and lead times to the Caledon plant ranged from three to five months. As a result, CCM was forced to keep a three-month supply of safety stock inventory on hand. Even with this precaution, supply shortages had threatened plant shutdowns on several occasions during the previous two years. With 50 percent of CCM's sales coming from four customers, changes in customer orders could have a significant effect on demand and inventories. To add to Sarah's frustration, BGK shipped only full container loads of 50 units, whereas production in some months was as low as 20 units.

Lastly, customer expectations for warranty and service were increasing, yet BGK was unwilling to extend its warranty coverage without an increase in price. The supplier referenced its quality data, which boasted the lowest failure rate in the industry at 0.5 percent. However, as margins on CCM's products shrank and customer demands grew, Sarah and her peers in the purchasing organization at IMC had become frustrated by the lack of responsiveness from their supplier and decided to test the marketplace.

SUPPLY OPTIONS

The decision was made in September to solicit RFQs for the combined gearbox volumes of CCM and IMC. Sarah led the RFQ process and identified five potential suppliers, including BGK, two of which were not invited to participate because they currently supplied product exclusively to Asia. The two new firms asked to participate were Moretti SpA and IGR Industries.

The RFQ specified a five-year contract for 100 percent of volumes for CCM and IMC, representing an annual volume of 2,800 to 3,300 units per year. Each supplier was asked to submit quotes in U.S. funds that included stable pricing for the term of the contract, warranty terms, and

distribution capabilities, including lead times and North American warehousing arrangements. Delivery would be FOB the London and St. Louis facilities.

IGR Industries was an Italian company, but its manufacturing operations were mainly in Eastern Europe and Asia. Revenues for IGR were approximately 1.5 billion euros, with sales concentrated primarily in Europe and Asia. It had a good reputation for quality, claiming that its failure rate was 1.0 percent. IGR did not currently supply product to North America, but proposed setting up a distribution facility in the Missouri region as part of their proposal. Under this arrangement, IGR promised just-in-time delivery to IMC and two-day delivery to CCM. IGR quoted a price of $3,400, with an annual adjustment for currency fluctuations, between the U.S. dollar and the euro, and steel pricing. It also offered a five-year warranty and 30-day payment terms.

Moretti SpA was also an Italian manufacturer with sales of approximately 1 billion euros. It had operations in 18 countries, including the United States. Approximately five years ago Moretti had experienced a quality problem with its gearbox, involving an oil leak. The oil leak problem became a major issue, as contractors had become increasingly sensitive to potential environmental problems at construction sites. However, according to company officials the oil leak problem had since been addressed and the company claimed that independent testing indicated a defect rate of 1.5 percent of its product after three years of operation. Moretti quoted a price of $3,200, with an annual adjustment for currency fluctuations between the U.S. dollar and the euro. The company also offered a five-year warranty and a consignment inventory arrangement. Under the consignment inventory system, Moretti would own the inventory at CCM and IMC until the gearboxes were assembled into the vehicle, at which point an invoice would be issued, with a 30-day payment term.

BGK's proposal was to extend the current supply arrangement, which included a price of $3,600 that was subject to annual adjustments and a standard one-year warranty. Lennart Wagner, the sales representative for BGK, indicated that the company was not prepared to set up a North American distribution facility. He indicated to Sarah that BGK was the world leader in gearboxes, and the high quality of their product should represent a significant selling feature of CCM's concrete mixers.

THE SUPPLIER SELECTION DECISION

Sarah had developed a supplier evaluation framework that ranked each supplier in eight areas: price, warranty

EXHIBIT 1
Supplier
Evaluations

Evaluation Criteria	Value	BGK		IGR		Moretti	
		Rating	Score	Rating	Score	Rating	Score
Price	15	7	105	8	120	9	135
Warranty	5	5	25	7	35	7	35
Lead time	20	3	60	9	180	7	140
Inventory cost	10	4	40	8	80	8	80
Logistics/Distribution	10	2	20	10	100	7	70
Order flexibility	15	3	45	8	120	7	105
Payment terms	10	5	50	8	80	8	80
Supplier financial stability	5	7	35	7	35	7	35
	90		380		750		680

(e.g., length of warranty), lead time, inventory costs (e.g., holding costs and need for safety stock), logistics/distribution (e.g., North American distribution capabilities), order flexibility (e.g., ability to make changes to orders), payment terms, and supplier financial stability. Each criterion was assigned a weight and suppliers were evaluated on scale of 1 (poor) to 10 (excellent). Exhibit 1 provides a breakdown of Sarah's rankings for the three suppliers.

As Sarah reviewed the data in the supplier evaluation framework, she wondered if it adequately represented the trade-offs among the three supply alternatives. Based on her analysis, IGR Industries would become the new gearbox supplier, which would mean ending their relationship with a supplier that had lasted more than three decades. She needed to finalize her recommendation before a planned conference call with Jon Del Rosario and the head of purchasing at the IMC in St. Louis the following week.

Case 7–3
Wentworth Hospital

Rebecca Hogan, manager of clinical engineering at Wentworth Hospital in Hamilton, Ontario, was considering her options to improve the quality and cost of repairs being made to the hospital's flexible endoscopes. It was Monday, April 8, and Rebecca wanted to prepare a recommendation to present at the monthly team meeting scheduled for April the 24th.

WENTWORTH HOSPITAL

Wentworth Hospital was one of the largest hospitals in the province, with approximately 600 beds and an annual budget of $500 million. The majority of the budget came from the Ontario Ministry of Health. Wentworth Hospital was part of a family of four large hospitals and a cancer center in the Northumberland Health Sciences (NHS) organization, which offered a complete range of acute and specialized health care services to more than 2 million residents

in southern Ontario. Each hospital in NHS had specific areas of expertise, and together they offered comprehensive health care services.

The biomedical engineering department was a team that focused on managing the hospital's medical technology. Its services included the purchase, maintenance, repair, and disposal of hospital equipment and assisting with the adoption of new technologies. The biomedical engineering department had an operating budget of approximately $3 million, and was also responsible for managing Wentworth Hospital's capital budget of approximately $5 million. Although most equipment repairs were covered by each individual department's budget, $45,000 of the capital budget was available for repairs costing more than $1,000.

The biomedical engineering department team was headed by Joseph Tai and was part of the medical operations division of Wentworth Hospital. Michael Pooley, Adam Schlegel, and Rebecca Hogan comprised the remaining members of the team. Michael, the equipment management coordinator, was responsible for financial management of repair budgets and medical equipment acquisition, working closely with the purchasing department in the NHS shared services organization. Adam managed technical concerns of the department, as technical supervisor. Rebecca, who held a degree in mechanical engineering and an MBA from the Ivey Business School, handled engineering- and technical-related issues.

ENDOSCOPY

Wentworth Hospital used flexible and rigid endoscopes in exploratory and corrective surgeries. An endoscopy was a simple medical procedure that involved examining the inside of a patient's body using an endoscope, which was a medical device consisting of a long, thin, flexible or rigid tube that contained a light and a video camera. Images of the endoscopy procedure could be seen on a screen and recorded if necessary. Endoscopy was commonly used to view areas such as the lungs, stomach, digestive tract, and major joints. Endoscopes could also be fitted with surgical instruments capable of performing a number of procedures, such as removing small tumors or gallstones, suction, and fluid exchange. Most endoscopes were flexible and could be manipulated using angulation knobs, which controlled the vertical and horizontal movement of the device. There were approximately 2,500 endoscopy procedures at Wentworth Hospital in the past year.

The advantages of an endoscopy were that the vast majority did not require a general anesthetic and they did not require a major incision. Most patients received a local anesthetic during the procedure. Common types of endoscopies include colonoscopy, laryngoscopy, and thoracoscopy.

Endoscopes were maintenance- and repair-intensive devices that involved extremely sensitive technology. The scopes were tested before and after each procedure, which included cleaning, leak testing, measuring of angulation ranges, and video testing. Despite careful maintenance, scopes sometimes broke down during surgery, which frequently meant aborting the operation and rescheduling the procedure, unless another endoscope was readily available.

Wentworth Hospital purchased two or three new flexible endoscopes each year at a cost of approximately $20,000 each and an additional $30,000 per year on related equipment. The hospital also purchased several rigid endoscopes each year, costing $5,000 to $10,000 each. Because of the cost of the endoscopes and supporting equipment, the four hospitals in NHS shared these resources as necessary.

The rigid endoscopes were often replaced if they needed a significant amount of repairs. Total spending by Wentworth Hospital the previous year on scope repairs was approximately $90,000.

ORIGINAL EQUIPMENT MANUFACTURERS

NHS bought and serviced all of their scopes from Robinson Surgical Products (Robinson) and Padzik Medical (Padzik). In selecting Robinson and Padzik, a cross-functional team was created, including representatives from purchasing in NHS shared services, physicians, and the biomedical engineering department. The biomedical engineering department had been responsible for assessing the technical and financial issues in the supplier selection process.

Robinson and Padzik provided endoscopes for use with specific procedures and most of the endoscopes used at Wentworth Hospital were supplied by Robinson based on the type of endoscope used at that hospital. Wentworth Hospital had developed a good relationship with Robinson and spent approximately $180,000 on their products and services annually. The services provided by Robinson included endoscope repairs. Since the original equipment manufacturers controlled the supply of specialized key endoscope components, they frequently were the logical option to provide repair services. There were third-party organizations that provided endoscope repair services, but they were not able to provide a full range of repairs because of difficulty obtaining parts from OEMs on a timely basis. Furthermore, warranties could be voided if the endoscope was repaired by an unapproved service provider. Some manufacturers had developed disposable scopes, but this technology was not viewed as a cost-effective option.

There was concern in the health care industry that the OEMs were charging unreasonable prices for endoscope repairs, and there were also some suspicions that occasionally unnecessary repairs were made. It was difficult to verify repair work since removing the sealed casing on an endoscope required specialized equipment. Furthermore, it often took as long as three weeks for an endoscope to be returned after being sent out for repairs.

IRVINE MEDICAL SERVICES

In mid-October last year, Rebecca was contacted by Steven Bowles, a representative from Irvine Medical Services (Irvine) in Vancouver, British Columbia. Steven met with Rebecca in her office and introduced Irvine as a new player in the endoscope repair industry. He claimed that they could provide repair service for 20 to 80 percent cheaper than the OEMs and provide a 24-hour free estimate and three- to five-day turnaround. Steven stressed that "we only repair what is broken and bill you accordingly."

In January, Rebecca decided to test Irvine's services and she sent them an endoscope that needed repairs. The endoscope was returned after three weeks and it was used 25 times over a four-week period, at which point one of the angulation wires snapped. Rebecca's intention was to send the endoscope back to Irvine for repair; however, it was inadvertently sent to Robinson. A few days later, Neha Khera, the technical representative from Robinson, brought the endoscope to Rebecca's office. The sealed casing had been removed to expose the inside of the endoscope and Rebecca was shocked by what she saw. She found it difficult to believe that anyone would intentionally damage the scope nor could she believe that anyone could be so incompetent as to do such an unprofessional repair job (see Exhibit 1). Neha explained that this is what Rebecca could expect when Robinson scopes were repaired by third-party repair companies.

Joseph Tai was travelling to Vancouver on business the following week and took the endoscope with him and visited Irvine. Steven Bowles was defensive and claimed to have no knowledge of the damage to the scope. After some persistence

by Joseph, Steven allowed him to speak with the technician that performed the repairs on the endoscope. The technician was insulted by Steven's suggestion that he might be responsible for the damage and threatened to resign.

The endoscope was left with Irvine and it took more than a month to be repaired—apparently due to difficulty in getting the necessary parts. When it was finally returned, it was put back in use and an angulation wire snapped during the first procedure.

Shortly thereafter, Rebecca received a strange invoice from Robinson for another endoscope that had been sent for normal repairs. The invoice included a charge for repairs that had resulted, according to Robinson, from a third party attempting to open the endoscope using improper tools.

IN-HOUSE REPAIRS

In November the previous year, Joseph Tai attended a conference organized by the Toronto Health Sciences Network, a consortium of seven hospitals in the Greater Toronto Area. One of the sessions at the conference explained how the Toronto Health Sciences Network had been successful combining their endoscope repair and moving it in-house, resulting in a savings of 40 percent.

Joseph felt that the biomedical engineering department should consider a similar initiative and had asked Rebecca

EXHIBIT 1 **List of Items Damaged on the Repair of the Endoscope**

1. Threaded attachment nut, used to seal the end of the body cover grip, was galled by attempted removal using improper tool.
2. Opening in forward body frame was damaged with the improper removal of an insert.
3. After the seal between the main housing and body cover grip was damaged, glue as used in an unsuccessful attempt to repair the seal.
4. Forward body trim nut to seal the forward body frame cover was also galled by attempting removal using improper tool.
5. The male threads on both the proximal and distal ends of the forward body frame were stripped.
6. An attempted remedy to correct the improper fit of the body cover grip due to stripped threads was to add large quantities of silicone onto the "O" ring.
7. An edge on the UD guide plate was filed down approximately 2 mm for no apparent reason.
8. A brass angulation wire guide was removed, possibly because the threaded mounting holes were stripped.
9. In place of the two missing screws, two new holes were drilled and tapped to secure the UD guide plate.
10. Metal filings from the filed-down section were still found in the housing.
11. A spare screw was found floating in the housing when the housing was opened.
12. Angulation wires appear to have neither been replaced nor repaired.
13. The field service report and accompanying documentation from Irvine did not indicate any difficulties in achieving a suitable repair.

to look into it and make a recommendation. The hospitals in NHS spent approximately $350,000 on endoscope repairs annually. Rebecca determined that there were four levels of service for an in-house repair operation: preventive maintenance, screening and providing repair estimates, minor repairs, and large repairs. Rebecca estimated that 80 percent of repair costs were in the first three levels, and currently the biomedical engineering department performed in the preventive maintenance level only. She was concerned that it would be extremely difficult to move level four repairs in-house due to a lack of technical capabilities. Recently, however, Robinson had been more responsive to assisting its customers with implementing levels 2 and 3.

Neha Khera had indicated that Robinson would supply parts for minor repair work and would provide a list

of the necessary tools, which would cost approximately $15,000. Furthermore, Robinson would provide training for two technicians, at a cost of $3,000. Rebecca felt that the technicians would be capable of performing all the minor repairs for NHS, which would have the advantage of reducing the turnaround time on endoscope repairs from two to three weeks to one or two days.

Rebecca knew that the endoscope repair situation at Wentworth Hospital needed to be resolved soon. Joseph wanted to focus on endoscopes at the monthly team meeting on the 24th, and Rebecca wanted to sort through the issues and make recommendations regarding the Robinson/Irvine matter and the possibility of setting up in-house scope repairs.

Quantity and Inventory

Key Questions for the Supply Decision Maker

Should we

- Change the way we forecast?
- Use vendor-managed inventories?
- Purchase our A items differently?

How can we

- Reduce our investment in supply chain inventories?
- Improve our inventory management?
- Initiate a services consumption management program?

Continuous improvement; speed to market; customer, employee, and supplier satisfaction; and global competitiveness require dedication to productivity and value-adding activities. These organizational goals drive management attitudes to quality, quantity, and delivery, with profound impact on the acquisition process. This is evident in supply management's focus on inventory reduction and shortened lead times. Both can be accomplished by increasing frequency of deliveries, while decreasing the amount delivered at one time. Accompanying efforts in setup time reduction, just-in-time (JIT) systems, vendor-managed inventory systems (VMI), order cost reduction, electronic data interchange (EDI), and e-commerce are all part of the same drive.

Managing the quantity of services acquired is also a supply concern. In many organizations, there are initiatives to standardize, simplify, and categorize services to aggregate demand and manage consumption.

For both goods and services, global events, including the Great Recession, the effects of climate change, and weather-related disasters in regions around the world, have focused supply attention on building resilient supply chains, meaning they have the ability to bounce back quickly and strongly. Likewise, increasing global demand for oil and uncertainty about long-term availability and price have led supply managers to consider slower supply chains that minimize cost and maximize energy efficiencies and to consider bringing back production of some products to the United States (sometimes referred to as "reshoring"). All of these factors influence quantity decisions.

In many organizations, the decisions of how much to purchase and when are made more important by the close relationship between purchase quantity and scheduled use. It is necessary to distinguish between how much to buy in an individual purchase or release and what portion of total requirements to buy from an individual supplier. This chapter deals only with individual order quantities and inventory management; the allotment to suppliers is discussed in Chapters 5, 12, and 13.

Three key questions are addressed in this chapter: (1) How much to acquire? (2) When to acquire? and (3) How to inventory effectively?

QUANTITY AND TIMING ISSUES

The decisions of *how much* to acquire and *when* logically follow clarification of *what* is required. The natural response is to say, "Buy as much as you need when you need it."

Such a simple answer is not sufficient, however. Many factors significantly complicate these decisions.

1. *Forecasts.* Managers must make purchase decisions before, often a long time before, actual requirements are known. Therefore, they must rely on forecasts, not only of future demand, but also of lead times, prices, and other costs. Such forecasts are rarely, if ever, perfect.
2. *Costs.* There are costs associated with placing orders, holding inventory, and running out of materials and goods or having a service be unavailable when it is needed.
3. *Availability.* Materials or services may not be available in the desired quantities without paying a higher price or delivery charge.
4. *Price-Volume Relationship.* Suppliers may offer reduced prices for buying larger quantities.
5. *Shortages.* Shortages may cause serious disruptions.

Quantity and Delivery

Quantity and delivery go hand in hand. Order less, deliver more frequently; order more, deliver less frequently. Every supplier performance evaluation scheme includes quantity and delivery as standard evaluation criteria. To ensure timely delivery, recognition needs to be given to the times required to complete each of the steps in the acquisition process discussed in Chapter 4. The ability to compress these times by doing them in parallel, by eliminating time-consuming and nonvalue-adding activities, by doing steps faster, and by eliminating delays can provide significant benefits. Much of the reengineering work in the supply area has focused on the acquisition process to make it more responsive and to reduce cycle times.

Time-Based Strategies

For the supply management function, the time-based strategies that are of importance in the quantity decision are ones that relate directly to the flow of materials and services, inventories (raw material, work-in-process, and finished goods), and related information and decisions. Competitive advantage accrues to organizations that can:

1. Successfully reduce the time it takes to perform activities in a process (reduce setup and cycle time).
2. Coordinate the flow of resources to eliminate waste in the system and ensure that materials and equipment arrive on time or just-in-time in economically sized batches.

Long lead times can occur in the design and development process, in the material acquisition to distribution of finished goods process, and in administrative support cycles (e.g., accounts payable, purchase order development/release cycle). Some of the causes of long lead times are waiting and procrastination, poorly engineered designs, the accumulation of batches prior to movement, inefficient and long physical flows with backtracking, and poor communication.

Long lead times can impact decisions about *how much* to buy. Compressed cycle times and coordination of material and information flows can result in materials arriving just-*on*-time (e.g., when they were scheduled to arrive) or just-*in*-time (just prior to actual use or need). Material requirements planning–type (MRP) programs or kanban (pull systems) can be used to plan the timing and quantity of purchased materials and internally manufactured materials.

There are many causes for poor material flow coordination, including late, early, or no deliveries; low fill rate; material defects; scrap; uneven batch sizes; long lead times; production schedule changes; downtime; long setup/changeover times; infrequent updates of MRP and/or ERP systems; forecasts; and on-hand inventory accounting systems. Greater coordination of material and information flows both within the buying firm and with its customers and between the buying firm and its suppliers (and their suppliers) can result in lower inventories and improvements in return on assets in the supply chain (see example in Chapter 1).

FORECASTING

Decisions about how much to order, when to order, and how to inventory effectively are also complicated by the rapidly changing environment within which order, inventory and supply planning is carried out. Inventories always seem to be too big, too small, of the wrong type, or in the wrong place. With changing economic conditions, what is too little in one period may easily become too much in the next.

Forecasting is very much a part of the supply management picture and directly affects both quantity and delivery. Forecasts of use, supply, market conditions, technology, price, and so on, are always necessary to make good decisions. The problem is how to plan to meet the needs of the future, which requires answers to questions such as:

- Where should the responsibility for forecasting future usage lie?
  - Should the supply management group be allowed to second-guess sales, production, or user forecasts?
  - Should other supply chain members be involved in a collaborative forecasting effort?
- If the forecast is wrong, who bears the risks?
  - Should suppliers be held responsible for meeting forecasts or actual requirements?
  - Should the supply manager be held responsible for meeting forecasts or actual requirements?
  - When should responsibilities for dealing with the results of inaccurate forecasts be outlined in the contract?
  - What role does negotiation play in resolving these issues?

In many organizations, the need for raw materials, services, parts, and subassemblies is usually derived from a sales forecast, which is the responsibility of marketing. In some service organizations and public agencies, the supply function often must both make forecasts and acquire items. In resale, the buyer may have to assess the expected sales volume (including volumes at reduced prices for seasonal goods), as well as make purchase commitments recognizing seasons. Whatever the situation, missed forecasts are quickly forgotten, but substantial overages or shortages are long remembered. Supply managers are often blamed for overages or shortages no matter who made the original forecast or how bad the forecast was.

Forecasting the consumption of services also may be difficult. Often there are numerous consumption points (for example, through web portals or service desks), and few controls on employee orders. If services spend management is widely dispersed throughout the organization, there may be multiple contracts with the same suppliers as well as multiple suppliers and different coding systems for the same service. In these situations, forecasting aggregate demand is difficult. On the selling side, forecasting service capacity is equally difficult. Many organizations use temporary or freelance labor as a means of mitigating the risks of poor forecasts of the demand for labor-intensive services. This tactic may backfire in a booming job market or if it leads to high turnover or lower-skilled workers than required.

The real problem with forecasts is their unreliability. Forecasts will usually be wrong, but will they exceed or fall short of actual requirements, and by how much? Continuous improvement methods can be applied to forecasting by tracking forecast accuracy and taking steps to eliminate root causes of forecast error.

To a supplier, a substantial variation from forecast may appear as a procurement ploy. If demand falls below forecast, the supplier may suspect that the original forecast was an attempt to obtain a favorable price or other concessions. Should demand exceed forecast, supplier costs may well increase because of overtime, rush buying, and changed production schedules. Purchasers need to share forecast uncertainty regularly with suppliers so that their quotations may take uncertainty into account. Such sharing is obviously impossible if buyers themselves are not aware of the uncertainty and its potential impact on the supplier. Forecasts also should be updated regularly.

Forecasting Techniques

There are many forecasting techniques that have been developed and an extensive literature that describes them. This section will review some briefly but will not describe any technique in detail.

Quantitative Forecasting

This approach uses past data to predict the future. One class of quantitative forecasting techniques, *causal models,* tries to identify leading indicators, from which linear or multiple regression models are developed. A carpet manufacturer might use building permits issued, mortgage rates, apartment and office vacancy rates, and so on, to predict carpet sales. A professional janitorial service might use the same leading indicators to predict demand. Standard computer programs are used to develop and test such models. Chosen indicators are usually believed to cause changes in sales, although even good models do not prove a cause-and-effect relationship. Indicator figures must be available far enough ahead to give a forecast that allows sufficient time for managerial decisions.

A second quantitative forecasting class assumes that sales (or other items to be forecast) follow a repetitive pattern over time. The analyst's job in such *time series forecasting* is to identify the pattern and develop a forecast. The six basic aspects of the pattern are constant value (the fluctuation of data around a constant mean), trend (systematic increase or decrease in the mean over time), seasonal variations, cyclical variations, random variations, and turning points. Time series forecasting techniques include simple moving averages, weighted moving averages, and exponential smoothing. These techniques might be used to forecast demand for tellers in a bank, traffic on a major communication switch, or frozen foods in a big box retailer.

Qualitative Forecasting

One of the most common classes is the *qualitative* approach of gathering opinions from a number of people and using these opinions with a degree of judgment to give a forecast. Market forecasts developed from the estimates of sales staff, district sales managers, and so on are an example. Such forecasts may also flow from the top down. The *Delphi technique* is a formal approach to such forecasting. Collective opinion forecasts lack the rigor of more quantitative techniques but are not necessarily any less accurate. Often, knowledgeable people with intimate market knowledge have a "feel" that is hard to define but that gives good forecasting results.

Collaborative Planning, Forecasting, and Replenishment (CPFR)

Better collaboration between trading partners is recognized as an efficient method for improving forecasts and service and reducing cost. Efforts at collaboration include JITII initiated by Bose, the audio system manufacturer, to co-locate key supplier's personnel at Bose facilities; Efficient Consumer Response (ECR) in the grocery industry, "Quick Response" in the American apparel industry, and vendor-managed inventory (VMI), co-managed inventory (CMI), and joint-managed inventory (JMI) programs between manufacturers and retailers and manufacturers and their suppliers.

CPFR (a trademark of VICS, the Voluntary Interindustry Commerce Solutions Association) is one example of a business practice in which multiple trading partners agree to exchange knowledge and share risks to generate the most accurate forecast possible and develop effective replenishment plans. CPFR links sales and marketing processes to supply chain planning and execution processes. Customers enjoy increased product availability. Partners benefit from increased sales, reduced inventories and cost, and higher service levels. Trading partners agree to mutual business objectives and measures, develop joint sales and operational plans, and electronically collaborate to generate and update sales forecasts and replenishment plans. When changes in demand, promotions, or policy occur, jointly managed forecasts and plans can be adjusted immediately, minimizing or eliminating costly after-the-fact corrections for both parties.

DETERMINING ORDER QUANTITIES AND INVENTORY LEVELS

In the following sections, some relatively simple theoretical models used to determine order quantities and inventory levels are discussed. The application of these models depends on whether the demand or usage of the inventory is dependent or independent.

- *Dependent demand.* The item is part of a larger component or product, and its use is dependent on the production schedule for the larger component. Hence, dependent demand items have a *derived demand.* For example, the demand for bottles and caps by an energy drink manufacturer depends on the number of finished bottles of drink scheduled for production.

- *Independent demand.* The usage of the inventory item is not driven by the production schedule. It is determined directly by customer orders, the arrival of which is independent of production scheduling decisions. The demand for the energy drink is determined by the consumer.

Fixed-Quantity Models

The classic trade-off in determining the lot sizes in which to make or buy cycle inventories is between the costs of carrying extra inventory and the costs of purchasing or making more frequently. The objective of the model is to minimize the total annual costs. In the very simplest form of this model, annual demand (R), lead time (L), price (C), variable order or setup cost (S), and holding cost percentage (K) are all constant now and in the future. When inventory drops to the reorder point (P), a fixed economic order quantity (Q) is ordered. Back orders and stockouts are not allowed.

Total cost is given as purchase cost, plus setup or order cost, plus holding cost, or

$$TC = RC + \frac{RS}{Q} + \frac{QKC}{2}$$

Using differential calculus, the minimum value of Q (also known as the economic order quantity or EOQ) is found at

$$Q_{opt} = \sqrt{\frac{2RS}{KC}}$$

This is the value at which order cost and carrying cost are equal. Figures 8–1 and 8–2 show how costs vary with changes in order size and how inventory levels change over time using

FIGURE 8–1
Material Carrying and Order Costs

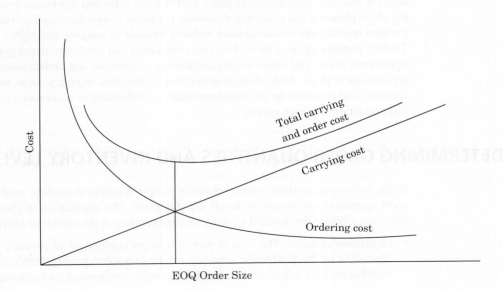

FIGURE 8–2
Simple Fixed Quantity Model

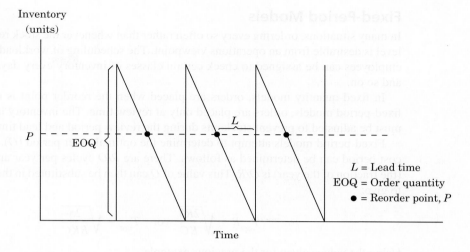

this model. As an example of the use of the model, consider the following:

R = annual demand   = 900 units
C = delivered purchase cost   = \$45/unit
K = annual carrying cost percentage = 25 percent
S = order cost   = \$50/order

$$Q_{opt} = \sqrt{\frac{2RS}{KC}} = \sqrt{\frac{2 \times 900 \times \$50}{.25 \times \$45}} = 89 \text{ units}$$

To determine the reorder point P, it is necessary to know the lead time L, which is 10 working days. Assuming 250 working days per year, the reorder point can be calculated as:

$$P = L \times \text{Daily demand} = L \times \frac{R}{250} = 10 \times \frac{900}{250} = 36 \text{ units}$$

This model suggests an order of 89 units whenever the inventory drops to 36 units. The last unit will be used just as the next order arrives. Average inventory will be 89/2 = 44.5 units. In practice, it might be advisable to keep some safety stock that must be added to the average inventory. Also, the bottom of the total cost curve (see Figure 8–1) is relatively flat (and asymmetric) so that there might be advantages in ordering 96 (eight dozen) or 100 units instead. In this case, these quantities would cost approximately an additional \$2.50 and \$6.25, respectively, out of a total annual cost of about \$41,500. These costs are the additional ordering and carrying costs resulting from the additional units ordered.

The assumptions behind the EOQ model place some rather severe restrictions on its general applicability. Numerous other models have been developed that take into account relaxation of one or more of the assumptions. However, the basic EOQ model is fairly robust and it will provide a reasonable estimate of the economic batch size even if one of the assumptions of the model is violated. The reader may wish to refer to books on inventory management for a more extensive discussion.

Fixed-Period Models

In many situations, ordering every so often rather than whenever the stock reaches a certain level is desirable from an operations viewpoint. The scheduling of workload is easier when employees can be assigned to check certain classes of inventory every day, week, month, and so on.

In fixed-quantity models, orders are placed when the reorder point is reached, but in fixed-period models, orders are placed only at review time. The inventory level, therefore, must be adjusted to prevent stockouts during the review period and lead time.

Fixed-period models attempt to determine the optimal order period (O). The minimum cost period can be determined as follows. There are R/O cycles per year and, therefore, T (the fraction of the year) is O/R. This value of O can then be substituted in the EOQ formula to give:

$$T_{opt}R = \sqrt{\frac{2RS}{KC}} \quad \text{or} \quad T_{opt} = \sqrt{\frac{2S}{RKC}}$$

Using the values given for the previous example:

$$T_{opt} = \sqrt{\frac{2 \times 50}{900 \times 0.25 \times 45}} = 0.1 \quad \text{or,} \quad 10 \text{ times per year}$$

For a year of 250 working days, this is 25 working days, or once every five weeks. The optimum order quantity, EOQ, is RT_{opt} or 90 units. This is the same result as before. Organizational procedures may make a review every four weeks or monthly more attractive. In this case, T would change to 0.08 and O to 72 at an additional cost of $23.77 per year over the optimum value.

Probabilistic Models and Service Coverage

The aforementioned models assume that all parameters are known absolutely and do not change over time. It is far more common to have some variability in demand, lead times, supply, and so on. Probabilistic lot size models take these variations into account. The models are more complex than the deterministic ones above, but the probabilistic approach gives more information on likely outcomes.

Buffer or Safety Stocks and Service Levels

For buffer or safety stocks, the major decision variable is how much buffer inventory to carry to give the desired service coverage. The service coverage can be defined as the portion of user requests served. If there are 400 requests for a particular item in a year and 372 were immediately satisfied, the service coverage would be 372/400 = 93 percent.

Service coverage also can be defined as the portion of demand serviced immediately. If the 372 orders in the above example were for one unit each and the 28 other unserviced ones, for five units each, the total yearly demand would be for 372 + 140 = 512 units. The service coverage would be 372/512, or 73 percent. It is obviously important to understand exactly what is meant by service coverage in an organization.

Holding a large inventory to prevent stockouts, and thus to maintain a high service coverage, is expensive. Similarly, a high number of stockouts are costly. Stockout costs are often difficult and expensive to determine but nevertheless real. Setting service coverage requires managers to make explicit evaluations of these costs so that the appropriate balance between carrying and stockout can be achieved.

Trade-offs between holding inventory and stocking out can be assessed quantitatively if accurate data are available, such as inventory holding costs, stockout costs, and demand or supply variability. However, because of the expense and difficulty of obtaining such costs and probability estimates for individual items, managers often set service coverage arbitrarily, typically about 95 percent, implying a ratio of stockout to holding costs of about 19 to 1.

In practice, setting and managing service coverage is difficult because of the complexity of item classification, function, and interdependence. Service coverage need not be as high on some items as on others, but an item that may be relatively unimportant to one customer may be crucial to another. If the customer is an assembly line, low service coverage on one component makes higher service coverage on others unnecessary. Also, some customers will tolerate much lower service coverage than will others. Within an organization, internal departments are sometimes regarded as customers, and service coverage attained is one measure of supply management's effectiveness. It is useful to stress that service coverage and inventory investment are closely related. It becomes expensive to achieve high service coverage, and a high service coverage expectation without the necessary financial backup can lead only to frustration. Supply is, of course, also interested in service coverage as it pertains to supplier performance.

Service coverage can be used to determine the appropriate level of buffer inventory. The situation is shown in Figures 8–3 and 8–4. Four situations can arise as shown from left to right in Figure 8–3.

1. Only some of the buffer inventory was used.
2. No buffer inventory remained, but there was no stockout.

FIGURE 8–3
Fixed-Order-Quantity Model Buffer Inventory and Variation in Demand

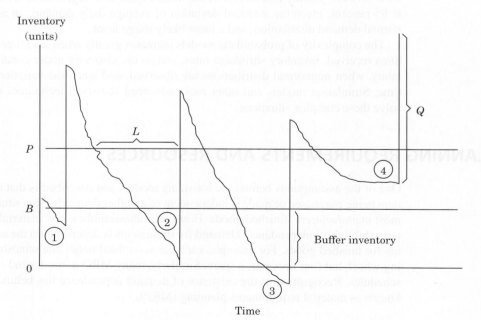

FIGURE 8–4
Determination
of Buffer
Inventory
to Achieve
Desired
Coverage

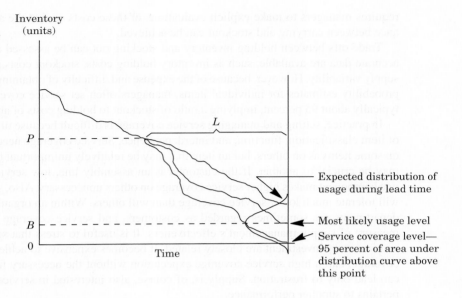

Inventory (units)

Expected distribution of usage during lead time

Most likely usage level

Service coverage level—95 percent of area under distribution curve above this point

3. There was a stockout.

4. All the buffer inventory remained.

Figure 8–4 starts with an EOQ model except that it is not certain how many units will be used between placing and receipt of an order. Figure 8–4 targets desired service coverage at 95 percent, given the standard deviation of average daily demand, an assumption of a normal demand distribution, and a most likely usage level.

The complexity of probabilistic models increases greatly when lead times, usable quantities received, inventory shrinkage rates, and so on, also vary under conditions of uncertainty, when nonnormal distributions are observed, and when the variations change with time. Simulation models and other more advanced statistical techniques can be used to solve these complex situations.

PLANNING REQUIREMENTS AND RESOURCES

One of the assumptions behind the lot-sizing models just described is that demand for the item being purchased or made is independent of all other demands. This situation is true for most manufacturers' finished goods. However, subassemblies, raw materials, and parts do not exhibit this independence. Demand for these items is dependent on the assembly schedule for finished goods. For example, each car assembled needs one windshield, one steering wheel, but four tires plus a spare. Similarly, many MRO items depend on maintenance schedules. Recognition of the existence of demand dependence lies behind the technique known as material requirements planning (MRP).

Material Requirements Planning (MRP)

MRP systems attempt to support the activities of manufacturing, maintenance, or use by meeting the needs of the master schedule. To determine needs, MRP systems need an accurate bill of materials for each final product or project. These bills can take many forms, but it is conceptually advantageous to view them as structural trees.

Not all organizations have been successful in implementing MRP systems. Implementation may take years and involve major investments in training, data preparation, and organizational adjustments as well as in computer software and hardware. However, most organizations with successfully implemented systems feel that the reduced inventory, lead times, split orders, and expediting; increased delivery promises met; and discipline resulting from MRP make the investment worthwhile. MRP systems allow rapid replanning and rescheduling in response to the changes of a dynamic environment.

MRP Inputs

There are three basic MRP inputs.

1. **Master production schedule.** The whole system is driven by the requirements forecast by time period (the master production schedule), which details how many end items are to be produced during a specified time period.
2. **Structured bill of materials (BOM).** The BOM uses information from the engineering and/or process records to detail the subcomponents necessary to manufacture one finished item.
3. **Inventory record.** This contains information such as open orders, lead times, and lot-size policy so that the quantity and timing of orders can be calculated.

The logic of MRP allows simultaneous determination of how much and when to order. The calculations hinge on the assumptions that all information is accurate and known with certainty and that material will be ordered as required. MRP systems can help production meet schedules, avoid equipment downtime, adjust to order quantity changes, and identify the need to expedite late orders.

MRP Lot Sizing

Lot-sizing rules must be assigned to each item before the MRP plan can be computed. The selection of a lot-sizing rule is important because it affects inventory holding costs and operations costs, such as setup costs.

The four basic lot-sizing rules are (1) lot-for-lot (L4L), (2) economic order quantity (EOQ), (3) least total cost (LTC), and (4) least unit cost (LUC).

1. **Lot-for-lot.** This is the most common technique. It does not take into account setup costs, carrying costs, or capacity limitations. Lot sizing is based on producing net requirements for each period.
2. **Economic order quantity (EOQ).** The EOQ lot-sizing technique balances inventory holding and setup (or order) costs. It uses the EOQ formula to set lot sizes, which requires estimates for annual demand, inventory holding costs, and setup (or order) costs.

3. **Least-total-cost (LTC).** The least-total-cost method compares the cost implications of various lot-sizing alternatives and selects the lot size that provides the least total cost. The LTC method is a dynamic lot-sizing technique.

4. **Least-unit-cost.** The least-unit-cost method is also a dynamic lot-sizing method. It factors inventory holding and setup (or order) costs into the unit cost.

Lot sizing is a difficult issue when using MRP. Because most lost-sizing techniques require cost and annual demand information, accuracy of the data used will determine the effectiveness of the decisions made.

MRP systems were designed for "push" systems where companies produced based on a forecast and then "pushed" the products on the market. In today's volatile global economy, "pull" systems produce based on real-time customer demand. MRP systems typically lack the agility to replenish global supply networks. This leads to chronic and frequent shortages in procurement, production, and fulfillment cycles. Demand-driven MRP is the next generation of MRP logic. Despite this effort, some lean and theory of constraints (TOC) implementations advocate removal of the formal MRP system.

Capacity Requirements Planning (CRP)

With advances in information systems technology, a number of improvements have been made to MRP systems that can help managers with planning and coordinating production and supply. One significant advance in MRP systems has been the addition of capacity requirements planning (CRP).

Capacity is how much work can be done in a set amount of time. CRP performs a similar function for manufacturing resources that MRP performs for materials. When the MRP system has developed a materials plan, CRP translates the plan into the required human and machine resources by workstation and time bucket. It then compares the required resources against a file of available resources. If insufficient capacity exists, the manager must adjust either the capacity or the master production schedule. This feedback loop to the master production schedule results in the term *closed-loop MRP* to describe this development.

The CRP module is often linked to a module that controls the manufacturing plan on the shop floor. The goal is to measure output by work center against the previously determined plan. This information allows identification of trouble spots and is necessary on an ongoing basis for capacity planning.

Manufacturing Resource Planning (MRP II)

MRP II links the firm's planning processes with the financial system. MRP II systems combine the capability of "what if" production scenario testing with financial and cash flow projections to help achieve the sales and profitability objectives of the firm.

Demand Driven MRP

The third edition of Orlicky's MRP book was published in 2011, called *Demand Driven MRP* (DDMRP), written by Carol Ptak and Chad Smith (Orlicky died in 1986). DDMRP revisits traditional MRP and adopts a multi-echelon demand and supply planning and execution approach with five key components: strategic inventory positioning, buffer profile and levels, dynamic adjustments, demand driven planning, and visible collaborative execution.[1]

DDMRP is best suited for manufacturing firms and combines aspects of traditional MRP, lean, and theory of constraints. Demand is driven largely by customer demand and the supply chain modeling process of DDMRP allows users to optimize inventory levels, determining where and when inventory should be held. The advantages of DDMRP include improved service levels while simultaneously reducing inventory levels.

Enterprise Resource Planning (ERP) Systems

Many companies use ERP systems, which include MRP modules, to integrate business systems and processes. ERP systems are software that allow all areas of the company—manufacturing, finance, sales, marketing, human resources, and supply—to combine and analyze information. ERP can provide a link from customer orders through the fulfillment processes. Therefore, fully implemented ERP systems allow supply to be aware of orders received by sales, manufacturing to be aware of raw material delivery status, sales to understand product or service lead times and availability, and financial transactions and commitments to be communicated directly into the financial accounting system. A thorough discussion of ERP and supply information systems is provided in Chapter 4.

Consequently, a modern MRP system is thus a lot more than simply a device to calculate how much material to obtain and when to do so. It is an information and communication system that encompasses all facets of the organization. It provides managers with performance measures, planned order releases (purchase orders, shop orders, and rescheduling notices), and the ability to simulate a master production schedule in response to proposed changes in production loading (for example, by a new order, delayed materials, a broken machine, or an ill worker). The integration required of such systems forces organizations to maintain highly accurate information, abandon rules of thumb, and use common data in all departments. The results are reduced inventory levels, higher service coverage, ready access to high-quality information, and, most importantly, the ability to replan quickly in response to unforeseen problems.

Supply Implications of MRP

The tight control required by MRP means that supply records regarding quantities, lead times, bills of material, and specifications must be totally accurate and tightly controlled. The on-time delivery required of MRP needs cooperation from suppliers. Purchasers, therefore, must educate their suppliers to the importance of quantity, quality, and delivery promises to the purchaser. Such education should enable purchasers to reduce their safety stock.

Many MRP systems have purchasing modules that perform many of the routine clerical supply tasks, making supply's job more analytical and strategic. The long-term nature of the MRP planning horizon, typically a year, means longer-term planning for supply and the negotiation of more long-term contracts with annual volume-based discounts. These contracts have more frequent order release and delivery, often in nonstandard lot sizes. Quantity discounts on individual orders become less relevant in favor of on-time delivery of high-quality product.

Purchasers must understand the production processes both of their own organizations and of their suppliers. The tighter nature of MRP-using organizations increases the responsibility of supply to be creative and flexible in providing assistance to minimize the

---

[1] www.demanddrivenmrp.com/, accessed March 3, 2014.

inevitable problems that will occur in supply lines. The MRP system provides purchasers with an information window to production scheduling so that they are better able to use judgment in dealing with suppliers. Because of the reduced resource slack that results from MRP, purchasers must incorporate deexpediting into their activities as well as the more usual expediting role. The integrating and forward-looking nature of MRP means an increase in specialization in the supply department. For example, the buyer-planner is a person who uses MRP to assure smooth functioning of the interface between the purchaser's and supplier's processes. Also, specialization will be based on finished product line outputs rather than on raw material inputs.

In contrast to MRP, just-in-time production methods can achieve many of the goals of MRP in conjunction with MRP or on a stand-alone basis.

FUNCTIONS AND FORMS OF INVENTORIES

Understanding where (and why) inventory should be positioned in the supply chain can improve customer service, lower total costs, or increase flexibility. Proper inventory management requires a thorough understanding of both the functions and the forms of inventory.

The Functions of Inventory

Many purchases cover repetitive items often held in inventory. Thus, inventory policy has a great influence on purchase quantity decisions. The questions of how much to order, when, and how much to carry in stock are key decisions subject to continuous improvement examination along with the focus on quality and customer, employee, and supplier satisfaction. It is important in making delivery, inventory, or purchase order size decisions to understand why inventories exist and what the relevant trade-offs are. Inventories exist for many purposes, including:

- To provide and maintain good customer service.
- To smooth the flow of goods through the productive process.
- To provide protection against the uncertainties of supply and demand.
- To obtain a reasonable utilization of people and equipment.

The following classification of inventory functions reveals the multipurpose roles played by inventories.

Transit or *pipeline inventories* are used to stock the supply and distribution pipelines linking an organization to its suppliers and customers as well as internal transportation points. They exist because of the need to move material from one point to another. Transit inventories are dependent on location and mode of transportation. A decision to use a distant supplier with rail transport will probably create a far larger raw materials transit inventory than a decision to use a local supplier with truck delivery.

In *just-in-time* (JIT) production, a variety of means are used to reduce transit inventories, including the use of local suppliers, small batches in special containers, and trucks specifically designed for side loading in small quantities.

Cycle inventories arise because of management's decision to purchase, produce, or sell in lots rather than individual units or continuously. Cycle inventories accumulate at various points in operating systems. The size of the lot is a trade-off between the cost of holding inventory and the cost of making more frequent orders and/or setups. A mathematical description of this relationship, the economic order quantity, has already been discussed. In JIT, the need for cycle inventories is reduced by setup cost and time reduction.

Buffer or *uncertainty inventories* or *safety stocks* exist as a result of variability in demand or supply. Raw material, purchased parts, or MRO buffer stocks give some protection against the variability of supplier performance due to shutdowns, strikes, lead-time variations, late deliveries to and from the supplier, poor-quality units that cannot be accepted, and so on. Work-in-process buffer inventories protect against machine breakdown, employee illness, and so on. Finished goods buffers protect against unforeseen demand or production failures.

Management efforts to reduce supply variability may have substantial payoffs in reduced inventories. Options may include increasing supply alternatives, using local sources, reducing demand uncertainty, reducing lead time, or having excess capacity. Buffer inventory levels should be determined by balancing carrying cost against stockout cost.

Buying in expectation of major market shortages is a longer time-frame variation of buffer inventory. It may require large sums and top management strategic review. Chapter 10 discusses forward buying more fully.

Another class of buffer stock is that purchased in anticipation, but not certainty, of a price increase. In this case, the trade-off is between extra carrying costs and avoidance of higher purchase cost. This trade-off can be structured as shown in Figure 8–5. Obviously, intermediate levels of price increase and the timing of increases also will be identified. Other buffer stock trade-offs can be structured similarly.

FIGURE 8–5
Decision to Inventory in Anticipation of a Possible Price Increase

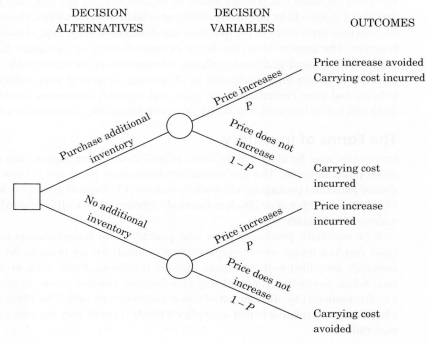

| DECISION ALTERNATIVES | DECISION VARIABLES | OUTCOMES |

Anticipation or *certainty inventories* are accumulated for a well-defined future need. They differ from buffer stocks in that they are committed in the face of certainty and therefore have less risk attached to them. Seasonal inventories are an excellent example. Stocking commodities at harvest time for further processing during the year is a typical example. Reasons for anticipation stocks may include strikes, weather, shortages, or announced price increases.

The managerial decision is considerably easier than with buffer stocks because the certainty of events makes probability estimates unnecessary. Unfortunately, in times of shortages and rapid price increases, organizations may not be able to commit enough funds to meet the clear need for more anticipation stocks. Public organizations working under preestablished budgets may not be able to obtain authorization and funds. Many organizations that are short of working capital may be similarly frustrated.

Decoupling inventories make it possible to carry on activities on each side of a major process linkage point independently of each other. The amounts and locations of raw material, work-in-process, and finished goods decoupling inventories depend on the costs and increased operating flexibility benefits of having them.

All inventories perform a decoupling function, whether they be transit, cycle, buffer, or certainty inventories. When the prime purpose is to decouple, and space and time have been designed into the process to accommodate them, it is appropriate to recognize decoupling inventory as a unique category of its own. It gives flexibility and independence to both parties and is an excellent area for negotiations. Many contracts specify that a supplier maintain a certain finished goods inventory. A finished goods inventory performs a decoupling function between the supplier's manufacturing process and the customers' process.

By examining the functions of inventory, it is clear that they are the result of many interrelated decisions and policies within an organization. At any time, any of the inventory functional types will be physically indistinguishable from the others. Frequently, a particular item may serve many of the functions simultaneously. Why, then, classify inventories by function? The answer lies in the degree of controllability of each class. Some inventories are essentially fixed and uncontrollable, whereas others are controllable. A management directive to reduce total inventories by 20 percent, combined with supply and marketing policies and prior commitments on cycle and seasonal inventories, could reduce decoupling and buffer inventories to nearly zero with potentially disastrous results.

The Forms of Inventory

Inventories may be classified by form as well as function; indeed, this classification is much more common. The five commonly recognized forms are (1) raw materials, purchased parts, and packaging; (2) work-in-process; (3) finished goods; (4) MRO items; and (5) resale items. Scrap or obsolete material, although technically regarded as inventory, is addressed in Chapter 16.

Raw materials, purchased parts, and packaging for manufacturers are stocks of the basic material inputs into the organization's manufacturing process. As labor and other materials are added to these inputs, they are transformed into work-in-process inventories. When production is completed, they become finished goods. In general, the forms are distinguished by the amount of labor and materials added by the organization. The classification is relative in that a supplier's finished goods may become a purchaser's raw materials.

For resource industries, service organizations, and public organizations, MRO inventories may be substantial. In resource industries, a significant portion of such inventory may be maintenance or repair parts to support the heavy capital investment base. In resale organizations, the main categories are goods for resale and inventories to maintain building and equipment. For many consumer goods industries, such as food and beverage, packaging represents a major purchase inventory category with substantial environmental implications.

Inventory Function and Form Framework

Combining the five forms and five functions of manufacturing inventory gives the 25 types of inventory that make up the inventory profile of an organization. They are presented in Figure 8–6 along with some of the managerial decision variables affecting each type. Not all inventory types will be present to the same extent in each organization; indeed, some may be completely absent. The 25 types make inventory control a more complex but a more easily focused task.

The behavior of inventories is a direct result of diverse policies and decisions within an organization. User, finance, production, marketing, and supply decisions can all have crucial influences on stock levels. Long-term fixed marketing or supply policies may render finished goods transit, raw materials transit, and cycle inventories quite inflexible, whereas short-term production scheduling may provide a great amount of flexibility of work-in-process inventories. Long-term supply contracts coupled with falling demand may lead to raw materials accumulation. Effective supply managers must recognize the behavior and controllability of each type of inventory in both the short and long terms. For effective supply management, they must also coordinate the policies and decisions of all functional areas.

Often managers use various informal rules of thumb in their decision making. A common one is turnover in number of times per year. The rule of thumb would dictate that as the use doubles, inventories should also double. However, a closer look must be taken at the components of that inventory.

Cycle inventories, produced in economic order lots (see earlier section), increase proportionally to the square root of demand, so, as demand doubles, cycle inventories should rise by a factor of only about 1.4. Ordering raw materials or storing them may have quite different cost structures from setting up machines, issuing production orders, or storing finished goods.

Transit inventories depend on supply and distribution networks. A change in the distribution system to accommodate extra volume could more than double or even reduce finished goods transit inventory. Anticipation stocks vary with the pattern of demand, not demand itself. Decoupling inventories may remain unchanged. Buffer inventories may increase or decrease in response to demand and supply instabilities. Many of these effects will balance each other out, but the point remains: Rules of thumb are crude ways of controlling inventory levels. Even if they seem to work, managers never know if they are the best available. Any set of rules must be interpreted intelligently and reevaluated and tested periodically.

Companies that have adopted lean supply practices achieve inventory reductions by eliminating the root cause for the purpose of holding the inventory. For example, cycle inventories are brought down by reducing setup times; decoupling inventories are reduced by better planning and better quality; and safety stocks are lowered because of lower supply and/or demand variability, reduced quality problems, or better on-time delivery performance. It is a continuing challenge to search for better ways to control inventories.

FIGURE 8–6 Inventory Forms and Function

Inventory Function	*Raw Materials, Purchased Parts, and Packaging* 1	*Work-in-Process* 2	*Finished Goods* 3	*MRO* 4	*Resale* 5
1 Transit (pipeline)	**Logistics Decisions**				
	Design of supply system, supplier location, transportation mode	Design of layout and materials handling system	Design of plant location and product distribution system	Supplier location, transportation mode, small shipments	Warehouse location, distribution, transportation mode
2 Cycle (EOQ, lots)	**Product/Process Design Decisions**				
	Order size, order cost	Lot size, setup	Distribution costs, lot sizes	OEM or not and order size	Order size and order cost
3 Buffer (uncertainty)	**Management Risk Level Decisions and Uncertainty**				
	Probability distributions of price, supply and stockout, and carrying costs	Probability distributions of machine and product capabilities	Probability distributions of demand and associated carrying and stockout cost	Probability distributions of breakdowns during use	Probability distributions of demand associated with carrying and stockout costs
4 Anticipation (price)	**Price/Availability/Decisions and Uncertainty, Seasonality, Capacity**				
(shortage)	Know future supply and demand price levels	Capacity, production costs of hire, fire, transfer, overtime, idle time, etc.	Demand patterns (seasonal)	Maintenance planning projects	Supply and demand patterns and price levels
5 Decoupling (interdependence)	**Production Control Decisions**				
	Dependence/independence from supplier behavior	Dependence/independence of successive production operations	Dependence/independence from market behavior	Stock at vendor or at user	Stock at vendor or buyer stock

INVENTORY MANAGEMENT

Along with the key decisions of how much and when to order is the question of how to inventory effectively. This is a challenge in most organizations. In this text we address several inventory management tools and techniques, including inventory costing; ABC classification; lean supply, JIT, and kanban systems; and supply chain inventory management.

Costs of Inventories

Because of the high cost of carrying inventory, many systems have been developed to reduce stocks. Japanese manufacturers have spearheaded lean supply chain practices, including just-in-time systems. Nevertheless, it is useful to understand the nature and costs of inventories so that appropriate policies and procedures can be developed for specific organizational needs. North American organizations have begun to rely heavily on material requirements planning systems that have similar goals of reducing inventories wherever possible by having accurate, timely information on all aspects of the users' requirements, thorough coordination of all departments, and rigorous adherence to the system.

For every item carried in inventory, the costs of having it must be less than the costs of not having it. Inventory exists for this reason alone. Inventory costs are real but are not easy to quantify accurately. The relevance of cost elements in a given situation depends on the decisions to be made. Many costs remain fixed when the order size of only one item is doubled, but the same costs may well become variable when 5,000 items are under consideration. The main types of inventory costs are described below.

Carrying, holding, or possession costs include handling charges; the cost of storage facilities or warehouse rentals; the cost of equipment to handle inventory; storage, labor, and operating costs; insurance premiums; breakage; pilferage; obsolescence; taxes; and investment or opportunity costs. In short, any cost associated with having, as opposed to not having, inventory is included.

The cost to carry inventory can be very high. For example, recent estimates of the annual cost to carry production inventory ranged from 25 to 50 percent of the value of the inventory. Many firms do not do a very good job of estimating carrying costs. While there are several methods for calculating inventory carrying costs, the basic elements are (1) capital costs, (2) inventory service costs, (3) storage space costs, and (4) inventory risk costs.

Once the firm has estimated its carrying costs as a percentage of inventory value, annual inventory carrying costs can be calculated as follows:

(carrying cost per year) = (average inventory value)
$$\times \text{ (inventory carrying cost as a \% of inventory value)}$$

Average inventory value = (average inventory in units) $\times$ (material unit cost)

$$CC = Q/2 \times C \times I$$

where

CC = carrying cost per year

Q = order or delivery quantity for the material, in units

C = delivered unit cost of the material

I = inventory carrying cost for the material, as a percentage of inventory value

Ordering or purchase costs include the managerial, clerical, material, telephone, mailing, fax, e-mail, accounting, transportation, inspection, and receiving costs associated with a purchase or production order. What costs would be saved by not ordering or by combining two orders? Header costs are those incurred by identifying and placing an order with a supplier. Line item costs refer to the cost of adding a line to a purchase order. Most orders will involve one header and several line item costs. Electronic data interchange (EDI) and Internet-based ordering systems try to reduce ordering or purchase costs significantly as well as reduce lead time at the same time.

Setup costs refer to all the costs of setting up a production run. Setup costs may be substantial. They include such learning-related factors as early spoilage and low production output until standard rates are achieved as well as the more common considerations, such as setup, employees' wages and other costs, machine downtime, extra tool wear, parts (and equipment) damaged during setup, and so on. Both the purchaser's and supplier's setup costs are relevant. It should be pointed out that the reduction of setup costs and times permits smaller production runs and hence smaller purchaser order quantities and more frequent deliveries, requirements for a just-in-time system.

Stockout costs are the costs of not having the required parts or materials on hand when and where they are needed. They include lost contribution on lost sales (both present and future), changeover costs necessitated by the shortage, substitution of less suitable or more expensive parts or materials, rescheduling and expediting costs, labor and machine idle time, and so on. Often, customer and user goodwill may be affected and occasionally penalties must be paid. The impact of stockouts on customers will vary. In a seller's market, an unsatisfied customer may not be lost as easily as in a buyer's market. In addition, each individual customer will react differently to a shortage.

In many organizations, stockout costs are very difficult to assess accurately. The general perception, however, is that stockout costs are substantial and much larger than carrying costs. Stockout costs, here discussed as they relate to inventory, are similar for late delivery or quantity shortfalls.

Variations in delivered costs are costs associated with purchasing in quantities or at times when prices or delivery costs are higher than at other quantities or times. Suppliers often offer items in larger quantities or at certain times of the year at price and transportation discounts. Purchases in small quantities or at other times may result in higher purchase and transportation costs, but buying in larger quantities may result in significantly higher holding costs. The quantity discount problem will be discussed in Chapter 10.

Many inventory costs may be hard to identify, collect, and measure. One can try to trace the individual costs attributable to individual items and use them in decision making. Usually such costs will be applicable to a broader class of items. A second approach is to forecast the impact of a major change in inventory systems on various cost centers. For example, what will be the impact on stores of a switch to systems contracting or vendor-managed inventories for some low-value items? Or what would be the impact of a just-in-time system on price, carrying, ordering, and stockout costs? Because most inventory models are based on balancing carrying, order, and stockout costs to obtain an optimal order and inventory size, the quality and availability of cost data are important considerations.

ABC Classification

A widely used classification of both purchases and inventories is based on monetary value. In the 19th century, the Italian economist Vilfredo Pareto observed that, regardless of the country studied, a small portion of the population controlled most of the wealth. This observation led to the Pareto curve, whose general principles hold in a wide range of situations. In materials management, for example, the Pareto curve usually holds for items purchased, number of suppliers, items held in inventory, and many other aspects. The Pareto curve is often called the 80-20 rule or, more usefully, ABC analysis, which results in three classes, A, B, and C, as follows when applied to inventory:

Class	Percentage of Total Items in Inventory	Percentage of Total Dollars Tied Up in Inventory
A	10	70–80
B	10–20	10–15
C	70–80	10–20

These percentages may vary somewhat from organization to organization, and some organizations may use more classes. The principle of separation is very powerful in materials management because it allows concentration of management efforts in the areas of highest payoff. For example, a manufacturer with total annual purchases or spend of $30.4 million had the following breakdown:

Number of Items	Percentage of Items	Annual Purchase Value	Percentage Annual Purchase Volume	Class
1,095	10.0%	$21,600,000	71.1%	A
2,168	19.9	5,900,000	19.4	B
7,660	70.1	2,900,000	9.5	C
10,923	100%	$30,400,000	100%	

A similar analysis of the organization's inventories would be expected to show a similarly high portion of total value from a relatively small number of items.

Purchase value is a combination of unit price and number of units, so it is not sufficient to classify either high-priced or high-unit-volume items as As on that basis alone. Annual value (Unit value × Annual value = Total annual value) must be calculated and a classification into three groups on this basis is a good starting point (see Figure 8–7).

How can a supply manager use such a classification? Far more managerial time and effort should be spent on A and B items than on C items. Because supply assurance and availability are usually equally important for all items, it is common to manage C items by carrying inventories, by concentrating a wide variety of requirements with one or a few suppliers, by arranging stockless buying agreements or systems contracting, by using procurement cards, by buying from e-catalogs, and by reviewing the items infrequently. These techniques reduce documentation and managerial effort (for most items) but maintain high service coverage.

FIGURE 8–7
ABC
Classification
of Inventory

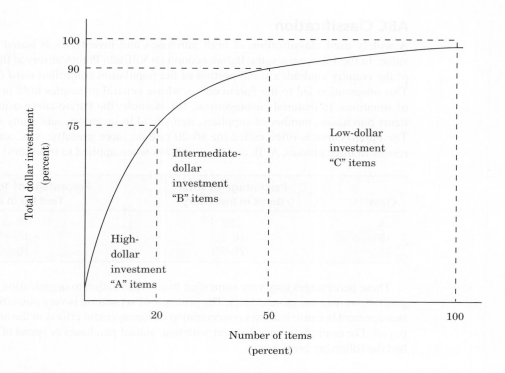

A items are particularly critical in financial terms and are, therefore, barring other considerations, normally carried in small quantities and ordered and reviewed frequently. B items fall between the A and C categories and are well suited to a systematic approach with less frequent reviews than A items. It should be noted that some B or C items may require A care because of their special nature, supply risk, or other considerations.

Vendor- or Supplier-Managed Inventory (VMI/SMI)

Supplier- or vendor-managed inventory, systems contracting, or stockless buying is a more sophisticated merging of the ordering and inventory functions than blanket contracts. Systems contracts rely on periodic billing procedures; allow nonpurchasing personnel to issue order releases; employ special catalogs; require suppliers to maintain minimum inventory levels, but normally do not specify the volume of contract items a buyer must buy; and improve inventory turnover rates.

This technique has been used most frequently in buying stationery and office supplies, repetitive items, and maintenance, repair and operating supplies (MRO). This latter class of purchases is characterized by many different types of items, all of comparatively low value and needed immediately when any kind of a plant or equipment failure occurs. The technique is built around a blanket-type contract that is developed in great detail regarding approximate quantities to be used in specified time periods, prices, provisions for adjusting prices, procedures to be followed in picking up requisitions daily and making delivery within a short time (normally 24 hours), simplified billing procedures, and a complete catalog of all items covered by the contract.

Generally the inventory of all items covered by a contract is stored by the supplier, thus eliminating the buyer's investment in inventory and space. Requisitions for items covered by the contract go directly to the supplier and are not processed by the purchasing department. The requisition is used by the supplier to pull stock, to pack, to invoice, and as a delivery slip. The streamlined procedure reduces paper-handling costs for the buyer and the seller and has been a help in solving the small-order problem.

Jointly managed inventory (JMI) is an extension of VMI in which the supplier and customer map out a more detailed business process and increase involvement in sales and order forecasting and in generating replenishment orders. The supplier may be more integrated into the customer's point of sale (POS) system and have access to real-time sales data.

Lean Supply, Just-in-Time (JIT), and Kanban Systems

Lean thinking is a management philosophy focused on creating value for the customer while eliminating seven forms of waste or nonvalue-adding activities:

1. Overproduction.
2. Waiting, time in queue.
3. Transportation.
4. Nonvalue-adding processes.
5. Inventory.
6. Motion.
7. Costs of quality: scrap, rework, and inspection.

Lean Supply

Lean supply is an approach in which relationships with suppliers are managed based on a long-term perspective to eliminate waste and add value. It is based on Japanese manufacturing concepts pioneered by Toyota. Lean systems have been adopted in many organizations, including high-tech companies like Apple, grocery retailers like Tesco, online distributors like Amazon, and health care providers like the Mayo Clinic. However, the Toyota production system is generally recognized as the best model of lean operations. Lean thinking was discussed in Chapter 7, "Quality". Lean tools such as just-in-time (JIT) and kanban systems that focus on eliminating waste cannot work unless quality levels are attained consistently. Decisions about quality and quantity of goods and services are inextricably linked.

Just-in-Time (JIT)

The most popular system that incorporates the lean philosophy is *just-in-time (JIT)*. Under a JIT system, components, raw materials, and services arrive at work centers exactly as they are needed. This feature greatly reduces queues of work-in-process inventory. The goals of JIT production are similar to those of MRP—providing the right part at the right place at the right time—but the ways of achieving these goals are radically different and the results impressive. Whereas MRP is computer based, JIT is industrial engineering based. JIT focuses on waste elimination in the supply chain, and there are many JIT features that are good practice in any operation, public or private, manufacturing or nonmanufacturing.

In JIT, product design begins with two key questions:

- Will it sell? and
- Can it be made easily?

These questions imply cooperation between marketing and operations. Once these questions have been answered positively, attention turns to design of the process itself. The emphasis is on laying out the machines so that production will follow a smooth flow. Automation (often simple) of both production and materials handling is incorporated wherever possible. Frequently, U-shaped lines are used, which facilitate teamwork, worker flexibility, rework, passage through the plant, and material and tool handling. In process design, designers strive to standardize cycle times and to run a constant product mix, based on the monthly production plan, through the system. This practice makes the production process repetitive for at least a month.

The ability to smooth production implies very low setup and order costs to allow the very small lot sizes, ideally one. JIT treats setup and order costs as variable rather than as the fixed costs implied by the EOQ equation. By continuously seeking ways to reduce setup times, the Japanese were the first to have managed impressive gains. Setups, which traditionally required three to four hours, have been reduced to less than a minute in some JIT facilities.

These dramatic improvements have been achieved by managerial attention to detail on the shop floor; the development and modification of special jigs, fixtures, tools, and machines; and thorough methods training. Setup simplification is aided by the willingness to modify purchased machines, acquire machines from only a few sources, and frequent manufacture of machines in-house—often special purpose, light, simple, and inexpensive enough to become a dedicated part of the process. Order costs, conceptually similar to setup costs, have similarly been reduced.

One of the necessary corollaries of having components and materials arrive just as they are needed is that the arriving items must be perfect. In JIT, a number of interrelated principles are used to ensure high-quality output from each step in the production process.

1. **Worker responsibility.** Responsibility for quality rests with the maker of a part, not with the quality control department. In addition, workers and managers habitually seek improvement of the status quo, striving for perfection. Quality improvements are often obtained from special projects with defined goals, time frames, and measures of achievement. Also, workers are responsible for correcting their own errors, doing rework, and so on.

2. **Build-in quality.** The use of production workers instead of quality control inspectors builds quality in rather than inspecting it in. This feature and the small lot sizes allow every process to be controlled closely and permit inspection of every piece of output. Workers have authority to stop the production line when quality problems arise. This aspect signifies that quality is a more important goal of the production system than output.

3. **Compliance to quality standards.** JIT insists on compliance to quality standards. Purchasers reject marginally unacceptable items and visit supplier plants to check quality on the shop floor for themselves. Because such visits are frequent, JIT manufacturers document their quality in easily understood terms and post the results in prominent places. This process forces the manufacturer to define quality precisely.

JIT control of quality is helped by the small lot sizes that prevent the buildup of large lots of bad items. JIT tends to have excess production capacity so that the plants are not stressed to produce the required quantities. Similarly, machines are maintained and checked regularly and run no faster than the recommended rates. Plant housekeeping is generally good. The quality control department acts as a quality facilitator for production personnel and suppliers, giving advice in problem solving. This department also does some testing, but the tests tend to be on final products not easily assignable to a single production worker, or special tests requiring special equipment, facilities, knowledge, or time not available to personnel on the shop floor. Automatic checking devices are used wherever possible. Where necessary, sample lots are chosen to consist of the first and last units produced rather than a larger, random sample. Analytical tools include the standard statistical techniques, often known by workers, and cause-and-effect diagrams to help solve problems.

JIT requires great dedication by both workers and managers to hard work and helping the organization. JIT workers must be flexible. They are trained to do several different jobs and are moved around frequently. The workers are responsible for quality and output. Workers continuously seek ways to improve all facets of operations and are rewarded for finding problems that can then be solved.

In summary, JIT is a mixture of a high-quality working environment, excellent industrial engineering practice, and a healthy focused factory attitude that operations are strategically important. The order and discipline are achieved through management effort to develop streamlined plant configurations that remove variability. The JIT system has often been described as one that "pulls" material through the factory rather than pushing it through. The use of a kanban system as a control device illustrates this point well.

Kanban Control Systems

Kanban is a simple but effective control system that helps make JIT production work. Kanban is not synonymous with JIT, although the term is often incorrectly so used and the two are closely related. *Kanban* is Japanese for *"card"*; the use of cards is central to many Japanese control systems, including the one at Toyota, whose kanban system has received much attention.

Kanban systems require the small lot size features of JIT and discrete production units. The systems are most useful for high-volume parts used on a regular basis. They are much less useful for expensive or large items that cost a lot to store or carry, for infrequently or irregularly used items, or for process industries that don't produce in discrete units.

Two types of kanban systems exist: single card and double card. In double-card systems, two types of cards (kanban) exist: conveyance (C-kanban) and production (P-kanban). Single-card systems use only the C-kanban. The two-card system's operation uses the following rules.

1. No parts may be made unless there is a P-kanban authorizing production. Workers may do maintenance, cleaning, or work on improvement projects until a P-kanban arrives rather than making parts not yet asked for. Similarly, C-kanban controls the transport of parts between departments.

2. Only standard containers may be used, and they are always filled with the prescribed small quantity.

3. There is precisely one C-kanban and one P-kanban per container.

The system is driven by the user department pulling material through the system by the use of kanban. The main managerial tools in this system are the container size and the number of containers (and therefore kanban) in the system. The control is very precise, flexible, and responsive. It prevents an unwanted buildup of inventory. For example, the actual assembly of parts into a complete finished product provides the "pull" for more parts to be produced.

JIT and Inventory Management

Inventories often exist to cover up problems in supply or inside the organization. For example, a buffer inventory can protect a user from poor quality or unreliable delivery from a marginal supplier. In JIT, the deliberate lowering of inventory levels to uncover such malpractices forces an organization to identify and solve the underlying problems or causes for high and undesirable inventories. This deliberate inventory reduction is often seen by some managers as a form of organizational suicide, a willingness to put continuity of supply, service, or operation at risk. However, enough organizations have experimented with this concept (and survived) to show the merits of this practice. Diagrammatically, the lowering of inventory levels is frequently shown as a seascape of inventory with sharp rocks of different heights underneath, representing the problems or malpractices that need to be exposed sequentially.

JIT Implications for Supply Management

JIT has become sufficiently entrenched as a concept that its applicability is not in question, only the extent to which it should be applied. Many companies are working closely with their suppliers to implement JIT.

There are a number of implications of JIT for supply management. First, suppliers must deliver high and consistent quality and with reliable delivery. This implies that concentrating purchases with fewer nearby suppliers may be necessary. The frequent delivery of small orders may require a rethinking of the inbound transportation mode. For example, it is normal to have a trucker in a specially designed side-loading vehicle follow a standard route daily to pick up small lots from 6 to 20 different suppliers. Delivering directly to the place of use eliminates double handling. Special moving racks designed for proper protection, ease of counting, insertion, and removal also help improve material handling. A lot of supplier training and cooperation is required to assist in the design and operation of an effective JIT system.

In the minimum sense, JIT can refer to arranging for delivery just before a requirement is needed. In this context, JIT has wide applicability beyond manufacturing—in public, service, and other nonmanufacturing organizations. Reliability of delivery reduces the need for buffer or safety stock, with the benefits that arise out of such inventory reduction.

In JIT there is a close cooperation between supplier and purchaser to solve problems, and suppliers and customers have stable, long-term relationships. In keeping with the JIT philosophy, suppliers, usually few in number, are often located close to their customers to facilitate communication, on-time delivery of small lots of parts, low pipeline and safety stocks, and low supply costs. The situation in many JIT companies is much like extensive backward vertical integration. The organizations have close coordination and systems integration that smooth operations. The job of a purchaser in the JIT environment is that of a facilitator, negotiator, communicator, and innovator.

Managing Supply Chain Inventories

Decisions regarding what inventory to have in the supply chain and where to have it have important implications for customer service, working capital commitments, and ultimately profitability. Companies such as Dell, Walmart, and Hewlett-Packard have demonstrated the opportunities to combine lean supply chains with high levels of customer service.

They have also demonstrated that supply chains are dynamic. HP embarked on a supply chain optimization initiative to streamline, simplify, and standardize procurement and product design, physical network and logistics, services and warranty, and process and IT applications. Dell and Walmart have worked to transform their supply chains after experiencing market setbacks. When Dell entered the retail market, it developed four supply chains—build-to-order for online, build-to-stock for popular products sold online, build-to-plan for retail, and build-to-spec for corporate clients. To reduce complexity and exploit economies of scale, it focuses on synergies in five areas: procurement, product design, manufacturing, planning, and order fulfillment.[2] Walmart's global expansion of physical stores and its cost-cutting strategy led to large stockouts in 2013 because of too few employees. It has also lagged in developing an efficient e-fulfillment network to compete with Amazon, the world's largest online retailer.

Supply chain inventory management involves managing information flows and establishing operational design of the physical flow of the goods and services. Managing information flows with supply chain partners is not an easy task. While information technology can be used to link customers quickly and efficiently, firms are frequently required to make major investments in new systems to ensure compatibility. (See Chapter 4 for a more detailed examination of information systems and information technology issues in supply chain management.)

However, coordinating information technology standards and software compatibility is just part of the challenge. Because most suppliers frequently deal with multiple customers, as opposed to focusing on a dominant downstream supply chain partner, issues relating to confidentiality must be addressed, affecting what information should be shared and when it should be communicated.

Operational design issues relate to production and fulfillment activities and can affect performance factors such as lead times, quality, and lot sizes. For example, flexible manufacturing processes that can respond quickly to customer orders may allow reductions in safety stock. Identifying appropriate modes of transportation is also important. Rail may provide the lowest cost, but trucking provides faster door-to-door service and opportunities to reduce transit inventories.

Finally, inventory fulfillment policies should take into account market conditions and the impact on supplier operations. Broad policies such as "We keep four weeks of inventory for all A items" ignores variability of demand or supply for product groups or families. It may be necessary to develop inventory level decision rules within group classifications to ensure that appropriate stocks are maintained.

Order policies based on percentage of total demand can lead to large fluctuations in demand from the retailer up the supply chain through the wholesaler, distributor, manufacturer, and raw materials supplier. This is known as the "bullwhip effect." It can be addressed by sharing actual consumer demand with suppliers so that they can plan production and have appropriate inventory available while keeping their costs low.

[2] D. Simchi-Levi, A. Clayton, and B. Raven, "When One Size Does Not Fit All," *MIT Sloan Management Review*, Winter 2013.

DETERMINING QUANTITY OF SERVICES

So far this chapter has addressed quantity decisions about tangible goods. Buyers of services also make decisions about how much of a service to acquire, when to acquire, and how to assure delivery of the specified services.

Aggregating Demand

As discussed in the forecasting section, forecasting aggregate demand for services is often more unreliable than forecasting demand for goods. Multiple users, specifiers, order placers, and supplier relationship managers often leads to multiple contracts at varying prices and terms with the same supplier. In these situations, organizationwide consumption management is impossible. This approach also challenges suppliers who must determine capacity requirements and project utilization rates.

Historically, supply has had a low involvement in managing services spend. Currently, two approaches to better management of services spend are evident. One, bring the services categories under the umbrella of supply management. Two, take professional buying tools and techniques to the users/consumers of services who have typically purchased services for themselves. Cooperative working relationships among buyers, users, and suppliers of services lead to clarity about requirements, consumption patterns, and opportunities to reduce costs and improve performance.

Managing Consumption

Managing consumption of services is a challenge in many organizations. When management first attempts to consolidate services spend for a particular category, it may take more time and human resources than anticipated just to make a reasonable estimate of aggregated demand by spend category. This task is complicated by widely geographically dispersed business units and local diversity. Nowhere is the tension between user desire for customization and buyer's goal of standardization and simplification more evident than the services spend.

Dimensions of Services and Quantity Decisions

The dimensions of services quality discussed in Chapter 7 can also be applied to discussions about quantity of services to acquire. These are degree of tangibility, direction of the service, production of the service, nature of demand, degree of standardization, and skills required.

Degree of Tangibility

Decisions about how much to order and when to order are influenced by the degree of tangibility. For a highly intangible service such as management consulting, the quantity decisions may be focused on how many people need to be on the consulting team, what qualifications they must have, and how long they need to be available. Determining the length of a project may be difficult for both buyer and seller, complicating the ability of the supplier to commit specific human resources to the project for its duration. Also, changes inside both organizations may mean changes to personnel in the middle of a project. Loss of personnel in either organization may change the timeline and quality of the service and lead to disagreements about cost. For some projects, such as an IT installation, it may be difficult to accurately predict the length of the project and therefore the quantity of IT professionals required. Contract terms may exacerbate the situation. Do contract terms reward suppliers for satisfactory installation with incentives for timely completion or do they allow the project time and cost to escalate?

Direction of the Service

When services are directed at people, quantity decisions may be made or heavily influenced by the special needs of those most affected by the service. The ultimate user (consumer of the service) likely will play a major role in the specification of the service. When services are directed at buildings or equipment, quantity decisions may be more impersonal, but in many cases humans are still affected by the decision. Consumption management efforts in any case may be met with resistance internally.

Production of the Service

Services can be produced by people or equipment, or a combination of both. For services with a high capital or asset component, potential suppliers can be assessed on asset capacity and availability as well as the state of their technology. For example, does a venue have adequate space for the number of people expected to attend each event at a multiday conference? For services with high labor intensity, a supplier's capacity and availability of people with the specified qualifications is the primary quantity concern.

Nature of the Demand

The demand for a particular service may be continuous, periodic, or discrete.

Continuous service: Insurance or a 365/24/7 around-the-clock security service or technical support.

Discrete or one-shot service: An interior decorator to suggest a new color scheme for an office complex.

Periodic service: May be regular, such as once a week or once a month, as with regular inspections, or it may vary with need, as in repair services.

The quantity of each type of service purchased impacts the price per service transaction and the total cost of ownership of the service. One of the first assessments of services spend is: How much of the service is acquired? In organizations with consumption management initiatives, the next question is: How much of the service provided is unnecessary?

This leads to additional questions and possible answers about the quantity of services required. For example, can a continuous service be reduced to a periodic service without loss of quality and with a cost reduction? Does the organization need technical support available 365 days a year, 24 hours a day, 7 days per week? What are the benefits compared to the costs of this level of service? If the number of times services were requested outside of normal business hours was small, perhaps a different contracting arrangement could be made for these situations such as a higher fee for other times and a flat fee for normal operating times.

Services bundled with goods may be a good place to review the quantity of services purchased. Is the organization paying for services that it never uses? Is there another way to approach this spend category? For example, reducing the number of times floors are waxed per year may be an excellent cost-cutting opportunity, but this must be compared to the impact of a dirtier floor on customers' perceptions of the organization as well as employee perceptions and morale. Scrutiny of quantity of services provided may be an excellent cost-cutting focus.

Degree of Standardization and Skills Required

In some organizations, categories of services have been placed along a continuum from commodity-type standardized services to highly customized ones. This approach allows the buying organization to streamline the acquisition process for services that are highly commoditized and focus more on customized services. In terms of quantity decisions, the internal user/specifier and the commodity manager may then develop standard descriptions of commoditized services and, in effect, assign a stock keeping unit (SKU) to each. A hiring manager can then designate quantities required by SKU much as he would for a good. While it may sound dehumanizing to have an SKU number on your forehead, it is an efficient and effective buying technique with quality and cost implications. Because the human element is critical in many services, users/specifiers may still want to interview candidates with the right SKU to determine best fit with their operation.

With highly customized services, the volume procured clearly has price and cost implications. These must be carefully assessed to ensure that customized services are not overspecified in the same way that buyers must watch out for overspecified goods.

Conclusion

Supply chain effectiveness is dependent on the assurance that quality, quantity, and delivery are consistently perfect. For goods, both quantity and delivery involve lot-sizing and inventory decisions that, in turn, affect costs, productivity, flexibility, and customer satisfaction. For services, both quantity and delivery involve a large "human component" that affects costs, productivity, flexibility, and customer satisfaction. Variability of supply, production, and demand complicate forecasting, planning, and inventory control. Despite differences between goods and services, opportunities exist to apply basic supply management principles to the acquisition of services.

Questions for Review and Discussion

1. Of what interest is ABC analysis?
2. What is a master production schedule and what role does it perform?
3. Why is it expensive to carry inventories?
4. In a typical fast-food operation, identify various forms and functions of inventory. How could total investment in inventories be lowered? What might be the potential consequences?
5. What are buffer inventories?
6. What is a kanban and why is it used?
7. What problems do inaccurate usage forecasts create for buyers? For suppliers?
8. What is the difference between JIT and MRP?
9. Why would anyone prefer to use a fixed-period reordering model over a fixed-quantity one?
10. How does intangibility of services affect quantity decisions?
11. Describe sources of variability in the supply chain. How does variability increase supply chain costs?

References   Bowersox, D.; D. Closs; and M. Bixby Cooper. *Supply Chain Logistics Management.* 4th ed. New York: McGraw-Hill, 2012.

Jacobs, F. R.; W. M. Berry; D. C. Whybark; and T. Vollman. *Manufacturing Planning and Control for Supply Chain Management.* New York: McGraw-Hill Professional, 2011.

Ptak, C., and C. Smith. *Orlicky's Material Requirements Planning,* 3rd ed. New York: McGraw-Hill Professional, 2011.

Krajewski, L. J.; L. P. Ritzman; and M. K. Malhotra. *Operations Management: Processes and Supply Chains.* 10th ed. Upper Saddle River, NJ: Prentice Hall, 2013.

Womack, J. P., and D. T. Jones. "From Lean Production to the Lean Enterprise." *Harvard Business Review* 27, no. 2 (1994), pp. 93–103.

Case 8–1

Lisa Caruso

Lisa Caruso, purchasing manager at Morrison, Inc., was very concerned about the company's stockroom operations. Faulty records, a rash of last-minute rush orders, and interference with production were troubles that she had become aware of since becoming manager nine months earlier. It was Thursday, November 6, and with volumes expecting to increase during the coming months, Lisa wanted to make a proposal to the president during their meeting the following week.

MORRISON, INC.

Morrison Inc., (Morrison) located near Philadelphia, Pennsylvania, manufactured loaders and accessories for the construction industry. Current sales were approximately $50 million. The owner-president of Morrison, David Morrison, was the son of the founder of the business. The company enjoyed an excellent reputation for a well-engineered, high-quality, sturdy product line. Morrison construction equipment was considered a premium brand in the industry, which differentiated itself from the large manufacturers on the basis of quality and reliability.

David Morrison believed in keeping overhead costs down and all aspects of the business as simple as possible. Sales were highly seasonal and cyclical, closely tied to the health of the construction industry. The peak manufacturing period ran between February and September. During this time, the company operated two 10-hour shifts (not including an unpaid 30-minute lunch break) Monday to Thursday, and two eight-hour shifts on Friday. Overtime was occasionally scheduled on weekends.

Most loaders were manufactured to customer order, with six to eight weeks' lead time. About 60 percent of the loaders and accessories (e.g., buckets and forks) were sold through distributors in the northeastern United States and Canada. Normally, distributors and customers did some final assembly themselves.

MANUFACTURING OPERATIONS

The major departments in the plant included the machine shop, fabrication and welding, assembly, and painting. The plant also had a maintenance and repair department, which included a repair parts storage room.

The company employed 140 nonunion hourly workers and 30 staff across six departments: engineering, manufacturing, human resources, accounting and finance, sales, and purchasing. Managers in each department reported directly to the president, but enjoyed a high degree of autonomy.

The company installed an ERP system several years prior, purchased from a local software provider. Purchasing modules in the system included inventory control, purchase orders, shipping and receiving, requisitions, and forecasting, planning, and scheduling. The information systems team reported to the CFO.

PURCHASING AND STORES

Lisa supervised a staff of six people: a buyer, three stockroom clerks, a shipper/receiver, and a materials planner. Total purchases were approximately $28 million. These purchases were received into inventory in one of two ways. Large expensive items, such as chassis, hydraulics, transmissions, steel, and forgings, which represented 83 percent of the dollar value of purchases, were individually inspected, entered into the inventory records, and allocated by job number as they were received. Chassis were stored in the yard until required for assembly. Transmissions and hydraulics were kept in a storage area adjacent to assembly, steel was stored in fabrication and welding, and forgings in the machine shop. A stockroom clerk took inventory counts of all high-value items every Friday.

The remaining items were sent from the receiving dock to the stockroom. This locked area contained 13,000 different parts, including all kinds of nuts and bolts, rubberized parts, gaskets, hoses, lights, and welding and machine shop supplies. It was staffed by three clerks. Normally one clerk worked days from 8:30 a.m. to 5:00 p.m., and another from 5:00 p.m. to 1:30 a.m. The third clerk would work either the first or second shift, depending on how busy it was.

Stores operated on a variation of a min/max system, with total inventory ranging from a low of $1.2 million to a high of $3 million. Order quantities varied on the time of year. In February, March, and April, purchasing paid particular attention to peak season requirements and the possibility of quantity discounts. Near the end of the season, however, Lisa was anxious to avoid carrying excess inventory and would try to order only in sufficient quantities to meet requirements until September. Past usage was used as a guide when determining order quantities.

A TYPICAL DAY'S OPERATION

The first production shift started at 7:00 a.m. The production supervisors, whose employee access cards opened the locked stockroom, collected and distributed trays to the workers, prepared the previous evening, with their parts requirements for the shift. If the tray was not prepared or incomplete, the supervisor would take the necessary items, often without bothering to record the removal in the inventory system.

At 8:30 a.m., the stockroom clerk opened the stores areas, handled requisitions as they arose, and, as time permitted, put away the parts trays from the previous night's shift and began assembly of new parts trays for the sec-

ond shift that day. In addition, the stockroom clerks were required to assemble kits of parts for finished loaders leaving the plant, which would be used by customers or distributors for final assembly. Normally, these kits were required to be available between 3:00 p.m. and 6:00 p.m. As shortages were noted in the stockroom bins, requisitions were completed and sent to the buyer.

All workers were required to return their parts trays to the stockroom at the end of the shift. This allowed unused parts to be returned to inventory and workers were held accountable for parts usage. Workers were also expected to order parts requirements for the following day at the end of their shift. Since it was not always clear what such requirements might be, because progress on the next shift could only be estimated, it was not unusual for workers to over- or under-order parts requirements.

The second production shift started at 5:30 p.m., 30 minutes after the second stockroom shift started. Parts trays were handed out to incoming workers and the stockroom continued the same routine as on the first shift. At 1:30 a.m. the stockroom clerk went off duty, while production continued until 3:30 a.m. The supervisors on the night shift opened the stockroom as required during the absence of the stockroom clerk, and, before locking up the plant at the end of the shift, they returned the parts trays and left lists specifying requirements for the shift the following evening.

PROBLEMS WITH THE CURRENT SYSTEM

Lisa Caruso had observed a variety of problems with the existing process. There were frequent discrepancies between inventory records and actual stockroom bin counts. Since inventory counts were only performed in the stockroom once per year, at audit time, discrepancies were normally only caught when inventory was depleted and the inventory record showed otherwise. Shortages resulted in an unusually large number of rush orders, which forced purchasing to buy parts at high prices, in small quantities, which strained supplier relations. The maintenance clerk occasionally "borrowed" parts for emergency requirements, without informing the stockroom clerks or entering the removal in the inventory system. Supervisors were complaining about how much time they and their workers were wasting on issues related to the stockroom.

Stockroom clerks were complaining about being overworked. They found it difficult keep up with the administrative demands to record inventory removals and process requisitions for replenishment. They were frequently forced to work overtime during the week or on Saturdays to catch up and take inventory of the high value items. However, discovering inventory shortages on Saturdays did little to address production problems for the following week.

Lisa realized that the stockroom problem was creating inefficiencies in the plant and disrupting administrative processes. After a discussion with the plant manager, both agreed to investigate and collect data. In meeting with the supervisors, she found that the average production worker spent two 10-minute periods, normally at the beginning and at the end of each shift, waiting at the stockroom. Lisa also estimated that the company was losing approximately $10,000 a month in higher parts prices, not including expediting costs and the value of capital tied up in loaders and accessories ready to be shipped but delayed due to missing parts.

The average rate of pay for the production workers was $22.00 per hour, not including benefits of approximately 30 percent. Wages of the stockroom clerks were $50,000 per year, plus benefits. Lisa realized that hiring an additional stockroom clerk was one potential solution, but she was concerned that this would not address the inventory control problem and avoid the price premiums due to rush orders. She wondered if there might be a more sensible solution under the circumstances.

In a recent management meeting, David Morrison announced that he expected sales to increase by 15 percent in the upcoming season. Lisa was anxious to resolve the stockroom issue before production began to ramp up in February. Knowing that it would likely take time to implement a solution to the problem, she wanted to get working on it right away.

Case 8–2
Throsel-Teskey Drilling

On Wednesday, June 12, Alison Burkett, purchasing manager at Throsel-Teskey Drilling Inc. (Throsel-Teskey) in Phoenix, Arizona, met with John Dietrich, the company's president. He said: "I am getting pressure from the board to address our inventory variance. It has been more than seven months since the merger, and we are not getting the synergies that we expected from purchasing. I know our sales are slightly higher than we expected, but inventory levels are more than twice what we had forecasted in our budget. Our new shareholder is irate—they expect a 25 percent return on their capital. I need you to come up with a plan that I can share with our board at the meeting here in Phoenix next Thursday." Alison got up from her chair and responded to John, "I will get you a report with my recommendations on Monday, so we can review it before the meeting."

THROSEL-TESKEY DRILLING

Throsel-Teskey was a mining services company that performed diamond drilling for underground and surface exploration. Based in Phoenix, Arizona, the company had more than 600 employees and approximately 145 surface

and underground drilling rigs operating at sites in the United States, Canada, Mexico, and South America. The company's customers were top-tier multinational and junior mining companies involved in the exploration and production of copper, zinc, and gold. Approximately 75 percent of the company's drilling rigs operated at sites in the southwestern United States.

Diamond drilling was required at each stage of mining operations: exploration, development, and production. Diamond core drilling utilized an annular drill bit with an industrial-grade diamond crown to cut a cylindrical core from solid rock. Core samples were extracted and analyzed to provide the mine operator with information about the mineral deposit. Throsel-Teskey paid its drill teams a base rate and an incentive bonus for achieving production targets. Production levels averaged 825 feet per week for each drill team, but varied substantially depending on conditions.

In the previous October, Throsel Drilling Inc. merged with Teskey-Dean Drilling Inc. (Teskey-Dean), which had its head office in Albuquerque, New Mexico. Both companies were approximately the same size with respect to total sales; however, Teskey-Dean specialized in underground drilling while Throsel's focus had been in surface drilling. Jongsma Equity Partners (Jongsma), a Chicago-based private equity firm, which owned Teskey-Dean, led the merger and financing of the transaction. John Dietrich, who had been CEO of Throsel, was appointed the president and CEO of the new company and operations were consolidated at Throsel's facilities located in Phoenix. Although Jongsma controlled Throsel-Teskey, John Dietrich maintained a substantial equity interest in the company.

Increases in commodity prices during the past two years had resulted in substantial increases in demand for drilling services as mining companies expanded output. As a result, Throsel-Teskey was operating at full capacity. John commented about the current market for his company's services: "Our bottlenecks are equipment and people. However, it is easier for me to buy more drilling rigs than to find qualified drillers. The pay is good, but it is hard work and it takes at least a year to get someone fully trained."

PURCHASING AND MATERIALS MANAGEMENT

Alison Burkett headed the purchasing department at Throsel-Teskey and was responsible for sourcing and materials management. She had worked for John in a similar role at Throsel Drilling for approximately three years. Reporting to Alison was Ken Jenner, materials manager, and Emerson Parrish, warehouse manager.

Alison estimated that Throsel-Teskey purchased $25 to $27 million in goods and services each year from approximately 400 suppliers. Major purchase categories—rods and casing, drill bits and reaming shells, wireline and drill parts (collectively referred to as "drilling supplies")—accounted for approximately one-half of the company's total spend. The Phoenix warehouse carried approximately 800 different stock keeping units (SKUs), across a variety of purchase categories, such as drilling supplies, tools, safety supplies, parts and equipment, motors, and hydraulic oil. For example, the company stocked eight different types of rods and five different types of diamond drill bits.

At the time of the merger the company purchased the majority of its drilling supplies from three companies. Subsequently, John and Alison negotiated a strategic sourcing agreement with a supplier, also located in Phoenix, who became the primary supplier for drilling supplies in return for a significant price discount. Implementation of the new sourcing agreement started in April, and the transition was expected to last six months. However, because of specific needs for certain equipment and drilling applications,

Alison expected that it would not be possible to standardize completely with one supplier.

The Phoenix warehouse had been expanded and renovated recently to accommodate the increased volume created by the merger. Shelving, racks, and bins had been added to store inventory. Ken Jenner was responsible for receiving, shipping, and inventory control at the Phoenix warehouse. Since the company's inventory system had not been updated since the merger, he physically reviewed inventory levels in the warehouse each Thursday and provided Alison with a written purchase requisition to replenish stock. In recent months, Alison had noticed that several suppliers were experiencing delivery problems and extending lead times as a direct result of an overall increase in demand for diamond drilling services by mining companies.

Shipments to drilling sites from Phoenix were made on a five-day schedule by an outside transportation service company. Site foremen faxed or e-mailed requests for materials and supplies to Ken two days in advance of the scheduled delivery run to their site. Ken supervised two people whose duties included picking and packing orders for the sites.

Employees were provided open access to the warehouse to obtain materials and supplies. Since several of the drilling sites were within a four hour drive to Phoenix, it was common for a foreman to arrive unexpectedly at the warehouse to pick up supplies.

Emerson Parrish supervised the warehouse in Albuquerque, where the company repaired its drills and equipment. This facility had been the central warehouse for Teskey-Dean prior to the merger.

CURRENT SITUATION

Completing the merger and integrating the two purchasing and materials management organizations had been an exhausting process for Alison and the other members of the organization. The business plan had savings built in from volume discounts and consolidating purchases with a limited number of suppliers. Overall inventories were expected to decline as a result of consolidating inventory management at the Phoenix warehouse. However, since the merger last October, sales had increased by approximately 40 percent while inventory levels had more than doubled from premerger levels of $5.990 million to $12.584 million in May (see Exhibits 1 and 2).

Alison commented on the current situation: "Our focus for the past seven months has been to keep the drill teams running and consolidate inventory in Phoenix. Part of the problem has been that I haven't had time to

EXHIBIT 1
Budget versus
Actual Results

Month	Inventory Budget	Inventory Actual	Sales
Jan.	4,976,613	9,643,700	4,616,411
Feb.	5,007,262	10,165,100	5,293,460
March	5,098,347	11,834,900	6,254,323
April	5,090,657	12,040,600	6,212,472
May	5,186,393	12,584,000	6,050,000

EXHIBIT 2
Inventory by
Category and
Location

Category	Phoenix	Albuquerque	Drill Sites	Total
Rods and casings	1,149,500	0	2,920,500	4,070,000
Drill bits and reaming shells	275,000	0	1,870,000	2,145,000
Wireline	550,000	0	825,000	1,375,000
Drill parts	1,210,000	671,000	297,000	2,178,000
Parts for equipment	275,000	385,000	165,000	825,000
Other	1,430,000	396,000	165,000	1,991,000
Total	$4,889,500	$1,452,000	$6,242,500	$12,584,000

scrutinize our purchases and inventory levels. The fact that our information system is cumbersome and the inventory records are not up to date is also a problem. We are putting in a new ERP system starting in August, but I expect it will be early next year before we can start to rely on accurate, timely data from our system. In the meantime our new shareholder is putting a lot of pressure on John to do something about the inventory problem, and I need a plan that will keep them satisfied while not compromising production."

Delivery

Chapter Outline

Key Questions for the Supply Decision Maker

Should we

- Designate delivery mode and carrier, or let the supplier do it?
- Use FOB (free on board) origin or FOB destination terms, or some other designation?
- Outsource some or all of the logistics function to a third party?

How can we

- Develop an effective delivery strategy for goods and services?
- Identify value-added logistics services that will reduce our overall costs?
- Ensure that we attain the optimum mix of reliability, cost, and service from delivery service providers?

Purchased goods must be transported from the point where they are grown, mined, or manufactured to the place where they are needed, when they are needed, with inventories held at a minimum amount to ensure production and customer service. Purchased services must also be delivered on time. Delivery of services often depends more on radio frequency waves and the Internet than trucks, trains, and planes. No matter which mode of transport is involved, on-time delivery is a critical element of both goods and services purchasing.

The emphasis on reducing costs and cycle times throughout supply chains highlights the importance of inventory velocity. This increases the need for competitive transportation and other logistics services as an alternative to maintaining costly inventories. Advances in information technology, coupled with the speed of Internet communications, have greatly enabled the flow of real-time information and the reduction of inventory throughout supply chains. (Technology issues are addressed in Chapter 4.)

Management must decide if results will be better if some or all logistics tasks are performed in-house or outsourced. No matter who is responsible and where logistics tasks are performed (e.g., in-house or outsourced), improved coordination of information and material flows can help to achieve economies of scale and economies of scope. (Outsourcing is discussed in Chapter 5.)

Decisions about how to assure on-time delivery are important due to the large number of dollars involved in the movement of goods into and out of an organization and the potential effect on profits. Two key decisions are addressed in this chapter: (1) How can we assure on-time delivery at lowest total cost? and (2) What mode(s) of transportation and supplier(s) should be selected for delivery?

LOGISTICS

Logistics is the management of inventory in motion and at rest. Logistics is defined by the Council of Supply Chain Management Professionals (CSCMP) as "that part of supply chain management that plans, implements, and controls the efficient, effective forward and reverse flow and storage of goods, services, and related information between the point of origin to the point of consumption in order to meet customers' requirements."[1]

---

[1] CSCMP Supply Chain Management, http://cscmp.org/about-us/supply-chain-management-definitions

According to the CSCMP, logistics management activities typically include inbound and outbound transportation management, fleet management, warehousing, materials handling, order fulfillment, logistics network design, inventory management, supply/demand planning, and management of third-party logistics services providers. Logistics costs can be divided into three categories—inventory carrying costs, administrative costs, and transportation—with transportation accounting for the bulk of the costs. Inventory was discussed in Chapter 8. Transportation is covered in this chapter.

Role of Logistics in the Economy

Logistics activities are a vital part of economies. Total business logistics costs in the United States in 2013 were estimated at $1.39 trillion up from $1.33 trillion in 2012, continuing an increase from $1.1 trillion in 2009. These costs were divided into inventory carrying costs, transportation costs, and administrative costs. While this is an impressive amount, business logistics costs in the United States have actually been declining over the past three decades as a percentage of gross domestic product (GDP). Logistics costs as a percentage of U.S. GDP dropped to 8.2 percent from 8.5 percent in 2011 and 2012 compared to a high of 16.2 percent in 1981. In comparison, logistics costs were 14 percent of Mexico's GDP, 14.5 percent of Chinas's, and 12.5 percent of India's.[2]

A number of factors have contributed to declining logistics costs, including deregulation of the transportation sector, technology advances and e-commerce, and greater emphasis in organizations on improving supply chain processes and practices. More recently, the global recession has severely affected the logistics industry.

Role of Supply in Logistics

Supply plays a vital role in delivery of goods and services in the supply chain. Supply may have direct functional responsibility for some logistics responsibilities, such as arranging in-bound transportation with suppliers or responsibility for supervising warehousing and stores. Meanwhile, others in the organization, such as marketing, may turn to supply to assist in establishing relationships with third-party logistics (3PLs) service providers to operate distribution facilities and warehouses. Consequently, supply's role in delivery can involve functional oversight and logistics services acquisition. (Also see Chapters 3 and 16 for more information about the role of supply in logistics.)

The purchase of logistics services demands a high degree of skill and knowledge if the costs of movement are to be minimized while at the same time meeting service needs. Due to the complexity of the logistics industry and the significantly larger number of alternatives available as a result of deregulation, getting the best value for an organization's transportation and logistics dollar involves much more than simply "getting the best rate."

TRANSPORTATION

Transportation accounts for the majority of logistics costs, approximately 62 percent in 2013. Depending on the type of goods being moved, transportation may account for as much as 40 percent of the total cost of the item, particularly if it is of relatively low value, bulky, and heavy, such as agricultural commodities or construction materials. But in the

[2] R. Wilson, *CSCMP's Annual State of Logistics Report,* June 17, 2014.

case of very high-value low-weight and low-bulk electronics goods, transport costs may be less than 1 percent of total purchase costs. It is not unusual in many firms to find that a significant percent of their purchase expenditures go for transportation costs. While target savings vary from firm to firm, many have found that only a modest effort to manage transportation services more efficiently will result in substantial savings.

If minimization of costs were the only objective in buying transportation services, the task would be easy. However, the transportation buyer must look not only at cost but also at service provided. For example, items are purchased to meet a production schedule, and the available modes of transport require different amounts of transport time. If items are shipped by a method requiring a long shipment time, inventory may be exhausted and a plant or process shut down before the items arrive. Also, reliability may differ substantially among various transportation companies or carriers; service levels, lost shipments, and damage may vary greatly between two different carriers. The buyer should use the same skill and attention in selecting carriers as used in selecting other suppliers. The effects of transportation deregulation have made the carrier selection and pricing decision far more important today.

In addition, just-in-time (JIT) purchasing systems (Chapter 8), global sourcing (Chapter 14), and outsourcing (Chapter 5) make logistics decisions more crucial. With JIT, deliveries must be on time, with no damage to the items in transit, because minimal inventories are maintained. Inventory cost savings should offset additional transportation costs from a supplier providing fast, reliable deliveries. When the transport buyer is sourcing globally, extended lead times and distance place additional pressure on the transport decision maker. The option to outsource some or all of the logistics function also adds complexity to the analysis of options and the management of inventory at rest and in motion.

With deregulation of the transportation industry and the development of intermodal service, the focus for the transport buyer has shifted from mode of transport to breadth of service, information systems, timeliness (reliability and speed), and rates. Breadth refers to the ability of a carrier to handle multiple parts of the logistics process, including transportation, warehousing, inventory management, and shipper–carrier relationships.

Because of the importance of speed—in terms of both providing reliable, consistent, on-time service and moving goods through the system quickly—shippers are seeking core carriers with whom they can develop closer relationships to reduce cycle time. The development of information systems and the application of e-commerce tools to both inbound and outbound transportation also contribute to timeliness and breadth of service. Shippers are demanding improved communications and information systems to facilitate order tracking and expediting. Because delays in the supply chain may lead to higher inventory levels and increased total cost, the whole logistics process is viewed as an area where cost avoidance and cost reductions will reap bottom-line rewards.

Outsourcing to Third-Party Logistics (3PLs) Service Providers

Outsourcing, or using third-party logistics (3PLs) service providers, has become increasingly popular as organizations downsize, focus on core competencies, and seek partnerships or alliances with key suppliers. The 3PL industry grew rapidly following deregulation of the transportation sector. In the *2013 Third-Party Logistics Study,* shippers reported that outsourcing accounted for 54 percent of their transportation spend and

39 percent of warehouse operations spend.[3] 3PLs provide a wide range of logistics services for their clients, with transactional, operational, and repetitive activities outsourced most frequently. These include international and domestic transportation, warehousing, freight forwarding, and customs brokerage. The less frequently used 3PL services tend to be more strategic, customer facing, and IT intensive, including order management and fulfillment, IT services, supply chain consultancy services, customer service, and LLP/4PL services.[4]

Transportation Regulation and Deregulation

Government regulation in the transportation sector in both the United States and Canada has been focused in two areas: economic and safety/environmental. For nearly 100 years, the U.S. and Canadian transportation sectors operated under a strict regulatory environment that controlled rates, routes, carrier services, and geographic coverage. These economic regulations were controlled at the federal, state, and provincial levels. While government policies evolved over time, the objectives were to ensure that transport services were available in all geographic areas without discrimination, establish rules for new forms of transportation, provide market stability and supply, and control prices and services in the face of monopoly power. Since the late 1970s, governments in Canada and the United States and elsewhere in the world have embraced a policy and legislative agenda of deregulation. Today, the U.S. and Canadian transportation sectors are essentially deregulated, with shippers able to negotiate rates, terms, services, and routes with service providers.

While economic regulations have been eliminated for the most part, carriers must adhere to an ever-increasing number and range of safety and environmental regulations, such as transportation of dangerous goods, vehicle emissions, and working conditions. Government regulation also has established new standards for security at airports and ports since the tragic events of 9/11. For example, the International Ship and Port Facility Code set new standards for ship verification, certification, and control to ensure that appropriate security measures are implemented.

As changes occur in the political, social, economic, and technological landscape, governments will continue to reassess transportation policies and regulations. Supply managers must keep abreast of actual and potential regulatory changes because of the potential significant impact on the organization's supply chain.

Supply's Involvement in Transportation

Involvement of the supply function in transportation decisions is significant and growing as a result of the added alternatives opened up by deregulation. Supply involvement is in two areas. The first is direct functional responsibility within the organization for any one or several logistical activities, such as transportation, warehousing, receiving, or inventory control. A CAPS Research study found that in 249 large organizations, inbound transportation reported to supply in 53 percent of the firms in 2011, compared to 56 percent in 2004, 51 percent in 1995, and 40 percent in 1987. In the case of the outbound transportation it reported to supply

---

[3] C. J. Langley, et al., *2013 Third-Party Logistics Study: The State of Logistics Outsourcing*, www .capgemini.com/resources/2013-thirdparty-logistics-study, p. 4.

[4] Ibid., p. 10.

in 51 percent of the firms in 2011, compared to 43 percent of the firms in 2003, which was up from the 39 percent that reported to supply in 1995 and 31 percent in 1987.[5]

A second area of supply involvement is working with managers from other functions, such as operations or marketing, in devising solutions with suppliers of logistics services to improve customer service, lower costs, increase flexibility, or improve quality.

TRANSPORTATION MODES AND CARRIERS

The delivery decision includes three questions: (1) What mode of transportation is most appropriate for a specific order? (2) What carrier is the best? and (3) Which supplier offers the best value? To answer these questions, the buyer must first understand modes and carriers.

A mode of transportation is the means by which people, freight, or information gain mobility. The three basic means of mobility are land (road, rail, and pipeline), water, and air. Radio frequency (RF) waves are a transportation mode that moves information instantaneously. Transportation trends include integrating modes (*intermodality*) and *linking* modes more closely into supply chain activities of production and distribution.

A carrier transports property or people by any means of conveyance (truck, auto, taxi, bus, railroad, ship, airplane), almost always for a charge. Carriers for RF waves are air (wireless), copper wire, and fiber optic cable. Once a mode (e.g., land) of transportation has been selected, the buyer must decide on a carrier (e.g., railroad) and a specific supplier (e.g., BNSF Railway).

Supply professionals need to understand the characteristics of each mode and carrier in order to assess trade-offs when making transportation decisions. A brief description of each follows.

Road

Motor carriers, or trucks, are the most flexible mode of transportation and account for approximately 80 percent of transportation expenditures by U.S. firms. This mode offers the advantage of point-to-point service, over any distance, for products of varying weight and size. Compared to other modes, service is fast and reliable, with low damage and loss rates. Consequently, motor carriers are the preferred mode for organizations operating under a just-in-time system with many suppliers in close proximity to the manufacturing facility.

Motor carriers can be divided into three categories: (1) less-than-truck-load (LTL), (2) truckload (TL), and (3) small parcel, ground. LTL shipments are typically of short haul compared to TL shipments, while the cost per hundredweight (cwt) is generally higher compared to TL shipments over the same distance. One of the biggest problems facing the trucking industry is the lack of drivers. The industry has an aging workforce, an inability to attract qualified younger and minority candidates, expensive driver training programs, and a federal focus on unsafe drivers. The Council of Supply Chain Management Professional's 24th annual "State of Logistics Report" identified regulatory issues that will likely affect productivity. These included the Federal Motor Carrier Safety Administration's Compliance, Safety, Accountability (CSA) initiative to enforce stricter qualifications, new health requirements, and hair follicle drug testing, which have reduced the pool of eligible

---

[5] P. F. Johnson and M. R. Leenders, *Supply's Organizational Roles and Responsibilities 2011* (Tempe, AZ: CAPS Research, 2012).

drivers; the prospect of electronic onboard recorders (EOBRs) for documenting hours of service; and the new *Hours of Service* rule that went into effect July 1, 2013.

Rail and Intermodal

Rail carriers once dominated the transportation sector, but their share of the transportation market has declined steadily since World War II. Rail carriers are relatively inflexible and slow and have higher loss and damage rates, compared to motor carriers. However, rail has the advantage of lower variable operating costs, which makes it attractive for hauling large tonnage over long distances.

In the United States, the oil and gas boom, along with the absence of pipelines, has led to dramatic growth in rail transport of oil. According to the Association of American Railroads, U.S. Class I railroads originated just 9,500 carloads of crude oil in 2008, 234,000 carloads in 2012, and around 400,000 in 2013. There has also been an increase in spills and accidents. According to the Pipeline and Hazardous Materials Safety Administration, from 1975 to 2012, railroads spilled 800,000 gallons of crude oil, and in 2013 they spilled 1.15 million gallons. Safety and environmental debates are ongoing between and among stakeholders, including the Association of American Railroads, the Railway Supply Institute, the U. S. Department of Transportation, pipeline proponents, and environmental and safety groups.

Intermodal freight services are divided between containers on flatcars (COFC) and truck trailers on flatcars (TOFC), sometimes referred to as piggyback systems. This segment allows carriers to take advantage of the relative strengths of two modes. For example, shipments can benefit from the long-haul economies of rail, while accommodating door-to-door service attributes of trucks. Additional benefits include shorter terminal delays and lower damage rates due to less handling. Since intermodal service was completely deregulated, attractive arrangements often are possible, and growth in this mode has been substantial.

Pipelines

Since pipelines can only transport products in either a liquid or gaseous state, the use of this mode of transport is quite limited. However, once the initial investment in the pipeline is recovered, the variable costs of operation are relatively low. The oil and gas boom in the United States and Canada has ignited a debate over building additional pipelines or transporting by rail. Both have advantages and disadvantages.

Air

The primary advantage of airfreight is speed. Airfreight is costly and also must be combined with trucks to provide door-to-door service. Consequently, products best suited for this mode are of high value and/or extremely perishable. Although airfreight volume has increased over the past two decades, most shippers still regard this mode as premium emergency service. Excess capacity plagues the air cargo industry as new cargo planes come onstream while passenger carriers are allocating more space for cargo.

Water

Although most international trade uses water carriers, referred to as international deep sea transport, this mode is also used domestically in inland water and coastal systems and lakes. Although inexpensive compared to other modes, water carriers are slow and inflexible. The risks of water transport include increased cost for added security such as X-ray facilities to monitor cargo and the expense of qualified security employees to detect and prevent terrorist attacks; effects of weather events and climate change on routes; piracy, especially off the coast of East Africa; fuel costs; a slow growing global economy; and environmental impact.

Similar to rail, waterway transportation is best suited for hauling large tonnage over long distances and is frequently used for bulk commodities such as coal, grain, and sand. Furthermore, compared to other modes, water carriers are disadvantaged because of the need for suitable waterways, ports, and handling equipment. For example, a third set of locks is being built in the Panama Canal to allow larger ships passage through the nearly 50-mile (80-kilometer) transoceanic cargo route. Originally scheduled to open in 2014, the project has been slowed by disputes over cost overruns. Weather and climate also impact water shipments. For example, drought in 2012 caused the lowest water levels in 50 years in the Mississippi River. Barges made more trips with lighter loads, meaning higher fuel costs and delays. The effects of climate change, including rising sea levels, melting ice, changes in weather patterns, and the corrosive effects of invasive species, have a direct effect on the shipping industry. This includes shipping patterns and the facilities used to move freight. New inland waterways might become available as well as new polar routes such as the Northwest passage and the Northern sea route around Russia.

Water carriers also must team up with motor carriers to provide door-to-door service. Many waterway shipments involve the use of containers. Containers also can be transported via truck or rail from the point of origin to the final destination.

Radio Frequency Waves

Radio frequency (RF) waves are a mode of transportation for information. Carriers for RF waves are air (wireless), copper wire, and fiberoptic cable. These telecommunication routes transport information instantaneously. Growth comes from the increasing size of the services sector of the economy, the increase in knowledge workers, and the importance of information sharing in all types of organizations. For example, software may be delivered via the Internet, and some movement of people may be replaced with information transport (e.g., telecommuting).

Telecommunication routes are practically unlimited. Constraints from land and ocean obstructions to laying cable are low. High network costs and low distribution costs characterize many telecommunication networks. Because radio frequency waves have limited range, they require repeaters or substations, such as cellular towers, to transmit information over distances. The limits on transmission speed and successful transmission come from hardware, such as servers and modems, and software.

Communications satellites in geostationary orbit occupy a single ring (Clarke Orbit) above the equator. Each satellite occupies a slot and requires a buffer of space to avoid radio-frequency interference. This buffer limits the number of slots available. Conflicts occur among densely populated countries at the same longitude (Americas, Europe, Africa) that require the same orbital slots and radio frequencies. Superiority in the ability to compress information gives a provider the advantage of transmitting more information on the same bandwidth as a competitor. Resolution of decompressed information may be a quality issue.

TYPES OF CARRIERS, PROVIDERS, AND SERVICE OPTIONS

While deregulation has reshaped the transportation sector, some terminology used to describe carriers is based on the legal designations under regulation. These are common carriers, contract carriers, exempt carriers, and private carriers. While these legal designations technically no longer exist, they still provide guidance in terms of the role and function of each group.

Types of Carriers

Common carriers offer transportation service to all shippers at published rates, in a nondiscriminatory basis, between designated points. Under deregulation, however, common carriers have considerable flexibility in establishing rates and routes.

A *contract carrier* is a for-hire carrier that provides service to a limited number of shippers and operates under specific contractual arrangements that specify rates and services. Generally, rates for contract carriers are lower than for common carriers because volumes are typically higher with individual shippers and scheduling is usually more predictable.

Exempt carriers are also for-hire carriers, but they are exempt from regulation of rates and services. This status was originally established to allow farmers to transport agriculture products on public roads, but this status has been broadened over the years to include a number of different products by a variety of modes. Under deregulation, most carriers can be considered exempt from rate restrictions.

A *private carrier* provides transportation for its company's own products and the company owns (or leases) all related equipment and facilities. In a regulated environment, private carriers had the advantages of not being restricted by regulations and the flexibility that this status offered. Today, common and contract carriers enjoy the same flexibility and many companies have chosen to outsource transportation services as a result.

Transportation Service Providers

There are a number of transportation service providers, including freight forwarders, brokers, and customs house brokers.

Freight forwarders buy dedicated space on scheduled carriers. The benefits are lower rates than the shipper might otherwise receive and one point of contact for shipments that may span two or more modes and carriers. Freight forwarders can specialize as domestic or international, or by mode, such as airfreight or surface transportation. Freight forwarders can provide a number of value-added services. For example, domestic surface freight forwarders consolidate small shipments into rail cars and piggyback trailers and arrange for motor carrier pickup and delivery.

Brokers charge shippers a fee for arranging transportation services with a carrier. The broker will act as the shipper's agent in negotiating rates and service arrangements. In instances where the shipper has limited familiarity with the transportation market and carrier options, brokers can provide the necessary expertise to oversee negotiations with carriers.

Customs house brokers are used for importing products. They ensure that documentation is accurate and complete and can provide a variety of other services, such as providing estimates of landed costs, payments to offshore suppliers, and insurance options available to shippers. These include expedited transportation, same-day service, freight forwarders, brokers, and customs-house brokers. The role and function of each service is described below.

Specialized Service Options

Expedited transportation refers to any shipment that requires pickup service and includes a specific delivery guarantee. In the United States, this is typically less than five days. Shipments may move via domestic air, ground parcel, less-than-truckload, or air-export services.

Under deregulation, competition for *small-shipment services* has become intense. Buyers now can use some of the standard supply techniques, such as systems contracts, aggressive negotiation, multiple sourcing, quotation analysis, target pricing, and supplier evaluation, to get better purchasing arrangements with carriers. Competition is intense among express carriers as they move to cross over into the heavy-lift air cargo market. The emerging integrated carriers, those with their own aircraft like Federal Express and UPS, are capturing a larger share of the market. Volume discounts, tracking systems, and ground networks are the distinguishing factors.

Another growth area is *same-day service,* which is being developed by express carriers such as DHL, UPS, and Federal Express. The same-day niche is growing rapidly and expanding into the international market. The users of same-day service range from the entertainment, advertising, and legal industries to manufacturers. The same-day service is used when the cost of not having a critical part or document is greater than the amount spent on same-day service. Amazon and Walmart have announced trial runs of same-day service in specific urban markets. This would push same-day delivery into the retail sector.

SELECTION OF MODE AND SUPPLIER

Normally, the buyer will wish to specify how purchased items are to be shipped; this is the buyer's legal right if the purchase has been made under any of the free-on-board (FOB) origin terms (defined later in this chapter). If the purchaser has received superior past service from a particular carrier, it then becomes the preferable means of shipment.

"Best Value" Delivery Decisions

As one would expect, shippers are most concerned that the carrier meet its delivery promises (deliver on schedule) without damaging the goods and at a competitive cost. On the other hand, if the shipper has relatively little expertise in the transportation area and the supplier has a skilled logistics department, it might be wise to rely on the supplier's judgment in carrier selection and routing. Also, in a time of shortage of transport equipment (e.g., railroad cars, trucks, or ocean freight), the supplier may have better information about the local situation and what arrangements will get the best results. And, if the item to be shipped has special dimensional characteristics requiring special rail cars, the supplier may be in a better position to know what is available and the clearances needed for proper shipment.

Each form of common carrier transportation—rail, truck, air, and inland water—has its own distinct advantages for shippers in respect to speed, available capacity, flexibility, and cost. Each mode also has inherent disadvantages. For example, comparing air with truck transport, air has the advantage in terms of speed; truck transport can accommodate greater volume and has lower rates and greater flexibility in terms of delivery points. The astute buyer must recognize such advantages/limitations and arrive at the best value considering the needs of the organization.

Key Selection Criteria

After the buyer has determined the mode (land, water, or air) and carrier (truck, rail, pipeline, ship, or airplane), a specific supplier and specific shipment routing must be determined. The factors to be considered when selecting mode of shipment, carrier, and routing include the following:

Required delivery time. The required date for material receipt may make the selection of mode of shipment quite simple. If two-day delivery from a distant point is needed, the only viable alternative probably is air shipment. If more time is available, other modes can be considered. Most carriers can supply estimates of normal delivery times, and the purchaser also can rely on past experience with particular modes and carriers. Time-definite services are in demand as organizations focus on time-based competition and JIT inventory management systems.

Reliability and service quality. While two carriers may offer freight service between the same points, their reliability and dependability may differ greatly. One carrier may, (1) be more attentive to customer needs; (2) be more dependable in living up to its commitments; (3) incur less damage, overall, to merchandise shipped; and (4) in general be the best freight supplier. The buyer's past experience is a good indicator of service quality.

Available services. As the demand for third-party logistics (3PLs) services grows, shippers want services like warehousing and inventory management in addition to transportation services. In addition, carriers and 3PLs may offer access to data that can be used to improve inventory management practices or to provide better customer service.

Type of item being shipped. If the item to be shipped is large and bulky, a particular mode of transportation may be required. Special container requirements may indicate only certain carriers that have the unique equipment to handle the job. Bulk liquids, for example, may indicate railroad tank car, barge, or pipeline. Also, safety requirements for hazardous materials may make certain carriers and routings impractical or illegal.

Shipment size. The postal service, and companies such as Federal Express and United Parcel Service, or airfreight forwarders can move items of small size and bulk. Larger shipments probably can be moved more economically by rail or truck.

Possibility of damage. Certain items, such as fine china or electronics equipment, by their nature have a high risk of damage in shipment. In this case, the buyer may select a mode and carrier by which the shipment can come straight through to its destination, with no transfers at distribution points to another carrier. It is part of the buyer's responsibility to ensure that the packaging of goods is appropriate for both the contents and mode of transport.

Cost of the transport service. The buyer should select the mode, carrier, and routing that will provide for the safe movement of goods, within the required time, at the lowest total transport cost. Also, the buyer may make certain trade-offs in purchasing transportation, just as trade-offs are made in selecting suppliers for other purchases.

Carrier financial situation. If any volume of freight is moved, some damages will be incurred, resulting in claims against the carrier. Should the carrier get into financial difficulty, or even become insolvent, collection on claims becomes a problem. Therefore, the buyer should avoid those carriers that are on the margin financially. While in an era of deregulation there are many new entrants in the transportation industry, there also are many exits, and the number of bankruptcies—combined with changes in the laws and regulations governing transportation—may cause shippers to receive undercharge bills years after the service was provided.

Handling of claims. Inevitably, some damage claims will arise in the shipment of quantities of merchandise. Prompt and efficient investigation and settlement of claims is another key factor in carrier selection.

Private fleets. One alternative to a common carrier is private or leased equipment. A private carrier does not offer service to the general public. Many companies have elected to contract for exclusive use of equipment; and some have established their own trucking fleet with either company-owned or leased tractors and vans.

The use of a private fleet is a type of make-or-buy decision. Maintaining a private fleet gives the firm greater flexibility in scheduling freight services. It can be economically advantageous, but unless the equipment can be fully utilized through planned back-hauls of either semifinished or finished goods, it may turn out to be more costly than use of the common carrier system.

FOB Terms and Incoterms

The term *FOB* stands for *free on board,* meaning that goods are delivered to a specified point with all transport charges paid. There are several variations in FOB terms, as Table 9–1 shows. Shipping terms and the responsibilities of buyer and seller in international contracts are covered by Incoterms (International Commercial Terms). Incoterms

TABLE 9–1 **FOB Terms and Responsibilities**

FOB Term	Payment of Freight Charges	Bears Freight Charges	Owns Goods in Transit	Files Claims (if any)	Explanation
FOB origin, or FOB freight collect	Buyer	Buyer	Buyer	Buyer	Title and control of goods passes to buyer when carrier signs for goods at point of origin
FOB origin, freight prepaid	Seller	Seller	Buyer	Buyer	
FOB origin, freight prepaid and charged back	Seller	Buyer	Buyer	Buyer	Seller pays freight charges and adds to invoice
FOB destination, freight collect	Buyer	Buyer	Seller	Seller	Title remains with seller until goods are delivered
FOB destination, freight prepaid	Seller	Seller	Seller	Seller	
FOB destination, freight prepaid and charged back	Seller	Buyer	Seller	Seller	Seller pays freight charges and adds to invoice
FOB destination, freight collect and allowed	Buyer	Seller	Seller	Seller	Buyer pays freight charges and deducts from seller's invoice

were developed in 1936 by the International Chamber of Commerce and most recently revised in 2010. (Incoterms are covered in more detail in Chapter 14.)

The selection of the FOB point is important to the purchaser because it determines four things:

1. Who pays the carrier.
2. When legal title to goods being shipped passes to the buyer.
3. Who is responsible for preparing and pursuing claims with the carrier in the event goods are lost or damaged during shipment.
4. Who routes the freight.

It is incorrect to claim that FOB destination is always preferable because the seller pays the transportation charges. Ultimately, the charges are borne by the buyer because they will be included in the delivered price charged by the supplier. In effect, if the buyer lets the supplier make the transportation decisions, then the buyer is allowing the supplier to spend the buyer's money.

In purchases from international suppliers, FOB is an Incoterm meaning *free on board (named port of shipment),* and the seller passes title to the goods to the buyer when the goods are on the vessel. The ocean carrier typically does not provide any insurance on goods in transit; therefore, it is important, when goods are bought FOB origin, for the buyer to ensure that adequate insurance coverage is provided.

According to Incoterms 2010, *CFR* and *CIF* should only be used with bulk sea shipment consignments and CPT and CIP should be used with all other types of shipments, including containerized sea shipments. CFR *(cost and freight)* is similar to FOB origin, with freight charges paid by the seller. However, under CFR the buyer assumes all risk and should provide for insurance. CIF *(cost, insurance, and freight)* means that the seller will pay the freight charges and provide appropriate insurance coverage. This is similar to FOB destination, freight prepaid. CPT *(carriage paid to named port of destination)* means that the buyer assumes all risk and should provide for insurance. CIP *(carriage and insurance paid)* means the seller pays for freight charges and insurance. In some instances, the buyer may wish to obtain equalization of freight charges with the nearest shipping point of the seller, or some competitive shipping point. Then the following clause can be used: "Freight charges to be equalized with those applicable from seller's shipping point producing lowest transportation cost to buyer's destination." For a more detailed discussion of Incoterms, see Chapter 14.

Rates and Pricing

The economic realities of transportation costs can be summarized succinctly. Transportation costs are influenced by distance, weight, density, stowability, handling, liability, and market. These realities are reflected in the carrier's rates and pricing arrangements.

The two categories of carrier rates are line haul rates and accessorial rates. *Line haul rates* are per-mile truckload pricing charged for moving products to a nonlocal destination and can be grouped into four categories: (1) class rates, (2) exception rates, (3) commodity rates, and (4) miscellaneous rates. *Accessorial rates* are charges for services not included in the negotiated line haul rate. These may include fuel surcharges, Sunday pickup or delivery, stop-off fee, layover, or loading and unloading. Today, most rates between shippers and carriers are negotiated, and the distinctions between rate classifications have become blurred.

As with other purchases, carriers offer lower rates if the quantity of an individual shipment is large enough. Both rail and motor carriers offer discounts for full carload (CL) or truckload (TL) shipments. These will be substantially less per hundred weight (cwt) than less-than-carload (LCL) or less-than-truckload (LTL) quantities. If the shipper can consolidate smaller shipments to the same destination, a lower rate may be available (called a *pool car*). In some instances, shippers may band together through a shippers' association to get pool car transport rates. Or a redistributor may consolidate LTL shipments from multiple customers to gain the advantages of a TL shipment. Shippers pay less than they would for an LTL shipment and the redistributor can still make a profit.

The *unit train* is another innovation by which the shipper gets a quantity discount. By special arrangement with a railroad, a utility company, for example, is provided one or more complete trains, consisting of 100-plus coal cars, that shuttle between the coal mine and the utility's place of use. This speeds up the movement and the materials are moved at an advantageous commodity rate.

Four basic types of rate discounts have developed; the buyer in some instances can take advantage of one or more of them and possibly enjoy substantial savings.

1. *Aggregate tender rates* provide a discount if the shipper will group multiple small shipments for pickup or delivery at one point.
2. *Flat percentage discounts* provide a discount to the shipper if a specified total minimum weight of less-than-truckload shipments is moved per month, encouraging the shipper to group volume with one carrier.
3. *Increased volume–increased discount percentage* is applied if a firm increases its volume of LTL shipments by a certain amount over the previous period's volume.
4. *Specific origin and destination points* provide a specified discount if volume from a specified point to a specified delivery point reaches a given level.

Demurrage charges (sometimes also called detention charges for motor carriers) often are incurred by shippers or receivers of merchandise. This simply is a daily penalty charge for a rail car or a motor van that is tied up beyond the normal time for loading or unloading. If demurrage were not charged, some firms would use the carrier's equipment as a free storage facility. In most instances, the daily demurrage rate becomes progressively higher the longer the car or trailer is tied up, until it gets almost prohibitive. A shipper can enter into an averaging agreement with a carrier, whereby cars or vans unloaded one day early may be used to offset cars that are unloaded a day late. In an averaging agreement, settlement is made monthly. If the shipper owes the carrier, payment must be made; if the carrier owes the shipper, no payment is made, but instead the net car balance starts at zero in the new month. The supply department should be aware of the normal number of rail cars or vans that can be unloaded each day and attempt to schedule shipments in so that they do not "back up" and result in payment of demurrage penalties.

Documentation in Freight Shipments

There are several kinds of documents used when shipping products.

The *bill of lading* is the key document in the movement of goods. It contains information about the products being shipped including weight and quantity, the origin of the shipment, contract terms between the carrier and shipper, and the final destination. Each shipment must have a bill of lading, which is the contract, spelling out the legal liabilities of all parties, and no changes to the original bill of lading can be made unless approved by the carrier's agent in writing on the bill of lading. Signed by both the shipper's and carrier's agents, the bill of lading is proof that shipment was made and is evidence of ownership. It is a contract and fixes carrier liability; normally it will be kept by the party that has title to goods in transit, for it must be provided to support any damage claims. As with most other documentation, electronic versions and online systems management are common in many organizations.

There are several variations on the bill of lading.

Uniform straight bill of lading. This is the complete bill of lading and contains the complete contract terms and conditions. The straight bill of lading–short form contains those provisions uniform to both motor and rail. Short bills are not furnished by carriers but instead are preprinted by shippers.

Unit bill of lading. This is prepared in four copies; the extra copy is the railroad's waybill. This waybill moves with the shipment and may be of assistance in expediting freight movement. A digital waybill is the electronic version.

Uniform order bill of lading. This is printed on yellow paper (the other bills of lading must be on white paper) and is called a sight draft bill of lading. It is a negotiable instrument and must be surrendered to the carrier at destination before goods can be obtained. Its primary use is to prevent delivery until payment is made for the goods. To obtain payment, the shipper must provide a sight draft, along with the original copy of the bill of lading, to its bank; when the draft clears, the bank gives the bill of lading to the shipper, who then can obtain delivery of the merchandise. May be issued electronically.

The *freight bill* is the carrier's invoice for services provided. In addition to providing the total charges for the shipment, the freight bill typically lists the origin and destination, consignee, items, and total weight. Carriers are not obligated to extend credit to shippers and freight bills can be prepaid or collect (e.g., freight charges paid upon arrival of the shipment).

A shipper must provide its carrier with a detailed description, in writing, of any loss or damage that occurs in a shipment. A *freight claim* is a document submitted to recoup financial costs from shipment loss or damage. There is not a standard freight claim form, but most of the information provided in the claim is available on the bill of lading.

The carrier's liability for loss and damage varies depending on the service provided and the contractual terms between the shipper and the carrier. Most freight claims must be submitted within nine months of delivery (or reasonable delivery in the event of loss), but the carrier contract terms could stipulate a different filing period.

If the merchandise is being shipped under any of the FOB origin terms, the buyer will have to pursue the claim. If the shipment is FOB destination, the supplier must process the claim, but because the merchandise is in the buyer's hands, the buyer will have to supply much of the information to support the claim.

Unconcealed loss or damage is referred to in situations when it is evident on delivery that loss or damage has occurred. Such damage or loss must be noted on the carrier's delivery receipt and signed by the carrier's delivering agent. If this is not done, the carrier may maintain that it received a "clear receipt" and not admit any liability. It is a good idea for the receiving department to have a camera available, take one or more photos of the damaged items, and have them signed by the carrier's representative.

In contrast, *concealed loss or damage* refers to situations in which merchandise is found short or damaged after the container is opened. The unpacking should be discontinued, photos should be taken, and the carrier's local agent should be requested to inspect the items and prepare an inspection report.

Concealed loss or damage claims often are difficult to collect because it is hard to determine whether the loss or damage took place while the shipment was in the carrier's possession or whether it occurred before the shipment was delivered to the carrier.

Expediting and Tracing Shipments

Expediting means applying pressure to a supplier, in this case the transportation carrier, in an attempt to encourage faster-than-normal delivery service. The carrier often can and will provide faster service to assist the shipper in meeting an emergency requirement, provided such requests are made sparingly. Expediting should be done through the carrier's general agent and, if at all possible, the carrier should be notified of the need for speed as far in advance of the shipment as possible.

Tracing is similar to follow-up, for it attempts to determine the status (location) of items that have been shipped but have not yet been received and thus are somewhere within the transportation system. Tracing also is done through the carrier's agent, although the shipper may work right along with the carrier's agent in attempting to locate the shipment. If tracing locates a shipment and indicates it will not be delivered by the required date, then expediting is needed.

With new technology tools, such as global positioning systems, Internet-based communications, and bar coding, tracing can be done faster and more accurately. The prevalence of online freight information systems makes it common for a carrier to have the ability to track shipment status in real time.

Freight Audits

Under regulation, it was common practice to hire *traffic consultants* or *rate sharks* to audit freight bills to uncover instances of overpayment to the carrier. Traffic consultants usually worked on a contingency basis, receiving a fee as a percentage of the costs recovered.

Today, with the ability of carriers to adjust fees based on market conditions and to negotiate fee structures directly with the shipper, the role of *freight auditors* has changed dramatically. It is common for firms to hire transportation consultants that handle a wide range of activities including carrier selection, rates and discounts, and liability. Sometimes referred to as "nonasset-based" third-party logistics (3PLs) providers, they provide many of the services of transportation brokers. They use a combination of a network of service providers and computer programs that helps to identify opportunities to optimize costs in the transportation network and take responsibility for billing accuracy. In contrast, "asset-based" 3LPs focus on their dedicated service offering and typically have long-term relationships with shippers for services such as transportation, warehousing and inventory control, and fulfillment.

DELIVERY OPTIONS FOR SERVICES

Service delivery can be thought of along the same lines as the delivery of goods. Delivery involves modes, carriers, and suppliers. Services are intangible products, typically information and/or activities directed at people, buildings, or equipment. Some services also include a tangible good. For example, lawyers provide legal services for client firms that may include a document such as a contract, an airline's kiosk provides check-in services and generates boarding passes for passengers, and an Internet service provider offers information transmission services to users who may then print output.

The modes (means of a service gaining mobility) are people, equipment, and radio frequency waves. Carriers (means of service conveyance) are the different service categories: For example, law firms are carriers of legal expertise, janitorial firms are carriers of cleaning expertise, and phone companies are carriers for information transmission. Suppliers include all of the companies providing a specific service: For example, Verizon, AT&T, and Sprint provide telecommunications services.

Innovation in services may come in the form of totally new services, or variations on a service or how the service is delivered. Think about the delivery of music—streaming music versus downloading versus buying CDs. Depending on the content, an in-person meeting may be replaced by a phone call, which may be replaced by an e-mail, which may be replaced by a text message or a web meeting. While there are serious considerations when selecting the mode and carrier, clearly there are several options.

How a service is delivered offers opportunities to both buyer and supplier. Are airplanes, trains, and cars the only carriers a consultant can use to enable the delivery of consulting services? Might some of the service be delivered via RF waves carrying information that travels through the modes of air (wireless) or land (copper wire or fiber optic cable)? To what extent can online meetings, conference calls, e-mail, and texting be used to deliver high-quality consulting services at a lower total cost?

Intermodality (using multiple modes of delivery) is also used in services delivery. For example, a janitorial service provides people and equipment to clean a building. The people or service providers require a means of transportation to travel to the building; they then require access to the building, which may be by way of a secured entry requiring keys, a swipe card or an access code; and they require the cleaning equipment and supplies necessary to actually deliver the cleaning service.

Members of supply chains that produce tangible products link modes closer together in production and distribution activities. These linking techniques are also used in the delivery of services. For example, a curriculum development team that is spread out geographically might use web-based meetings, e-mail, and texting to replace or supplement face-to-face meetings with subject matter experts, teachers, students, parents, and other stakeholders through all phases of instructional design, delivery, assessment, and feedback. Even the delivery of the educational service may involve multiple modes and linkages: people—teachers and students together in a classroom using web-based materials (RF waves), an off-site teacher communicating via the web with students in one location accessing web-based materials, or an off-site teacher and students in dispersed locations using web-based materials.

Buyer Location versus Supplier Location

The nature and place of service delivery may have significant acquisition repercussions. For example, if the delivery of the service occurs on the premises of the purchaser, the contract agreement may have to address a number of provisions. For example, in construction or installation services, questions of security, access, nature of dress, hours of work, applicability of various codes for health and safety, what working days and hours are applicable, and what equipment and materials are to be provided by whom are all issues that need to be addressed as part of the contract.

On the other hand, when the service is provided on the supplier's premises or elsewhere, many of these concerns may not arise, provided the service is not directed at personnel of the purchaser.

On-premise versus Off-premise/Web-Based IT Delivery

Technology issues were discussed in Chapter 4, "Processes and Technology." How application software is delivered relates to this discussion of delivery options. On-premise delivery means that a company purchases a software package; pays a licensing fee; and installs, operates, and maintains that software at the company location. The total cost of this approach includes purchase price, licensing fee, and internal IT capability. Off-premise application service providers (ASP) house the software in one location and multiple users access it. For example, Gmail users are all accessing Google's e-mail software from their individual locations. The lower costs of this model enable smaller and medium-sized organizations to use software that might be prohibitively expensive to purchase.

TRANSPORTATION AND LOGISTICS STRATEGY

Every supply organization must deal with logistics and transportation. Purchased goods must be transported to the purchaser's facilities where they are stored prior to consumption. A recent study of Fortune 500 companies found that 68 percent of respondents gave responsibility for transportation and logistics to supply.[6] The changes in the regulatory environment of transportation, advances in information management systems, and the growing concern with managing both upstream (suppliers) and downstream (end customers) in supply networks have brought rapid and continuous change to logistics management. The same principles of effective purchasing and supply management for the acquisition of goods can and should be applied to logistics services. Development of a transportation and logistics strategy should include:

Value analysis of alternatives. A service requirement value analysis may turn up totally adequate lower-cost transport arrangements.

Price analysis. Rates vary substantially and decisions should be made only after consideration of all possibilities. Competitive quotes should be obtained. Negotiation of big-ticket transportation is possible.

Consolidation of freight, where possible. Volume discounts may reduce transport costs substantially. Systems contracts and blanket orders may be advantageous. If JIT purchasing is in use or being implemented, consolidation of several JIT suppliers may be cost-effective.

Analysis and evaluation of suppliers. Carrier selection and evaluation systems can provide data needed for better decision making. Four areas to evaluate are (1) financial, (2) management, (3) technical/strategic, and (4) relational, or overall corporate relationship between carrier and shipper.

Reassessment of the possibilities of using different transport modes. This would include using private trucking and intermodal transportation, such as piggybacking. The savings often are substantial.

---

[6] Johnson and Leenders, *Supply's Organizational Roles and Responsibilities.*

Development of a closer relationship with selected carriers. Data that enable better planning of transport requirements should be shared to take advantage of the specialized knowledge of both buyer and carrier. A reduced carrier base and partnerships or logistics alliances might be considered.

Cost analysis/reductions. Long-term contracts; partnerships; third-party involvement; freight consolidation; demurrage; packaging; and service, quality, and delivery requirements offer opportunities for cost reductions.

Outsourcing, third-party logistics, contracting out. As organizations downsize, focus on core competencies, and face time-based competition, the decision to contract with a company or several companies to provide complete logistics services should be considered.

Safety considerations. Safety issues may be related to downward pressure on driver's income since deregulation, and to shipper demands that may result in shippers and carriers agreeing to unrealistic, legally unattainable delivery schedules. These pressures may lead to drivers falsifying log books to conceal violations of hours worked and miles driven, and to accidents involving commercial vehicles. Avoidance of safety problems should be a key element in the strategy.

Environmental factors. Growing concerns over clean air and water, the transport of hazardous materials, and fuel/energy consumption also must be taken into account.

ORGANIZATION FOR LOGISTICS

In many firms, especially larger ones, management has decided that it can improve customer service and reduce costs by outsourcing multiple logistics functions. Other large firms have decided there are benefits to having a separate in-house logistics services department. This department has specialists in areas such as selection of carriers and routing, expediting, packaging, and handling claims in the case of loss or damage to goods during shipment.

In the very large firm, the logistics function may be specialized even further, based on the purpose of shipment. For example, an automobile producer may have three separate departments: one concerned with incoming materials shipments, one making the decisions on in-plant and interplant materials movement, and the third concerned with the shipment of finished goods through the distribution channels to customers. In an organization operating under the materials management concept, the transportation or logistics manager may have responsibility for all types of materials movement. This person must recognize that storage, handling, and shipping of raw materials and finished goods does not add value to the product. Instead, it is a key cost element in the operation of the firm and should be managed to minimize costs, within the parameters of needed service.

In the medium-sized and smaller organization, the number of logistics decisions may not be large enough to warrant a full-time logistics specialist and the volume of business may make outsourcing too costly. The buyer or supply manager may be responsible for logistics decisions. In this case, the buyer must have enough knowledge to make decisions on preferred free on board (FOB) terms, selection of carriers and routing, determination of freight rates, preparation of necessary documentation, expediting and tracing of freight shipments, filing and settling of claims for loss or damage in transit, and payment procedures for transport services received. These decisions must be made in light of their impact on other areas such as inventory levels, carrying costs, and the use of capital.

Conclusion

Transportation costs represent a significant expense at most organizations and, in a deregulated environment, there is a wide range of service options available. Not only do logistics and transportation services represent a significant cost; they also affect customer service levels through availability of products, investments in infrastructure such as warehouse networks and trucks, and responsibilities within the supply chain for activities such as expediting and filing claims for loss or damaged goods.

Supply has a dual role in managing transportation and logistics activities. In many companies, supply has functional responsibility for logistical activities such as inbound transportation, warehousing, and packaging. Supply also is expected to work with others in the organization, such as marketing and operations, in managing outsourced agreements with third-party logistics suppliers. Astute supply managers, therefore, should be familiar with the basic concepts of transportation and logistics in order to appreciate the implications of their decisions, such as arranging transportation of raw materials from suppliers or negotiating logistics outsourcing contracts with a 3PL.

Questions for Review and Discussion

1. Which logistics activities are most commonly outsourced to 3PL providers and why?
2. What factors should be considered in selecting a mode of transportation? A carrier?
3. How do firms organize to handle the logistics function?
4. Why might an organization decide to outsource all or some of its logistics activities to a third party?
5. What types of transportation damage might occur and how should each be handled?
6. What kinds of shipping needs are best met by a courier and why?
7. What are the use and significance of the bill of lading?
8. What does FOB mean? What variations are there in FOB terms?
9. Why should a buyer audit payments for freight purchases?
10. What strategies should be developed to effectively manage the logistics function?
11. How would logistics decisions be affected by a JIT purchasing arrangement?
12. Under what circumstances might a buyer prefer each of the following carriers: TL, LTL, air, water, rail, intermodal?
13. What is the difference between on-premise and off-premise delivery of IT services?
14. What are the key issues when deciding how a service is delivered?

References

Bowersox, D. J.; D. J. Closs; and M. B. Cooper. 4th ed. *Supply Chain Logistics Management.* New York: McGraw-Hill/Irwin, 2012.

Coyle, J. J.; E. J. Bardi; and C. J. Langley Jr. *The Management of Business Logistics: A Supply Chain Perspective.* 9th ed. Toronto, Canada: Thomson, 2013.

Incoterms 2010. New York: International Chamber of Commerce (ICC) Publishing Inc., 2010.

Langley, C. J. 2013. *Third-Party Logistics Study: The State of Logistics Outsourcing, Results and Findings of the 17th Annual Study*, Capgemini, 2012, www.capgemini.com /resources/2013-thirdparty-logistics-study

Murphy Jr., P. R., and Wood D. F. *Contemporary Logistics.* 10th ed. Upper Saddle River, NJ: Prentice Hall, 2010.

Ramburg, J. *ICC Guide to Incoterms 2010.* New York: International Chamber of Commerce (ICC) Publishing Inc., 2010.

Case 9–1

Penner Medical Products

Neil Bennett, warehouse manager at Penner Medical Products (Penner), in Rockford, Illinois, was concerned about rising costs and delays associated with shipments arriving from an important Canadian supplier. Ken McCallum, the general manager, had asked Neil to look into the situation and get back to him with recommendations. It was Monday, April 14, and Neil knew that Ken expected to see his plan by the end of the week.

PENNER

Penner was a medical supplies distributor and retailer, supplying small and medium-sized medical practices for more than 50 years. Company sales were $30 million and Penner employed approximately 120 people. Management expected a 10 percent increase in sales over the following five years. Penner sold a wide range of products, such as blood pressure gauges, tongue depressors, scalpels, and specialized furniture. Customers could purchase products either through Penner's five retail locations, all of them within a 200-mile radius of Rockford, or order directly from its central warehouse. The company took orders from customers either over the phone or through its website.

Although Penner was a family-owned business, retirement of key family members resulted in the hiring of several professional managers to run the company. Ken McCallum had been with the company for less than one year and was anxious to exploit opportunities to improve profitability.

Penner's main warehouse was a 30,000-square-foot building, normally filled with merchandise in excess of $2 million. The warehouse was staffed by a manager, two receivers, two drivers for local deliveries to customers, two shippers, and two stock pickers, one of whom was

also occasionally asked to drive the company's two-ton truck, the biggest delivery vehicle available. Warehouse workers were paid an average of $15 per hour.

Neil Bennett started with Penner as a stock picker and was able to progress though the organization as a result of his effort and dedication. He was promoted to warehouse manager eight months earlier.

STINSON DISTRIBUTION COMPANY

Rising costs and missed delivery dates from Stinson Distribution Company (Stinson), an important supplier in Ontario, Canada, had been a concern for some time. A medium-sized company, Stinson had a long-term relationship with Penner, supplying a wide variety of specialized equipment for medical offices. Stinson produced high-quality products and was Penner's only supplier of this equipment.

Missed delivery dates and incomplete orders from Stinson were resulting in customer complaints and lost sales. Furthermore, transportation costs were well over budget and senior management viewed inventory levels as excessive. The controller indicated to Neil that inventory holding costs were 15 percent.

Two days per week, Penner's two-ton truck was sent to Stinson, traveling across the border at Detroit. Under ideal conditions, the one-way trip took 9 to 10 hours, and the truck, although empty in the first leg of the trip, was typically fully loaded with approximately $15,000 in goods on its way back to Rockford. The controller indicated that the cost of operating the two-ton truck was $55 per hour, including fuel, insurance, and administrative overhead. Neil observed that fuel costs had increased dramatically lately. He had tried to share the trips to Ontario with other local businesses to cut down transportation costs, but such efforts had been sporadic.

Concerns regarding security since 9/11 had resulted in delays at the Detroit border crossing, extending shipping times and costs for Penner. The duration and timing of delays at the border were highly variable and could last anywhere from 30 minutes to several hours. Furthermore, incomplete paperwork could add to these problems, since customs officials had become very thorough when reviewing documentation. Neil estimated that approximately 25 percent of the goods from Stinson were delayed as a result of paperwork problems.

The two-ton truck was also in demand to supply materials to Penner's customers, making scheduling deliveries increasingly difficult. Neil had recently resorted to

using United Parcel Service (UPS) to handle rush orders from Stinson, with an appreciable cost premium. He observed that: "At least UPS never messes up the paperwork and gets the product here on time." Penner was also currently paying $1,000 per month to rent space at a warehouse in Windsor used to prepare shipments to cross the border.

EVALUATING OPPORTUNITIES

Neil recognized that his meeting with Ken McCallum was still five days away but wanted to get started working on the problem right away. Ken had indicated, "This problem is costing us a lot of money every day we let it continue. I want a plan in place at the end of the week that will convince me that the problem is going to get fixed quickly."

Case 9–2
Russel Wisselink

"Have a plan ready for me by 9:00 a.m. tomorrow morning" was the instruction Russel Wisselink, senior buyer for Trojan Technologies in London, Ontario, Canada, received from Randy Haill, Trojan's materials manager. In the morning of March 12, Russel Wisselink had received an e-mail from China stating that Trojan's UV4 crystal glass sleeves requirements would not be met because of a governmental ban on the use of its raw material. Russel, aware of the consequences of stockouts on this critical part, had immediately notified Randy.

TROJAN TECHNOLOGIES

Trojan Technologies Inc. (Trojan) was a leading water treatment technology company with the largest installed base of ultraviolet water treatment systems in operation around the world. Trojan specialized in the design, manufacture, and sale of pressurized and open-channel, ultraviolet disinfection and water treatment systems for industrial, municipal, commercial, and residential applications. Trojan's head office was in London, Ontario, Canada. The company had sales of $140 million, employed approximately 400 people in offices around the world, and served its customer base through an extensive network of dealers and representatives.

Trojan was owned by Danaher Corporation (Danaher), which had acquired the company in 2004. Danaher was a

diversified global manufacturer, with businesses in professional instrumentation, industrial technologies, and tools and components. Sales revenues were $6.8 billion with a net profit of $746 million, and Danaher employed approximately 37,000 people. Management used its Danaher Business System (DBS) of continuous improvement to guide and measure operations and business activities.

Trojan's current product line consisted of 10 systems across its five markets: (1) residential water treatment, (2) municipal drinking water, (3) municipal wastewater, (4) environmental contaminant treatment, (5) and industrial process. Systems for commercial and government customers ranged from approximately $50,000 to more than $1 million. These systems, which typically had a product life cycle of 7 to 10 years before being replaced with a new design, were designed and manufactured at the London facility and modified to meet individual customer requirements. In a typical year, Trojan manufactured 500 to 600 systems for its commercial and government customers.

LOW-COST REGION SOURCING PROJECT

Following its acquisition of Trojan, Danaher implemented several new initiatives aimed at improving corporate performance. One area targeted was low-cost region sourcing

(LCR)—an initiative originally championed by Russel's boss, Randy Haill. Russel had been given responsibility for the LCR sourcing project in January after his predecessor left the company.

One of the products critical for Trojan's UV water treatment and purification systems was a crystal quartz sleeve that acted as an ultratransparent barrier between the water and the UV lamp. These sleeves were built to custom specifications for size and optical transparency for each of Trojan's product applications, making them very expensive and difficult to procure. Depending on the system, several crystal quartz sleeves could be required for each unit. The company had traditionally sourced its crystal quartz sleeves from Advanced Material Solutions, Inc. (AMS), located in Dearborn, Michigan, approximately 150 miles from Trojan's plant in London, Ontario. AMS produced the sleeves from various types and purities of silica sand.

While there were a number of locations that could have supplied the silica sand used for manufacturing crystal quartz sleeves, China was selected as the primary location for LCR sourcing for three reasons. First, China had a good supply of both regular quartz sand for standard sleeves, and uncontaminated crystal sand for UV4 sleeves. Second, Danaher already had an established sourcing group in China and as a result Trojan would not have to do much of the work to locate suppliers. Third, Trojan had been developing plans to establish its own manufacturing operations center in China to service the region. These plans were ready for implementation but had been stalled due to slowing demand in the Asia-Pacific region.

AMS's pricing for crystal quartz sleeves for Trojan's UV4 model (part number GA-311) was $51 per unit, and the delivery lead time was approximately two weeks. Trojan's annual requirement for the UV4 sleeves was about 10,000, which represented roughly 15 percent of Trojan's total sleeve orders, but approximately 30 percent of total sleeve costs. Very few places in the world had crystal sand resources of sufficient quality (e.g., very low levels of impurities) to produce sleeves with the necessary optical transparency for UV4 applications. After Trojan's careful screening of potential suppliers, Juntao was chosen in May the previous year to be the primary Chinese supplier. The net cost savings to Trojan on the sleeves would be 70 percent. However, the delivery lead time from Juntao would be extended to eight weeks due to longer lead times for production and shipping.

Once the sourcing relationship was established, it took approximately six months for Juntao to begin accepting orders from Trojan because of communication problems, which Russel found particularly frustrating. The first shipment of sleeves from Juntao arrived at Trojan in February.

DELIVERY PROBLEMS

The original procurement plan developed by Russel's predecessor was to use an 80/20 production ratio with Juntao and AMS respectively. However, when AMS became aware that Trojan was going to source from China they issued an ultimatum: "Keep 100 percent of the business with us or the pricing for sleeves will increase to $77 per sleeve. Furthermore, delivery lead time will be extended to 12 weeks because we will no longer stock sleeves for Trojan." This development led Trojan to decide to source 100 percent of the sleeves from Juntao. Russel felt that AMS believed that they would ultimately lose all of Trojan's business to off-shore suppliers, and thus they wanted to extract a premium price from Trojan.

On March 12, Russel received an e-mail stating that new regulations imposed by the Chinese government temporarily banned all uncontaminated crystal sand mining because government officials wanted to establish regulations for usage of natural resources. According to the e-mail, it was uncertain how long the ban would be in place and what the new regulations would entail.

Trojan had not received any warning or indication regarding the change in government regulations. However, this new development meant that Juntao would be unable to provide the crystal sleeves for Trojan once their existing supply of crystal sand was depleted. Because Trojan did not stock the crystal sleeves, any disruption in supply would rapidly lead to negative impacts on customer orders and projects.

IDENTIFYING OPTIONS

As soon as Russel received the e-mail he informed Randy, who asked him to put together a list of viable options and to make a recommendation. Top among Randy's concerns was to minimize the financial impact while ensuring no disruptions to Tojan's customers. Juntao only had a small supply of the crystal sand on hand, which meant that Trojan would face a sleeve shortage in approximately 30 days.

Juntao had offered to import crystal sand for use in sleeve production; however, this alternative would require time to run tests to ensure that the new crystal sand would meet the purity requirements for making UV4 sleeves. It was unlikely that the samples using the new imported sand would be available within the next month. Furthermore, importing raw material would add to Juntao's costs, which would represent doubling of its prices, increasing to approximately $28 per sleeve.

Russel felt he could order just the crystal sleeves on an as-needed basis from AMS and keep all other sleeve production with Juntao, but the downside to this option would be the premium cost of $77 per sleeve and the extended lead times. Alternatively, Russel had an option to sign a one-year contract with AMS at $51 per sleeve on the condition that AMS provided 100 percent of Trojan's UV4 sleeve requirements.

Another option was to investigate alternative suppliers of crystal quartz sleeves in China who might have raw material stockpiles in reserve. Russel felt that dual sourcing would help reduce Trojan's risk exposure, provided supply from China eventually returned to normal.

Russel knew that a plan needed to be put in place quickly to ensure continuous supply. However, Randy was expecting that Russel would address both the long-term sourcing strategy for crystal quartz sleeves as well as the short-term supply issue.

Case 9–3
Cameron Power Equipment

Tim Peterman, director of logistics at Cameron Power Equipment in Charlotte, North Carolina, was evaluating the future of the company's warehouse in Atlanta, Georgia. The vice president of logistics, Kelly Armstrong, described the situation to Tim in a meeting the previous day: "Our largest competitor is able to handle its U.S. distribution with half the number of warehouses that we use. Head office is telling me we need to reduce our costs, and I think we should target closing at least two warehouses. Get back to me with a plan next week with how you want to proceed."

The lease for the Atlanta warehouse was due to expire in two months, and Tim felt it would be a logical candidate to consider for closure. It was Tuesday, April 22, and Tim wanted to prepare a recommendation to present to Kelly at their next meeting.

CAMERON POWER EQUIPMENT

Established in 1922, Cameron Power Equipment (Cameron) was a leading manufacturer and distributor of outdoor power products, including lawn mowers, garden tractors, snow blowers, chain saws, and trimmers. Headquartered in the United Kingdom, Cameron had annual revenues of $2.5 billion, with operations in Europe, North America, Central and South America, Asia, and Australia. Cameron sold more than 300 different models of outdoor power equipment around the world. Its products were sold through a network of more than 10,000 power equipment retailers (also referred to as "dealers") in the United States. The average margin on products sold by Cameron to dealers was 30 percent of full manufactured costs for

products sourced from the company's global manufacturing operations and 50 percent for parts and accessories sourced from suppliers.

Company operations in the United States included its head office and distribution center (DC) in Charlotte, North Carolina, and a manufacturing facility in Columbia, South Carolina. The Columbia plant employed 1,500 people and was one of several facilities in the Cameron global manufacturing network. It produced high-quality, handheld outdoor power equipment, including blowers, trimmers, and chain saws. Direct variable manufacturing costs of Cameron products typically represented 80 percent of full cost.

THE DISTRIBUTION NETWORK

The Charlotte DC was a 250,000 square foot facility that handled approximately 30,000 stock keeping units (SKUs), including parts and accessories. The DC received goods from Cameron manufacturing facilities and suppliers, and distributed the products to its U.S. warehouse network or directly to dealers. Direct shipments to dealers from the DC were limited to full truckload shipments, typically to large dealers. Tim was responsible for managing the network of the eight warehouses that comprised the U.S. distribution network. These facilities ranged in size from 15,000 to 20,000 square feet.

Warehouses handled distribution of equipment, parts, and accessories to the dealers in their regions. The power equipment industry was subject to seasonal demand, with the spring and summer representing the peak sales periods, and fast, reliable deliveries to dealers was essential.

The targeted service level to dealers was 99 percent with 48-hour lead times, but actual performance was a service level that averaged 97 percent.

Inventory levels at the warehouses were maintained at an average of 30 days. Tim commented on the balance between inventory holding costs and customer service: "We have found that keeping inventory levels at 30 days provides adequate customer service levels. I hired an MBA student on a summer internship last year and I asked her to evaluate our inventory holding costs. She provided an estimate of 16.5 percent, which included the cost of capital at 9.5 percent, plus 7 percent for storage and handling costs, including warehouse rent, labor, insurance, taxes, and obsolescence."

THE ATLANTA WAREHOUSE

The Atlanta warehouse was a 15,000 square foot facility that serviced dealers in the Southeast, including Georgia, Alabama, Mississippi, Tennessee, and Louisiana. The total cost to operate the warehouse was $5,250 per month plus $6,500 per month in salaries, wages, and administrative expenses.

In order to minimize transportation costs, full truckload shipments were used to ship products to the Atlanta warehouse. Although the number of shipments varied each month, on average, eight shipments were made from Charlotte and four shipments were made from the Columbia plant. Freight charges were $725 per load from Charlotte and $625 per load from Columbia.

Since the Charlotte DC was not set up to support small-order fulfillment, Tim spoke to Cameron's current transportation service provider in Atlanta, Merwin Logistics, about setting up a cross-docking shipping process. Under this arrangement, Cameron would make daily shipments to Merwin's Atlanta terminal, where the loads would be cross-docked, consolidated, and sent to the dealers in LTL loads. Merwin quoted a fee of $7,000 per month to provide the cross-docking service and agreed to provide 200 square feet of space for transit storage at the terminal. There were no changes in the delivery costs to the dealers.

In order to maintain service levels to the dealers, Tim would need to make shipments to Merwin's terminal in Atlanta each day, which was 250 miles from the Charlotte DC. Shipments normally sent directly to Atlanta from Columbia would instead be sent to Charlotte and consolidated with other SKUs on the daily shipments. The cost to ship from Columbia to Charlotte was $260 and would continue to be made in full truckloads four times per month. Freight costs from Charlotte to Atlanta remained unchanged.

The Atlanta warehouse maintained an average inventory of $400,000, valued at full cost. Tim felt that if the Atlanta warehouse was closed, they would realize a one-time systemwide reduction in inventory of approximately 50 percent of the value of inventory in the Atlanta warehouse.

The hurdle rate used for capital expenditures was set at 30 percent by head office, so Cameron leased its warehouses in order to provide operating flexibility and to avoid capital outlays. Leases for the warehouses were typically signed for a three-year period, and the leases for all eight warehouses were due to expire with the next 24 months, including three that were up for renewal in the next 9 months (including Atlanta).

PHASING OUT THE ATLANTA WAREHOUSE

Tim was attracted to the opportunities to eliminate the costs of operating the Atlanta warehouse and reducing inventory levels. However, the phase-out of the Atlanta warehouse did have uncertainties and potential problems. Daily shipments from Charlotte would be an additional cost and service levels would have to be maintained. In some cases, deliveries to dealers would be extended by a day, depending on time of day their order was received and the available capacity on the truck. However, Tim was hopeful that service levels could be maintained at their current level under the proposed distribution model.

It was clear that Kelly Armstrong felt that costs could be reduced by closing at least two of the eight warehouses. Tim wanted to carefully analyze the situation at the Atlanta warehouse before making his recommendation about its future.

Price

Chapter Outline

Key Questions for the Supply Decision Maker

Should we

- Use competitive bidding as our principal means of price determination?
- Take advantage of a volume or cash discount offered by a supplier?
- Use forward buying?

How can we

- Spot and combat price fixing?
- Use the futures market to hedge the purchase of raw materials?
- Know when to allow price changes during a contract?

Determination of the price to be paid is a major supply decision. The ability to get a "good price" is sometimes held to be the prime test of a good buyer. If "good price" means greatest value, broadly defined, this is true. Three key decisions are addressed in this chapter: (1) What is the right price to pay? (2) What represents best value? and (3) How can we assure we are paying the right price?

While price is only one aspect of the overall supply job, it is extremely important. The purchaser must be alert to different pricing methods, know when each is appropriate, and use skill in arriving at the price to be paid. There is no reason to apologize for emphasizing price or for giving it a place of importance among the factors to be considered. The purchaser rightly is expected to get the best value possible for the organization whose funds are spent.

While competitive bidding can be used for some purchases, purchasing in the commodities market requires a much different approach and buyer skill set. This chapter examines how suppliers set prices and techniques that can be used to establish and adjust prices. Chapter 11 complements the material covered in this chapter by addressing supplier cost analysis and negotiation.

RELATION OF COST TO PRICE

Every supply manager believes the supplier should be paid a fair price. But what does "fair price" mean? A fair price is the lowest price that ensures a continuous supply of the proper quality where and when needed.

A "continuous supply" is possible in the long run only from a supplier who is making a reasonable profit. The supplier's total costs, including a reasonable profit, must be covered by total sales in the long run. Any one item in the line, however, may never contribute "its full share" over any given period, but even for such an item the price paid normally should at least cover the direct costs incurred.

A fair price to one seller for any one item may be higher than a fair price to another or for an equally satisfactory substitute item. Both may be "fair prices" as far as the buyer is concerned, and the buyer may pay both prices at the same time.

Merely because a price is set by a monopolist or is established through collusion among sellers does not, in and of itself, make that price unfair or excessive. Likewise, the prevailing price need not necessarily be a fair price, as, for example, when such price is a "black" or "gray" market price or when it is depressed or raised through monopolistic or coercive action.

The supply manager is called on continuously to exercise judgment about what the "fair price" should be under a variety of circumstances. In part, accuracy in weighing the various factors that culminate in a "fair and just price" depends on capitalizing on past experience and thorough knowledge of production processes for goods and services and associated costs, as well as logistics costs such as storage, transportation, service delivery, and other relevant costs.

Meaning of Cost

Assuming this concept of a fair price is sound, what are the relationships between cost and price? To stay in business over the long run, a supplier must cover total costs, including overhead, and receive a profit. Otherwise, eventually the supplier will be forced out of business. This reduces the number of sources available to the buyer and may cause scarcity, higher prices, less-satisfactory service, and lower quality.

But what is to be included in the term *cost?* At times it is defined to mean only direct labor and material costs, and in a period of depressed business conditions, a seller may be willing merely to recover this amount rather than not make a sale at all. Or cost may mean direct labor and material costs with a contribution toward overhead. If the cost for a particular item includes overhead, is the latter charged at the actual rate (provided it can be determined), or is it charged at an average rate? The average rate may be far from the actual rate.

Most knowledgeable businesspeople realize that determining the cost of a particular article or service is not a precise process. There are two basic classifications of costs: *direct* and *indirect.*

Direct costs can be specifically and accurately assigned to a given unit of production or a specific identifiable task performed by a service provider. For example in manufacturing, direct material is 10 pounds of steel or direct labor is 30 minutes of a person's time on a machine or assembly line. For a service provider that has inventory, direct material costs are parts and supplies used to provide the service, for example cleaning supplies in a janitorial service. Direct labor costs are the wages paid to the professionals and fees paid to contract or freelance labor to deliver the service. However, under accepted accounting practices, the actual price may not be the cost included in determining direct material costs. Because the price paid may fluctuate over a period of time, it is common practice to use a standard cost. Some companies use the last price paid in the immediately prior fiscal period. Others use an average price for a specific period.

Indirect costs are incurred in the operation of a production plant or process or service organization, but normally cannot be related directly to any given unit of production or service provided. Some examples are rent, property taxes, machine depreciation, expenses of general supervisors, data processing, power, heat, and light. Indirect costs often are referred to as *overhead.* They may be fixed or variable.

Classification of costs into variable, semivariable, and fixed categories is a common accounting practice and necessary for any meaningful analysis of price/cost relationships. Most direct costs are **variable costs** because they vary directly and proportionally with the units produced. For example, a product that requires 10 pounds of steel for one unit will require 100 pounds for 10 units.

Semivariable costs may vary with the number of units produced but are partly variable and partly fixed. For example, more heat, light, and power are used when a plant is operating at 90 percent of capacity than when operating at 50 percent, but the difference is not directly proportional to the number of units produced. In fact, there would be some costs (fixed) for heat, light, and power if production were stopped completely for a period of time.

Fixed costs generally remain the same regardless of the number of units produced. For example, real estate taxes will be the same for a given period of time regardless of whether one unit or 100,000 units are produced. Several accounting methods can be used to allocate fixed costs. A common method is to apply a percentage of direct costs in order to allocate the cost of factory overhead. Full allocation of fixed expenses will depend on an accurate forecast of production and the percentage used. Obviously, as full production capacity is reached, the percentage rate will decline.

Factory overhead often is based on some set percentage of direct labor cost because, historically, labor represented the largest cost element. Although rarely true now, standard cost accounting often has not changed. Selling, general, and administrative expense is based on a set percentage of total manufacturing cost or services cost. The following example illustrates the typical product cost buildup in a manufacturing setting:

Direct materials	$ 5,500
+ Direct labor	2,000
+ Factory overhead*	2,500
= Manufacturing cost	**$10,000**
+ General, administrative, and selling cost	1,500
= Total cost	**$11,500**
+ Profit	920
= Selling price	**$12,420**

*Factory overhead consists of all *indirect* factory costs, both *fixed* and *variable*.

Costs can be defined as dollars and cents per unit based on an average cost for raw material over a period of time, direct labor costs, and an estimated volume of production over a period of time on which the distribution of overhead is based. Cost of services or cost of revenue includes all expenses that occur only when services are sold or expenses that increase or decrease as sales of the service increase or decrease. Expenses commonly included in the cost of services are sales commissions, fees or wages for professionals and contract labor paid by projects, transportation costs to deliver services, and rental costs for equipment or tools that occur only when services are sold.

If this definition of cost is acceptable, then a logical question is: Whose cost? Some manufacturers are more efficient than others. Usually all sell the same item at about the same price. But should this price be high enough to cover only the most efficient supplier's costs, or should it cover the costs of all suppliers? Furthermore, cost does not necessarily determine market price. A seller's insistence that a price must be a given amount because of costs is not justified. Goods are worth and will sell for what the market will pay.

Moreover, no seller is entitled to a price that yields a profit merely because the supplier is in business or assumes risk. If so, every business automatically would be entitled to a profit regardless of costs, quality, or service. A seller that cannot efficiently supply a market with goods that are needed and desired by users is not entitled to get a price that even covers costs.

HOW SUPPLIERS ESTABLISH PRICE

Depending on the commodity and industry, the market may vary from almost pure competition to oligopoly and monopoly. Pricing varies accordingly. For competitive reasons, most firms will not disclose how prices are set, but the two traditional methods are the cost approach and the market approach.

The Cost Approach

The cost approach means that price is a certain amount over direct costs, allowing for sufficient contribution to cover indirect costs and overhead and leaving a certain margin for profit. This provides the purchaser with opportunities to seek lower-cost suppliers, to suggest lower-cost manufacturing or service alternatives, and to question the size of the margin over direct costs. Negotiation, used with cost-analysis techniques, is a particularly useful tool.

The Market Approach

The market approach implies that prices are set in the marketplace and may not be directly related to cost. If demand is high relative to supply, prices are expected to rise; when demand is low relative to supply, prices should decline. This, too, is an oversimplification. Some economists hold that large multinational, multiproduct firms have such a grip on the marketplace that pure competition does not exist and that prices will not drop even though supply exceeds demand.

In the market approach, the purchaser either lives with prevailing market prices or finds ways around them. If nothing can be done to attack the price structure directly, it still may be possible to select suppliers willing to offer nonprice incentives, such as holding inventory, technical and design service, guaranteeing specific people as part of a service contract, superior quality, excellent delivery, transportation concessions, and early warning of impending price and product changes. Negotiation, therefore, may center on items other than price.

Many economists hold that substitution of like but not identical materials or products is one of the most powerful forces preventing a completely monopolistic or oligopolistic grip on a market. For example, aluminum and copper may be interchanged in a number of applications. The aluminum and copper markets, therefore, are not independent of one another. The purchaser's ability to recognize these trade-offs and to effect design and use changes to take advantage of substitution is one determinant of flexibility. Make or buy (or outsource or in-source) is another option. If access to the raw materials, technological process, and labor skills is not severely restricted, one alternative may be for an organization to make its own requirements to avoid excess market prices. When buying services, substitutability of one service provider for another may hinge on the perceived value of the service provider's expertise.

Sometimes purchasers use long-term contracts to induce the supplier to ignore market conditions. This may be successful in certain instances, but suppliers normally find ways around such commitments once it becomes obvious that the prevailing market price is substantially above that paid by their long-term customers.

GOVERNMENT INFLUENCE ON PRICING

The government's role in establishing price has changed dramatically. The role of government has been twofold. The government can have an active role in determining prices by establishing production and import quotas and regulating the ways that buyers and sellers are allowed to behave in agreeing on prices. Because other governments are active in price control and have, in a number of situations such as natural gas prices in Russia, created dual pricing for domestic use and exports, it is difficult to see how the U.S. and Canadian governments will be able to ignore their position. Prices may be determined by review or control boards or by strong moral suasion. They are likely to be augmented by governmental controls such as quotas, tariffs, and export permits.

Governments influence prices of utilities that offer common services, such as electricity and water, and set prices on licenses and goods and services provided by government-run organizations, such as postal services. Energy deregulation is still in its infancy but will be an interesting and challenging area for purchasers to watch.

The U.S. Postal Service, a quasi-governmental organization, also is undergoing changes as it forges alliances with private-industry competitors such as FedEx and UPS. Despite receiving no tax dollars for operating expenses, key decisions, including prices and fees charged, services offered, and the pension coverage calculation, are made by various government entities while the Postal Service relies on the sale of postage, products, and services to fund its operations.

Other nations have taken various steps to introduce competition into their national postal service. For example, Germany privatized Deutsche Post in 2000, and now DHL is part of the world's leading postal and logistics Group, Deutsche Post DHL. What these changes will mean in terms of pricing and negotiation opportunities remains to be seen.

Legislation Affecting Price Determination

While there are differences in United States and Canadian laws related to pricing, both federal governments have taken an active interest in how a buyer and seller agree on a price.

United States

The government has largely played a protective role by preventing the stronger party from imposing too onerous conditions on the weaker one or preventing collusion so that competition is maintained.

The two most important federal laws affecting competition and pricing practices are the Sherman Antitrust and Robinson-Patman acts. The **Sherman Antitrust Act** of 1890 states that any combination, conspiracy, or collusion with the intent of restricting trade in interstate commerce is illegal. It is illegal for suppliers to get together to set prices (price fixing) or determine the terms and conditions under which they will sell. For example, following a three-year investigation by the U.S. Department of Justice Antitrust Division, 26 Japanese companies in the automotive parts industry pleaded guilty of bid-rigging and price-fixing. By February 2014, the companies had agreed to pay criminal fines of over $2 billion. Twenty-eight individuals were also charged.[1] Buyers cannot get together to set the prices they will pay.

Over 120 countries have antitrust laws of some sort to protect competition. There is increasing cooperation in investigating international cartels, and many multinational mergers are reviewed by antitrust agencies.

The Robinson-Patman Act (Federal Anti-Price Discrimination Act of 1936) says that a supplier must sell the same item, in the same quantity, to all customers at the same price. It is known as the "one-price law." Some exceptions are permitted, such as a lower price (1) for a larger purchase quantity, providing the seller can cost justify the lower price through cost accounting data; (2) for moving distress or obsolete merchandise; or (3) for meeting the lower price of local competition in a particular geographic area. It is also illegal for a buyer to *knowingly* induce or accept a discriminatory price. However, the courts have held that it is the buyer's job to get the best possible price, and as long as a buyer does not intentionally mislead the seller into giving a more favorable price than is available to other buyers of the same item, the law is not being violated.

A buyer can file a charge detailing the alleged violation to the Federal Trade Commission (FTC), which investigates alleged improprieties. Bringing a seller's actions to the government's attention has few advantages for a buyer. Typically, the government's reaction is relatively slow; the need for the item may be gone and conditions may be substantially changed by the time the complaint is decided. Most sellers view a complaint as an unfriendly act, making it difficult to maintain a reasonable future relationship with that particular supplier. For this reason, complaints are not common, and most are lodged by public buying agencies rather than corporations.

Canada

Canadian federal pricing legislation differs from U.S. legislation, but it has essentially the same intent. It prohibits certain pricing practices in an attempt to maintain competition in the marketplace and applies to both buyers and sellers. Violation of the statute is a criminal offense. Suppliers or buyers may not "conspire, combine, agree, or arrange with another person" to raise prices unreasonably or to otherwise restrain competition. It does not prevent the exchange of data within a trade or professional association, providing it does not lessen price competition. Bid rigging is a per se violation, which means that the prosecution need only establish the existence of an agreement to gain a conviction; there is no requirement to prove that the agreement unduly affected competition. It is also illegal for a supplier to grant a price concession to one buyer that is not available to all other buyers (similar to the U.S. Robinson-Patman Act).

Quantity discounts are permitted, as are one-time price cuts to clear out inventory. As in the United States, the Canadian buyer who knowingly is on the receiving end of price discrimination also has violated the law. With regard to price maintenance and the purchase

---

[1] www.justice.gov/opa/pr/2014/February/14-at-157.html

of goods for resale, it requires that a supplier should not, by threat or promise, attempt to influence how the firms that buy from it then price their products for resale.

TYPES OF PURCHASES

Analysis of suppliers' costs is by no means the only basis for price determination. What other means can be used? Much depends on the type of product being bought. As discussed in Chapter 6, there are seven general classes:

1. *Raw and semiprocessed materials.* This includes *sensitive commodities,* such as copper, wheat, and crude petroleum, but also steel, cement, and so forth. The Wedlock Engineered Products case at the end of this chapter provides an example of a supplier selection decision that involves raw material.

2. *Parts, components, and packaging.* This includes nuts and bolts, many forms of commercial steel, valves, and tubing, whose prices are fairly stable and are quoted on a basis of "list price with some discount."

3. *Maintenance, repair, and operating (MRO) supplies and small-value purchases (SVP).* Some organizations require a huge variety and number of MRO and SVP items. Effort to check price prior to purchase is not justified.

4. *Capital assets.* Capital assets are long-term assets that are not bought or sold in the regular course of business, have an ongoing effect on the organization's operations, have an expected use of more than one year, involve large sums of money, and generally are depreciated. Assets may be tangible or intangible. Historically, tangible assets (land, buildings, and equipment) have been the primary focus of managerial attention because they were the key drivers of wealth. Today, intangible assets (patents, copyrights, ideas, knowledge, and people) are important generators of wealth. Intangible assets are especially challenging because traditional accounting procedures do not include valuation methods for intangibles.

5. *Services.* This category is broad and includes many types of services, such as advertising, auditing, consulting, architectural design, legal, insurance, personnel travel, copying, security, and waste removal.

6. *Resale.* This category can be subdivided into two groups:

   a. Items that formerly were manufactured in-house but have been outsourced to a manufacturing supplier. For example, a major appliance maker markets a microwave oven but, instead of manufacturing the product, buys it under its own brand name. The decision process for these items is the same as presented in this book.

   b. Items sold in the retail sector, such as clothing sold in general-line department stores; food sold through supermarkets; tools sold in hardware stores; and tires, batteries, and accessories sold in gasoline/filling stations.

   The dollar amount involved in the purchase of these resale items is tremendous. The people who buy these items, merchandise managers, make their buying decisions based on the forecast of consumer demand. There is no detailed coverage of merchandise buying in this text, although many of the same supply principles and practices apply.

7. *Other.* This includes custom-ordered items and materials that are special to the organization's product line.

Raw and Semiprocessed Materials

Raw materials and commodities are normally quoted at market prices, which fluctuate daily. The price at any particular moment probably is less important than the trend of the price movement. The price can be determined readily in most instances because many of these commodities are bought and sold on well-organized markets. Prices are reported regularly online and in print in many of the trade and business journals and on websites, such as *American Metal Market (*www.amm.com)*, ICIS,* the world's largest petrochemical market information provider (icis.com), *Bloomberg.com,* and *The Wall Street Journal* (wsj.com). These quoted market prices can be useful in developing prices-paid evaluation systems and price indexes for use in price escalator clauses.

To the extent that quoted prices are a fair reflection of market conditions, the current cash price is known and is substantially uniform for a given grade. Such published market quotations usually are on the high side, and the astute buyer probably can get a lower price. A company's requirements for these commodities usually are sufficiently adjustable that purchase can be postponed if there is a downward price trend.

While the price trend is of importance in the purchase of any commodity, it is particularly important for this group. Insofar as "careful and studious timing" is essential to getting the right price, both the type of information required as a basis for such timing and the sources from which the information can be obtained differ from those necessary in dealing with other groups of items. Commodity study research, discussed in Chapter 17, is particularly useful in buying these items.

Parts, Components, and Packaging

The prices of parts, components, and packaging are comparatively stable and likely to be quoted on a basis of list-less-certain-discounts. This includes a range of items commonly obtainable from multiple sources. The inventory problems are largely routine. Changes in price do occur, but they are moderate and far less frequent than with raw materials. Prices usually are obtained from online or hard-copy catalogs or similar publications of suppliers, supplemented by periodic discount sheets.

Still price quotes should be examined carefully because annual dollar volume may be high and price per unit may be worth attention. If the material has been regularly or recently purchased, an up-to-date price record and catalog file give information about potential and current suppliers and prices paid. This enables the buyer to order without extended investigation. However, if the buyer thinks the information is incomplete, a list of available suppliers can be assembled from supplier files, catalogs, the Internet, and other sources and quotation requests issued. Online auctions (seller-initiated) or reverse auctions (buyer-initiated) are also used by some organizations to more efficiently purchase standard items (see Chapter 4).

Sales representatives are good sources for current prices and discounts. Few manufacturers rely wholly on catalogs (online or hard copy) for sales, but follow up such material with visits by their salespersons.

A sales representative may quote the buyer a price while in the buyer's office, and the buyer may accept by issuing a purchase order (PO). There likely will be no problem, although legally the salesperson probably doesn't have agency authority, and the offer made by the salesperson does not legally commit the selling company *until* it has been accepted by an officer of the selling company. If the buyer wishes to accept such an offer, and to know that the offer is legally binding, he or she should ask the salesperson to furnish a letter, signed by an officer of the selling company, stating that the salesperson possesses the authority of a sales *agent* (see Chapter 15).

Maintenance, Repair, and Operating Supplies (MRO) and Small-Value Purchases (SVPs)

MRO includes items of small comparative value, and prices are typically competitive so no special effort is required to analyze price. Every supply department buys MRO items, yet they do not justify a catalog file, even when such catalogs are available, nor do they represent enough money to warrant requests for quotations. The pricing problem is handled in a variety of ways; the following constitutes an excellent summary of these procedures.

As discussed in Chapter 4, MRO items may be procured through e-procurement systems. While the actual transaction is handled electronically, most of the advantages come from applying good supply practices, such as consolidating and standardizing requirements and reducing the number of suppliers.

Other common practices include sending out unpriced orders and indicating on the order the last price paid or buying on a cost-plus basis with suppliers who have the materials in inventory and then conducting price checks. Procurement cards allow internal customers to purchase small-value items from designated suppliers. Perhaps a more effective way to buy items of small value, such as those included in the MRO group, is to use the systems-contracting, vendor-managed inventory (VMI), and third-party supplier techniques described in Chapters 4 and 8.

Typically, sources of supply for small-value items are local, and current prices often are obtained online or by telephone or fax. Prices are included on the purchase order so they become a part of the agreement. The most common practice is to rely on the integrity of the suppliers and omit detailed price checking. The supply manager's goal when purchasing small-value items is to minimize the cost of acquisition, that is, the ordering process costs. Spot-checking is often used to control prices for small-dollar items. Discovery of unfair or improper prices is a reason for discontinuing the source of supply.

Similar to the small-value purchase problem is the emergency requirement. For example, with equipment breakdown, time may be of much greater value than money, and the buyer may wish to get the supplier started immediately even though price has not been determined. The buyer may decide merely to say "start" or "ship" and issue an unpriced purchase order. If the price charged on the invoice is out of line, it can be challenged before payment.

Capital Assets

As addressed in Chapter 6, "Need Identification and Specification," capital assets include equipment, IT, real estate, and construction. Because of the high-dollar amount and the long-term consequences of many capital projects, purchase price is often a small percentage of total cost of ownership. The application of tools and techniques such as enterprisewide spend analysis; standardization of equipment, including hardware and software; globalization of processes; and cost visibility are important. Price determination tools range from request for proposals (RFP) to competitive bidding to negotiation.

Services

Pricing in services may be fixed or variable, by the job or by the hour, day, or week. Prices may be obtained by competitive bid if the size of the contract warrants it; enough competitors are available; and adequate, specific, consistent specifications can be prepared.

Negotiation is commonly used to establish prices and may be the only option in sole-source situations. Volume and size can be used effectively as leverage by the knowledgeable supply manager. Understanding the cost structure of the service is helpful in revealing negotiation opportunities. For example, if a service provider has offshored high-paid service providers such as research analysts, engineers, or computer animators to lower-labor-cost countries, how does this change the service provider's cost structure? Depending on the relative strength of each party, the changed cost structure might be a negotiating point.

It is not unusual to estimate professional time required without committing to a specific figure. Most supply managers probably would prefer such contracts to have a "not to exceed limit." Some professionals, such as architects, may quote their fee based on a percentage of the total job cost. But from a supply standpoint, this removes the incentive for the architect to seek the best value for the total job.

Resale

Merchandise managers must determine a fair price to pay for resale items that allows both the supplier and the merchandiser to make a profit. As discussed in Chapter 6, the largest single cost for a reseller who takes ownership of the goods it resells is what it paid for the goods or services. Although resale is not covered specifically in this text, many of the concepts and practices of price and cost management apply.

Other

Other items include the large variety of purchased parts or special materials peculiar to the organization's end product or service. Make or buy is always a significant consideration because of the proprietary nature of these items. Prices normally are obtained by quotation because published price lists are unavailable. Subcontracts are common, and the availability of compatible or special equipment, skilled labor, and capacity may be significant factors in determining price. Because large differences may exist between suppliers in terms of these factors and their desire for business, prices may vary substantially. Each product is unique and may need special attention. A diligent search for suppliers willing and able to handle such special requirements, including an advantageous price, may pay off handsomely.

THE USE OF QUOTATIONS AND COMPETITIVE BIDDING

Quotations normally are secured when the size of the proposed commitment exceeds some minimum dollar amount, for example, $1,000. Governmental purchases commonly must be on a bid basis; here the law requires that the award be made to the lowest *responsible* and *responsive* bidder. In the private sector, organizations may solicit quotations and negotiate the final price.

The use of competitive bidding for price determination varies widely. It is a common practice for buyers of routine supplies, purchased from the same sources time after time, to issue unpriced orders or to order automatically through an e-procurement system. The same thing occasionally happens in a very strong seller's market for some critical item when prices are rising so rapidly that the supplier refuses to quote a fixed price. Whenever possible, however, price should be indicated on the purchase order. In fact, from a legal point of view, a purchase order *must* contain either a price or a method of its determination for the contract to be binding. With competitive bids, the following are required: a careful initial selection of dependable, potential sources; an accurate wording of the request to bid; submission of bid requests to a sufficient number of suppliers to ensure a truly competitive price; proper treatment of quotations; and a careful analysis prior to award.

Steps in the Bidding Process

The first step is to screen sources of supply and select potential suppliers from whom quotations will be solicited. It is assumed that the bidders must (1) be qualified to make the item in accordance with the buyer's specifications and to deliver it by the desired date, (2) be sufficiently reliable, (3) be numerous enough to ensure a truly competitive price, but (4) not be more numerous than necessary. The first two issues were considered in our discussion of sources. The *number* of suppliers to whom inquiries are sent is largely a matter of the buyer's judgment. Ordinarily, at least two suppliers are invited to bid. More often, three or four are. Multiple bidders do not ensure a competitive price, although under ordinary circumstances it is an important factor if bidders are comparable and each is sufficiently reliable and the buyer would purchase from them.

The buyer normally will exclude from the bid list those firms with whom it is unlikely to place an order even though their prices are low. Sometimes bids are solicited solely for the purpose of price checking or for inventory-pricing purposes. It costs a company to submit a bid. Suppliers should not be asked to bear this cost without good reason. Moreover, the receipt of a request to bid is an encouragement to the supplier and implies that an order is possible. Therefore, purchasers should not solicit quotations unless placement of a purchase order is a possibility.

Off-line Process

After selecting the companies to be invited to bid, the purchaser in an off-line process sends a general inquiry that includes a complete description of the item(s), the delivery date, and the due date for bids. A telephone inquiry may be substituted for a formal request to bid.

Between mailing an inquiry and awarding the contract, bidders want to know how their quotations compare with competitors. Because sealed bids, used in governmental/public purchasing, are not commonly used in private industry, the purchaser is in a position to know how the bids, as they are received, compare with one another. However, if the bids are examined on receipt, it is important that this information be treated in strictest confidence. Indeed, some buyers deliberately keep quotations secret until they are ready to analyze the bids; thus, they are in a position to tell any inquiring bidder truthfully that they do not know how the bid prices compare. Even after the award is made, it probably is the better policy not to reveal to unsuccessful bidders the amount by which they failed to meet the successful bid.

Electronic Process

In both the public and private sectors, the entire bid process may be automated. For example, the federal governments in the United States and Canada (http://www.tpsgc-pwgsc.

gc.ca) have well-established electronic procurement systems. On the U.S. FedBizOpps site (fbo.gov), more than 20,000 active federal opportunities were listed in early 2014.

Beginning in 2009, the Mexican government modernized its procurement methods, eliminated obsolete regulations, built in methods for transparency, and created an on-line platform to ensure transparency and ease of access. This reduced execution time by 95 percent. Within three years, small and medium enterprises increased their participation in the federal procurement system by 36 percent, and the government saved $1 billion USD. Bid packages and specifications are made available online, bidders submit their bid and proposals online, and the bid opening and award are communicated electronically. The cycle time reductions and other cost savings can be great if the automated process is efficient.

This process is similar to an online bid. In an online auction, the potential sources are prequalified and invited to participate. The auction, or event, is set for a specific date and time period much like the deadline and bid opening deadlines in an off-line process. Auction success depends on the quality of the bid specifications and the ability of the person and process to prequalify suppliers. Bidders can see, online, the actual bid amounts but not who the bidders are (see Chapter 4).

Firm Bidding

Bid price information is treated confidentially because buyers often face "firm bidding." Most organizations have a policy of notifying suppliers that original bids must be final (firm) and that revisions will not be permitted under any circumstances. Exceptions are made only in the case of obvious error.

When prices are falling and suppliers need orders, suppliers try to ensure that their bids will be the lowest. Frequently, suppliers are encouraged by purchasers who have acceded to requests that revisions be allowed. Unfortunately, it is also true that there are buyers who deliberately play one bidder against another and who even seek to secure lower prices by relating imaginary bids to prospective suppliers. The responsibility for deviations from a policy of firm bidding lies with the purchaser as well as the supplier.

A policy of firm bidding is sound and should be deviated from only under the most unusual circumstances. This is the practice followed in many organizations. The advantage of firm bidding as a general policy is that it is the fairest possible means of treating all suppliers alike. It tends to stress the quality and service elements in the transaction instead of the price factor. Assuming that bids are solicited only from honest and dependable suppliers and that the buyer is not obligated to place the order with the lowest bidder, it removes from suppliers the temptation to try to use inferior materials or workmanship once their bid has been accepted. It saves the purchaser time by removing the necessity for constant bargaining with suppliers over price.

An exception to the firm bidding approach is one in which the buyer wants both parties (seller and buyer) to have the flexibility to clarify and define specifications and prices further after the initial bids are received. The buyer will notify all the sellers in the bid request that, after the initial bids are received, the buyer may enter into discussions with one or more of the bidders, and then request best-and-final-offers (BAFOs). Some public buying agencies also use this approach.

Occasionally the buyer may notify bidders that all bids are being rejected and another bid request is being issued, or that the item will be bought through a means other than competitive bidding. This is done if it is obvious that the bidders did not fully understand the specifications, if collusion on the part of the bidders is suspected, or if it is felt that all prices quoted are unrealistically high.

Determination of Most Advantageous Bid

Typically, a bid analysis arrays the bids or they are viewed electronically in real time during an online auction. The lowest bid customarily is accepted. The objective of securing bids from various sources is to obtain the lowest price, and the purpose of supplying detailed specifications and statements of requirements is to ensure receipt of the same items or services from any bidder. Governmental contracts must be awarded to the lowest bidder unless very special reasons can be shown for not doing so.

Sometimes the lowest bidder may not receive the order. This occurs when the buyer discovers that the lowest bidder is unreliable, the lowest bid is higher than the buyer believes justifiable, or there is reason to believe bidders colluded. Also, users such as plant management, engineering, or marketing may prefer a certain supplier's product. A slight difference in price may not compensate for the confidence in a particular supplier's product or service, or satisfaction with a long-term supplier. Yet the bid process may be essential in ensuring proper price treatment.

Selecting the supplier is not a simple matter of listing the bidders and picking out the one whose price is apparently low, because the obvious price comparisons may be misleading. Of two apparently identical bids, one actually may be higher than the other. One supplier's installation costs may be lower than another's. If prices quoted are FOB origin (buyer pays freight charges), the transportation charges may be markedly different. One supplier's price may be much lower because it is trying to break into a new market or is trying to force its only real competitor out of business. One supplier's product may require tooling that must be amortized. One supplier may quote a fixed price; another may insist on an escalator clause that could push the price above a competitor's firm bid. These and other factors render a snap judgment on comparative price a mistake.

The Coral Drugs case at the end of this chapter and the Carson Manor case in Chapter 6 are examples of organizations facing complex supplier selection decisions following a bidding process.

Collusive Bidding

A buyer also may reject all bids if it is suspected that the suppliers are acting in collusion with one another. The proper policy is often difficult to determine, but there are various possibilities. Legal action is possible but seldom feasible because of the expense, delay, and uncertainty of the outcome. Often, unfortunately, the only apparent solution is to accept the situation because there is nothing the buyer can do about it anyway. Another possibility is to seek new sources of supply either inside or outside the area in which the buyer customarily has purchased materials or services. Using substitute materials, temporarily or permanently, may be an effective solution. Another possibility is to reject all the bids and then try to negotiate with one supplier to reduce the price. If negotiation is the most feasible alternative, a question of ethics is involved. Some supply managers believe that supplier collusion means it is ethical for them to attempt to force down prices by means that ordinarily would not be adopted.

Public-Sector Bidding

The process for bidding in the public sector is similar to the private sector, but there are a few important differences. Public statutes normally provide that the award of purchase contracts should be made on the basis of open, competitive bidding. The goal is to ensure that all qualified suppliers who are taxpayers or who employ personnel who are taxpayers, have an equal opportunity to compete for the sale of products or services needed to operate government. Since bids are open to public inspection, it is difficult for the public buyer to show favoritism to any one supplier. This system tends to put a heavy weight on price as the basis for supplier selection because it might be difficult for the buyer to defend selecting a higher-priced supplier. Providing a list of weighted criteria for bid evaluations in the invitation to bid allows the buyer to consider nonprice factors (see Chapter 13).

Either by law, statute, or regulation or as a matter of normal operating policy, public purchasers in North America and Europe are required to advertise upcoming purchases in specified newspapers or online. The advertisement informs interested suppliers how to access or receive a request for bid for a particular requirement. The buyer then determines whether the supplier meets the minimum supplier qualifications. Advertising ensures that purchasing is not conducted under a veil of secrecy.

The public buyer generally must be willing to consider any supplier who requests to be put on the bid list if the supplier meets the minimum standards for a responsible bidder in measurable terms. However, public purchasers should be aggressive in ferreting out new potential supply sources. Public purchasers are required to award contracts to the lowest "responsible" and "responsive" bidder. A *responsible* bidder is fully capable and willing to perform the work; a *responsive* bidder submits a bid that conforms to the invitation for bid.

In some public agencies, a purchase award cannot be made unless at least some minimum number of bids (often three) have been received. If the minimum number is not received, the requirement must be rebid, or the buyer must justify that the nature of the requirement is such that it is impossible to obtain bids from more suppliers.

Use of Bid Bonds and Deposits

There may be a legal or policy requirement for bidders to submit a bond at the time of the bid, especially for large-dollar bids or construction. Or the bidders are required to submit a certified check or money order in a fixed percentage amount of the bid. If the selected bidder does not agree to sign the final purchase contract or does not perform according to the terms of the bid, this amount is retained as liquidated damages for nonperformance. The bid bond or bid deposit is designed to discourage irresponsible bidders from competing. In high-risk situations, the extra cost of the bid bond, which in some way will be passed back as an extra cost to the buyer, is warranted; in the purchase of standard, stock items available from several sources, the use of a bond is questionable.

There are three general types of bonds. Most bidders purchase each, for a dollar premium, from an insurance company, thus effectively transferring some of the risk to the insurance carrier:

1. The *bid (or surety) bond* guarantees that if the bidder wins it will accept the purchase contract. If the supplier refuses, the extra costs to the buyer of going to an alternative source are borne by the insurer.

2. The *performance bond* guarantees work will be done according to specifications and in the time specified. If another supplier does rework or completes the order, purchasing is indemnified for these extra costs.

3. The *payment bond* protects the buyer against liens that might be granted to suppliers of material and labor to the bidder, in the event the bidder does not make proper payment to its suppliers.

In a multiple-year contract or one with high initial costs, the purchaser may want to break the performance bond into periods or stages of completion to avoid having the surety write the bond too high and increase the cost of the contract too much.

Bid Opening, Evaluation, and Award

In an off-line system, at the hour and date specified in the bid instructions, the buyer opens and records all bids. Usually, any interested party can attend the bid opening and examine any of the bids. The original bids are retained for later inspection by any interested party for a specified time period (often 12 months). In an e-procurement system these steps are done electronically. For example, many U.S. government opportunities and awards are processed through fedbizopps.gov. Most U.S. states and Canadian provinces have a similar e-procurement system.

After the bid opening, the buyer analyzes the bids for conformance to bid requirements and prepares a recommended purchase action. Large-dollar purchases may require council approval in a municipality or cabinet approval for a federal or state procurement.

If multiple bid criteria apply and if two or more responsible bidders meet the specifications and conditions, the supplier with the best rating is selected. Other actions by the buyer must be justified. If identical low bids are received, and the buyer has no evidence or indication of collusion or other bid irregularities, then the buyer must find an acceptable way of resolving this issue.

The public buyer has no obligation to notify unsuccessful bidders because the bid opening was a public event and the bid and award documents are retained and may be viewed. In an e-procurement system, bidders can access the information online.

Bid Errors

If the successful low bidder notifies the buyer of an error after the bid has been submitted, but before the award of the purchase order has been made, normally the bid may be withdrawn. However, the buyer makes note of this, since it reflects on the responsibility of the bidder.

A much-more-serious problem arises if the bidder, claiming a bid error, attempts to withdraw the bid *after* it has been awarded. A bid bond helps protect the buyer. If no bid bond exists, the buyer must decide on court action to force performance or collect damages or go to the closest other successful bidder (who now may no longer be interested) or go through the bid process again. Legally, if the mistake was mechanical in nature, a mathematical error, the courts probably will side with the supplier. However, if it was an error in judgment—for example, the supplier misjudged the rate of escalation in material prices—then the courts generally will not permit relief to the supplier. Also, for the supplier to gain relief in the courts, the supplier must show that once the error was discovered, the buying agency was notified promptly.

If the buyer receives a bid that commonsense and knowledge of the market indicates is unrealistic, the bid should be rechecked and the bidder requested to reaffirm that it is a bona fide bid. In the long run, such action likely will be cheaper than a protracted legal battle with an uncertain outcome.

Competition Concerns

Since public purchasers share bid information with each other, they are in a unique position to watch for illegal trade practices by suppliers. Collusion may be evident from artificially high prices, identical prices, unwillingness to bid, the rotation of low bidder among a small group of bidders, the apparent favoring of a particular bidder on a specific requirement area, and so on. Every country has an agency or bureau that investigates anticompetitive practices and prosecutes perpetrators. The antitrust division of the U.S. Department of Justice and the Competition Bureau in Canada perform these tasks.

The Problem of Identical Prices

It is not unusual to receive identical bids from various sources. This may indicate intensive competition or discrimination or collusion. Identical or parallel prices are suspect when:

1. Identical pricing marks a novel break in the historical pattern of price behavior.
2. There is evidence of communication between sellers or buyers regarding prices.
3. There is an "artificial" standardization of the product.
4. Identical prices are submitted in bids to buyers on complex, detailed, or novel specifications.
5. Deviations from uniform prices become the matter of industrywide concern—the subject of meetings and even organized sanctions.

There are four types of action to discourage identical pricing. First, encourage small sellers who form the nonconformist group in an industry and are anxious to grow. Second, allow bids on parts of large contracts if bidders feel the total contract is too large. Third, encourage firm bidding without revision. Fourth, choose award criteria that discourage future identical bids.

If identical bids are received, the buyer can reject all bids and then either call for new bids or negotiate directly with one or more specific suppliers. If the contract is going to be awarded, it may be given to:

1. The smallest supplier.
2. The one with the largest domestic content.
3. The most distant firm, forcing it to absorb the largest freight portion.
4. The firm with the smallest market share.
5. The firm most likely to grant nonprice concessions.
6. The firm whose past performance has been best.

Competitive bidding is used to obtain a fair price; the forces of competition are used to bring the price down to a level at which the efficient supplier will be able to cover only production and distribution costs, plus make a minimum profit. If a supplier wants the order, that supplier will review and improve the offer and give the buyer an attractive quote. This places a good deal of pressure on the supplier.

Several conditions are necessary for the bid process to work efficiently: (1) there must be at least two, and preferably several, qualified suppliers; (2) the suppliers must want the business (competitive bidding works best in a buyer's market); (3) the specifications must be clear, so that each bidder knows precisely what it is bidding on, and so that the buyer can easily compare quotes; and (4) there must be honest bidding and the absence of collusion. When any of these conditions is absent—that is, a sole-source situation, a seller's market, specifications that are not complete or subject to varying interpretations, or suspected supplier collusion— then negotiation is the preferred method of price determination (see Chapter 11).

DISCOUNTS

Discounts represent a legitimate and effective means of reducing prices. The most commonly used types of discounts are cash discounts, multiple discounts, quantity discounts, and cumulative or volume discounts. They may be offered by suppliers or negotiated by purchasers.

Cash Discounts

Cash discounts are granted by virtually every seller of industrial goods. The actual discount terms are determined by individual trade custom and vary considerably. The purpose of a cash discount is to secure the prompt payment of an account.

For example, a 2/10 net 30 cash discount means a discount of 2 percent if payment is made within 10 days, with the gross amount due in 30 days. This is the equivalent of earning an annual interest rate of approximately 36 percent. If the buying company does not pay within the 10-day discount period but instead pays 20 days later, the effective cost for the use of that money for the 20 days is 2 percent (the lost discount). Because there are approximately 18 20-day periods in a year, $2\% \times 18 = 36\%$, the effective annual interest rate.

Most sellers expect buyers to take the cash discount. The net price is commonly fixed at a point that will yield a fair profit to the supplier and is the price the supplier expects most customers to pay. Those who do not pay within the time limit are penalized and are expected to pay the gross price. However, variations in cash discount amounts frequently are used merely as another means of varying prices. If a buyer secures a cash discount not commonly granted in the past, the net result is merely a reduction in the price. A reduction in the size of the cash discount is, in effect, an increase in the price.

Cash discounts sometimes raise difficult questions about price policy. If the same terms and practices are granted to all buyers, then the supply department's major interest in cash discounts is bringing them to the attention of financial managers. The purchaser ordinarily cannot be held responsible for a failure to take cash discounts because this depends on the financial resources of the organization and is, therefore, a matter of financial rather than supply policy. The purchaser should, however, be very careful to secure such cash discounts as customarily are granted. The buyer is responsible for ensuring prompt inspection and acceptance and expeditious document handling so discounts may be taken.

The exact date by which payment must be mailed or electronically transferred to take the discount must be established. Some purchase orders specify that "determination of the cash discount payment period will be calculated from either the date of delivery of acceptable goods, or the receipt of a properly prepared invoice, whichever date is later."

Some customers will take the cash discount even when they are paying after the discount date. Part of the buyer's responsibility is to ensure that his or her organization lives up to the terms and conditions of the contract. This means working with other functional areas to ensure that payment is made in a timely manner.

Trade Discounts

Trade discounts are granted by a manufacturer to a particular type of distributor or user. They aim to protect the distributor by making it more profitable for a purchaser to buy from the distributor than directly from the manufacturer. Manufacturers use distributors in territories where the distributors can sell more cheaply than the manufacturer. The distributor is granted a trade discount approximating the cost of doing business to move goods through the channel.

Trade discounts may be used improperly when protection is granted to distributors not entitled to it, because the services they provide to manufacturers and customers are not commensurate with the discount. Generally speaking, buyers dealing in small quantities who secure a great variety of items from a single source or who depend on frequent and very prompt deliveries are more likely to obtain their supplies from wholesalers and other distributors receiving trade discounts. Manufacturers are more likely to sell directly to large accounts, even though they may reserve the smaller accounts in the same territory for the wholesalers. Some manufacturers refuse to sell to accounts below a stipulated minimum annual volume.

Discounts often are available to a buyer who also purchases aftermarket requirements (replacement parts for units already sold). The supplier may put the buyer who wishes to buy items that will be sold to the aftermarket into one of several price classifications: (1) an OEM (original equipment manufacturer) class, (2) a class with its distributors, or (3) a separate OEM aftermarket class. Aftermarket suppliers often do special packaging, part numbering, or stocking, which may justify a special price schedule. The buyer needs to know what price classifications the supplier uses and the qualifications for placing the buyer in a particular classification.

Multiple Discounts

In some industries and trades, prices are quoted on a multiple discount basis. For example, 10, 10, and 10 means that, for an item listed at $100, the actual price to be paid by the purchaser is ($100 − 10%) − 10%($100 − 10%) − 10%[($100 − 10%) − 10%($100 − 10%)] = $100 − $10 − $9 − $8.10 = $72.90. The 10, 10, and 10 is, therefore, equivalent to a discount of 27.1 percent. Tables are available listing the most common multiple discount combinations and their equivalent discount.

Quantity Discounts

Quantity discounts apply to particular quantities and vary roughly in proportion to the amount purchased. Sellers grant such discounts because volume purchases result in savings to the seller, enabling a lower price to the buyer. These savings may be marketing or distribution expense or production expense.

Marketing or distribution savings occur because it may be no more costly to sell a large order than a small one; the billing expense is the same; and the increased cost of packing, crating, and shipping is not proportional. A direct quantity discount not exceeding the difference in cost of handling the small and the large order is justified. Transport savings (e.g., truckload [TL] versus less-than-truckload [LTL]) is a classical example of quantity discounts.

Production cost savings occur because setup costs may be the same for a large order as a small one or material costs may be lower per unit.

For the buyer, quantity discounts are intimately connected with inventory policy. Larger order sizes may mean lower unit price, but carrying charges on larger inventory are more costly. Hence, the savings on the size of the order must be compared against the increased inventory costs.

The Price-Discount Problem

Accepting a price discount for ordering larger quantities leads to higher levels of anticipation inventory. Marginally, the question is, Should we increase the size of our inventory so that we obtain the benefits of the lower price? This can be analyzed as a return on investment (ROI) decision. The simple EOQ model is not of much assistance here because it cannot account for the purchase price differential directly. It is possible to use the EOQ model to eliminate some alternatives, however, and to check the final solution (see Chapter 8). Total cost calculations are required to find the optimal point.

The following problem is illustrative of the calculation:

$R = 900$ units (annual demand)

$S = \$50$ (order cost)

$K = 0.25$ or 25 percent (annual carrying cost)

	100	200	400	800
Total annual price paid	$40,500	$38,700	$37,350	$36,000
Carrying cost	562	1,075	2,075	4,000
Order cost	450	225	112	56
Total cost	41,512	40,000	39,537	40,056
Average inventory	$2,250	$4,300	8,300	16,000
EOQ (units)	89	92*	93*	94*

* Not feasible.

$C = \$45$ for 0–199 units per order

$\$43$ for 200–399 units per order

$\$41.50$ for 400–799 units per order

$\$40$ for 800 and more units per order

A simple marginal analysis shows that in moving from 100 per order to 200, the additional average investment is $4,300 - \$2,250 = \$2,050$. The saving in price is $\$40,500 - \$38,700 = \$1,800$, and the order cost saving is $\$450 - \$225 = \$225$. For an additional investment of $\$2,050$, the savings are $\$2,025$, which is almost a 100 percent return and is well in excess of the 25 percent carrying cost. In going from 400 to 800, the additional investment is $7,700 for a total price and order savings of $1,406.25. This falls below the 25 percent carrying cost and would not be a desirable result. The total cost numbers show that the optimal purchase quantity is at the 400 level. The largest single saving occurs at the first price break at the 200 level.

The EOQs with an asterisk are not feasible because the price range and the volume do not match. For example, the price for the second EOQ of 92 is $45. Yet for the 200 to 400 range, the actual price is $43. The EOQ may be used, however, in the following way. In going from right to left on the table (from the lowest unit price to the highest price), proceed until the first valid EOQ is obtained. This is 89 for the 0 to 199 price range. Then the order quantity at each price discount around this EOQ is checked to see whether total costs at the higher order quantity are lower or higher than at the EOQ. Doing this for the example shown gives us a total cost at the valid EOQ level of 89 of:

Total annual price paid	$40,500
Carrying cost	500
Order cost	500
Total cost	$41,500

Because this total cost at the feasible EOQ of 89 units is above the total cost at the 200 order quantity level and the 400 and 800 order levels as well, the proper order quantity is 400, which gives the lowest total cost of all options.

The discussion so far has assumed that the quantity discount offered is based on orders of the full amount, forcing the purchaser to carry substantial inventories. The buyer prefers to take delivery in smaller quantities, but still get the discounted price. This might be negotiated through annual contracts, cumulative discounts, or blanket orders. This type of analysis also can identify what extra price differential the purchaser might be willing to pay to avoid carrying substantial stocks.

Quantity Discounts and Source Selection

The quantity discount question is also of interest because all quantity discounts, and especially those of the cumulative type, tend to restrict the number of suppliers, thereby affecting the choice of source.

The buyer should obtain discounts whenever possible. Ordinarily they come through the pressure of competition among sellers. Furthermore, an argument may be advanced that such discounts are a matter of right. The buyer is purchasing goods or merchandise, not crating or packing materials or transportation. The seller presumably should expect to earn a profit, not from those wholly auxiliary services, but rather from manufacturing and selling the merchandise processed. These auxiliary services are necessary, they must be performed, they must be paid for, and it is natural to expect the buyer to pay for them. But the buyer should not be expected to pay more than the actual cost of these auxiliary services.

When quantity discounts are justified because they contribute to reduced production costs by providing a volume of business large enough to reduce overhead expenses, more cautious reasoning is necessary. It is true that in some lines of business the larger the output, the lower the overhead cost per unit of product. It also may be true that without the volume from the large customers, the average cost of production would be higher. However, the small-volume buyers may place a greater total proportion of the seller's business than do the large-volume ones. For production costs, therefore, the small-volume buyers may contribute even more toward that volume so essential to the per-unit production cost than does the larger buyer.

Large customers may contend that ordering early in the season or prior to actual production justifies higher discounts because their orders keep the facility in production. While early season ordering may justify a lower price than later ordering, it should be granted to every order regardless of its size. This would properly be called a time discount, not a quantity discount.

Cumulative or Volume Discounts

A cumulative discount varies in proportion to the quantity purchased. It is based on the quantity purchased over a period of time not on the size of any one order. It is an incentive for continued patronage and the concentration of orders with a single supplier. Typically, distributing one's orders over many sources is uneconomical and costly. The supplier may pay more attention to the buyer's requirements if it is getting the larger portion of the purchaser's business.

The use of cumulative discounts must meet the same cost justification rules under the Robinson-Patman Act as other quantity discounts. However, as long as the buyer is not knowingly accepting or inducing discriminatory quantity discounts, the responsibility for justification rests solely with the seller.

Cumulative discounts, if provided in the form of a payment by the supplier after the specified contract date, can provide tangible evidence of purchasing savings, especially if the discounts were not included in budgets or standard costing systems.

It may be easier for a supplier to provide a discount to a purchaser than a lower price. This allows the supplier to keep established list prices unchanged and distinguish between various classes of purchasers.

CONTRACT OPTIONS FOR PRICING

Four contract options for pricing are firm-fixed-price (FFP), cost-plus-fixed-fee (CPFF), cost-no-fee (CNF), and cost-plus-incentive-fee (CPIF).

Firm-Fixed-Price (FFP) Contract

The price set is not subject to change, under any circumstances. Buyers prefer this type of contract, but if the delivery date is some months or years away and if there is substantial chance of price escalation, a supplier may feel that there is far too much risk of loss to agree to sell under an FFP contract. In services, it is often difficult to agree on a firm fixed price because of the historical practice of hourly billing and the fear that scope creep will erode the margin built into the fixed price. A detailed scope of work includes customers' responsibilities as well as supplier's, time lines, progress payment schedule, and how work outside the scope will be handled.

Cost-Plus-Fixed-Fee (CPFF) Contract

If it is unreasonable to expect a supplier to sell at a firm fixed price, the CPFF contract can be used. This occurs if the item is experimental and the specifications are not firm, or if costs in the future cannot be predicted. The buyer agrees to reimburse the supplier for all reasonable costs incurred (under a set of definite policies under which "reasonable" is determined) in doing the job or producing the required item, plus a specified dollar amount of profit. A maximum amount may be specified for the cost. This contract type is far superior to the old "cost-plus-percentage" type, which encouraged the supplier to run the costs up as high as possible to increase the base on which the profit is figured. While the supplier bears little risk under the CPFF, since costs will be reimbursed, the supplier's profit percentage declines as the costs increase, giving some incentive to the supplier to control costs.

Cost-No-Fee (CNF) Contract

If the buyer can argue persuasively that there will be enough subsidiary benefits to the supplier from doing a particular job, then the supplier may be willing to do it provided only the costs are reimbursed. For example, the supplier may be willing to do the research and produce some new product if only the costs are returned, because doing the job may give the supplier some new technological or product knowledge, which then may be used to make large profits in some commercial market.

Cost-Plus-Incentive-Fee (CPIF) Contract

Both buyer and seller agree on a target cost figure, a fixed fee, and a formula under which any cost over- or underruns are shared. For example, assume the agreed-on target cost is $100,000, the fixed fee is $10,000, and the incentive-sharing formula is 50/50. If actual costs are $120,000, the $20,000 cost overrun would be shared equally between buyer and seller, based on the 50/50 sharing formula, and the seller's profit would be reduced by $10,000, or to zero in this example. On the other hand, if total costs are only $90,000, then the seller's share of the $10,000 cost underrun would be $5,000. Total profit then would be $10,000 + $5,000, or $15,000. This motivates the supplier to be efficient because the benefits of greater efficiency (or the penalties of inefficiency) accrue in part, based on the sharing formula, to the supplier.

Provision for Price Changes

Many long-term contracts contain provisions for price changes. The contract normally provides for no price changes for a fixed period of time, after which a price change may become possible with a minimum notice period (for example, see the Loren case in Chapter 12). There are several options for price changes.

Guarantee against Price Decline

For recurring purchases and for raw materials, the contract may be written at the price in effect at the time the contract is negotiated. Provision is made for a reduction during a subsequent period if there is a downward marketplace price movement. The contract specifies how a price change is determined, typically by a specific business or trade publication or website. Buyers prefer this provision when it overcomes their reluctance to buy because of fear that prices are likely to drop still further.

Price Protection Clause

In a long-term contract for raw materials or other key purchased items with one or more suppliers, the buyer may want to keep open the option of taking advantage of a lower price offered by a different supplier. This might be done by either buying from the noncontract supplier or forcing the contract supplier(s) to meet the lower price available from the noncontract suppliers. A price protection clause may be incorporated into the contract specifying that "If the buyer is offered material of equal quality in similar quantities under like terms from a responsible supplier, at a lower delivered cost to the buyer than specified in this contract, the seller on being furnished written evidence of this offer shall either meet the lower delivered price or allow the buyer to purchase from the other supplier at the lower delivered price and deduct the quantity purchased from the quantity specified in this contract."

Escalator Clauses

The actual wording of many escalator clauses provides for either an increase or decrease in price if costs change. Escalator clauses came into common use during the hyperinflation years in the 1970s when suppliers believed that the uncertainty of future costs made firm quotation either impossible or, if covering all probable risks, so high as to make it unattractive, and perhaps unfair, to the buyer.

There are several general and many specific problems with escalator clauses. These include determining the proportion of the total price subject to adjustment; the particular measures of prices and wage rates to be used in making the adjustment; the methods to be followed in applying these averages to the base price; the limitations, if any, on the amount of adjustment; and the methods for making payment.

When prices are stable, escalation usually is reserved for long-term contracts in which certain costs may rise and the seller has no appreciable control over this rise. When prices are unstable, with inflation, shortages, and sellers' markets, escalation becomes common on even short-term contracts as sellers attempt to ensure the opportunity to raise prices and preserve contribution margins. Changes in material and direct labor costs generally are tied to one of the published price and cost indexes, such as those of the Bureau of Labor Statistics or one of the trade publications, such as *Iron Age* or *ICIS* for chemical, energy, and fertilizer prices. It can be a problem finding a meaningful index to use. Because most escalation is automatic, it is important to carefully determine the index, the portion of the contract subject to escalation, the frequency of revision, and the length of contract.

The following is an illustrative escalator clause:

Labor

Adjustment with respect to labor costs shall be made on the basis of monthly average hourly earnings for the (Durable Goods Industry, subclass Machinery), as furnished by the Bureau of Labor Statistics (hereafter called the Labor Index). Adjustments shall be calculated with respect to each calendar quarter up to the completion date specified in contract. The percentage increase or decrease in the quarterly index (obtained by averaging the Labor Index for each month of the calendar quarter) shall be obtained by comparison with the Labor Index for the base month. The base month shall be_____ 201_____. The labor adjustment for each calendar quarter as thus determined shall be obtained by applying such percentage of increase or decrease to the total amount expended by the contractor for direct labor during such quarter.

Materials

Adjustment with respect to materials shall be made on the basis of the materials index for Group VI (Metals and Metal Products), as furnished by the Bureau of Labor Statistics (hereafter called the Materials Index). Adjustments shall be determined with respect to each calendar quarter up to the completion date specified in the contract. The percentage of increase or decrease in the quarterly index (obtained by averaging the Materials Index for each month of the calendar quarter) shall be obtained by comparison with the Materials Index for the base month. The base month shall be____ 201____. The material adjustment for each calendar quarter shall be obtained by applying to the contract material cost the percentage of increase or decrease shown by the Materials Index for that quarter.

A buyer who uses escalator clauses must remember that one legal essential to any enforceable purchase contract is that it contains either a definite price or the means of arriving at one. No contract for future delivery can be enforced if the price of the item is conditioned entirely on the will of one of the parties. The clauses cited earlier would appear to be adequate. So too are clauses authorizing the seller to change price as costs of production change, provided that these costs can be reasonably determined from the supplier's accounting records.

Most-Favored-Customer Clause

Another price protection clause (sometimes referred to as a "most-favored-nation clause") specifies that the supplier, over the duration of the contract, will not offer a lower price to other buyers, or if a lower price is offered to others, it will apply to this contract as well.

Contract Cancellation

Cancellations usually occur during a period of falling prices. At such times, some buyers find loopholes and technicalities in the purchase order or sales agreement to reject merchandise. One can have sympathy for the buyer with a contract at a price higher than the market price. There is little justification, however, for the purchaser who follows a cancellation policy under this situation. A contract should be considered a binding obligation. Canceling a contract because of falling market prices is not justified. Sometimes the buyer knows when the purchase order is placed that the customer for whose job the materials are being bought may unexpectedly cancel the order, thus forcing cancellation of purchase orders for materials planned for the job. This is a common risk when purchasing materials for use on a government contract, for appropriation changes often force the government to cancel its order, which results in the cancellation of a great many purchase orders by firms that were to have been suppliers to the government under the now-canceled government contract. Or severe changes in the business cycle may trigger purchase-order cancellations. If cancellation is a possibility, the basis and terms of cancellation should be agreed on and included in the terms and conditions. Problems such as how to value and what is an appropriate payment for partially completed work on a now-canceled purchase order are best settled before the situation arises.

FORWARD BUYING AND COMMODITIES

Forward buying is the commitment of purchases in anticipation of future requirements beyond current lead times. An organization may buy ahead because of anticipated shortages, strikes, or price increases. As the time between procurement commitment and actual use of the requirement grows, uncertainties also increase. One common uncertainty is whether the actual need will be realized. A second concern is with price. How can the purchaser ascertain that the price currently committed is reasonable compared to the actual price that would have been paid had the forward buy not been made?

Commodities represent a special class of purchases frequently associated with forward buying. Almost all organizations purchase commodities in a variety of processed forms. For example, an electrical equipment manufacturer may buy a substantial amount of wire, the cost of which is significantly affected by the price of copper. Many organizations buy commodities for further processing or for resale. For them, the way they buy and the prices they pay for commodities may be the single most important factor in success. Prices for selected commodities are reported daily in *The Wall Street Journal,* Bloomberg.com, and many other sources, in hard copy or on the Internet.

Managing Risk with Production and Marketing Contracts

Marketing and production contracts in agriculture are substitutes for spot market (cash) sales. Marketing contracts outline the terms of exchange, including the product to be delivered; the quantity, location, and time window for delivery; and a price or pricing formula. Production contracts govern an entire production process—farmers are paid a fee to grow an animal or crop for a contractor who provides some production inputs and who removes the product from the farm for processing or marketing at the close of the production cycle.

Contracts can help farmers manage price and production risks, they can elicit the production of products with specific quality attributes by tying prices to those attributes, and they can smooth flows of commodities to processing plants, thus encouraging more efficient use of farm and processing capacities. The downsides of contracts include introducing new and unexpected risks for farmers—in some circumstances, they can extend a buyer's market power—and they can effect fundamental changes in how farming is organized and carried out. The attractiveness of contracts depends on multiple factors, including government farm programs, price behavior of noncontract agricultural commodities, and the specificity of buyers' quality requirements. Thus, farmers turn to contracts when they perceive the efficacy of spot markets to be inadequate in handling their risks, and processors turn to contracts as a way to encourage farmers to produce specific products at desired times.

In 2008, the USDA reported that production and marketing contracts covered 39 percent of the value of U.S. agricultural production, up from 28 percent in 1991 and 12 percent in 1969. Contract use is more common on large farms and the use has stabilized in recent years. Marketing contracts are reached prior to crop harvest and production contracts before the completion phase for livestock. Contracts are now the primary method of handling sales of many livestock commodities, including milk, hogs and broilers, and of major crops such as sugar beets, fruits, and tomato processing. Farms with $1 million or more in sales have nearly half their production under contract.

Forward Buying versus Speculation

All forward buying involves some risk. In forward buying, purchases are confined to actually known requirements or to carefully estimated requirements for a limited period of time in advance. The essential controlling factor is need. Even when the organization uses order points and order quantities, the amount to be bought may be increased or decreased in accordance both with probable use and with the price trend, rather than automatically reordering a given amount. Temporarily, no order may be placed at all.

This may be true even when purchases have to be made many months in advance, such as seasonal products like wheat, or those that must be obtained abroad, such as cocoa or coffee. The price risk increases as the lead time grows longer, but the basic reasons for these forward commitments are assurance of supply to meet requirements and price.

Speculation seeks to take advantage of price movements. At times of rising prices, commitments for quantities beyond anticipated needs would be called speculation. At times of falling prices, speculation would consist of withholding purchases or reducing quantities purchased below the safety limits, thereby risking stockouts as well as rush orders at high prices, if the anticipated price decline did not materialize.

At best, any speculation, in the accepted meaning of the term, is a risky business, but speculation with other people's money has been cataloged as a crime. It is supply's responsibility to provide for the known needs to the best advantage possible at the time and to keep the investment in unused materials at the lowest point consistent with safety of operation. Purchasers can buy forward, but should not speculate or gamble.

Organizing for Forward Buying

The organization's size, financial strength, and the percentage of total cost represented by volatile commodities influences how the company organizes to determine and execute policy on long-term commodity commitments. In some instances, the CEO exercises complete control, based almost wholly on personal judgment. In other cases, although the CEO assumes direct responsibility, a committee provides assistance.

Some organizations designate a person, other than the supply manager, whose sole responsibility is price-sensitive materials and who reports directly to top management. Often, the supply manager controls the commodity inventory. Or an outside agency specializing in speculative commodities executes policy. The soundest practice for most organizations appears to be to place responsibility for policy in the hands of a committee consisting of the top executive or general manager, an economist, a risk manager, and the supply manager. Actual execution of the broad policy should rest with the supply department.

Control of Forward Buying

Safeguards should be set up to ensure that commodity commitments will be kept within proper bounds. For example, a leather company established the following safeguards: (1) Forward buying must be confined to those hides that are used in the production either of several different leathers or of the leathers for which there is a stable demand. (2) Daily conferences are held among the president, treasurer, sales manager, and hide buyer. (3) Orders for future delivery of leather are varied in some measure in accordance with the company's need for protection on hide holdings. Because the leather buyer is willing to place orders for future delivery of leather when prices are satisfactory, this company follows the practice of using unfilled orders as a partial hedge of its hide holdings. In general, the policy is to have approximately 50 percent of the total hides the company owns covered by sales contracts for future production of leather. (4) A further check is provided by an operating budget that controls the physical volume of hides rather than the financial expenditures, and that is brought up for reconsideration whenever it is felt necessary. (5) There is a final check that consists of the use of adequate and reliable information, statistical and otherwise, as a basis for judging price and market trends.

This particular company does not follow the practice of hedging on an organized commodity exchange as a means of avoiding undue risk, though many companies do. Nor does this company use any of the special accounting procedures, such as last-in, first-out, or reproduction-cost-of-sales, in connection with its forward purchases.

These various control devices, regarded as a unit rather than as unrelated checks, should prove effective. They are not foolproof, nor do they ensure absolutely against the dangers inherent in buying well in advance. However, flexibility in the administration of any policy is essential, and, for this one company at least, their procedure combines reasonable protection with flexibility.

In organizations requiring large quantities of commodities whose prices fluctuate widely, the risks involved in buying ahead, under some circumstances, may be substantially minimized through the use of the commodity exchanges.

The Commodity Exchanges

The prime function of an organized commodity exchange is to furnish an established marketplace where the forces of supply and demand may operate freely as buyers and sellers carry on their trading. An exchange that has facilities for both cash and futures trading also can be used for hedging operations. The rules governing the operation of an exchange are concerned primarily with procedures for the orderly handling of the transactions negotiated on the exchange, providing, among other things, terms and time of payment, time of delivery, grades of products traded, and methods of settling disputes.

In general, the purposes of a commodity exchange will be served best if the following conditions are present:

1. The products traded are capable of reasonably accurate grading.
2. There are a large enough number of sellers and buyers and a large enough volume of business so that no one buyer or seller can significantly influence the market.

In order for a commodity exchange to be useful for hedging operations, the following conditions also should be present:

1. Trading in "futures"—the buying or selling of the commodity for delivery at a specified future date.
2. A fairly close correlation between "basis" and other grades.
3. A reasonable but not necessarily consistent correlation between "spot" and "future" prices.

All of these conditions usually are present on the major grain and cotton exchanges, and in varying degrees on the minor exchanges, such as those on which hides, silk, metals, rubber, coffee, and sugar are traded. Financial futures also permit a firm to hedge against interest rate fluctuations, which are one of the strongest factors affecting exchange rate fluctuations.

One of the most easily accessed sources of information about futures and options prices is the commodities section of Bloomberg.com and the *Wall Street Journal* (wsj.com). They report prices from the major exchanges, from North/Latin America (e.g., Chicago Board of Trade [CBOT], ICE Futures Canada [formerly the Winnipeg Commodity Exchange], Mexico Bolsa [MEXBOL], and Brazil BOVESPA); Europe/Africa (e.g., NYSE Euronext, NYSE Liffe [formerly the London International Financial Futures Exchange], South Africa Futures Exchange [SAFEX]); and Asia/Pacific (e.g., Tokyo Commodity Exchange [TOCOM], Hong Kong Exchanges and Clearing [HKFE], and the Australian Securities

Exchange [ASX]). Each of the major commodity trading exchanges has a website that provides real-time information for quotes, charts and historical data, and news.

The commodities traded on the exchanges vary; if the volume is not large enough, a given commodity will drop off the exchange either temporarily or permanently. However, the following agricultural items, metals, petroleum products, and currencies normally are among those listed on any given day: corn, oats, soybeans, soybean oil, wheat, canola, cattle, hogs, pork bellies, cocoa, coffee, sugar, cotton, orange juice, copper, gold, platinum, silver, crude oil, heating oil, gasoline, natural gas, Japanese yen, Euro, Canadian dollar, British pound, Swiss franc, Australian dollar, U.S. dollar, and Mexican peso.

In most cases, the prices quoted on the exchanges and the record of transactions completed furnish some clue, at least, to the current market price and to the extent of the trading in those commodities. They offer an opportunity, some to a greater extent than others, of protecting the buyer against basic price risks through hedging.

Limitations of the Exchanges

There are limitations to these exchanges as a source of physical supply for the buyer. In spite of a reasonable attempt to define the market grades, the grading often is not sufficiently accurate for manufacturing purposes. The cotton requirements of a textile manufacturer are likely to be so exacting that even the comparatively narrow limits of any specific exchange grade are too broad. Moreover, the rules of the exchange are such that the actual deliveries of cotton do not have to be of a specific grade but may be of any grade above or below basic cotton, provided, of course, that the essential financial adjustment is made. This also holds true for wheat. Millers who sell patented blended flours must have specific types and grades of wheat, which normally are purchased by use of a sample.

There are other reasons why these exchanges are not satisfactory for the buyer endeavoring to meet actual physical commodity requirements. On some of the exchanges, no spot market exists. On others there is a lack of confidence in the validity of the prices quoted. Crude rubber, for example, is purchased primarily by tire manufacturers, a small group of very large buyers. On the hide exchange, on the other hand, a majority of hides sold are by-products of the packing industry, offered by a limited number of sellers. An increase or a decrease in the price of hides, however, does not have the same effect on supply that such changes might have on some other commodities.

It is not asserted that these sellers use their position to manipulate the market artificially any more than it is asserted that the buyers of rubber manipulate the market to their advantage. In these two cases, however, the prices quoted might not properly reflect supply and demand conditions.

Hedging

The commodity exchanges provide a manufacturer an opportunity to offset transactions, and thus to protect, to some extent, against price and exchange risks. This commonly is done by *hedging*.

A hedging contract involves a simultaneous purchase and sale in two different markets, which are assumed to operate so that a loss in one will be offset by an equal gain in the other. Normally this is done by a purchase and sale of the same amount of the same commodity simultaneously in the spot and futures markets.

Hedging can occur only when trading in futures is possible. A simple example follows:

In the Cash Market	In the Futures Market
On September 1: Processor buys 5,000 bushels of wheat shipped from country elevator at $4.00 per bushel (delivered Chicago)	Processor sells 5,000 bushels of December wheat futures at $4.10 per bushel
On October 20: Processor sells Flour based on wheat equivalent of 5,000 bushels priced at $3.85 per bushel (delivered at Chicago)	Processor buys 5,000 bushels of December wheat futures at $3.95 per bushel
Loss of 15¢ per bushel	Gain of 15¢ per bushel

In the example, it is assumed that the cash or spot price and the futures price maintained a direct correlation, but this is not always the case. Thus, there may be some gain or loss from a hedging operation when the spread between the spot price and the futures price does not remain constant. *Hedging can be looked on as a form of insurance, and, like insurance, it is seldom possible to obtain 100 percent protection against all loss, except at prohibitive costs.* As the time between the spot and future declines, the premium or discount on the future declines toward zero (which it reaches when spot = future). On seasonal commodities, this decline in price differential usually begins six to eight months in advance. Under certain circumstances, this phenomenon can make "risk-free" speculation possible. For example, when the speculator has access to a large amount of money, at least three times the value of the contract, and when a six- to eight-month future premium exceeds the sum of contract carrying cost and inventory and commission cost, the "speculator" can buy spot and short the future with a precalculated profit. Volume on the exchange should be heavy for this kind of operation.

While there are other variations of the techniques used in hedging, the one simple example is sufficient for the present discussion of forward and speculative buying.

Successful hedging on an exchange requires skill, experience, and capital resources. This may limit small organizations. It also explains why organizations using large amounts of a certain commodity often own memberships on the relevant exchange. A representative may then be constantly watching for advantageous opportunities for placing, withdrawing, or switching hedges between months and can translate this judgment into immediate action. To be successful, the actual procedure of hedging calls for the close observation of accumulating stocks of the commodity, the consequent widening or narrowing of the spreads between prices quoted on futures contracts, and the resulting opportunities for advance opening and closing of trades. These factors are constantly shifting on the exchanges. The skill of the hedger is reflected in the ability to recognize and grasp these momentary opportunities.

Hedging may not always be helpful or advantageous to the purchaser. One obstacle to a wider use of the exchanges is the lack of understanding by potential users about when and how to use them. Another limitation is the vacuum effect when one of the relatively few large commodity brokers goes bankrupt, pulling some clients along. Hedging is common in some industries, such as international airlines hedging fuel costs and insurance companies hedging interest rate risk, equity risk, foreign currency risk, and credit risk.

Moreover, most brokers have not shown extensive interest in the industrial market. Most brokers probably will admit that they can barely afford to service a straight hedger because they may have to send out six monthly position statements and four or more margin calls for a single round turn commission, while their faithful "traders" will often maintain a substantial cash account and net them several round turn commissions per month with a minimum of bookkeeping.

Furthermore, many managers still view futures trading with suspicion and tend to blame past mistakes on the system rather than managerial errors of judgment. The large variations in commodity prices in recent years may well have sensitized a number of managers to the opportunities in futures trading, where before there seemed little need to be involved.

Sources of Information Regarding Price Trends

There are five general sources of price trend information: creditworthiness ratings, commodity exchanges, government data, expert data, and purchasing manager indexes (PMIs). All have limitations on their value and dependability.

One source of information consists of companies that provide credit ratings, research, and risk analysis, such as Moody's Investors Service (moodys.com), S&P (standardandpoors.com), Fitch (fitchratings.com), and A.M. Best (ambest.com). A second source is the commodity exchanges, (e.g., the London Commodity Exchange [LCE] and the New York Mercantile Exchange [NYMEX]), which typically provide historical information about prices and volumes. Most exchanges also provide access to reports by government agencies and some analysts. Commodity exchanges exist worldwide in Africa, the Americas, Asia, Europe, and Oceania.

The third source includes a wide variety of governmental and other published data, such as the *Federal Reserve Bulletin* (federalreserve.gov), the Bureau of Economic Analysis's *Survey of Current Business* (bea.gov/scb), *Bloomberg BusinessWeek* (businessweek.com), *Bloomberg.com, Barron's* (barrons.com)*,* and *The Wall Street Journal* (wsj.com). Trade magazines also are helpful in particular industries and are typified by such publications as *Iron Age* (ironagemag.com) and *Chemical Market Reporter* (ICIS.com).

Probably the most-watched indicator of industrial purchase prices is the producer price index (PPI) compiled and released monthly by the Bureau of Labor Statistics (bls.gov/ppi/). It previously was called the wholesale price index (WPI). The PPI is a family of indexes that measure the average change over time in selling prices received for their output by over 650 U.S. industries in the mining, forestry, utility, construction, manufacturing, and service sectors of the economy. As of January 2014, the Bureau of Labor Statistics (BLS) transitioned from the Stage of Processing (SOP) to the Final Demand-Intermediate Demand (FD-ID) aggregation system. The new system incorporates PPIs for services, construction, government purchases, and exports. Over 75 percent of in-scope domestic production is covered. The FD-ID index for final demand measures price changes for goods, services and construction sold to final demand (personal consumption, capital investment, government purchases, and exports). Intermediate demand is price changes for goods, services, and construction sold to business as input to production. The FD-ID system treats intermediate demand in two ways: (1) by commodity type that includes aggregate indexes for processed goods, unprocessed goods, and services; and (2) by production flow or a stage-based system of price indexes where price changes for goods, services, and construction can be studied as they move through the production chain to the final demand.

A companion measure, also produced monthly by the Bureau of Labor Statistics, is the thousands of consumer price indexes (CPIs). A CPI is based on the prices from the perspective of the end purchaser. The two most widely watched CPIs are the headline or All Items CPI, which includes food and energy, and the CPI-U or core CPI, which does not. Food and energy prices are volatile and subject to price shocks that monetary policy cannot dampen. The methods used by the U.S. Bureau of Labor Statistics are also widely used by nations in the OECD and the European Union.

The fourth source comprises the highly unscientific—but nevertheless valuable, if properly weighted—information derived from sales representatives, other buyers, and others with whom the buyer comes in daily contact.

The fifth source of information is the purchasing manager indexes (PMI), which are leading near-term economic indicators derived from monthly surveys of purchasing managers about actual company conditions. PMIs present a composite reading in a number of areas. For manufacturing, these include prices, inventory levels, lead times, new orders, production, and employment. For services, these include business activity, new business, backlogs of work, prices charged, input prices, employment, and expectations for activity in services.

A PMI is a diffusion index. A composite reading of 100 means that all respondents reported improvement on a variable, zero means all reported a decline, 50 means no changes, above 50 means expansion, and below 50 means contraction. For example, the Manufacturing Index from ISM was 56.5 in December 2013 and 51.3 in January 2014. This means manufacturing was growing in January 2014, but at a slower rate of growth than in December 2013. For the nonmanufacturing sector, the ISM PMI was 53.0 in December 2013 and 54.0 in January 2014, indicating that this sector was growing and at a faster rate of growth. PMI data can be used to assess underlying business conditions, gauge general price trends, and feed forecasts.

Each month in the United States, ISM releases the Manufacturing *Report on Business* (ROB) and the Nonmanufacturing ROB; and in Canada, the Ivey Purchasing Managers Index is released. JPMorgan and Markit, in association with ISM and the International Federation of Purchasing and Supply Management (IFPSM), generate a monthly global manufacturing and services PMI. Markit also surveys more than 20,000 companies in manufacturing, services, construction, and retail monthly across over 30 major developed and emerging economies, including the Eurozone, Brazil, China, Germany, Hong Kong, India, Japan, Saudi Arabia, the United Arab Emirates, and the UK. The data are collected using identical methods in all countries so that international comparisons may be made.

Conclusion

Price determination can be a tricky issue. The method of price determination should be influenced by what is being bought and the characteristics of the supply market at that particular point in time relative to the strategic goals of the organization. Discounts offer an interesting opportunity for buyers and sellers to achieve their price objectives. Knowing how to set prices, establishing appropriate strategies for price adjustments, and managing supply price risk are important skills for supply managers. Buyers who rely on competitive bidding and one-year contracts for every purchase may miss opportunities for achieving lower total costs.

Price is one critical element in cost management, the focus of the following chapter. Cost analysis and total cost or life-cycle cost management take price into a bigger picture of what supply managers must think about. Negotiation is one of the most important skills for supply managers and will also be discussed in the Cost Management chapter.

Questions for Review and Discussion

1. What is the significance of the Sherman Antitrust and the Robinson-Patman acts to the industrial buyer?

2. What disadvantages does the competitive bid process have as a method of price determination?

3. How is supplier cost related to supplier price?

4. What are the various ways by which prices are determined?

5. What methods can the buyer use to establish price for (*a*) raw materials, (*b*) professionals services, (*c*) parts, components, and packaging, and (*d*) MRO supplies?

6. Distinguish between direct and indirect costs. How can the buyer analyze these costs?

7. What can the buyer do if he or she suspects collusion on the part of suppliers?

8. What are cash discounts, quantity discounts, trade discounts, and cumulative discounts? Should the buyer attempt to use these discounts? How?

9. Why might a buyer wish to hedge a commodity purchase? How would the buyer do that?

10. Does hedging remove all risk? Why or why not?

11. What is the difference between forward buying and speculation?

References

An Antitrust Primer for Agents and Procurement Officials. U.S. Department of Justice, Antitrust Division, www.justice.gov/atr/public/guidelines/disaster_primer.pdf

Asian Development Bank et al., *Multilateral Development Bank: International Survey of E-procurement Systems,* May 2007, http://ec.europa.eu/internal_market /publicprocurement/docs/eprocurement/mdb_egp_survey_en.pdf.

Baker, R. J. *Implementing Value Pricing: A Radical Business Model for Professional Firms,* Hoboken, NJ: John Wiley & Sons, Inc., 2011.

MacDonald, J. M., and P. Korb. *Agricultural Contracting Update: Contracts in 2008.* EIB-72. U.S. Dept. of Agriculture, Econ. Res. Serv., February 2011.

Zsidisin, G. A. "Managing Commodity Pricing and Availability Volatility." *Critical Issues Report.* Tempe, AZ: CAPS Research, February 2012.

Zsidisin, G. A., and J. L. Hartley. *Managing Commodity Price Risk: A Supply Chain Perspective.* New York: Business Expert Press, 2012.

Case 10–1

Wedlock Engineered Products

Cynthia Gao, procurement manager for Wedlock Engineered Products in Buffalo, New York, was reviewing a proposal recommending that the company change suppliers for a critical raw material. It was June the 3rd, and Cynthia needed to decide before the end of the day how she would respond to the proposal.

WEDLOCK ENGINEERED PRODUCTS

Wedlock Engineered Products (Wedlock) manufactured and distributed hydraulic, power-assisted, air-powered, and standard mechanical dock levelers, and dock seals and shelters, and vehicle restraints. Wedlock had profits of $50 million on sales of $450 million in the most recent fiscal year ending December 31. The company had enjoyed double-digit growth over the previous decade, supported mainly through an aggressive acquisition strategy.

Wedlock's growth masked cost pressures the company was facing in its key markets. The company's annual report indicated that financial results were lower than expected due to price erosion. In February, the CEO, Dmitry Barsukov, announced a corporate cost-reduction initiative aimed at improving the company's competitive position. As part of the announcement, Barsukov specifically mentioned "opportunities for supply chain savings through coordination of purchasing between operating units and divisions."

The Buffalo plant manufactured hydraulic dock levelers that were installed in shipping and receiving areas in manufacturing facilities, distribution centers, retail operations, and other facilities required to accommodate loading and unloading of highway transport trailers. It produced a standard product that was sold in the replacement and new construction markets under the Sloan Leveler brand. The Wedlock plant in Cleveland, Ohio, also manufactured hydraulic levelers, under the brand name Cole Dock Levelers. The Cole line of levelers targeted the customized market, for customers with unique material handling requirements.

PURCHASING AT THE BUFFALO PLANT

Cynthia Gao, along with Garett MacDonald, buyer, and Adam McEniry, materials planner, comprised the procurement group at the Wedlock plant in Buffalo. Total purchases were $23 million.

Cynthia worked closely with Robert Scobie, her counterpart at the Cleveland plant, to coordinate purchases and identify opportunities for costs savings. The Cleveland plant was similar in size to the Buffalo plant, with approximately $25 million in annual purchases. Cynthia and Robert had committed to savings of $1.5 million in the current fiscal year as part of the corporate cost-reduction initiative. They had documented approximately $500,000 so far, measured by year-over-year price reductions from suppliers and based on forecasted annual usage.

STEEL TUBING

The Buffalo and Cleveland plants purchased 3-inch steel tube with a combined total value of $1.1 million annually. The tubing was used on the loading dock platform to support the hinge connected to the lip of the platform that allowed it to lay flat or unfold, in order to connect or disconnect from the transport trailer. The tubing was required to meet specific metallurgical standards or else the tubing would warp or crack, causing the loading dock to malfunction.

The current supplier for 3-inch tubing was Marandi Steel (Marandi). Located near Buffalo, Marandi distributed a wide range of carbon, stainless, alloy, and aluminum tubing; pipe products in round, square, and rectangular shapes; and steel plate to manufacturing companies in the eastern United States and Canada. Marandi had been a supplier to the Wedlock Buffalo plant for approximately 15 years and provided excellent service. Cynthia had a strong working relationship with the general manager at Marandi and could recount several occasions when they reacted quickly to material shortages at the Buffalo plant that helped keep production going. Marandi currently supplied several products, including tubular steel, shapes, and plate, to both the Wedlock Buffalo and Cleveland plants. The supply arrangement with Marandi to the Buffalo plant included just-in-time delivery arrangements, which helped to keep inventory levels at a minimum. Total annual purchases from the supplier were approximately $3 million for the Buffalo plant and $2.5 million for the Cleveland plant.

In order to test the pricing for 3-inch tubing, Robert Scobie issued a request for quotations (RFQ) the previous month from several steel tubing distributors, including Marandi. The RFQ indicated the expected term of the contract would be two years and include 100 percent of the requirements for both the Buffalo and Cleveland plants. The two lowest quotes were from Vergis Tubing (Vergis), located in Erie Pennsylvania, and Marandi. The quote submitted by Vergis represented an annual cost savings of approximately $24,000 compared to the incumbent supplier.

REVIEWING OPTIONS

Robert felt that Vergis should be awarded the contract to supply 3-inch tubing for the Buffalo and Cleveland plants and was urging Cynthia to accept the proposal. However, Cynthia had concerns. Vergis had attempted unsuccessfully on several other occasions to secure business from Wedlock, and she was worried that Vergis did not have any history with either the Buffalo or Cleveland plants. Delivery and quality performance for 3-inch tube was critical for the Buffalo plant, and the performance of Marandi in these areas had been outstanding. A check of

Vergis's references found that they had a good reputation and there were no problems uncovered.

Cynthia was also concerned about the effect of abandoning a long-standing relationship, which might have other cost implications and jeopardize service provided by Marandi. Marandi supplied a number of other products to the Buffalo plant, and Cynthia wondered how awarding

the 3-inch tube contract to Vergis would affect the relationship with Marandi.

Robert was expecting a decision from Cynthia the following morning regarding which supplier she felt should be awarded the contract for 3-inch tubing. Cynthia knew that she would need strong arguments if she decided not to support his recommendation to switch to Vergis.

Case 10–2

Coral Drugs

Shirley Black glanced at her watch. It was 1 p.m. on January the 25th, and only two hours remained before her meeting about Coral Dandruff Shampoo with the vice president of purchasing. As merchandise group coordinator at Coral's head office in Columbus, Ohio, Shirley was trying to decide whether to recommend switching from a large shampoo manufacturer to a small local supplier.

CORAL DRUGS

Coral Drugs was founded in 1962. Since that time, the company had steadily expanded its chain of retail drug stores throughout the state. Currently, Coral operated 114 stores and planned to add an additional 8 to 10 stores over the next five years. Coral's retail outlets sold both prescribed and over-the-counter pharmaceutical products as well as other drugstore items. This private company's strategy was focused on the further expansion of its successful retail operations. Coral had a strong financial position and intended to pursue any opportunity that had potential to increase its bottom line and was related to its retail operations.

CORAL PRIVATE-LABEL PRODUCTS

One such opportunity was the development of Coral private-label products. Since 1980, the company had aggressively developed a line of products carrying the Coral name. Currently, Coral stocked over 200 different private-label products. Coral was proud of its ability to bring a product to its shelves that was comparable in quality to the national brands, but offered at least a 25 percent price savings to the consumer. The company was able to sell at a

better price than the national brands because it was buying directly from the manufacturer and its advertising expenditures were significantly lower. Examples of successful products included Coral Acetaminophen Tablets and Coral Vitamin Supplements.

Coral private-label products were attractive to the company for several reasons. First, the margin on these products averaged 40 percent as compared with 25 percent on national brands. Also, the product line was virtually hassle-free. Apart from the initial supplier approval, the sourcing agreement left the manufacturer responsible for all aspects of product development and investment. Consequently, Coral intended to pursue any growth opportunities this private labeling offered in the future.

SOURCE SELECTION FOR PRIVATE-LABEL PRODUCTS

Coral private-label products were purchased from 26 different suppliers. Several sourcing agreements were in contract form, while others were simply an understanding between Coral and the manufacturer. The process for developing a sourcing agreement began with an internally generated idea for a potential private-label product. Once the product idea was approved, Coral announced that it was accepting bids from manufacturing operations that wanted to produce the product. Coral carefully analyzed the potential suppliers to ensure that they were able to provide a consistent product that was comparable in quality to the leading national brands and at a price that would provide satisfactory margins. When the bid was accepted, Coral and the manufacturing company worked together to develop the final product.

Sourcing agreements left the manufacturer responsible for almost all aspects of product development. Based on specifications provided by Coral, these manufacturers generated the artwork for the product, designed the packaging, invested in any necessary equipment, and performed quality assurance. Once the product received final approval from Coral, the company simply placed an order for the product when stock was required. The order was then delivered FOB to Coral's central warehouse and shipped from there to the retail stores. Consequently, this high level of supplier autonomy made annual reevaluation of the sourcing arrangements necessary.

SWITCHING THE SOURCING AGREEMENT FOR CORAL DANDRUFF SHAMPOO

In December, Shirley had reviewed the performance of the company that produced Coral Dandruff Shampoo—Twinney Inc. After several requests from Coral to improve delivery terms, Twinney had indicated that it would not alter the terms originally agreed upon. Many of Coral's concerns were directly related to the location of Twinney's manufacturing plant 600 miles to the east. Consequently, in early January, Coral announced that it was accepting bids on the future production of the product. A product specification document was sent to manufacturers that were known to have the capability to produce similar products. Twinney was notified prior to the announcement and was asked to submit a bid along with the others.

TWINNEY INCORPORATED

Under the current sourcing agreement, Coral had to order full skids when purchasing its private-label dandruff shampoo from Twinney. Each skid held 4,000 units. Although the shampoo was considered an excellent product, volumes for the regular, fragranced, and trial-sized products averaged only about 20,000 units each annually. Shirley knew that the inventory carrying cost at Coral was around 2 percent a month, and felt that the company had too much money tied up in such a low-volume product. Furthermore, the three- to four-week lead time required when placing an order had been causing problems. On several occasions, the Coral central warehouse had been stocked out of the products while waiting for a skid to arrive.

Shirley could not understand why a large company like Twinney would be so unwilling to accommodate Coral's requests for improved shipping terms. Although there had never been any problems with the consistency or quality of the shampoo Coral received, Shirley Black felt that perhaps more beneficial terms could be offered by a manufacturer located closer to Coral's warehouse. It seemed like a perfect opportunity because Twinney's injection mold for the product had just broken down and the artwork was due for revision soon. The Twinney sourcing agreement was not in contract form and, therefore, Shirley Black believed Coral was not legally obligated to continue purchasing from Twinney.

GORMAN AND IRIZAWA LTD

Out of the many bids received, the most attractive terms were offered by a young local company, Gorman and Irizawa Ltd. (G & I). The bidder agreed to similar responsibilities as those in the existing Twinney agreement, as well as the same payment terms of 2 percent/10, net 30, FOB Coral's warehouse. G & I also offered several additional advantages.

The first benefit was the cost of the product. As illustrated in Exhibit 1, G & I undercut the price Twinney was offering on all three products. This cost differential was made even more attractive by the fact that the prices quoted were for 7-ounce bottles of regular and fragranced product and 3-ounce trial-sized bottles. The leading national brand was offered in similar sizes. The existing agreement with Twinney called for the production of smaller 6-ounce and 2-ounce bottles. Coral's retail selling price was $1.49 for the regular and fragranced shampoo and $0.89 for a trial-size bottle. Shirley believed this was an excellent opportunity to pass on more value to the consumer.

The second advantage was G & I's shipping flexibility. Under the terms of the proposed agreement, the company

EXHIBIT 1 **Coral Drugs Price and Size Comparison for Coral Dandruff Shampoo**

	Size	Twinney	Size	Gorman & Irizawa
Regular	6 oz.	0.72	7 oz.	0.70
Fragrance	6 oz.	0.85	7 oz.	0.75
Trial	2 oz.	0.47	3 oz.	0.35

offered next-day delivery service with no minimum order quantity. G & I was able to offer such favorable terms because its manufacturing facility was located near Coral's central warehouse.

Shirley believed this was an opportunity to support a small local company. If Coral agreed to source its dandruff shampoo from G & I, the account would be one of G & I's largest. In a recent tour of the G & I plant, Shirley was impressed by the cleanliness of its manufacturing facilities; however, she could not help comparing the relatively small-scale operation to Twinney's large shampoo factory.

SHIRLEY'S RECOMMENDATION

Shirley had discussed the dandruff shampoo sourcing issue with the vice president of purchasing in December and knew he was expecting a recommendation from her at the January 25th meeting at 3 p.m. She was well aware that Coral Drugs had a reputation for long-term relationships with its private-label product suppliers. She was, therefore, still unsure about which supplier to recommend for Coral Dandruff Shampoo.

Case 10–3

Price Forecasting Exercise*

You and ____ other members of the class have been asked to forecast the price of a commodity on ____. So that your organization may take the most advantageous procurement action possible, your organization needs $5 million worth of this commodity for delivery between ____ and ____. The amount—$5 million worth—is based on the spot price of this commodity on ____. Your report must address the following four questions:

Question 1. What is the current ____ spot price of this commodity, based on what quotation? What is the specification of the commodity, and what is the minimum amount of purchase required for the quoted price to hold? How much in weight or volume does $5 million represent?

Question 2. What are the current futures for ____?

Question 3. What spot price do you forecast for this commodity on ____? Why?

Question 4. In view of your forecast, what recommendations would you make to the executive committee of your organization with regard to the purchase of this commodity? Would you advise buying now and taking delivery now, or later? Would you hedge? Would you delay purchase? Anything else? What savings do you forecast from your recommendation?

QUALIFICATIONS

1. The commodity selected may not be a pegged price in the market in which you are purchasing. It must be a freely fluctuating price, and it must be traded on a recognized commodity exchange. Prices must be reported daily in an accessible news source.

2. Approval for a selected commodity must come from the instructor. No two teams may select the same commodity. Commodity selection is on a first-come, first-served basis.

3. Foreign exchange rates may be an important consideration in your decision.

4. This report has four parts:
   a. A written report (in at least two copies) to be handed in on ____ before 4:30 p.m.
   b. A five-minute class report to be presented orally during class on ____.
   c. A written evaluation report (in at least two copies) to be handed in before 4:30 p.m., ____, including the ____ actual spot price. The evaluation should compare a savings (loss) estimate in view of the recommended action for the weight calculated in the report.

* Your instructor will supply the missing information, dates, and so forth.

Chapter Eleven

Cost Management

Chapter Outline

Strategic Cost Management
Sources of Competitive Advantage
Frameworks for Cost Management

Cost Management Tools and Techniques
Total Cost of Ownership
Target Costing
The Learning Curve or Experience Curve
Value Engineering and Value Analysis
Activity-Based Costing

Negotiation
Negotiation Strategy and Practice
Framework for Planning and Preparing
for Negotiation

Conclusion

Questions for Review and Discussion

References

Cases

Key Questions for the Supply Decision Maker

Should we

- Use target pricing?
- Negotiate with our suppliers or accept their existing terms and conditions?
- Estimate total cost of ownership for all our purchases?

How can we

- Understand what it costs our suppliers to manufacture their products or deliver their services?
- Make a cost analysis on all our large-dollar purchase items?
- Achieve our objectives in a negotiation with an important supplier?

The profit leverage effect of supply (discussed in Chapter 1) lays the foundation for the role of supply in helping the firm meet strategic goals of continuous improvement, customer service, quality, and increased competitiveness. Leveraging the potential of supply requires fully exploiting all opportunities to reduce, contain, or avoid costs, resulting in the lowest total cost of ownership and, hopefully, leading the organization to becoming the low-cost producer of high-quality goods and services. Cost analysis and cost management are important whether the source of competitive advantage for a specific product or service is product leadership (higher perceived product or service differentiation and lower customer price sensitivity) or cost leadership (lower perceived product or service differentiation and higher customer price sensitivity).

Supply management can contribute to attainment of low-cost-producer status by its management of internal and external costs. Methods of streamlining the acquisition process and reducing internal costs associated with acquisition were discussed in Chapters 3 and 4. This chapter focuses on managing external costs.

As the status of the supply function in well-managed companies has increased in importance, a more professional attitude has developed in the people responsible for the operation of the function. As the professional competence of the personnel has increased, greater use has been made of the more sophisticated tools available to the business decision-making executive. Negotiation and cost management techniques are prime examples of this developing professionalism.

In the long run, companies need suppliers that provide the lowest total costs, not necessarily the lowest prices. Consequently, a focus on costs, as opposed to prices, allows purchasers to make informed decisions and identify opportunities to reduce waste in the supply chain. However, understanding "what the numbers tell us" is only part of the battle. Effective buyers also need to understand how and when to use information effectively in a negotiation setting with important suppliers and key internal stakeholders. This chapter addresses supply's role in strategic cost management, describes cost management techniques, and explains basic negotiation concepts. Cost management and negotiation represent a powerful combination for supply professionals.

Two key decisions are addressed in this chapter: (1) How can cost management and negotiation tools help identify opportunities and assure value? (2) How can we determine the supplier's costs? deliverer's cost? our own use costs? and disposal costs?

STRATEGIC COST MANAGEMENT

Strategic cost management is an externally focused process of analyzing costs in terms of the overall value chain. Cost analysis can be used to measure and improve cost performance by focusing attention on specific cost elements. Cost management systems can be designed that depend on strategic partnering to achieve competitive advantage. Cost management is a major opportunity area for strong supply leadership and management. Cost management is a continuous improvement process. The focus is essentially on applying tools and techniques to sustain cost savings year over year. Supply leaders and managers must develop a cost culture rather than a price culture with multiple internal stakeholders and externally with suppliers. Cost management should be part of the standard operating procedure in every supply management organization.

The actual cost management process in any organization depends on context. What is the strategic positioning of the organization and how sophisticated is the supply organization in terms of price and cost analysis? If little attention has been paid to spend, then the opportunities may come from spend aggregation and price-volume leverage, supply base rationalization, and better terms and condition. As supply develops expertise in cost management, attention turns to avoiding, eliminating, or reducing costs through design and redesign of products/services, and process improvements internally within the supplier's processes and in joint processes.

Sources of Competitive Advantage

Sources of sustainable competitive advantage are: (1) product or service differentiation (wherein customers have low price sensitivity), (2) low cost (wherein customers have high price sensitivity), and (3) a combination of product or service differentiation and cost leadership. While an organization may be positioned strategically in one category, it may have products or services in both. For example, a technical support center may offer customized support 365/24/7 for a relatively high price and also offer basic online diagnostics and reporting as part of a standard package. Or a fast-food restaurant chain may compete fiercely on price with value menus while also offering relatively highly priced specialty hamburgers.

Frameworks for Cost Management

Supply professionals must understand their own organization's strategic positioning (overall and by product or service) and that of their suppliers. Cost analysis and cost management approaches can then be adapted and applied appropriately. Various tools discussed in this text provide a framework for cost management. These include ABC (Pareto) analysis (Chapter 8) and portfolio analysis (Chapter 11).

ABC or Pareto Analysis and Cost Management

ABC analysis assigns items to either the A, B, or C category. A items are high-dollar items, B are medium-dollar, and C are low-dollar items. From a cost management perspective, more time and managerial attention is directed toward A items because of the percent of annual spend consumed by the purchase of these items. The supply manager would focus on understanding the supplier's cost structure to identify opportunities for either the supplier or a joint buyer-supplier initiative to eliminate, reduce, or avoid costs in any of a number of cost elements, including materials, services, labor, and overhead. Thinking about the supplier's strategic positioning, A items might be either differentiated products (customized) or low-cost commodity type items. If they are customized, then the source of cost reductions might come from decisions inside the buying organization such as specification or design changes. If the items are commodity-type items meaning they are standard off-the-shelf goods or services with substitutes available, then the cost reductions might come from inside the supplier's organization and be from its supply chain, production process, or distribution network.

Portfolio or Quadrant Analysis and Cost Management

Portfolio analysis enables a supply management team to place each major spend category on a spend map based on the risks to acquire in the marketplace and the value of the category to the organization. Figure 11–1 provides typical characteristics of each quadrant. The x-axis represents the assessment of risk to acquire or how easy or hard is it to acquire a specific spend category (good or service) in the marketplace. (Also see strategy development in Chapter 12). The Delphi Corporation case in Chapter 13 shows how the company uses a similar framework as part of its strategic sourcing process.

FIGURE 11–1   Characteristics of Spend Categories

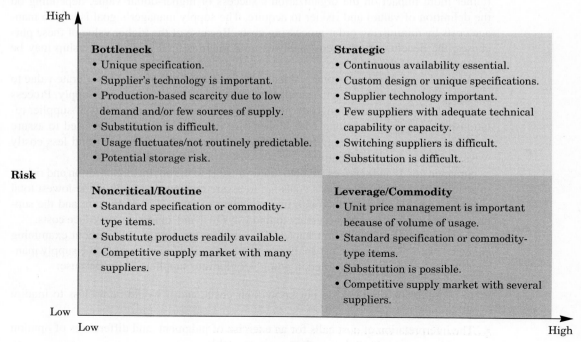

Bottleneck
- Unique specification.
- Supplier's technology is important.
- Production-based scarcity due to low demand and/or few sources of supply.
- Substitution is difficult.
- Usage fluctuates/not routinely predictable.
- Potential storage risk.

Strategic
- Continuous availability essential.
- Custom design or unique specifications.
- Supplier technology important.
- Few suppliers with adequate technical capability or capacity.
- Switching suppliers is difficult.
- Substitution is difficult.

Noncritical/Routine
- Standard specification or commodity-type items.
- Substitute products readily available.
- Competitive supply market with many suppliers.

Leverage/Commodity
- Unit price management is important because of volume of usage.
- Standard specification or commodity-type items.
- Substitution is possible.
- Competitive supply market with several suppliers.

Source: Adapted from Peter Kraljic, "Purchasing Must Become Supply, Management," *Harvard Business Review, 1983.*

The analyst should locate the spot on the map that represents the best analysis of two dimensions. This is done by first analyzing and determining the point on one axis, then doing the same for the other axis, and then locating the point of intersection on the map. For example, not all leverage items behave the same. A leverage item in the upper-right corner of that quadrant is both of greater value to the organization and higher risk (harder to acquire in the marketplace) than a leverage item (good or service) located in the lower-left corner of the leverage quadrant.

Portfolio analysis provides a framework for developing strategic plans for spend categories and for applying price and cost management tools. The price analysis tools discussed in Chapter 10 are primarily used when purchasing lower risk commodity-type items of lower total value to the organization. The cost tools discussed in this chapter are primarily applied to higher-risk and higher-value purchases. A key decision in this process is the definition of value. The original intent was for value to be defined as impact on the organization. In practice, many users define value as percent of annual spend.

Commodity-type items of low value to the organization (noncritical or routine) are essentially commodities. If a supplier has positioned a good or service as a cost leader, it is essentially selling a commodity and price must be competitive. To compete aggressively on price, the supplier must focus on continually reducing its costs. For a manufacturer these might be production costs, carrying costs, and raw materials costs. For a service provider, these might be labor costs or process costs. The buyer's cost management approach might be to minimize acquisition or order process costs and rely on market competition to keep prices competitive.

Commodity-type goods and services in the leverage quadrant are both higher value (either more impact on the organization's success or higher-dollar value, depending on the definition of value) and riskier to acquire. The supply manager's goal is still to manage costs by minimizing order processing costs. Because of the higher value of these purchases, the benefits of other cost analysis tools such as total cost of ownership may be worth the cost of the process.

As goods and services become riskier to acquire while still of low to moderate value to the organization (bottleneck), the supply manager's goal may be to assure supply. Process costs related to negotiating longer-term contracts and building stronger buyer–supplier relationships may increase along with higher carrying costs if inventory is used to assure supply. Longer-term costs may be incurred to conduct value analysis to find less costly ways to deliver the same function.

Strategic goods and services are both more valuable to the buying organization and riskier to acquire. The supply manager's goals are to assure continuous supply at the lowest total cost of ownership. A more thorough understanding of internal cost structure and the supplier's cost structure may be necessary to find ways to avoid, eliminate, or reduce costs.

Price analysis, addressed in Chapter 10, examines price proposals without examining elements of cost and profit. Cost analysis reviews actual or future costs. Some supply managers believe they are not justified in going very far into suppliers' costs because:

- In many cases, suppliers do not know their costs, and it would be useless to inquire about them.
- The interpretation of cost calls for an exercise of judgment, and differences of opinion would arise even if all the numbers were available.
- Some suppliers will not divulge cost information.

- The seller's costs do not determine market prices.
- The buyer is not interested in the supplier's costs anyway; the primary concern is getting the best price consistent with quality, quantity, delivery, and service.
- If a seller offers a price that does not cover costs, either in ignorance or with full recognition of what it is doing, the matter is the seller's problem and not the buyer's.

However, unless a buyer has some idea of a supplier's costs, at least in a general way, it is difficult to judge the reasonableness of the supplier's prices. Furthermore, the position that the buyer is neither concerned with, nor responsible for, suppliers who offer merchandise below cost must recognize two things: First, good suppliers need to cover their costs to survive and prosper; and, second, prices may subsequently rise materially above cost as suppliers fight for financial survival.

The party in the strongest position in a negotiation session is the one with the best data. Recognizing the importance of cost, it is common practice for the purchaser to make the best estimate possible of the supplier's costs as one means of judging the reasonableness of the price proposed. Many larger firms have cost analysts within the supply area to assist in analyzing supplier costs in preparation for negotiation. Some companies use cost-based pricing, a cost modeling system used by purchasers to determine total cost. These cost estimates must be based on such data as are available.

COST MANAGEMENT TOOLS AND TECHNIQUES

Five cost management techniques are addressed in this section: total cost of ownership (TCO), target pricing, the learning curve, value engineering and value analysis, and activity-based costing.

Total Cost of Ownership

The purchaser should estimate the total cost of ownership (TCO) before selecting a supplier. Broadly defined, total cost of ownership for noncapital goods acquisition includes all relevant costs, such as administration, follow-up, expediting, inbound transportation, inspection and testing, rework, storage, scrap, warranty, service, downtime, customer returns, and lost sales. The acquisition price plus all other associated costs becomes the total cost of ownership. A total cost approach requires the cooperation of engineering, quality, manufacturing, and supply to coordinate requirements such as specifications and tolerances that affect the supply decision. A similar approach may be applied when describing the required service in the statement of work (SOW). Early supplier involvement also is essential to ensure cost-effectiveness.

TCO models attempt to determine all the cost elements, thereby revealing opportunities for cost reduction or cost avoidance for each cost element, rather than merely analyzing or comparing prices. The difficulty lies in identifying and tracking these cost elements and using the information appropriately to compare different suppliers.

In TCO analysis, acquisition price is merely one part of the costs associated with owning a good or procuring a service. While the most obvious reason for using TCO is to identify the actual cost of the supply decision, TCO also can be used to:

1. Highlight cost reduction opportunities.
2. Aid supplier evaluation and selection.

3. Provide data for negotiations.
4. Focus suppliers on cost reduction opportunities.
5. Highlight the advantage of expensive, high-quality items.
6. Clarify and define supplier performance expectations.
7. Create a long-term supply perspective.
8. Forecast future performance.

There are a number of methods for estimating the total cost of ownership. Each firm must develop or adopt a method of cost modeling that best fits the needs of the organization. In close buyer–supplier relationships, the seller may willingly share cost data with the buyer. In other situations, the buyer or sourcing team may have to develop its own cost model to prepare for negotiations. There are many approaches to cost modeling, from informal ones to highly sophisticated, complex computer models. Firms typically use either *standard cost models,* which are applied to a variety of supply situations, or *unique cost models,* which are developed for a specific item or situation.

One way of analyzing cost elements is demonstrated by a model developed by Ellram that refers to three cost components: (1) pretransaction costs (e.g., identifying need, qualifying sources, and adding supplier to internal systems); (2) transaction costs (e.g., purchase, inspection, and administrative costs); and (3) post-transaction (e.g., defective parts, repairs, and maintenance). The acquisition price is broken down into the individual cost elements from which the price is derived. Each of these cost elements then can be analyzed by the buyer for areas of reduction or avoidance. Cost elements are both tangible and intangible, meaning that many are difficult to estimate.

Manufacturing Cost Elements

The following section addresses the typical cost elements of a manufactured product and provides suggestions for estimating the cost of each.

The prices of *raw material* entering into the product are commonly accessible and the amounts required are also fairly well known. Material costs can be estimated from a bill of material, a drawing, or a sample of the product. The buyer can arrive at material costs by multiplying material quantities or weight per unit by raw material prices. Sometimes a material usage curve will be helpful. The purpose of the curve is to chart what improvement should occur from buying economies and lower scrap rates as experience is gained in the manufacturing process. Use of price indexes and maintenance of price trend records are standard practice. For *component parts,* catalog prices often offer a clue. *Transportation costs* are easily determined.

Overhead costs generally consist of indirect costs incurred in the manufacturing, research, or engineering facilities of the company. The buyer's own engineers should provide data on processing costs. Equipment depreciation typically is the largest single element in manufacturing overhead. It is important to know how these overhead costs are distributed to a given product. If overhead is allocated as a fixed percentage of direct labor costs and there is an increase in labor costs, overhead costs can be unduly inflated unless the allocation percentage is changed. General overhead rates can be approximated.

The growing tendency for industry to become more capital intensive has increased the relative percentage of overhead versus direct labor and materials. Because some items in the overhead, such as local real estate taxes, are attributable to the location of the supplier and others are properly seen as depreciation or investment at varying technological and economic risk levels, the analysis and allocation of these costs to individual products are particularly difficult.

Both *tooling costs* and *engineering costs* often are included as a part of general manufacturing overhead, but it is wisest to pull them out for analysis as separate items since each may account for a relatively large amount of cost. The buyer wants to know what it should cost a reasonably efficient supplier to build the tooling and own the completed tooling, what its life expectancy (number of units) is, and whether the tooling can be used with equipment other than that owned by the supplier. Only with such information can the buyer guard against being charged twice for the same tooling.

General and administrative expense includes items such as selling, promotion, advertising, executive salaries, and legal expense. Frequently there is no justification for the supplier to charge an advertising allocation in the price of a product manufactured to the buyer's specifications or after entering into a long-term buyer-supplier partnering relationship.

Direct labor estimates are not made as easily as material estimates. Even though labor costs are normally labeled direct for machine operators and assembly-line workers, in reality they tend to be more fixed than most managers care to admit. If an organization's management prefers not to lay off personnel, then inventories and overtime may be used to smooth fluctuations in demand and labor cost becomes at least semivariable and subject to allocation. The management of many organizations prefers to reduce direct labor cost by relying on contract, freelance, or temporary labor, domestic or offshore, thereby eliminating or greatly reducing the costs of salaries, wages, and benefits.

Product mix, run sizes, and labor turnover may affect labor costs substantially. The greater the mix, the shorter the lot size produced, and the higher the turnover, the greater the direct labor costs will be. These three factors alone may create substantial cost differences between suppliers of an identical end product. Geographical considerations also play a large part because differences in labor rates do exist between plant locations. Such differences may change dramatically over time, as the rapid increases in direct labor rates in Japan and Germany demonstrated in the 1950s and in China and India currently. The astute cost analyst will estimate the supplier's real labor costs, taking the above considerations into account.

Services Cost Elements

As addressed in Chapter 6 "Need Identification," services are intangible products that may or may not be bundled with a good. A service provider does not have costs of manufacturing and the accompanying carrying costs for raw materials, work-in-process, and finished goods inventory. The primary cost elements for a service provider are direct and indirect labor depending on whether the service is high or low labor intensive.

Overhead costs generally consist of indirect costs incurred in the design, development, delivery, and operational facilities of the company. The buyer's own operations should provide data on processing costs. Depending on the type of service provider, equipment depreciation may be a very small part of overhead. Labor intensity will affect the relative percentage of overhead versus direct labor.

General and administrative expense includes items such as selling, promotion, advertising, executive salaries, and legal expense. Frequently there is no justification for the supplier to charge an advertising allocation in the price of a service designed to the buyer's specifications or after forming a long-term buyer-supplier partnering relationship.

Transportation costs, in the form of Travel and Entertainment (T&E), may be high depending on the amount and geographical range of travel in support of sales and customer relationship management. These costs may be easily determined if the service provider has consolidated and manages this spend category. Or these costs may be hidden if responsibility for travel spend is highly decentralized. While travel spend is often targeted for cost reduction, starkly different perspectives on cost-cutting opportunities are likely to be offered by users and cost-cutters.

Direct labor for a service contract includes the supplier's employees whose time is directly engaged to perform an identifiable task required under the terms of the contract. This task may or may not result in a tangible output, for example an architectural drawing, depending on the nature of the service provided. If an organization's management prefers not to lay off personnel, and there are strong pressures to keep the so-called direct labor force reasonably stable and employed then overtime often is used to smooth fluctuations in demand and labor cost becomes at least semivariable and subject to allocation. Companies in the service sector are also relying more on freelance, contract, and temporary labor, domestic and offshore, to eliminate or reduce labor costs.

In high labor intensity services, the cost of managing multiple sources for the same service or the costs of switching suppliers may be very high. These costs include resolving contractual issues, knowledge-transfer costs, licensing fees, initial setup and training costs with a new supplier, and the internal resources to manage the process. These costs may be underestimated when initial sourcing decisions are made.

Services mix, length of service contract, location of service provision (supplier's site or buyer's site and onshore, near shore, or offshore) and labor turnover may affect labor costs substantially. The greater the mix, the shorter the contract term, the higher the labor rate, and the higher the turnover, the greater the direct labor costs will be. Geographical considerations also play a large part because differences in labor rates exist between locations. Labor savings is a prime driver of the trend to outsource and offshore a growing variety of services including legal, medical test reading, research analyst, and software developer. Labor differentials may change dramatically over time. Recent rapid increases in direct labor rates in certain job categories such as IT and call centers in India and China, have led to some industries moving to lower-cost sections of a country such as inner or western China or to lower-cost countries such as the Philippines, Vietnam, and Pakistan. The same thing occurred in Japan and Germany in the past. The astute cost analyst will estimate the supplier's real labor costs, taking the above considerations into account.

There are several opportunities for buyers of services to reduce, contain, and avoid cost in services contracts. These include:[1]

1. Usurping procurement leverage.
2. Hidden cost adders.
3. Cost of money.
4. Billing and calculation errors.
5. Substitution of lower-skilled staff or inputs.
6. Providing levels of service below commitment.

[1] Lisa M. Ellram, Wendy L. Tate, and Corey Billington, "Understanding and Managing the Services Supply Chain," *The Journal of Supply Chain Management* 40, no. 4 (2004), p. 17.

7. Bundling of services with other services or goods.
8. Summary invoicing.

Based on this list, many of the cost-saving, reduction, and avoidance opportunities in services come from improving operating efficiency and productivity rather than better design.

Frequently, in highly professional services the cost of the professional service may be relatively low compared to the benefit expected. For example, a good design may increase sales substantially; a good architect may be able to design a low-cost but effective structure; and a good consulting recommendation may turn around a whole organization. It often is difficult to deal with this trade-off between the estimated costs for the job versus the estimated benefits. Some supply managers are working to develop cost models for highly skilled service providers to better understand the service providers' cost structure and identify opportunities to lower costs.

Services involving largely lower- to medium-skilled people may focus more on cost minimization and efficiency. Services requiring highly skilled individuals may require the purchaser to distinguish between levels of professional skill and may require extensive ongoing communication between requisitioner and supply manager through all phases of the acquisition process. It is important to clearly define the quantity of each skill level required for successful delivery of the service and to match that skill level with the price and total cost of the project. For example, if a paralegal can perform the service at the quality level desired, then there may be no reason to pay the hourly cost of a partner in a high-level law firm.

Cost management of services often starts with demand management, also referred to as consumption management in some industries. An internal review analyzes consumption patterns to determine what, if any, changes can be made to consumption of the service. These include: eliminate the service, reduce the volume of the service, reduce the frequency of the service, change the specification; find a substitute; improve the purchasing process to eliminate maverick or off-contract buying; reduce overconsumption, rationalize the supply base; consolidate spend; and standardize the price, terms, and conditions.

Understanding the cost structure of professional service providers is important as more highly professional service providers offshore aspects of their business. For example, U.S. law firms offshore legal work, consulting firms offshore analytical work, and hospitals offshore the interpretation of medical tests. Should a client of these service providers share in the labor savings realized by these decisions? Do these offshoring decisions raise other issues about quality and costs?

Life-Cycle Costing and Capital Goods Acquisition

Life-cycle costing (LCC) is the term for TCO used in capital acquisitions. It is an appropriate decision approach to capital investments in which the price of the capital good may be dwarfed by the other costs associated with owning, operating, and disposing of the item. The philosophy behind LCC is the same as TCO. The total cost of a piece of equipment goes well beyond the purchase price or even its installed cost. What is really of interest is the total cost of performing the intended function over the lifetime of the task or the piece of equipment. Thus, an initial low purchase price may mask a higher operating cost, perhaps occasioned by higher maintenance and downtime costs, more skilled labor, greater material waste, more energy use, or higher waste processing charges. Since the low bid would favor a low initial machine cost, an unfair advantage may accrue to the supplier with possibly the highest life-cycle cost equipment.

It is the inclusion of every conceivable cost pertaining to the decision that makes the LCC concept easier to grasp theoretically than to practice in real life. Since many of the costs are future ones, possibly even 10 to 15 years hence and of a highly uncertain nature, criticisms of the exactness of LCC are well founded. Fortunately, IT solutions are available varying from simple accounting programs, which compute costs from project life cycles, to Monte Carlo simulation of the equipment from conception to disposal. The software allows for testing of sensitivity, and, when necessary, inputs can be changed readily. In one total cost of ownership study for a multimillion-dollar piece of equipment, 139 different cost elements were identified for the computer simulation of the process.

LCC is a serious and preferable alternative to emphasizing the selection of low bids, particularly in governmental purchasing. The experience with LCC has shown in a surprising number of instances that the initial purchase price of equipment may be a relatively low percentage of LCC. For example, the price paid for computers seldom accounts for over 50 percent of LCC, and most industrial equipment falls into the 20 to 60 percentage range.

However, price is often the major factor in an acquisition decision. This is easy to understand when the number and variety of cost elements and the difficulty in calculating these costs are considered. The fundamental questions about cost elements for capital goods include the following:

- Is the equipment intended for replacement only or to provide additional capacity?
- What is the installed cost of the equipment?
- What will start-up costs be?
- Will its installation create problems for plant layout?
- What will be the maintenance and repair costs?
- Who will provide repair parts and at what cost?
- Are accessories required and, if so, what will their costs be?
- What will be the operating costs, including power and labor?
- What is the number of machine-hours the equipment will be used?
- Can the user make the machine or must it be purchased?
- At what rate is the machine to be depreciated?
- What financing costs are involved?
- If the equipment is for production, what is the present cost of producing the product compared to the cost of obtaining the product from a supplier?
- If the equipment is for production, what is the projected cost of producing the product compared to the cost of obtaining the product from a supplier?

For example, in the semiconductor industry, capital equipment purchases normally represent the largest single percentage category of all purchase dollars. At Intel the goal is to tie capital equipment purchasing and equipment service to performance-based contracting. Thus, the supplier gets paid for uptime and quality output. The more the running time exceeds agreed-to output goals, the greater the rewards for the supplier. Future plans are driven by the need for continuous improvement in cost per wafer and number of wafers per year per machine. Only a few key supplier partners are included in Intel's longer-range technology road maps planning process—looking five years out. Total cost of ownership, not just the cost of the equipment itself, drives future technology decisions. Obviously, the corporate team approach is required to manage this process, and exceptionally capable individuals need to represent supply on the corporate team.

Target Costing

In target costing, a management team establishes the price at which it plans to sell its finished product, then subtracts out its normal operating profit, leaving the target cost that the organization seeks. The formula is Target Cost = Estimated Selling Price − Desired Profit. The target cost is then further subdivided into appropriate cost sectors, such as manufacturing process, overhead, materials, and services. Supply becomes responsible for working with suppliers to achieve the materials and services target. Target costing is typically used in new product development. Target pricing focuses the attention of everyone in the organization on designing costs out of products and services rather than on eliminating costs after production has begun or services have been delivered. This concept is a logical extension of the quality movement's basic premise that it makes sense to build something right the first time.

For example, if the end product is a manufactured item that will be sold for $200, and purchased goods represent 60 percent of each dollar in sales revenue, then supply would be responsible for $120 of the $200 selling price. If it is determined that a 10 percent reduction in price is desirable because of the expected impact on sales revenue, then supply would be responsible for securing a 10 percent reduction in its portion of the costs ($120) of the item, or $12. This means purchased materials, on a unit basis, should not exceed $108. This becomes the target materials cost in the pricing structure. See the example in Figure 11–2.

Target pricing results in companywide cost reductions in:

1. Design to cost, on the part of design engineering.
2. Manufacture to cost, on the part of production.
3. Purchase to cost, on the part of supply.

FIGURE 11–2
Target Pricing Example

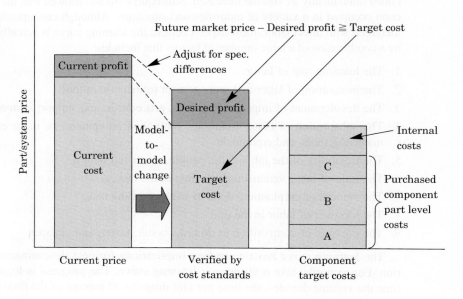

Implications for Supply Management

For supply, target pricing can be beneficial by providing a means of documenting specific price reductions needed from suppliers, demonstrating supply's contribution to the pricing goals of the firm, and documenting supply's contribution on a product-by-product basis. To be effective, target pricing works best when the customer has clout or leverage in the supply chain; when there is loyalty between buyer and seller, as in a partnering arrangement or alliance; and when the supplier also stands to benefit from the cost reductions.

The cost reductions on the part of the supplier conceivably can come from several areas: The supplier can seek reductions in overhead expenses and/or general, selling, and administrative expenses; the supplier can improve efficiencies in labor as measured by the learning curve; or the supplier can seek labor cost reductions and material cost reductions from its supply chain. This last option requires the supplier to pass down these techniques to *its* suppliers in the supply chain.

Overall, target pricing provides supply with:

1. A measurable target for supply performance.
2. A yardstick for measuring cost reductions.
3. A means of measuring the supplier's efficiency.

As with all cost analysis tools, the expected benefits from the target-costing process must exceed the costs associated with conducting the analysis. To be successful, the effort requires cross-functional team efforts, early supplier and early supply involvement, concurrent engineering, and value engineering.

The Learning Curve or Experience Curve

The learning curve provides an analytical framework for quantifying the commonly recognized principle that one becomes more proficient with experience. Its origins lie in the aircraft industry in World War II when it was empirically determined that labor time per plane declined dramatically as volume increased. Subsequent studies showed that the same phenomenon occurred in a variety of industries and situations. Although conceptually most closely identified with direct labor, most experts believe the learning curve is actually brought about by a combination of a large number of factors that includes:

1. The learning rate of labor.
2. The motivation of labor and management to increase output.
3. The development of improved methods, procedures, and support systems.
4. The substitution of better materials, tools, and equipment, or more effective use of materials, tools, and equipment.
5. The flexibility of the job and the people associated with it.
6. The ratio of labor versus machine time in the task.
7. The amount of preplanning done in advance of the task.
8. The turnover of labor in the unit.
9. The pressure of competition to do tasks better, faster, and cheaper.

The learning curve has tremendous implications for cost determination and negotiation. For example, take a 90 percent learning curve. The progress is logarithmic. Every time the volume doubles, the time per unit drops to 90 percent of the time per unit at half the volume. Suppose we wish to purchase 800 units of a highly labor-intensive, expensive product that will be produced by a group of workers over a two-year period. The 100th unit has been produced at a labor time of 1,000 hours. With a 90 percent learning curve, the labor time for the 200th unit would drop to 900 hours and the 400th unit to 90 percent of 900 hours, or 810 hours per unit.

Do service firms exhibit learning curves? Is there a significant association between experience-based knowledge and productivity increases in services? While the application of learning curve theory to services has not been well-researched, it is an interesting concept in a service economy.

It is important to recognize that the choice of learning curve, be it 95, 90, 85, or 80 percent or any other figure, is not an exact science. Normally, fairly simple tasks, like putting parts into a box, tend to have a learning curve close to 95 percent. Medium-complexity tasks often have learning curve rates between 80 and 90 percent, while highly complex tasks tend to be in the 70 to 80 percent range.

The learning curve implies that improvement never stops, no matter how large the volume becomes. The potential of the learning curve in supply management has not yet been fully explored. It is a powerful concept. Progressive discounts, shortened lead times, and better value can be planned and obtained through its use. The learning curve is used along with target costing to set progressively lower price targets for future deliveries.

Value Engineering and Value Analysis

Value methodology is a systematic approach to analyzing the functions of a product, part, service, or process to satisfy all needed quality and user requirements at optimum total cost of ownership. Value can be expressed as:

$$\text{VALUE} = \frac{\text{Function}}{\text{Cost}}$$

Function is defined in a noun-verb combination: for example, "holds liquid." The goal is to perform a function at the same or an improved level while reducing costs. The focus is on functional analysis. Unnecessary costs, those that do not provide quality, extend product or service life, or provide features desired by customers, can be avoided or eliminated.

Value engineering (VE) refers to the application of this analytical process to the design stage of a product or service; *value analysis (VA)* to the redesign of a product or service. By focusing on function and cost in the design stage, unnecessary costs can be avoided. In the redesign stage, the organization has already incurred costs that must now be reduced or eliminated. Lower total cost of ownership is achieved when a cost management focus starts in design.

Activity-Based Costing

Traditional cost accounting introduces distortions into product costing because of the way it allocates overhead on the basis of direct labor. In the past, when labor costs often were the largest cost category, this allocation made sense. However, as the cost of materials has eclipsed labor costs as the single largest cost factor, accountants have looked for other ways to allocate overhead.[2] Basically, *activity-based costing (ABC)* tries to turn indirect costs into direct costs by tracking the cost drivers behind indirect costs.

[2] The section is drawn largely from John C. Lere and Jayant V. Saraph, "Activity-Based Costing for Purchasing Managers' Cost and Pricing Determinations," *International Journal of Purchasing and Materials Management,* Fall 1995, pp. 25–21.

One of the biggest hurdles in ABC is the cost of tracking indirect costs and translating them into direct costs, compared with the benefits of being able to assign these costs to specific products more accurately. In ABC, manufacturing overhead is divided into costs that change in response to unit-level activities (in proportion to the number of units produced), batch-level activities (in proportion to the number of batches produced), and product-level activities (that benefit all units of a product). The remainder are true fixed costs and are allocated the same way as in traditional cost accounting.

It is easy for those trying to apply the ABC concept to collect too much detail and be unable to make much sense out of it. Even so, it is a powerful tool that has many implications for supply management.

Implications for Supply Management

Buyers can use activity-based costing as a tool to reduce supplier costs by:

- Eliminating nonvalue-adding activities.
- Reducing activity occurrences.
- Reducing the cost driver rate.

To accomplish these goals, buyers must collect data from suppliers on activities (specific tasks), cost drivers (a metric to measure activity), cost driver rates (rate at which cost is incurred), and units of cost driver (the amount of activity). Buyers then can determine which activities add value and should occur, and which do not add value and should be eliminated. Even if an activity is deemed value-adding, it may be possible to reduce the number of times the activity occurs, thereby reducing cost.

For example, receiving inspection may be rated as nonvalue-adding and targeted for elimination, or it may be deemed value-adding but the number of receipts requiring inspection may be reduced, thereby reducing costs. Lastly, the cost of the activity itself may be targeted as an area for improvements in efficiency through value analysis and system redesign.

Assigning cost estimates to activities is often difficult. It is essential, however, to enable comparison of activities and activity levels and to determine where improvements contribute most to organizational performance. Competing goals and objectives of different functional areas may increase the difficulty of using ABC as a decision-making tool. In the example above, receiving may use ABC to decrease incoming inspections and improve receiving department performance. Quality assurance, however, may want to increase incoming inspection to reduce acceptance rates of nonconforming product.

NEGOTIATION

Negotiation is the most sophisticated and most expensive means of price determination. Negotiation requires that the buyer and supplier, through discussion, arrive at a common understanding on the essentials of a purchase/sale contract, such as delivery, specifications, warranty, prices, and terms. Because of the interrelation of these factors and many others, it is a difficult art and requires the exercise of judgment and tact. Negotiation is an attempt to find an agreement that allows both parties to realize their objectives. It must be used when the buyer is in a single- or sole-source situation; both parties know that a purchase contract will be issued, and their task is to define a set of terms and conditions acceptable to both.

Because of the expense and time involved, true negotiation normally will not be used unless the dollar amount is quite large.

Negotiating a fair price should not be confused with *price haggling*. Supply managers generally frown on haggling and properly so, for in the long run the cost to the buyer far outweighs any temporary advantage. For a purchaser to tell a sales representative that he or she has received a quotation that was not, in fact, received or that is not comparable; to fake telephone calls in the sales representative's presence; to leave real or fictitious bids of competitors in open sight for a sales representative to see; to mislead as to the quantity needed—these and similar practices are illustrations of those unethical actions so properly condemned by the codes of ethics of the Institute for Supply Management (ISM), the Supply Chain Management Association (SCMA) of Canada, and other supply associations around the world.

Negotiation need not result in a lower price. Occasionally, there may be revision upward of the price paid, compared with the supplier's initial proposal. If, in the negotiation, it becomes clear that the supplier has either misinterpreted the specifications or underestimated the resources needed to perform the work, the buyer will bring this to the supplier's attention so the proposal may be adjusted accordingly. A good contract is one that both parties can live with, and under which the supplier should not lose money, providing its operation is efficient. When a purchaser cooperates in granting increases not required by the original supplier proposal, the buyer then is in a position to request decreases in prices if unforeseen events occur that result in the supplier's being able to produce the material or product at a substantial savings.

Negotiation Strategy and Practice

Reasonable negotiation is expected by buyer and seller alike. It is within reasonable bounds of negotiation to insist that a supplier:

1. Operate in an efficient manner.
2. Keep prices in line with costs.
3. Not take advantage of a privileged position.
4. Make proper and reasonable adjustment of claims.
5. Be prepared to consider the special needs of the buyer's organization.

While negotiation normally is thought of as a means of establishing the price to be paid, and this may be the main focus, many other areas or conditions can be negotiated. In fact, *any* aspect of the purchase/sale agreement is subject to negotiation.

The discussion of some of the elements and considerations that affect the price of an item makes it obvious that negotiation can be a valuable technique to use in reaching an agreement with a supplier on the many variables affecting a specific price. This is not to say that all buying/selling transactions require the use of negotiations. Nor is the intention to indicate that negotiation is used only in determining price. Reaching a clear understanding of time schedules for deliveries, factors affecting quality, and methods of packaging may require negotiations of equal or greater importance than those applying to price.

A list of some of the various kinds of purchasing situations in which the use of negotiations should prove valuable follows:

1. Any written contract covering price, specifications, statement of work, terms of delivery, and quality standards.

2. The purchase of items made to the buyer's specifications. Special importance should be attached to "first buys," because thorough exploration of the needs of the buyer and the supplier often will result in a better product at a lower price.

3. When changes are made in drawings, specifications, or statement of work after a purchase order has been issued.

4. When quotations have been solicited from responsible bidders and no acceptable bids have been received.

5. When problems of tooling or packaging occur.

6. When changing economic or market conditions require changes in quantities or prices.

7. When problems of termination of a contract involve disposal of facilities, materials, or tooling or ownership of copyright or coding.

8. When there are problems accepting any of the elements in cost-type contracts.

9. When problems arise under the various types of contracts used in defense and governmental contracting.

10. When cost analysis shows a significant gap between market price and costs.

Framework for Planning and Preparing for Negotiation

Success in negotiation largely is a function of the quality and amount of planning that has been done. Figure 11–3 presents a model of the negotiation process.

The basic steps in developing a strategy for negotiation are as follows:

1. Develop the specific objectives (outcomes) desired from the negotiation. This is done by gathering relevant information and then generating, analyzing, evaluating, and selecting alternatives.

2. Gather pertinent data. Here is where cost analysis comes into play.

3. Determine the facts of the situation. A fact is defined as an item of information about which agreement is expected. For example, if the supplier's cost breakdown states that the direct labor rate is $20.10 per hour, and you agree, that is a fact.

FIGURE 11–3
Model of the Negotiation Process

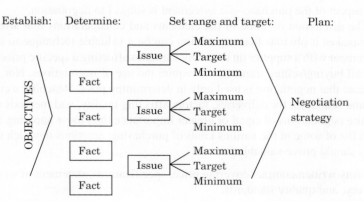

4. Determine the issues. An issue is something over which disagreement is expected. The purpose of negotiation is to resolve issues so that a mutually satisfactory contract can be signed. For example, if the supplier claims the manufacturing burden rate is 300 percent of direct labor costs, but your analysis indicates a 240 percent burden rate is realistic, this becomes an issue to be settled through negotiation.

5. Analyze the positions of strength of both (or all) parties. For example, what are the supplier's capacity, backlog, and profitability? How confident is the supplier of getting the contract? Is there any time urgency? The process of analyzing strengths helps the negotiator establish negotiation points, helps avoid setting unrealistic expectations, and may reveal ideas for strategies. The negotiator (or team) should be able to generate a list of 12 to 24 points for either side through a brainstorming process.

6. Set the buyer's position on each issue and estimate the seller's position on each issue based on your research. What data will be used to support the buyer's position? What data might support the seller's position? Two questions should be asked after analyzing positions of strength: (*a*) "Whose position is stronger?" and (*b*) "Which points give each side the most strength?" The answer to the first question should help determine how realistic the objectives are and if they need to be changed or clarified. The answer to the second question tells the negotiator what his or her key points will be in the negotiation and what to expect from the other side. If done well, this information allows the negotiator to prepare counterarguments.

By estimating the range of acceptable results for both buyer and seller, the negotiator can determine, first, if there is a zone of overlap, meaning negotiation is feasible and likely to result in an agreement; or, second, if there is a gap between the objectives of the parties (see Figure 11–4). If there is a gap, the negotiator must determine if it can be closed, and if not, whether negotiation even makes sense in this particular situation.

FIGURE 11–4
The Zone of Negotiation

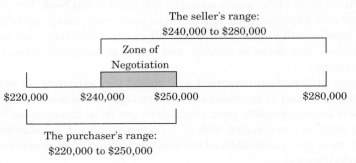

1. The seller and purchaser overlap.

The seller's range:
$240,000 to $280,000

Zone of Negotiation

$220,000 $240,000 $250,000 $280,000

The purchaser's range:
$220,000 to $250,000

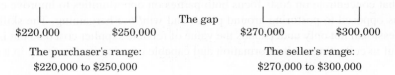

2. The seller and purchaser do not overlap.

$220,000 $250,000   The gap $270,000 $300,000

The purchaser's range: The seller's range:
$220,000 to $250,000 $270,000 to $300,000

7. Plan the negotiation strategy. Which issues should be discussed first? Where is the buyer willing to compromise? Who will make up the negotiation team (it frequently is composed of someone from both engineering and quality control for a good, or the primary internal consumer for a service, headed by the buyer)? Establishing a range and a target for each objective sets reasonable objectives that the negotiator feels can be achieved. The tactics used in the actual negotiation may mean starting out at a more extreme position than the negotiator truly believes is achievable. The decision about tactics should be based on the negotiator's understanding of the situation and the parties involved in the negotiation. If the goal of negotiation is performance, then the *way* negotiation is conducted is important because it affects the intention to perform. If the tactics used leave the other party feeling negative toward the negotiator or the results, there may be little commitment to the agreement or to solving any problems that might arise during the life of the contract.

8. Brief all persons on the team who are going to participate in the negotiations.

9. Conduct a dress rehearsal for the people who are going to participate in the negotiations.

10. Conduct the actual negotiations with an impersonal calmness.

All negotiation has an economic as well as a psychological dimension. It is important to satisfy both of these dimensions to achieve a win-win result. The trends toward teaming, single sourcing, partnering, and empowerment reinforce the need for supply personnel to be superior negotiators, both with suppliers and with others in their own organization. Actually, negotiations inside one's own organization to obtain cooperation and support for supply initiatives may be more challenging than those with suppliers.

Conclusion

The notion that an attempt should be made to identify and analyze all costs of ownership drives many of the supply strategies discussed in this book. For example, long-term collaborative buyer–supplier relationships; partnering arrangements and alliances; and early supplier and supply involvement all can facilitate total cost modeling, improve negotiations and decision making, and result in increased competitiveness for the organization.

Supply professionals concerned with contributing effectively to organizational goals and strategies need to be concerned with managing costs instead of prices. Haranguing suppliers for unreasonable price concessions can be as damaging as "leaving too much on the table" in a negotiation with an important supplier. Understanding where and how supply chain costs can be reduced or eliminated can represent an opportunity to gain competitive advantage.

Negotiation and supplier cost analysis complement each other. Cost analysis identifies the opportunity and secures the result. Costs drive pricing. Negotiations with suppliers that concentrate on costs focus both parties on opportunities to improve competitiveness as opposed to posturing around prices and win/lose bargaining. The skilled supply professional not only understands the value of reliable supplier cost data but is also resourceful in collecting such information and capable of using it effectively in a negotiation.

Questions for Review and Discussion

1. What is cost-based pricing? How and why is it used?

2. What are the major cost categories that you would include when estimating a supplier's cost for a manufacturing item? How would you estimate such costs if the supplier was either unwilling or unable to provide a detailed cost breakdown?

3. What are the major cost categories that you would include when estimating a supplier's cost for a service? How would you estimate the cost if the supplier was either unwilling or unable to provide a detailed cost breakdown?

4. When and how is negotiation used, and what can be negotiated?

5. What is a learning curve and how can it be used?

6. Why do firms use target costing? How are target costs established?

7. What is activity-based costing (ABC), and how can the buyer use ABC to reduce costs?

8. What is total cost of ownership (TCO), and how is it determined?

9. What is the difference between "managing costs" as opposed to "managing prices"?

10. Please comment on the following statement: Target costing can only be used for manufactured items and cannot be applied to services.

References

Anklesaria, J. *Supply Chain Cost Management: The AIM and DRIVE Process for Achieving Dramatic Results.* New York: AMACOM, 2007.

Boone, T.; R. Ganeshan; and R. L. Hicks. "Learning and Knowledge Depreciation in Professional Services." *Management Science* 54, no. 7 (July 2008), pp. 1231–1236.

Cooper, R., and R. Slagmulder. *Target Costing and Value Engineering.* Portland, OR: Productivity Press, and Montvale, NJ: The IMA Foundation for Applied Research Inc., 1997.

Ellram, L. M.; W. L. Tate; and C. Billington. "Understanding and Managing the Services Supply Chain." *The Journal of Supply Chain Management* 40, no. 4 (2004), p. 17.

Ellram, L. M. "The Implementation of Target Costing in the United States: Theory versus Practice." *The Journal of Supply Chain Management* 42, no. 1 (2006) pp. 13–26.

Ellram, L. "A Taxonomy of Total Cost of Ownership Models." *Journal of Business Logistics* 15, no. 1 (1994), pp. 171–91.

Fisher, R.; W. Ury; and B. Patton. *Getting to Yes: Negotiating Agreement Without Giving In.* New York: Penguin Books, 2011.

Flynn, A. E. *Consumption and Specification Management at Bristol Myers Squibb. Practix,* Tempe, AZ: CAPS Research, 2005.

Lewicki, R. J.; B. Barry; and D. M. Saunders. *Negotiation.* 6th ed. Burr Ridge, IL: McGraw-Hill/Irwin, 2010.

Shank, J. K., and Govindarajan, V. *Strategic Cost Management: The New Tool for Competitive Advantage.* New York: Free Press, 2008.

Ury, W. *Getting Past No: Negotiating Your Way from Confrontation to Cooperation.* New York: Bantam Books, 1993.

Case 11–1

Deere Cost Management

On Wednesday, February 18, Jim Elsey, cost management specialist at Deere & Company in Moline, Illinois, received a call from Glen Lowery, sales manager in the Agricultural Products Division:

> Jim, I need you to look into our costs on the gatherer chain. Our margins have really shrunk and we need to do something about this problem. Get back to me and let me know what you think.

THE GATHERER CHAIN

Deere & Company (Deere) manufactured and distributed a full line of agriculture equipment as well as a broad range of construction, turf, and forestry equipment. Additional supporting businesses were Financial Services, Power Systems, Parts Services, and the Intelligent Solutions Group. The company had annual sales of $35 billion with operations in more than 160 countries.

A popular product sold by the Agricultural Products Division was a conveyor system. Materials placed on the front end of the conveyor sat on the gatherer chain, which carried the material to the opposite end. The gatherer chain was joined together in links, fastened by pins, and included small hooks that helped to carry the material. It sat on rollers that required regular lubrication to keep the conveyor system in good working condition.

The Agricultural Products Division had produced the conveyor system for several years, with only slight modifications in its design. As standard practice for each product, Deere sold replacement parts, including gatherer chains, through its dealer network. It was the intention of management to ensure that its aftermarket products were price competitive. As a result, the sales department regularly benchmarked pricing for its products.

Jim learned that the gatherer chain was purchased from Saunders Manufacturing (Saunders), a supplier located in Decatur, Illinois. Saunders was a family-owned business run by Wayne Saunders, the son of the company's founder. Saunders had a long-term relationship with Deere, and Wayne had a reputation as a tough, successful businessman who had grown the company to the point where it now employed approximately 300 people.

Reviewing the sales margin for the gatherer chain, Jim could see why Glen was concerned. Over the past three years, the sales revenue and margin had been declining steadily (see Exhibit 1). The budgeted selling price for the current year was based on the need to match the price set by a major competitor.

FINANCIAL ANALYSIS

Jim arranged a meeting the following day with Susan Tessier, from purchasing, and Jose da Costa, from engineering. During the meeting, Jim laid a gatherer chain on the conference room table and asked Jose to estimate the raw material content. After a little bit of work, Jose estimated that the product consisted of approximately 11.6 pounds of steel and 46 pins that joined the links. He also expected that Saunders would have approximately a 20 percent scrap rate, for steel only, as part of their normal production cost. Jose also commented that Saunders could use general-purpose equipment for the manufacturing and assembly process.

Susan then pulled out her material cost file and made the following observations:

> We just finished negotiations with our steel suppliers and expect to pay approximately $28.00 per hundredweight for this type of material. I am also buying the same pins for a couple of our divisions, and I figure Saunders is paying about 3.5¢. Don't forget that for this part we pay

EXHIBIT 1
Profitability Analysis for Gathered Chain

	Two Years Ago	Last year	Current Year Budget
Aftermarket price	$ 40.00	$ 36.25	$ 30.00
Purchase cost	$ 21.25	$ 22.61	$ 24.12
Cost–price ratio	53%	62%	80%
Unit sales	475,000	410,000	350,000

the freight, which usually costs about 3 percent of the purchase price, and they pay the packaging.

We have looked around for other suppliers for this part and haven't been able to find anyone that capable of beating the current price. Saunders has been a good supplier. Their quality and on-time delivery performance have been excellent. I wouldn't want to lose them as a supplier.

Following the meeting, Jim examined the Annual Survey of Manufactures, published by the U.S. Department of Commerce. Within the report was a breakdown of manufacturing costs, as a percentage of sales, for U.S. companies in Saunders's industry code. According to data from the previous year, the breakdown was material, 42 percent; direct labor; 13 percent; indirect labor, 6 percent; and overhead, 20 percent.

SUPPLIER NEGOTIATION

Glen felt that the budgeted cost–price ratio for the gatherer chain was unacceptable and was anxious to see what could be done to address the problem. He remarked to Jim, "The competition is pretty strict about maintaining a 50–50 cost–price ratio on their product lines. Why is it they can sell this product for $30.00 and we can't match their cost structure?"

Jim felt that he had gathered enough information to do some preliminary analysis. However, he was aware that he needed to think about how he could use the information in his negotiation with the vendor. Susan had indicated that Wayne Saunders had been a tough negotiator, with a "take it or leave it" attitude regarding pricing, and had been unwilling to share any specific cost information to justify his requests for price increases.

Case 11–2
McMichael Inc.

Art Flynn, packaging buyer for McMichael Inc. (MI), was working on an import substitution project involving a local minority supplier. He was concerned, however, that his efforts would be fruitless because his original proposal had been flatly rejected by the plant manager as too expensive.

McMichael Inc., a medium-sized company, had over the years specialized in prescription skin-care products, a market niche in which it had developed an excellent reputation. About three years ago, after extensive testing, MI had introduced a new facial cream in a special package that allowed for precise measurement of the quantity dispersed. The container, manufactured by a French firm for a different application, was fairly expensive at an FOB MI's factory cost of $0.36. What concerned Art Flynn even more, however, were the quality and delivery problems encountered. Communications with the manufacturer were difficult, and Art had the impression the manufacturer did not seem to care much about MI's business, which, as Art knew, was only a small proportion of their total volume produced.

With the cooperation of MI's marketing, engineering, production, and quality control personnel, Art had found a local minority supplier who appeared capable of meeting MI's requirements. This custom molding firm, OSA Inc., was owned by Bert Wood, a bright engineer, who had purchased the firm several years earlier when the previous owner wished to retire. OSA Inc. had its own tool and die manufacturing operation as well as its own molding shop. It depended heavily on automotive contracts, a situation Bert Wood wished to correct by acquiring more nonautomotive business. In conjunction with MI's engineers, Bert Wood had worked out a mold design for the cream dispenser and included several suggestions for minor improvements. The cost of the mold was $56,000, an investment Bert Wood was in no position to make and that MI would have to absorb up front. Bert Wood quoted a unit price of $0.27 based on purchase quantities of 30,000 units at a time and an annual volume estimated at 300,000 units. Bert Wood had submitted a cost breakdown of this quote as follows:

Resin	16¢
Labor	3¢
Overhead*	8¢
	27¢

*Overhead breakdown:	
Power	1¢
Depreciation	1¢
Interest	3¢
Space, insurance, light and heat, taxes, supervision	3¢

When Art submitted this quote along with the request for a $56,000 mold investment up front, the plant manager and treasurer both turned it down, arguing that the 24-month payback on the mold was far too long and that the company had better investment opportunities with a 12-month payback.

Art was disappointed, because he had hoped this project would assist in helping him meet his savings target for the year. When he talked the idea over with his manager, Louise Moffat, she suggested he give it another try. She said, "I am sure that if you can get the mold payback down to 15 months, you will get a warmer reception. There are not that many deals around this company that pay for themselves in one year." She also suggested that Art talk to marketing to see if some other products could use the same packaging, and to the production scheduling group to check if different production quantities could be ordered.

When Art talked to the marketing people, he found out that the package was ideal for another product to be introduced shortly and with an annual demand estimated at 100,000 units. Marketing had been uneasy about using the French package because of the difficulties encountered with it and assured Art that if he could get a reliable domestic source, this option would be highly attractive.

The scheduling group, for a number of years, had used a modified MRP system. When Art discussed the new package idea with them, they told him that if the new product and the older one were to be packaged in the same package, a total package requirement of about 40,000 units would make sense and that the master production schedule could easily be adjusted to run the two products in conjunction.

Art also discussed the situation with the resin supplier, who indicated that his quote to Bert Wood had been based on the lot size of 30,000 packages, but that a 40,000 unit lot would fall into a new price bracket 5 percent lower than the originally quoted price.

Art wondered just what effect all of this new information would have on his original proposal. He knew that Bert Wood had been adamant about his $0.27 quote. Bert Wood had said, "I know I am classified as a minority supplier. But I don't want to hide behind that fact. I want no special favors from any of my customers. Nor am I in a position to make special gifts to anyone else. I have had to borrow at what I consider to be ridiculously high interest rates to buy this company. Now I have to make it pay off. My $0.27 price is as low as I can go, as far as I can see."

Case 11–3

Carmichael Corporation

Amanda Tellford, purchasing manager for Carmichael Corporation, became increasingly concerned about the purchase of MS-7, a special ingredient used in Stimgro, one of her company's new products. It appeared that a major cost increase might threaten the product's profitability, and Amanda was anxious to explore any alternatives that promised at least some cost relief.

CARMICHAEL CORPORATION

Carmichael Corporation was the U.S. subsidiary of Carmichael International, a UK-based producer of veterinary products and feed additives. Total U.S. sales were expected to be about $20 million with profits before taxes of about $1.2 million. Carmichael occupied a special niche in the market, offering small-volume specialty products that the bigger producers considered uneconomical. However, if sales of these products grew, the possibility existed that a larger producer might become interested. Carmichael had an exclusive distribution agreement with three distributors who covered all parts of the United States. Each distributor sold Carmichael products to feed stores, cooperatives,

and farm supply stores, which, in turn, sold to the farmer. For Stimgro the pricing structure through the distribution chain was approximately as follows:

Stimgro Carmichael $\xrightarrow{\$360}$ Distributor $\xrightarrow{\$520}$ Feed Store $\xrightarrow{\$780}$ Farmer

The Carmichael plant located in Chicago employed about 70 hourly rated people. The premises were leased and primary activities involved the mixing of ingredients and the bottling and packing of finished products. About half of the $8 million worth of ingredients was imported from the UK parent; the remainder and all packaging were purchased in the United States. The executive team consisted of Tim Paterson, president and treasurer; Charles Godfrey, sales manager; Amanda Tellford, manager of accounting and purchasing; and Andrew Hartwick, plant manager.

Carmichael Corporation concentrated on poultry medicines and feed additives. Three years earlier, Carmichael had introduced Stimgro, a feed additive for young turkeys, which had shown unusual promise in promoting rapid, healthy development in birds less than one month old. Shortly there-

EXHIBIT 1
Stimgro manufacturing

	(cost/kg)
MS-7 (500 grams)	$ 100
Other ingredients (500 grams)	48
Packaging	4
Labor	8
Overhead	20
Total	$ 180

after, a competitor, Brisson, introduced a similar product. Because Brisson, like Carmichael, had its own exclusive distributors, Brisson's entry into the market did not result in lower Stimgro sales for Carmichael. Small specialty producers like Carmichael and Brisson did not compete on price or manufacturing cost. Their big concern was finding new products to sell and making sufficient profit before the product was taken over by a larger company or lost its market appeal. Carmichael and Brisson had about equal shares in the Stimgro market with annual sales of about $1.4 million each.

Carmichael imported the two primary ingredients for Stimgro from its UK parent and mixed and packaged them in the Chicago plant. The manufacturing cost for Stimgro is shown in Exhibit 1. Carmichael's selling price of Stimgro was $360 per kilogram. Amanda Tellford had tried to find a North American source for MS-7 over the past few years but had found that all potential sources, pharmaceutical, and specialty chemical firms had declined serious interest. They claimed the volume was far too low, and the price would have to be at least $800 per kilogram before they could be persuaded to manufacture MS-7.

BRISSON

Brisson Corporation was a U.S.-owned manufacturer of products similar to those marketed by Carmichael. Brisson's range of products was greater than Carmichael's, and its annual sales volume was about $24 million. Brisson had originally obtained its MS-7 from a UK competitor of Carmichael International, but in the spring of the current year it had placed orders for equipment to manufacture its own MS-7. This action had surprised Amanda Tellford because, like Carmichael, Brisson had been relatively poorly prepared to take this step. For example, the North American market demand for MS-7 was limited to its use by Carmichael and Brisson. Although future growth might show a healthy increase, total current market demand certainly did not warrant the $1 million investment Brisson had to make.

Moreover, MS-7 was tricky to produce, requiring very careful temperature, pressure, and timing control. The main equipment item was a large glass-lined autoclave ingeniously instrumented and constructed to deal with the unusual demands of MS-7 production. The autoclave was normally a fairly general-purpose type of equipment in the chemical industry. However, the special conditions required for the manufacture of MS-7 made this reactor a special-purpose tool, certainly overdesigned and overengineered for the other uses to which Brisson might apply it. MS-7 manufacture was a batch production process, and the expected capacity of the equipment was about 40,000 kilograms per year based on two-shift operation.

In Amanda Tellford's eyes, Brisson's action affected her own purchases of MS-7, which up to this point had been at an advantageous transfer price from the UK parent. Although the exact impact was still not entirely clear, she expected at least a 40 percent increase in her laid-down cost. Amanda had no doubt that Brisson would aggressively seek customs protection from undervalued MS-7 imports and that at least a 20 percent duty would be applied on the American selling price.

Amanda Tellford, therefore, requested information from the parent company concerning manufacturing costs of MS-7. She added several other data from her own knowledge and prepared the following summary:

Summary of MS-7 cost and price data	
Minimum equipment outlay installed	$1 million
Delivery on equipment	9–12 months
UK normal market price	$224/kg
Our laid-down current cost from Carmichael, UK	$200/kg
Carmichael (UK) out-of-pocket cost (material, labor, and variable overhead)	$160/kg
Estimated minimum laid-down cost in Chicago after Brisson starts production	$280/kg

Amanda Tellford went to see Charles Godfrey, Carmichael's sales manager, to discuss possible sales requirements for the future. Charles said, "It's really anybody's guess. First, it depends on the popularity of turkeys. We are banking on continued growth there. Second, as soon as the feed companies can develop a suitable substitute for our product, they will go for it. We appear to be very expensive on a weight basis, although research and actual results show we represent excellent value. It takes such tiny quantities of Stimgro to improve the overall quality of a mix that it is difficult to believe it could have any impact. More competition can enter this market any day. We are just not large enough in the U.S. market to have any strong promotional impact. Each of our product lines is specialized, of relatively small volume, in an area where the big firms choose not to operate. Should a larger firm enter this market, they could flatten us. Now you tell me how to turn this into a reasonable forecast."

Amanda Tellford replied, "I'm glad that's your problem and not mine, Charles. Anytime you feel you're ready to put some figures down, please let me know, because it may become very important for us in the near future."

In looking over past figures, Amanda estimated that the second half of this year's requirements would total about 1,000 kilograms of MS-7. Amanda decided that she had better think out the effect that Brisson's decision to make MS-7 might have on her future purchasing strategy.

Supplier Selection

Chapter Outline

Key Questions for the Supply Decision Maker

Should we

- Use cross-functional sourcing teams to select suppliers?
- Use one, two, or more suppliers for a specific requirement?
- Switch from informal to formal supplier evaluation?

How can we

- Reach agreement with internal business partners on evaluation criteria and weighting?
- Balance financial and nonfinancial factors when selecting suppliers?
- Be sure that we choose the best supplier available?

THE SUPPLIER SELECTION DECISION

"If you choose the right suppliers, all of your supply problems will be solved" is old supply wisdom. It is at the supplier selection stage that all of the preparation in understanding and specifying organizational needs comes to fruition. The supply professional's key challenge is to match the organization's needs to what the market can supply. The critical decision is which supplier(s) to select. Honda of America's basic purchasing policy is that it "will buy from the most competitive suppliers in order to fulfill customer satisfaction." To do this, suppliers are required to be competitive along the dimensions of quality, cost, delivery, development, and management.[1]

This chapter will first discuss the identification of potential suppliers, where to find them, and the collection of information. The next topics include whether to select single or multiple sources, deal directly with manufacturers or go through distributors, and choose small or large suppliers and domestic or offshore ones. If no satisfactory source can be found, supplier development provides an alternative to routine supplier selection. This will be followed by how potential suppliers are evaluated according to the three levels of criteria described in Chapter 6 and how to rank them.

The decision to place a certain volume of business with a supplier should always be based on a sound set of criteria. The art of good supply management is to make the reasoning behind this decision as sound as possible. Historically, when purchasing decisions were largely viewed as operational rather than strategic, the analysis of the supplier's ability to meet quality, quantity, delivery, price/cost, and service objectives governed the supplier selection decision. Some of the more important supplier attributes related to these prime criteria may include past history, facilities and technical strength, financial status, organization and management, reputation, systems, procedural compliance, communications, labor relations, and location. The nature and amount of the purchase will influence the weighting attached to each objective and hence the evidence needed to support the decision. For example, quality and rapid delivery are of greater significance than price when ordering a small quantity of circuit boards to be used by engineers in a new

[1] www.hondasupplyteam.com/j_pstat/html/honda_howto_supplier.htm

FIGURE 12–1

A Simple One-Stage Supplier Selection Decision

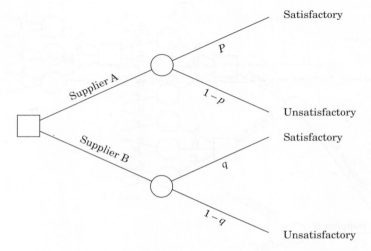

product design or engineering services to support the new product design process. The supplier should probably be local for ease of communication with the design engineers and have good technical credentials. Likewise, a janitorial service for the engineering offices would be local with good references. However, for a large printed circuit board order for a production run, price would be one key factor, and delivery should be on time, but not necessarily unusually fast. Thus, even on requirements with identical technical specifications, the weighting of the selection criteria may vary. It is this sensitivity to organizational needs that separates the good supply manager from the average. The one result every supply professional wishes to avoid is unacceptable supplier performance. This may create costs far out of proportion to the size of the original purchase, upset internal relationships, and strain supplier goodwill and final customer satisfaction.

Decision Trees

The supplier selection decision can be seen as a decision made under uncertainty and can be represented by a decision tree. Figure 12–1 shows a very simple one-stage situation with only two suppliers seriously considered and two possible outcomes. It illustrates, however, the uncertain environment present in almost every supplier choice and the risk inherent in the decision. To use decision trees effectively, the supply professional must identify the options and the criteria for evaluation and assess the probabilities of success and failure. This simple tree could apply to a special one-time purchase without expectation of follow-on business for some time to come.

The more normal situation for future repetitive purchases is shown in Figure 12–2. Whether the chosen source performs well or not for the current purchase under consideration, the future decision about which supplier to deal with next time around may well affect the present decision. For example, if the business is placed with supplier C and C fails, this may mean that only A could be considered a reasonable source at the next stage. If having A as a single source, without alternatives, is not acceptable, choosing C as the supplier at the first stage does not make any sense. If, however, the business is placed with supplier A and A fails, then the buyer has three options: Stay with A and fix things or switch to B or C.

FIGURE 12–2
Simplified
Three-Stage
Decision Tree
for Supplier
Selection

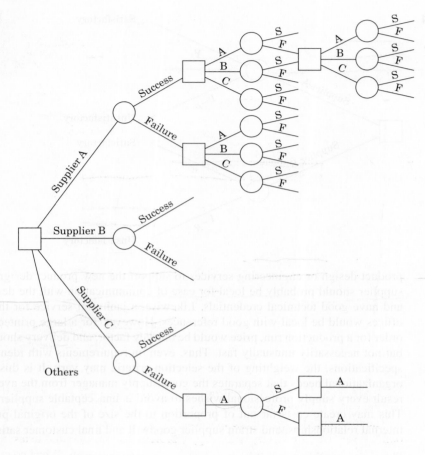

It is necessary to consider the selection decision as part of a chain of events, rather than as an isolated instance. This addition of a time frame—past, present, and future—makes the sourcing decision even more complex. However, as long as the objective of finding and keeping good sources is clearly kept in mind, the decision can be evaluated in a reasonable business context.

IDENTIFYING POTENTIAL SOURCES

There are three potential supply options for any new need/requirement of an organization. The make option or doing it in-house may be realistic for some needs but not for others. These decisions have already been discussed in Chapter 5 under make or buy, insourcing, and outsourcing. The second option is to acquire the new need from a current supplier of other requirements. Most supply professionals would prefer to pursue this option. There is already a record of past performance and communication and logistics requirements are in place.

Assuming past dealings with the current supplier have been satisfactory, the expectation would be that additional business might secure an even better value proposition on the total set of requirements supplied. Therefore, current good or superior suppliers have a right to

FIGURE 12–3 **Identification of Potential Sources for a New Need/Requirement**

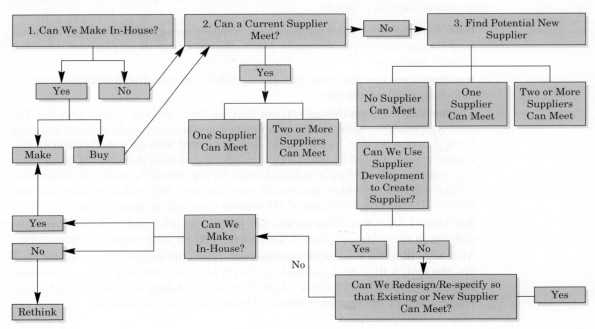

expect additional volumes of business as a reward for their performance on current and past business. Both purchaser and supplier stand to benefit from this understanding.

The third option is to engage in a search for potential suppliers, assuming the first two options were not satisfactory or the supply professional was anxious to test the market. Figure 12–3 diagrams the three options and the potential outcomes. When no suitable supplier can be found, the supply professional still has the option of using supplier development (discussed later in this chapter) or redesign or respecification to see if a suitable source can be found or developed. There is a remote chance that, despite all efforts, no solution is found. Then the supply professional and the requisitioner need to see if an alternative or substitute solution can be found.

Information Sources

The identification of potential sources is a key driver of the ultimate success or failure of the supplier selection effort. Every supply professional is always on the alert for potential new sources.

Knowledge of sources is therefore a primary qualification for any effective supply manager. Online searches, e-catalogs, and company websites are the most common tools used today. Other sources include trade journals, advertisements, supplier and commodity directories, sales interviews, colleagues, professional contacts, and the supply department's own records.

Online Sources

The Internet provides a rapidly growing and ever-changing body of information for supply professionals. The challenge is not just finding information, but identifying, sorting, analyzing, and using relevant information. The following list contains web addresses for some sites of interests to supply.

D&B www.dnb.com D&B provides basic company reports online for a fee, and company's location and products gratis. D&B offers a variety of supplier risk, loss, and viability predictors.

Kompass www.kompass.com provides a global B2B portal with a database of 11+ million companies worldwide.

Thomas Register www.thomasNet.com Supplier Discovery and Product Sourcing. The most comprehensive online resource for finding companies and products manufactured in North America. Services include online order placement, viewing and downloading millions of computer-aided design (CAD) drawings, and viewing thousands of online company catalogs and websites. It includes listings for over 610,000 qualified manufacturers, distributors, MRO providers, and custom manufacturers; 100 million products, and millions of 2D and 3D downloadable CAD modules from leading manufacturers.

Ziff Davis LLC www.ziffdavis.com Ziff Davis is an all-digital media company specializing in the technology market. This is a resource for information on e-commerce.

McRAE's Blue Book www.mcraesbluebook.com With three industrial market leaders, MacRAE'S Blue Book and the Canadian Trade Index, InfoMex Mexican Industrial Directory, the MacRAE'S Owen Media Network specializes in delivering high-value, unique company information to industrial buyers and sellers worldwide.

Catalogs

A well-managed purchasing and supply department must have catalogs (online, hard copy, or both) of the commonly known sources of supply, covering the most important materials in which a company is interested. The value of catalogs depends largely on presentation form, accessibility, frequency and extent of use. Electronic catalogs (discussed in Chapter 4) are increasingly used. The advantage of eCatalogs is that both buyers and internal customers have ready access to them and they can be customized to include the prices and other terms and conditions negotiated by the buyer with the seller. Management of eCatalog content is as serious an issue as management of hard-copy catalogs. Advances in online catalog management continue to increase the ease of access and improve the form of presentation.

The accessibility of catalog content is driven by the manner in which it is indexed and filed, a not-so-simple task even with online catalogs. Hard-copy catalogs are issued in all sorts of sizes and formats that make them difficult to handle. Proper indexing of catalogs is essential. Some companies still use microfilm files and loose-leaf binders with sheets especially printed for catalog filing; others use a form of card index. Indexing should be according to suppliers' names as well as products listed. It should be specific, definite, and easily understandable. The sort and search function of an eCatalog can make a catalog more or less userfriendly. Distributors' catalogs contain many items from a variety of manufacturing sources and offer a directory of available commodities within the distributors' fields. Equipment and machinery catalogs provide information about specifications and the location of a source of supply for replacement parts as well as new equipment. Catalogs frequently provide price information, and many supplies and materials are sold from standard list prices or by quoting discounts only. Catalogs are also used as reference books by internal customers.

Trade Journals

Trade journals also are a valuable source of information about potential suppliers. The list of such publications is very long, and the individual items in it vary in value. Yet in every field there are worthwhile trade magazines, and buyers read extensively those dealing with their own industry and with those industries to which they sell and from which they buy. These journals are utilized in two ways. The first use is to gain general information from the articles that might suggest new products and substitute materials as well as information about suppliers and their personnel. The second use is a consistent perusal of the advertisements to stay current on offerings.

Trade Directories

Trade directories are another useful source of information. They vary widely in their accuracy and usefulness, and care must be exercised in their use. Trade registers, or trade directories, are online or hard-copy volumes that list leading manufacturers, their addresses, number of branches, affiliations, products, and, in some instances, their financial standing or their position in the trade. They also contain listings of the trade names of articles on the market with names of the manufacturers and classified lists of materials, supplies, equipment, and other items offered for sale, under each of which is given the name and location of available manufacturing sources of supply. These registers are organized by commodity, manufacturer, or trade name. Standard directories include the Thomas Register (thomasnet.com), MacRAE's Blue Book (macraesbluebook.com) and Kompass publications (kompass.com).

Trade directories of minority- and women-owned business enterprises can assist purchasers with a goal or requirement to increase the percentage of contracts awarded to these firms. For example, the System for Award Management (sam.gov) simplified the U. S. federal contracting process by creating an integrated database that consolidated the capabilities of the Central Contractor Registration (CCR)/Federal Registration (FedReg), Online Representations and Certifications Application (ORCA). It is a Federal Acquisition Regulation (FAR)-mandated web-based system that streamlines the solicitation and award process for both vendor and government by collecting vendor representations and certifications of business information that is required by law for contract award. The Excluded Parties List System (EPLS) is an electronic, web-based system that identifies those parties excluded from receiving federal contracts, certain subcontracts, and certain types of federal financial and nonfinancial assistance and benefits. The EPLS keeps its user community aware of administrative and statutory exclusions across the entire government and individuals barred from entering the United States. Searches can be based on North American Industry Classification System (NAICS, pronounced NAKES) Codes, keywords, location, quality certifications, business type, and ownership race and gender. Diversity Information Resources (www.diversityinforesources.org) fosters economic development through the publication of directories of minority, women, veteran, service-disabled, Gay, Lesbian, Bisexual, and/or Transgendered (GLBT)-owned businesses, and HUBZone suppliers. A number of organizations also certify businesses as minority- and women-owned, including the Women's Business Enterprise National Council (WBENC) (wbenc.org); the National Women Business Owners Corporation (NWBOC) (nwboc.org); the National Minority Supplier Development Council (NMSDC) (www.nmsdc.org); and in the public sector, the Office of Small Disadvantaged Business Utilization (OSDBU) (www.sbu.gov/GC/OSDBU.html) which also certifies Asian, Black, Hispanic, and Native American business enterprises.

Sales Representation

Sales representatives may constitute one of the most valuable sources of information available, with references to sources of supply, types of products, and trade information generally. One challenge for supply personnel is balancing the need to meet with sales representatives with other responsibilities and time constraints. It is essential to develop good supplier relations that begin with a friendly, courteous, sympathetic, and frank attitude toward the supplier's salesperson. After contact, relevant information should be captured in a format that can be easily accessed and used effectively. Some organizations develop routing mechanisms on their web sites to alleviate the time pressure on buyers and sellers by providing information about how to do business with the organization and routing callers to the appropriate person or portal for RFQs, RFPs, and invitations to bid.

Supplier and Commodity Databases

Information from any source, if of value, should be captured. For example, an index of catalogs makes it easy to access a needed catalog. Two common databases are of suppliers and commodities. The supplier database includes information on each active supplier, including locations and contact information, open orders and past orders, supplier performance scorecards, and other pertinent information that might be of value to future decisions. Supplier databases may be managed online, in a simple computer file, or in a card file.

 A commodity database classifies material on the basis of the product and includes information related to the sources from which the product has been purchased in the past, perhaps the price paid, the point of shipment, and a link or cross-reference to the supplier database. Miscellaneous information is also given, such as whether specifications are called for, whether a contract already exists covering the item, whether competitive bids are commonly asked for, and other data that may be of importance. Accompanying files dealing with sources are those relating to price and other records. Some of these have already been discussed in earlier chapters, and others will be discussed later. The information management aspects of enterprise resource planning (ERP) systems and e-procurement systems are discussed in Chapter 4.

Visits to Suppliers

Some supply managers feel that visits to suppliers are particularly useful when there are no difficulties to discuss. The supply manager can talk with higher-level executives rather than confining discussion to someone who happens to be directly responsible for handling a specific complaint. This helps to cement good relationships at all levels of management and may reveal much about a supplier's future plans that might not otherwise come to the buyer's attention. Such a visitation policy does raise certain problems not found in the more routine types of visits, such as who should make the visits, how best to get worthwhile information, and the best use of the data once obtained. Experience has indicated that the best results come from (1) developing, in advance, a general outline of the kinds of information sought; (2) gathering, in advance, all reasonably available information, both general and specific, about the company; and (3) preparing a detailed report of the findings after the visit. When the visits are carefully planned, the direct expense incurred is small compared with the returns.

Samples

In addition to the usual inquiries and a plant visit, samples of the supplier's product can be tested. This requires thinking about the "sample problem." Frequently a sales representative for a new product urges the buyer to accept a sample for test purposes. This raises questions about what samples to accept, how to ensure a fair test of those accepted, who should bear the expense of testing, and whether or not the supplier should be given the results of the test. (See "Sampling, Inspection and Testing" in Chapter 7.)

Colleagues

Frequently, internal business partners are valuable sources of information about potential sources of supply. Purchase requisitions may invite the requisitioner to identify potential sources.

References

Often buyers will include a request for references in the RFQ, RFP, or RFB/invitation to bid. To get the most useful information possible, it is the job of the interviewer to set the parameters for the interview. First, make sure that the reference is a company of similar size and objectives. Second, talk to people with firsthand knowledge of the supplier's performance. Third, ask open-ended questions that allow the reference to describe the performance of the supplier and the relationship. For example, a new customer might be asked about the implementation process: "Did it go smoothly? Tell me about a time things weren't going according to plan. How did the supplier deal with the problem or change?" A veteran customer might be asked about the supplier's actions to stay competitive or to continuously improve: "Tell me about a time when the supplier initiated an improvement that also benefited you (the customer)?" Past customers might be asked about the transition process to another supplier: "When you switched suppliers, how did the original supplier handle the transition of information? materials? and so forth?" Potential sources need to be evaluated.

Standard Information Requests

Additional information from the supplier is usually sought during the identification of potential suppliers stage and before supplier selection takes place. As described in Chapter 4, the nature of these communications takes a variety of forms.

The Request for Information (RFI)

The request for information or expression of interest serves several purposes. It signals that the supply professional has identified a supplier as a potential source of supply. It is also an opportunity for the supplier to indicate its willingness to enter into a potential business relationship. Although the content of the RFI may vary considerably from technical data to interest in receiving an invitation to bid, it is clear to both parties that the RFI does not commit either party to future business. If the information collection process could result in significant additional expense for the supplier, it is appropriate for the supply professional to offer reimbursement of some or all of these costs.

The Request for Quotation (RFQ) or Request for Bid (RFB) or Invitation to Bid or Tender

These requests represent a serious inquiry of the supplier on a specific requirement or a variety of requirements. The RFQ and its equivalents ask the supplier to declare at what price and what terms they are prepared to supply. In the public sector, it is often an organizational requirement that all requirements exceeding a certain dollar amount be put out to bid and that the lowest bidder will be awarded the contract. Bidders are required to submit their bids by a certain deadline and meet all of the conditions stated in the invitation to bid or tender.

Suppliers are invited to attend a public opening of bids and, thus, each bidder knows exactly what prices have been quoted by all bidders or to review the awards online. After the public opening, public supply professionals usually require some additional time to examine all bids for compliance with conditions and to deal with possible exceptions. Fair as this process may appear, it is still occasionally abused. Various bidders may collude to rig prices. A recent example involving road construction contracts in Montreal had a group of bidders, reported to be Mafia related, deciding on the lowest bid beforehand and who was allowed to be the lowest bidder. This resulted in an elevation of construction costs exceeding 10 percent.

In the private sector, there is no public opening of bids and the lowest bid may not be accepted if, in the opinion of the supply professional, a higher bid represents better value. Because the preparation of a bid always entails costs for the supplier and may raise expectations, it is deemed ethical practice to invite only those suppliers to bid who have a serious chance of receiving the business.

In the RFQ, RFB, and Invitation to Bid, the assumption is that requirement specifications are sufficiently descriptive and standard so that multiple suppliers can meet these requirements. Therefore, the price and terms quoted differentiate among suppliers.

The Request for Proposal (RFP)

An RFP allows more latitude to the supplier than an RFQ when it is difficult to describe a requirement, or the supply organization lacks the ability to create an RFQ or the supply professional expects that innovation or creativity in the market might result in a superior solution. The RFP permits the supplier to fit the proposal to its strengths. For the supply professional, comparison of RFPs received is considerably more difficult than an RFQ evaluation and may involve a lot of judgment. Also, the preparation of an RFP is often more expensive for the supplier than an RFQ, and the issue of reimbursement for supplier costs incurred in its preparation needs to be resolved. Moreover, if the RFP contains proprietary technical or commercial information, protection of confidentiality is critical. Often the RFP is used as the first stage of a two-stage process in which only certain suppliers are invited to quote on the business or enter into negotiations for the final round.

ADDITIONAL SUPPLIER SELECTION DECISIONS

The discussion on supplier selection in this chapter has thus far focused on the identification of potential suppliers and information about them. There are, however, additional decisions that need to be identified and five, in particular, are highlighted here:

1. Should we use a single source, dual sources, or more than two?
2. Should we buy from a manufacturer or a distributor?
3. Where should the supplier be located?
4. Relative to our organization, should the supplier be small, medium, or large?
5. If no supplier can be found, should we use supplier development?

Single versus Multiple Sourcing

Should the supply professional choose a single supplier or utilize several? The answer to this question must be the very unsatisfactory one: "It all depends."

Table 12–1 lists the main arguments for placing all orders for a given item with one supplier and Table 12–2 provides the main arguments for multiple sourcing:

TABLE 12–1
Single Sourcing

1. Prior commitments, a successful past relationship, or an ongoing long-term contract with a preferred supplier might prevent even the possibility of splitting the order.
2. The supplier may be the exclusive owner of certain essential patents or processes and, therefore, be the only possible source.
3. A given supplier may be so outstanding in the quality of product or in the service or value provided as to preclude serious consideration of buying elsewhere.
4. The order may be so small as to make it not worthwhile to divide it.
5. Concentrating purchases may make possible certain discounts or lower freight rates that could not be had otherwise.
6. The supplier will be more cooperative, more interested, and more willing to please if it has all the buyer's business.
7. When the purchase of an item involves a die, tool, mold charge, or costly setup, the expense of duplicating this equipment or setup is likely to be substantial.
8. Deliveries may be more easily scheduled.
9. The use of just-in-time production, stockless buying, or systems contracting.
10. Effective supplier relations require considerable resources and time. Therefore, the fewer suppliers the better.
11. Single sourcing is a prerequisite to partnering.

TABLE 12–2
Multiple Sourcing

1. It has been traditional practice to use more than one source, especially on the important requirements.
2. Knowing that competitors are getting some of the business may keep the supplier more alert to the need for giving good value.
3. Assurance of supply is increased. Should fire, strikes, breakdowns, or accidents occur to any one supplier, deliveries can still be obtained from the others for at least part of the needs.
4. The supply organization has developed a unique capability of dealing with multiple sources.
5. To avoid supplier dependence on the purchaser.
6. To obtain greater flexibility, because the unused capacity of all the suppliers may be available.
7. Even in situations involving close and cooperative supplier relationships, it is possible to make backup arrangements so that supplier X specializes in product Q and backs up supplier Y, who specializes in product R and backs up supplier X.
8. Strategic reasons, such as military preparedness and supply security, may require multiple sourcing.
9. Government regulations may insist that multiple suppliers, or small or minority sources, be used. If there is high risk associated with a small or single-minority source, multiple sourcing may be necessary.
10. Sufficient capacity may not be available to accommodate the purchaser's current or future needs.
11. Potential new or future suppliers may have to be tested with trial orders, while other sources receive the bulk of the current business.
12. Volatility in the supply market makes single sourcing unacceptably risky.

Genuine concern exists among supply executives about how much business should be placed with one supplier, particularly if the supplier is small and the buyer's business represents a significant portion of the seller's revenue. It is feared that sudden discontinuance of purchases may put the supplier's survival in jeopardy, and yet the purchaser does not wish to reduce flexibility by being tied to dependent sources. One rule of thumb is that no more than a certain percentage, say 20 or 30 percent, of the total supplier's business should be with one customer.

If a decision is made to divide an order among several suppliers, then the question is how to divide the business. Actual practice varies widely. One method is to divide the business equally. Another is to base the allocation on geographical coverage. Another is to place the larger share with a favored supplier and give the rest to one or more alternates. In the chemical industry, as in a number of others, it is common practice to place business with various suppliers on a percentage of total requirements basis. Total requirements may be estimated, not necessarily guaranteed, and there may not even be a minimum volume requirement. Each supplier knows what its own percentage of the business amounts to, but may not be aware who the competition is or how much business each competitor received if the number of sources exceeds two. There is no common practice or "best" method or procedure. There was renewed interest in single sourcing in conjunction with the quality movement, partnerships, and strategic sourcing. Interest in dual or multisourcing as a risk mitigation strategy is renewed each time there is an event that disrupts global supply chains. Recent events include the Great Recession, the earthquake and tsunami in Japan, and a factory fire at a Chinese factory making almost one-sixth of the world's supply of DRAM chips. The allocation of business between and among suppliers is a key component of building resilient supply chains.

Manufacturer versus Distributor

Should a supply professional deal with the manufacturer directly or through some trade channel such as a wholesaler, distributor, or even a retailer? Occasionally, various types of trade associations pressure supply professionals to patronize the wholesaler, distributor, or mill supply house. The real issue is often closely related to buying from local sources.

The justification for using trade channels is found in the value-added services rendered. If wholesalers are carrying the products of various manufacturers and spreading marketing costs over a variety of items, they may be able to deliver the product at a lower cost, particularly when the unit of sale is small and customers are widely scattered or when the demand is irregular. Furthermore, they may carry a stock of goods greater than a manufacturer could afford to carry in its own branch warehouse and therefore be in a better position to make prompt deliveries and to fill emergency orders. Also, they may be able to buy in car- or truckload lots, with a saving in transportation charges and a consequent lower cost to the buyer.

Local sentiment may be strongly in favor of a certain distributor. Public agencies are particularly susceptible to such influence. Sometimes firms that sell through distributors tend, as a matter of policy, to buy, whenever possible, through distributors.

On the other hand, some large organizations often seek ways of going around the distributor, particularly when the buyer's requirements of supply items are large, when the shipments are made directly from the original manufacturer, and when no selling effort or service is rendered by the wholesaler. Some manufacturers operate their own supply houses to get the large discount. Others have attempted to persuade the original manufacturers to establish quantity discounts—a practice not unlike that in the steel trade.

Still others have sought to develop sources among small manufacturers that do not have a widespread distribution organization. Some attempts have been made to secure a special service from a chosen distributor, such as an agreement whereby the latter would add to its staff "two people exclusively for the purpose of locating and expediting nuisance items in other lines." A similar arrangement might place a travel agent directly on the purchaser's premises to improve service or require corporate travelers to use a designated online travel booking tool. Systems contracting and stockless purchasing systems depend heavily on concentrating a large number of relatively small purchases with a highly capable distributor.

Ultimately, every participant in the value chain needs to add value. This guiding principle should apply also to the selection of nonmanufacturers in the distribution network.

Geographical Location of Sources

Where should an organization's suppliers be located—onshore or offshore? If onshore, should they be local, regional, or national suppliers? If offshore, how far offshore?

Onshore: Local, Regional, or National

Onshore sources are domestic suppliers. They may be local, regional, or national. For example, a company in Vancouver may prefer to do business with suppliers in Vancouver (local), or Western Canada (regional), or Canada (national).

While there have been varying degrees of global trade throughout history, onshore or domestic sourcing was standard operating procedure for most buyers until the mid-1980s. The difficulties and expense of communications and transportation made onshore sourcing more practical even with the labor rate differential. Historically, the advantages of local sourcing have been more dependable service: for example, shorter distances and fewer dangers of transport interruptions; knowledge of the purchaser's specific requirements and the seller's special qualifications; greater flexibility in meeting the purchaser's requirements; and equal facilities, know-how, and financial strength compared to offshore sources. Thus, there may well be sound economic reasons for preferring a local source to a more distant one. However, transformations in communications and transportation, improvements in infrastructure, education, and legal frameworks have made it easier to extend the advantages of local sourcing to offshore locations.

In just-in-time and lean production systems, proximity of the supplier's plant to that of the purchaser is vital. For example, automotive manufacturers encourage suppliers to locate plants close to automobile assembly operations. In 2012, Honda had nine manufacturing plants in the United States and spent $22 billion with U.S. suppliers, including over 500 original equipment manufacturers (OEM) in 34 states and 13,500 MRO suppliers (honda.com).

A second basis for selecting local sources rests on equally sound, although somewhat less tangible, grounds. The organization owes much to the local community. The facility is located there, the bulk of the employees live there, and often a substantial part of its financial support, as well as a notable part of its sales, may be local. The local community provides the company's personnel with their housing, schools, churches, and social life.

An argument can be made that participating in the local community, in part by doing business with or developing local suppliers, is part of corporate social responsibility.

One complication is the difficulty in defining *local*. Is *local* the buyer's city, county, or state/province? If a company has operations with employees and customers in many parts of a country, might *local* mean national? And if a company has employees and customers in many countries, does *local* mean global? Increasingly, global companies generate larger portions of their revenue and profits from offshore customers. For example, in 2013 U.S.-based Yum! Brands (KFC, Pizza Hut, and Taco Bell) reported that almost 70 percent of its profits came from outside the United States compared to 20 percent in 1997 (yum.com). To reflect the shift in growth potential, in 2014, the company reorganized into five divisions: Yum! China, Yum! India, KFC, Taco Bell, and Pizza Hut with the latter three divisions covering all other locations by brand (113 countries, including the United States).

Regional sourcing means doing business with suppliers in a geographic area, the Northeastern United States, for example. National sourcing means buying from suppliers located in the same country as the buyer. These distinctions are also blurred by trade agreements. For example, regional might also refer to countries in a regional trade pact such as NAFTA (Canada, Mexico, and the United States); or the European Union (EU) with 28 member countries; or ASEAN, a trade bloc of 10 countries, including Singapore, Thailand, Vietnam, and Indonesia, or one of the other multination trade blocs. One of the purposes of these pacts is to reduce or eliminate trade barriers and essentially to extend domestic treatment to what are physically offshore locations. To what extent do regional trade blocs blur the definition and boundaries of *region* and even *nation*?

Bilateral trade negotiations may also blur national boundaries. For example, Canada and the United States negotiate exceptions to legislation restricting federal procurement spend to domestic suppliers. There is a quid pro quo in the negotiations that enable Canadian suppliers to bid on U.S. government contracts in exchange for U.S. suppliers bidding on similarly valued Canadian federal contracts. Negotiators also seek to flow down these allowances to Canadian provincial and territorial spend and U.S. city, state, and municipality spend.

Offshore: Near Shore and Far Shore

Offshore means suppliers are located in another country. Near shore refers to a location that is closer in terms of travel time and time zones. For example, the United States, Mexico, and Canada are near shore relative to each other. Far shore entails longer transit times across more time zones: for example, the United States to countries in Asia. Offshoring is not the same thing as outsourcing. For example, most large organizations outsource the operation of in-house dining. The foodservice provider may be a local, regional, national, or an international company, but the employees are onshore.

Organizations also outsource and offshore. Many organizations have shut down in-house business processes, from call centers to legal to IT, and outsourced them to India, the Philippines, and other countries. The same is true for manufacturing and assembly. Nike, Inc. subcontracts all of its footwear production to independently owned and operated offshore suppliers. Roughly 90 percent of the parts in an iPhone are outsourced offshore, including advanced semiconductors from Germany and Taiwan, memory from Korea and Japan, display panels and circuitry from Korea and Taiwan, chipsets from Europe, rare metals from Africa and Asia, and assembly in China. Apple's iPhones are sold in 100 countries. The company has 100 local markets.

Honda, on the other hand, has an operational strategy of building products close to its customers. It owns and operates (a make decision in make or buy) offshore manufacturing facilities in the United States, Mexico, Europe, South America, China, India, New Zealand, Turkey, Thailand, and Indonesia as well as onshore facilities in Japan. When Honda first started manufacturing in the United States, most components were sourced from Japan. Today Honda of America sources the majority of inputs from U.S. suppliers.

Companies all over the world face the same question of where to source goods and services. Hon Hai Precision Industry (trade name Foxconn), a primary assembler for Apple, announced in January 2014 that it is assessing the feasibility of building a manufacturing plant in the United States to produce liquid display screens larger than 60 inches to overcome the difficulties of shipping large TV screens to the United States from Asia.

Reshoring

To a certain degree, no location decision is a final decision. The supplier location decision may change as internal organizational and external market conditions change. The cost of switching from one location to another, and from one supplier to another, must be assessed. Recently, a number of organizations have, or are considering, bringing some supply back to their home country (reshoring). For example, while call centers are still outsourced to India and, increasingly, to the Philippines, there is growth in the United States of virtual call centers using home-based agents. Caterpillar is opening a new factory in Texas to make excavators, but has also just announced that it will expand its research and development activities in China. Lenovo, a Chinese company, is bringing back computer-making to North Carolina to enhance its reputation and gain direct business benefits. The location decisions made by an organization are a critical part of organizational as well as supply strategy. (See Chapter 17 for additional discussion of this trend.)

Supplier Size

If a supply professional has the option of buying from a large, medium, or small supplier, which size of supplier should be favored? How does the size of the purchasing organization affect the decision? A matrix of relative sizes can be developed (see Figure 12–4). The size and nature of the requirement may also affect the decision, because it is general wisdom

FIGURE 12–4
Relative Purchaser and Supplier Size

Purchaser Size	Supplier Size
Small	Small
	Medium
	Large
Medium	Small
	Medium
	Large
Large	Small
	Medium
	Large

that the larger the requirement, the larger the supplier should be. Generally, smaller suppliers tend to be local for those smaller requirements where flexibility, speed of response, and availability tend to be more important than price. Larger suppliers tend to be more appropriate for high-volume requirements where technology, quality, and total cost of ownership may be critical; medium suppliers fall in between. The trouble with generalizations is that exceptions abound. Small suppliers tend to fill niches that the larger ones cannot or may have chosen not to cover. According to *Hispanic Business* magazine, the leaders of its fastest-growing 100 companies focus on a strategy of focusing on, and filling, one niche in the marketplace.

Historically, small suppliers have shown a loyalty and service deemed impossible from larger suppliers. Many larger organizations are trying to reverse this perception by developing a strong customer service focus. Small suppliers tend to depend on the management of a key owner-manager, and this person's health and attitude will affect the risk of doing business. Larger organizations tend to have greater stability and greater resources, reducing the day-to-day risk of supplier performance.

Interest in diversity of customers, employees, and suppliers has renewed interest in the large purchaser–small supplier interface and the role of education, assistance, and continuing watchfulness on the part of supply to help the supplier succeed.

SUPPLIER DEVELOPMENT/REVERSE MARKETING

In supplier selection the assumption has so far been made that at least one suitable and willing supplier already exists and that the purchaser's problem is primarily one of determining who is the best supplier. It is possible, however, that no suitable source is available and that the purchaser may have to create a source. Reverse marketing or supplier development implies a degree of aggressive procurement involvement not encountered in supplier selection. For example, it places a supply manager in a position where a prospective supplier must be persuaded to accept an order. In this no-choice context, the purchaser does not initiate supplier development as an appropriate technique or tool; it is the only alternative other than making the part or producing the service in-house.

Reverse marketing/supplier development also has a broader point of view. It defines the need for developing new or existing suppliers as follows: The purchaser is aware that benefits will accrue to both the supplier and the purchaser, benefits of which the supplier may not be aware. These benefits may be limited to the particular order at hand, or they may include more far-reaching aspects, such as technical, financial, and management processes, skills, or quality levels; reduction of marketing effort; use of long-term forecasts or permitting smoother manufacturing levels and a minimum of inventory; and so on.

It is the aggressiveness and initiative by the supply professional that makes the difference (see Figure 12–5). In the normal market context, the purchaser responds to marketing efforts. In reverse marketing, the purchaser, not the supplier, has the initiative and will predetermine prices, terms, and conditions as part of the aggressive role. Taking the initiative requires extensive research on the part of the supply professional to understand fully the organization's short- and long-term needs, operationally and strategically, and assess the supplier's capability to meet these needs so that a win-win proposal can be made. This is why the term *reverse marketing* has been chosen as a synonym for supplier development.

FIGURE 12–5
Supplier Development Initiative with the Purchaser

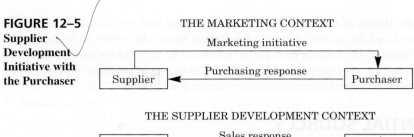

THE MARKETING CONTEXT

Marketing initiative

Supplier ← Purchasing response ← Purchaser

THE SUPPLIER DEVELOPMENT CONTEXT

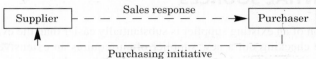

Supplier – – – Sales response – – → Purchaser

Purchasing initiative

Numerous examples show that high payoffs are possible from this supply initiative and that suppliers of all sizes may be approached in this fashion.

A further reason for reverse marketing is that there are bound to be deficiencies in the normal industrial marketing process in which the marketer traditionally takes the initiative. Even when a supplier and a purchaser have entered into a regular buyer–seller relationship, often neither party is fully aware of all the opportunities for additional business that may exist between them. This might arise because of salesperson and supply professional specialization, a lack of aggressiveness by the salesperson, or a lack of inquisitiveness by the purchaser.

If gaps are evident even where an established buyer–seller relationship exists, there must be even greater shortcomings where no such relationship has yet been established. For example, a supplier may be unable to cover its full market because of geography, limited advertising, or lack of coverage by its sales force, distributors, or agents. Most suppliers have lines of products that receive more management attention and sales push than other products also made or sold by the same company. It is always difficult to keep entirely up to date. A time lag may exist between the time of product or service introduction and the time the supply manager finds out about it. By filling these gaps through aggressiveness, the supply professional effectively strengthens this whole process.

One of the most important arguments in favor of reverse marketing not yet mentioned arises from future considerations. If the supply role is envisaged as encompassing not only the need to fill current requirements but also the need to prepare for the future, reverse marketing is valuable in assuring future sources of supply.

There are at least three outside forces that suggest the increasing necessity for purchaser initiative in the creation of future sources of supply. One of these forces is technological. The increasing rate of development of new products, materials, and processes will tend to make the industrial marketing task even more complex and more open to shortcomings. In addition to this, the increase in international trade will tend to widen supplier horizons and may create a need for purchaser aggressiveness in the development of global sources of supply. One of the most demanding and important tasks of management of a subsidiary in a less economically developed country is the problem of supplier development. Lastly, new management concerns with extracting competitive advantage from the supply chain require purchasers to be more aggressive with suppliers and to develop sources to their expectations.

For example, Honda of America developed a program to help reestablish strong, financially stable tool and die manufacturers in the United States after years of decline in the U.S. tooling industry. By helping their partners more efficiently design and manufacture their products and by providing financial support through new purchase orders, Honda helped their partners become more competitive locally and globally.[2]

EVALUATING POTENTIAL SOURCES

The evaluation of an existing supplier is substantially easier than the evaluation of a new source. Since checking out a new supplier often requires an extensive amount of time and resources, it should be done only for those suppliers that stand a serious chance of receiving a significant order. Where such a potential supplier competes with an existing supplier, the expected performance of the new source should, hopefully, be better than that of the existing one. The use of trial orders has been mentioned as a popular means of testing a supplier's capability, but it still fails to answer the question about whether the trial order should have been placed with a particular source at all. Even though a supplier may complete a trial order successfully, it may not be an acceptable source in the long run.

The evaluation of potential sources, therefore, attempts to answer one key question:

1. Is this supplier able to supply the purchaser's requirements satisfactorily, both strategically and operationally in the short and long term?

The question must be assessed on the basis of the three levels of need criteria described in Chapter 6. It is useful to repeat the three levels of need criteria and, hence, supplier evaluation and selection criteria here: level 1—strategic; level 2—traditional: quality, quantity, delivery, price, and service; and level 3—current additional: financial, risk, environmental, regulatory, social, and political. The following sections will address supplier evaluation according to these criteria.

Level 1—Strategic

Effective sourcing decisions form the basis of sound supply for any organization. These decisions should be driven by a sourcing strategy that is directly linked to organizational strategy, goals, and objectives. Many organizations have adopted the term *strategic sourcing* to capture the linkage between sourcing strategy and organizational strategy. A strategic sourcing process considers suppliers and the supply base integral to an organization's competitive advantage. It is important to define clearly the term *strategic* and establish what makes a purchase or a supplier strategically important to the organization. Typically, a strategic purchase is one that is mission critical. The good or service has the potential to either help or hinder the attainment of the organization's mission. Categorizing purchases into strategic and nonstrategic buckets is a first step in the strategic sourcing process. This type of categorization drives the decisions throughout the sourcing and selection process, including the allocation of resources to any specific buy. Without this categorization, the

[2] www.honda.com/newsandviews/local_news_content/[5032]_Honda_in_America.pdf.

supply manager or sourcing team may overinvest resources, time, and attention in tactical or operational purchases and underinvest in strategic ones.

Linking Sourcing with Strategy

From various sources of information, the supply professional is able to make up a list of available suppliers from whom the necessary items can be acquired. The first level of analysis is finding out which suppliers might be able to meet the buying organization's requirements. The second level of analysis is determining which of these the supply manager or sourcing team is willing to consider seriously as a source. For items that are high risk and high value, the investigation may be drawn out and extensive, requiring the collaboration of supply, internal users, and technical experts such as engineering, operations, quality control, systems, and maintenance on a formal or informal team. The cost of analysis greatly outweighs the advantages for items that are inexpensive and consumed in small quantities.

It is not possible to separate risk assessment from strategy development. Therefore, risk assessment and strategy development are discussed jointly as level 1 valuation criteria. Although the same argument can be applied for the other level 2 and 3 criteria, they will be discussed later.

Risk Assessment

Every organization's management makes decisions about the risks it is willing to take in light of the expected returns. It takes actions to avoid, mitigate, transfer, insure against, limit, or explicitly assume risk. For the supply manager, it is essential to consider each decision in the context of the organization's risk profile.

Research into risk assessment behavior of supply professionals shows that the perceived risk of placing business with an untried and unknown supplier is high. Likewise, the perceived risk associated with routine, repetitive purchases is much less than the risk of new or less standard acquisitions. In general, the risk is seen to be higher with unknown materials, parts, equipment or services, or suppliers and with increased dollar amounts. Commodity managers can take a number of actions to avoid, mitigate, transfer, limit, or insure against risk. For example, a supply professional may attempt to transfer risk by asking for advice, such as engineering judgment, or by seeking additional information, including placing a trial order, or hedging in the commodities market. He or she may require bid bonds, performance bonds, or payment bonds to insure against risk, or avoid risk by not doing business with suppliers in certain countries, or mitigate risk by dual or multiple sourcing rather than single sourcing. It is possible to limit risk by negotiating payment terms that allow progress payments when certain milestones are met, but withholds a percentage of the payment until completion and acceptance of the service provided. When a supply professional takes an action such as selecting a supplier, or switching suppliers, or agreeing to certain terms and conditions, he or she should take these actions with the explicit understanding of both the risk at which the decision puts the organization, the return expected, and the balance between the two.

Loss Exposure.   There are selective buying situations in which the specifications may well expose the buying organization to risk. Robert S. Mullen, director of purchasing at Harvard University, cited the instance of a purchase of fireproof mattresses, costing only

acquisition of strategic purchases and management of strategic spend historically have been handled by many people outside of the supply organization. For example, jet fuel for an airline or energy supplies for certain manufacturing concerns may represent both high-dollar and high-value purchases, and those with primary ownership of these purchase categories were business specialists with technical rather than supply management skills. The trend is toward joint ownership of strategies, goals, objectives, metrics, and accountability for these purchases. Supply brings expertise such as supply base knowledge, negotiating skill, contract development and management skill, and the ability to build and manage a long-term relationship to complement the technical knowledge of the internal business partner. The tools and techniques applied to strategic purchases include total cost modeling, value analysis and engineering, cross-functional teams, and strategic alliances. Many of the efficiency tools and process improvements described in this text free up time for supply personnel to focus resources and human talent on the acquisition and management of strategic purchases.

Another strategic option is the potential to use supply expertise and leverage in the market of the buying organization to purchase goods and services for suppliers, customers, or other supply chain members. Typically, this is the acquisition of direct materials, parts, and/or packaging for first-tier suppliers, giving the supply professional cost and quality control.

In certain industries in which purchasers are much larger companies than suppliers, the supply professional may have the power to direct small suppliers to use specific sources of supply. Under this kind of arrangement the supplier receives a processing fee and an administrative margin. Automotive suppliers of stampings commonly work under this kind of arrangement for steel supply.

Level 2—Traditional

Applying the traditional level 2 evaluation criteria of quality, quantity, delivery, price, and service is still a fundamental assessment task in evaluating potential suppliers. For a manufactured good, these are typically evaluated on the basis of the technical, engineering, manufacturing, and logistics strengths of potential suppliers. For a service, these are typically evaluated on the basis of service design, operations, and delivery strengths of the potential suppliers.

Technical, Engineering, Manufacturing, and Logistics Strengths

Technical and engineering capability, along with manufacturing strength, impinges on a number of supply concerns. The most obvious factor is the quality capability of the supplier. It is possible, however, that a company capable of meeting current quality standards may still lack the engineering and technical strengths to stay current with technological advances. Similarly, manufacturing may lack capacity, or the space to expand, or the flexibility to meet a variety of requirements. Presumably, the reason for selecting one supplier over another is that of greater strengths in areas of importance to the purchaser. The evaluation of the supplier, therefore, should focus not only on current capability, but also on the supplier's future strengths. Only in very large organizations might the supply group have sufficient technical strength to conduct such supplier evaluations on its own. Normally, other functions such as engineering, manufacturing, internal users, or quality control provide expert assistance to assess a potential supplier on technical and manufacturing strengths.

Should the supplier be a distributor, the stress might be more on logistics capability. The nature of the agreements with the distributors' supplying manufacturers, their inventory policies, systems capability and compatibility, and ability to respond to special requirements would all be assessed, along with technical strengths of the personnel required to assist the supply professional to make the right choices among a series of acceptable options. A number of distributors have developed strong supplier-/vendor-managed inventory programs, permitting organizations the option of outsourcing the total MRO supply function and reducing the total supply base significantly.

Service Design, Operations, and Delivery

Service design, operations, and delivery impinge on a number of supply concerns. First, the quality capability of the supplier is determined to a large extent on its ability to design services that meet the quality standards of the users as defined in the statement of work (SOW). Just as with manufacturing, a service provider may not have the capability to meet future quality standards either because the supplier is not able to attract and retain high-quality employees or it fails to upgrade its technology. For example, there is a persistent gap between shippers' IT expectations and third-party logistics providers' capabilities. While some of this is because 3PLs are slow to upgrade their IT, some of it is also because shippers lack adequate information about their supply chains. Similarly, a supplier's service operations and service delivery system may lack the capacity to expand or the flexibility to meet a variety of requirements. For example, a management consulting company may need to have a presence in specific countries with staff fluent in specific languages and cultures for the buying organization's current and future operations. Presumably, one service provider is selected over another because its strengths match the buyer's needs. The evaluation of the supplier, therefore, should focus not only on current capability, but also on the supplier's future strengths. Normally, for services, other functions such as internal users and budget owners provide expert assistance to assess a potential service supplier on its capabilities. For example, the human resources department, legal, and compliance may be on a team with supply for purchases of services related to benefits.

Management and Financial Evaluation

As the tendency toward greater reliance on single sources for a longer period of time continues, along with greater interest in lean operations, lean supply, and strategic sourcing, a potential supplier's management strengths take on added significance. From the supply point of view, the key question is this: Is the management of this supplier a corporate strength or a weakness? This will require a detailed examination of the organization's mission, values and goals, its structure, qualifications of managers, management controls, the performance evaluation and reward system, training and development, information systems, and policies and procedures. It is also useful to have an explanation about why the supplier's management believes it is managing well and an indication of its most notable successes and failures. A functional assessment of strengths and weaknesses in areas like marketing, supply, accounting, and so on will substantiate the overall picture. For example, in a contract in which the supplier spends a substantial percentage of total volume on raw materials and parts with suppliers or subcontractors, the supply group of the buying organization would be best suited to evaluate the supplier's procurement system, organization, procedures, and personnel. This is especially important when assessing supply chains that consist of multiple tiers of suppliers.

Supplier documentation and personal visits by the sourcing team are typically required. For large contracts in large organizations, the sourcing team's formal report detailing the management strengths and weaknesses of potential suppliers will be the deciding factor in the selection process.

The financial strengths and weaknesses of a supplier affect its capability to respond to the needs of customers. The supply professional must determine the extent of the financial assessment appropriate for each purchase. As discussed earlier in this chapter, the critical question is this: Is the product or service strategic? If so, then the supplier is strategically important and a full financial analysis is necessary. While short-term alternatives may lessen the risks, the strategic nature of the purchase indicates the need for complete understanding of the long-term risks and opportunities from the supplier's financial situation. Many supply managers focus on early warning systems to alert them to changes in the financial situation of key suppliers that may affect the buying organization. This allows them to step in and work with the supplier or strengthen their contingency plans if the supplier's situation worsens.

There are often substantial opportunities for negotiation if the purchaser is fully familiar with the financial status of a supplier. For example, the offer of advance payment or cash discounts may have little appeal to a cash-rich source but highly attractive to a firm short of working capital. A supplier with substantial inventories may be able to offer supply assurance and a degree of price protection at times of shortages that cannot be matched by others without the materials or the funds to acquire them.

Individual financial measures that may be examined include, but are not limited to, credit rating, capital structure, profitability, ability to meet interest and dividend obligations, working capital, inventory turnover, current ratio, and return on investment. Presumably, financial stability and strength are indicators of good management and competitive ability. Financial statements, therefore, are a useful source of information about a supplier's past performance. Whether the supplier will continue to perform in the same manner in the future is an assessment the purchaser must make, taking all available information, including the financial side, into account. Some of the financial ratios that a buyer may want to take a look at include profit and loss, inventory turnover, account receivables turns, and current ratio. This information is available from a variety of sources including Dun & Bradstreet (www.dnb.com) and Hoovers (www.hoovers.com). For privately held companies, the buyer may have difficulty accessing sufficient financial information depending on the buyer's strength in the relationship.

There is general agreement among supply executives that a supplier's management capability and financial strength are vital factors in source evaluation and selection. Even after a satisfactory evaluation of management, financial, and technical strengths of a supplier has been completed, the question remains about what weight should be accorded to each of the various dimensions. Also, should the supply manager take the initiative in insisting that the supplier correct certain deficiencies, particularly on the management or financial side?

Many examples exist that illustrate the need for supplier strength. These are normally related to the long-term survival of the company. Small suppliers are frequently dependent on the health, age, and abilities of the owner-manager. Every time this individual steps into an automobile, the fate of the company rides along. The attitudes of this individual toward certain customers may be very important in supply assurance.

Most long-term and significant supplier–buyer relationships are highly dependent on the relationships and communication channels built by the respective managers in each organization. Unless each side is willing and able to listen and respond to information supplied by the other side, problems are not likely to be resolved to mutual satisfaction.

Level 3—Current Additional

In the following section, the current additional criteria which includes financial considerations, environmental impact, innovation, regulatory compliance, and social and political factors will be addressed. All of these potentially impact the strategic aspects of supply, and risk has already been discussed in that context.

Financial Considerations

Financial considerations other than price may impact the supplier selection decision. The financial health of the supplier has already been discussed as part of the normal supplier assessment process when the prime concern is the supplier's viability as an ongoing enterprise in the long term.

In this additional context an opportunistic perspective is used to find potential ways of strengthening the purchasing organization's financial statements beyond obtaining a lower price. For example, is it possible to have the supplier manage and own inventories so that they do not show up on the financial statements of the purchasing organization? Can capital purchases be timed to achieve tax savings? Can judicious use of international finance experts facilitate global supply agreements in terms of trade credit, payment, guarantees, and inventory financing?

Environmental Impact

Sustainability is the ability to achieve economic prosperity while protecting the natural systems of the planet and providing a higher quality of life for present and future generations. To accomplish this, decision makers must consider the role of four types of capital: financial capital (cash, investment, and monetary instruments), manufactured capital (infrastructure, machines, tools, and factories), human capital (labor and intelligence, culture, and organization) and natural capital (resources, living systems, and ecosystem services). Supply managers play a key role in an organization's sustainability initiatives in product or service design, sourcing and contracting, and asset or investment recovery. Consequently, supply's role in helping to achieve this goal needs to be examined carefully.

The first issue is, How can our organization design products and services that directly or indirectly contribute to sustainability? The second issue is, How can our organization purchase materials, products, or equipment that directly or indirectly contributes to sustainability? How can the supply group raise sustainability questions when others in the organization fail to do so? The third issue is, How can we purchase from sources, domestic or international, that we know are committed to sustainability and sound practices? These are not easy questions answered glibly out of context. It is possible to evade the issue by putting government in the control seat, saying, "As long as government allows it, it must be all right." A practical consideration is that government may shut down a polluting supplier with little notice, endangering supply assurance.

Environmental supply chain strategies range from merely trying to avoid violations to including environmental considerations from the design stage forward. The preferred hierarchy is (1) source reduction—design or use less, (2) reuse—multiple use of same item such as a package or container, (3) recycle—reprocess into raw material, (4) incinerate—at least extract energy, but create CO_2 pollution at a minimum, (5) landfill—require space and transportation to store with potential impact on land and water. The introduction of gas-electric hybrid vehicles and the development of fuel cell technology are examples of source reduction initiatives. "Designing for recycling" requires manufacturers of appliances and automobiles to design products for ease of disassembly to allow for recovery of useful materials. In the automobile industry, this represents a particularly difficult challenge. Much of the weight-reduction emphasis to improve government-required fuel ratings has come about by the substitution of lightweight, but difficult to retrieve and recycle, plastics for heavier but easily recycled metal parts.

Suppliers can aid substantially in addressing these priorities to minimize the environmental impact of purchasers' and their customers' requirements. In many organizations, supply's role as an information link between environmentally affected individuals, internal functions, and suppliers in the handling of waste and hazardous materials has been established already. Government regulations stipulate precautions for the use, transport, storage, and disposal of hazardous materials. For example, in the United States, the Department of Transportation, the Occupational Safety and Health Administration, and the Environmental Protection Agency all have regulations pertaining to hazardous goods. In Canada, there are federal and provincial regulations related to hazardous goods.

There are many organizations and programs available to support the efforts of supply managers. For example, since 1982, Rocky Mountain Institute (RMI) has worked with corporations, governments, communities, and citizens to help solve problems, gain competitive advantage, increase profits, and create wealth through the more productive use of resources. RMI's Research & Consulting team helped a semiconductor manufacturer improve its buildings and equipment in ways that also radically reduced energy costs and carbon emissions; showed urban planners how to spur economic development through better building design and water infrastructure; and helped conceive a successful floor-covering service utilizing resource-efficient, closed-loop industrial processes with an innovative business model.

The U.S Environmental Protection Agency (www.epa.gov) offers programs and tools that contribute to sustainability in the areas of planning and practices, scientific tools and technology, and measuring progress. Its publications, *Sustainable Materials Management* and *The Lean and Green Supply Chain: A Practical Guide for Material Managers and Supply Chain Managers to Reduce Costs and Improve Environmental Performance,* illustrate the efficiency-enhancing opportunities that arise when companies incorporate environmental costs and benefits into mainstream materials and supply chain management decision making. The Office of Policy (OP) works with participating trade associations; EPA programs; and regions, states, and other groups to find sensible solutions to sector-specific problems. The U.S. National Recycling Coalition (www.nrcrecycles.org) represents all the diverse interests committed to the common goal of maximizing recycling to achieve the benefits of resource conservation, solid waste reduction, environmental protection, energy conservation, and social and economic development.

Internationally, the ISO 14000 certification, developed along the lines of ISO 9000, is a process for certifying the environmental management system of an organization. Benefits of certification may include reduced cost of waste management, savings in consumption of energy and materials, lower distribution costs, and improved corporate image among regulators, customers, and the public.

Strategic supply management is all about maximizing opportunities and minimizing risks. In the area of environmental impact and sustainability, there are many opportunities for supply managers who are at the forefront of environmental awareness. By being ahead of, rather than behind, legislative requirements, supply managers may find that opportunities to tap government financial support and public recognition for innovative experiments may exist. The simple fact is that almost every supplier selection decision is likely to be impacted by environmental considerations.

Innovation

Assessing a supplier's potential for innovation requires evidence of continuing improvement and managerial and technical competence. Also references from existing customers are relevant in this regard. Where innovation is a strategic issue, the skills required to assess a supplier's potential go well beyond those of the typical supply professional. Strategic innovation acquisition may involve mergers and acquisitions, patents, licensing, and contracts. These specialized areas are well beyond the scope of this text. Suffice it to say here that even the more common innovation initiatives of continuous improvement, suggestions from both purchaser and supplier involving each other's operations, and a conviction that the status quo is not acceptable for the future are vital to effective innovation.

Regulatory Compliance

The supply professional does not want supply arrangements to be sidetracked because of a lack of supplier attention to regulatory compliance. Therefore, it is appropriate to assess a potential supplier in terms of compliance. What evidence can the supplier provide to assure the supply professional that compliance will not become a future issue? The lack of citations can be seen as one sort of evidence. So can the speed of correction in case of citations. The very broad range of regulations regarding trade, employee treatment, financial dealings, the environment, international business, workplace safety and health, and so forth requires a comprehensive approach to compliance valuation.

Social and Political Factors

Noneconomic factors may have a significant bearing on sourcing decisions. These include social and political concerns. In a CAPS Research study, Carter and Jennings defined the supply manager's involvement in the socially responsible management of the supply chain as "a wide array of behaviors that broadly fall into the category of environmental management, safety, diversity, human rights and quality of life, ethics, and community and philanthropic activities."[3]

---

[3] Craig R. Carter and Marianne M. Jennings, *Purchasing's Contribution to the Socially Responsible Management of the Supply Chain* (Tempe, AZ: Center for Advanced Purchasing Studies, 2000), p. 7.

Social.   Most organizations recognize that their existence may affect the social concerns of society. Some social problems can be addressed through supply policy and actions. For example, it is possible to purchase certain services or goods from social agencies employing recovering addicts, former prisoners, or the physically and mentally handicapped. It is possible to purchase from suppliers located in low-income areas or certain geographical areas of high unemployment. Government legislation requiring suppliers on government contracts to place a percentage of business with designated service-disabled veteran-, minority-, or woman-owned businesses has forced many purchasers to undertake searches for such suppliers. Many supply managers have initiated assistance and educational programs to make their minority sourcing programs work. For example, the secretary of the Department of Energy (DOE) established a mentor-protégé program in which prime contractors help energy-related small minority businesses increase their capabilities in return for subcontracting credit and other incentives. In one sense these early reverse marketing efforts provided useful insights into the process of developing partnerships with larger suppliers as well.

Companies in the private sector often engage in these actions voluntarily out of a sense of corporate social responsibility and to gain strategic advantage. For example, Ford, General Motors, and Toyota Motor North America have positioned supplier diversity as a strategic advantage because they see the connection between from whom they buy and to whom they sell. By helping to develop the economy of the ethnic community through its supplier development programs it is also increasing the purchasing power of the community's members.

There are problems and opportunities when exercising purchasing power in the social area. Balancing the often conflicting goals of the organization (lowest total cost with social responsibility) and assessing and mitigating the risks presented by supplier diversity programs adds a level of complexity to what may already be a complex sourcing decision. Most supply managers agree that the "deal" must make good business sense. There are a number of resources and publications available to link buyers and minority and women business owners including the following:

- The U.S. Small Business Administration (SBA) (www.sba.gov).
- The National Minority Supplier Development Council and its regional Purchasing Councils, (www.nmsdc.org).
- *Minority Business Entrepreneur (MBE)* magazine, www.mbemag.com.
- *Hispanic Business* magazine, www.hispanicBusiness.com.

Political.   The basic question in the political area is, Should the acquisition area be seen as a means of furthering political objectives? Public agencies have long been under pressure of this sort. "Buy local" is a common requirement for city and state purchasing officials. "Buy American" is a normal corollary requirement. The attempt by the Canadian government to spread purchases across the country, approximately in line with population distribution, is another example. For military purposes, the U.S. government has a long-standing tradition of support and development of a national supply base to afford security protection in the case of conflict and, recently, to reward other countries for their support of U.S. initiatives.

The question always arises about how much of a premium should be paid to conform with political directives. Should a city purchasing agent buy buses from the local manufacturer at a 12 percent premium over those obtainable from another state or other country? The debate over offshore outsourcing has raised the political stakes, and many public entities are passing legislation to prevent offshore outsourcing that results in a loss of jobs domestically. Politics aside, whether this behavior is good for the economy in the long run is an ongoing debate.

For private industry, political questions are also present. Should the corporation support the political and economic aims of the governing body? Governments have little hesitation on large business deals to specify that a minimum percentage should have domestic content. In the aerospace and telecommunications industry, for example, international orders are often contingent on the ability to arrange for suitable subcontracting in the customer's home country. It is interesting that governments have no fear to tread where private industry is forbidden to walk. Multinationals often find themselves caught in countries with different political views. U.S. companies for over 50 years have not been allowed to trade with Cuba, yet their subsidiaries in other countries face strong national pressure to export to Cuba the same products that the U.S. parent is not allowed to sell from U.S. soil. The same holds for purchasing from countries with whom trade is not encouraged by the government. American subsidiaries frequently find themselves caught between the desire of the local government to encourage local purchases and the U.S. government, which encourages exports from the parent company or its suppliers. The growing role of government in all business affairs is likely to increase difficulties of this kind in the future. Their resolution is far from easy and will require a great deal of tact and understanding.

Chapter 17 also covers the role of supply in corporate social responsibility.

Level 3 Criteria Conclusion

The supplier's performance according to level 3 criteria has become a matter of considerable concern in supplier selection. What environmental programs does the supplier have in place to assure compliance with current environmental regulations? What plan does the supplier have to meet future requirements, and what is management's attitude towards the environment? What is the supplier's attitude to corporate social responsibility? In the early 1990s, Nike's share value was significantly discounted because it was found to be using shoe manufacturers in underdeveloped countries where child labor and poor working conditions were prevalent. Starting in 1996, in response to weak demand and unrelenting criticism, Nike upgraded factory and employee standards, started a nonprofit to conduct audits, and began publishing audit data, including conditions and pay in its factories. Thus, suppliers do affect the reputation of the purchasing organization and the potential reputational risk is high.

The belief that in any organization, customers, employees, and suppliers should be treated equally leads to the conclusion that organizations with similar values make for good customers and suppliers of each other. This shows up in leadership, attitude towards innovation and continuing improvement, concern for the environment and society, as well as employee, customer, and supplier satisfaction. Although the full evidence of compatibility may not be forthcoming until well after a trading relationship has been established, significant clues can be extracted in face-to-face meetings between corporate leaders, examination of corporate publications, and reactions from customers.

RANKING POTENTIAL SUPPLIERS

During the first two stages of the acquisition process, need identification and description, it is important to establish which of the three levels of selection criteria are most relevant for this particular requirement. This will not only assist in identifying potential suppliers but also in evaluation of bids and ultimate supplier selection. Because many purchasing organizations use formal supplier performance evaluations for existing and new suppliers, the criteria used for selection and subsequent actual performance should be similar.

Letting suppliers know how bids will be evaluated and what weights will be used to compare competitive bids is considered good practice. Thus, in the traditional context, quality might be assigned 60 points, price 30 points, and delivery 10 points for a particular purchase. Even in such a simple three-factor, no strategy, or level 3 consideration, judgment is required to establish these weightings and how to assign points for differing bids.

The Caledon Concrete Mixers case in Chapter 7 illustrates an example of a company that uses a supplier evaluation system that weights different aspects of supplier bids using a point system. If more than one potential supplier is available, the supply professional's ranking of each supplier in relation to one another and the selection interview will determine the best available source. Almost all of the cases in this text require this kind of judgment.

A recent multimillion dollar purchase of paper at the World Bank resulted in supply's rethinking of how to measure the environmental impact of this requirement. This resulted in a new set of seven environmental evaluation criteria: fiber type, transportation pulp to mill and mill to Bank, chemical processing, certifications when sourcing, energy source at the mill, packaging, and compliance and other sustainability considerations. A low environmental score disqualified potential suppliers, even though their traditional offering in terms of quality, quantity, delivery, price, and service would have been deemed acceptable in prior years. In the supplier ranking scheme of 100 points, 70 points were assigned to the technical environmental evaluation criteria mentioned above. A total of 30 points was assigned to total annual cost, with the full 30 points given to the lowest bidder. The highest points assigned on the technical side were below 40, suggesting either lots of further improvement potential for the future or the need for a recalibration of point assignment.

The next chapter on supplier evaluation and relationships describes ranking systems. Therefore, the coverage in this chapter is brief.

Conclusion

The most critical decision for the supply professional deals with the selection of suppliers. Based on his or her understanding of the organization's strategic and operational needs, short and long term, the supply manager has to find the best way of matching the marketplace to these needs. Finding potential suppliers and gathering relevant information about them are standard tasks prior to supplier selection. Options of in-house, existing supplier, and new supplier need to be considered as well as single and multiple sourcing, dealing with manufacturers or distributors, domestic or offshore supplier, and small or large supplier. Whether supplier development should be used operationally or strategically is also a consideration. Evaluating potential sources according to the three levels of acquisition criteria requires a disciplined and reasoned approach. There is always a risk that actual supplier performance will not match expectations and risk management is intricately linked with the supplier selection decision.

Questions for Review and Discussion

1. Why might a supply manager prefer to look for a new supplier rather than place additional business with an existing supplier? Why not?

2. What challenges do you see in assessing a supplier's environmental performance?

3. Why is the trend toward single sourcing? What are the disadvantages to this trend?

4. What are standard supply risks? How might they be mitigated?

5. Why might it be preferable to buy from a distributor or wholesaler rather than directly from the manufacturer?

6. What are the advantages of purchasing from large, global sources?

7. When might it be appropriate to conduct a formal, rather than an informal, supplier evaluation?

8. What are the similarities and differences between evaluating new and existing sources of supply?

9. Why is supply focusing more attention on a supplier's management as part of the evaluation process? How might this evaluation be conducted?

10. How might social or political issues impact a supplier selection decision?

References

Carter, C. R.; and M. M. Jennings. *Purchasing's Contribution to the Socially Responsible Management of the Supply Chain*. Tempe, AZ: CAPS Research, 2000.

EPA. Sustainable Materials Management. Washington:D.C.: EPA, 2009, www.epa.gov/wastes/conserve/smm/pdf/vision2.pdf

Flynn, A. E. "Knowledge-Based Supply Management." Chap. 7. In *The Purchasing Handbook*. 7th ed., eds. J. L. Cavinato; A. E. Flynn; and R. G. Kauffman. New York: McGraw-Hill, 2006.

Gottfredson, M.; R. Puryear; and S. Phillips. "Strategic Sourcing: From Periphery to the Core." *Harvard Business Review* 83, no. 2 (2005), pp. 132–139.

Nelson, D. P. E. Moody; and J. R. Stegner. *The Incredible Payback: Innovative Sourcing Solutions That Deliver Extraordinary Results*. New York: AMACON, 2006.

Sako, M. "Supplier Development at Honda, Nissan and Toyota: Comparative Case Studies of Organizational Capability Enhancement." *Industrial and Corporate Change* 13, no. 2 (2004), pp. 281–308.

Thornton, L. M.; C. W. Autry; D. M. Gligor; and A. B. Brik. "Does Socially Responsible Supplier Selection Pay Off for Customer Firms? A Cross-Cultural Comparison." *Journal of Supply Chain Management* 49 (2013), pp. 66–89.

Case 12–1

Loren Inc.

On June 15, Brent Miller, raw materials buyer, had to prepare his recommendation for Loren's annual hexonic acid requirements. Four suppliers had submitted substantially different bids for this annual contract to commence August 1. Brent knew his recommendation would involve a variety of policy considerations and wondered what his best option would be.

COMPANY BACKGROUND

Loren (Canada) was the Canadian subsidiary of a larger international chemical company. The company sold both consumer and industrial products and had over the years established an excellent reputation for quality products and marketing effectiveness. This was evidenced by a substantial growth in total sales and financial success. Total Canadian sales were approximately $800 million and after-tax profits were $40 million. Raw material and packaging costs were about 50 percent of sales.

PURCHASING

Brent Miller, a recent graduate of a well-known business school, knew that purchasing was well regarded as a function at Loren. The department was staffed with 12 well-qualified persons, including a number of engineering and business graduates at both the undergraduate and master levels. The department was headed by a director who reported to the president. It was organized along commodity

lines, and Brent Miller had recently been appointed raw materials buyer reporting to the manager of the chemicals buying group. The hexonic acid contract would have to be approved by his immediate supervisor and the director of the department.

Brent was aware that several Loren purchasing policies and practices were of particular importance to his current hexonic contract decision. The purchasing department had worked very hard with suppliers over the years to establish a single-bid policy. It was felt that suppliers should quote their best possible offer on their first and only quote, and all suppliers should be willing to live with the consequences of their bid. Long-term supplier relations with the best possible long-term opportunities were considered vital to the procurement strategy. Assured supply for all possible types of market conditions was also of prime concern. Multiple sources were usually favored over single sources where this appeared to be reasonable and where no strong long-term price or other disadvantages were expected. Frequent supplier switching would not be normal, although total volumes placed with suppliers might change depending on past performance and new bids. Brent recognized that any major departure from traditional practice would have to be carefully justified. Exhibit 1 shows the four prime objectives of the purchasing department and Exhibit 2 contains excerpts from the company's familiarization brochure for new suppliers.

EXHIBIT 1	The basic objectives for the Loren purchasing department are:
Purchasing Objectives	A) *Assurance of Material Availability.* The major objective of purchasing must be the guarantee of sufficient supply to support production requirements.
	B) *Best Value.* Loren recognizes that value is a combination of price, quality, service, and that maximum profitability can only be obtained through the purchase of optimal value on both short- and long-term basis.
	C) *An Ethical Reputation.* All dealings must respect all aspects of the law and all business relationships must be founded on a sound ethical approach.
	D) *Gathering of Information.* Purchasing involves a constant search for new ideas and improved products in the changing markets. A responsibility also exists to keep the company informed on industry trends including information on material supply and costs.

EXHIBIT 2   Excerpts from Brochure for New Suppliers

The purpose of the information contained herein is to give our suppliers a better understanding of certain policies and practices of Loren. We believe it is important that we understand our suppliers and, in turn, that they understand us. As you know Loren believes in free enterprise and in competition as the mainspring of a free enterprise system. Many of our basic policies stem from a fundamental belief that competition is the fairest means for Loren to purchase the best total value. However, the policies and practices we want to outline here for you relate to Loren's business ethics and the ethical treatment of suppliers. In brief, fair dealing means these things to us:

1. We live up to our word. We do not mislead. We believe that misrepresentations, phantom prices, chiseling, etc., have no place in our business.

2. We try to be fair in our demands on a supplier and to avoid unreasonable demands for services; we expect to pay our way when special service is required.

3. We try to settle all claims and disputes on a fair and factual basis.

4. We avoid any form of "favored treatment," such as telling a supplier what to quote to get our business or obtaining business by "meeting" an existing price. In addition, all suppliers that could qualify for our business are given identical information and an equal opportunity to quote on our requirements.

5. We do not betray the confidence of a supplier. We believe that it is unethical to talk about a supplier with competitors. New ideas, methods, products, and prices are kept confidential unless disclosure is permitted by the supplier.

6. We believe in giving prompt and courteous attention to all supplier representatives.

7. We are willing to listen to supplier complaints at any level of the buying organization without prejudice concerning the future placement of business.

We also do not believe in reciprocity or in "tie-ins" which require the purchase of one commodity with another.

We believe that supplier relationships should be conducted so that personal obligations, either actual or implied, do not exist. Consequently, we do not accept gifts and we discourage entertainment from suppliers. Similarly, we try to avoid all situations which involve a conflict of personal interest.

HEXONIC ACID—RECENT MARKET HISTORY

Loren expected to use approximately 3,000 tons of hexonic acid in the following year. Requirements for the past year amounted to 2,750 tons and had been supplied by Canchem and Alfo at 60 and 40 percent, respectively.

Hexonic acid was a major raw material in a number of Loren products. Its requirements had grown steadily over the years and were expected to remain significant in the years to come. The availability of this material in the marketplace was difficult to predict. The process by which it was produced yielded both hexonic and octonic acids and the market was, therefore, influenced by the demand for either product.

Two years previously there had been major shortages of hexonic acid due to strong European and Japanese demand. Furthermore, capacity expansions had been delayed too long because of depressed prices for hexonic and octonic acid over the previous years. During this period of shortage, both of Loren's suppliers, Alfo and Canchem, were caught by the market upsurge. Alfo had just shut down its old Windsor plant and had not yet brought its new Quebec City plant up to design capacity. At the same time, Canchem was in the midst of converting its process to accommodate recent chemical improvements, and they, too, found themselves plagued with conversion problems. Both companies were large multiplant companies in Canada and had supplied Loren for many years. The parent companies of both Alfo and Canchem had been faced with too high a demand in the United States to be able to afford any material to help meet the Canadian commitments of their subsidiaries. As a result, both Canadian suppliers were forced to place many of their customers on allocation. However, through considerable efforts both were able to fulfill all of Loren's requirements. The increased prices charged throughout this period

EXHIBIT 3
Hexonic
Acid—Purchase
History

Period	Total Volume Purchased	Canchem Percent Delivered/Cost	Alfo Percent Delivered/Cost
Three years ago	1,800 tons	50% $828 / ton	50% $828 / ton
Two years ago	2,200 tons	50% $1,176 / ton	50% $1,084 / ton
Last year	2,750 tons	60% $1,384 / ton	40% $1,296 / ton

fell within the terms of the contracts and were substantially lower than those that would have been incurred if Loren would have had to import offshore material. Quotations on such imports had revealed prices ranging from $1,920 to $2,880 per ton.

The past year was relatively stable with both producers running almost at capacity. Loren again had contracted its requirements with Alfo and Canchem, both of whom continued to perform with the same high quality and service to which Loren had become accustomed over the years.

For the past year, Brent's predecessor had recommended a split in the business of 60 percent to Canchem and 40 percent to Alfo based on a number of factors. Important to the decision at the time was the start-up of the new Alfo plant. Alfo's quotation of $1,292 per ton delivered offered a lower price per ton than Canchem's at $1,384 per ton, but it had been uncertain whether the new plant would be able to guarantee more than 40 percent of Loren's hexonic acid requirements. Currently, however, Alfo had brought their plant up to capacity and could certainly supply all of the 3,000 tons required, if called on (see Exhibit 3 for a recent history of hexonic acid purchases).

Brent thought that recently the hexonic acid cycle had turned around. Hexonic acid demand had eased and now it was octonic acid that was in high demand by the booming paint industry. Recent plant expansions by a number of suppliers had been completed. The overall result seemed to be a building of excess hexonic acid inventories. Brent believed this would be reflected in a buyer's market in the coming year and looked forward to aggressive quotes from all potential sources.

MEETINGS WITH HEXONIC ACID SUPPLIERS

An important part of the buyer's job at Loren was to become an expert in the materials purchased. Among other things, this meant keeping an open ear to the market and building strong relationships with suppliers. It was the buyer's responsibility to assure that all information between buyer and seller would be completely confidential.

The director of purchasing believed it was important to build a reputation so that suppliers could trust Loren purchasing personnel. On May 14, Brent sent out the hexonic acid inquiry to the four suppliers he believed had a chance of quoting competitively on the needs of the Hamilton plant. The two current Canadian suppliers, Alfo and Canchem, were included as well as two American companies. The deadline for bids was June 7 at 4 p.m. Brent knew that on receipt of the inquiry, supplier sales representatives would be eager to discuss it. Actually, he had two contacts before the inquiry was sent out.

MEETING WITH ALFO

Mr. Baker, sales representative of Alfo, met with Brent on April 20. He said that Alfo had unfilled capacity at its new Quebec City plant and he appeared eager to receive an indication of Loren's future hexonic acid requirements. Mr. Baker informed Brent that he was aware of low-priced hexonic acid on the European market, but also made sure to emphasize that it would be uncompetitive in the Canadian market after the cost of duty and freight were added. Brent said it was a published fact that inventories were building in the United States as other hexonic acid users showed signs of easing their demands.

The meeting ended with the assurance from Brent that Mr. Baker would again receive an invitation to quote on the next period's business.

PHONE CALL BY MICHIGAN CHEMICAL

Mr. Wallace, sales representative of Michigan Chemical, assured Brent over the telephone on April 30 that his company would be a contender this year. He said that Michigan Chemical would be represented by their Canadian distributor, Carter Chemicals Ltd., located in Niagara Falls, Ontario. Brent remembered that Michigan Chemical had a good record with Loren (U.S.). According to the U.S. raw materials buying group, Michigan Chemical had supplied close to 99 percent of its commitment in the recent period of shortage. Brent emphasized to Mr. Wallace over the telephone that the present suppliers held the advantage and that he would have to offer better value in order for Loren to swing any business away from them. Brent said at the end of the call that Michigan Chemical would receive an inquiry and that their quote would be seriously considered.

MEETING WITH CANCHEM

On June 3, Mr. Aldert, sales representative for Canchem, personally brought in his company's quotation and presented the terms to Brent with a distinct air of confidence. Mr. Aldert explained that although his delivered price of $1,384 per ton was the same as that which Loren was currently paying for delivered Canchem material, it remained a competitive price. Brent could not help showing his disappointment to Mr. Aldert, and he said that he had expected a more aggressive quote. However, he assured Mr. Aldert that every consideration would be given to Canchem once all the quotations were in by the June 7 deadline.

MEETING WITH AMERICAN CHEMICAL INC. (AMCHEM)

On the morning of June 7, two representatives from AMCHEM delivered their hexonic acid quotation and explained its contents to Brent. AMCHEM had recently completed a plant expansion at its Cleveland plant and clearly had the ability to supply many times Loren's total requirements. Brent thought the quote of $1,204 per ton appeared attractive and noted that the price per ton depended on the specific volume allocated to AMCHEM. The price of $1,204 applied to an annual volume to 1,050 tons. For a volume of 2,250 tons per year, the delivered price would be lowered to $1,192.

When the representatives had left, Brent searched the hexonic acid material file for any information about past dealings with AMCHEM. He found that Loren had been supplied with AMCHEM hexonic acid seven years previously. At that time, AMCHEM apparently had quoted a price below Canchem and Alfo and, as a result, had been allocated a portion of the business. This had the result of sparking aggressiveness into the two Canadian suppliers during the next inquiry. Both fought to gain back the tonnage that had been taken away from them. Apparently, neither Canchem nor Alfo had been aware who their competitor was at the time.

Brent also telephoned the purchasing department of Loren (U.S.) in an effort to draw any information about their experience with AMCHEM. Supplier information like this flowed quite freely within the corporation on a need-to-

know basis. The U.S. buyer informed Brent that AMCHEM did at one time supply the parent with hexonic acid and that quality and service were excellent. However, he did caution Brent that during the recent period of shortage, AMCHEM did place Loren (U.S.) on allocation and as a result fell short of its commitment by a considerable extent.

MEETING WITH ALFO

Mr. Baker, sales representative of Alfo, presented his company's quote to Brent at 3 p.m., the afternoon of June 7. He explained that the contractual terms and $1,296 delivered price offered were the same as those under the current contract with Alfo. Brent thanked Mr. Baker for his quotation and told him he would be informed in late June when a decision had been made.

QUOTATION BY CARTER CHEMICAL

The quotation from Carter Chemical arrived in the afternoon mail on June 7. The $1,268 per ton FOB destination quote was a pleasant surprise to Brent. He thought that Michigan Chemical had been right when they had said that their distributor would make an aggressive offer. Brent now had received two quotes that offered a better laid-down cost than the two current suppliers.

VISIT OF CANCHEM

At 3:45 p.m. on June 7, Brent received another visit from Mr. Aldert of Canchem, who had apparently been disheartened after his earlier meeting on June 3. He had gone back to his management, for he now had a new quotation prepared. His new quote offered Loren hexonic acid on a three-year contract for $1,192 per ton. With freight included, this price appeared to be equal to the lowest bid that had been received. Brent realized that he had probably inspired Mr. Aldert to resubmit his quotation by the feedback he had given him during their June 3 meeting. With this in mind, Brent was wary of accepting this quotation for fear he would be setting a bad precedent. He told Mr. Aldert that he might not be in a position to accept his bid, but would let him know subsequently. The following day Brent discussed the situation with his superior, Mr. Williams. Mr. Williams retraced the steps Brent had gone through. It had been normal practice at Loren to open quotes as they were received. It had also been standard policy not to give suppliers any feedback on their quote until all quotes had been received. Mr. Williams told Brent to think the situation over in his own mind and to make a recommendation on

EXHIBIT 4 Quotation Summary: Hexonic Acid

	Price			Terms
	Spot	Contract		
Alfo	$1,296.00 / ton	$1,296.00 / ton		Min. period: 1 year Min. volume: — Price protection: 90 days Notice: 15 days
Canchem	**Bid 1** $1,384.00 / ton	$1,384.00 / ton		Min. period: 3 years (Bid 2) Min. volume: 1,000 tons
	Bid 2 $1,192.00 / ton	$1,192.00 / ton		Price protection: 30 days Notice: 30 days
American Chemicals		*Min. 1,050 tons*	*Min.2,250 tons*	Min. period: 1 year Min. volume: Stated
	$1,607.72 / ton	$1,204.00 / ton	$1,192.00 / ton	Price protection: Firm Notice: —
Carter Chemicals		*Min. 750 tons*		Min. period: 1 year Min. volume: 750 tons
(Michigan Chemical Material)	$1,268.00 / ton	$1,268.00 / ton		Price protection: 90 days Notice: 15 days

how Canchem's second bid should be treated as part of his hexonic acid contract deliberations.

QUOTE SUMMARY

Brent prepared a quote summary to put all bids on an equal footing (see Exhibit 4). To be able to compare quotes fairly, it was necessary to examine the laid-down cost of each of the four options. Brent realized he did not have much time left and the unusual situation surrounding Canchem's second bid gave him further concern. Mr. Williams was expecting his written analysis and recommendation no later than June 17.

Case 12–2
Kettering Industries Inc.

In late February, Victoria Jackson, supply manager at Kettering Industries Inc. in Dayton, Ohio, needed to decide which glass supplier(s) to choose. She was not sure whether her past approach to buying glass would still be appropriate in future.

KETTERING INDUSTRIES INC.

Kettering Industries Inc. (KII) competed in the regional window market in the Midwest home remodeling industry. The plant initially manufactured low-cost products such as storm doors, storm windows, school bus windows, and low-end replacement aluminum windows. Over the

years, storm door and replacement aluminum window production was eliminated and vinyl window production was initiated. The 86,000 sq. ft. facility manufactured vinyl windows (800/day), storm windows (200/day), and school bus aluminum windows (50/day). A total of 160,000 windows was produced last year.

Sales were approximately $25 million. Sales of vinyl windows were seasonal with primary demand in the warmer months, from May to October. The company sold its high-priced, high-quality vinyl windows through a number of branches located across the Midwest. The delivery goal to customers was 10 days from the date the order was received at the plant.

In order to maintain competitiveness and increase returns to shareholders, KII was committed to becoming a world-class manufacturer. Programs were developed and implemented to meet goals of improved quality, delivery performance, customer responsiveness, and better engineered products.

VINYL WINDOW PRODUCTION

All production at KII was based on custom orders. Windows were usually manufactured and shipped on the same day, reducing the need for work-in-process inventory.

Due to cost and performance advantages of vinyl over wood and aluminum windows, management projected that demand would continue to grow, and production, as measured by total blocks of glass used, would double over the next five years. All of this growth was expected to be in low energy glass windows.

Vinyl windows could be made with either clear glass or low energy glass; both types of glass were available in thicknesses of each 3 mm or 4 mm. Low energy glass was a special glass with an invisible metal coating that reduced penetration of infrared rays and decreased heat loss. Currently, low energy glass windows accounted for about 22 percent of the plant's vinyl window production. Low energy glass window production, as a percentage of total vinyl window production, was increasing monthly.

PURCHASING OF GLASS

Last year, KII purchased a total of $1.15 million of clear and low energy glass from four different suppliers (Exhibit 1). Glass was purchased by the block with each block consisting of 40 sheets for 4 mm glass and 50 sheets for 3 mm glass. Due to the nature of the glass-cutting equipment that the company used, 3 mm glass had

EXHIBIT 1
Kettering Industries Inc. Last Year's Glass Consumption

Supplier	3 mm Clear	4 mm Clear	3 mm Low Energy	4 mm Low Energy	Total
Ross Industries					
666 blks	541,090				$541,090
Clear View Distributors					
94 blks	77,812				
8 blks		5,618			
110 blks			234, 882		
12 blks				16,631	$334,943
Travers Glass Ltd.					
104 blks	85,902				
42 blks		29,494			
36 blks			76,822	0	$192,218
West Bend Glass					
36 blks	0	0	76,046		
4 blks				7,073	$83,119
Blks Total	**$704,804**	**$35,112**	**$387,750**	**$23,704**	**$1,151,370**
Clear Glass Total	872	blocks		$739,916	
Low Energy Glass Total	198	blocks		441,454	
TOTAL	**1,070**			**$1,151,370**	

to be ordered in sheets of 72″ × 96″ and 4 mm glass in sheets of 60″ × 96″.

Glass sheet order quantities were determined based on historical usage reports and sales forecasts. In order to take advantage of quantity discounts and obtain the best possible price, Victoria usually ordered by the truckload. Truckload size could vary between 8 to 18 blocks depending on the capacity of the truck, the packaging, and weight restrictions.

The amount of glass that could be held in inventory was constrained by a storage capacity of 32 blocks. During the past year, to maintain production during peak periods (May through October), six blocks of glass per day were required. Only 13 blocks of glass per week were needed for the November through April period. Each week an inventory count was undertaken so that orders could be adjusted as necessary. Last year raw material glass inventory turned about 14 times.

KII occasionally manufactured products using obscure glass instead of clear or low energy glass. Rather than stocking the obscure glass in inventory it was only ordered as required.

SELECTING SUPPLIERS

Victoria wanted one or more suppliers to be able to meet forecasted needs. The company had set a goal of increasing raw material inventory turns from 14 times a year to 30–35 times a year within two years. In addition to requiring less working capital, increased inventory turns would free up floor space that was needed for other production activities. A Vendor Certification Program was also being implemented to assist in the setup of long-term relationships with suppliers in a partnership mode to encourage delivery of on-time, zero-defect materials to the plant.

KII's president had asked Victoria to research four potential suppliers and recommend the arrangements the company should make for purchasing glass. Victoria had asked several suppliers to submit quotes, from which she had narrowed the alternatives to three of last year's suppliers and one former supplier, Jackson Glass Co. She summarized these quotes in her bid summary as shown in Exhibit 2.

SUPPLIER ALTERNATIVES

Ross Industries. Ross Industries was a glass manufacturer that had provided KII with excellent service and good quality glass for 20 years. Their low energy glass did not meet KII's testing standards and, therefore, mixed truckloads of clear and low energy glass were not possible. To get the quoted 3 mm clear glass truckload price of $.3278/sq. ft./blk delivered, a minimum of 12 blocks had to be

EXHIBIT 2
Bid Summary and Past Year Prices Paid (in dollars per square foot)

	Clear				Low Energy	
	3 mm (822 blocks 2400 ft²/bl)		**4 mm (50 blocks 1600 ft²/bl)**		**3 mm (234 blocks 2400 ft²/bl)**	**4 mm (124 blocks 1600 ft²/bl)**
Ross Ind.	.3278 .33 [.3384][1]	12 min 1 min	.4371 .44			
Clear View	.33 [.3449]	8 min	.44 [.3489]		.8920 [.8900]	1.142 [1.135]
Travers	.3172 [.3445]	12 min	.4389 [.4389]		.8830	1.160
Jackson	.33	6 min	.44			1.092
West Bend[2]					0.8794	

[1] Brackets indicate last year's actual prices.
[2] Because West Bend Glass was a Canadian manufacturer and unable to price its glass competitively in the United States, it was not asked to submit a quote for either clear glass for the current year.

ordered at one time. If quantities of less than 12 blocks were ordered, the delivered price was $.33/sq. ft./blk. The Ross plant was located 150 miles from Dayton and lead time was one week. They had access to an associated supplier in Illinois as an alternate source of glass if they were unable to meet KII's demands.

Clear View Distributors.   Clear View Distributors was a small local glass distributor that had supplied KII for three years. They had provided consistent, on-time delivery of low energy glass. They had also built sealed units for KII, but there had been problems with some units. Both clear glass (made by Ross Industries) and low energy glass (made by West Bend Glass) were available on a mixed eight-block truck. Delivery was available daily, if requested, and they were willing to stock inventory for KII.

Travers Glass Ltd.   Travers Glass Ltd. was a glass distributor about twice the size of Clear View Distributors. They had provided KII with service for 15 years and had been an excellent backup service for Ross Industries. They offered clear glass (made by Jackson Glass Co.) at the lowest delivered price of $.3172/sq. ft./blk in a straight or mixed truckload of at least 12 blocks with low energy glass (made by West Bend Glass). The quote for 4 mm clear glass was $.4389/sq. ft./blk. For low energy glass their quote was $0.6734/sq. ft./blk for 3 mm and $0.9512/sq. ft./blk for 4 mm glass. Clear glass made by Ross Industries was also available at a higher price than the clear glass made by West Bend Glass. Their distribution centre was located 135 miles from Dayton. Lead time was two to three days and they could deliver three to four times a week. They were willing to stock inventory for KII.

Jackson Glass Co.   Jackson Glass Co. was a glass manufacturer that had been one of several suppliers to KII in the past. They were very interested in doing business with KII again. Their glass quality was good and they would supply 3 mm clear glass at a delivered price of $.33/sq. ft./blk for a minimum order of six blocks. Jackson's quote for 4 mm clear glass was $.44/sq. ft./blk. Their low energy glass would require KII's testing lab's approval. The Jackson distribution center was located about 130 miles from Dayton and lead time was one week. They were aligned with a Canadian supplier that could provide an alternate source of glass if required.

Now that she had gathered the necessary information, Victoria needed to proceed with her analysis. She knew that she would have to make her recommendation soon.

Case 12–3

Plastic Cable Clips

In mid-September Robyn Pemberton, purchasing officer in the laundry division of Fisher & Paykel Limited, located in Auckland, New Zealand, was wondering which procurement option made most sense for the plastic cable clips requirements for the new line of washing machines.

THE LAUNDRY DIVISION

Fisher & Paykel Limited was the largest home appliance manufacturer in New Zealand with sales of its major appliances amounting to $135,000,000 and total sales of $270,000,000 for the fiscal year ending March 31, including $36,000,000 of export sales and royalty income. It comprised eight operating divisions, one of which was the laundry division employing over 500 people to produce washing machines and dryers. Currently, the laundry division produced about 50,000 washing machines, solely for the domestic market.

THE NEW WASHING MACHINE

For the last two years, the laundry division had been developing a new line of automatic washing machines. The planning and development of the new machine was conducted by a seven-person committee of engineers, production, and marketing people as well as a purchasing coordinator.

The new machine, designed entirely by F&P, used electronic controls. It was believed to be technologically advanced by world standards. Its manufacturing process would be highly automated, featuring considerable part rationalization and cost reduction over the old production line. In fact, maintaining costs at the lowest possible level was one of the key priorities of the planning committee.

With good opportunities for export and royalty income, the laundry division hoped to produce between 75,000 and 100,000 new washing machines a year. However, 50,000 machines were planned for the first full year of production. The first production run was scheduled for the beginning of next April.

PLASTIC CABLE CLIPS

The old washing machine used about 20 different plastic cable ties for a total of about 250 ties in each machine. At the moment, the laundry division bought nearly $1,250,000 a year worth of plastic cable ties: about $500,000 from Olson Plastics, a New Zealand manufacturer; $500,000 from Barry Cleaver and Sons, a local agent importing mostly from Japan; $200,000 from G. T. Rollman, another local agent importing from Australia; and at most $50,000 from Plastic Distributing, a relatively new and smaller multisource New Zealand agent.

The ties to be used in the new machine required new specifications because of the automated production process. None of the existing ties suppliers actually had in stock the kind of parts required.

A year earlier, Robyn Pemberton, who was the purchasing coordinator for the new washing machine, managed to convince the planning committee to draw on the technical expertise of Barry Cleaver, the New Zealand agent currently supplying some of the plastic ties. As a result of Barry Cleaver's input, the number of ties required was reduced to half a dozen new parts for a total of about 45 plastic clips to be used in each new machine. Robyn Pemberton made it very clear to Barry Cleaver that all current plastic ties suppliers would be asked to submit quotations as soon as all the specifications on the new clips were finalized and that his involvement would not give him any preferential treatment over the others.

SUPPLIER SELECTION

Because of design changes, the specifications for the new cable clips were not confirmed until early July. Robyn promptly sent letters asking for quotations to the four existing plastic ties suppliers (see Exhibit 1).

OLSON PLASTICS

Olson Plastics, the only New Zealand manufacturer of plastic ties, clips, and rivets, had been supplying F&P for many years. Robyn Pemberton believed that F&P would be among its top five customers. With occasional quality and service problems, Robyn felt the quality of Olson's products was not as high as that of the other ties suppliers.

EXHIBIT 1
Quotation Request Letter Sample

5 July

The following new parts are required, commencing next March. Please advise price, minimum quantity, and delivery details.

Part	Description	Qty/Annum
816549	Clip snap .125M × .5	30,000
816553	Clip snap .250M × .75	30,000
817709	Clip-tie HM FT	60,000
817803	Clip-lock HBX	165,000
817923	Clip-tie HM FT (SS)	650,000
817975	Clip-tie HM RS.2	135,000

Samples would be appreciated when possible.
Awaiting your reply with interest.

Yours faithfully,
FISHER & PAYKEL LIMITED

Robyn Pemberton
Purchasing Officer
Laundry Division

Olson's prices for certain parts were twice as high as prices for imported parts. But deliveries were Robyn's major area of concern with this supplier. Even with a six-to-eight-month lead time, deliveries were unreliable and Robyn had to chase every order. She believed Olson had capacity problems although they did not wish to admit it.

However, Olson enjoyed government protection in the sense that, under normal circumstances, a New Zealand agent could not import products that could be made domestically.

BARRY CLEAVER AND SONS

Barry Cleaver and Sons, a New Zealand agent for three generations with an excellent reputation, was receiving about $2 million a year worth of orders from F&P. Its prices and service were normally excellent. Delivery was good, providing adequate lead time of six to eight months was given. Barry Cleaver was getting F&P plastic parts from Japan and, during seller's markets, would have difficulty obtaining supply because of the relative low importance of its orders.

However, Robyn was concerned about the long-term availability of the imported parts because the agent's license could be revoked if it was proven that a domestic supply alternative existed. F&P was legally free to buy from any agent in New Zealand. It was up to the agent to justify its stance with the Department of Trade and Industry. However, Robyn was well aware of the department's licensing policy (see Exhibit 2), because she remembered vividly a problem encountered with plastic rivets and a few cable ties in May.

Barry Cleaver had been supplying F&P with Japanese rivets and cable ties until Olson complained to Trade and Industry. As a result, Barry Cleaver not only had to stop importing and start purchasing from Olson at three times the former price, but he was also having a terrible time meeting F&P volume requirements and had to deliver some of the parts on a daily basis. After F&P started noticing that the rivets purchased from Barry Cleaver came in Olson's boxes, Robyn asked Olson for quotes on the rivets, but was subsequently surprised to discover that Olson's prices were higher than Barry Cleaver's.

G. T. ROLLMAN

G. T. Rollman was a large New Zealand agent importing from Australia. Although the prices were high, the service was excellent and the delivery was good. The average lead time was three to four months but, in urgent

EXHIBIT 2
New Zealand Government Standard Licensing Policy[1]

The following policy applies to all item codes except those for which specific policies are set on the following pages.

1. Goods of Types Not Produced in New Zealand
   Licenses will generally be granted to meet reasonable requirements for goods of types not produced in New Zealand.
   Licenses will not be issued under this provision unless it is quite clear that the goods to be imported are not substitutable for domestic alternatives.
   The applicants will need to provide adequate evidence that suitable alternatives are not available from New Zealand manufacturers.
   In considering applications Trade and Industry will assess the extent to which established licensing provisions have been and are being used to import the goods concerned. The aim of this is to ensure that domestic production is not detrimentally affected by the consequential availability of license to import directly competitive goods.
2. All Other Goods
   Licenses may be granted in special circumstances such as:
   - Established trading patterns arising from continuing special licensing provision.
   - Shortfalls in normal domestic supply.
   - Special provision for the requirements of new manufacturers.
   - Applications under general policies and provisions set out in Annex III.

   Note: Item Codes which fall under Industry Development Plans are subject to any special import licensing provisions of those plans.

[1] This policy does not apply to Australian-made products.

situations, it could supply within six weeks by airfreighting the stock.

Robyn Pemberton was also conscious of the advantage of Australian sourcing due to the Closer Economic Relations Agreement between New Zealand and Australia. She knew that a higher New Zealand and Australian content in the new washing machine would permit F&P free or minimum duty access to the Australian market. Although she had to inform the costing department of the country of origin of each part purchased, she did not know at what level some price reduction on a part would offset a duty increase. She had tried to find out more information on this subject, but no one had been very explicit. With the labour government in power, a considerable amount of uncertainty existed. All she knew was that the group purchasing department of F&P was pushing for as much New Zealand and Australian content as possible.

PLASTIC DISTRIBUTING

Plastic Distributing was a local agent with annual sales under $1 million that imported plastic products from a number of countries. This young company was eager to obtain orders but offered little technical backup. In the past, Robyn had given it the odd order, especially when supply was tight. She had asked this agent to quote on the new plastic clips mostly for comparison purposes.

SELECTION DECISION

Quotes started arriving on July 10 with Barry Cleaver's response. But it was not until September 12 that she obtained Olson's prices (see Exhibit 3 for a summary of quotes). In mid-September Robyn called Barry Cleaver and asked for a meeting. Barry Cleaver came with a technical expert to meet with Robyn and her supervisor, John Wardrop. Barry made clear that the recent problem encountered with the supply of rivets and cable ties was in the process of being solved, because they had been able to regain their importing license from Trade and Industry by proving that Olson did not have sufficient capacity to meet the demand. Barry Cleaver assured Robyn and John that he felt there would be no problem to import all the new plastic clips required for the new washing machines.

Robyn was wondering what to do. In light of Deming's philosophy adopted by Fisher & Paykel as a whole, she felt some pressure toward single sourcing. However, she was not convinced of the soundness of single sourcing in the context of this purchase. She was also wondering to what extent Olson Plastics realized what their situation would be once the old washing machine was phased out, should she choose to go with Barry Cleaver. She was debating whether she should call on Olson for further consultation. In any event, she knew a decision had to be reached quickly in view of the lead time involved, with the first production run scheduled for next April.

EXHIBIT 3
Summary of Quotes/Prices per 1,000

Part No	Description	Barry Cleaver	Olson	Plastic Dist.	Rollman
816549	Clip snap 1.25M × .5	76.00	54.00	99.95	—
816553	Clip snap .250M × .75	76.00	119.80	99.95	—
817709	Clip-tie HM FT	25.20	36.80	28.26	—
817803	Clip-lock HBX	39.20	61.82	—	134.40
817923	Clip-tie HM FT(SS)	23.06	20.40	28.12	—
817975	Clip-tie HM RS.2	38.40	50.00	63.22	—

Chapter **Thirteen**

Supplier Evaluation and Supplier Relationships

Key Questions for the Supply Decision Maker

Should we

- Change the way we evaluate supplier performance?
- Have annual top executive meetings with our key suppliers?
- Have more or fewer partnerships and alliances?

How can we

- Reduce the number of unacceptable suppliers?
- Improve our relationships with suppliers?
- Find out how satisfied our suppliers are with us as a customer?

Supplier performance evaluation and supplier relationship management are integral parts of the acquisition process. Performance evaluation ensures adherence to the contract and enables continuous improvement of both buyer and seller. Supplier relationship management, like customer relationship management, contributes to long-term organizational stability.

There are two key decisions in this chapter: (1) How do we evaluate supplier performance? and (2) How do we manage our supplier relationships? Obviously, these two questions are interrelated. How we relate to a supplier may affect its performance and the reverse, how the supplier performs may affect our relationship. Supplier performance evaluation is addressed first.

MEASURING SUPPLIER PERFORMANCE

Collection and analysis of performance data are the basis for determining how good a job the supplier is doing. This information also allows for intelligent decisions about sources for rebuys and useful feedback to current suppliers about areas of improvement. Normally, the performance of the supplier is assessed regularly to reveal cycle time reductions, opportunities for process improvements, cost reduction, and quality and service improvements. Regular performance assessment is a catalyst for continuous improvement.

There are many metrics that may be included in a supplier performance measurement system. Some organizations use a few critical metrics while others develop systems that track dozens. There should be a clear link between data and decisions to avoid expending excessive resources capturing information that is never used by decision makers. Some of the more common metrics are discussed in the following section.

Key Performance Indicators (KPIs)

Direct measures quantify supplier performance at the time work is completed. Examples are on-time delivery, number of rejects, increase in sales after a marketing campaign, and cycle time to develop a specific product/service/technology in a development stage. Automation of real-time metrics such as quality, quantity, price, and on-time delivery and careful selection of more time-consuming data collection activities help to reduce the time spent measuring results.

The supplier scorecard may include a summary statement of the supplier's cost, quality, and timeliness performance and a compilation of satisfaction surveys, real-time metrics, variance of invoice amounts to estimates or contract negotiated rates, and other contract-related terms.

Most supply professionals tend to separate suppliers into two categories: new and current. A new supplier is one about which no track record is yet available. This is a supplier new to the buying organization and in the process of attempting to meet its obligations under its first contract. The new supplier can be considered probationary and will normally be watched closely to ascertain whether preselection expectations warranted awarding the business. For current and longer-term suppliers who have already proven in the past that their performance meets minimum expectations, at least, the evaluation of their performance may be more routine.

EVALUATION METHODS

The supplier evaluation process can be informal or highly structured and formalized depending on the nature of the acquisition. In this section, several methods are discussed, including informal and semiformal, categorical, and weighted point evaluations.

Informal Evaluation and Rating

Informal evaluation includes assessments of the supplier by internal users and others anywhere in the buying organization where supplier contact takes place. "How are things going with supplier X?" is a typical question that can and should be asked by supply personnel when in contact with others in their own organization. Similarly, information gleaned from conversations at professional meetings, conferences, and from the media can be useful in checking out and comparing such personal impressions. An experienced supply professional will have accumulated a wealth of such information on suppliers and will always be on the alert for signs that new information may affect the overall assessment of a supplier. In fact, in most small organizations almost all evaluation of current sources is carried out informally. When users and supply managers are in daily personal contact and feedback on both satisfactory and unsatisfactory supplier performance is quick, such informality makes a lot of sense.

In larger organizations, however, communication lines are stretched, supply personnel and internal users may be in different locations, and large contracts may be negotiated by a centralized supply group or a prime contractor located at a primary facility, while daily supplier contact is handled at various locations. If suppliers are also large, requirements in different locations of the country or the world may be met with varying degrees of success by different plants or offices belonging to the same supplier. As the buyer–supplier network grows in complexity, the need to have a more formal system for evaluating current sources also increases.

Semiformal: Executive Roundtable Discussions

One simple semiformal supplier evaluation tool is the regular, annual discussion between top executives in the buying organization and those of the supplier. Normally, these top-level discussions are confined to suppliers of strategic or critical requirements. The presence of top executives of both sides lends weight to the occasion and permits discussion of past performance; future expectations; economic, social, and technological trends; long-term plans; and so on, in a high-level context. The chief supply officer (CSO) normally takes the lead in organizing and facilitating such sessions and invites the appropriate executives to take part. These roundtable discussions can help cement relationships between the two organizations at a high level, and when repeated over time can provide invaluable information for both sides. They would normally, but not exclusively, take place at the buying organization.

The number of such high-level sessions must be limited. Equivalent lower-level sessions for suppliers further down the priority list also have considerable merit and permit a regular update in a broader context than the normal supplier–purchaser contacts geared to specific current orders.

Formal Supplier Evaluation and Rating

Accompanying the trends of supply base rationalization, strategic sourcing, and closer relationships with key suppliers is the growing sophistication in supplier performance rating. Often, continuous improvement is tracked along with more traditional factors such as quality, quantity, delivery, and price. In other cases, suggestions for product or service redesign, value-chain improvements, willingness to work on supply chain teams, assistance in investment recovery or disposal, or the development of anything that would provide better value for the ultimate customer may be tracked and recorded. In evaluating current sources, the question is, How well did the supplier do? To use this information in future supplier selection decisions, the key question is, What is this supplier's performance likely to be in the future?

Most formal supplier rating approaches attempt to track actual performance over time. Advances in supply process software allow for easier tracking on a real-time basis and greater performance visibility. As orders are delivered, quality, quantity, delivery, price, and service objectives and other terms and conditions are tracked. Thus, corrective action can be taken as needed on the existing contract. Also, when it is time to place another order, the past record can be used to assess whether the same supplier should again be considered or not. A simple scheme for smaller organizations might include a notation only as to whether these factors were acceptable or not for specific orders received. More detailed evaluations include a summary of supplier performance over time.

It is normal to track a supplier's quality performance closely and in sufficient detail to pinpoint corrective action. In many organizations, only certified suppliers are considered for potential future business, and extensive evaluations on quality and other dimensions of supplier attributes and performance are carried out accordingly.

Categorical Evaluation and Rating

Delivery performance of a current supplier is fairly easily tracked if good records exist of delivery promises and actual receipts and few modifications have been made on an informal basis. In a JIT mode, nonperformance on delivery is just as critical as unsatisfactory quality, and actual delivery is closely monitored. In the example below, different levels of delivery performance are described and assigned a category rating (excellent, good, fair, poor).

Excellent:	a.	Meets delivery dates without expediting.
	b.	Requested delivery dates are usually accepted.
Good:	c.	Usually meets shipping dates without substantial follow-up.
	d.	Often is able to accept requested delivery dates.
Fair:	e.	Shipments sometimes late, substantial amount of follow-up required.
Poor:	f.	Shipments usually late, delivery promises seldom met, constant expediting required.

Quantifying the assessment is often preferred because it signifies an attempt to remove subjectivity from the process. Some performance areas, such as delivery, are more easily quantified than others such as service. For example, the on-time delivery window might be defined by a particular company as anywhere between two days early and zero days late as committed by master scheduling. Deliveries are tracked and performance is rated according to a preestablished rating system. For example, delivery may be worth 15 out of 100 points, which means that delivery performance carries 15 percent of the weight of the decision. Points for on-time delivery might be allocated as follows:

15 points	> 98 % on-time
10 points	95–97.9% on-time
5 points	90–94.9% on-time
0 points	< 90% on-time

Actual price performance of a supplier is easily tracked, as discrepancies between agreed-to prices and those actually invoiced by suppliers should normally be brought to supply's attention anyway. Price ratings of suppliers are, therefore, often of a comparison type, actual price versus target, or actual price versus lowest price received from other suppliers supplying the same requirement. Assessment of total cost of ownership from one supplier to another is more difficult to track, and often far more important than year-over-year price savings. Estimating total cost of ownership for a potential supplier rather than a current one is even more difficult and adds a level of complexity to the decision process.

It is in the service area that perhaps the most judgment is called for. Opinions need to be collected on the quality of technical assistance, supplier attitude and response time to requests for assistance, support staff qualifications, and so on. It is normal, therefore, to have a relatively simple rating scheme for service, such as outstanding, acceptable, and poor, along with explanations regarding specific incidents to explain these ratings. Efforts should be made to create objective assessments of service performance including clearly defined service levels and metrics. A key driver in satisfactory service performance is clear and unambiguous descriptions of the required service level included in the statement of work.

It is even more difficult to establish metrics to assess supplier performance or projected performance in areas of strategic importance such as innovation. Measures of innovation at an organizational level might include the percentage of sales attributable to new products or services, the number of new patents or new products successfully introduced, or gross margins from new products compared to gross margins from existing products. Measuring supply and suppliers' direct and indirect contribution to these metrics is an ongoing challenge.

Weighted Point Evaluation Systems

Many organizations rate suppliers by assigning points and scales to each factor and each rating. Where several sources supply the same goods or services, such schemes permit cross-comparisons. Outstanding performance of a supplier can then be rewarded with additional business, while poor performance may result in the development and implementation of a performance improvement plan, or lead to less business with the supplier, or possibly dropping a supplier altogether.

The APC case at the end of this chapter provides a good example of a weighted point evaluation system and how it applies to a specific supplier.

The typical process for developing a weighted point evaluation system is to: (1) identify the factors or criteria for evaluation, (2) determine the importance of each factor, and (3) establish a system for rating each supplier on each factor.

The relevant factors or decision criteria should be determined in the context of the purchase and the sourcing strategy for that item. Most organizations track major suppliers more closely than those sources deemed to have less impact on organizational performance. Some organizations use annual dollar volume as a guide toward such categorization (for example, identifying A, B, and C sources), much the same as inventories can be classified using the Pareto distribution. Some organizations add a special category of "critical" or "strategic" goods or services regardless of dollar volume, in which unsatisfactory performance by a supplier might result in serious problems for the organization and good supplier performance provides strategic opportunities. The purpose of such categorization is to fit each category with an appropriate supplier rating scheme. For example, for a high-value, high-volume purchase over a long-term contract, the buyer may include factors such as the supplier's management, human resources, and information systems fit. For a C-item (low-dollar value, high-volume), the critical factors may be delivery, availability, convenience, and price. There are a number of ways to assign weight to the factors. One is to assign percentages to each factor for a total of 100 percent.

The selection of the factors, weights, and form of measurement will require considerable thought to ensure congruence between the organization's priorities for this product class and the rating scheme's ability to identify superior suppliers correctly. For different product classes, different factors, weights, and measures should be used to reflect varying impact on the organization.

In an electronic procurement system, all supplier performance data is entered as orders are received, and the buyer (and the supplier in some cases) has online access to be able to discuss the supplier's performance at any time. Suppliers need to be informed about how they stand on the rating scale. Improved performance on the part of the supplier often results from the knowledge that its rating is lower than some competitor's or falls short of a set target.

SUPPLIER RANKING

If supplier performance is measured fairly and regularly, it is possible to rank suppliers on a scale from unacceptable to exceptional.

Unacceptable Suppliers

Unacceptable suppliers fail to meet operational and strategic needs of the buying organization. Discontinuing business with unacceptable suppliers and substituting better ones are the normal actions required. A special case exists when such a discontinuance may create even greater problems for the purchasing organization. A typical example is a sole-source situation such as a patented or OEM part where the supplier takes undue advantage of its privileged position. Discontinuance in the short term may not be feasible, but in the long term it may be, if the supply organization has diligently worked on finding an appropriate substitute or developing another source of supply. Another exception is a new source of supply that is still learning how to satisfy the purchasing organization's requirements and is assiduously working to achieve significant improvement.

Acceptable Suppliers

Acceptable suppliers meet current operational needs as required by contract. Acceptable suppliers provide a performance that other purchasers could easily match and, hence, acceptable suppliers provide no basis for competitive edge.

Preferred Suppliers

Purchasers have a system or process orientation with preferred suppliers and this integration avoids unnecessary duplication and speeds up transactions that normally are handled on an electronic basis. Both parties work toward mutual improvements to eliminate nonvalue-adding activities. Preferred suppliers meet all operational and some of the strategic needs of the buying organization. Preferred suppliers react positively to initiatives of the purchaser to improve the current situation.

Exceptional Suppliers

Exceptional suppliers anticipate operational and strategic needs of the purchaser and are capable of meeting and exceeding them. With exceptional suppliers, mutual breakthroughs may be a source of significant competitive advantage. Exceptional suppliers, like exceptional customers, need to be treasured. They can serve as an example of what is possible: an opportunity to experiment with new and different approaches to supply base management and as an early indicator of future supply management and supplier relationship direction and goals.

It requires a substantial amount of work on the part of both the supplier and the purchaser to obtain the big rewards of mutual breakthrough. Patience and persistence are required to sustain the investment in relationship building. The lack of evidence of substantial reward in the earlier stages may be disappointing for those who are interested only in the short term.

SUPPLIER RELATIONSHIPS

The key strategic decisions in supply management center on which supplier to pursue and what kinds of relationships to maintain with suppliers. Strategic supply management is founded on the conviction that a significant competitive edge can be gained from the suppliers an organization has developed and its supply systems and supplier relationships. Any organization's desire to satisfy its customers and to provide continuing improvement in its customer service is dependent on its suppliers to help it accomplish this goal. (See Figure 13–1.)

Supplier performance has a greater impact on the productivity, quality, and competitiveness of the organization than most managers realize. Recent trends to buy instead of make, to outsource instead of continuing to make, to improve quality, to lower inventories,

FIGURE 13–1
Customer Satisfaction Depends on Supplier Performance

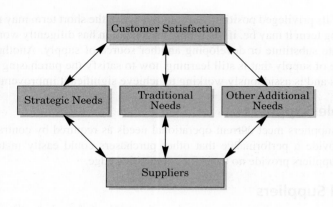

FIGURE 13–2
Simplified Supply Chain Perspective Showing the Three Core Links

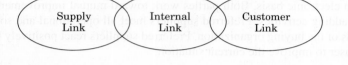

to integrate supplier and purchaser systems, and to create cooperative relationships such as partnerships have underlined the need for outstanding supplier performance.

In the supply chain management perspective, the link between the buying organization and its direct suppliers (upstream) is one of the two primary external ones. The other link, between the buying organization and its customers (downstream), continues the chain on the exit, or distribution, side. The ability of any organization to connect these two external links through its internal organization will, to a large extent, determine the effectiveness of its supply chain. Figure 13–2 provides a simplified overview of these links. Since, in any chain, the weakest link determines the strength of the whole chain, it is important that the strength of each link be equal and congruent. It is also a relatively simple perspective that greater strength in any one link can create a customer-dominant, internally dominant, or supplier-dominant chain. The prime objective in supplier relationships is, therefore, to develop a supply link that will provide a short- and long-term strategic competitive advantage.

Supplier Relationship Context

The criticality or impact of the supplier choice may vary and the acquisition process and final decision may change depending on the nature of the purchase, whether it is a repeat, a modified repeat, or a new requirement, the size of the dollar amount involved, and the market conditions. Whereas in the past most buyers felt that the supplier selection decision should be purchasing's domain, today's trend to team procurement recognizes that it is necessary to bring together key organizational resources outside and inside of the supply area to achieve sound supplier choices. Moreover, the trend to fewer suppliers, longer-term contracts, e-procurement, and continuing improvement in quality, delivery, price, and service requires much closer coordination and communication between various people in both the buying and selling organizations. Therefore, improving buyer–seller relationships is a key concern.

Outstanding supplier performance normally requires extensive communication and cooperation between various representatives of the buying organization and the selling organization over a long period of time. In full recognition of this, progressive supply organizations are pursuing ways and means of limiting their total number of suppliers and maximizing the results from fewer key suppliers. Bringing new suppliers onstream is expensive and is often accompanied by a period of learning and aggravation for both sides. Frequent supplier switching for the sake of a seemingly lower price may not result in obtaining the best long-term value. As quality improvement programs and lean production efforts take hold, proximity of the supplier's premises to those of the purchaser becomes a significant consideration. An imaginative and aggressive supplier development effort, both with existing and new sources, holds high promise as a review of existing suppliers discloses gaps and as new technology evolves into new requirements. System and philosophical compatibility between purchaser and supplier has become more vital as ways and means are found to shorten the time taken from requisition to actual receipt of the order.

These exciting new approaches to supplier choice and relationships between suppliers and purchasers are in stark contrast to the old-fashioned, hard-nosed way of procurement. It used to be reasonably common that suppliers were dropped with little notice when they failed to provide the lowest quote on an annual contract. The ideas of sharing information and assisting suppliers to improve their performance are no longer seen as novel, but more as a necessity for world-class performance. The challenge is implementation.

When one organization supplies another with goods or services, the nature of the relationship between the two organizations is a major influencer of the ultimate value and customer satisfaction achievable. Supply management is, therefore, not simply engaged in the exchange of money for goods and services, but also in the management of the buyer–seller relationship.

In this section, the nature of supplier goodwill is discussed along with the qualifications of good and preferred suppliers, partnerships, and strategic alliances.

Supplier Goodwill

Good sources of supply are one assurance of desired quality. Progressive thinking and planning is a further assurance of improved quality tomorrow. Superior sources of supply, therefore, are an important asset to any organization.

It has long been considered sound marketing policy to develop goodwill on the part of customers toward the seller. Goodwill has been cultivated through the development of trademarks and brands, service satisfaction, utility satisfaction (goods and services are available at the right quality), extensive advertising, regular calls by sales personnel, fairness, relationship commitment and all the emotional, nontangible aspects of a professional relationship that lead the customer to see the seller as a partner and not a supplier. These days these efforts are often lumped together under the term *relationship marketing*. Sellers are jealous of this goodwill, considering it one of their major assets. It has real commercial value and is so recognized by courts of law.

Goodwill between a purchasing organization and its suppliers needs to be just as carefully cultivated and just as jealously guarded. When purchasers are as aggressive in their attempts to maintain proper and friendly relationships with suppliers as marketing managers are in their relations with customers, congruence in supply chain linkage may be achieved. Since strategic plans are so often based on the assumption that supply sources will be cooperative, it makes sense to ensure that such cooperation will be forthcoming.

Progressive companies have started to measure supplier goodwill on a regular basis using third-party research organizations to conduct surveys. The president of one electronics firm flatly stated, "No company can be world class if it does not measure on a regular basis the satisfaction level of its key suppliers and try to improve constantly on its relationships with its suppliers."

One of the interesting outcomes of supplier satisfaction surveys is the general finding that suppliers believe that the best purchasers are those who know more about the supplier's business than the supplier's own employees.

The Purchaser–Supplier Satisfaction Matrix

One of the major assessments a purchaser must make is whether the current relationship with a supplier is a satisfactory one or not. This relationship is highly complex, and different people inside the purchasing organization may have different perceptions of it. For a new supplier of a small order where no deliveries have been made, the perception of satisfaction may be based on an assessment of the agreement and the buyer's impression of the salesperson. For a long-term supplier of major needs, the assessment will be based on past and current performance, professional relationships with a number of personnel in both organizations, and even future expectations. Such assessments may well change as a result of competitive action in the marketplace. What may look like a good price deal today may not look so attractive when information comes to light that a fully competent competitor could have supplied the same materials or services for substantially less.

The matrix in Figure 13–3 provides a simple framework for clarifying the current purchaser–supplier relationship in terms of satisfaction and stability. The assumptions behind it are:

1. That satisfaction with a current supplier relationship can be assessed, whether it is satisfactory or not.
2. That an unsatisfied party (seller or purchaser or both) will attempt to move to a more satisfactory situation.
3. That attempts to move may affect the stability of the relationship.
4. That attempts to move may fall in the win-lose, as well as the lose-lose, lose-win, and win-win categories.
5. That purchaser and seller may well have different perceptions of the same relationship.
6. That many tools and techniques and approaches exist that will assist either party in moving positions and improving stability.

Obviously, any purchaser–supplier relationship could fall into any of the four quadrants in the matrix. However, only quadrant A represents a desirable region in which a reasonably stable relationship can be maintained. In each of the other quadrants attempts by purchaser or supplier or both to increase satisfaction may worsen the satisfaction of the other, thereby lowering stability in the relationship. Clearly, quadrant D, with both parties dissatisfied, represents a highly undesirable and unstable relationship.

The diagonal in the diagram may be seen as a "fairness or stability" line. As long as positions move along this line, both purchaser and supplier are at least equally well off. Its end

FIGURE 13–3
**A Simple
Purchaser–
Supplier
Satisfaction
Matrix**

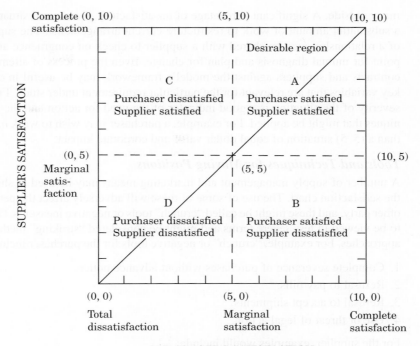

points of (0, 0) and (10, 10) represent two extremes. The (0, 0) position is completely undesirable from either standpoint. The (10, 10) position represents a utopian view rarely found in reality. It requires a degree of mutual trust and sharing and respect that is difficult to achieve in our society of "buyer beware" and where competition and the price mechanism are supposed to work freely. However, in some partnerships a relationship close to the (10, 10) state has been developed. Buyers are willing to share risks and information with the seller, and the seller is willing to open the books for buyer inspection. Risks and rewards are allocated between buyer and seller. Problems are resolved in an amicable and mutually acceptable manner, and both parties benefit from the relationship.

The middle position of (5, 5) should really be considered as a minimum acceptable goal for both sides, and few agreements should be reached by the purchaser without achieving at least this place. Adjustments in positions should, hopefully, travel along the diagonal and toward the (10, 10) corner. Substantial departures from the diagonal raise the difficulty that the agreement may be seen as less beneficial to one party than the other, with the possibility of jealousy and the attempt by the less-satisfied party to bring the other down to a more common denominator. The region of greatest stability will, therefore, lie close to the (5, 5) to (10, 10) portion of the diagonal line.

This model becomes more complex when the perceptions of both parties are considered, both with respect to their own position and the other side's. For example, the purchaser's perception may be that the relationship is in the A region. The supplier's perception may or may not match this view.

From a supply point of view, it is possible to assess the total package of current supplier relationships and to determine how many fall inside the desirable region and how many outside. A significant percentage of unsatisfactory or marginal situations will mean a substantial amount of work to restructure current arrangements. The supply perception of a relationship may be shared with a supplier to check on congruence and as a starting point for mutual diagnosis and plan for change. Even the process of attempting to assess contracts and suppliers against the model's framework may be useful in establishing the key variables that are relevant for the particular requirement under study. Furthermore, the severity of the situation is a good indicator of the need for action and the tools and techniques that might be applied. For example, a purchaser may wish to work harder at a (1, 5) than a (5, 5) situation of equal dollar value and corporate impact.

Tools and Techniques for Moving Positions

A number of supply management and marketing means may be used to shift positions on the satisfaction chart. The use of some of these will adversely affect the perceptions of the other party, and these might be called "crunch" tools or negative measures. Others are likely to be viewed in less severe terms and might be considered "stroking" methods or positive approaches. For example, "crunch" or negative tools for the purchaser include:

1. Complete severance of purchases without advance notice.
2. Refusal to pay bills.
3. Refusal to accept shipments.
4. Use or threat of legal action.

For the supplier, examples would include:

1. Refusal to send shipments as promised.
2. Unilateral price increase without notice.
3. Insistence on unreasonable length of contract, take or pay commitments, onerous escalation clauses, or other unreasonable terms and conditions and use of take it or leave it propositions.

"Stroking" or positive techniques by the purchaser would include:

1. Granting substantial volumes of business, long-run commitments, or 100 percent requirements contracts.
2. Sharing internal information on forecasts, problems, and opportunities to invite a mutual search for alternatives.
3. Evidence of willingness and ability to work toward changed behavior in the purchasing organization to improve the seller's position.
4. Rapid positive response to requests from suppliers for discussions and adjustments in price, quality, delivery, and service.

On the supplier side, examples could be:

1. Willingness and ability to make rapid price, delivery, and quality adjustments in response to purchase requests without a major hassle.
2. Invitation to the purchaser to discuss mutual problems and opportunities.
3. Giving notice substantially in advance of pending changes in price, lead times, and availability to allow the purchaser maximum time to plan ahead.

It is interesting that "stroking" techniques are more likely to be used in the A region, further strengthening the stability of the relationship, whereas the use of "crunch" tools may well accomplish short-term objectives but may impair future chances of a desirable stable relationship.

The perception of a relationship is based on both the results obtained and the process by which they have been achieved. For example, a price concession grudgingly granted by a supplier and continually negatively referred to by a supplier's personnel may create less satisfaction for the purchaser than one more amicably reached. Crunch methods pleasantly applied may be far more palatable than the same tool used in a hard-nosed way. For example, an unavoidable price increase can be explained in person by a supplier's sales manager well in advance more palatably than by a circular letter after the increase has been put into effect. A supply manager can visit a supplier's plant to determine ways and means of solving a quality problem and explain that no deliveries can be accepted until the problem is solved, instead of sending back shipment after shipment as unacceptable. The results–process combination puts a heavy emphasis on managerial judgment and capability to accomplish change effectively.

Supplier Relationship Management

The satisfaction-stability matrix underlines the need for extensive communications between both parties in the buying–selling relationship. The art of supplier relationship management from a supply perspective is to bring both sides into an effective working relationship. This requires substantial coordination work inside the purchaser's organization to ensure that the people most vitally concerned with a particular supplier's performance are fully involved in the planning and execution of a program leading to the desired long-term relationship. Therefore, the team approach to long-term supplier relationships is probably the only reasonable option. In such team acquisition, the buyer or supply manager usually plays the coordination and project manager role.

Without internal cooperation and a congruent strategic internal approach to the improvement of supplier relationships, supplier relationship management is impossible. The members of the internal team are the ones who have to deal directly with their appropriate counterparts on the supplier side. Good management of this interface is required. Immediate and concerted action needs to be taken when either side detects problems or sees opportunities. Awareness of the full details of each side's situation, aspirations, strengths, and weaknesses is necessary for any team member to be able to assess the impact of changes, problems, or opportunities on the other side. Simply stated, the seller's and purchaser's personnel need to understand their own and the other's organization very well so that both sides can work on continuing improvement for mutual benefit. Such understanding can come only through exposure, discussion, mutual problem solving, and willingness to investigate every aspect of a meaningful relationship frankly. Given that in many organizations it is difficult for individual employees in different functional areas to work well together toward a common goal, it is easy to appreciate the challenge posed by adding the tier 1/direct supplier's organization to this set. Managing relationships with the tier 1 supplier's key suppliers (tier 2) and through the tiers of suppliers may be extremely difficult. It may well be that the development of superior supplier relationships will be the most critical challenge for supply managers in the decades ahead.

Moreover, the ability to develop effective working relationships with suppliers will be dependent on supply's ability to develop effective working relationships internally. Thus, supply's status within the organization and the availability of qualified and credible supply personnel will be key determinants of the organization's ability to get the most out of its supplier force.

PARTNERSHIPS AND ALLIANCES

In the last three decades, many organizations have created partnerships and alliances with their suppliers. The term *partnership* gives lawyers discomfort because in the legal sense it has certain obligations that are not necessarily part of a standard purchaser–seller partnership. Unfortunately, considerable confusion exists regarding the meaning of partnership. The selling community has further compounded these difficulties by making it a part of a standard sales pitch to any customer. Likewise, some in the buying community have labeled every relationship a partnership, often to force concessions from suppliers. To avoid some of this confusion, some purchasers have chosen the term *preferred suppliers*.

The interest in supplier partnerships was fanned in the 1980s by the study of Japanese companies that maintained close relationships with their suppliers. This was seen as one of the key elements in the achievement of quality, fast delivery, and continuous improvement. Early adopters in North America included companies like Xerox, Honeywell, Polaroid, Motorola, and IBM. These buyer–supplier partnerships represented a substantial shift from the traditional buying–selling mode. A summary of some of the key differences is shown in Figure 13–4.

In the 1990s, buyer–supplier partnerships were focused on collaborating for mutual benefit. Many partnerships were operational. Operational goals might include standardizing and consolidating volume for standard goods, such as MRO, and forming longer-term contracts with a single source. Strategic alliances were partnerships that targeted strategic goods and services for joint programs related to quality, cost, and continuous improvement. The goals were linked to buyer and supplier competitive advantage.

FIGURE 13–4
View of Buyer–Supplier Relationship

Traditional	Partnership	
Lowest price	Total cost of ownership	
Specification-driven	End customer-driven	
Short term, reacts to market	Long term	
Trouble avoidance	Opportunity maximization	
Purchasing's responsibility	Cross-functional teams and top management involvement	
Tactical	Strategic	
Little sharing of information on both sides	Both supplier and buyer share short- and long-term plans	
	Share risk and opportunity	
	Standardization	
	Joint ventures	
	Share data	

In the 2000s, partnerships and alliances became network oriented with an emphasis on building efficient and effective multi-tiered supply chains and global networks. The focus shifted to building and maintaining resilient and sustainable supply chains.

Early Supplier/Supply Involvement (ESI)

The opportunity to affect value in the acquisition process is significantly greater in the early stages (need recognition and description) than in the later ones. Involving the supplier and the buyer in these early stages can lead to improvements in processes, design, redesign, or value analysis activities. The drive to cut cycle time, improve competitiveness, and reduce cost compels some organizations to include supplier(s) on cross-functional teams.

A supplier may participate with the hope of securing the business, or as part of an ongoing partnering/alliance relationship. Confidentiality issues often must be dealt with up front, and it must be clear to the supplier(s) if involvement guarantees the business or not.

The benefits from partnering come from intercorporate closeness. The philosophy is similar to design for manufacturability or design for assembly, in which internal barriers are removed between design, marketing, manufacturing engineering, quality assurance, procurement, and operations to avoid functional suboptimization. By removing functional barriers associated with "throwing the design over the wall," new products and services may be designed and introduced faster, thereby achieving significant quality and cost improvements. By making supply and suppliers part of the process—it could be called "design for procurability." Others call it "early supply/supplier involvement" or ESI. Moreover, if suppliers involve their suppliers in the process, the supply organization has access to a wide pool of talent all focused on the needs of its customers. The supplier may then consider the customer/partner's future needs while making decisions about investments, hiring, new products, processes, or systems. It is this latent potential for improvement that the partnership tries to tap.

Partnerships may be seen as an alternate solution for the make option in the make-or-buy decision. Similarly, a partnership could be a substitute for vertical integration. A partnership attempts to unlock the benefits from shared information without the disadvantages of ownership.

Partnerships require hard work on both sides to make them effective. They require a tolerance of mistakes and a real commitment to make the relationship work. The key idea is that each partner might enhance its own competitive position through the knowledge and resources shared by the other.

Partner Selection

When selecting potential partners, soft and hard factors are considered. All of the traditional hard factors of quality, delivery, cost, environment, safety and continuing improvement, financial and management stability, risk reduction, and technological accomplishment are relevant. Soft factors also become important: for example, congruence of management values on issues like customer satisfaction, concern for quality, employee involvement, supplier relationships, and personal compatibility between functional counterparts. Vital questions are: Can we work well together? Can we respect and trust each other? Do we like each other? Questions like these are not answered easily and quickly. It is, therefore, more likely that potential partners are found among the organization's best current suppliers. (See Figure 13–5.) Developing partnerships takes time and

FIGURE 13–5
Some Indicators of a Successful Partnering Effort

- Formal communication processes
- Commitment to our suppliers' success
- Mutual profitability
- Stable relationships, not dependent on a few personalities
- Consistent and specific feedback on supplier performance
- Realistic expectations
- Employee accountability for ethical business conduct
- Meaningful information sharing
- Guidance to supplier in defining improvement efforts
- Nonadversarial negotiations and decisions based on total cost of ownership

Source: SEMATECH.

some organizations may be ill prepared for the amount of time it does take before seeing the desired results.

Types of Partnerships and Alliances

Partnerships and alliances come in many forms and are structured for many purposes. Two types of relationships are common: operational and strategic.

Operational Partnerships

Operational partnerships are typically formed around leverage items in portfolio analysis where the attainment of the desired levels of quality, quantity, delivery, price, and service are achieved at the lowest total cost of ownership. Often operational partnerships focus on acquisition process improvements as a means of achieving the goal of lowest acquisition cost, a component of total cost of ownership. By partnering with a single source or more, depending on the risk assessment and strategy for risk mitigation, the commodity or category manager can focus on lowering total cost primarily through acquisition process improvements, consumption management techniques such as simplification and standardization, and streamlining inventory and delivery systems. For example, an e-procurement system might be used to automate orders, and a vendor-managed inventory system might be implemented to shorten lead times and reduce the amount of inventory in the supply chain.

One potential outcome of a partnering effort may be co-location of a supplier in the buyer's organization. As organizations look for ways to do more work with fewer people and achieve the productivity and competitiveness goals of the firm, they are increasingly looking to suppliers for expertise and assistance. Having a key supplier locate personnel in a department in the buying organization who can function as buyer, planner, and salesperson can improve buyer–seller communications and processes, absorb work typically done by the firm's employees, and reduce administrative and sales costs.

Strategic Partnerships and Alliances

A strategic buyer–supplier partnership or alliance makes a strategic difference to both buyer and seller and attempts to seek sustainable competitive advantage. Buyer and seller share the conviction that it is in the interest of both to formalize the relationship beyond the standard mode of trade. As cornerstones of corporate strategy, these alliances are of major concern to top management and reinforce the perspective that suppliers and supplier relationships are of strategic concern to any organization. These alliances are often technology based and require substantial investment of both buyer and seller to achieve major market breakthroughs.

The success of strategic alliances depends on many factors, including alignment between the organization's management in terms of quality, continuous improvement, and customer service; commitment and involvement at multiple levels of both organizations (C-suite, operational functions), the implementation and use of appropriate technology applications, negotiated agreement on goals, key performance indicators, allocation of risks and rewards, and a commitment to problem-solving and continuous improvement. The key driver of competitiveness will drive the alliance, which is one means of achieving quality, continuous improvement, and innovation.

Strategic alliances are long-term relationships focused on mutual strategic and tactical goals and may include customer/supplier team support to promote mutual success and profitability. Continuing improvement is an objective, and evidence of accomplishments must exist. The partners must have a passion to help each other succeed; place a high priority on the relationship; and include shared risks, opportunities, strategies, and technology road maps. It is expected that most organizations would have a limited number (6 to 20) of strategic alliances and each would normally have a top executive assigned to it. This executive would interact several times per year with his or her counterpart in the selling organization. Together they monitor internal progress on joint projects and smooth the way for changes necessary for success. Regular contact via various media between buyer and seller representatives manages one level of the relationship. There will also be frequent contact by operational project team members who perform and manage operational tasks related to the goals of the alliance. A substantial number of people from various functions in the buying and selling organizations will have some role to play in the alliance.

The Longer-Term Perspective

Another interesting question is what happens over a longer period of time. Do benefits continue to accelerate, or does the law of diminishing returns set in? Companies like Honda that have maintained partnerships with some suppliers since the late 1970s have clearly found a way to continue generating benefits for both parties. Whether all companies can sustain the relationship over the long term probably depends on many variables, including what the original goals of the partnership were, the level of commitment of both sides to continuing to develop the relationships, and the specific situation of the companies and industry. Thinking about the longer term at the initial stages of the relationship may help to prevent dissatisfaction in the long run.

Concerns about Partnerships and Alliances

There are serious concerns about partnerships and alliances. Buyer–supplier relationships range from transactional to cooperative to collaborative. Not all supply professionals believe that collaborative or even cooperative relationships are better than the competition-based culture upon which most traditional procurements tools and techniques are based. One concern is that at least one partner might wish to take advantage of the preferred status and let the commitment and relationship deteriorate. In a technology-driven world, intellectual rights to new technology are extremely valuable and the preservation of secrecy a vital concern. It is critical for purchasers and suppliers to assess if the other can be trusted with information that might shape competitive strategy in years to come.

Similarly, whether cutting off the option to "shop around" is in the best long-term interest of the purchaser will depend on its customer-satisfaction-driven strategies. The decision to enter into a partnership is an organizational commitment, not just a procurement one. It is either of operational or strategic importance depending on the nature of the relationship.

Often partnerships or strategic alliances involve single or sole sourcing a particular requirement so the risk may be high. For the buyer, one danger in single sourcing lies in becoming puppets of suppliers. Suppliers know that customers depend on them, and they may charge excessively, let quality or delivery slip, or slow down or stop continuing improvement programs. For the supplier, one danger is becoming overly dependent on the buying organization for a major portion of revenue. Buyers know that these suppliers depend on them. They may demand unreasonable concessions on price or quality and stop sharing necessary information or benefits. This is where careful supplier relationship management becomes important. It requires an understanding and identification of value. Value is the ultimate long-term life-cycle cost and benefit to the user of the product or service acquired. It does not necessarily mean lowest purchase price, or lowest investment in inventory, or fastest delivery time, or lowest delivery cost, or longest life, or highest disposal value, or even the highest attainable quality; it is an optimal amount cutting across all of these. The purchase price frequently is one important part of this total. It is the duty of the supply manager to make sure that the purchase represents exceptional long-term value. Moreover, in the establishment of preferred suppliers or partnerships, it is normal to agree on future quality, delivery, and price goals, in full recognition of learning curve theory and the commitment of both buyer and seller to continuous improvement.

Another danger in single sourcing is that an unpredictable event such as the tsunami in Japan, Hurricane Katrina in New Orleans, political upheaval, a factory disaster, or an act of terrorism will severely disrupt supply chains. Supply managers, under considerable internal and external pressure, are focused on designing and maintaining resilient supply chains, meaning the supply chain is capable of resisting disruptive forces and, when it is not, it is capable of returning to full function with little damage.

Multi-tier Supplier Relationships

The length and complexity of supply chains or networks compound the issues and challenges of partnerships and alliances. While a lean supply network may make relationship management more feasible, it also increases the risk of supply disruptions. Supply chain organizations often struggle with extending the business philosophy and practice of partnerships and alliances beyond their direct, first-tier suppliers to their key suppliers. Long, complex supply networks have many global suppliers of various sizes and maturity on multiple aspects, including management, IT, human capital, and supply management. This increases the difficulties of sharing the values, goals, and processes of the partnership or alliance.

Partners are in a dynamic supply network where power, position, revenue, and cost savings shift as they work together to achieve quality, cost, resiliency, and sustainability.

Conclusion

Supplier evaluation is an integral part of the acquisition process. There has to be a check to ensure that the contractual arrangement is adhered to by the supplier. Methods for evaluation range from informal to formal and have to suit the criteria established for supplier selection. Suppliers may be ranked from unacceptable to acceptable, preferred, and exceptional.

Supplier relationship management is just as important to the organization as customer relationship management. Therefore, although supplier relations are a prime responsibility for supply professionals, they also represent a responsibility for other functions and top management. To gain satisfaction for each side, it is the goal of relationship management to assure long-term stability. Partnerships require a high degree of satisfaction and a degree of closeness and cooperation among purchaser and seller not present in normal supplier relationships. Strategic alliances represent a special form of partnership in which both parties exploit an opportunity that may provide a sustainable competitive advantage. Extending the relationship to multiple tiers in a global supply chain or network is an ongoing challenge for supply managers.

Questions for Review and Discussion

1. What is a weighted point evaluation system? Why is it used?
2. When might it be appropriate to conduct a formal, rather than an informal, supplier evaluation?
3. What are the similarities and differences between evaluating new and existing sources of supply?
4. Why is purchasing focusing more attention on a supplier's management as part of the evaluation process? How might this evaluation be conducted?
5. Why are buyer–supplier relationships important?
6. Why create a partnership?
7. What is a strategic alliance and why is it used?
8. What are the goals of early supplier involvement (ESI)? How does ESI fit in with cross-functional teams?
9. What are the differences between an operational alliance and a strategic alliance?
10. What is the relationship between satisfaction and stability in buyer–supplier relations?

References

Forrest, W. "McDonald's Applies SRM Strategy to Global Technology Buy." *Purchasing* 135, no. 12 (2006), pp. 16–17.

Krause, D. R.; R. B. Handfield; and B. B. Tyler. "The Relationship Between Supplier Development, Commitment, Social Capital Accumulation and Performance Improvement." *Journal of Operations Management* 25, no. 2 (2007), pp. 528–545.

Leuschner, R.; D. S. Rogers; and F. F. Charvet. "A Meta-Analysis of Supply Chain Integration and Firm Performance." *Journal of Supply Chain Management,* 49, no. 2 (2013) pp. 34–57.

Liker, J. K., and T.Y. Choi. "Building Deep Supplier Relationships." *Harvard Business Review* 83, no. 1 (2004), pp. 104–113.

Mena, C.; A. Humphries; and T. Y. Choi. "Toward a Theory of Multi-Tier Supply Chain Management." *Journal of Supply Chain Management* 49, no. 2 (2013), pp. 58–77.

Oke, A.; D. I. Prajogo; and J. Jayaram. "Strengthening the Innovation Chain: The Role of Internal Innovation Climate and Strategic Relationships with Supply Chain Partners." *Journal of Supply Chain Management,* 49 (2013), pp. 43–58.

Robitaille, D. *Managing Supplier-Related Processes.* Chico, CA: Paton Professional, 2007.

Reuter, C.; K. Foerst; E. Hartmann; and C. Blome. "Sustainable Global Supplier Management: The Role of Dynamic Capabilities in Achieving Competitive Advantage." *Journal of Supply Chain Management* 46 (2010), pp. 45–63.

Teague, P. E. "How to Improve Supplier Performance." *Purchasing* 136, no. 4 (2007), pp. 1–32.

Case 13–1

APC Europe

On Thursday, October 5, Maggie Agnelli, the packaging purchasing manager for APC's European division in Utrecht, the Netherlands, wondered what she should say in the next day's meeting with the plant manager of Branco, a custom packaging supplier. In the last three quarters, Branco's quality performance rating had shown a steady decline. Maggie believed it was essential to get the plant manager's cooperation to avoid future problems.

APC

APC, a diversified international manufacturing organization headquartered in the United States, offered a wide range of products to both industrial and consumer markets. Its Utrecht plant employed approximately 400 people. European sales were €150 million a year and the company had a long-standing track record of successful business performance.

Each division operated within a set of corporate guidelines and was responsible for its own financial performance.

QUALITY CONTROL

Contributing to the success of APC was a commitment to strict quality standards in purchasing. Coordination between each supplier and APC's plant was crucial to avoid production slowdowns. Contact was maintained directly between plant personnel and sales representatives. When a problem in the manufacturing plant arose due to the supplier's product, the appropriate sales representative was immediately notified by email via a standard form called "Nonconformance

Action Report" completed by the plant operator closest to the problem. The sales representative was required to return, by email a standard "Feedback Form" to acknowledge the problem and explain how it was to be solved.

Supplier deviations from standard, as reported on the Nonconformance Action Report, were also forwarded to each purchasing manager. The supply assistant compiled these forms, together with information collected on a number of other supplier performance criteria, such as accuracy of the quantity delivered, shipments on time, and accuracy of paperwork (see Exhibit 1). Each quarter, each purchasing manager used the information collected to compute a "Supplier Performance Rating." Suppliers were all rated on the same scoring criteria.

The criteria and scoring system implemented by APC (Europe) had been developed by the headquarters supply group in North America several years earlier and reflected the key aspects of supplier performance deemed to be important by APC management. Suppliers received a copy of the scoring criteria so that they were fully aware of how they were evaluated. At the end of each quarter, they were advised of their rating. APC (Europe) maintained detailed documentation of supplier activity and variance from norms.

The rating criteria included three categories: quality, delivery, and continuous performance, with quality accounting for the largest portion—50 percent of the total rating. Within each category was a list of items. Each item was scored according to the supplier's provision of that item, on a scale from 0 to 4. Scores were then weighted

EXHIBIT 1 Supplier Performance Scoring Criteria

Quality		
Item	**Grade**	**Criteria**
Rejected and Nonconforming	4	No rejected or nonconforming shipments.
	3	Up to 5% of shipments nonconforming.
	2	>5–10% of shipments nonconforming.
	1	>10–20% of shipments nonconforming.
	0	>20% of shipments nonconforming.
Process Capability, Data/Samples	4	Less than 1% outside control limits and samples/data received for all shipments.
	3	Up to 5% outside limits and 90–99% of shipments have samples/data.
	2	5–10% outside limits and 80–90% of shipments have samples/data.
	1	10–20% outside limits and 70–80% of shipments have samples/data.
	0	More than 20% outside limits and <70% of shipments have samples/data.

Delivery		
Item	**Grade**	**Criteria**
Quantity	4	All correct quantities (within tolerance).
	3	Up to 5% shipments incorrect (within tolerance).
	2	>5–10% shipments incorrect (within tolerance).
	1	>10–20% shipments incorrect (within tolerance).
	0	>20% shipments incorrect (within tolerance).
Time	4	All shipments on time (within tolerance).
	3	Up to 5% of shipments outside tolerance.
	2	>5–10% of shipments outside tolerance.
	1	>10–20% of shipments outside tolerance.
	0	>20% of shipments outside tolerance.
Paperwork	4	No missing lot numbers, packing lists, invoice errors, or other required documentation.
	3	Up to 5% of shipments have errors.
	2	>5–10% of shipments have errors.
	1	>10–20% of shipments have errors.
	0	>20% of shipments have errors.
Shipment Condition	4	All shipments received in expected condition.
	3	Up to 5% of shipments have damaged pallets, inadequate packaging, or damaged cartons.
	2	>5–10% of shipments are damaged as above.
	1	>10–20% of shipments are damaged as above.
	0	>20% of shipments are damaged as above.

(Continued)

EXHIBIT 1 **Supplier Performance Scoring Criteria (*Continued*)**

Continuous Improvement		
Item	**Grade**	**Criteria**
Corrective Action	4	CA response and implementation within 30 days.
	3	CA response and implementation within 31–60 days.
	2	CA response within 30 days.
	1	CA response within 31–60 days.
	0	No response within 60 days.
Cost, Lead Time, Lot Size Reduction	4	Major reduction in unit cost, lead time, and lot size.
	2	Minor reduction in unit cost, lead time, and lot size.
	0	No reduction in unit cost, lead time, and lot size.

and totaled. A total performance rating for the quarter was derived by summing categories (see Exhibit 2 for Branco's scoring sheet). The supplier's maximum possible score was 4. An overall rating of 3 was considered the minimum acceptable performance rating.

BRANCO

Maggie had been watching Branco's performance ratings for the last three quarters with some concern. Although the problems incurred each quarter were rectified by Branco, the next quarter brought even more problems. As a result, Branco's performance rating had dropped further each quarter. Finally, in the most recent quarter, Branco's rating dropped below the minimum acceptable standard of 3 (see Exhibits 2 and 3). When Branco's sales representative, Hil Damsma, received the rating, she had called Maggie immediately, and she was just as concerned. They agreed that a meeting was necessary right away, and that APC's production manager, Eric Koendeeile, and Branco's plant manager, Ruael Mooij, should also attend. They agreed to meet at APC on Friday, October 6, at 2 p.m.

Branco, located near Amsterdam, was the supplier of packing cartons for APC's custom products. These packing

EXHIBIT 2 **Branco Performance Rating July 1–September 30**

Category	Item Description	Time Score	Weight	Category Score	Weight	Total Score
Quality	Rejected and nonconforming	3	0.65	1.92		
	Process capability, data/samples	2	0.35	0.70		
				2.65	0.50	1.33
Delivery	Quantity	4	0.30	1.20		
	Timely deliveries	4	0.30	1.20		
	Paperwork	4	0.20	0.80		
	Shipment condition	4	0.20	0.80		
				4.00	0.30	1.20
Continuous improvement	Corrective action response	3	0.50	1.50		
	Cost, lead time, lot size reduction	0	0.50	0.00		
				1.50	0.20	0.30
TOTAL						2.83

EXHIBIT 3
Branco's Performance Rating (July 1– September 30)

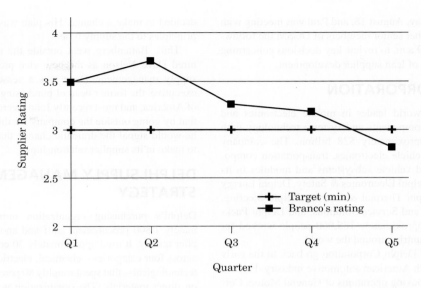

cartons were odd sizes and required custom specifications. Custom packaging was required for special orders, promotion, and unique customer requirements. Many orders involved small lots and specifications changed frequently. As a result, it had been necessary for Branco to customize production operations to meet the unique requirements of APC. Branco had become the only supplier of all custom packing cartons to APC (Europe). Therefore, Maggie could not source a custom product from a different supplier easily or quickly. Branco delivered on a daily basis and its yearly sales to APC (Europe) amounted to about €500,000. Custom work required a substantial commitment from both parties. The relationship of trust between APC (Europe) and Branco had taken eight years to solidify.

Quality problems were costly for APC (Europe). A number of Branco's orders had included defective cartons due to overlapping flaps. Nonconformance problems such as this were typically not identified until a production run had started, and equipment stalls occurred. Production used a fully automated line process, and a stall at one end resulted in a slowdown throughout. Because the defective cartons would not affect the end product to

the customer, the plant continued the run in order to meet customer deadlines. However, the last Branco shipment of defective packing cartons resulted in a 30 percent production loss for an entire day's (two shifts) production. At full production, the plant ran 2,000 cartons per hour, with three operators at €28 per hour each.

THE MEETING WITH BRANCO

Over the last few years, Maggie felt things had changed drastically in the industry. At one time, as a purchaser, she might have demanded that the supplier make changes "or else." This was no longer the case. Maggie reflected, "In such a tight market, you just don't drop suppliers. Relationships are everything."

In the meeting scheduled for the next day, Maggie felt it was essential that she impress upon Hil and Ruael her desire to continue a strong relationship. Yet she would somehow have to convince Ruael that something had to change at his end, without confronting him. Maggie wondered, "What should my agenda be for this meeting? What should I say?"

Case 13–2
Delphi Corporation

Paul Brent, director, lean purchasing operations at Delphi Corporation, was preparing for his meeting the following week with Dave Nelson, vice president, global supply

management. Dave had recently appointed Paul to head the new supplier development initiative in the Delphi global supply management (DGSM) organization. It was currently Tuesday, August 18, and Paul was meeting with Dave and the other senior members of DGSM the following Monday at 9 a.m. to review key decisions concerning implementation of lean supplier development.

DELPHI CORPORATION

Delphi was a world leader in mobile electronics and transportation components and systems technology with revenues of approximately $28 billion. The company manufactured vehicle electronics, transportation components, integrated vehicle subsystems and modules in its six divisions: Delphi Electronics & Safety, Delphi Energy & Chassis, Delphi Thermal & Interior, Delphi Steering, Delphi Product and Service Solutions, and Delphi Packard Electric. Approximately 185,000 people worked for Delphi in 38 countries around the world.

The roots of Delphi Corporation go back to the early days of the North American automotive industry. Formed from the parts making operations of General Motors Corporation (GM) in 1991, Delphi was incorporated in 1998 and became independent in 1999 following its initial public stock offering (NYSE: DPH).

THE DELPHI MANUFACTURING SYSTEM

J. T. Battenberg III, former chairman and CEO of Delphi, launched the Delphi Manufacturing System (DMS) in 1996. This initiative was modeled after the principles of the Toyota Production System and represented the cornerstone of the company's drive to become a lean enterprise. DMS focused on six interdependent elements aimed at eliminating waste: employee environment and involvement, workplace organization, quality, operational availability, material movement, and flow manufacturing. During the decade that followed the introduction of DMS, Delphi received 23 Shingo Awards for Manufacturing Excellence.

DMS was, however, focused exclusively on Delphi plants and manufacturing facilities. The company's approach to supplier cost reductions involved the traditional industry practice of negotiating annual price reductions for purchased goods and services. Although this approach provided a steady source of cost savings that were important to the company's overall financial well-being, it only delivered low single-digit cost reduction performance.

In 2002, facing continuing significant cost pressures from its customers, Battenberg examined opportunities to step up Delphi's cost-reduction efforts. Recognizing that approximately 60 percent of Delphi's costs were represented by the purchase of parts and materials, Battenberg decided to make a change. His plan was to extend DMS principles to the supply base.

Thus, Battenberg went outside the organization and hired Dave Nelson as the new vice president of global supply management. Dave was a seasoned purchasing executive, the former head of purchasing at TRW, Honda of America, and most recently John Deere. Battenberg felt that by going outside the company for this important post he would signal the dramatic change that Delphi needed to make in its supplier relationships.

DELPHI SUPPLY MANAGEMENT STRATEGY

Delphi's purchasing organization numbered approximately 1,800 procurement staff and another 500 in supplier quality. It used approximately 30 commodity teams, across four categories—chemical, electrical, metallic, and technological—that spent roughly 80 percent of the dollars on direct materials. The organization was a centralized-hybrid structure, matrixed by divisions and regions. Divisional purchasing directors, regional purchasing directors, and commodity directors reported to Dave Nelson and to the divisional and regional presidents. The commodity team leaders were divisional buyers, and typically included cross-functional representation, depending on the need, from areas such as quality, manufacturing, and product engineering. Staff was largely located in the business units, with 50 people at the head office.

The Delphi goals for supply were to take a total cost focus, adopt strategic sourcing, extend lean principles to suppliers, and establish deep supplier relationships. To accomplish these goals, Dave Nelson wanted to shift from a price to a cost focus and launch lean into the supply base. He proposed creating teams to focus on three key areas: strategic sourcing (including global sourcing) for direct and indirect purchases, cost management, and lean supply development. He commented on the challenge:

> With a total spend of approximately $14 billion in direct purchases and $3 billion in indirect purchases, our global supply management team should play a major role in achieving the objective of significantly reducing costs within Delphi manufacturing and our supply base. We need to help our suppliers better understand the significant cost pressures facing Delphi because of customer demands for annual price reductions. So we need to work much more closely with our suppliers to get and keep costs out—not merely push them onto someone else.
>
> I identified nine key elements of the Delphi's lean supply transformation (see Exhibit 1). All nine elements need to be integrated to provide the maximum benefits.

EXHIBIT 1
Delphi Lean Supply Management Strategies: Nine Elements Working in an Integrated Way

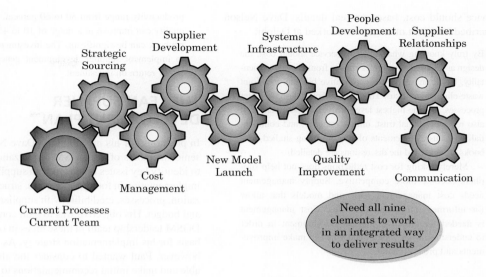

Strategic Sourcing

Supplier Development

Systems Infrastructure

People Development

Supplier Relationships

Current Processes Current Team

Cost Management

New Model Launch

Quality Improvement

Communication

Need all nine elements to work in an integrated way to deliver results

EXHIBIT 2
Delphi Strategic Sourcing Framework

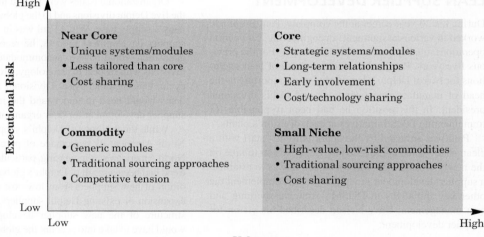

High

Low

Executional Risk

Near Core
• Unique systems/modules
• Less tailored than core
• Cost sharing

Core
• Strategic systems/modules
• Long-term relationships
• Early involvement
• Cost/technology sharing

Commodity
• Generic modules
• Traditional sourcing approaches
• Competitive tension

Small Niche
• High-value, low-risk commodities
• Traditional sourcing approaches
• Cost sharing

Low

High

Value

STRATEGIC SOURCING

When Dave Nelson arrived at Delphi, the company had a global supply base of nearly 7,000 suppliers. Believing that working with substantially fewer suppliers would make Delphi more agile and reduce costs, Dave Nelson was vehement in his vision to right-size the supply base (see Exhibit 2 for the Delphi strategic sourcing framework):

> Our vision is that components with high value and complexity are core and ultimately will be sourced to a group of *strategic suppliers* with whom we will have

close and deep relationships. Lower-value materials that still have high complexity will be sourced to *near-core suppliers*. *Niche suppliers* would be those with unique products or with patents that restrict Delphi's ability to compete. Commodities with low value and less complexity will be sourced using a more conventional approach.

COST MANAGEMENT

Effective cost management required the ability to develop and manage cost standards that determined what a part or service should cost, based on real details. Dave Nelson described how cost management worked at Delphi:

> By truly knowing what a part or service should cost, the design and sourcing dynamics change from an auction mentality, based on aggressive competitive bidding, to a joint waste-elimination focus. This leads to better designs, better processes, and the highest level of true competitiveness. It also requires mutual trust, utmost integrity, and confidentiality because all elements of cost are being studied—the books are open and the discussions are detailed.

> Merely asking for cost reductions does not help suppliers become more competitive. Supply management needs cost management tools and models that allow for informed purchasing decisions. Cost management is needed for effective supplier development in order to understand what, where, and when to make improvements and process changes.

LEAN SUPPLIER DEVELOPMENT

During his 30-year career at the company, Paul Brent had worked in various assignments in engineering, production operations, quality, and as a plant manager. For the previous five years, Paul had been the director of lean operations for two of Delphi's largest divisions, reporting to the head of manufacturing operations and to his divisional president. In this position he had been responsible for implementing DMS initiatives at each division's plants.

Paul was attracted by the opportunity to "start with a clean slate" when approached by Dave Nelson to take on the newly created role. Dave's objective was to establish a supplier development group that would complement the other key initiatives in DGSM—strategic sourcing and cost management. Dave Nelson described his vision for supplier development:

> Supplier development requires the expertise of engineers dedicated to enabling suppliers to achieve the best levels of lean manufacturing in their plant operations. I want to put together a group of Delphi supplier development engineers who will work directly with suppliers, in their plants, on initiatives designed to eliminate waste in areas such as process improvements, operational productivity and efficiencies, product quality, and delivery.

> My experience has been that the magnitude of cost savings opportunities can be dramatic with suppliers who are involved—when they experience the exact same double-digit improvements as Delphi's manufacturing operations achieve through DMS. Reduction in people costs range from 20 to nearly 50 percent, increases in

productivity range from 30 to 60 percent, and first-time quality can improve in a range of 10 to 45 percent. The payback can be significant. The investment in resources to implement supplier development generally yields a 3-to-1 return on investment.

THE LEAN SUPPLIER DEVELOPMENT PLAN

In preparing for his meeting with Dave Nelson and other senior members of the DGSM organization, Paul wanted to identify key issues related to lean supplier development implementation in four general areas: structure and organization, processes, credibility with suppliers, and resources and budget. His objective was to gain consensus from the DGSM leadership team in these areas in order to form the basis for his implementation strategy. As a starting point, however, Paul wanted to consider the alternatives available and make initial recommendations to the group.

Organizational issues were related to differences among the five Delphi divisions and to the global nature of the company's supply base. While Paul was in favor of a common supplier development process, he recognized that his organization would have to accommodate differences across divisions with respect to technology, processes, product life cycle, and customer base. Divisional and regional presidents would need to understand the implications of lean supplier development for their organization and suppliers.

While the majority of Delphi's suppliers were based in North America, its percentage of purchases from outside North American was increasing, particularly from Asia. This trend had been a result of Delphi's global expansion, the addition of new suppliers from low-cost regions, and global expansion of existing Delphi suppliers. Consequently, the structure of the new supplier development organization would have to take into account the global reach of Delphi's operations. How quickly should he expand supplier development to international suppliers? Should he create supplier development offices in key regions around the world?

In addition, there was also the matter of where Paul would get his supplier development engineers. Delphi had developed a significant depth of lean manufacturing knowledge through DMS implementation at its plants. Paul also had a strong network in the company that he could tap. However, Paul wanted to set some guidelines concerning what percentage of his group would be recruited internally and what target percentage would come from outside the company.

A second and related issue was the need to establish a lean supplier development process. Paul wanted to identify the steps that would be used to implement lean supplier development, starting with supplier selection and ending with implementation of a plan agreed to with the supplier. However, Paul had a number of questions concerning how this process would work. For example, how would suppliers be selected to participate? Would they be nominated by someone in DGSM, by someone outside the DGSM group, such as a plant, or could suppliers volunteer to participate? Criteria needed to be established regarding when a supplier represented a good opportunity for development. In addition, what steps would be followed concerning meetings, assessment, and implementation—who would be involved from Delphi and the supplier and when?

Paul was especially concerned with how suppliers would receive Delphi's supplier development initiative. He commented on the history:

> After years of being pounded on with the heavy-handed approach, they may not muster the faith, will, or commitment to shift to this new lean paradigm—even when it means larger profits, higher quality, and enhanced competitiveness for them. They may not trust Delphi because of bad experiences in the past with customers who promise trust but fail to deliver on commitments and responsibilities. We must change this viewpoint held by some suppliers.

How would benefits be shared between Delphi and its suppliers? Dave Nelson had indicated to Paul in their first meeting, "Conceptually, Delphi's value proposition is to share gains on a 50/50 basis with suppliers, but each situation should evaluated individually." Paul wanted to establish specific ground rules concerning how savings would be shared.

A final issue was related to the budget and resources. Dave Nelson had already indicated to Paul that he expected the supplier development group would grow to 50 engineers. Paul estimated that each person would cost approximately $100,000 per year in salary and benefits, plus related expenses such as travel. How fast Paul grew the number of supplier development engineers would be influenced by a number of factors, such as supplier acceptance and payback from the initiative.

Paul also recognized that a primary measure of the performance of his new group would be cost reductions. Consequently, he would not only have to set targets on headcount, but also savings. However, identifying savings was not always a simple task. For example, how long would cost reductions be counted? Would it accumulate over the life of the contract, the life of the component, or for the current fiscal year only? Would cost avoidance and cost reductions both be measured, or would only year-over-year piece price reductions be measured?

As Paul sat down at his desk to prepare for his meeting the following Monday, he began to appreciate the complexity of the challenge that lay ahead. While lean supplier development represented a significant opportunity for Delphi, implementation would need to be carefully planned and executed to avoid potential problems with the company's divisions and their key suppliers.

Case 13–3
Northeastern Hospital

On Tuesday, October 7, Kathy Cheung, senior buyer at Northeastern Hospital in Newton, Massachusetts, was examining three supplier proposals for recycling and waste transfer services. Hospital policy required supplier contract reviews every five years, and Kathy needed to prepare a recommendation that would be considered at the sourcing team meeting the following day.

NORTHEASTERN HOSPITAL

Northeastern Hospital (Northeastern) was one of largest acute-care teaching hospitals in Massachusetts, dedicated to excellence in patient care, teaching, and research. Physicians, residents, and staff numbered nearly 15,000, and the hospital provided care for more than one million patient visits each year. Newton was located in the Boston metropolitan area, which had a population of approximately 4.5 million people.

Northeastern was committed to environmental stewardship and to reducing the hospital's dependence on nonrenewable energy and waste sources through five key environmental programs: energy conservation, waste management, sustainable transportation, procurement, and an awareness and education campaign. The hospital's waste and recycling program included a collection of glass, newspaper, fine paper, cardboard, mixed plastic, aluminum, and organic materials. In the previous year, Northeastern collected and recycled approximately 200 tons of co-mingled products, 240 tons of paper products, 290 tons of cardboard, and 230 tons of organic waste.

Purchasing played a critical role in Northeastern's recycling and waste management initiative. It was responsible for managing the infrastructure and suppliers involved with recycling activities.

THE RECYCLING CONTRACT

Northeastern had a policy of limiting contracts with suppliers to a maximum of five years, and most contracts were awarded for one, three, or five years. When contracts expired, purchasing would issue request for quotations (RFQs) or request for proposals (RFPs) to identify opportunities for improved quality, service, and lower total costs. The RFP and RFQ process was typically managed by a sourcing team that involved purchasing and representatives from key stakeholder groups who would be impacted by the sourcing decision. Along with Kathy, Sam Griffiths, supervisor of grants, and Riccardo Cosentino, facility manager, sat on the sourcing team for the recycling and waste management RFP. The expectation was that the recycling and waste transfer services contract would be awarded for five years.

As part of the process to create and review RFPs, the team was required to create a rating system that included set criteria and a point system, which would be used to evaluate each proposal. To develop the rating system for the recycling RFP, the team evaluated the current situation and identified key components of the contract. The committee considered past contractual issues to ensure that previous problems or missing components were addressed. The point system was also expected to reflect the overall strategic direction of the hospital. Northeastern set several high-level criteria, including best value-based pricing, service, and specification, and a site visit evaluation. The purpose of the site visit was to see the location, staffing, equipment, and capacity of each potential supplier. Points were allocated to specific items within each section and then each section was weighted based on importance. Once the criteria were established, the committee created the RFP, which outlined the scope of work, bidder instructions, terms and conditions of the contract, service and pricing specifications, and clarification of what Northeastern was looking for from proposals overall. Exhibit 1 provides details for selected sections of Northeastern's recycling and waste transfer services RFP.

The RFP was posted on Northeastern's purchasing department website on September 3. Two weeks later,

Kathy hosted a day for potential suppliers to visit the hospital and examine its operations, and proposals were due on September 26. Proposals were submitted by Murray Brothers Ltd. (MBD), Newton Waste Management Services Inc. (NWMS), and Universal Waste Management and Recycling (UWM).

Once the RFP responses came in, the committee evaluated each based on their RFP response, financial data, and reference checks. Supplier site visits were conducted on October 2 and 3.

THE MURRAY BROTHERS DISPOSAL LTD. PROPOSAL

MBD was the current supplier for recycling and waste transfer services at Northeastern, originally awarded the contract five years prior. The company was a regional firm with a good reputation. It handled waste and recycling contracts for several of the municipalities in the area.

Although MBD offered the best recycling rebate (see Exhibit 1), their price was 25 percent higher than what NWMS offered. Kathy expected that the recycling rebate offered by MBD would offset the price differential with NWMS. The MBD proposal was not very detailed, offering to extend the contract for the current services provided, without any changes. Kathy did not consider MBD to be particularly innovative, but she had not received any major complaints about their services during the past five years.

The site visit revealed that MBD was undergoing a construction project that would consolidate all of their facilities into a single location, including a new building. MBD seemed to have the staff, equipment, capacity, and capability to handle the Northeastern contract. However, there was minimal evidence of formal systems and processes in areas such as equipment maintenance, material handling, and training.

THE NEWTON WASTE MANAGEMENT SERVICES INC. PROPOSAL

NWMS was a new company, founded by two local businesspeople two years prior. NWMS offered the lowest price and all other proposals were measured against its price. The proposal provided minimal information, with many sections omitted. In some cases, Kathy was unable to determine if NWMS agreed to the terms and conditions set out in the RFP. Financial statements were also missing.

EXHIBIT 1
Selected
Sections of
RFP

2.1   Proponents are invited to submit proposals for recycling and waste transfer services as required by the grounds department. The spend for the most recent year at Northeastern Hospital is estimated to be greater than $200,000. The annual spend figures are furnished for Proponents to assess the total annual base value of the contract. Northeastern Hospital cannot guarantee the purchase volumes/values indicated in this RFP.

2.2   Northeastern Hospital's recycling and waste transfer program includes:
   (a)   Paper: paper products: boxboard (i.e., cereal, detergent, cracker, and tissue boxes); cardboard (i.e., clean pizza boxes, packing boxes); catalogs, magazines, newspaper, phone books, paper egg cartons, and miscellaneous paper products such as flyers, envelopes, and writing paper.
   (b)   Co-mingled: rigid food, beverage, and liquid containers, milk and juice cartons, drink boxes, aluminum and steel containers, empty paint cans, aluminum foil and pie plates, glass bottles and jars, and plastic bottles and tubs.

2.3   The successful Proponent shall be required to provide the necessary equipment to handle the recycling program: a compactor for paper, 30 yard bins or other suitable transfer systems, and cardboard gaylords containers on a trailer.

2.4   Northeastern Hospital is looking for the successful Proponent to suggest/or identify alternative methods that would provide greater efficiencies and/or cost savings initiatives that would benefit Northeastern Hospital.

4.6   The lowest-cost Proposal or any other Proposal may not necessarily be accepted.

6.1   Northeastern Hospital is interested in participating with the successful Proponent in any initiatives that are mutually beneficial and can give Northeastern Hospital strategic or economic advantages in the areas of administration, health, research, or teaching. Bidders should provide any evidence of previous "partnering" arrangements where they have collaborated on mutually beneficial initiatives with clients providing them with strategic or economic value beyond the narrow scope of the supply arrangement.

8.1   Northeastern Hospital is looking for a rebate program, payable on a monthly basis, which will be applicable when the value of the goods recycled represents a positive return. Credits will be based on fair market value of the recycled goods minus processing fees and handling costs incurred. Proponents must identify in their proposals the method to be used to:
   (a)   calculate fair market value;
   (b)   establish the date of the fair market value; and,
   (c)   calculate processing fees and handling costs incurred by the proponent.

When the sourcing team arrived for the site visit at NWMS, they were surprised that the processing operations were not busy and there were only about 15 people working in the operation, plus a small office staff. NWMS had very little processing and material handling equipment at the site, and Kathy was concerned about the supplier's ability to handle the capacity generated by Northeastern. The general manager at NWMS, who conducted the tour, indicated that his organization had plans to invest in additional equipment if it was successful in securing the contract from Northeastern.

THE UNIVERSAL WASTE MANAGEMENT AND RECYCLING PROPOSAL

UWM was a Fortune 500 company that was one of the largest environmental solutions providers in North America. The proposal from UWM was the most expensive of the three, at 50 percent higher than the cost of the MBD proposal. Furthermore, the rebate proposed by UWM set commodity prices so low that any rebate payments

EXHIBIT 2   Evaluation of RFPs for Recycling and Waste Transfer Services

	Total Possible score	Weight	NWMS Proposal	UWM Proposal	MBD Proposal
Section A: Best value including pricing • Includes: Best value based on pricing, rebate offered, no additional charges, financial stability of supplier, etc.	75	50%	52	33	50
Weighted Supplier Score:			35.67%	22.00%	33.33%
Section B: Service and Specification • Includes: Similar contracts, guarantee of services, references, ability to implement as per RFP, etc.	45	30%	12	42	40
Weighted Supplier Score			8.00%	28.00%	26.67%
Section C: Other • Includes: Compliance with terms and conditions, submissions that are clear and easy to understand, other value-added services, certifications, etc.	20	10%	2	20	16
Weighted Supplier Score			1.00%	10.00%	8.00%
Section D: Site visit • Includes: Capacity to handle Northeastern's requirements, staff, equipment, overall appearance of site, location of site, etc.	25	10%	5	25	19
Weighted Supplier Score			2.00%	10.00%	7.60%
Total	**165**	**100%**	**46.67%**	**70.00%**	**75.60%**

would be negligible. The proposal also placed additional charges for use of the compactor and trailer. In all other areas, however, UWM seemed exceptional. It provided excellent references, with evidence of a track record of excellent service to its customers. All sections of the RFP were thoroughly completed, including a section on the company's strategic initiatives and environmental solutions capabilities. UWM also suggested additional programs that it recommended Northeastern consider as part of a comprehensive sustainability program.

The site visit further impressed the sourcing team. It was evident that UWM had the capacity to handle additional work from Northeastern, the staff was knowledgeable, and the equipment was in excellent condition, supported by on-site maintenance. Overall, the operation was very professional.

EVALUATION OF THE PROPOSALS

Kathy evaluated each supplier proposal using the predetermined rating system (see Exhibit 2). According to her evaluation, MBD came out on top, slightly ahead of UWM. However, after the site visits, Kathy was much more impressed by UWM and felt that this supplier was a better fit with Northeastern. Although UWM's cost was higher, it excelled in the other three areas in the evaluation system. She remained concerned, however, that ignoring the results of the rating system violated Northeastern's establish purchasing practices and wondered what recommendation she should make at the sourcing team meeting schedule for the afternoon of October 8.

Global Supply Management

Key Questions for the Supply Decision Maker

Should we

- Source more goods and services globally?
- Establish regional or global purchasing offices?
- Buy directly from the supplier or through an intermediary?

How can we

- Locate and evaluate global suppliers?
- Organize for effective global supply management?
- Overcome the potential problems faced in supply from offshore suppliers?

Supply is becoming more global. Since the end of World War II, many different events and forces have relaxed barriers to world trade. Geopolitical events of the past two decades, such as the creation of the European Union (EU), the disintegration of the USSR, the reunification of Germany, the North American Free Trade Agreement (NAFTA), the emergence of China and India as global economic powers, and the growth of other emerging economies such as Brazil, the Russian Federation, Mexico, the Philippines, and Malaysia have created major opportunities for the global economy. Furthermore, changes to the global political landscape are continuing at a rapid pace.

To seize opportunities in the global marketplace, companies are deploying their organizations on a global scale. For supply managers, this represents the opportunity to deliver improved value to end-customers by developing world-class supply relationships in terms of cost, quality, delivery, and performance. Global supply for many companies is a competitive necessity. Managing global supply networks presents a number of challenges in areas such as source identification and evaluation, international logistics, communications and information systems, and risk management, especially security and environmental loss exposure.

Two key decisions are addressed in this chapter: (1) How do we select and manage offshore suppliers? (2) How do we assure value from our global supply network?

THE IMPORTANCE OF GLOBAL SUPPLY

The world has grown a good deal smaller, figuratively, in the last 60 years, with the increased speed of transportation and communication. The Internet has accelerated the trend to global supply, making it easier for source selection and reducing communication problems. While trading patterns and partners shift depending on a number of economic factors, the clear trend is toward more trade globally. The value of worldwide merchandise trade imports grew by a factor of 95 times between 1948 and 2001.[1] Between the fall of 2008 and the spring of 2009, global trade collapsed by 20 percent in volume. International merchandise trade registered its greatest plunge since the Second World War. According to the

---

[1] World Trade Organization, *International Trade Statistics 2013,* p. 183.

United Nations Conference on Trade and Development, the global crisis appears to have left a marked impact on the dynamism of global trade, keeping the volume of global trade well below its pre-crisis growth trajectory.[2]

The total value of world merchandise imports in 2012 was $18.6 trillion and the value of exports was $17.9 trillion. World merchandise includes agricultural products, fuels and mining products, and manufactures. In 2008, China overtook Germany as the leading exporter of manufactured goods (not total merchandise exports). In 2012, the top five merchandise exporters represented 36 percent of world exports. The percentages for each were as follows: China (11.4 percent), the United States (8.6), Germany (7.8), Japan (4.5), and the Netherlands (3.7). Growth of merchandise exports was greater in the BRIC (Brazil, Russia, India, China), rising by 4.5 percent in 2012, than in NAFTA (North American Free Trade Agreement) or the European Union.

However, international trade is not restricted to goods alone. World commercial services imports in 2012, such as transportation, construction, communications, computer and information, insurance, and financial services, were $4.1 trillion.[3]

Reasons for Global Purchasing

The reasons for sourcing from other countries are many and vary with the specific requirement. However, the underlying summary reason for using an offshore supplier is that better value is perceived to be available from that source than from a domestic one. A supplier's ability to be competitive is influenced by the overall competitiveness of the country. Therefore, embarking on a global sourcing strategy requires a level of country knowledge and analysis beyond that for a domestic supplier.

The specific factor that makes the international buy look attractive will vary. Technological know-how can shift from one country to another over time; the ability and willingness to control quality can change; and, from time to time, a stronger U.S. dollar makes the price of offshore goods more attractive. There are at least 10 specific reasons an offshore supplier may be selected as the preferred source.

1. Unavailability of Items Domestically

The first and oldest reason for international trade has been that domestic sources were unavailable. For example, cocoa and coffee, certain spices and fruits, chrome, palladium, and rare earth elements are available only from certain countries.

As comparative economic advantage shifts, the location of manufactured products shifts. For example, the United States no longer manufactures televisions, and 90 percent of footwear is imported compared to only 2 percent in the 1960s. The manufacture of electronics parts, audio and telecommunications equipment, and computer and office equipment has moved from Japan and South Korea as manufacturers set up facilities in lower-cost countries such as China, India, and the Philippines or outsource to contract manufacturers in these countries.

Global supply chains include numerous tasks from design to manufacturing to assembly and marketing. Intermediate unfinished goods often cross borders several times before final assembly. The World Trade Organization reports increasing trade in intermediate goods. Consequently, for many organizations, global supply has become a necessity.

[2] Global Trade Trends, UNCTAD, http://dgff.unctad.org/chapter1/1.1.html

[3] Unless otherwise noted, all the data in this section came from the World Trade Organization, *International Trade Statistics 2013*, www.wto.org

2. *Price and Total Cost*

Most studies show that the ability of an offshore supplier to deliver product in the United States or Canada at a lower overall cost than domestic suppliers is a key reason to buy globally. While it may seem surprising that an offshore supplier can produce and ship an item several thousand miles at lower cost, there are several reasons why this may be the case for a specific commodity.

A. The *labor costs for manufacturing* offshore may be substantially lower than domestically. Many manufacturers in North America, Japan, and Korea have found that wage rate differences are great enough to offset other costs associated with offshore sourcing. Many manufacturers have either set up manufacturing facilities in lower-cost countries or outsourced to contract manufacturers.

Historically, manufacturers have chased low labor costs. When the export-led growth in Japan drove up wage rates for low-end, labor-intensive sources, the operations moved to Korea and Taiwan, and from there to Southeast Asia and, more recently, the coastal provinces of China. As wage rates increase in coastal China, movement is into the interior of China or lower-cost countries such as Vietnam, Indonesia, and the Philippines. And, as the gap closes between wage rates in China and Mexico, the closer proximity of Mexico to end product consumers means the lower shipping costs outstrip the lower Chinese wages. However, when evaluating labor costs, factors such as productivity and quality also must be taken into account.

For example, average pay for Mexican manufacturing workers in 2012 was only slightly higher than for Chinese ones. The lessening pay differential coupled with days of transit time versus months makes Mexico increasingly attractive. Cost drivers, including currency value and exchange rates, the cost of freight (largely influenced by fuel costs), and labor rates will continue to influence decisions about locating manufacturing.

The *labor costs for services* also may be substantially lower in countries outside of North America, Western Europe, Japan, and Korea. Highly educated and capable professionals including lawyers, doctors, software developers, engineers, and professors reside in lower-cost countries. Enabled by technology, many buying organizations are outsourcing (buying instead of making in-house) and offshoring (sourcing from nondomestic suppliers) professional services.

For example, professional services that may be outsourced and offshored include legal research to India and the Philippines; medical services such as transcription, billing, coding, and insurance claims processing to India; interpretation of medical tests to radiologists in India, the Philippines, or Australia; and software development to India, China, and Uruguay. Some services are multisourced and multishored to ensure coverage 24 hours a day, 7 days a week, 365 days a year.

B. The *exchange rate* may favor buying offshore. When the U.S. dollar gets progressively stronger, as was the case in the late 1990s, it effectively reduces the selling price of products bought from offshore suppliers. A weakened dollar makes imports more expensive and less attractive.

C. The *equipment and processes* used by the international supplier may be more efficient than those used by domestic suppliers. This may be because their equipment is newer or because they have been putting a greater share of their gross domestic product into capital investment. A good example of this is the steel industry in the Far East.

A more recent example is Korean dominance in the dynamic random access memory (DRAM) market. With increasing Taiwanese and Chinese sales growth, other memory suppliers are forming alliances to compete. Because there are many more Taiwanese and Chinese companies that can invest in such a capital-intensive industry, Korean manufacturers may have difficulty maintaining long-term leadership despite superior technology and operational excellence.

D. The international supplier may be concentrating on certain *products, and pricing* export products at particularly attractive levels to gain volume. One practice is dumping, which occurs when a product is sold in another country for less than either (a) the price in the domestic market, or (b) the cost to make the product. Dumping is illegal in some countries for certain products because the government wants to protect the domestic producer from what is perceived as unfair competition. While there are many attempts to prevent dumping practices, control of this is complex and has never been particularly effective. Some countries and regions have developed infrastructures and supply networks that support the efficient production of certain goods; for example, integrated circuits, computers, and computer parts in Malaysia; clothes and shoes in China; and wire and cable assemblies in Mexico.

Industry clusters may develop in a country. For example, the Monterrey, Mexico, industrial cluster has attracted many of the world's top manufacturers of industrial, commercial, and home refrigeration, heating, and air conditioning equipment. LG has been there since 1988. It has also attracted parts and components suppliers. The largest producer of precision copper tube, China's Golden Dragon Precise Copper Tube Group, is there. A second cluster is growing around the aerospace industry and a third around automobile manufacturing.[4]

The Trojan Technologies case at the end of this chapter illustrates how a company wants to achieve cost savings through a low-cost country sourcing plan. The challenge for Joyce Guo in the case is to develop a global sourcing process and decide which parts are best suited for sourcing in Asia.

3. *Government Pressures and Trade Regulations*

North American firms produce many goods that are sold (exported) around the world. The United States exported $1.59 trillion in goods and $683 billion in services in 2013.[5] Canadian exports reached $477.3 billion.[6] It makes sense to consider buying from suppliers in customer countries. Many executives accept the social responsibility to help develop the economies of the countries in which they operate.

Additionally, many nations insist as a condition of sale of a major product—for example, aircraft—to their country that the seller agree to buy a specified value of goods or services in that country. These types of arrangements, called *offset agreements*, are covered in more detail later in this chapter.

Also, trade incentives or restrictions may influence decisions about source location. For example, China's market share of textiles increased rapidly after the United States lifted

---

[4] Adam Thomson, "Investors Shrug Off Mexican Drugs Violence, The Financial Times, July 29, 2011.

[5] U.S. Census Bureau, U.S. Bureau of Economic Analysis, *U.S. International Trade in Goods and Services: Annual Summary, 2013,* www.bea.gov

[6] www.statcan.gc.ca/

quotas on textile imports. Decision makers must consider various combinations of sourcing locations and destinations for inputs (goods and services) and products in relation to bilateral trade agreements to identify savings opportunities.

4. Quality

While the quality level of the offshore sources generally is not higher than that of domestic suppliers, on some items it is more consistent. This is due to several factors, such as newer, better capital equipment; better quality control systems; and the offshore supplier's success in motivating its workforce to accept responsibility for doing it right the first time (the zero-defects concept). Also, some firms buy globally to round out their product line, with domestic suppliers furnishing "top-of-the-line" items and international suppliers filling in some of the "low-end" holes, and vice versa.

5. Faster Delivery and Continuity of Supply

Because of limited domestic capacity, in some instances the offshore supplier can deliver faster than the domestic supplier. The offshore supplier may even maintain an inventory of products in North America, available for immediate shipment.

Some countries have made investments in infrastructure (roads, ports, and power) that support strong supply lines. For example, China invests heavily in the rapid development and expansion of infrastructure.

Cycle time can also be compressed by automating compliance processes. For example, with Importer Security Filing—"10 + 2"—now in effect in the United States, companies must be prepared to deliver customs paperwork electronically. Electronic filing is now a requirement for the efficient reporting and archiving of all trade transactions, including third-party ones. This expedites cross-border trade and reduces or eliminates the time and cost of shipping and warehousing paper files.

Also, a Global Trade Management (GTM) IT system enables a virtual network of partners including suppliers and government agencies. A GTM speeds up compliance requirements such as product screening and foreign trade zone support. They enable faster information gathering and more data transparency. With the availability of Software as a Service (SaaS), these solutions are more affordable (see Chapter 4).

6. Better Technical Service

If the offshore supplier has a well-organized distribution network in North America, better supply of parts, warranty service, and technical advice may be available than from domestic suppliers. Offshore suppliers in locations with a large pool of people fluent in American English and Latin American Spanish along with technical knowledge may also provide superior call center and customer service experiences.

7. Technology

Increasingly, as domestic and offshore organizations specialize, technological know-how in specific lines varies. Particularly in the case of capital equipment, such as for the primary metals industry (steel and aluminum), offshore suppliers may be more advanced technologically than their North American counterparts.

On the services side, communications technology advancements and the availability of technologically sophisticated workers at lower wage rates than their domestic counterparts make offshoring attractive for software development, engineering and accounting services, technical support, customer support center operations, and some legal and medical services. For example, India has advantages in industries that rely on *soft* infrastructure (intangible assets) and excels at software and biotechnology.

Often governments encourage the development of *technology clusters or corridors.* India, China, and Mexico do this, but in different ways. These areas attract investment and create employment. They may include co-located science or business parks as well as colleges or training centers. They become magnets for outsourced IT work, including IT, business processes, automotive, and aerospace, which can lead to overstressed infrastructure, escalating real estate costs, and a shortage of skilled professionals.

8. *Marketing Tool*

To sell domestically made products in certain countries, it may be necessary to agree to purchase specified dollar amounts from suppliers in those countries. (See countertrade later in this chapter.)

9. *Tie-in with Offshore Subsidiaries*

Many firms operate manufacturing, distribution, or natural resource-based companies in other countries. A conscious decision may be made, particularly in the case of emerging markets and the least-developed economies, to support the local economy by purchasing there for export to the home country.

10. *Competitive Clout*

Competition tends to pressure the domestic supplier to become more efficient, to the long-term benefit of both the supplier and the buyer. Purchasers use imports or the threat of imports as a lever to pressure concessions from domestic suppliers.

Partnering with an offshore supplier may also improve competitiveness of both when neither nation is able to dominate both invention and low-cost manufacturing. There are hybrid organizations in the clean energy sector. For example, Missouri-based Peabody Energy purchased a stake in GreenGen, a Chinese high-tech, low-emissions coal-fired plant slated for a 2011 opening. In return, Peabody obtains data from, and lends expertise to, a cutting-edge Chinese power plant.

Potential Problem Areas

While it is not possible in this chapter to give a complete discussion of all the potential problem areas faced in global sourcing and the methods for minimizing the impact of each, the major ones can be highlighted. The same principles of effective supply discussed throughout this book apply to global supply, but some unique problems arise when dealing across country boundaries.

Seventeen potential problem areas are highlighted. The astute buyer will recognize that he or she must consider the total cost of ownership, not just the initial purchase price, when evaluating an offshore source.

1. *Source Location and Evaluation*

The key to effective supply is selecting responsive and responsible suppliers. Globally, this is sometimes difficult because obtaining relevant evaluation data is both expensive and time consuming. However, the methods of obtaining data on international suppliers essentially are the same as for domestic suppliers (discussed in Chapter 12). In addition to gathering background data (discussed later in this chapter under "Information Sources for Locating and Evaluating Suppliers"), certainly the best method of obtaining detailed data is an on-site supplier visit. Because a visit to a supplier(s) in another country is expensive and time consuming, it must be well planned. If the dollars and risk involved are great, the on-site visit is a necessity. Firms doing a great deal of international buying will make frequent visits to offshore sources; for example, in a firm buying millions of dollars' worth of electronics equipment, the responsible supply manager spends a significant percent of his or her time in the Far East visiting and negotiating with potential or actual suppliers.

There are alternatives to personal on-site visits, such as the use of consultants and local third-party purchasing organizations. The Internet has made information on potential sources more readily available, and e-mail, text messaging, and web meetings represent cost-effective methods of communication.

2. *Lead Time and Delivery*

Improvements in transportation and communications have reduced the lead time for offshore purchases. However, there are four areas in which the buyer should anticipate additional lead time:

A. Establishing credit for a first-time international buyer often involves obtaining a letter of credit, which is a document that assures payment.

B. Even with improvements in transportation, the buyer may still experience delays, particularly with inland carriers in the supplier's country.

C. Delays in domestic customs are also possible. Proper documentation and customs bonds help expedite shipments through customs. The customs bond allows goods to be released after inspection and lets the buyer pay duties later. Delays due to increased security or security-related emergencies should also be anticipated.

D. The time goods are in port, for both outbound and inbound, also depends on the number of ships in line for unloading, hours of port operations, and additional security measures.

Selecting the mode of transport is an important decision in international sourcing because of long supply lines and greater risk of loss or damage. High-value, low-weight items may move by airfreight, and delivery time may be almost as short as from domestic suppliers. High-weight items that are costly to transport should move by ocean shipment. Lead time may be several weeks.

For high-bulk, high-weight, low-value commodities, such as steel, the buying firm must do a much longer-range planning job (which is possible in most firms) and must notify the offshore supplier promptly of any schedule changes. Also, the selection of the transportation carrier must be done with great care. To compensate for transport uncertainty, the buyer may insist that the supplier maintain a safety stock inventory in North America. Some type of performance bond also might be required.

Most large transportation services companies and international freight forwarders have information systems that allow shippers to track and trace shipments. Such information can be useful in inventory planning and can help identify potential problems, such as stockouts or production shortages.

3. Expediting

Expediting is the process of speeding up production or delivery. Because of distance, expediting an offshore supplier's production/shipment is more difficult. This places a premium on knowing a supplier's personnel and ensuring that they are responsive. Some firms also arrange to have an expediter on contract in the offshore country or to use personnel from a company-owned subsidiary closer to the supplier to assist with expediting problems.

4. Political, Labor, and Security Problems

Depending on the country in which the supplier is located, the risk of supply interruption due to governmental problems—for example, change in government or trade disputes—may be quite high. Disruptions may also be caused by unsafe buildings and equipment, poor working conditions, violation of child labor laws, strikes, or environmental events. Often these events are related to weak or nonexistent health, safety, and environmental laws and regulations, noncompliance with existing laws and regulations, or corruption.

The heightened risk of supply chain disruptions from terrorist acts, counterfeit goods, or unsafe products increases the time and cost of offshore sourcing. Every importer and exporter must have the knowledge and records about its products, where they were sourced, and how they were transported, because governments continue to increase their requirements for safety standards and compliance reporting. The cost of correction for a product recall or scandal, including the cost of brand or image degradation, can be huge.

Risk management strategies and contingency planning are of even greater importance in the global economy. The supply manager must assess risks, establish a monitoring system, and communicate in time to implement a contingency plan.

5. Hidden Costs

When comparing an offshore source with a domestic source, it is easy to ignore some of the costs in the offshore purchase. The buyer must compare total cost of ownership before opting for an offshore supplier. The following checklist of cost factors provides some examples of hidden costs.

- Currency exchange premiums.
- Commissions to customs brokers.
- Terms of payment costs and finance charges: letter of credit fee, translation costs, exchange rate differentials.
- Foreign taxes imposed.
- Import tariffs.
- Extra safety stock/buffer and transit inventory, plus inventory carrying costs due to longer lead times.
- Extra labor for special handling.
- Obsolescence, deterioration, pilferage, and spoilage.
- Additional administrative expenses.
- Packaging and container costs.
- Business travel.
- Fees for freight forwarders, consultants, or inspectors.

- Marine insurance premium.
- Customs documentation charges.
- Transportation costs, including from manufacturer to port, ocean freight, from port to company plant, freight forwarder's charges, port handling charges, warehouse costs.
- Additional security measures.

6. Currency Fluctuations

Should payment be made in the buyer's currency or that of the country in which the purchase is made? If payment is to be made in a short period of time, the currency exchange rate may be less of a problem. However, if payment is not due for several months or if the supply relationship lasts for a long time, the exchange rates could change appreciably, making the price substantially higher or lower than at the time the agreement was originally signed.

Most significant world exchange rates float freely, and sometimes change rather rapidly, due to economic, political, and psychological factors. This means that the buyer, when contracting, also must make a forecast of how the exchange rates likely will move between now and the time of payment. In addition, certain countries sometimes impose restrictions and controls on the use of their currency. This requires that the buyer have a good source of financial advice. For example, the ongoing discussions between the United States and China over Chinese currency valuation have the potential to impact supply decisions.

Probably the most conservative approach is to price in U.S. dollars, for the buyer then knows exactly what the cost will be, but this denies the advantage of a lower price if the dollar increases in exchange value between the time the contract is written and the time when payment is made. Various approaches are possible, such as pricing in the supplier's currency with a contractual limit to the amount of exchange rate fluctuation permitted, up or down. Or the really knowledgeable buyer may protect against an unfavorable rate change by dealing in foreign currency options. It is important that supply cooperate closely with finance to assure that the corporation manages its currency risks and cash flows effectively.

7. Payment Methods

The method of payment often differs substantially in international sourcing than in domestic. In some instances, the offshore supplier may insist on cash with the order or before shipment.

Suppliers with whom the buyer has established a long-term relationship may be willing to ship on open account. But the seller may insist that title to goods does not pass until payment is made. The instrument used in this case is a *bill of exchange (draft)*, which the seller draws on the buyer and to which it attaches the shipping document before handing it to its bank for collection. The bank, in turn, sends the documents to a bank in the buyer's country, together with instructions covering when the documents are to be released to the buyer—normally at time of presentation—a *sight draft*.

Commercial letters of credit (CLCs) are the most actively used structured payment instruments in global trade. Their purpose is to provide secure, efficient, and prompt payment. The CLC is drawn by the buyer's bank at the buyer's request, and guarantees that the bank will pay the agreed-on amount when all prescribed conditions, such as satisfactory delivery, have been completed. Discrepancies in the complying documents provided by the seller may result in lengthy delays in payment and create misunderstandings between buyer and seller.

8. Quality

It is extremely important that there be a clear understanding between buyer and seller of the quality specifications. Misunderstandings can be quite costly, due to the distances and lead times involved. Also, there could be a problem in interpretation of drawings and specifications. In addition, it is important that both buyer and seller agree on what quality control/acceptance procedures are to be used.

As more services are offshored, all the challenges of defining and assuring quality services are increased by distance, language, and cultural diversity. A clear and unambiguous statement of work (SOW) is the foundation of quality services. For an example of purchasing services on a global basis, see the Marc Biron case at the end of this chapter. In the case, Marc Biron has been asked to manage the global marketing spend for a large financial services firm.

9. Warranties and Claims

In the event of rejection for quality reasons, what are the responsibilities of both parties? Due to distances, return and replacement of items is complex and time consuming. Are there provisions for the buyer reworking the items? Who pays for rework, and how are rework costs calculated? These areas should be agreed to in advance of the purchase.

For services, it may be even more difficult to resolve differences over perceived quality levels with an offshore supplier than a domestic one. Clearly defined expectations are a critical success factor in services contracts.

10. Tariffs and Duties

A *tariff* is a schedule of duties (charges) imposed on the value of the good imported (or, in some cases, exported) into a country. While, theoretically, the world is moving to eliminate tariffs through the various World Trade Organization agreements, tariffs still exist. The buyer must know which tariff schedule(s) applies and how the duties are computed. Additionally, the contract should make it clear who pays the duty—buyer or seller.

A *Certificate of Origin,* issued by a proper authority in the exporting country, is the document used to certify the origin of materials or labor in the manufacture of the item. It is used to obtain preferential tariff rates, when available. For example, the North American Free Trade Agreement (NAFTA) has rules relating to origin. The United States has adopted the Harmonized Tariff Schedule to provide a uniform, updated international coding system for goods moving in international trade.

The cost of noncompliance with import regulations can be staggering. In a case where containers are marked with incorrect country of origin, the costs can include delayed receipt of goods, charges for freight forwarders or attorneys to get the goods released from customs, remarking, storage, and time to fix the problem. For more serious offenses, fines may apply, legal action may be required, and seizure, and possibly forfeiture, of goods may occur.

11. Administration Costs

Global supply requires additional documentation, mainly for duty and customs, logistics activities, payment, and financial transactions. Even with developments such as electronic funds transfers and Internet-based communications systems, the administrative costs in international buying pose a major problem.

12. Legal Issues

If potential legal problems are a risk in domestic buying, they are several times greater in international buying. If delivery time is critical, a penalty or liquidated-damages clause for late delivery may be advisable. Also, a performance bond may be required or a bank guaranty to ensure payment in case of specified nonperformance. Litigation is time consuming and expensive; therefore, it is increasingly common to agree to settle international trade disputes by international arbitration.

The UN Convention on Contracts for the International Sale of Goods (CISG) went into effect January 1, 1988. The CISG applies only to the sale of goods and does not apply to services. As of September 26, 2013, 80 countries, including Canada, Mexico, the United States, China, Germany, and Japan had adopted the CISG. The goal of the CISG is to create a uniform international law for the sale of goods. There are several key differences between the Uniform Commercial Code (UCC) and the CISG, and purchasers should be aware of them:

A. Under the UCC, the terms of a contract may vary in the acceptance from the proposed contract, and a contract still may exist. Under the CISG, however, no contract is created if the terms of acceptance differ from the proposed terms.

B. Under the UCC, the statute of frauds requires a written agreement if the value of the goods exceeds $500. Under the CISG there is no dollar limit.

C. Under the UCC, there are implicit warranties, such as warranty of merchantability, and a warranty of fitness for purpose. Under the CISG, there are additional warranties.

Purchasers should consider carefully the laws under which an international contract is governed. If trading with a company in a country where the CISG has been adopted, the CISG governs the contract and the buyer should understand the differences between the CISG and the UCC. CISG allows the parties to "opt out" and agree on other relevant law to govern the contract. However, unless another body of law specifically is stated and agreed upon, the CISG will apply automatically if both nations have adopted the CISG. Likewise, if the other party is from a country that has not adopted the CISG and wants to have its domestic law apply, the U.S. purchaser may try to get agreement on using the CISG instead.

Rotterdam Rules.   The United Nations Convention on Contracts for the International Carriage of Goods Wholly or Partly by Sea, known as the Rotterdam Rules, has been signed by 21 nations (including the United States) representing over 25 percent of 2008 world trade volume. Ratification by parliamentary and legislative bodies of 20 countries puts them into force.

The rules establish a uniform and modern global legal regime governing the rights and obligations of stakeholders in the maritime transport industry under a single contract for door-to-door carriage. The convention builds upon and provides a modern alternative to earlier conventions governing the international carriage of goods by sea, as well as codifying important industry practice. The rules provide a legal framework that accounts for the many technological and commercial developments in maritime transport, including the growth of containerization, the need for door-to-door transport under a single contract of carriage, and the development of electronic commerce.

Services. There is no international common law of contracts. The choice of law will depend on the countries represented in the deal. The supplier is likely to want to apply the laws of its country; the U.S. courts may prefer U.S. federal laws. The two (or more) parties may agree to defer to U.S. state law. Or the parties to the agreement may agree to apply the UN CISG if it is a mixed contract and the services portion does not form the preponderance of the contract.

The parties should agree on what laws apply, where a dispute will be resolved, and in what language. As with domestic services purchasing, the statement of work (SOW) is critical to forming a contract that guides performance of supplier and buyer. Also, service specific clauses should be included in the contract to clearly define risks and reward allocation between buyer and supplier.

Other U.S. laws affecting international transactions are the Exxon-Florio Amendment to the Omnibus Trade Competitiveness Act, the International Traffic-in-Arms Regulations (ITAR), antiboycott legislation, and the Foreign Corrupt Practices Act.

13. *Logistics and Transportation*

Logistics presents some of the biggest problems for buyers involved in international sourcing. The trend toward integrated logistics on the domestic side is mirrored by a similar move in global supply. Integrated logistics refers to the coordination of all the logistics functions—the selection of modes of transportation and carriers, inventory management policies, customer service levels, and order management policies. Logistics companies that provide a wider base of services, thereby allowing firms to coordinate logistics functions, should enable more cost-effective and competitive international sourcing.

Many firms outsource logistics activities to third-party logistics (3PL) providers. Deregulation and globalization have resulted in a series of mergers and alliances in the third-party logistics industry as service providers attempt to provide a global presence for their major customers. International freight forwarders are increasingly diversified, offering a number of value-added services, such as payment of freight charges, tracing and expediting, making routing recommendations, issuing export declarations, and preparing certificates of origin. The growth of one-stop service providers is likely to continue and appears to be in congruence with intermodalism (e.g., air-sea, rather than all air) and outsourcing.

14. *Language*

Words mean different things in different cultures. An American word (legitimate or slang) may have a different connotation in the United Kingdom or in South Africa (both English-speaking countries). Consider then the difficulties of communicating with someone who does not speak your language, when everything must go through a translator. Often, the buyer may not even know what connotations the words used by the translator have.

Because of these language difficulties, some firms insist that a supply manager who is going to have repeated dealings with suppliers whose native language is different from theirs be multilingual or take a language course. The buyer still will have to use an interpreter, but may be a bit more comfortable. Language difficulties may be compounded by the prevalent use of electronic communications such as e-mail and texting. Writing in a second or third language may prove even more difficult than face-to-face communication.

15. *Communications*

Many supply managers worldwide are used to instant communication when dealing with their domestic supply network partners. Communicating with offshore suppliers is easier than ever with online video conferencing such as Cisco WebEx and Skype, which are cheap, easy to set up, and accessible by most Internet connections. Text messaging, instant messaging, e-mail, phone, and fax all help make communication fast, inexpensive, and reliable. Texting, which is widely used globally for personal communication, is increasingly used in business dealings. Security, confidentiality, reliability, and speed are critical. Some organizations use service level agreements (SLAs) to define reliability and quality parameters.

Still, global supply can involve problems with communication. These relate to time zone differences and problems with the communication network itself. When dealing with suppliers several time zones away, purchasers cannot simply pick up the phone and talk with their supplier any time of the day or night. Because of the time differences, some communication must be done in the evening or early hours of the morning. Furthermore, long-distance telephone calls add to the costs of global supply. Poor reliability of communication networks in some regions of the world also may create difficulties in some circumstances. Proximity to the supplier may be an advantage if the supplier and buyer are in the same time zone. For example, the majority of Mexican cities are in the same time zone as Chicago. On-site visits are easier because there are frequent direct flights from multiple U.S. cities. Language is less of a barrier because many Mexican managers speak English, and more people from the States are conversant in Spanish. These considerations must be factored into the sourcing analysis, especially the total cost analysis.

16. *Cultural and Social Customs*

Even in North America, business customs vary from area to area: for example, Boston or New York City compared with Houston or Birmingham or Monterrey with Mexico City. Certainly business/social customs vary even more widely in other countries. Good purchasers do not focus only on the economic transaction but also on the noneconomic needs of their supply network partners. Furthermore, problems caused by cultural misunderstandings can lead to higher supply chain costs. Therefore, purchasers need to have cross-cultural skills and must adjust to their suppliers' customs if they are to be effective in communicating and negotiating with suppliers.

In general, learn about the history, culture, and customs of the country you are traveling to, paying close attention to simple actions and behaviors that are considered rude or inappropriate. Many cultures are more formal than U.S. culture, so start out using last names and formal titles. Get cultural advice from professionals or colleagues familiar with the country. Make sure your interpreter understands the issues you will be discussing. Even if your counterparts speak your native language, remember to speak slowly, avoid jargon, and use graphics to illustrate points. Document decisions and key points of discussions. Be prepared to spend time getting to know people as part of the negotiation process. Even as business practices become more homogenized across cultures, adapting to cultural norms may improve the chances of a successful business relationship.

17. *Ethics and Social Responsibility*

Because of perceived problems involving U.S. firms dealing with offshore customers or suppliers, Congress passed the Foreign Corrupt Practices Act (FCPA) in 1977. Basically, this law prohibits U.S. firms from providing or offering payments to officials of foreign governments to obtain special advantages. The FCPA distinguishes between transaction bribes and "variance" or "outright" purchase bribes.

The FCPA does allow transaction bribes or facilitating payments ("grease") to persuade foreign officials to perform their normal duties, such as getting a phone installed or processing papers. The types of actions that might trigger an investigation into outright or variable bribes are payments of large commissions, payments to individuals who do not render substantial services, and payments made in cash and labeled miscellaneous. If the North American supply professional has little experience with a particular environment, it is essential that he or she become familiar with the FCPA, the Omnibus Trade Act of 1988, and individual country customs.

As more companies commit to, and report on, their corporate social responsibility, formal monitoring and measurement are required for global trade and supply chain practices. Companies want to ensure their goods are manufactured with appropriate testing and without the use of child labor or other unethical practices. Environmental impact is also of increasing importance in supply chain design and management. Supply chain visibility and accountability are increasingly important to importers. (See Chapter 17.)

SELECTING AND MANAGING OFFSHORE SUPPLIERS

Selecting and managing offshore suppliers requires an organizational infrastructure that can compensate for the challenges of offshore sourcing and optimize the opportunities of a globally networked supply base. Decisions must be made about (1) the structure of the global sourcing group, (2) the role of third-party intermediaries, and (3) how potential sources will be identified and researched.

Global Sourcing Organizations

The structure of a global supply organization is influenced by the location of key suppliers and company operations and the overall corporate organizational structure. Companies with a decentralized organization structure give business unit and/or local supply staff responsibility for international supply. In a centralized or hybrid structure, global supply activities can be coordinated through several organizational models, including (1) regional purchasing offices, (2) a global commodity management organization, and (3) international purchasing offices (IPO).

Regional Purchasing Offices

One approach is to create regional purchasing offices, such as the approach taken by Unisys. The global supply organization at Unisys has a chief purchasing officer for each of its four regions—the United States; Europe, the Middle East, and Africa; Asia and the Pacific; and Latin America and the Caribbean—each reporting to the corporate vice president of global procurement. Furthermore, the structure in each region is identical. The vice president of global procurement believed that some procurement activities, such as customer sales support, process management, and supplies and services, required close geographic proximity.

However, commodity management represented one area where geographic location was not always important. While it was necessary to negotiate local and regional supply agreements for many commodities, responsibility was divided between the European and U.S. commodity purchasing organizations for its global suppliers. Discussions between the corporate vice president of global procurement and the commodity management directors for the United States and Europe led to consensus regarding lead responsibility for global commodities. Such decisions were based on supplier location, previous experience of the United States and European purchasing staff with the commodities in question, and staff availability.[7]

Global Commodity Management Organization

Another approach is the creation of a global commodity management organization. This makes sense when there are a large number of common requirements across facilities or business units and the supply base is not always located in the same geographic area as the buying company's operations. The global commodity managers are responsible for identifying world-class suppliers for important requirements common to the company's global operations. Meanwhile, local supply managers are allowed to focus on identifying capable local suppliers for requirements unique to their operation.

For example, French electronics and media services company Thomson (known as the RCA brand in North America), which had its main operations in North America and Europe, relied heavily on suppliers in Asia. Given the large number of common requirements and suppliers, along with the geographical spread of manufacturing and laboratory facilities, the vice president of worldwide sourcing deemed it essential to increase the staffing of global commodity management. Therefore, a number of global commodity coordinators positions were created, each assigned worldwide responsibility for a specific group of common requirements.[8]

International Purchasing Office (IPO)

A third approach to global sourcing is the creation of international purchasing offices (IPOs). International purchasing offices can be focused on the basis of commodities, such as important raw materials, or on the basis of projects, such as large capital projects. Typically, IPOs are used when the company does not have a presence in the same geographic region where important suppliers are located. The logic of establishing IPOs is that the local presence of supply personnel can provide better access to suppliers and lower total costs. IPOs facilitate activities such as local sourcing and review, supplier development, materials management, quality control, and payment and can employ local personnel

---

[7] M. R. Leenders and P. F. Johnson, *Major Changes in Supply Chain Responsibilities* (Tempe, AZ: CAPS Research, 2002).

[8] Ibid.

thoroughly familiar with the language, culture, and way of doing business in that country or geographic area.

For example, when John Bradshaw became vice president of global procurement at Godiva Chocolatier in New York in 2007, he changed the name of purchasing to procurement and took the organization global. He assigned individuals to work in procurement in offices in regions where Godiva had operations—Brussels, Hong Kong, Tokyo, and Shanghai.[9]

Intermediaries

Should purchases be made direct from the supplier or through an intermediary? This depends on factors such as how much specialized international buying knowledge is available in the supply department and the volume and frequency of sourcing expected. Many firms use intermediaries for some or all of their global purchasing. The following list describes some of the options available.

Import brokers and agents.   For a fee (usually a percentage of purchase value—and it can be as high as 25 percent), the broker or agent will assist in locating suppliers and handling required documentation. In most situations, title passes directly to the buying organization. The buyer, of course, must make sure the fee is reasonable with regard to the services performed.

Import merchant.   The import merchant makes a contract with the buyer and then buys the product in its name from the offshore supplier, takes title, delivers to the place agreed on with the buyer, and then bills the buyer for the agreed-on price. The buyer pays a fee (buried in the price paid) for the buying services provided.

Seller's subsidiary.   Purchasing from the North American subsidiary of an offshore supplier is a common approach. The subsidiaries provide the benefits of having a better location (right time zone), conducting business in English, and accepting payments in U.S. dollars. They also may provide credit terms.

Sales representatives.   Some companies hire sales agents to represent them in various regions of the world. Typically, sales representatives handle low-volume-value contracts and are paid a commission by the supplier that is included in the price of the goods.

Trading company.   A trading company is typically a large firm that normally handles a wide spectrum of products from one or a limited number of countries. Trading companies are used extensively by Japanese firms to move products into North America. The advantages to the buyer of using a trading company are (1) convenience; (2) efficiency; (3) often lower costs, due to volume; (4) reduced lead times because it often maintains inventory in North America; and (5) greater assurance of the product meeting quality specifications because the trading company inspects in the producing country before shipment. But, as with any supplier, the buyer should assess the trading company carefully.

---

[9] S. Avery, "Godiva Transforms Purchasing into Global Procurement," *Purchasing,* January 14, 2010, www.purchasing.com/article/443489-Godiva_transforms_purchasing_into_global_procurement.php

In global sourcing, the task of locating and evaluating potential suppliers, and selecting and managing chosen suppliers is more difficult than in domestic source selection. Also, decisions must be made about how to organize the supply process/function for efficient and effective global sourcing.

Information Sources for Locating and Evaluating Offshore Suppliers

Similar types of information sources are available to the global buyer as the domestic buyer. They are as follows:

1. The *Internet* can be used to gain access to websites for companies and government organizations. Most large and medium-sized companies have websites that describe their main products and services. Many governments have extensive websites that provide a variety of information, such as trade statistics and assistance for importing and exporting goods and services.

2. A number of *government sources* are available. The U.S. Department of Commerce can supply current lists of names and addresses of offshore suppliers, by general types of products produced. The district offices, located in most major U.S. cities, can be helpful in obtaining this information.

Almost all countries of the world maintain an embassy in Washington, D.C. The major industrial nations (and many of the lesser economically developed countries) maintain trade consulates in the United States and Canada (typically in Washington, D.C., or Ottawa, but many also have an office in other major cities, such as New York, Toronto, Miami, New Orleans, Chicago, San Francisco, or Los Angeles). Their role is to promote exports from their country so they will supply names of suppliers and background information.

3. The *chambers of commerce* located in major cities in the United States, Canada, and around the world will help buyers locate sources. The International Chamber of Commerce has contacts through its country branches around the world and will supply leads to possible sources.

4. Typically, the *supply department* of a company with experience in offshore sourcing is willing to share that information with other buyers, providing they are not direct competitors. The *local associations* of the Institute for Supply Management (ISM) and the Supply Chain Management Association of Canada (SCMA) often can facilitate such an information exchange. Many countries have comparable purchasing, supply, and supply chain organizations that might be of assistance. The International Federation of Purchasing and Supply Management (IFPSM), made up of member nation associations, maintains a list of contacts in many countries. These are buyers and supply managers who have agreed to supply to buyers in other nations information on suppliers in their own countries.

5. There are a variety of *supply chain partners* that can help locate sources. Current domestic suppliers often are in a position to supply information and leads on noncompetitive suppliers. Almost all major banks have an international trade department. In addition to supplying information on currency, payment, documentation procedures, and governmental approval procedures, a bank's international trade department can assist in locating potential sources.

Customers also can assist with locating international suppliers. This source of information can be especially useful when the customer also has international operations or markets for its products.

6. Every major industrial country has at least one *supplier locator directory*, similar to the commonly used *Thomas Register* (thomasnet.com) for North American manufacturers. The foreign trade consulate or embassy of any nation should be able to refer you to the appropriate directory for their country. Dun & Bradstreet (D&B) also has offices in many countries and can supply a D&B report on many firms.

7. *Importers and foreign trade brokers* stay informed about developments in the supply base of the countries with which they deal, and they can give the buyer a great deal of useful information.

The evaluation of a specific supplier's capabilities is more difficult than locating the supplier. Two key sources of evaluation information are the shared experiences of other supply people, which usually can be obtained simply by asking, and the supplier visit, which was discussed earlier in this chapter.

If a supplier visit is not made, the buyer should at least ask the potential supplier for information such as (1) a list of present and past North American customers, (2) payment procedures required, (3) banking reference, (4) facilities list, (5) memberships in quality specification-setting associations, and (6) basic business information, such as length of time in business, sales and assets, product lines, and ownership.

INCOTERMS

Shipping terms and responsibilities are more complex in international sourcing than in domestic transportation. The International Chamber of Commerce has created Incoterms (International Commercial Terms) as a uniform set of rules to clarify the costs, risks, and obligations of buyers and sellers in an international commercial transaction. Incoterms provide globally accepted definitions that avoid disputes over what the terms mean. They determine who pays the freight, who pays the carrier, who handles the import clearance and export clearance, and two of the terms address insurance. Almost any international purchase or sale contains a reference to Incoterms.

These rules were first published in 1936 and are modified periodically. The most current version is Incoterms 2010. The latest revisions reclassified the rules into two classes (rules for any mode of transport and rules for sea and inland waterway transport only), applied the rules to domestic and international trade, developed two terms to replace four from the 2000 rules, clarified that only the first seller will be responsible for shipping the goods when commodities are sold multiple times during transit, clearly allocated terminal handling charges to avoid potential double exposure for the buyer, allocated insurance responsibility and security-related obligations, allowed electronic communication in lieu of paper where agreed or customary, and reiterated that parties should refer to Incoterms 2010 (or whichever version is preferred) expressly in their sales contract.[10]

The 13 Incoterms have been grouped into two categories:[11]

[10] S. Shepherd and T. Graham. *New Incoterms 2010: A Summary of the Principal Changes to Incoterms 2000*, www.ince.law.com, 2011.

[11] Edward G. Hinkelman, Dictionary of International Trade, 10th ed., Novato, CA: World Trade Press, 2012.

Rules for Any Form of Transport

1. EXW: Ex Works (*named place*). The seller/exporter makes the goods available at his or her premises and the buyer assumes all costs and risks from the seller's "named place" of business. The seller does not clear the goods for export and does not load the goods for transport. This arrangement places the greatest responsibility on the buyer, who assumes all risks from the time when the seller has made the goods available.

2. FCA: Free Carrier (*named place*). The seller clears the goods for export and delivers them to the carrier specified by the buyer at the named location, where the buyer takes possession. The "named place" is domestic to the seller and the carrier can be a shipping line, an airline, a trucking firm, a railway, or an individual or firm that undertakes to procure carriage by any of these methods of transport, including intermodal, such as an international freight forwarder. The buyer assumes all risk of loss or damage from the time the goods have been delivered to the carrier.

3. CIP: Carriage and Insurance Paid (*named place of destination*). The seller clears the goods for export, delivers them to the carrier, and is responsible for paying for carriage and insurance to the named port of destination. The seller is also responsible for the costs of unloading, customs clearance, duties, and other costs if included in the cost of carriage, such as in small package delivery.

4. CPT: Carriage Paid To (*named place of destination*). The seller clears the goods for export and delivers them to the carrier and is responsible for paying carriage to the named port of destination. The seller is also responsible for the costs of unloading, customs clearance for import, and duties where such costs are included in the cost of carriage, such as small package courier. The buyer is responsible for all additional costs, such as procuring and paying for insurance coverage.

5. DDP: Delivered Duty Paid (*named place of destination*). The seller clears the goods for export and is responsible for making them available to the buyer at the named place of destination, including customs clearance for import. Therefore, the seller assumes all responsibilities for all costs associated with transportation to the named place of destination, including duties and other costs payable upon import. The buyer is responsible for unloading. DDP can be used for any mode of transport and the buyer assumes all risks from the time the goods have been made available at the "named place of destination."

6. DAT: Delivered at Terminal (*named place of destination*). The seller covers all transport costs and assumes all risks until the goods, having been unloaded from the arriving means of transport, are placed at the buyer's disposal at a named terminal at the named port or place of destination. DAT requires the seller to clear the goods for export where applicable, but the seller has no obligation to clear the goods for import, pay any import duty, or carry out any import customs formalities. DAT addresses the case of containers that might be unloaded and then loaded into a container stack at the terminal, awaiting shipment.

7. DAP: Delivered at Place (*named place of destination*). The seller clears the goods for export and is responsible for making them available to the buyer on the arriving vehicle at the named place of destination. The buyer is responsible for unloading and

clearing the goods for import. The buyer assumes all risks from the time the goods have been made available at the place of destination.

Rules for Sea and Inland Waterway Transport Only

1. FAS: Free Alongside Ship (*named port of shipment*). The seller clears the goods for export and places them alongside the vessel for loading. The buyer takes possession at the dock of the port of export.

2. FOB: Free on Board (*named port of shipment*). The seller clears the goods for export and is responsible for the costs and risks of delivering the goods on board at the named port of export. Title passes once the goods are on board. It should not be confused with the conventional North American term *F.O.B.*

3. CFR: Cost and Freight (*named port of destination*). The seller is responsible for clearing the goods for export, delivering the goods on board at the port of shipment, and paying the costs to transport the goods to the named port of destination. The buyer assumes responsibility for risk of loss or damage and additional transportation costs once the goods are on board at the port of shipment.

4. CIF: Cost, Insurance, and Freight (*named port of destination*). The seller clears the goods for export, is responsible for delivering the goods on board at the port of shipment, pays the costs associated with transport of the goods to the port of destination, and procures and pays for marine insurance in the buyer's name for the shipment. The buyer assumes responsibility for risk of loss or damage once the goods are on board at the port of shipment. The seller also contracts for insurance cover against the buyer's risk of loss of or damage to the goods during the carriage. The seller is required to obtain insurance only on minimum cover. For more coverage, the buyer will need to either agree with the seller or purchase its own extra insurance.

It is possible, and in some cases desirable, to agree to add wording to the Incoterms that specifies buyer, seller, and carrier responsibilities. For example, agreeing to DDP terms obligates the seller to pay for import duties, but using the term "DDP VAT Unpaid" means that the seller is not responsible for paying value-added taxes.[12]

Incoterms do not (1) apply to contracts for services; (2) define contractual rights and obligations other than for delivery; (3) specify details of the transfer, transport, and delivery of the goods; (4) determine how title of the goods will be transferred; (5) protect either party from risk of loss; (6) cover the goods before or after delivery; or (7) define the remedies for breach of contract.[13]

In addition, packaging and insurance decisions in international supply are much more complex than in domestic buying situations. Although it is the responsibility of the seller to provide packaging, it is important that the buyer and seller agree on arrangements for packaging in the contract. Although many Incoterms do not obligate either the buyer or the seller to procure insurance, both parties should recognize the risks and make arrangements for suitable coverage.

---

[12] Ibid.
[13] Ibid.

TOOLS FOR GLOBAL SUPPLY

There are a number of tools available to the supply manager when sourcing globally. These include (1) countertrade, (2) foreign trade zones (FTZ), (3) bonded warehouses, temporary importation bonds (TIBs), and duty drawbacks.

Countertrade

Countertrade is a fancy term for a barter agreement, but with some twists. Barter has been around for years and takes place when payment between buyer and seller is made by the exchange of goods rather than cash. U.S. firms, in times of shortage, often swap merchandise; for example, a utility trades fuel oil to another utility in exchange for copper cable, as a matter of expediency. However, the complexities of international trade, particularly with developing countries, have brought some new variations, with supply right in the middle of the action. There are five principal variations of countertrade.

Barter/Swaps

Barter involves the exchange of goods instead of cash. Typically, barter takes place when a country, which is short of hard currency, agrees to exchange its product for another country's product. This normally is a rather clean transaction, for the firms (countries) are exchanging equivalent dollar values. If goods of the same kind—for example, agricultural items or chemicals—are exchanged to save transportation costs, the arrangement is called a *swap*.

In a mixed barter, the seller ships product of a certain value—for example, motors—and agrees to take payment in a combination of cash and product—for example, wheat. It then is up to supply to resell the product for cash or to barter it to someone else. A commodity that changes hands twice is referred to as a *two-corner trade*. If it changes hands three times, it is a *three-corner deal*. Supply often gets involved in situations where working out the particular barters or swaps is both difficult and time consuming.

Offset Arrangements

Offsets are distinguished by the condition that one part of the countertrade be used to purchase government and/or military-related exports. Under these agreements, in order to make the sale, the selling company agrees to purchase a given percentage of the sales price in the customer country. The negotiation usually starts at 50 percent and then goes up or down from there. Whatever the figure agreed to, it then is up to supply to figure out how it can spend the specified amount for worthwhile goods or products. In some instances, the goods purchased later are resold, putting the supply department largely in the role of a trading company. Such resale occurs when supply cannot locate a supplier of suitable, needed merchandise in the customer country and simply makes a purchase of goods (that hopefully later will be salable) to complete the deal. Even if specific deals are unprofitable, firms engaging in countertrade usually are looking for long-term, meaningful, and mutually advantageous relationships with the other country.

When other countries buy North American–produced merchandise, they often push hard for offsets to gain access to technology, to get U.S. dollars, to increase employment, and/or to help maintain political stability by protecting jobs and domestic producers.

Counterpurchase

Counterpurchase agreements require the initial exporter to buy (or to find a buyer for) a specified value of goods (often stated as a percentage of the value of the original export) from the original importer during a specified time period.

Buyback/Compensation

In buyback agreements, the selling firm agrees to set up a producing plant in the buying country or to sell the country capital equipment and/or technology. The original seller then agrees to buy back a specified amount of what is produced by the plant, equipment, or technology. Buyback agreements can span 10 or more years.

Switch Trade

In switch trades, a third party applies its "credits" to a bilateral clearing arrangement. The credits are used to buy goods and/or services from the company or country in deficit. Usually a broker or trading house handles the switch.

Countertrade is used in situations where a country has a shortage of foreign exchange or a shortage of credit to finance its desired trade flows, wishes to diversify its foreign exchange earnings, or is encouraging the development of the domestic economy by promoting labor-intensive exports. The number of countries participating in countertrade has increased steadily and includes most of the United States' main trading partners, such as Canada, the United Kingdom, and China.

The World Trade Organization, the International Monetary Fund and governments, including the United States, Germany, and the UK, generally view countertrade as contrary to an open free-trading system. The U.S. government, however, does not oppose participation by U.S. companies. The Bureau of Industry and Security (BIS) reports annually to Congress on the impact of offsets in the defense trade on defense preparedness, industrial competitiveness, employment, and U.S. trade. U.S. firms entering into foreign defense sales contracts must report all offset transactions in excess of $5 million in contracts for the sale of defense articles or services, and offset transactions completed that were valued in excess of $250,000.

The exact value of international countertrade transactions is not known—secrecy surrounding the transactions typically prevents collection of these data. However, in 2011, U.S. firms reported 745 offset transactions (transactions conducted to fulfill offset agreement obligations) with 31 countries with an actual value of $4.01 billion, and an offset credit value of $5.18 billion.[14]

Countertrade is also used in civilian government procurement projects, such as the sale of civilian aircraft, telecommunications, and technology systems. In the competitive global marketplace, the ability to meet countertrade requirements in a cost-effective manner offers a competitive advantage. Supply has a legitimate role in managing countertrade arrangements and should be involved early in the process. Supply can provide feedback on cost implications, the status of the countertrade market, sourcing information, and the availability of suppliers and opportunities for barter.

Unfortunately, supply is not always involved in the decision to engage in countertrade, but becomes involved after the decision has been made, at the stage where potential

---

[14] U.S. Department of Commerce, Bureau of Industry and Security, *Offsets in Defense Trade, Sixteenth Study,* December 2012, p. i.

counterpurchases are being evaluated. Given the risks of countertrade—the possibility of poor-quality goods and services, the development of unprofitable deals, and the acceptance of goods and services that do not match marketing channels—the supply function should be consulted in the proposal evaluation stage.

Often, countertrade obligations present complex problems for supply managers. However, they may also provide the opportunity to develop lower-cost sources of supply in the world marketplace.

Because countertrade is a "way of life" for many supply professionals, several guidelines are suggested:

1. Decide whether countertrade is a viable alternative. If a company does not have the organization to do the international sourcing required, it might contract with a third-party service provider to manage the process or refuse to participate.
2. Build the cost of countertrade into the selling price.
3. Know the country—its government, politics, and regulations.
4. Know the products involved and what is available.
5. Know the countertrade negotiation process—offset percentage, penalties, and time period.

The Global Offset and Countertrade Association (G.O.C.A.) (formerly the American Countertrade Association—ACA) includes over 100 globally based companies engaged in countertrade and offset. The purpose of G.O.C.A. is to promote trade and commerce between companies and their foreign customers through a greater understanding of countertrade and offset (www.globaloffset.org).

Foreign Trade Zones

Foreign trade zones (FTZ) are special commercial and industrial areas in or near ports of entry, designed to avoid, postpone, or reduce duties on imported goods. Foreign and domestic merchandise, including raw materials, components, and finished goods, may be brought in without paying customs duties. FTZs are the U.S. version of what are known internationally as free trade zones. Merchandise brought into these zones may be stored, sold, exhibited, repacked, assembled, sorted, graded, cleaned, or otherwise manipulated prior to reexport or entry into the national customs territory.

U.S. FTZs are restricted-access sites in or near ports of entry. They are licensed by the Foreign Trade Zone Board and operate under the supervision of the U.S. Customs and Border Protection Service. Zones are operated under public utility principles to create and maintain employment by encouraging operations in the United States that might otherwise have been carried on abroad.

There are two categories of FTZs: general-purpose zones and subzones.

General purpose zones handle merchandise for many companies and are typically sponsored by a public agency or corporation, like a port authority.

Subzones are special-purpose zones, usually located at manufacturing plants. Subzones are usually preexisting manufacturing sites that operate under the guarantee of a local general-purpose site. There are no legal differences in the types of activities that can be undertaken at zones or subzones. According to government data, the value of shipments into zones was $732 billion in 2012. This has been the pattern for 15 years. In 2012 there were 174 FTZs, with 276 active manufacturing/production operations.[15]

Each FTZ differs in character depending upon the functions performed in serving the pattern of trade peculiar to that trading area. The six major functions that may be conducted within a zone are the following:

Manufacturing. Manufacturing involving foreign goods can be carried on in the zone area. Foreign goods can be mixed with domestic goods and, when imported, duties are payable only on that part of the product consisting of foreign goods. In some circumstances, the final assembled product may qualify for reduced duties, or might have no duties imposed if it has more than 50 percent U.S. content of labor or components. Such merchandise can be classified as "American made" for purposes of export under NAFTA. Besides reduced duties, there is a saving on interest, because duty payments are not due until the merchandise leaves the FTZ and enters the United States.

Transshipment. Goods may be stored, repacked, assembled, or otherwise manipulated while awaiting shipment to another port, without the payment of duty or posting a bond.

Storage. Part or all of the goods may be stored at a zone indefinitely. This is especially important for goods being held for new import quotas or until demand and price increase.

Manipulation. Imported goods may be manipulated, or combined with domestic goods, and then either imported or reexported. Duty is paid only on imported merchandise.

Refunding of duties, taxes, and drawbacks. When imported merchandise that has passed through customs is returned to the zone, the owner immediately may obtain a 99 percent drawback of duties paid. Likewise, when products are transferred from bonded warehouses to foreign trade zones, the bond is canceled and all obligations in regard to duty payment and time limitations are terminated. Also, exporters of domestic goods subject to internal revenue taxes receive a tax refund when products move into a foreign trade zone.

Exhibition and display. Users of a zone may exhibit and display their wares to customers without bond or duty payments. They can quote firm prices (because they can determine definite duty and tax rates in advance) and provide immediate delivery. Duty and taxes apply only to goods that enter customs territory.

If the company has large offshore suppliers or is contemplating importing substantial amounts of dutiable products, savings can be realized on duties or drawbacks, and on the cost of shipping both imported materials to plants in the hinterland and manufactured products back to the same port for export. The functions actually performed in any zone depend on the inherent nature of the trading and commercial community and demands made by users of zone facilities.

Avoiding, postponing, or reducing duties on imported goods makes them more competitive in the U.S. marketplace and creates economic benefits for the local community through job creation. The potential disadvantages of the FTZ are (1) the additional labor costs and operating and handling costs associated with its use and (2) the uncertainty of its long-term use due to changes in international trade agreements that are reducing and eliminating import duties.

[15] U.S. Department of Commerce, *74th Annual Report of the Foreign-Trade Zones Board,* 2012.

Maquiladoras

Mexico's maquiladoras are examples of the foreign trade zone concept or industrial parks. Non-Mexicans can own the maquila, or plant, in the maquiladora in order to take advantage of low Mexican labor costs. Maquilas are best suited to labor-intensive assembly. Parts and supplies enter Mexico duty free, and products exported to the United States are taxed only on the value added in Mexico. According to the maquiladoras's industry association (index.org.mx), exports and foreign investment each grew by more than 50 percent between 2009 and 2012, to $196 billion and $7.4 billion, respectively. Employment, which fell sharply after the global financial crisis, rebounded by 25 percent to just over $2 million, slightly above the average for 2007–08.[16]

Much assembly work was shifted to lower-cost countries such as China. As the wage differential decreases, companies from the United States and elsewhere are looking to the maquilas to do more sophisticated manufacturing and product design. Since the maquilas originally did assembly, there is a limited supply base in proximity to the maquilas. Industry clusters in automotive and aerospace are growing.

Bonded Warehouses

Bonded warehouses are utilized for storing goods until duties are paid or goods are otherwise properly released. Ownership is approved by the Treasury Department. They are under bond or guarantee for the strict observance of the revenue laws of the United States. The purpose of bonded warehousing is to exempt the importer from paying duty on foreign commerce that will be reexported or to delay payment of duties until the owner moves the merchandise into the host country. Goods can be stored for three years. At the end of the period, if duty has not been paid, the government sells the goods at public auction.

All merchandise exported from bonded warehouses must be shipped in the original package unless special permission has been received from the collector of customs. Any manufacturing must be conducted under strict supervision and the resulting items must be reexported.

Temporary Importation Bond (TIB) and Duty Drawbacks

A temporary importation bond (TIB) permits certain classes of merchandise to be imported into the United States. These are articles not for sale, such as samples, or articles for sale on approval. A bond is required, usually for an amount equal to twice the estimated duty. While there is a fee for the TIB, the net effect is that no duty is paid on the merchandise, provided it is reexported. The TIB is valid for one year, with two one-year extensions possible. However, if the goods are not exported on time, the penalty can be twice the normal duty, which is why the TIB must be for twice the normal duty.

Duty drawback permits a refund of duties paid on imported materials that are exported later. The buyer enters into a duty drawback contract with the U.S. government, imports the material for manufacture, and pays the normal duty. If the final manufactured or processed product is exported within five years of import, duty drawback can be obtained. There are three main types of duty drawback: direct identification drawback, substitution drawback, and rejected merchandise drawback. Provisions for duty refunds differ slightly under each type.

---

[16] "Mexico's Maquiladoras: Big Maq Attack," *The Economist* (October 26, 2013).

REGIONAL TRADING AGREEMENTS

Efforts to eliminate trade barriers result in bilateral, regional, and global trade agreements. Supply managers should know who the major trading partners with their countries are, what trade agreements are in place, and what opportunities exist in emerging economic markets.

Several major regional trading agreements are described in the following sections. Data on trading patterns of the majority of the countries in the world or regional trading blocks are available from the World Trade Organization (wto.org). The WTO hosts an interactive database of international trade statistics from 1948 to the present.

North American Free Trade Agreement (NAFTA)

In 1994, the North American Free Trade Agreement (NAFTA) took effect for the United States, Canada, and Mexico to eliminate tariffs and nontariff barriers to trade of goods and services. The final NAFTA provisions were implemented on January 1, 2008. NAFTA created a free trade area of 444 million people producing $17 trillion worth of goods and services. Canada and Mexico are the two largest importers of U.S. exports and the second and third largest suppliers to the United States. They purchase nearly one-third of U.S. merchandise exports. U.S. exports of goods and services to Canada and Mexico have tripled since NAFTA entered into force and U.S. imports from Canada and Mexico have also risen substantially.[17] Since the agreement, merchandise trade between the NAFTA countries has grown dramatically.

Actions that would build upon NAFTA include improved cooperation in the trade of intermediate goods and supply chains; improved border infrastructure to reduce the disruptions in production chains caused by post–9-11 security that cause unpredictable and extended delays; and the possibility of creating a customs union, a free trade area with a common set of external tariffs.

Buyers must adhere to NAFTA's rules of origin for products eligible for preferential reduced tariff rates. Other goods are taxed as if they were from any other country. Filling out and filing the certificate of origin is a major problem for many importers and a cost driver because of inconsistent and product-specific rules and documentation. Purchasers can file an annual blanket certificate if they anticipate buying the same goods more than once a year. Common external tariffs would enable the NAFTA countries to eliminate the agreement's rules of origin.[18]

The European Union (EU)

Efforts to increase cooperation economically and politically began in Europe after World War II. In 1993 four freedoms were agreed to: freedom of movement of goods, services, people, and money. In 2002, the euro became the sole currency of the EU member states, allowing easier price comparisons and lower foreign currency transaction costs. Currently the debate is over whether or not a European constitution is needed, and if so, what form it should take.

---

[17] U.S. Census Bureau, Foreign Trade Division, and U.S. Department of Commerce, Bureau of Economic Analysis.

[18] www.ustr.gov/trade-agreements/free-trade-agreements/north-american-free-trade-agreement-nafta.

As of 2013, the EU included 28 member states, 24 official and working languages, a total population of more than 500 million people, and EU GDP in 2012 of €12,945,402 million. With just 7 percent of the world's population, the EU's trade with the rest of the world accounts for around 20 percent of global exports and imports.[19]

ASEAN

The Association of South East Asian Nations (ASEAN) was established in 1967. Today it includes 10 South East Asian countries (Brunei Darussalam, Cambodia, Indonesia, Lao PDR, Malaysia, Myanmar, Philippines, Singapore, Thailand, and Vietnam). The ASEAN Free Trade Area (AFTA) was created in January 1992 to eliminate tariff barriers. ASEAN has a 2015 target to integrate the ASEAN economies into a single production base creating a regional market of 592 million people. ASEAN had a combined GDP of US$1.492 billion in 2009.[20]

Mercosur

Mercosur (El Mercado Común del Sur) was established in 1991 and encompasses Argentina, Brazil, Paraguay, Uruguay, Venezuela, and Bolivia in a customs union. As associate members, Chile, Colombia, Ecuador, Peru, Guyana, and Surinam can join free trade agreements but are not part of the customs union. Often referred to as the Common Market of the South, Mercosur is four times as big as the EU in area, encompasses more than 275 million people, and accounts for more than three-quarters of the economic activity on the continent (2011 combined GDP of US$3.3 trillion).[21]

Andean Community

The Andean Community (Spanish: Comunidad Andina de Naciones or CAN) includes Bolivia, Colombia, Ecuador, and Peru. CAN originated in 1969 with the ultimate aim to create a Latin American common market. A free trade area was established in 1993 and a common external customs tariff in 1994. CAN has a combined population of 103 million and a GDP in 2010 of US$902.8 billion.

CAN and Mercosur, the two main South American trading blocs, agreed in 2008 to form the Union of South American Nations (unasur.org). In 2012, the EU signed a trade agreement with Colombia and Peru and continues to consider expanding it to Ecuador and Bolivia.[22]

China's Trade Agreements

According to the China FTA Network (http://fta.mofcom.gov.cn), the Chinese Government sees Free Trade Agreements (FTAs) as a way to further open up to the outside world, to speed up domestic reforms, to integrate into global economy, to strengthen economic cooperation with other economies, and to supplement the multilateral trading system. China has 14 FTA partners, including ASEAN, Pakistan, Chile, and New Zealand, comprising 31 economies. The Chinese government has also created a mechanism for collectively interacting with groups of nations. In 2000, the Forum on

[19] www.europa.eu

[20] www.aseansec.org

[21] www.mercosur.int

[22] www.comunidadandina.org

China-Africa Cooperation (FOCAC) with 54 African countries was created. In 2014, the Community of Latin American and Caribbean States (CELAC) agreed to create a mechanism for collectively interacting with China.

The World Trade Organization (WTO)

The WTO was formed on January 1, 1995 following the Uruguay Round of trade negotiations. It replaced the General Agreement on Trade and Tariffs (GATT), which had been in existence since 1947.

In 2013, the WTO had 159 member countries, which account for more than 90 percent of world trade. Its overriding objective is to help trade flow smoothly, freely, fairly, and predictably. The WTO accomplishes this objective by administering trade agreements, acting as a forum for trade negotiations, handling trade disputes, monitoring national trade policies, assisting developing countries in trade policy issues, and cooperating with other international organizations. While GATT dealt mainly with trade in goods, WTO also has new agreements on trade in services and intellectual property rights.[23]

EMERGING MARKETS

Although there is no common definition of an emerging market, generally speaking it refers to countries undergoing a high growth rate and rapid economic liberalization. One assessment of emerging markets is the MSCI Emerging Markets Index (msci.com). In early 2014, emerging markets by region were the Americas (Brazil, Chile, Columbia, Mexico, and Peru); Europe, the Middle East, and Africa (Czech Republic, Egypt, Greece, Hungary, Poland, Russia, South Africa, Qatar, Turkey, and the United Arab Emirates); and Asia (China, India, Indonesia, Korea, Malaysia, Philippines, Taiwan, and Thailand). These, and other emerging economies, represent huge opportunities for sourcing and supply management.

How does a supply manager identify and assess the risks and opportunities of any particular emerging market? What questions should be asked? and Where can the answers be found? There are many resources at the national and international level to assist supply professionals engaged in global trade. These include departments in the United Nations, the World Bank, the International Monetary Fund, and the World Trade Organization. GlobalEdge (globaledge.msu.edu) at Michigan State University is an excellent source of global business knowledge. Three resources published annually that provide a good starting point for gaining a better understanding of global opportunities and challenges are *The Global Competitiveness Report, The World Factbook,* and *The Corruption Perceptions Index.* A fourth resource, the *Bribe Payers Index,* is updated every few years.

The *Global Competitiveness Report* published by the World Economic Forum defines competitiveness as the set of institutions, policies, and factors that determine the level of productivity of a country. Every country is measured on 12 pillars of competitiveness: institutions, infrastructure, macroeconomic stability, health and primary education, higher education and training, goods market efficiency, labor market efficiency, financial

---

[23] www.wto.org

market sophistication, technological readiness, market size, business sophistication, and innovation.[24]

The *World Factbook*, produced by the U.S. Central Intelligence Agency, contains all vital information and statistics for most countries around the world, including geography, people, government, economy, communications, transportation, transnational issues, and military.

Transparency International (transparency.org) produces numerous reports on global transparency. The annual *Corruption Perceptions Index* measures the perceived levels of public-sector corruption in 177 countries based on expert opinion. Countries are scored from 0 (highly corrupt) to 100 (very clean). On the 2013 index, 69 percent of countries score less than 50, with wide regional differences. Transparency International advocates stricter implementation of the UN Convention against Corruption, the only global initiative that provides a framework for putting an end to corruption.

The organization also produces the *Bribe Payers Index,* which is based on the views of business executives about countries they have a business relationship with as a supplier, client, partner, or competitor. The index ranks the likelihood of companies from 28 leading economies to win business offshore by paying bribes. These indexes provide indicators of the business climate that may be factored in the assessment of risk and total cost of doing business in various countries. Determining the risks and opportunities in a country requires a level of knowledge and analysis beyond what is required for domestic sourcing. Assessments in these reports and surveys may aid supply decision makers in identifying opportunities and risks in emerging economies.

Conclusion

In our global economy, it is nearly impossible for most companies to rely on the domestic supply base for 100 percent of purchased goods and services. For many organizations, global supply management has become a reality, as they are forced to seek out world-class suppliers to maintain their competitive position. The benefits of global procurement extend beyond simple price and cost advantages. Firms may purchase products and services abroad to gain access to better technology, secure items not available domestically, or purchase better-quality products.

While managing a global supply network can represent an important opportunity, it does provide a number of significant challenges. Consequently, the capability of managing global supply chains effectively can be a source of competitive advantage.

[24] K. Scwab, *The Global Competitiveness Report 2013–2014* (Geneva: World Economic Forum, 2013), pp. 1–9.

Questions for Review and Discussion

1. What are the factors/forces that have caused the increase in global trade? What changes do you think will occur in the next 10 years?

2. Why have North American firms outsourced and offshored the manufacture of goods and delivery of services?

3. What do firms see as the principal advantages to be gained when they buy globally? What are the principle disadvantages?

4. How can the buying firm minimize the problem areas connected with global buying? Which do you feel are most serious?

5. How can the buyer best get a list of potential international sources? Evaluate potential suppliers?

6. What are the pros and cons of buying direct versus using some form of intermediary?

7. What are the forms of countertrade, and what problems do they cause for the buyer? How can the buyer help make countertrade work?

8. How can the buyer make effective use of foreign trade zones?

9. What advantages are there for buyers affected by the North American Free Trade Agreement (NAFTA)? What is a certificate of origin? Why does the buyer need to be concerned with this?

10. What are Incoterms? What factors should be considered when selecting an Incoterm?

References   Daniels. J. D.; L. H. Radebaugh; and D. P. Sullivan. *International Business: Environments and Operations.*14th ed. Upper Saddle River, NJ: Prentice Hall, 2012.

Fishman, T. C. *China Inc.* New York: Scribner, 2005.

Hinkelman, E. G. *Dictionary of International Trade.* 10th ed. Novato, CA: World Trade Press, 2012.

Kamann, D. J., and V. Van Nieulande. "A Four-Filter Method for Outsourcing to Low-Cost Countries." *Journal of Supply Chain Management* 46 (2010), pp. 64–79.

Leenders, M. R., and P. F. Johnson. *Major Changes in Supply Chain Responsibilities.* Tempe, AZ: Center for Advanced Purchasing Studies, 2002.

Oshri, I.; J. Kotlarsky; and L. Willcocks. *The Handbook of Global Outsourcing and Offshoring.* 2nd ed. London: Palgrave Macmillan, 2011.

"Reshoring Manufacturing: Coming Home." *The Economist*, January 19, 2013.

Schwab, K., et al. *The Global Competitiveness Report, 2013–2014.* Geneva: World Economic Forum, 2013.

The *World Factbook* 2013–14. Washington, D.C.: Central Intelligence Agency, 2013. https://www.cia.gov/library/publications/the-world-factbook/index.html.

The 2013 Corruption Perceptions Index. Transparency International, http://cpi .transparency.org/cpi2013/

World Trade Organization. *Global Competitiveness Report 2013–2014,* www.weforum.org /issues/global-competitiveness

World Trade Organization. *International Trade Statistics 2008.* www.wto.org.

World Trade Organization Interactive Statistics Database. www.wto.org/english/res_e /statis_e/statis_e.htm

Case 14–1

Trojan Technologies

As Joyce Guo, senior buyer at Trojan Technologies Inc. in London, Ontario, Canada, finished her presentation, Randy Haill, materials manager, made the following comments to her:

> It appears there is a lot of opportunity and I want to proceed to the next step. Joyce, I need you to lay out an implementation plan for low-cost region sourcing that we can take to the president for his approval. Our plan will have to include the sourcing process, a schedule and timeline for implementation, a budget and the expected savings. We will also have to identify the risks and our contingency plans. Get to work on this and let's meet Friday morning next week to follow-up.

It was Thursday, February 23 and, as Joyce packed up her laptop and notes, she recognized that she had a lot more work to do before her meeting with Randy the following week.

TROJAN TECHNOLOGIES

Trojan Technologies Inc. (Trojan) was a leading water treatment technology company with the largest installed base of ultraviolet water treatment systems in operation around the world. Trojan specialized in the design, manufacture, and sale of pressurized and open-channel, ultraviolet disinfection and water treatment systems for industrial, municipal, commercial, and residential applications. Trojan's head office was in London, Ontario, Canada. The company had sales of $140 million and employed approximately 400 people in offices around the world, and served its customer base through an extensive network of dealers and representatives.

Trojan was owned by Danaher Corporation (Danaher), which had acquired the company in 2004. Danaher was a diversified global manufacturer, with businesses in professional instrumentation, industrial technologies, and tools and components. Sales revenues were $6.8 billion with a net profit of $746 million, and Danaher employed approximately 37,000 people. Management used its Danaher Business System (DBS) of continuous improvement to guide and measure operations and business activities.

Trojan's current product line consisted of 10 systems across its five markets: (1) residential water treatment, (2) municipal drinking water, (3) municipal wastewater,

(4) environmental contaminant treatment, and (5) industrial process. Systems for commercial and government customers ranged from approximately $50,000 to more than $1 million. These systems, which typically had a product life cycle of 7 to 10 years before being replaced with a new design, were designed and manufactured at the London facility, and modified to meet individual customer requirements. In a typical year, Trojan manufactured 500 to 600 systems for its commercial and government customers.

THE PURCHASING ORGANIZATION

Trojan's purchasing organization had seven buyers responsible for six commodity groups:

1. Lamps, quartz sleeves, and ballast.
2. Electrical parts and panels.
3. Stainless steel fabrication parts.
4. Machined and plastic parts.
5. Hydraulic parts and sensors.
6. MRO.

Purchases in the first two commodity groups accounted for approximately 60 percent of Trojan's $45 million spend on direct materials. However, most of these components were high-technology items and were locked up in strategic sourcing agreements. The remaining 40 percent comprised approximately 400 SKUs that were sourced primarily to North American suppliers.

THE LOW-COST REGION SOURCING PROJECT

Following its acquisition of Trojan, Danaher implemented several new initiatives aimed at improving corporate performance. One area targeted was global sourcing—an initiative Randy was asked to champion.

Randy turned to Joyce to lead a project investigating potential opportunities at Trojan for global sourcing and to recommend what action, if any, the company should take. Joyce had joined Trojan, approximately one year prior following completion of her MBA at the Richard Ivey School of Business, as senior buyer for stainless steel fabrication parts. With her background as a purchasing manager for a state-owned enterprise in China before returning to school

EXHIBIT 1
Parts List of Potential Candidates for Global Sourcing

Part Number	Description	Piece Price ($)	Annual Volume
PJ - 224	Stainless Steel Tray	13.31	2,000
PJ - 245	Stainless Steel Tray	6.11	10,000
ML - 092	Metal Disk	2.37	72,000
ML - 667	Clamp	1.65	15,000
RK- 376	Spring	1.07	20,000
LM - 144	O-Ring	0.18	20,000
GA - 136	Quartz Sleeve	27.62	15,000
GA- 208	Quartz Sleeve	18.57	18,000
GA - 659 - 1	Quartz Sleeve	6.19	700
GA - 659 - 2	Quartz Sleeve	5.85	1,000
GA - 659 - 3	Quartz Sleeve	8.66	11,000
GA - 024	Quartz Sleeve	27.62	2,000
RR - 061	Ceramic Disk	1.87	70,000
JH - 625	Machined Collar	139.15	500
DM - 354 - 01	Weldment	52.03	6,000
DM - 354 - 02	Weldment	63.03	1,000
TB - 024 - 01	Wire Harness	9.47	2,500
TB - 024 - 02	Wire Harness	13.27	2,500
TB - 024 - 03	Wire Harness	17.15	2,500
TB - 024 - 04	Wire Harness	21.37	2,500
PB - 554	PS 120/130V 50W	46.20	250
ML - 174	Metal Bracket	15.95	1,050

at Ivey, Randy felt that Joyce had the perfect credentials to lead the low-cost region sourcing project.

In her report to Randy on February 23, Joyce indicated that

- Trojan's global sourcing was not part of the company's purchasing strategy. Presently, international purchases were limited only to those components that were otherwise not available to North America.

- By not engaging in global sourcing, Trojan was missing potential opportunities for lower costs, higher quality, and improved product availability.

- Companies using global sourcing had been able to reduce costs substantially for some products and services.

- Several Danaher businesses sourced components globally and the company had set up an international purchasing office in China, staffed by five people: a sourcing manager, a buyer, and three engineers.

- China appeared to offer Trojan the best opportunities for low-cost sourcing, and Joyce suggested that the company start its global sourcing initiative there.

As part of her report to Randy, Joyce also identified a preliminary list of purchased components that she considered potential candidates for global sourcing that were not part of strategic sourcing agreements (see Exhibit 1).

IMPLEMENTATION PLAN

In preparation for her meeting with Randy, Joyce wanted to prepare a thorough plan for implementing low-cost region sourcing. Joyce expected that if the project went ahead, Randy would put her in charge and she wanted to make sure it would be a success.

As a starting point, Joyce wanted to create a process that Trojan would use for low-cost region sourcing. She expected that people from the engineering and quality departments would be involved, and Joyce wanted to identify the specific steps that would be used to source each component. Joyce wanted to identify the approximate time to complete each step in order to estimate the sourcing cycle time.

Starting the low-cost region sourcing process would require clear criteria on which to select components and evaluate their suitability. Joyce wanted to establish guidelines for components that could be used to identify parts that provided the greatest opportunity and probability for success.

A major consideration for Joyce was setting expectations for cost reductions that Trojan could achieve through low-cost region sourcing. Based on the information that she collected so far, Joyce found that while global sourcing provided opportunities for substantial reductions in piece prices, there were also additional costs. For example, Trojan would have to pay 8 percent duties for products imported from China. She also learned that, based on the experience of other Danaher businesses, inventories could increase by 25 percent and transportation premiums averaged 5 percent. In addition, Joyce believed that there would be other administrative and travel costs she would need to budget.

Not only would Joyce have to provide an estimate to Randy concerning what Trojan could save each year through low-cost region sourcing, but also set guidelines regarding when piece price reductions justified the costs and efforts to switch suppliers. In preparing her cost savings estimate, Joyce would have to take into account that Trojan's standard costs were adjusted each January the 1st. Consequently, savings could only be claimed for the year in which purchases were made.

A final concern was risk management and contingency planning. Trojan was enjoying strong sales growth and Joyce wanted to avoid supply shortages or quality problems. Consequently, Joyce wanted to establish appropriate policies that would address low-cost region sourcing supply risks.

Case 14–2

Marc Biron

MARC BIRON

"I want you to see how supply can add value to our global marketing spend. You've got a couple of months to come back to me with a plan." Marc Biron, supply manager at BCI, one of the world's largest financial institutions, headquartered in Paris, France, pondered the new assignment just given to him by Pierre Jardin, the vice president of supply at BCI.

BCI

BCI, started as a small commercial bank over a hundred years earlier, had grown over the years to offer a large variety of financial services, including commercial and retail banking, asset management, and retail and wholesale insurance. Over the past two decades BCI had expanded its international presence significantly by acquisition of regional financial institutions in all major countries around the world. With revenues in excess of $200 billion a year, BCI was considered a major global giant in the industry.

SUPPLY AT BCI

Until five years ago, supply at BCI had been decentralized with each local or regional business unit responsible for managing its own supply requirements. A review of supply by a major consulting firm pointed out that a centralized supply function might be able to achieve considerable savings by consolidating world requirements and bringing professional supply expertise to the acquisi-

tion of BCI requirements. For example, the consultants pointed out that in their estimate IT expenditures with suppliers might exceed $6 billion per year and that major improvements in process and spend should be possible. BCI's senior management board followed the consultant's advice and hired Pierre Jardin, who had managed the supply function at one of BCI's competitors, to establish a central procurement organization. Pierre had personally started on the IT spend in Europe, while building up a group of supply professionals at head office. In the first two years, Pierre had succeeded in saving about $1 billion on Europe's IT spend with suppliers, and he then hired Marc Biron to take over IT acquisition. Having spent three years in IT supply worldwide, Marc had learned how each of the international business units operated. He was also well aware that business unit managers prized their local independence and were wary of head office involvement in their units. Nevertheless, Marc was successful in negotiating IT supply contracts that provided an additional $1 billion in annual savings.

THE NEW BCI PRESIDENT

Two years ago, a new president took over at BCI. With a strong marketing background, the new president insisted on worldwide brand recognition for BCI, with all business units displaying the corporate logo in all of their communications, promotion, and advertising. In addition, a major increase in marketing spend was initiated to grow the brand. For the first two years, there was no supply involvement in any country on the media spend as local and regional marketing managers had free reign on how to spend their budgets.

MARC BIRON'S ASSIGNMENT

Pierre Jardin had made reasonable progress in improving BCI's spend with suppliers for certain categories. In addition to the IT spend on hardware, software, and IT services, he had made progress in increasing supply involvement in corporate travel, furniture, and paper purchases. In each category, resistance from local managers with strong preference for local and, in many cases, multiple suppliers had been strong.

Aware that marketing's spend was large, although Pierre did not know the exact amount, he decided that this category might represent an opportunity for the supply function. Not only might BCI achieve considerable savings, but here was a category spend where, even in those business units that had a local supply manager, there had been no supply involvement at all historically. Therefore,

working with and through local supply managers was not even an option.

Although Pierre was reluctant to pull Marc Biron out of his IT assignment, he felt that Marc had the international experience, skills, and personality to tackle marketing's spend as a category. He, therefore, called Marc into his office and explained why he wanted Marc to drop his IT work and take on the marketing spend challenge. He gave Marc two months to come up with a plan.

THE MARKETING SPEND

Marc Biron had no marketing spend experience. He agreed with Pierre that this category was one of BCI's largest spends and if IT experience was any indicator, potentially an area of major savings opportunities. He knew that this was a major test for him and that success in this task would impact favorably on his future career. On the other hand, finding a successful way of gaining meaningful involvement for supply in this category would be difficult. He wondered how he should use the next two months that Pierre had granted him to come up with a plan and what that plan would be.

Case 14–3

Sarin Pharmaceuticals Ltd.

Alan Mannik, director of procurement for the Sarin Pharmaceuticals Ltd. (Sarin) Animal Health Division plant in Vancouver, British Columbia, was planning for the transfer of eight products from the company's plant in France. He had a conference call with Francois Simpson from the Sarin facility in Arras, France, on June 11 to discuss details of the transfer. It was Monday, June 2, and Alan needed to prepare for the meeting, which was set up to review purchasing transition issues. He was particularly concerned with the supply of raw materials and packaging.

SARIN PHARMACEUTICALS LTD.

Founded in 1865, Sarin was headquartered in New York and had a reputation for excellence and innovation in the discovery, development, and manufacturing of medicines for people and animals. In the most recent year, company revenues were $12 billion, with net income of $1.4 billion. The company employed more than 45,000 people who worked in 60 countries.

Sarin was organized into four segments: pharmaceuticals, vaccines, consumer health, and animal health. The Pharma-

ceutical Division accounted for approximately 70 percent of company revenues, while the Vaccine, Consumer Health, and Animal Health Divisions represented 13 percent, 10 percent, and 7 percent of Sarin's revenues respectively. The Pharmaceutical Division developed and manufactured medicines for the treatment of a variety of serious and chronic diseases, such as cancer, epilepsy, and heart disease. The Vaccine Division produced pediatric and adult vaccines to prevent a range of infectious diseases, including hepatitis A and B, polio, and influenza. The Consumer Health Division focused on a wide range of consumer health products in the areas of skin care, wellness, oral care, and nutrition. The smallest division, Animal Health, developed and produced medicines for livestock, poultry, and pets.

Sarin focused on its strategic mission of discovering, developing, and bringing to market health care products in an effective manner that fulfilled unmet medical needs. As a result, the company had recently divested a number of operations that did not align with the company's strategy. A number of businesses that complemented Sarin's strategy had recently been acquired, and additional acquisitions were expected to be announced during the coming year.

ANIMAL HEALTH DIVISION

The Animal Health Division was facing major changes. The company recently purchased Milway-Kitsch Animal Health (MKAH), which would push Sarin to the number one position in the world in animal health products. Sarin had traditionally held a leading position in medicines for large animals, plus a strong presence in Latin America and Asia. MKAH, on the other hand, had strong product lines in the pet market in North America and in vaccines worldwide. They also had superior organizational strength in Europe and Australia. It was planned that the merger of these two firms would lead to the creation of a single, integrated unit that would place Sarin in a position to achieve the vision for the Animal Health Division: "We will be the driving force in the animal health industry." The number of manufacturing facilities for the combined company numbered 46 in 35 different countries.

PROCUREMENT

The manufacturing process for animal health products required the acquisition of a wide variety of chemical compounds, syringes, bottles, packaging materials, and labels. Most of the products manufactured by Sarin were subject to stringent regulatory requirements, such as content, scale for the unit of measurement, language, and dosage, that varied by country. The procurement organization at the Vancouver plant was responsible for sourcing more than 1,600 raw material and packaging items with a total annual value of $22 million (Canadian). Each item had to be purchased from an approved Sarin supplier. The approval process involved a series of tests and reviews that could take a year to complete and involved the following steps:

1. A copy of the standard operating procedures for the product had to be provided and approved by Sarin.

2. A certificate of analysis of a sample lot had to be provided, manufactured according to the process established in the standard operating procedure.

3. Three random samples from different lots were required for testing, along with a certificate of analysis. These samples were tested by Sarin and the results compared to the certificate of analysis.

4. The supplier processes and capabilities needed to meet acceptable standards in the areas of product development, quality control, and manufacturing.

5. A pilot batch would be run at Sarin, using materials from the supplier, and tested.

6. Only after the supplier had successfully passed steps 1–5 could the product be used in production. The first three lots shipped by the supplier were to be tested by Sarin. Only if all three lots were approved would the supplier be approved. Future shipments would be subject to periodic testing.

CLOSURE OF THE FRENCH PLANT

It was announced in March that Sarin's only Animal Health plant in France would be closing by May the following year. The eight products manufactured there would be transferred to the Vancouver plant on a phased basis starting in December and commencing full production a year later. It was planned that the French plant would increase production sufficiently to provide sufficient inventory to satisfy demand until the Vancouver plant could provide adequate supply. The addition of the eight products to the Vancouver portfolio would increase production by 30 percent (see Exhibit 1). Capacity was not an issue.

EXHIBIT 1
Products to Be Transferred from France to Vancouver

Product Name	Number of Formulations	Sizes	Number of Label Languages
Tetratex (injection)	1	1	8
Vetracil (tablets)	2	2	9
Baxotil (suspension)	1	2	3
Baxotil (paste for dogs)	1	2	14
Baxotil (paste for cats)	1	2	14
Federex (paste)	1	1	1
Vitopax (1% paste)	1	1	2
Vitopax (10% paste)	1	2	2

By late May, it had become apparent that the French plant would not be able to increase production for sufficient inventory to last for the phase-in period due to low-productivity rates and morale issues. Also, French regulations restricted the ability of the plant to run overtime. It was clear that the transition to the Vancouver plant would have to be achieved earlier than planned to avoid product shortages.

The approximately 300 approved suppliers for the French plant consisted of both large and small operations that were located all over Europe. A sample of some of the suppliers were as follows:

Company name: E. Durand
Location: Metz, France
Size: Approximately 400 employees
Product: Chemicals

Company name: P.J. Laurent
Location: Metz, France
Size: Family firm, 3 employees
Product: Printing barrel syringes

Company name: Union Plastics
Location: St. Didier-En-Valley, France
Size: Approximately 100 employees
Product: Syringe barrels and plungers for syringes

Company name: Loffler AG
Location: Freyung, Germany
Size: Approximately 500 employees
Product: Chemicals

As Alan contemplated his moves over the next six months, he wondered how he could ensure that the Vancouver plant had all the necessary supplies for production in an efficient and timely manner.

Legal and Ethics

Key Questions for the Supply Decision Maker

Should we

- Put all purchase agreements in writing?
- Develop and support a set of principles of social responsibility?
- Use alternative dispute resolution in large-dollar purchase agreements?

How can we

- Minimize the organization's legal and ethical exposure?
- Minimize our own personal liability for purchase actions?
- Avoid legal disputes with suppliers?

All supply communications, agreements, and understandings internally and externally have ethical and legal implications. In Chapter 4, purchasing was defined as the exchange of money (the buyer's responsibility) for goods and services (the supplier's responsibility). From a legal perspective, the obligation of the seller is to transfer and deliver and that of the buyer is to accept and pay in accordance with the contract. This chapter addresses three key decisions: (1) How can we assure that the legal record reflects the commercial agreement? (2) How can we confirm the legal record? (3) How can we assure that supply personnel deal ethically and in conformance with regulatory requirements as well as organizational values?

First and foremost, it must be realized that the courts are a place of last resort. *Seldom will either buyer or seller resort to the courts to enforce a purchase contract or assess financial damages.* In those infrequent situations in which formal legal action is taken, the legal costs can be high and the outcome uncertain. *The competent purchaser wishes to avoid such situations and will take legal action only as a last resort.* Knowledge of the law of contracts and common law helps the supply manager both to avoid legal involvement and position the organization to successfully pursue, or defend itself against, such lawsuits.

While professional supply managers do not require the training of a lawyer or an ethicist, they should understand the basic principles of commercial law and ethics. This will help them recognize problems and situations that require professional counsel. It will also provide knowledge to avoid pitfalls in day-to-day operations. As a strategic player in the organization, the supply manager must continually look to maximize opportunities and minimize risks for the organization. Monitoring the legal and ethical horizons is one way supply professionals can contribute to the organization.

Another way supply managers contribute to the organization is by ensuring that the supply process is conducted ethically and in a socially responsible manner. Recent events have once again put ethical behavior in the spotlight. Ethical purchasing and supply behavior will help avoid ethical breaches and position the organization to capitalize on its reputation.

LEGAL AUTHORITY OF BUYER AND SELLER

Making sure that the right people are entering into the commercial agreement in the first place is the starting point for aligning the commercial agreement and the legal agreement. The legal authority of the buyer and the seller is different. It is important for everyone in both organizations to understand who has the legal authority to commit an organization's funds and who has the authority to accept an order. This is especially important if buying off-contract or circumventing the supply process is prevalent in an organization because these actions may put the buying organization at legal risk.

Legal Authority of the Buyer

What is the supply officer's legal status? According to the law of agency, he or she has the authority as an agent of the organization to attend to the business of supply in accordance with the instructions given by his or her employer. This legal authority may be actual (express or implied) or apparent.

Actual Authority (Express and Implied)

The law assumes that an agreement exists between the agent (employee) and the principal (employer) about the employee's scope of authority. This authority may be express or implied.

Express authority includes the acts that the agent is expressly and directly authorized to perform. This might be the duties and responsibilities defined by a job description. (See Figures 3–3 and 3–4 for sample job descriptions.) It might be the levels of authority laid out in a policy and procedure manual.

Implied authority is all other authority that is necessary, usual, and proper to carry through to completion the express authority conferred. The extent of the agent's implied authority is determined from the nature of the business to be transacted. Implied authority is broad in the case of a general agent or manager.

Third-party role. It is the duty of the third party (e.g., a supplier's representative) to ascertain the scope of an agent's authority. The supplier cannot only rely on statements of the agent about the extent of his or her powers. If the third party knows of limitations on the agent's power, he or she is bound by them. A supplier may request documentation from a buying organization clarifying an individual's level of authority. In practice, it is in the best legal and commercial interests of the supply organization to clarify roles and responsibilities of department employees for its supply base. Also, if a salesperson knows that someone in the buying organization is acting outside his or her scope of authority, the salesperson is legally bound to operate within the legal scope of authority of that individual.

Apparent Authority

A person's apparent authority is that which he or she appears to have. This appearance of authority is created when the words or actions of the principal (employer) lead a reasonable person to believe that authority has been granted.

For example, as an agent of the company, the supply officer has the *right* to bind the company within the limits assigned (that is in accordance with the actual authorization). The *power* to bind the principal, however, is defined by the *apparent* scope of authority. For most supply officers apparent authority is rather broad. In fact, the power of an agent to bind the principal may greatly exceed the right to do so.

For nonsupply personnel who have not been delegated any agency status, apparent authority is the only kind they might have. For example, an engineer agrees to buy something from a salesperson. The engineer is not a legal agent of the company. The goods are received, the invoice arrives, and payment is made. The engineer acquired apparent authority when the company ratified the purchase by receiving the goods and paying for them. Legally, the engineer now has indefinite apparent authority to buy similar products from the same supplier for similar dollar amounts.

Each time the company ratifies an unauthorized purchase, a valid contract is created and apparent authority is created.

Apparent Authority and Maverick Buying

People within an organization who spend company money on the basis of apparent authority are commonly referred to as maverick buyers. They typically buy off-contract or circumvent the purchasing policy and procedures to make their own buying decisions.

In many organizations, the number of people with *apparent* authority and the volume of dollars spent by them is great enough to undermine the integrity of the supply process and jeopardize supply's relationship with suppliers.

Several process efficiency measures discussed in Chapter 4 rein in maverick buying. These include better spend category management, e-procurement systems, and procurement card programs. P-card programs give limited authority to nonpurchasers, set spending limits, and designate what can and cannot be purchased. A P-card is an effective and legal means of giving limited authority to persons outside the supply department. This allows supply professionals to focus on more critical goods and services.

Personal Liability

The supply officer may be held personally liable under certain conditions when signing contracts. These conditions include instances when an agent:

1. Makes a false statement about his or her authority with intent to deceive or when the misrepresentation has the natural and probable consequence of misleading.
2. Performs a damaging act without authority, even though he or she believes he or she has such authority.
3. Performs an illegal act, even on authority from the employer.
4. Willfully performs an act that results in damage to anyone.
5. Performs a damaging act outside the scope of his or her authority, even though the act is performed with the intention of rendering the employer a valuable service.

Agent's Liability to Seller

In each case, no valid contract existed between the seller and the principal (purchasing firm). Therefore, the supplier ordinarily has no recourse to the company employing the agent. The only recourse the supplier has is to the agent personally.

The purchaser also may be answerable to the seller on three grounds: (1) The purchaser engaged in deceit. (2) The purchaser is the real contracting party. (3) The purchaser breached the warranty that he or she had actual authority in this instance.

Lawsuits have also been brought by sellers against supply managers when their principal (employer) was unable to pay the account. This has occurred when:

1. The employer became insolvent or bankrupt.
2. The employer tried to avoid the legal obligations to accept and pay for merchandise purchased.

3. The employer became involved in litigation with the seller, whose lawyers decided that the contract price could be readily collected personally from the supply manager.

Principal's Liability to Seller

The principal may still be held legally liable in some instances: if the purchaser acted within apparent scope of authority but outside actual scope and if the seller did not know that there were limitations on the actual authority. Under these circumstances, the purchaser probably is in the wrong and is answerable to the principal.

Agent's Liability to the Principal

The supply officer becomes liable to the principal (employer) when damage occurs through active fault or through negligence. It is difficult to define what negligence is, although in general it may be said to constitute an "omission of due care under given circumstances."

The supply officer also has an obligation to inform the employer about specific actions taken to perform the purchasing function and report results. Proper documentation and accounting must also cover any funds or property handled. If these obligations are not met, the employer may sue for damages.

Antitrust acts (discussed in detail later in this chapter) apply to buyers as much as to sellers. The U.S. Supreme Court has held that these acts are applicable to all attempts to restrain trade, even though the restraint is exercised on those not engaged in the same line of business and is based on purchasing activities rather than selling activities—provided that the net result of the act is to restrain competition. Although a supply officer should never attempt to perform the duties of a competent lawyer, he or she should keep informed about court decisions and changes in laws that affect his or her actions. Trade publications normally report court decisions and major changes in laws that impact supply management.

Authority of Suppliers' Representatives

The authority of the sales representative is different than that of a supply manager. A salesperson's ordinary authority is simply to solicit orders and to send them to his or her employer for ratification and acceptance. The U.S. courts have consistently held this distinction between a buyer's and a seller's legal authority. An employer is bound by all the acts of an agent acting within the scope of the employment, and a salesperson only solicits orders. Therefore, the supply officer should determine definitely whether or not a salesperson has the authority to conclude a contract without referring it to the company for acceptance. The purchaser may request a letter, signed by an officer of the supplier firm, specifying that the salesperson has the authority of a sales agent.

However, the courts tend to view agreements between a purchaser and a salesperson as valid. This is true even if a supplier has not authorized its salesperson to enter into binding contracts and the company has done nothing to lead others to believe that its representative has such power. A contract results because the conduct of the seller is interpreted as acceptance. Behavior matters! To invalidate this agreement, the seller must notify the buyer within a reasonable time that the salesperson has exceeded his or her authority.

A contract may be voidable if the seller or its representative makes false statements about the character of the merchandise. The other party may exercise this option. There are relevant laws and rulings for voiding a contract on this basis for both goods and services. Aside from any legal question, the seller may make substantial concessions because it wants to protect its reputation and goodwill.

THE UNIFORM COMMERCIAL CODE

In most countries, the actions of buyers and sellers occur within a framework of laws that govern transactions. In the United States, the Uniform Commercial Code (UCC), as it is adapted and adopted by each state, governs the transaction of goods. In this section, the UCC is addressed in detail. The next section addresses common law that governs the purchase of services.

Purpose of a Uniform Commercial Code

The purpose of a uniform commercial code is to facilitate fair and efficient transactions. A flexible code is adaptable to the needs of commerce as business practices and supporting technologies change. The challenge for code developers is combining and balancing fairness and efficiency with flexibility.

This flexibility is evident in the terms used. According to Article 1, Section 201, "*Record* means information that is inscribed on a tangible medium or that is stored in an electronic or other medium and is retrievable in perceivable form." "*Signed* includes using any symbol executed or adopted with present intention to adopt or accept a writing." These simple changes bring under the UCC new technology such as electronic documents and electronic signatures (Section 2-201).

A uniform body of law governing the sale of goods within a country and between countries minimizes the risks associated with the acquisition process and facilitates fair and efficient trade. Uniform laws:

- Provide a set of rules for making and interpreting contracts.
- Clarify rights, obligations, and remedies of parties to the contract.
- Provide a more efficient and economical way to buy and sell raw materials, commodities, and manufactured goods.
- Provide buyers and sellers a framework within which to mold their contracts to their specifications.
- Reduce uncertainty and doubt about which rules apply.
- Reduce disputes.

Efforts to develop uniform laws occur at the country and international level. Examples include the following:

United States: The American Law Institute and the National Conference of Commissioners on Uniform State Laws jointly sponsor the revisions and preparation of the Uniform Commercial Code (UCC). The UCC is a comprehensive modernization of various statutes relating to commercial transactions.

Canada: The Uniform Law Conference spearheads the Commercial Law Strategy, which is designed to modernize and harmonize commercial law in Canada. The goal is to create a comprehensive framework of commercial statute law to make it easier to do business in Canada. Quebec, similar to Louisiana in the United States, has its own set of laws dealing with property and civil rights based on the Napoleonic Code.

United Nations: At the international level, the UN Convention on Contracts for the International Sale of Goods (CISG) serves the same purpose. The CISG typically applies if both countries have adopted it and no other law is specified. Or the contract may specify the law of the buyer's country or of the seller's country.

UCC Article 2

In the United States, many federal, state, and local statutes govern purchasing practice. Article 2 of the UCC (as adopted and adapted by each state legislature) covers most of the transactions involving the purchase and sale of goods. The UCC resulted from the joint efforts of the American Law Institute and the National Conference of Commissioners on Uniform State Laws. Since first published in 1952, the UCC has undergone numerous revisions and refinements with the latest in 2012. The UCC applies only to legal situations in the United States related to the sale of goods (not services).

All or some of the UCC has been enacted in all 50 states, the District of Columbia, the U.S. Virgin Islands, and Puerto Rico. There is substantial uniformity of commercial law in the United States. Even Louisiana, whose law is based on the Napoleonic Code, not English common law, has adopted most of the UCC.

Supply managers should understand the UCC adopted by whichever state the contract is in. Also, they may want to include separate terms relating to the goods portion of a contract covering goods and services so that the UCC applies to the goods portion of the contract.

The Purchase Order Contract

Article 2 of the UCC applies to transactions in goods (Section 2-102). A buyer is a person who buys or contracts to buy goods, and a seller is a person who sells or contracts to sell goods (Section 2-103).

According to Section 2-204, "a contract for sale of goods may be made in any manner sufficient to show agreement, including conduct by both parties that recognizes the existence of such a contract."

A valid contract is based on four factors:

1. Competent parties—either principals or qualified agents.
2. Legal subject matter or purpose—no illegal activities or violations of existing laws.
3. An offer and an acceptance.
4. Consideration—bargained-for exchange, typically money for goods or services.

Offers

An offer may be made by either a buyer or a seller. Offers can be modified or revoked before acceptance. The courts generally have held that advertisements and price lists do not constitute legal offers unless specifically directed to the buyer or unless an order placed on the basis of the advertisement or price list is specifically accepted by the supplier.

A *purchase order (PO)* generally contains the buyer's *offer. Acceptance* by the supplier makes it a legal contract. Purchase orders (paper or electronic) often include provision for acknowledgment or acceptance.

An offer can be equally valid if made by a seller either in writing or orally. Acceptance by the buyer creates a legal contract. Under the UCC, if a seller makes a firm offer to sell, but no time period is stated, it generally must be held open for a "reasonable" time period (Section 2-205). *Reasonable* is defined as three months ("in no event may such period of irrevocability exceed three months"), unless a shorter period is stated by the seller in the offer. Also, if a seller's offer includes an assurance that the price will remain firm for a specified period, the price may not be revoked prior to the expiration of the period.

Terms and Conditions (Ts and Cs) on the PO.   There is no universal agreement on how detailed the terms and conditions on a purchase order should be. Three options exist:

1. *Boilerplate or a framework agreement.* Some companies include the complete terms and conditions that apply to *any* transaction.
2. *Specific Ts and Cs.* Some include detailed terms and conditions applying to that *specific* order.
3. *Basic Items.* Others provide only the basic items necessary for a valid offer and depend on the provisions of the UCC for proper legal coverage.

The supply manager should rely on company legal counsel to determine the policy to be followed.

Acceptance of Offers

It is important to know when an offer of sale or purchase has been accepted. Legally this is important because an offer and an acceptance is one of the four elements of a valid contract. According to Section 2-206, "Unless otherwise unambiguously indicated by the language or circumstances, (a) an offer to make a contract shall be construed as inviting acceptance in any manner and by any medium reasonable in the circumstances." This language allows for electronic acceptance of a contract. (Section 2-206)

Acceptance of goods occurs when the buyer (a) after a reasonable opportunity to inspect, signifies that the goods are either conforming or acceptable in their nonconformity, (b) fails to reject after a reasonable opportunity to inspect, or (c) the buyer behaves as if the seller no longer owns the goods. Acceptance of a part of any commercial unit is acceptance of that entire unit. Often the buyer will require a supplier acknowledgment to facilitate internal planning and operations.

The purchase order form or the sales contract is intended to include all the essential conditions of the transaction. Typically, the documentation includes a statement such as "Acceptance of this order implies the acceptance of conditions contained thereon." This provision is intended to warn that conditions are attached to the contract, make all conditions legally binding, and to prevent the seller from later arguing lack of awareness. Similar statements are found in most purchase agreements.

Method of Acceptance

The offeror may include a contract clause requiring that acceptance be indicated in a specific manner. The U.S. federal E-Sign law allows a "written" response to mean any reasonable form such as a written signature or an electronic form. The buyer may stipulate a means of acceptance such as a written signature or an e-mail or a tweet. This should be specified by a clause that stipulates this: "This order must be acknowledged on the enclosed (if paper) or in the following manner (if electronic)." In e-procurement systems, both the purchase order and the acknowledgment are transmitted electronically.

When the answer is electronically transmitted, faxed, or posted, the acceptance is communicated and the contract is completed from the moment the electronic document, complete with a digital signature is sent, or the fax is transmitted or the letter is mailed. The increased use of electronic data interchange (EDI), digital signatures, and web-based purchasing systems to send bids, purchase orders, and contracts requires buyers and sellers to agree on procedures, terms, and conditions to prevent disputes that might end up in court.

Conflicting Conditions

Sometimes the supplier uses its own acknowledgment that includes conditions that conflict with some stated in the purchase order. After comparing the conditions stated in the offer with those in the acceptance, the buyer and supplier may negotiate to resolve differences. Or they may rely on the UCC for resolution. Section 2-207 states that "A definite and seasonable expression of acceptance or a written confirmation which is sent in a reasonable time operates as an acceptance even though it states terms additional to or different from those offered or agreed upon, unless acceptance is expressly made conditional on assent to the additional or different terms." This statement is designed to reduce or eliminate the "battle of forms" that may occur when the Ts and Cs on the forms of the buyer and seller conflict.

Subject to Section 2-207, the additional terms are considered proposals. They become part of the contract unless (1) the offer expressly limits acceptance to the terms of the offer; (2) they materially alter it; or (3) notification of objection to them has already been given or is given within a reasonable time after notice of them is received.

Furthermore, "Conduct by both parties which recognizes the existence of a contract is sufficient to establish a contract for sale although the writings of the parties do not otherwise establish a contract. In such case the terms of the particular contract consist of those terms on which the writings of the parties agree, together with any supplementary terms incorporated under any other provisions of this Act" (Section 2-207).

Purchases Made Orally—Statute of Frauds

Orders are occasionally placed by telephone or orally in person. Section 2-201 of the UCC specifies that:

1. Except as otherwise provided in this section a contract for the sale of goods for the price of $500 or more is not enforceable by way of action or defense unless there is some writing sufficient to indicate that a contract for sale has been made between the parties and signed by the party against whom enforcement is sought or by his authorized agent or broker. A writing is not insufficient because it omits or incorrectly states a term agreed upon but the contract is not enforceable under this paragraph beyond the quantity of goods shown in such writing.

2. Between merchants if within a reasonable time a writing in confirmation of the contract and sufficient against the sender is received and the party receiving it has reason to

know its contents, it satisfies the requirements of subsection (1) against such party unless written notice of objection to its contents is given within 10 days after it is received.

When an alleged oral agreement is partially performed—for example, 1 of 10 lots is delivered and then the purchaser cancels—the partial performance can validate the contract, but only for the amount accepted. A valid contract also exists for goods when goods have been received and accepted or payment has been made and received (Section 2-206.)

However, if one party "relied to its detriment" on the promises made by the other party, the entire contract may be validated. Both the buyer and seller may rely on the doctrine of *promissory estoppel,* which is an exception to the statute of frauds. This means that even if there is no record, the entire contract may be valid (a) if the goods are specially manufactured for the buyer and not suitable for sale to others; and (b) if the seller has substantially begun manufacturing or committed for their procurement.

To avoid misunderstandings during a conversation with a supplier, say, "This is not an order" if seeking information only; instruct suppliers not to begin work without authorization; and document all changes made after the purchase order has been issued.

Inspection

The buyer has a right to inspect goods before acceptance to determine if they comply with the contract description. According to Section 2-513, "The buyer has a right before payment or acceptance to inspect them at any reasonable place and time and in any reasonable manner. When the seller is required or authorized to send the goods to the buyer, the inspection may be after their arrival."

Inspection before Contracting

If a buyer inspects goods *before* entering into a contract of sale, he or she is expected to use his or her own judgment with respect to quality, quantity, and other characteristics of the merchandise. The UCC states that "when the buyer before entering into the contract has examined the goods or the sample or model as fully as desired or has refused to examine the goods after a demand by the seller there is no implied warranty with regard to defects which an examination ought in the circumstances to have revealed to the buyer" (Section 2-316).

This means the buyer cannot raise an issue about quality or quantity after inspecting and accepting merchandise. Also, a seller cannot be held responsible if equipment fails to perform the work that the buyer expects if the buyer merely provides material specifications. For the seller to be held responsible for equipment performance, the buyer has to indicate the purpose of the equipment or goods.

Payment before Inspection

In some purchase contracts, payment may be required before the buyer has an opportunity to inspect the goods (Section 2-512). For example, payment may be made before the seller actually ships the goods. Payment in this case does not constitute an acceptance of the goods or impair the buyer's right to inspect or any of the buyer's remedies on breach of contract. In a JIT or ship-to-stock arrangement wherein goods are not inspected, the buyer needs to specify in the written contract a time frame for notification of defects, since the UCC does not cover these situations completely.

The courts generally have held that if a purchaser is not sufficiently experienced to be able to judge adequately the goods inspected, or if he or she relies on a fraudulent statement made by a seller and purchases in consequence of that fraudulent statement, the buyer then may rescind the contract or hold the seller liable for damages.

Acceptance and Rejection of Goods

The acceptance of goods means the buyer becomes the owner of the goods. Any words or acts that indicate the buyer's intention to become the owner of the goods are sufficient. If the buyer keeps the goods and exercises rights of ownership over them, acceptance has taken place, even though the buyer may have expressly stated that the goods are rejected (Section 2-606).

Notice of Breach of Contract

If the goods tendered do not comply with the sales contract, the buyer is under no duty to accept them. Even if the buyer accepts nonconforming goods, the right to damages still exists for the seller's breach of contract. The seller must be notified of the breach within a "reasonable" time (Section 2-607) or be barred from any remedy.

A "reasonable time" is determined by normal commercial standards (Section 2-201). Recent legal rulings indicate that if the buyer tells the supplier about a problem, but fails to specifically give notice "of breach," the supplier may have room for legal negotiating even if the supplier tries to fix the problem. An amendment to this section replaced the requirement for providing notice of breach with a requirement for "timely notice" (Section 2-607).

Options for Nonconforming Goods

In the event the seller delivers goods or the tender of delivery fails in any way to conform to the contract, the buyer has the option to (1) reject the whole shipment, (2) accept the whole shipment, or (3) accept part of the shipment and reject the balance (Section 2-601). Rejection, of course, must be within a reasonable time after delivery and the seller must be notified promptly. The buyer must hold the goods, using reasonable care, until the seller has had sufficient time to remove them (Section 2-602).

There are a variety of reasons and remedies for rejecting goods. For instance, the goods may be late, may have been delivered in the wrong amount, or may fail to meet the specifications. Ultimately, the purchaser wants the goods. Therefore, a lawsuit is undesirable, even though the buyer may be granted any one of the commonly recognized judicial remedies for breach of contract, such as money damages or insistence on performance. Legal action is uncertain and often costly, may take a great deal of time, and may cause the loss of a good supplier. A negotiated resolution is often preferable.

Actions in Event of Breach

Several options are available. If the breach of contract is not too serious, a simple warning to the supplier may be adequate. If the goods received are usable for some purpose, even though not quite up to specifications, a price adjustment may satisfy both parties. Sometimes the goods may be made usable by the supplier, or by the purchaser at the supplier's expense. If the goods are component parts, they may be replaced by the supplier. If the purchase is equipment or even processed material that is incapable of being efficiently used in its present form, the supplier may correct the defects at the user's plant; or, as a last resort, the goods may be rejected and shipped back to the supplier, usually at the supplier's expense.

In some cases, purchasers use a full-payment check to settle a dispute. The purchaser sends a check for what he or she believes covers the goods, less the cost of the defect, and writes the words "Payment in Full" to indicate that this is a settlement. The supplier, under the UCC, can cash the check and write "under protest" or "without prejudice" to protect its rights to try to collect the balance due.

Recent court rulings indicate there is an offer and acceptance, hence a valid contract, if the check and notice were sent to a specific person who knowingly cashes the check. If, however, the check was sent to accounts receivable or some other routine processing area of the supplier's company, there would not be a real acceptance, and the supplier would still have rights to try to collect or settle the balance with the buyer.

Warranties

The rules governing warranty arrangements between buyer and seller have advanced from *caveat emptor* (let the buyer beware) to the legal provisions of the UCC, which recognize four types of warranties:

1. Express warranty (Section 2-313).
2. Implied warranty of merchantability; usage of trade (Section 2-314).
3. Implied warranty of fitness for a particular purpose.
4. Warranty of title and against infringement (Section 2-312).

Express Warranties

Express warranties to the *buyer* include affirmation of facts, promises, description, sample, or model pertaining to the goods that are the subject of the negotiation (Section 2-313).

Implied Warranty of Merchantability

Implied warranty of merchantability or usage of trade means that the goods fit the *ordinary* purpose for which goods of that description are used in the trade. Accepted trade standards of quality, fitness for the intended uses, and conformance to promises or specified fact made on the container or label are all used as measures of merchantable quality (Section 2-314). Under this section, the serving for value of food or drink to be consumed either on the premises or elsewhere is a sale.

Implied Warranty of Fitness for a Particular Purpose

Implied warranty of fitness for a particular purpose occurs when the seller, at the time of contracting, has reason to know any particular purpose for which the goods are required. The buyer is relying on the seller's skill or judgment to select or furnish suitable goods and the seller knows this. Unless excluded or modified, there is an implied warranty that the goods shall be fit for such purpose (Section 2-315).

Warranty of Title and Against Infringement

Warranty of title and against infringement ensures that there are no liens against the title to the goods and the goods are free from "any security interest or other lien or encumbrance of which the buyer at the time of contracting has no knowledge" such as patent or copyright infringement (Section 2-312).

This warranty is especially important for supply managers because the type of description in the purchase order affects who is responsible in case of infringement. When a purchase is from a seller that is a merchant regularly dealing in these kinds of goods, the seller warrants that they are not infringing on the rights of any third party. If, however, a buyer furnishes specifications to the seller, then the buyer must hold the seller harmless against any such claim that arises out of compliance with the specifications. The buying organization is responsible for ensuring its specification does not infringe on the rights of any third party.

Disclaimers or Exclusions to Warranties

Under the UCC, suppliers may write disclaimers or exclusions to warranties (Section 2-316).

- To exclude express warranties, suppliers may include a clause that "no express warranties have been made by the supplier except those specifically stated in this contract."
- To exclude implied warranties, suppliers must put the disclaimer in writing in a conspicuous place. Typical language is, "No implied warranties of merchantability or fitness for a particular purpose accompany this sale."
- A general disclaimer may be made by labeling the sale "as is" or "with all faults." Also, if the buyer examines goods before the sale, the buyer is bound by all defects found and those the buyer should have found.

Title to Purchased Goods

It is important for the buyer to know when the title of goods passes from the seller to the buyer. Normally, there will be an agreement on the FOB (free on board) point, and the buyer receives title at that point. UCC Sections 2-401 through 2-403 cover the legal obligations. Generally, the UCC provides that "title to goods passes from the seller to the buyer in any manner and on any conditions explicitly agreed on by the parties." Sections 2-319 through 2-324 deal with delivery terms, including FOB, FAS, CIF, and C&F. Chapter 14, "Global Supply Management," discusses international commercial terms (INCOTERMS) in detail. With capital goods it is particularly important for tax and depreciation reasons to establish title before the tax year ends.

If the buyer specifies a particular carrier, the seller must follow the buyer's instructions. This is part of the contract, subject to any substitution necessary because of the failure of the specified carrier to provide adequate transportation services. The seller must promptly notify the buyer of substitutions.

Or the buyer may allow the seller to choose a carrier, routing, and other arrangements. Whether or not the FOB term requires the buyer to pay for shipment, the seller must see to any reasonable arrangements, such as refrigeration, watering of livestock, protection against cold, and selection of specialized cars.

Sometimes the buyer is given possession of the goods prior to the passing of a legal title. This is known as a *conditional sales contract*. The full title passes to the buyer only when final payment is made. This procedure permits a buyer to obtain needed material or equipment now and pay at some future time.

Protection against Price Fluctuations

Cancellations can be the direct result of two actions by the buyer: (1) to avoid losing money and (2) to take advantage of a price decline.

Cancel to Avoid Loss

First, the buyer cancels because if compelled to live up to the agreement, the company would lose money. Conditions may have changed or sales may have dropped. The market price may have dropped and the buyer could now buy the goods for less money. Either way, the buyer no longer wants the goods.

To justify cancellation, the buyer becomes extremely watchful of deliveries and rejects goods that arrive even a day late. Inspection is tightened, and failure to meet any detail in the specifications is seized on as an excuse for rejection. Such methods should never be followed by a good supply officer. Longer term these practices undermine the credibility of the supply organization.

Cancel due to Market Change

Second, the buyer cancels because of a clause in purchase contracts that seeks to guarantee against price decline. If goods are subject to price fluctuations, it is in the interest of the buyer to be protected against unreasonable price changes.

Open Price

Occasionally a long-term contract is drawn up that leaves the determination of the exact price open until deliveries are called for. To meet these conditions, a clause such as the following may be incorporated in purchase contracts:

> Seller warrants that the prices stated herein are as low as any net prices now given by seller to any customer for like materials, and seller agrees that if at any time during the life of this order seller quotes or sells at lower prices similar materials under similar conditions, such lower prices shall be substituted for the prices stated herein.

These stipulations against price decline are not confined to purchase agreements. Under some circumstances the buyer may receive price reductions on the seller's initiative. An example of this type of clause is the following:

> Should the purchaser at the time of any delivery, on account of this contract, be offered a lower price on goods of equal quality and in like quantity by a reputable manufacturer, it will furnish the seller satisfactory proof of same, in which event the seller will either supply such shipment at the lower price or permit the buyer to purchase such quantity elsewhere, and the quantity so purchased elsewhere will be deducted from the total quantity of this contract. Should the seller reduce its prices during the terms of this contract, the buyer shall receive the benefit of such lower prices.

Such clauses are legally enforceable and frequently work to the buyer's advantage. However, the administrative problems of enforcement mean these clauses are often ignored.

Cancellation of Orders and Breach of Contract

Both buyers and sellers are expected to adhere to the terms of a contract. Occasionally one or the other seeks to cancel the contract. Ordinarily this is a more serious problem for the seller than it is for the buyer.

Seller Cancels

Occasionally a seller may wish to avoid complying with the terms of an agreement such as refusing to manufacture the goods or delaying the delivery beyond the period stipulated in the agreement. The rights of the purchaser under these circumstances depend on the conditions surrounding the transaction. The seller is likely to be able, without liability, to delay delivering purchased goods when the buyer orders a change in the original agreement that may delay the seller in making delivery.

The purchaser may refuse to accept (without obligation) a later delivery if the seller fails to meet the contracted delivery date. However, it may be difficult to secure what the buyer might consider reasonable damages for the breached sales contract. The courts have difficulty establishing guiding rules for the jury to use in estimating the damages justly allowed a buyer who sustains financial losses resulting from a seller's failure to fulfill a contract of sale.

Damages

If there is a general rule (Section 2-713), it is that the allowable damages are measured by the difference between the original contract price and the market value of the merchandise at the time for tender under the contract and at the place where the goods should have been delivered, together with any incidental and consequential damages provided in Section 2-715, but less expenses saved in consequence of the seller's breach.

However, in a very strong seller's market, where the breach of contract by the seller is related to failure to deliver on a promised date or even to abide by the agreed price, the practical alternatives open to the buyer are almost nil. The buyer still wants the goods and may be unable to acquire them from any other supplier on time or at any better price.

Actually, this is true even where the contract provides the buyer the option to cancel. The purchaser wants goods, not damages or the right to cancel. Since the chances of getting the goods as promptly from any other supplier are slight, the buyer is likely to work with the original supplier to ensure delivery. If the supplier acted in bad faith on price or delivery, the buyer may work harder to find an alternate supplier.

Buyer Cancels

Sometimes the buyer attempts to cancel a contract. Sellers often include a clause: "This contract is not subject to cancellation." The inclusion of such a clause has little practical effect, unless it is intended to indicate to the purchaser that if he or she attempts to cancel, a suit for breach of contract may be expected.

The Rocky Plains Brewing case at the end of this chapter describes a situation in which the buyer has canceled a contract with a supplier of labels and the supplier retaliates by threatening to withhold shipments, which would potentially shut down production. Mike Pearson, packaging materials manager for Rocky Plains Brewery, has to decide how to resolve the supply problem and avoid production interruptions.

COMMON LAW AND THE PURCHASE OF SERVICES

The UCC does not address contracts for services. Common law governs the purchase of services. This includes (1) contracts solely for services and (2) contracts wherein services and goods are bundled and the service portion equals more than 50 percent of the value of the contract.

Origins of Common Law

Common law originated in England and became the foundation of U.S. law in the original 13 colonies. It is not based on written rules of law. It is based on the law of the courts as expressed in judicial decisions. Common law develops over time as courts make decisions on a case-by-case basis, developing what is known as "case law."

When deciding cases, judges look to prior judicial decisions for established precedents. They make adaptations only to account for changing conditions and societal needs. Judicial precedents derive their force from the doctrine of *stare decisis* (Latin for "stand by the decided matter"). Courts cite *stare decisis* when an issue has been previously brought to the court and a ruling already issued. Generally, courts will adhere to the previous ruling, though this is not universally true.

The common law system has both flexibility and stability. *Flexibility* comes as changing conditions make decisions inapplicable except as analogy. Then the courts turn to other English-speaking (common law) judicial experiences. *Stability* derives from general acceptance of certain authoritative materials. When the courts fail to address changing conditions, statutes are enacted that supersede common law. Typically, however, in statutory interpretation, the courts have recourse to the doctrines of common law.

Implications for Supply Managers

Supply managers who contract for services must understand that while common law provides them with general guidelines for contracting for services, it does not offer much in terms of performance obligations. Because the parties to a service contract cannot refer to a set of rules to govern performance, they must ensure that each and every performance requirement and expectation is clearly defined in the contract. Many service contracts start with a performance-based specification (statement of work). The process of writing the specification should lead to the development of clear performance obligations in the contract.

Contracting for Services

The purchase agreement for services usually is called a service contract or contract for services. It may be short or long term, a standard or custom document. Services lend themselves to a large variety of contract types, including fixed price, unit price, cost-plus-percentage-fee, cost-plus-fixed-fee, or incentive contracts.

Many professional service providers try to use standard contracts agreed to by their professional association. Frequently, the associations even have guidelines about appropriate fee structures and contracts for a particular kind of work. However, a purchaser is not compelled to accept these contracts as they are.

Most organizations develop a wide range of contracts, each with its own service-specific language. Thus, a security service contract will appear totally different from a contract for corporate maintenance, food service, or marketing consulting. Suppliers in each service area will suggest the use of their own contracts. In the case of low-value services, using such a standard contract may be the simplest and least expensive solution. For many professional services a custom contract may be needed to adequately address key issues.

Types of Services Contracting Methods

Several types of contracting methods are used in services purchasing. These include service level agreements (SLA), milestone deliverables, time and materials (T&M), volume of service (VoS), cost, and cost plus. Each is described in the following section.

Service Level Agreement (SLA): An SLA is a document that details the means, method, organization, and processes along with material requirements.

Milestone Deliverables: This method requires that specific activities be completed by a prescribed date, or that the supplier(s) prepare and deliver to the buyer documentation that reports on the current status of ongoing projects or activities. The requirements for providing milestone deliverables are detailed in the contract.

Time & Materials (T&M): Acquiring services on the basis of (1) direct labor hours at specified fixed hourly rates that include wages, overhead, general and administrative expenses, and profit; and (2) materials at cost, including, if appropriate, material handling costs as part of material costs.

Volume of Service (VoS): Generally imbedded in Service Level Agreements and related contracts, the volume of service refers to the predetermined services that will be provided over a specified period of time. Volume of service agreements may be more project oriented, wherein the buyer can specify the number of temporary workers needed to satisfy the needs of the project. The scope of work and level of services are usually structured for periods of one year or longer.

Cost and Cost Plus: These are cost reimbursement types of contracts that provide for payment of allowable incurred costs, to the extent prescribed in the contract. These contracts establish an estimate of total cost for the purpose of obligating funds and establishing a ceiling that the supplier(s) may not exceed (except at their own risk) without the approval of the buyer. Cost reimbursement type contracts are generally used when a reasonable basis for firm contract pricing may not exist.

Aligning Commercial and Legal Agreements

One of the key decisions this chapter addresses is, How can the supply manager assure that the legal agreement accurately reflects the commercial agreement? For services, this is especially difficult because of their intangibility. Efforts to link the provisions of the statement of work to the contractual provisions force both the buyer and the seller to clarify expectations, develop specific language, and appropriate metrics.

Service Level Agreements (SLAs) and Contractual Provisions

A service level agreement includes each important aspect of the service and the metrics used to determine level of performance of the service provider. SLAs are frequently used for repetitive services such as software or equipment maintenance, call centers, and professional services.

Linking the SLA provisions with contract clauses helps align the commercial agreement with the legal agreement. The goal is to drive performance. The buying organization must clarify its expectations of service performance and distill these expectations into measurable performance targets. Likewise, the selling organization (the services provider) must clarify its performance assertions and distill these into measurable deliverables.

The first step is to define variables and metrics. Variables are the indicators of performance. For example, response time may be a variable of interest. The metric is the definition of acceptable response time. For example, the supplier commits to having a service technician on-site within two hours of a service request 98 percent of the time. This service level can then be incorporated into contract clauses to strengthen the contract by avoiding ambiguity.

The resulting contract should capture accurately the expected performance of both parties and drive behavior toward achieving that performance. It will also clarify the actions that will be taken if either party fails to live up to its commitment. Again, it is worth remembering that both buyers and sellers prefer to use the courts as the last, not the first, resort. A strong services contract is a good court avoidance measure.

Typical Provisions in a Services Contract

The specific provisions in a service contract vary depending on whether the service is strategic or nonstrategic and repetitive or nonrepetitive spend, and whether it is a short- or long-term agreement, and with the nature and location of the service provided.

There are a number of provisions that are typical in contracts for many types of services (see Figure 15–1). Several items are discussed in the following section.

Terms and Conditions of Services Contracts

The terms and conditions of a services contract, like that of a contract for goods, are designed to clearly and unambiguously describe the quality, quantity, delivery, price/cost, and service agreed to by both parties. It should specifically address the price, changes to price,

FIGURE 15–1
A Typical Table of Contents for a Generic Service Contract

Source: P. O'Reilly, D. H. Garrison, and F. Khalil, "Service Contracts" in *NAPM InfoEdge,* May 2001.

1. Definitions and Rules of Construction	9.1. Key Supplier Personnel
2. Scope of Services [refers to the Statement of Work]	9.2. Limitations on Transfers of Key Supplier Personnel
3. Term of Agreement	9.3. Replacement of Supplier Personnel
4. General Provisions	9.4. Qualifications of Supplier Personnel
4.1. Entire Agreement	9.5. No Solicitation of Employees of Other Party
4.2. Notices	10. Buyer Responsibilities
4.3. Governing Law	11. Supplier's Representatives and Warranties
4.4. Confidentiality	11.1. Supplier Warranties and Additional Covenants
4.5. Audit Rights	11.2. Disclaimer of Warranties
4.6. Access	12. Indemnities
4.7. Severability	13. Limitation of Liability
4.8. Media Releases	14. Request for Renegotiation
4.9. Right to Engage in Other Activities	15. Documents Incorporated by Reference
5. Service Level Agreements	16. Appendices
5.1. Service Levels in General	16.1. Scope of Services [Statement of Work]
5.2. Periodic Reviews and Revisions to Service Levels	16.2. Service Level Agreements/Performance Credits
5.3. Measurement and Monitoring Tools for Service Levels	16.3. Charges, Measures of Utilization, and Financial Responsibilities
6. Termination	16.4. Travel Guidelines and Policy
6.1. Termination by Buyer for Cause	16.5. Technology Standards
6.2. Termination by Supplier for Cause	16.6. Reporting and Meeting Requirements
6.3. Termination for Convenience	16.7. Approved Subcontractors
6.4. Service Level Termination Event	16.8. Procedures Manual
7. Charges	
8. Invoicing and Payment	
9. Personnel Matters	

actions if market prices fluctuate or how price will be determined as well as bonus or incentive arrangements, the payment schedule including discounts or interest for late payment, delivery time (may be start and stop time, frequency, etc.), and location of service delivery. Quality is often addressed in service level agreements discussed later in this section.

A detailed discussion of each provision is outside the scope of this book. However, several provisions that are typically addressed in service contracts for all types of services are discussed in detail in the following sections.

Request for Renegotiation

A renegotiation clause may require both parties to agree to renegotiate in good faith if any party believes that compensation or other requirements of the agreement no longer meet the essential purpose of the contract. In a long-term agreement, if business conditions change or if one party might be taking advantage of the other party, this clause might be useful. Rights under this provision should be mutual. The provision only requires that the parties come to the bargaining table and negotiate in good faith.

Dispute Resolution

Alternative dispute resolution clauses may help parties in a dispute reach resolution without resorting to the courts. These methods are discussed later in this chapter.

Termination for Cause

This provision defines what constitutes a default that is sufficient cause for the buyer to terminate the contract. It may also describe the rights the supplier has under the contract to correct the cause. Service level agreements may be used to specifically identify events that will trigger termination with cause. A Service Level Termination Event clause might read, *"A Service Level Termination Event will occur if Seller fails to meet any Service Level for two consecutive months or six times in any twelve-month period. A Service Level Termination Event will be considered as a termination under the Termination for Cause provision of this Agreement."*

Termination for Convenience

A Termination for Convenience clause is common in government contracts and increasingly in private contracts. If a prime contract contains the clause, so should any related subcontracts. Also, there should be complimentary payout amounts under both the prime and subcontract provisions.

Determining if a termination was improper has typically rested on determining if it was made in bad faith or constituted a clear abuse of discretion. If the termination for convenience clause is exercised in bad faith, the termination may be a breach of contract. For example, if an owner chooses to exercise the termination for convenience clause when work was 90 percent complete to avoid paying the balance of the profit on the remaining contract work, the termination could be held to be a bad faith termination and constitute a breach of contract.

However, it is difficult to prove bad faith or clear abuse of discretion. Court rulings have restricted the use of the bad faith or discretion test starting with a 1982 case in which it was ruled that the clause could not be used to avoid paying anticipated profits unless there was a change of circumstances that warranted the use of the clause.

Clauses Related to On-Premise Service Delivery

Several clauses may be needed to address issues that might arise if the service occurs on the purchaser's premises. For example, in construction or installation services, clauses may cover security, access, nature of dress, hours of work, applicability of various codes for health and safety, what working days and hours are applicable, and what equipment and materials are to be provided by whom.

Clauses Related to Professional Services

More organizations are outsourcing (and offshoring) professional services, including legal, engineering, software development, medical, and so on. Certain clauses are typically included in these professional services contracts.

For example, when contracting for consulting services, the contract might include a key personnel clause, warranty clause, an independent contractor clause, a work product clause, and a nondisclosure clause.

Key Personnel. This is included if the success of the service depends on specific individuals. This provision (1) allows the customer to approve of key personnel assigned to the project, (2) requires that the supplier keep the specified key personnel assigned as needed (e.g., full time) to the project, and (3) gets the customer's approval before transferring key personnel.

Warranty Clause. Depending on the clarity of functional requirements and the availability of objective criteria for assessing performance, the buyer may be able to negotiate a warranty for the service provider's work. If the work is unacceptable, the clause may require the consultant to redo it at no additional charge until it is acceptable. If the functional requirements are vague, the service provider probably will not agree to this clause.

Independent Contractor Clause. To protect the buying organization, it is important to meet the IRS requirements for hiring an independent contractor and to include a clause stating that the contractor is independent and therefore responsible for filing his or her own taxes.

Work Product Clause. This assigns the ownership of the work product to the buying organization. While large service providers may not be willing to agree to this, many smaller ones will. Even if ownership does not pass to the buying organization, the contract should require documentation of the work product to avoid future problems.

Indemnification. To indemnify means to secure against future loss, damage, or liability. An indemnification clause is used to protect the buyer against all claims, costs, and expenses that arise from the supplier's breach of its obligations. This includes claims of patent, copyright, or trademark infringement against the supplier.

Nondisclosure Clause. The contractor should be contractually obligated to keep the buying organization's information confidential. For example, consultants sell their services to many companies, some of whom may be competitors, and this clause can provide a remedy short of going to court.

Subcontractor Clause. This clause either allows or disallows the use of subcontractors. If allowed, the buyer may retain approval before subcontractors are selected. As more services are offshored, the buyer may wish to expand or restrict the supplier's use of offshore subcontractors.

Errors When Drafting Services Contracts

The most common error when drafting contracts for services is vagueness. This follows somewhat naturally from the intangible nature of many services and the difficulty in clearly and unambiguously describing some service requirements.

Vagueness may apply to any area listed in Figure 15–1. Because most of the quality and cost are driven in during the need recognition and description stages of the acquisition process, these are the areas to focus on in services acquisition. The buying team should develop a clear and unambiguous scope of work, measurable performance specifications (included in service level agreements), and clear accountability for buyer and supplier.

Improving the ability to draft effective statements of work and services contracts may be one of the greatest opportunity areas for supply management.

SOFTWARE CONTRACTS

"Software is characterized by novel speed, copying, and storage capabilities, and new inspection, monitoring, and quality challenges," according to the American Law Institute. Consequently, "the law governing the transfer of hard goods is inadequate to govern software transactions."

Compounding these inherent challenges are the differences in licensing open source software and commercial software and the growth in cloud computing. A study identified six major issues when negotiating contracts for cloud computing:

1. exclusion or limitation of liability and remedies, particularly regarding data integrity and disaster recovery;
2. service levels, including availability;
3. security and privacy, particularly regulatory issues under the European Union Data Protection Directive;
4. lock-in and exit, including term, termination rights, and return on data on exit;
5. providers' ability to change service features unilaterally; and
6. intellectual property rights.[1]

The Principles of the Law of Software Contracts was approved by the American Law Institute (ALI) in 2009. The principles are meant to clarify the ambiguity created by conflicting legal decisions and the application of multiple laws to software licenses, such as intellectual property law (including, most importantly, copyright), Article 2 of the Uniform Commercial Code, and various consumer laws (especially warranty acts). The principles address issues including contract formation, the relationship between federal intellectual property law and private contracts governed by state law, the enforcement of contract terms governing quality and remedies, the meaning of breach, indemnification against infringement, automated disablement, and contract interpretation.

There is concern in the software industry about provisions in the principles, especially in two areas: (1) perceived limitations on negotiating the terms of software licenses for business, and (2) the "nondisclaimable warranty" and hidden material defects in software, where the definitions of hidden and defects may be unclear.

---

[1] W. K. Hon, C. Millard and I. Walden. "Negotiating Cloud Contracts: Looking at Clouds from Both Sides Now," *Stanford Technology Law Review*, 16 Stan. Tech. L. Rev. 79 (2012).

Software licensors need to deal with the likelihood that the courts will be influenced by the principles and need to review their agreements and processes. Supply managers responsible for software contracts should also be aware of how the principles influence case law, statutes, or interpretations of UCC Article 2, and the impact court rulings have on their approach to negotiations and contract formation.

E-COMMERCE AND THE LAW

The growth of e-commerce has led to both hope and despair in many quarters. Some fear that it will lead to a greater divide between the haves and have-nots, both between and within nations. Many companies, governments, and nongovernmental organizations are focused on broadening access to technology. This means integrating technology into people's lives by making it available and equipping people with the tools to use it.

Many policy makers believe that e-commerce will lead to wider economic growth and have endorsed general principles focusing on facilitating the market-driven development of electronic commerce. For example, in the late 1990s a number of joint statements (e.g., United States-EU, United States-Japan) were issued in support of electronic commerce as an engine of growth.

The growth of e-commerce also raised the question of whether or not existing laws sufficiently address the legal ramifications of e-commerce. The governments of many countries as well as the World Intellectual Property Organization (wipo.int), the UN Commission on International Trade Law (UNCITRAL) and the European Union have focused on the legal aspects.

In some countries, it is believed that a legal structure must be developed first before the government allows and encourages the spread of e-commerce. In other countries, such as the United States, e-commerce was quickly adopted by many businesses and the law came later.

Electronic Signatures

One critical issue in e-commerce transactions is the legality of electronic or digital signatures for contractual purposes. The term *digital signature* is used generically to mean electronic authentication of documents.

The United Nations Commission on International Trade Law (UNCITRAL) provided the Model Law on Electronic Signatures in 2001. Most countries, including Canada, Japan, China, India, Brazil, the Russian Federation, Malaysia, and the United States, have electronic signature laws, though they vary in complexity. The European Union Signature Directive provides an in-depth legal framework for electronic signatures and their validity inside and between EU countries. Each of the 28 member countries must incorporate this into their legislation, so additional layers of complexity are added by some countries. Electronic signatures may not apply across borders. Applicability with specific trading partners should be verified.

The U.S. E-Sign Act

In the United States, most states have passed legislation on electronic signatures. The passage of the Electronic Signatures in Global and National Commerce Act, Public Law No. 106–229 (E-Sign Act) in June 2000 was an attempt to develop uniform rules across the country.

The E-Sign bill was introduced to regulate interstate commerce by electronic means by permitting and encouraging the continued expansion of electronic commerce through the operation of free market forces and for other purposes. This statute grants online legal or financial agreements signed with a digital signature or chain of electronic code equivalent legal status with handwritten signatures and paper documents. It also included electronic recordkeeping provisions. As discussed earlier in this chapter, the UCC has been amended to reflect the legality of electronic signatures and records.

The important features are (1) technology neutrality and (2) party autonomy. Technology-neutral standards prevent governments from legislating a specific type of technology. Parties entering in electronic contracts can choose the IT system to use to validate an online agreement. Party autonomy is the right of businesses to "freedom of contract" in determining the terms and conditions specified in a transaction.

U.S. Uniform Electronic Transactions Act

The Uniform Electronic Transactions Act (UETA) was approved and recommended for enactment by the National Conference of Commissioners on Uniform State Laws in July 1999. UETA validates the use of electronic records and electronic signatures. Forty-seven states, the District of Columbia, Puerto Rico, and the Virgin Islands have adopted UETA. Illinois, New York, and Washington have not adopted the uniform act, but have statutes pertaining to electronic transactions.

The federal E-Sign Act allows a state to preempt the act if it has enacted UETA. UETA and the E-Sign Act bear many similarities and in some situations the language of UETA was borrowed by the authors of the E-Sign bill. However, there are differences. UETA is more comprehensive than E-Sign and addresses some topics differently. UETA contains provisions for the following issues that are not dealt with in the E-Sign Act:

- *Attribution.* An electronic record or signature is attributed to a person if it was an act of that person.
- *Effect of other state law.* UETA recognizes that an electronic signature is just as effective, valid, and enforceable as paper. However, questions of authority, forgery, and contract formation are determined by other state law.
- *Effect of party agreement.* The parties to the contract are free to enter into agreements concerning their use of electronic media.
- *Send and receive.* UETA ties the determination of when an electronic record is sent or received to the communications systems used by the parties to the contract.
- *Effect of change or error.* E-Sign does not contain provisions for dealing with mistakes in electronic communications, while UETA does contain such provisions for breaches in security procedures and mistakes made by an individual dealing with an electronic agent. Unless otherwise specified, the rules of mistake apply.
- *Admissibility.* UETA specifies that electronic records cannot be excluded as evidence solely because they are in electronic format.[2]

---

[2] Patricia Brumfield Fry, "A Preliminary Analysis of Federal and State Electronic Commerce Laws," UETA Online, www.nccusl.org/update/whatsnew-article1.asp

INTELLECTUAL PROPERTY LAWS

In the Knowledge Age, more and more wealth is derived from intellectual capital. According to the World Intellectual Property Organization (wipo.int), intellectual property (IP) refers to creations of the mind: inventions, literary and artistic works; designs; and symbols, names and images used in commerce. IP is protected in law through patents, copyright, industrial designs, and trademarks. Intellectual property is divided into two categories.

Industrial property includes inventions (patents), trademarks, industrial designs, and geographic indications of source. *Copyright* includes literary and artistic works such as novels, poems, and plays; films; musical works; artistic works such as drawings, paintings, photographs, and sculptures; and architectural designs. Rights related to copyright include those of performing artists in their performances, producers of sound recordings, and those of broadcasters in their radio and television programs.

Emerging Global Issues in Intellectual Property Rights

According to the World Intellectual Property Organization (WIPO), the emerging issues in intellectual property range from the Internet to health care to nearly all aspects of science and technology and literature and the arts. The legal issues of who actually owns intellectual capital are of great concern globally. New technology enables the rapid and widespread duplication and transfer of information. However, should access give unlimited rights when intellectual property interests are involved? What is fair use? Does existing domestic and international law adequately address the challenges caused by new technology?

WIPO is an international organization dedicated to promoting the use and protection of intellectual property. Headquartered in Geneva, Switzerland, WIPO is one of the 16 specialized agencies of the United Nations. It has 186 nations as member states and administers 23 international treaties dealing with different aspects of intellectual property protection. The World Trade Organization also has agreements on trade in services and intellectual property rights.

WIPO research has dealt with intellectual property issues related to access to drugs and health care, small and medium-sized enterprises, electronic commerce programs and activities, Internet domain disputes, genetic resources, and traditional knowledge and folklore.

Copyright Law

The U.S. Copyright Act is federal legislation enacted by Congress to protect the writings of authors. As technology has changed, the term "writings" has expanded and the Copyright Act now reaches architectural design, software, the graphic arts, motion pictures, and sound recordings.

A copyright gives the owner the exclusive right to reproduce, distribute, perform, display, or license his or her work. The owner also receives the exclusive right to produce or license derivatives of his or her work with limited exceptions for types of "fair use," such as book reviews. A Copyright is a form of protection provided to the authors of "original works of authorship" including literary, dramatic, musical, artistic, and certain other intellectual works, both published and unpublished. The 1976 Copyright Act generally gives the owner of copyright the exclusive right to reproduce the copyrighted work, to prepare derivative works, to distribute copies or phonorecords of the copyrighted work, to perform the copyrighted work publicly, or to display the copyrighted work publicly.

To be covered by copyright, a work must be original and in a concrete "medium of expression." Under current law, works are covered whether or not a copyright notice is attached and whether or not the work is registered. The Copyright Office of the U.S. Library of Congress administers the act. One hundred sixty-seven countries have ratified the Berne Convention, the leading international treaty dealing with copyright, which is administered by WIPO.[3]

Patents

A patent is a property right that provides the inventor/developer the sole rights of making, using, and selling the item in question—and denying others the right to also do so, unless the inventor decides to sell the patent rights. An invention must be novel, useful, and not of an obvious nature.

Patents are granted by national (e.g., the U.S. Patent and Trademark Office) or regional (e.g., the European Patent Office) government agencies for rights within that jurisdiction. The Patent Cooperation Treaty (PCT), administered by WIPO, is an international treaty between 148 countries that makes it possible to seek patent protection simultaneously in member countries by filing a single "international" patent application instead of filing several separate national or regional patent applications. The granting of patents remains under the control of the national or regional patent offices. The PCT assists applicants internationally, helps patent offices with granting decisions, and facilitates public access to relevant technical information. Applications may be filed electronically through e-PCT. The PCT is used by the world's major corporations, research institutions, and universities. For example, LG Electronics has filed more than 8,000 applications since the Republic of Korea joined the PCT in 1984. LG is among the top PCT filers worldwide.

Types of Inventions. Utility patents are issued for four general types of new and useful inventions/discoveries: (1) machines, (2) manufactures, (3) compositions of matter, and (4) processes. Changing technology has led to an ever-expanding understanding of what constitutes a human-made product. This has led to additions to the Patent Act for design and plant patents.

Patent Infringement and Liability. In the United States, *utility patents* are normally issued for a nonrenewable period of 20 years, measured from the date of application. *Design patents* last 14 years from the date the patent is granted. There is an implicit warrant that a supplier's regular products do not infringe against the patent rights of any third party. A contractual clause may transfer this responsibility to the buyer.

When the buyer orders goods to be assembled, prepared, or manufactured to the buyer's specifications, then the buyer warrants that there is no infringement of patent or trademark. If there is a charge of infringement of a patent or trademark, the buyer may be liable to legal action. There is a tacit representation on the part of the buyer that the seller will be safe in manufacturing according to the specifications, and the buyer then is obliged to indemnify the seller for any loss suffered (UCC Section 2-312).

If a charge of patent infringement is made against the buyer, the supplier should be notified promptly so that the charge can be defended, or settlement made, in a timely manner. Also, if a seller attempts to include a patent disclaimer clause in the sales contract, the

---

[3] World Intellectual Property Organisation (WIPO), www.wipo,int/treaties/en/ip/berne/

buyer should be extremely cautious in accepting such a clause, since there may be costly litigation if patent infringement has occurred.

Protection Clause.   Sometimes a buyer contracts with a supplier to manufacture an item, to the buyer's specifications, that includes a new idea, process, or product that has not yet been awarded patent protection. This often happens in high-technology industries. To guard against losing the right to the new development and possible subsequent financial rewards, the buyer includes a protection clause in the contract.

Recent Developments.   The 2011 Leahy-Smith *America Invents Act* (AIA) made major changes to U.S. patent law. Some changes relate to patenting business methods such as tax strategy, and others were designed to reduce litigation. The two changes with the broadest impact were the following:

1. The United States converted from a first-to-invent system to a first-to-file system, which is used by most countries. This simplifies and reduces the cost of disputes when multiple applications are filed for similar inventions. However, it favors large organizations with the resources to file early for a patent and then refile if required after final design versus smaller companies that typically file after they know an invention works.
2. A "prior commercial user" defense was established for inventors who commercially use certain inventions at least one year before another inventor files a patent on the same invention or discloses it publicly. This protects inventions that a company uses, but does not want to patent such as an invention that is invisible to the customer.

Trademarks

A trademark is a logo, brand name, or design that is new or distinctive enough to market or represent a company or its goods and services. It protects the owner of the mark by ensuring the exclusive right to use it to identify goods or services, or to authorize another to use it in return for payment. The protection period varies but a trademark can be renewed indefinitely for a fee. Trademark protection is enforced by the courts, which in most systems have the authority to block trademark infringement.

The trademark system facilitates global trade. It promotes initiative and enterprise worldwide by rewarding the owners of trademarks with recognition and financial profit. If enforced, it also hinders unfair competitors, such as counterfeiters, from using similar distinctive signs to market inferior or different products or services.

The manufacture and sale of counterfeit goods is a problem in some industries. In some, such as aerospace, counterfeit parts of inferior design, material, and manufacture may cause loss of life. In others, such as shoes, clothing, and accessories, the loss is a degradation of brand as well as financial losses. The lack of international intellectual property laws exacerbates this situation. What is illegal in one country is a perfectly acceptable sector of the economy in another.

Counterfeiting has been affecting trade for 2,000 years and most countries have been involved at one time or another: from the British cotton mills in Manchester forging American trademarks, to the U.S. textile industry copying the English water-spinning frame, to Korean's hawking high-end handbags, to the Chinese copying almost everything. Counterfeiting typically occurs in developing economies with a low-cost manufacturing base, weak IP laws, and limited enforcement. Intellectual property laws develop with the economy and harmonize over time nationally and internationally through bilateral and multilateral agreements.

China, for example, first introduced modern copyright, patent, and trademark laws in the late 1970s. Under pressure from the United States, China updated IP laws in the 1980s, the 1990s, and again in 2001 prior to joining the World Trade Organization (WTO). While China now has a multipronged approach to enforcement, two obstacles remain: (1) an administrative and judicial inability or unwillingness to enforce IP laws and (2) an overall lack of administrative and judicial transparency. As Chinese companies grow and innovate, they too want to protect their IP and many predict that Chinese IP laws and enforcement will strengthen.

The Anti-Counterfeiting Trade Agreement (ACTA) signed in 2011 by Australia, Canada, Japan, Korea, Morocco, New Zealand, Singapore, and the United States is an example of a multilateral trade agreement related to IP. The purpose of the ACTA is to strengthen the international legal framework for effectively combating global proliferation of commercial-scale counterfeiting and piracy. The agreement calls for strong legal frameworks and provides innovative provisions to deepen international cooperation and to promote strong intellectual property rights (IPR) enforcement practices. Representatives of the European Union, Mexico, and Switzerland, the remaining negotiating parties, confirmed their preparations to sign the agreement as soon as practicable. The agreement will enter into force following the deposit of the sixth instrument of ratification, acceptance, or approval.

Industrial Design

An industrial design is the ornamental or aesthetic aspect of an article. This includes its three-dimensional features, such as the shape or surface of an article, or two-dimensional features, such as patterns, lines, or color. Industrial designs are applied to a wide variety of products of industry and handicraft such as clinical and medical instruments, luxury items, housewares, electrical appliances, vehicles, and architectural structures. To be protected under most national laws, an industrial design must appeal to the eye. It does not protect any technical features of the article to which it is applied.

Geographical Indication

A geographical indication is a sign used on goods from a specific geographical origin that possess qualities or a reputation due to its origin. It may be used for a variety of agricultural products, such as "Tuscany" for olive oil produced in a specific area of Italy, or "Roquefort" for cheese produced in France, or "Champagne" for sparkling wine produced in that region of France. Yes, that is why California bubbly is called sparkling wine, not champagne.

PRODUCT LIABILITY

From lead paint on toys to e-coli on spinach to melamine in milk and pet food, keeping products safe for consumers is an ongoing challenge across industries and countries. Product liability refers to the liability of any or all parties along the manufacturing supply chain for damage caused by that product. This includes the manufacturer of component parts, an assembling manufacturer, the wholesaler, and the retail store owner. Liability suits have been filed over inherent defects in products that harmed consumers.

Product safety and product liability considerations have become more important for several reasons: (1) Lawsuits, large settlements, and greater public awareness have occurred when government regulations and oversight increase and judicial interpretations of the existing laws favor plaintiffs; (2) a reduction or elimination of either regulations or oversight leads to lax control within and among supply chains, resulting in large product recalls; (3) the growth of global supply chains and the inherent difficulties of managing all aspects of safety and quality across borders and across legal and regulatory systems increase the risk of harm to consumers.

The definition of product liability has expanded from tangible goods to include intangibles (gas), naturals (pets), real estate (house), and writings (navigational charts). The move to create a body of law covering software is largely focused on liability issues. The supply managers' role and responsibility increases as firms attempt to reduce the financial threat of product and service liability problems.

Claims can be based on negligence, strict liability, or breach of warranty of fitness.

Strict Liability

Product liability is generally considered a strict liability offense. This means that the defendant is liable when it is shown that the product was defective. No amount of care on the part of the manufacturer exonerates it from its legal liability if it is demonstrated that the product was defective.

There are three types of relevant product defects: design defects, manufacturing defects, and defects in marketing. *Design defects* occur when a product may perform its function but is inherently dangerous due to a design flaw. *Manufacturing defects* occur during the construction or production of the item. *Marketing defects* result from improper instructions and failures to warn consumers of latent dangers in the product.

The United States does not have a federal products liability law. State statutes apply. However, the U.S. Department of Commerce promulgated a Model Uniform Products Liability Act (MUPLA) for voluntary state use. The law of products liability is found mainly in common law (case law) and in Article 2, Sections 314–315, of the UCC, which deal with implied and express warranties of merchantability.

Implications for Supply. Part of the strategic role of supply managers is to minimize organizational risk. Taking a more active role in designing for procurability and sustainability is one way for supply managers to be more strategic. Considering potential risks and associated costs throughout the life of a product can help the organization avoid product liability suits. In the sourcing, evaluating, selecting, contracting, and receiving stages, there are opportunities to recognize and deal with potential product liability. The earlier in the process this is done, the lower the cost to financials and reputation or brand. This requires close internal relationships with design, engineering, quality control, manufacturing, and marketing to ensure that the organization is not being unreasonably exposed to product liability lawsuits. It also requires a close relationship and involvement with top management to ensure that the costs of failure are fully understood and included in organizational risk management.

The increased application of strict liability tests and the lack of federal product liability laws mean that an organization may assume greater liability based on the actions of the purchaser. Supply managers must ensure defect-free materials and components capable of performing a full range of applications and uses, in compliance with relevant standards, tests, and criteria for product safety.

ALTERNATIVE DISPUTE RESOLUTION

If legal action is the last resort in disputes with suppliers, alternative dispute resolution (ADR) may be seen as the next to the last resort. ADR is any means of settling disputes outside of the courtroom, including arbitration, mediation, early neutral evaluation, and conciliation. Packed court dockets, the rising cost of litigation, and time delays encourage the use of ADR. Some programs are voluntary; others are mandatory. All provide an opportunity to reach negotiated settlements and maintain working professional relationships.

Title 9 of the U.S. Code establishes federal law supporting arbitration based on Congress's plenary power over interstate commerce. Where it applies, its terms prevail over state law. There are also numerous state ADR laws. Thirty-five jurisdictions have adopted the Uniform Arbitration Act as state law, and in similar form in 14 others. Thus, the arbitration agreement and the arbiter's decision may be enforceable under state and federal law. In 1970, the United States joined the UN Convention on the Recognition and Enforcement of Foreign Arbitral Awards.

The two most common forms of ADR are arbitration and mediation.

Commercial Arbitration

Regardless of the type of contract, disputes will arise. While annoying, these disputes usually cost too much in time and money to go to court. Most are settled by buyers and sellers through negotiation. Arbitration clauses are included in contracts to avoid litigation when a negotiated agreement cannot be reached. An impartial arbitrator, or panel of arbitrators, listens to the evidence and renders a judgment. Both parties have agreed in advance to accept without appeal. This is less costly and time consuming than court action. Arbitration is a simplified version of a trial involving no discovery and simplified rules of evidence.

To select an arbiter, both sides may agree on one, or each side may select one arbitrator and the two arbitrators elect the third to comprise a panel. Arbitration hearings usually last only a few hours and the opinions are not public record. Arbitration has long been used in labor, construction, and securities regulation; and its use is growing in other business disputes.

Standard arbitration clauses exist that are valid, irrevocable, and enforceable under arbitration laws of certain states. For matters under the jurisdiction of the federal courts, there is the Federal Arbitration Law. Even in states without such laws, it is possible to demand arbitration if provision is made in the contract, and if there is a statute making *future* disputes" the subject of binding arbitration agreements.

Arbitration clauses in contracts are a reasonable measure of protection against costly litigation. The following questions will help ensure that the clause is sound:

1. Is the clause in the proper form under the appropriate arbitration laws? Unless properly drawn, it may not be legally valid, irrevocable, and enforceable.

2. Does the clause fully express the will of the parties or is it ambiguous? If it is uncertain in its terms, the time and expense involved in determining the scope of the clause and the powers of the arbitrators under it may destroy its value or increase costs.

3. Does the clause ensure the appointment of impartial arbitrators? If a person serving as arbitrator is an agent, advocate, relative, or representative of a party, or has a personal interest in the matter being arbitrated, the award rendered may be vacated by the court on the ground of evident corruption or partiality on the part of an arbitrator.

4. Does the clause provide adequately, by reference to the rules of an association or otherwise, for a method of naming arbitrators, thus safeguarding against deadlocks or defaults in the proceedings? If not, the actual hearing of the dispute may be unduly delayed, and the practical value of the arbitration defeated.

Mediation

Mediation is a less formal alternative to litigation than arbitration. Mediators are individuals trained in negotiations. They bring opposing parties together and attempt to work out a settlement or agreement that both parties accept or reject. Mediation is used for a wide range of case types.

Internal Escalation

A third form of alternate dispute resolution is internal escalation. It may be agreed by both buyer and seller that if a dispute arises, the first round of resolution will fall to the purchaser and sales representative. If they cannot resolve the matter, their supervisors will get together and so on, with the final round between the top executives of both organizations. Only if they fail to agree will other forms of dispute resolution be pursued.

REGULATORY REQUIREMENTS

There are a wide range of regulations that affect business. Some are industry specific and some apply across industries. Three are addressed here: Dodd-Frank, the Sarbanes-Oxley Act, and Environmental Regulations.

The Dodd-Frank Act and Conflict Minerals

Conflict minerals, as defined in Section 1502(e)(4) of the Dodd–Frank Wall Street Reform and Consumer Protection Act (2010), include tantalum, tin, tungsten, and gold or any other mineral or derivative determined by the U.S. Secretary of State to be financing conflict in the Democratic Republic of the Congo (DRC) or an adjoining country. Adjoining countries share an internationally recognized border with the DRC and include Angola, Burundi, Central African Republic, Republic of the Congo, Rwanda, South Sudan, Tanzania, Uganda, and Zambia. Conflict minerals are used in a wide range of products, including mobile phones, computers, digital cameras, video game consoles, jewelry, light bulbs, pipes, electronic circuits, and automobiles.

U.S. publicly traded companies are required to confirm annually that their supply chains are free of conflict minerals and to provide a description of the measures taken to exercise due diligence on the conflict minerals' source and chain of custody. Due diligence must follow a nationally or internationally recognized framework. The OECD's "Due Diligence Guidance for Responsible Supply Chains of Minerals from Conflict-Affected and High-Risk Areas" is currently the only recognized framework available for use.

According to the OECD Due Diligence Guidance, the mineral supply chain refers to the system of all the activities, organizations, actors, technology, information, resources. and services involved in moving the mineral from the extraction site downstream to its incorporation in the final product for end consumers. The process of bringing a raw mineral to the consumer market involves multiple actors and generally includes the extraction, transport, handling, trading, processing, smelting, refining and alloying, and manufacturing and sale of end product.

The OECD guidance recommends five key steps to establish a due diligence program to prevent and detect sourcing of conflict minerals:

1. Establish strong company management systems.
2. Identify and assess risk in the supply chain.
3. Design and implement a strategy to respond to identified risk.
4. Carry out independent third-party audit of the supply chain (e.g., audit high-risk suppliers or smelters).
5. Report on supply chain due diligence internally to management.

Compliance will likely require a cross-functional team, including representatives from sales, purchasing/procurement, legal, senior management, customer service, engineering, investor relations, quality and environmental, and health and safety functions. The amount of time required for a due diligence program depends on the size of the supply chain; volume of conflict minerals being used; the cost, accessibility, availability, and quality of alternate supply sources or materials; the stockpile of minerals already in the supply chain; and the company's commitment to the effort.

The SEC standards are focused on reasonable design and good faith effort because the rule requires cooperation by a company's suppliers, and it may be difficult to force supplier cooperation. The Reasonable Country of Origin Inquiry (RCOI) should include an understanding of the issuer's supplier/sub-supplier population, a framework or process for evaluating responses from suppliers, and sufficient knowledge of the issuer's supply chain to be able to identify potential red flags in suppliers' responses. Companies may need to work with industry/trade organizations, negotiate cooperation into contracts, or use their buying power leverage to force the issue. This may be difficult for smaller companies with less leverage. Suppliers may move toward compliance in response to the broad applicability of the rule.

In its eighth *Supplier Responsibility 2014 Progress Report*, issued in January 2014, Apple announced that it would cease using conflict minerals. It reported that its entire supply of tantalum, a rare metal used in the production of capacitors, is provided by certified conflict-free smelters. Apple's approach is to verify a critical mass of suppliers to influence demand while also supporting verified supply lines and economic development in the region. However, conflict-free smelter certification programs are not well developed. The Global e-Sustainability Initiative (GeSI) and the Electronic Industry Citizenship Coalition (EICC) updated their Conflict-Free Smelter program to incorporate the OECD guidelines. Participating companies must implement the OECD guidelines, conduct a third-party review of their supply chains to verify compliance, and obtain documentation from smelters about the mines of origin for all materials supplied.

In March 2014, the EU proposed voluntary rules to prevent European companies from importing conflict minerals. The rationale is that U.S. legislation has led many U.S. companies to stop sourcing these minerals in Africa rather than going through the onerous certification process. The biggest hindrance according to the EU's trade commission is that only about 20 percent of smelters and 40 percent of refiners conduct due diligence with their supply chain. The EU imports about 25 percent of the global trade in tin, tungsten, and tantalum and about 15 percent of gold.[4]

---

[4] C. Oliver, K. Manson, and J. Wilson, "EU Plans Voluntary Rules on Conflict Mineral Imports," *Financial Times*, March 5, 2014.

The Sarbanes-Oxley Act

The Sarbanes-Oxley Act (2002) is the public company accounting reform and investor protection act. Several sections of the act might impact supply management.

Section 401a requires off-balance-sheet transactions and obligations to be listed. For supply management this might include long-term purchase agreements such as multiyear supplier-managed inventory programs, cancellation and restocking charges, and lease agreements.

Section 404 requires the creation and maintenance of viable internal controls that the SEC has ruled include policies, procedures, training programs, and other processes beyond financial controls. For supply management this might include insecure and unreliable communications such as e-mails used to communicate with trading partners, poor purchase commitment visibility, and inventory write-offs.

Section 409 requires timely reporting of material events that impact financial reporting. Supply events that might meet the threshold of materiality include late supplier deliveries, ERP system crashes that disrupt shipments, and poor inventory accuracy.

Environmental Regulations

Why are environmental issues of concern to supply managers, especially U.S. supply managers? For one thing, the people of the United States consume approximately 25 percent of the world's resources despite representing less than 5 percent of the world's population. China's explosive growth has, like most industrial revolutions, come with severe environmental problems. Both business and government leaders should consider the impact of these numbers.

The U.S. and Canadian governments have enacted a number of important regulations, and many of these affect the supply function. Important among these regulations in the United States are four pieces of federal legislation: (1) the Resource Conservation and Recovery Act, (2) the Toxic Substances Control Act, (3) the Comprehensive Environmental Response, Compensation and Liability Act, and (4) the Clean Air Act. In Canada, the major pieces of environmental legislation are the Environmental Protection Act and the Water Resources Act.

Among the implications of government environmental legislation for supply is that

1. Purchasers contracting for waste disposal may want to (*a*) ensure that a disposal supplier is competent and reputable and has an EPA permit, (*b*) require the supplier to warrant that employees are trained in handling the specific waste, and (*c*) insist on the right to inspect the facility and the EPA permit.
2. Purchasers should require suppliers to warrant that any chemical or chemical mixture they provide is listed by the EPA.
3. Purchasers must track the amount and type of chemicals that enter and leave the plant and consult the Material Safety Data Sheets (MSDS).
4. Purchasers can choose environmentally friendly products; establish criteria for supplier selection that limit purchases from suppliers that sell damaging products; and be alert to alternatives, substitutes, or new technology that may help their companies meet the goals of government legislation.

The U.S. government provides details of its major environmental laws on the Environmental Protection Agency (EPA) website (www.epa.gov).

Environmentally Preferable Purchasing

Recognizing that the U.S. government is one of the largest consumers of goods and services in the world, the EPA developed the Environmentally Preferable Purchasing (EPP) program. EPP requires all federal procurement officials to assess and give preference to products and services that are environmentally preferable. A database of environmental attribute information for a wide range of products exists. Although developed for federal agency procurement, commercial purchasers may find the information useful.

Environmentally Preferable Purchasing (EPP) helps the federal government "buy green" and use the federal government's buying power to stimulate market demand for green products and services. This site can help green vendors, businesses of all sizes, and consumers to

• Find and evaluate information about green products and services.
• Identify federal green buying requirements.
• Calculate the costs and benefits of purchasing choices.
• Manage green purchasing processes (www.epa.gov/epp).

Voluntary Compliance Programs

The EPA is developing a more comprehensive program designed to hold down the costs of environmental continuous improvement. The goals are to develop an industry-by-industry approach, coordinate rule making, simplify recordkeeping and reporting requirements, permit streamlining, and review enforcement/compliance objectives. Toward those goals, the EPA has developed a wide range of voluntary compliance programs (www.epa.gov/compliance/incentives).

ETHICS

Ethics comes from a Greek work *ethika,* which means "character" or "custom." It relates to the principles or standards of human conduct, sometimes called *morals* (Latin *mores,* "customs"). Ethics, as a branch of philosophy, is considered a normative science. It is concerned with norms of human conduct. Each individual makes decisions out of an ethical framework. Each organization creates an ethical framework as part of its organizational culture that drives and constrains behavior.

Numerous factors influence ethics, including family, education, religion, peers, gender, age, socioeconomic status, culture, and experience. When a group of diverse people is brought together in one organization, it is important to consciously create an ethical culture. This culture is documented by the standards of conduct in a code of ethics. It is brought to life by the attitude, behavior, and practices of company leaders as well as each individual in the organization. This is especially true when ethical challenges occur. It is reinforced by the procedures put in place to monitor ethical behavior and by the language used in the course of doing business.

Purchasing represents the exchange of money for goods and services. Often, a very large amount of money is involved in this exchange. It is, therefore, vital that the transactions associated with this process be carried out at the highest ethical level. Unfortunately, temptation is always present where large amounts of money are involved. Sometimes suppliers will go to considerable lengths to secure business and resort to unethical practices, such as bribes or large gifts. Sometimes unscrupulous purchasers take advantage of their privileged position to extract personal rewards that are unethical as well as illegal.

Clearly, both suppliers and purchasers are responsible for ensuring that unethical conduct is not tolerated. Both the Supply Chain Management Association (SCMA) of Canada and the U.S.-based Institute for Supply Management (ISM) have codes of ethics and principles and standards of purchasing practice that guide the professional behavior of their members. (See Figure 15–2 and 15–3.)

International Federation of Purchasing and Supply Management (IFPSM) is the union of 48 National and Regional Purchasing Associations worldwide. About 250,000 supply

FIGURE 15–2   **Excerpts from SCMA Code of Ethics**

SCMA CODE OF ETHICS

A. Standards of Conduct

Members will conduct themselves in a manner that a reasonable and informed third party would conclude as being appropriate to a professional in supply chain management.

1. *Avoidance of conflicts of interest.* Members should exercise professional judgment and discretion in order to avoid any apparent or actual conflict of interest when performing their duties.
2. *Protection of confidential or sensitive information.* Where a member has been privy to confidential or sensitive information, it is their responsibility to ensure that it remains so.
3. *Business relationships.* Members should maintain relationships with suppliers and third parties in a manner that contributes to and promotes fair competition in the market and protects the interests and reputation of his or her employer.
4. *Gifts, gratuities, and hospitality inducements.* When permitted by employing organizations, members must ensure that the objectivity of their decisions is not compromised or unduly influenced by the acceptance of gifts, gratuities, or hospitalities of any kind.
5. *Environmental and social responsibilities.* Members shall exercise their responsibilities in a manner that promotes and provides opportunities for the protection and preservation of the natural environment.

B. Professional Principles

Members will perform their roles and duties based on the following principles of professional practice:

1. *Professional competency.* To maintain their professional competency by staying informed of, and complying with, the best supply chain management practices, and for SCMP designation members to retain their professional certification in good standing.
2. *Professionalism.* To provide professional advice to their employer or any other impacted party to the best of their knowledge, recognizing that any final decision is the prerogative of the senior authority within the employing organization; to act with courtesy and due consideration in dealings with other professional members and in all business relationships.
3. *Honesty and integrity.* To maintain an unimpeachable standard of integrity and honesty in all their business relationships both inside and outside the organizations in which they are employed.
4. *Responsible management.* To optimize, without prejudice, the use of resources for which they are responsible so as to provide the maximum value as defined by the organizations they represent.
5. *Serving the public good.* To use their position to advance the interests and well-being of society; to denounce all forms of business practice which may compromise value or bring discredit to the organization and/or society.
6. *Compliance with legal obligations.* Members must not engage in or condone any activity or attempt to circumvent the clear intention of the law.

FIGURE 15–3 ISM Principles and Standards of Ethical Supply Management Conduct

INTEGRITY IN YOUR DECISIONS AND ACTIONS
VALUE FOR YOUR EMPLOYER
LOYALTY TO YOUR PROFESSION

From these principles are derived the ISM standards of supply management conduct:

STANDARDS

1. **Impropriety.** Prevent the intent and appearance of unethical or compromising conduct in relationships, actions, and communications.
2. **Conflicts of Interest.** Ensure that any personal, business or other activity does not conflict with the lawful interests of your employer.
3. **Influence.** Avoid behaviors or actions that may negatively influence, or appear to influence, supply management decisions.
4. **Responsibilities to Your Employer.** Uphold fiduciary and other responsibilities using reasonable care and granted authority to deliver value to your employer.
5. **Supplier and Customer Relationships.** Promote positive supplier and customer relationships.
6. **Sustainability and Social Responsibility.** Champion social responsibility and sustainability practices in supply management.
7. **Confidential and Proprietary Information.** Protect confidential and proprietary information.
8. **Reciprocity.** Avoid improper reciprocal agreements.
9. **Applicable Laws, Regulations, and Trade Agreements.** Know and obey the letter and spirit of laws, regulations, and trade agreements applicable to supply management.
10. **Professional Competence.** Develop skills, expand knowledge, and conduct business that demonstrates competence and promotes the supply management profession.

Adopted: 01/2012

professionals are members of these associations. The IFPSM facilitates the development and sharing of the practice of the purchasing and supply management profession through its network of member organizations. The IFPSM has adopted a Code of Ethics. (See Figure 15–4.)

Most large organizations deal specifically with standards of behavior of supply personnel and their relationships with suppliers in their policies and procedures. Many organizations are moving to a congruent position that equates the treatment of customers, employees, and suppliers as identical. Simply stated, "Every customer, employee, and supplier of this organization is entitled to the same level of honesty, courtesy, and fairness." Buyers are urged to behave in a manner that reflects the organization's wishes.

Several areas help establish and maintain the reputation of the supply group and the organization. These are perceptions, conflict of interest, gifts and gratuities, relationships with suppliers, and reciprocity.

Perceptions

Perception is often as important as reality. If a buyer's action is perceived by others to be inappropriate, then both the buyer's and the buying organization's reputations may be harmed. Because of this danger, everyone in supply must think about how an action will appear to others.

FIGURE 15–4 IFPSM Code of Ethics

Precepts

Members shall not use their authority or office for personal gain and shall seek to uphold and enhance the standing of the purchasing and supply management profession and the Federation by:

A. Maintaining an unimpeachable standard of integrity in all their business relationships both inside and outside the organizations in which they are employed;

B. Fostering the highest standards of professional competence amongst those for whom they are responsible;

C. Optimizing the use of resources for which they are responsible so as to provide the maximum benefit to their employers;

D. Complying with the letter and the spirit of:

    I. The laws of the country in which they practice;

    II. The Federation's 'guidance' on professional practice as outlined below and as may be issued by the Federation from time to time; and

    III. Contractual obligations.

E. Rejecting and denouncing any business practice that is improper; and

F. Enhancing the proficiency and stature of the profession by acquiring and maintaining current technical knowledge.

Guidance

In applying these precepts, members should follow the guidance set out below:

A. Declaration of interest. Any personal interest which may impinge or might reasonably be deemed by others to impinge on a member's impartiality in any matter relevant to their duties should be declared to their employer.

B. Confidentiality and accuracy of information. The confidentiality of information received in the course of duty must be respected and should not be used for personal gain; information given in the course of duty should be true and fair and not designed to mislead.

C. Competition. While considering the advantages to the member's employer of maintaining a continuing relationship with a supplier, any arrangement which might, in the long term, prevent the effective operation of fair competition, should be avoided.

D. Business gift. To preserve the image and integrity of both the member and the employer, business gifts should be discouraged. Gifts, other than items of very small intrinsic value, should not be accepted.

E. Hospitality. Moderate hospitality is an accepted courtesy of a business relationship. However, the recipients should not allow themselves to reach a position whereby they might be or might be deemed by others to have been influenced in making a business decision as a consequence of accepting such hospitality. The frequency and scale of hospitality accepted should not be significantly greater than a recipient's employer, through the recipient's expense account, would be likely to provide in return.

F. When in doubt of what is acceptable in terms of gifts and hospitality, the offer should be declined or advice sought from the member's superior.

Source: www.ifpmm.org/About/Ethics.cfm

Conflict of Interest

Conflict of interest touches on the issue of perception. There are situations where two parties cannot agree on the existence of a conflict. Often, the person involved truly believes that he or she can remain objective despite having conflicting interests. It may never be proven otherwise, but others may perceive that the business interest was sacrificed for personal interest.

For example, a supply professional may be in a decision-making position that involves a friend or family member's business. No matter how thorough a job the person does, some observers will always believe the business was won on personal and not professional relationships.

Gifts and Gratuities

Supply personnel can avoid ethical entanglements through conscious behavior. Whether or not to accept entertainment, gifts, and gratuities is related to perceptions. Many purchasers argue that their decisions are not swayed by a free lunch. Others argue that even if the buyer knows the entertainment did not influence the decision, others (especially rejected bidders and personnel in other functions) may not be so sure.

There is also concern that any perceived imbalance in a relationship will subconsciously motivate the parties to move to parity. For example, after accepting several dinner invitations, most people feel a sense of obligation to return the favor. How does one know for sure that one can remain objective after receiving gifts and entertainment from a salesperson?

Targets of Unfair Influence.   Supply personnel are not the only targets of attempts to influence decisions unfairly. Executives, managers, supervisors, and others in production, marketing, information systems, engineering, or elsewhere may be targeted. Anyone with direct responsibility for, or large influence on, decisions about procurement may be approached. Even when the buyer is not directly influenced, the buyer's task is affected. If undue influence is considered a serious issue, all employees can be prohibited from receiving any gift, no matter how trivial, from any supplier, actual or potential.

In some organizations nonsupply personnel are allowed to receive or extend entertainment and gifts and supply personnel are not. This policy may undermine the integrity of the supply process. Sales representatives focus their attention on nonsupply personnel who they believe can influence the decision. An astute sales representative can quickly determine who the real decision maker is and how serious the buying organization is about following its own processes. The impact on total cost of ownership is often overlooked by those who argue that there is no harm done in accepting gifts and entertainment.

The Sales Perspective.   A salesperson's job is to influence and persuade decision makers. This can be done most effectively by knowing the product or service and the potential customer's needs and wants and presenting proposals that represent good value. People learn about others and their situation by spending time with them. They also build a relationship and a foundation of trust. The easiest way is to spend time together in a social setting.

Maintaining a Professional Relationship.   The challenge is finding ways to foster the development of trust and mutual understanding of the goals and objectives of each other's organization while maintaining a professional relationship. In buyer–supplier partnerships or strategic alliances, this issue is even more pronounced. Now the supplier may be a single source in a long-term deal that brings together people from the two organizations on a regular, sometimes daily, basis. Special attention is required to ensure that the business focus is maintained.

How, then, shall the supply manager deal with the problem of excessive entertainment and gifts in any one of its varied and subtle forms? This practice is designed to influence the decision maker by creating a sense of obligation through gifts, entertainment, and even open bribery. It is, of course, often difficult to distinguish between legitimate expenditures by suppliers in the interest of goodwill and illegitimate expenditures made in an attempt to place the buyer under some obligation to the supplier. In these borderline cases, only a clearly written code of conduct and ordinary common sense can provide the answer.

The code of ethics of most supply professional associations strongly condemns gratuities beyond token gifts of nominal value. However, every year a small number of cases is uncovered of individuals who do not abide by this code, thereby placing the whole profession under suspicion.

Part of the blame must clearly lie with those who use illegal enticements to secure business. For example, a salesperson calls on a purchaser and extends an invitation to lunch so they may discuss a transaction without losing time or as a matter of courtesy. Such action is presumed to be in the interests of goodwill, although the cost of the lunch must be added to the selling price. An attractive but inexpensive gift may be given by the supplier's company to adorn the desk of the buyer. The supplier's name appears on the gift, and therefore it is construed as advertising. The sales representative may send a bottle of wine or sporting event tickets after a deal has been completed.

The custom of giving simple gifts may develop into providing much larger ones. It is difficult to draw the line between these different situations. In some organizations, the supply manager or buyer frequently refuses to allow salespeople to pay for luncheons or insists on paying for an equal number.

Commercial Bribery

Aside from its economic aspects, commercial bribery is the subject of many legal cases. Fundamentally, the rulings on commercial bribery rest on the doctrine of agency. The agent is recognized by law as keeping a fiduciary position. Any breach of faith on the part of the agent is not permitted. Therefore, the agent's acceptance of a bribe to do anything in conflict with the interests of its principal is not permitted by law.

The evils of commercial bribery are more far-reaching than first imagined. Although originating with only one business, it may quickly become an industry practice. No matter how superior the quality of goods or how low its price, a producer will have difficulty competing with businesses that practice bribery. The behavior of the buyer who accepts bribes will change. He or she will likely pay higher prices than normal. Defects in workmanship or quality are likely to be hidden. Materials from other manufacturers may be deliberately damaged or destroyed. The total cost of ownership rises as a result of commercial bribery.

Even though bribery is outlawed in almost every country in the world, it often flourishes, legally or not. The spectacular revelations about the bribery involved in the UN-sponsored oil for food program in Iraq were a sad reminder of the pervasiveness of such practices.

In the last 10 years, both international organizations and individual countries have passed and begun to enforce antibribery and anticorruption laws. Multiple laws and jurisdictions bring greater transparency to employees' actions and greater force behind refusals to engage in bribery in countries where it has been prevalent. However, it also adds complexity in terms of knowing and abiding by the applicable laws.

In the United States, enforcement of the Federal Corrupt Practices Act (FCPA) has increased dramatically as have the assessed penalties. Money laundering, fraud and tax issues, and enforcement around exports to banned countries are also receiving increased enforcement action. Similarly, new regulations that govern private business, including hedge funds and financial products like derivatives, could extend to foreign activities.

For the supply executive team formulating global ethics policy and procedures, there are three key questions to ask:

1. What did you do to stay out of trouble?
2. What did you do when you found out?
3. What remedial action did you take?

Appropriate answers are

1. The company has systems in place such as a company code of conduct and the policies and procedures present to implement the code companywide, as well as an anonymous hotline. The company provided training on these policies and processes. They were used actively in business. For example, the company used due diligence on business partners, agents, distributors, and suppliers.
2. After an FCPA/compliance issue arose or was discovered, the company launched an investigation. No persons involved with the underlying matter were involved in running the investigation. Or the investigation was handled by an outside agency or law firm.
3. After completing the investigation, the company disciplined the persons involved in the FCPA/compliance violation. The company voluntarily disclosed the matter to the Department of Justice (DOJ). The company cooperated with the DOJ in the ongoing investigation.[5]

Promotion of Positive Relationships with Suppliers

Most organizations have policies and procedures about relationships between the supply organization and suppliers' representatives. Purchasing and supply management associations in many countries around the world have adopted their own codes of ethics governing the relationship between supplier and purchaser. As mentioned earlier, the International Federation of Purchasing and Supply Management (IFPSM) has a code of ethics for all member associations and their members. All codes are based on the requirement that seller and buyer deal ethically with one another to ensure a sound basis for business dealings.

Thus, courtesy, honesty, and fairness are stressed. Buyers are urged to behave in the highest professional manner. Normally, this includes a long list of behaviors: see suppliers without delay; be truthful in all statements; cover all elements of procurement to ensure complete understanding; do not ask suppliers to quote unless they have a reasonable chance at the business; keep specifications fair and clear and competition open and fair; respect the confidence of suppliers with regard to all confidential information; do not take improper advantage of sellers' errors; cooperate with suppliers to solve difficulties; and negotiate prompt and fair adjustment in cases of dispute. It is also expected that a buyer will be courteous in stating rejection of bids with reasonable explanations, but not betray confidential information; answer inquiries promptly; and handle samples, tests, and reports with prompt, complete, and truthful information. Lastly, all codes of ethics stress a need to avoid all obligations to sellers except strict business obligations.

[5] D. B. Henriques, "F.B.I. Charges Arms Sellers with Foreign Bribes," *New York Times*, January 21, 2010, www.nytimes.com/2010/01/21/business/21sting.html?th&emc=th Jan. 21, 2010 p. A3 in print version.

Occasionally, sales representatives attempt to bypass supply because they believe it may be to their advantage to do so. If the supplier secures an order without the knowledge and agreement of purchasing, internal dissension may be created, as well as resentment against the sales representative. The short-term gain may turn into a long-term loss.

Supply personnel are expected to be well acquainted with the organization's operations, equipment, materials, and varied requirements. They should be qualified to share the practicality of supplier's technical suggestions and proposals. However, the supply manager often is not a technical expert (engineer, scientist, and so on). Cross-functional sourcing teams bring together the supply expert and the technical expert. Team members may manage the supplier relationship for their primary area of expertise. The team approach lessens the fears of individual members that others will make decisions that are not in their best interests.

In a partnering relationship or buyer–supplier alliance, there is a substantial amount of regular direct contact between supplier personnel and nonsupply people in the buyer's organization. Direct contacts are essential to the effective execution of the contract and maintenance of a superior working relationship.

Reciprocity

Reciprocity is "the practice of giving preference in buying to those suppliers who are customers of the buying company as opposed to suppliers who do not buy from the company." Under what circumstances, if at all, shall trade relations or reciprocity be practiced? From a supply management perspective, reciprocity is unacceptable when it involves purchasing items under conditions that will result in higher prices or inferior service. It is also debatable how much it should be practiced, *assuming that conditions of price, service, and quality are substantially the same.*

The case against any general use of reciprocity is that the practice is at variance with the sound principles of either buying or selling. The sale of a product or service must be based on product qualities and the accompanying service. There is only one permanent basis for a continuing customer–supplier relationship: (1) the buyer's conviction that the product or service of a particular seller is the one best adapted to the need and is the best all-around value available, and (2) the seller's conviction that the buyer will act in good faith with the best interest of both parties in mind. As long as the sales department concentrates its attention on this appeal, it will find and retain permanent customers.

Few purchasers would object to reciprocal buying on the basis that quality, service, and price must be equal. In practice, abuse is practically certain. For instance, buyers are urged to buy from X, not because X is a customer, but because X is Y's customer, Y is our customer, and Y wants to sell to X.

The normal expectation of a seller using reciprocity as an argument is that the purchaser is willing to grant price, quality, or delivery concessions. In North America, reciprocity is on shaky legal grounds, and the U.S. Supreme Court has upheld the Clayton Act under Section 7 that reciprocity is restrictive to trade and creates unfair competition.[6]

As discussed in Chapter 14, "Global Supply Management," a form of reciprocity is practiced widely by governments who insist on "offsets." For example, a seller gets a contract

---

[6] The case is *FTC v. Consolidated Foods*, 380 U.S. 592 (1965).

in another country based on the condition that it meet stringent local content requirements. Thus, the supplier is forced to develop new sources, often at substantial cost, to secure the business. Furthermore, such foreign contracts often involve barter in which the buyer pays with raw materials or locally manufactured goods instead of currency.

CORPORATE SOCIAL RESPONSIBILITY (CSR)

Organizations are more conscious today of their responsibilities to protect the natural environment (e.g., sustainability) and to ensure that they conduct business in a manner that is socially responsible. Supply has a significant role in sustainability initiatives and establishing codes of conduct for managing suppliers. Chapter 16 covers issues related to investment recovery and disposal, and Chapter 17 covers supply's role in corporate social responsibility and sustainability. These topics certainly have implications for the ethical conduct of the organization and its supply function.

Conclusion

Supply professionals play both a strategic and an operational role in the organization. The strategic role is to maximize opportunities and minimize risks for the organization. The operational role is to execute the strategies in the most efficient and effective way possible.

Monitoring the legal and ethical environment is one area in which supply contributes strategically and operationally. The supply manager is well positioned to identify potential legal and ethical opportunities and risks.

Questions for Review and Discussion

1. What is counterfeiting and how does this issue affect supply managers?
2. Under what conditions is it realistic for a buyer to cancel a contract for goods? For services? For a seller to cancel a contract for goods? For services?
3. Does a supplier have to accept a PO exactly as offered by the buyer to create a legally binding contract?
4. What is alternative dispute resolution? When and how should it be used?
5. Does a salesperson have basically the same legal authority as a buyer? If not, how is it different?
6. What are the legal rights of the buyer if goods delivered by a supplier do not measure up to the specifications?
7. Under what conditions might purchasers be personally liable for contracts they enter into?
8. Is an oral contract legally enforceable? Under what conditions?
9. What authority does a supply manager have to make decisions that are binding on the principal? What responsibility do purchasing agents have for the consequences of their decisions?
10. What actions can the supply manager take to protect intellectual property rights and avoid legal action?

11. What can supply managers do to minimize the company's risk of a product liability lawsuit?

12. What legal issues would you want to consider before setting up an e-procurement system in a company?

13. What are the liability issues when contracting for software?

14. Where does the borderline fall between gratuities and bribery?

References American Arbitration Association. *Dispute-Wise^{SM} Business Management: Improving Economic and Non-Economic Outcomes in Managing Business Conflicts.* 2006. www.adr.org.

American Arbitration Association. *Drafting Dispute Resolution Clauses: A Practical Guide* 2013. www.adr.org.

BSR: Business for Social Responsibility. www.bsr.org.

Franklin, J. *The e-RG: International Intellectual Property Law,* American Society of International Law, last updated February 8, 2013. www.asil.org/.

Global Reporting Initiative. www.globalreporting.org.

ICDR Guide to Drafting International Dispute Resolution Clauses. International Centre for Dispute Resolution, 2011. www.icdr.org.

OECD Due Diligence Guidance for Responsible Supply Chains of Minerals from Conflict-Affected and High-Risk Areas. 2nd ed. Paris: OECD Publishing, 2013. dx.doi .org/10.1787/9789264185050-en.

Towle, H. K. "Modern Contracts: Boilerplate Needs an Overhaul for the Information Age." *Electronic Commerce and the Law Publication of the Bureau of National Affairs, Inc.* 14, no. 42 (November 4, 2009).

Wang, F. F. *Law of Electronic Commercial Transactions: Contemporary Issues in the EU, US and China.* 2nd ed., New York: Routledge, 2014.

Uniform Commercial Code: Official Text and Comments 2013–2014 edition. Philadelphia, PA: American Law Institute and the Uniform Law Commission, Thomas West Publishing Company, 2013.

World Intellectual Property Organization (WIPO), www.wipo.int/.

Wydick, R. C. *Plain English for Lawyers.* 5th ed. Durham, NC: Carolina Academic Press, 2005.

Zimmerman, A., and P. E. Chaudhry. *Protecting Your Intellectual Property Rights: Understanding the Role of Management, Governments, Consumers, and Pirates.* New York: Springer, 2013.

Case 15–1

Rocky Plains Brewing Ltd.

On April 21, Mike Pearson, packaging materials manager for Rocky Plains Brewery Ltd. (Rocky Plains), in Billings, Montana, received a call from Gerald Gilpin, owner and president of Gilpin Printing Inc (Gilpin), a local label supplier. Two days earlier Mike had notified Gerald that Rocky Plains was terminating the label contract with Gilpin as of May 30 and expected payment of a contractual rebate of $690,000. Gerald told Mike he refused to pay the rebate and demanded a $4.4 million wire transfer the next day in order to continue supply.

ROCKY PLAINS BREWING LTD.

Rocky Plains was more than 100 years old and was one of the most recognized beer brands in the United States. The company had a reputation for producing products of exceptional quality, supported by high standards for raw materials, proven brewing methods, and rigorous production processes. After operating for more than 80 years as a family business, the company was presently owned by a large multinational brewery. The Billings facility brewed three to four million barrels of beer per year and employed approximately 500 people.*

GILPIN PRINTING

Gilpin was a family-owned business and its president, Gerald Gilpin, was the son of the company's founder. Gilpin had been Rocky Plains primary label supplier for approximately 15 years, and Mike considered Gilpin's performance in the areas of quality and service to be good. Mike estimated that sales to Rocky Plains represented 45 percent to 50 percent of Gilpin's total annual revenues.

Gilpin provided Rocky Plains with three-day service— typically orders for labels were placed on Thursday for delivery on Monday morning. As a result, Gilpin carried substantial raw material safety stock, and Rocky Plains carried minimal inventories for its labels.

Rocky Plains used "cut and stack" labels exclusively for its products, of which approximately 80 percent were metallised labels and the balance were paper labels. The majority of high-volume labels supplied by Gilpin were produced through a rotogravure printing process, which used a printing plate to stamp the ink on to the paper. Rotogravure printing required the label design to be etched onto a copper cylinder, which typically required a four-week lead time to create. Litho-offset printing was the second method used for Rocky Plains labels, typically for speciality and low-volume brands. In contrast to rotogravure printing, litho-offset used etched rubber cylinders.

CONTRACT REVIEW

Rocky Plains' supply contract with Gilpin was to expire on May 30 and, after consultation with Mike's boss, Brian Evans, director of purchasing, the decision had been made in November to test the market. Mike's intention was to probe the market for better pricing,

* 1 barrel = 13.8 cases of beer with 24 bottles per case.

EXHIBIT 1 Summary Financial Information for Gilpin Printing Inc. (*in thousands of dollars*)

Sales	$34,296
Profit before tax	(1,014)
Write-downs	13,715
Net profit (loss)	(14,729)
Current assets	9,222
Noncurrent assets	9,953
Current liabilities	12,239
Long term debt	21,471
Shareholders equity (deficit)	(14,535)

materials, and print methods. A major concern for Mike and Brian was ongoing financial problems at Gilpin (see Exhibit 1 for a summary of Gilpin's financial statements). Gilpin had been unsuccessful in efforts to stem its financial losses during the past two years, and Mike had heard rumors that Gerald Gilpin was attempting to sell the business.

Requests for proposals (RFP) for a three-year contract were sent to eight potential suppliers, including Gilpin, and five responses were submitted prior to the December deadline. Mike's analysis of the proposals included financial stability of the supplier, protection for raw materials price increases, currency and foreign exchange exposure, freight costs, print run sizes, and label cutting options. Mike narrowed the field to two suppliers in February: Gilpin and Stiles Printing. Stiles was a large printer located in Billings with a solid reputation.

Gilpin offered a continuation of its current pricing for a three-year period, which included continuation of an annual rebate payable July 31 each year. The rebate was based on total purchases for the 12-month period between June and the following May each year, and ranged from a minimum of 3 percent to a maximum of 5 percent. Mike estimated that the rebate for the current year would be approximately 4.4 percent of total purchases from Gilpin.

The proposal from Stiles identified a variety of cost reduction opportunities through initiatives to use white paper with metallised ink, elimination of trim outs/ square cut labels, size optimization, and freight saving opportunities. Stiles also committed that it would not increase prices in the second year of the contract, and price increases for the third year would be capped at 3 percent. In addition, the company indicated that any future reductions in cost drivers, including raw material costs, would be passed directly to Rocky Plains. Mike estimated that the Stiles proposal represented savings of approximately $2.5 million in the following year compared to the proposal submitted by Gilpin.

NEGOTIATIONS WITH GILPIN

Due to the long-standing relationship with Gilpin and concerns that losing the contract could push the company into bankruptcy, Mike allowed the company to submit a second proposal. In his meeting with Gerald Gilpin on February 19, Mike indicated: "If you want to keep the business, we need a solid proposal with specific recommendations that will reduce our costs substantially."

Gilpin's second proposal, received on March 25, provided an overall annual price reduction of $2.0 million and did not include specific information regarding measures to support the lower pricing. During the meeting between Mike and Gerald Gilpin when the second proposal was presented, Gerald confirmed that he intended to sell the business, although a buyer had not yet been identified.

THE DECISION

Under the existing circumstances, Mike felt compelled to recommend awarding the label supply contract to Stiles. He based his decision on the better pricing offered by Stiles and concerns regarding the financial stability of Gilpin. Mike toured the Stiles facility in Billings the first week of April and a procurement audit had been completed the following week. Brian Evans concurred with Mike's recommendation, and in a meeting on April 19, Gerald Gilpin was notified that his company's label supply contract would expire on May 30 and it would not be renewed.

Meantime, Mike had been working with Pat Schofield, project manager at Stiles, to create a transition plan. The major tasks were:

- Create rotogravure print cylinders for high-volume brands (total of 285 cylinders)—completion date May 15.
- Production trials and qualifications of labels at Stiles—to be completed May 22.
- Production line trials with high-volume brand labels at Rocky Plains (led by Rocky Plains Brewery Support Group)—completion June 15.
- Implement Stiles pricing in Rocky Plains ERP system—completion June 1.

RESPONSE FROM GILPIN

On the morning of Friday, April 21, Mike Pearson received a call from Gerald Gilpin informing Mike that Gilpin was refusing to pay the contractual rebate due on July 1 and demanding $4.4 million for printed stock inventory, pending orders, and outstanding invoices. Gerald indicated that he expected a wire transfer in their account before the end of the next business day; otherwise he would cut off supply immediately.

Mike checked the computer system to see where Rocky Plains stood with Gilpin immediately after Gerald Gilpin's call. He estimated that Gilpin would owe Rocky Plains approximately $690,000 for its annual rebate in July, accounts payable to Gilpin were $442,398, pending orders were $583,165 and total label inventories at Rocky Plains were $846,835. A major concern, however, was potential production problems caused by label shortages, and Mike expected that production interruptions could start as early as Tuesday, April 25. Recognizing the significance of the problem, Mike knew he needed to come up with a plan quickly.

Case 15–2

Sinclair & Winston

Mr. Carter, vice president of supply for Moren Corporation, had just received a legal opinion from Sinclair & Winston regarding the cross arm failure on a new power line. Moren had run into major problems during the erection phase of the new ornamental tubular poles, and

Mr. Carter was anxious to assure early safe operation of the line. He was not sure on how to proceed with recovery of additional costs since three different suppliers had participated in the project.

CROSS ARM PROBLEMS

At the time of the cross arm failure, it was not clear what caused the problem. Only after extensive engineering tests that lasted almost three months was the prime cause found. Had the conductors been strung immediately or had the insulators been installed, as had been normal practice in all other tubular steel pole erections in this country, failure of the arms within a month of installation would not have occurred. However, the tests also showed that a long-term failure would occur because of galloping of the lines.

Mr. Carter had advised all three suppliers involved of the difficulties as soon as they arose. All three expressed concern and all claimed their part of the job could not have been responsible and that all work had been done to specifications. All offered to be of any assistance they could and gave a number of suggestions throughout the research phase. All of the work on the lines was halted until the reason for the failure was clear. Once the real cause was found, engineering was able to make recommendations for repair and strengthening that would prevent recurrence of the same difficulties (see Exhibit 1). Purchasing had obtained preliminary estimates showing an additional cost of about $5.4 million.

SINCLAIR & WINSTON

Mr. Carter had written a letter to Moren's legal firm, Sinclair & Winston, summarizing the situation to date. Sinclair & Winston met with Mr. Carter five days later and confirmed their statements in this meeting by letter the following day (see Exhibit 2).

Twenty-six months had passed since the beginning of the three-year project (see Exhibit 3). Moren Corporation was facing tremendous demand pressures for more power and simultaneously had not received particularly favorable treatment with rate increase requests. Mr. Carter was not sure where the extra funds to repair the cross arms would come from. The very high demand for capital in the corporation made it imperative that every avenue be explored to recover the extra costs to be incurred on the line. Workers had expressed fear about working near and with the poles. Since on-time completion and safety were also both of the highest priority, Mr. Carter wondered what action to take next.

EXHIBIT 1 **Moren Corporation, Transmission Engineering Department**

Re: Replacement of Henry Nelson Company—345 kV Cross Arms—Addison-Smithfield-Mesa Valley

It is required that all the groundwire and conductor cross arms on the line be removed and replaced with modified or new cross arms. It is the purpose of this correspondence to review the problems that have occurred and to outline a specific specification for the handling of these damaged cross arms. We will also continue the procedures for the installation of new cross arms on poles already erected and on new poles that have not been erected.

Through an extensive engineering research program, it was determined that the existing Nelson Company cross arms have low fatigue properties. First, the existing cross arm will fail by low velocity wind induced (aeolian) vibration, which can cause a fatigue failure in less than a month. Second, the cross arm can fail by fatigue over a period of approximately 15 years by the continuing reversal of stresses due to the galloping of the conductors.

The problem of aeolian vibration can be resolved by the use of dampening devices mounted on the ends of the cross arms. Examples would be the use of insulator strings on the conductor cross arms and stockbridge dampers on the groundwire cross arms. The problem of designing for galloping requires the reduction of the stress level at the weldment of the cross arm shaft to the cross arm baseplate. This can be accomplished by the use of stiffener bars on existing cross arms that have been fabricated but not erected. It can be accomplished on the damaged arms by the use of new thicker baseplates for the conductor cross arms. On new cross arms to be fabricated, there will be some of both of the types previously described.

Summary of estimates

Damaged arm repair:	
1,310—Structures Canadian	$1,492,504
Nondamaged arm repair:	
1,245—Structures Canadian	929,176
3,007—Hendy Nelson	1,256,860
Contractor—remove and replace	1,280,000
Research costs	400,000
Total	$5,358,540

EXHIBIT 2   Sinclair & Winston Attorneys and Counselors

Mr. John Carter
Vice President of Supply
Moren Corporation

Dear Mr. Carter:

Re: 345 kV Transmission Pole Failures

This is to confirm our opinion as expressed at the meeting held in your office on Monday. As you will recall, two basic legal matters were discussed, to wit the possible bases of liability of the three parties involved and whether the company would jeopardize its rights by proceeding to repair the poles without first consulting any of those parties.

Concerning the latter, if the company is entitled to recover from anyone, it can reasonably expect to recover the cost of correcting the problem. The cost of doing so must be reasonable, and the repair must also be reasonably likely to correct the problem. In other words you cannot recover for a "gold plating" job, nor can you recover the cost of a repair that does not correct the problem. This right to recover is not affected by a failure to negotiate in advance with any party against which a claim might be made. If, however, any such party is consulted in advance of the commencement of a repair program and is given a chance to participate in determining the repair to be used, the chances of later being required to defend either the necessity of that repair or its cost would be greatly reduced.

With respect to the liabilities of each party, the contracts and related documents have been reviewed in detail on the basis of the company's findings that the cause of the damage to the pole arms was wind vibration, which can be substantially avoided by dampening the arms with conductors, rather than letting the bare arms stand. As stated at the meeting, the bases for potential liability of each party can be set out, and the company can then assess the value of each on the basis of the known facts.

McTaggart Construction Company performed its services pursuant to a detailed contract that covered the work to be done but did not provide any specific rights or remedies for a situation like the one now faced. In order to recover from McTaggart, whether on a theory of breach of contract or of negligence, it will be necessary to show that in erecting the poles, McTaggart did not exercise the degree of care, skill, and diligence that a reasonably competent contractor, purporting to be able to erect poles and lines, would have exercised. The McTaggart contract does not, in our opinion, impose any burden on McTaggart for engineering or design adequacy.

(Continued)

EXHIBIT 2 Sinclair & Winston Attorneys and Counselors (*continued*)

As for Henry Nelson Company, their contract consists of a purchase order with detailed specifications attached thereto. There are no commercial terms, such as warranties, in the contract that relate directly to the arm failure problem. There are, however, four (4) possible bases of liability, which are

1. *Faulty design:* This would require that Nelson be shown to have had general design responsibility and that the current problem is a result of faulty design. The principal problem in this area is that the contract appears to give Nelson the burden of designing to Pettigrew Associates' specifications only.
2. *Breach of warranty:* If Nelson had reason to know the use to which the poles would be put and to know that Moren was relying on Nelson's skills and ability to produce a product fit for that purpose, then there would be in the contract an implied warranty that the poles would be fit for the purpose for which they were intended to be used. The primary weakness here is that the poles may well be fit for their ultimate intended use, and it would be necessary to show that Nelson knew or had reason to know that the poles would be erected and left standing without conductors
3. *Failure to detail assembly procedures:* Section 14 of the Pettigrew specification indicates in part that "the Vendor shall provide sketches indicating assembly procedures and the most desirable attachment points for raising the structures." With the benefit of hindsight, it can be argued that this includes the responsibility to direct that the arms be hung with conductors, although there seems to be general agreement that this is not necessarily what 14 was intended to cover.
4. *Failure to comply with the National Electrical Safety Code:* 24 of the Pettigrew specifications require compliance with the NESC, and it appears that here may be some basis for asserting that Nelson did not comply. This depends, as I understand it, largely upon whether the relevant section of the NESC can be construed as covering poles erected without conductors.

Finally, as regards Pettigrew Associates, the company has a contract pursuant to which Pettigrew is selected ". . . to perform the engineering and design services in connection with (the) Addison-Smithfield-Mesa Valley 345 kV Transmission Line Project." Article 1 provides that Pettigrew will ". . . furnish complete project administration for coordinating and expediting the Work" and is to perform services ". . . of the highest professional character . . ." with Pettigrew being ". . . fully responsible to Moren for the correctness of the engineering design and related data . . .," which included pole design. In addition, Pettigrew evaluated all bids, including designs offered, and recommended the award to Henry Nelson. If it can be shown either that the engineering design and related data were not correct or were not of the highest professional quality, then the company should have a sound cause of action against Pettigrew. I might add that the term "incorrect" can readily be construed to include omissions. As for the professional quality ground, it would be necessary to introduce expert testimony or evidence, or both, to establish that a top-quality engineer would have at least considered the wind vibration problem.

Depending on the facts that you are able to establish, the company may have a cause of action against one or more of the parties involved. We would be pleased to assist you further, should you so request, in progressing any claim the company may wish to make.

Yours very truly,
W. N. Sinclair

EXHIBIT 3   **Moren Corporation Timetable for the New Addison-Smithfield-Mesa Valley Power Line**

Year 1

March	Management approves use of ornamental tubular steel poles for the 140-mile line.
April–July	Preliminary work and search for engineering consultant.
August	Pettigrew Associates selected as consulting engineers to prepare pole specifications, line layout, and assist in selection of manufacturer and erection.

Year 2

March	Pettigrew Associates submit pole specification and line layout.
April–July	Engineering and purchasing evaluation of manufacturing of poles for the first half of the line.
July	Henry Nelson selected as the pole manufacturer.
June–September	Engineering and purchasing evaluation of foundation and erection contractors.
September	McTaggart Construction chosen for both foundation and erection of the new line.
October	Delivery of test poles by Henry Nelson. Tests prove poles meet specifications.
January	Installation starts. New poles draw favorable employee and public attention.
February 20	Henry Nelson completes manufacture of poles for Addison-Smithfield section.
February 24	First cross arm failure noted. Purchasing notifies all three suppliers. All deny blame
February 26	All project work halted.

Year 3

March–April	Continuing pole cross arm failures. Engineering searches for causes.
May 11	Engineering determines reason for failure.
May 25	Purchasing determines repair costs.
May 25	Mr. Carter sends memo to Sinclair & Winston for a legal opinion.
May 30	Sinclair & Winston representatives meet with Mr. Carter.
May 31	Letter from W.N. Sinclair confirming legal opinion.

Year 4

April 30	Project deadline.

Chapter **Sixteen**

Other Supply Responsibilities

Chapter Outline

Key Questions for the Supply Decision Maker

Should we

- Attempt to use scrap, surplus, and excess materials in-house?
- Arrange for our raw material suppliers to purchase scrap materials?
- Give supply responsibility for accounts payable?

How can we

- Improve the investment recovery process?
- Make improvements to our receiving process?
- Work effectively with operations and sales and marketing to achieve better supply chain integration?

As discussed in Chapter 3, supply management is broader than traditional procurement activities involving supplier selection and the acquisition of goods and services. Supply has significant involvement in a wide range of supply chain activities, such as warehousing, transportation, and logistics. In addition, many organizations involve supply in major corporate activities, such as mergers and acquisitions. The level of supply involvement in what is acquired, supply chain activities, and corporate activities can vary significantly from organization to organization, depending on factors, including industry, organizational size, customer requirements, and the competitive environment.

The focus of this chapter is on the many supply chain activities that the supply function may be either involved in or for which it may have direct responsibility. A list of responsibilities is provided in Table 3–3 in Chapter 3. This chapter covers six activities that fall under supply at many organizations: receiving, logistics and warehousing, inbound and outbound transportation, production planning, accounts payable, and investment recovery. Because several of these topics are also addressed in other chapters (e.g., production planning in Chapter 8 and transportation and logistics in Chapter 9), significant emphasis is placed on investment recovery, which does not have coverage in other chapters.

RECEIVING

Receiving is the first step in the internal supply chain and is a critical part of the acquisition process (see Chapter 4). It represents the point in the supply chain at which there is closure of the contract with the supplier and the buying firm accepts responsibility for the goods.

Receiving involves inspection, physical handling of goods, and processing of information. Receiving inspection ensures that the goods arrive in the quantity and condition as set out in the purchase order. Most organizations use a *receiving report* to identify the activities in the receiving process. The receiving report may involve checking quantity shipped, confirmation that the goods are the correct product, product number or model, and a quality test. For example, receipt of a shipment of steel may involve weighing the incoming shipment, reviewing mill specifications, and testing the material to confirm metallurgical specifications. Chapter 7 describes quality control techniques that can be used as part of the receiving process.

Information included with goods typically includes a packing slip and bill of lading. Internal receiving forms may include a quality inspection form or a discrepancy report. The use of technology in the receiving process, such as bar codes, can help improve efficiency and accuracy.

The *packing slip* is produced by the supplier and provides information such as a description of the goods and quantity. It will also refer to the customer purchase order number and, in some cases, a tracking number. The packing slip can be used to confirm that the actual quantity shipped matches the quantity ordered. Therefore, the receiving clerk can use the packing slip to compare the actual quantity shipped to the purchase order quantity to determine if the supplier over- or under-shipped.

The *bill of lading* is the contract between the shipper and carrier. It contains information about the quantity shipped, origin, and final destination. (See Chapter 9 for more information about the bill of lading.)

Service receipt is much more varied and may involve personnel from the organization in the process. Some services, such as electronic funds transfers or training of staff, may be done off-site and without the physical presence of receiving personnel.

Supply will most likely be involved in the resolution of issues that arise from the receiving process, such as quality concerns or discrepancies in volumes or prices.

LOGISTICS AND WAREHOUSING

As described in Chapter 1, supply can involve a wide range of logistics activities because of the need to control inventory levels and to coordinate material availability. These activities include inventory control, materials movement, scheduling and planning, and warehousing.

Following receipt, inventory must be stored. Specific personnel are typically assigned to manage raw material and work in progress inventory (WIP), and to transport it to the point of use. This is often the responsibility of stores and material handling personnel. The key decisions for stores and material handling are, Should it be stored? How and where should it be stored? How should it be moved? and, How should the inventory be tracked? Chapter 8 covers inventory management techniques.

Warehousing and inventory storage can either be an internal function or outsourced to a third-party logistics firm (3PL). Consequently, supply can be involved with direct accountability for warehouse personnel or for supplier selection and oversight. The trend in many organizations has been to outsource logistics activities.

Logistics activities occur throughout every organization—service or manufacturing, public or private sector—from material receipt to shipment of finished goods. Supply may be responsible for some or all of these activities. For example, supply involvement may include raw materials planning and storage, while sales may take responsibility for finished goods' storage and distribution. Chapter 9 covers the role of logistics in the supply chain and FOB terms. Chapter 14 covers Incoterms.

INBOUND AND OUTBOUND TRANSPORTATION

An integral part of acquiring goods and services is ensuring proper, cost-effective delivery. In some organizations, transportation costs can be one of the largest cost components. It is not unusual for suppliers to be responsible for delivery (e.g., FOB destination). In other circumstances, either company-owned fleets or dedicated carriers handle inbound transportation. Just-in-time delivery systems require frequent, small-lot deliveries. Consequently, supply frequently has input or direct control over inbound transportation. Chapter 9 covers transportation and delivery.

Coordinating inbound and outbound transportation helps to reduce costs and improve utilization of transportation-related resources. Consequently, a single transportation department within the supply organization may be responsible for both inbound and outbound transportation.

PRODUCTION PLANNING

Production planning involves short-, medium-, and long-term schedules for controlling inventory and production schedules. Since planning requires coordinating the delivery and storage of key raw materials with suppliers, some organizations designate responsibility for production planning to supply.

Production planning relies heavily on forecasts from sales and marketing to anticipate demand for products and services. Furthermore, operations is responsible for implementing the plan. Supply must, therefore, work closely with other key functions when developing production plans. Chapter 8 covers forecasting and planning techniques.

ACCOUNTS PAYABLE

Terms and conditions of the purchase contract spell out when payment will be made. Problems arise when changes are made to the original order (e.g., engineering changes) or when paperwork (e.g., bill of lading and purchase order) does not match. Unfortunately some organizations finance short-term working capital requirements by delaying payments to suppliers.

Some organizations today are giving supply the responsibility for processing accounts payable, a practice once considered unacceptable for reasons of control. The potential benefits are familiarity with the supplier and order, opportunities to reduce transaction costs and headcount, and ability for supply to ensure that payments for suppliers are made on time.

The Ross Wood case at the end of this chapter provides an example of the potential benefits of combining supply and accounts payable. The case describes opportunities to improve process effectiveness while simultaneously reducing headcount.

INVESTMENT RECOVERY

An area closely related to corporate social responsibility and sustainability is investment recovery, which represents the effective, efficient, and profitable recovery and disposal of scrap, surplus, obsolete, and waste materials and assets generated within the firm. In recent years, disposal problems have become more complex and important as companies face increasingly stringent environmental regulations and rising disposal costs. The focus on the end-to-end supply chain means that managers must look for return loops to recapture their initial materials investment through remanufacturing, repair, reconfiguration, and recycling. Added to this is the need to develop and use new methods for avoiding the generation of solid waste products in the first place and better means of disposing of wastes that are discharged into the air and waterways, causing pollution. Supply plays a critical role in investment recovery activities.

Not only does the proper sale of scrap, surplus, and waste result in additional income for the seller, but it also reduces the organization's environmental footprint by preventing pollution and conservation of raw material resources and energy. For example, every ton of iron and steel scrap recycled saves one-and-one-half tons of iron ore, one ton of coke, and one-half ton of limestone, plus the energy required to convert the raw materials into virgin product. Scrap steel is collected for beneficial reuse, conserving impressive amounts of energy and natural resources in the recycling process.

Thus, investment recovery requires attention to environmental issues and regulations (e.g., hazardous waste disposal) and the ability to identify opportunities to recover revenues or reduce costs (e.g., through recycling or new means of disposal). In many organizations, investment recovery is the responsibility of the supply function.

The emphasis on managing a network of supply chain partners leads to a number of cost-reduction opportunities in areas that may have been previously neglected by management. Environmental safety and health is one such area. Some of the ways in which supply can simultaneously achieve cost reductions and make improvements in environmental performance are (1) reducing the obsolescence and waste of maintenance, repair, and operating (MRO) supplies through better materials and inventory management; (2) substantially reducing the costs from scrap and materials losses; (3) lowering the training, handling, and other expenses for hazardous materials; (4) increasing revenues by converting wastes to by-products; (5) reducing the use of hazardous materials through more timely and accurate materials tracking and reporting systems; (6) decreasing the use and waste of chemicals, solvents, and paints through chemical service partnerships; and (7) recovering valuable materials and assets with efficient materials recovery programs.

Scrap is often a potential source of profit, and, therefore, the most obvious contribution of properly managed disposal activities is cost recovery. Directing residuals to landfills is an expensive disposal option, with tolling costs at landfills exceeding $100 per ton in some regions. Furthermore, associated costs, such as handling and transportation, make using landfills even more expensive. Firms can reduce their costs or avoid cost increases by examining ways to reduce or reuse their scrap materials.

Disposition costs are often ignored by managers who prefer to concentrate on more traditional cost areas, such as direct labor and raw material costs. In situations where firms produce a high volume of scrap, regular examination of plant investment recovery activities can lead to cost-reduction initiatives. Managers should examine scrap handling processes, segregation activities, logistics costs, and fees charged by dealers, brokers, and processors.

Categories of Material for Disposal

No matter how well a company is managed, every organization has some waste, scrap, surplus, and/or obsolete material. Companies try, of course, to keep such material to a minimum. But try as it may, this never will be wholly successful. The existence of this class of material is the result of a wide variety of causes, among which are overoptimism in the sales forecast, changes in design and specifications, errors in estimating usage, inevitable losses in processing, careless use of material by factory personnel, and overbuying resulting from attempts to avoid the threat of rising prices or to secure quantity discounts on large purchases.

We are not presently concerned with the methods by which excess, waste, scrap, or obsolete material may be kept at a minimum; these already have been discussed in previous chapters in connection with proper inventory, standardization, quality determination, value analysis, and forward buying. The immediate problem has to do with the disposition of these materials when they do appear. We first need to distinguish among the six categories of material for disposal.

Excess or Surplus Materials

Excess (or surplus) material is stock that is in excess of a reasonable requirement of the organization. It arises because of errors in the amount bought or because anticipated production did not materialize. Such material may be handled in various ways. In some cases it can be stored until required, particularly if the material is of a nonperishable character, if storage costs are not excessive, and if there is a reasonable expectation that the material will be required in the future. Occasionally it may be substituted for more active material. Or if the company operates a number of plants, it may be possible to transfer the excess to another plant.

There are times, however, when these conditions do not exist and when prompt sale is desirable. The chances for change in the style or design may be so great as to diminish considerably the probability that this particular material may be required, or it may be perishable. Factory requirements may be such as to postpone the demand for large amounts of this material so far into the future that the most economical action is to dispose of it and repurchase at a later date.

The Raleigh Plastics case at the end of this chapter describes a situation in which the director of purchasing has to dispose of surplus plastic resin. The supplier will take back the resin, but only at a substantial discount. Holding on to the material in the hope of future opportunities to use it is also not attractive.

Obsolete Material or Equipment

Obsolete material differs from excess stock in that, whereas the latter presumably could be consumed at some future date, the former is unlikely ever to be used inside the organization that purchased it. For example, material can become obsolete as a result of a change in the production process or when some better material is substituted for what was originally used. Once material has been declared obsolete, it is wise to dispose of it for the best price that can be obtained.

Although material or equipment may be obsolete to one user, this need not mean that it is obsolete to others. For example, a company could replace old machines with others that are more modern and more productive. However, the discarded machines may still have value for some other manufacturer in the same type of business or in some other industry, representing a profit-making opportunity for the company wanting to dispose of the obsolete equipment. Similarly, an airline may decide to discontinue using a certain type of airplane. This action makes not only the plane but also the repair and maintenance parts inventory obsolete. But both may have substantial value to other airlines or users of planes.

Rejected End Products

Because of the uncertainties of the production process, or because of complex end-product quality specifications, a certain percentage of completed products may be rejected by outgoing quality control as unsatisfactory. In some instances, these finished products can be repaired or reworked to bring them up to standard, but in other instances it is not economical to do so. The semiconductor industry is a good example; because of the technological complexities of the process, the "yield" on a particular production line may be such that only 70 percent of the finished devices measure up to end-product specifications.

The rejected products may then be sold to users who do not require the normal quality in purchased items. These might be classified as factory seconds. One problem is that if the end product is identified with a name or trademark, unscrupulous buyers may then turn around and remarket the item as one that measures up to the stated quality requirements for the original item. To avoid this, the sales contract may include a statement that "the buyer agrees and warrants that the product will not be resold in its present form or for its original usage application." If the seller does not feel this contract clause provides adequate protection, then the firm may find it necessary to destroy the rejected items (as is done in the pharmaceutical industry), remove the distinguishing mark or identification, or melt the product down to recover any valuable metal content.

Scrap Material

Scrap material differs from excess or obsolete stock because it cannot properly be classified as new or unused. *Scrap* is a term that may be applied to material or equipment that is no longer serviceable and has been discarded. Another form of scrap is represented by the many by-products of the production process, such as fly from cotton spinning; warp ends from weaving; ferrous and nonferrous metal scrap from boring, drilling, and stamping machines; flash metal from the foundry process; or paper cuttings from the binding process, as when this book was bound.

Start-up adjustment scrap is frequently significant, and in industries like papermaking, paper converting, printing, and polyethylene pellet manufacturing, it is one major reason for a significant price increase for small custom orders. The faster and the more automated the equipment, the higher the start-up scrap will be as a percentage of the total material used in small orders. Commonly, items of this class, which are a normal part of the production process, are considered a form of scrap; such material frequently may be salvaged. In the metal industries, the importance of scrap in this form has a definite bearing on costs and prices. For instance, a selection from among forgings, stampings, or castings may depend on the waste weight. The waste weight to be removed in finishing plus labor costs of removing it may make a higher-priced article the better value. In turning brass parts, the cost of the raw material (e.g., the brass rod) may be greater than the price of the finished parts because the recovered brass scrap is such an important element in the cost. Indeed, scrap is so valuable as an element in cost that it is not unusual for the purchase contract on nonferrous metals to include a price at which the scrap will be repurchased by the supplier.

Scrap metals normally are separated into ferrous and nonferrous categories. *Ferrous* includes those products conceived from iron that generally are attracted by the scrapman's Geiger counter (an ordinary magnet). The ferrous group consists of scrap steel, cast iron, white iron, and so on. The nonferrous group includes four broad families: (1) red metals, which are copper based; (2) white metals, which are aluminum, tin, lead, or zinc based; (3) nickel alloys; and (4) precious metals—for example, gold, silver, and palladium—known as exotics. Industry standards have been established for the grading of ferrous and nonferrous scrap materials, such as copper, steel, glass, and paper.

There are some 1,500 scrap dealers and brokers in the United States who buy, broker, and/or process scrap commodities, including metals, paper, plastics, glass, rubber, and textiles. The dealer or broker acts as an intermediary between the seller (normally the supply department) and the final buyer (such as a steel mill). These organizations can be an important service provider to manufacturing companies that generate a large amount of scrap and by-products as part of the normal manufacturing process by installing in-plant equipment for residual handling, hauling the material, and selling the scrap.

Waste

Waste is material or supplies that have been changed during the production process and, through carelessness, faulty production methods, poor handling, or other causes, have been spoiled, broken, or otherwise rendered unfit for further use or reclamation. There is a form of waste not due to obsolescence and yet not a result of carelessness or poor handling. Waste, for example, may occur by the fact that the material is not up to specifications because of faulty machinery or breakdowns, or because of unforeseen chemical action.

In some instances, waste can be defined simply as the residue of materials that results from the normal manufacturing process and that has no economic (resale) value (unlike scrap, which does have value). An example is the smoke produced by burning fuel, or cutting oil that has become so badly contaminated as a result of the normal manufacturing process that it cannot be reclaimed. However, what is waste today and has no current economic value may change tomorrow. For example, years ago the natural gas produced in crude oil production was waste and was flared off in the oil fields because it had no sales value; today it has substantial economic value.

Hazardous Waste

Hazardous waste is discarded material that exhibits certain specific hazardous characteristics, such as toxic, ignitable, corrosive, or dangerously reactive substances. Because of supply's role in the acquisition of materials and the disposal of waste, purchasers should consider the total cost of hazardous waste for the company. These costs include direct cleanup costs, disposal costs (rapidly rising due to a landfill shortage), administrative and legal costs, and new plant and equipment costs (to reduce waste and deal with contaminated plants).

The U.S. Department of Transportation regulates all hazardous materials transported under the Hazardous Materials Transportation Act (HMTA). In Canada, the Federal Department of Transport is responsible for administration of the Transportation of Dangerous Goods Regulations. Purchasers play a key role in transferring information required by the Hazard Communication Standard (HCS) or "right-to-know" law developed by the Occupational, Safety, and Health Administration (OSHA). Material safety data sheets (MSDS) provide the information necessary to recognize potential health hazards to employees and the community at large. The purchaser should request an MSDS from the manufacturer or supplier, perform a hazard evaluation considering the need for the chemical against the potential hazard to employees and the community, and, if necessary, develop sourcing and usage alternatives. The MSDS should be kept on file.

Laws and regulations for hazardous materials also cover packaging and movement of hazardous materials. The HMTA requires facilities to follow certain packaging, labeling, loading, routing, and emergency planning requirements.

Differences of opinion may exist about the exact definitions of scrap, excess, and waste. From the standpoint of the supply manager who has to dispose of the material, these differences are secondary. The objective is to realize as large a return as possible from the safe disposal of these items.

Responsibility for Material Disposal

The question of who bears the responsibility for the management of material disposal in an organization has more than one answer. In large companies where substantial amounts of scrap, obsolete, surplus, and waste materials and equipment are generated, a separate department may be justified. The manager of such a department may report to the general manager or the production manager. In some companies there is, within the manufacturing department, a separate investment recovery, salvage, or "utilization" division to pass on questions about possible reclamation. Indeed, the place of "investment recovery" in the organization is well established among many large firms. It is primarily a manufacturing responsibility, concerned with such duties as the development of salvage processes; the actual reclamation of waste, scrap, or excess material; and the reduction of the volume of such material. Most companies depend on the supply department to handle disposal sales.

A study of purchasing organizational relationships, conducted by CAPS Research, found that supply was responsible for scrap/surplus disposal/inventory recovery in 45 percent of firms and had responsibility for equipment for resale in 43 percent of firms.[1] Legitimate reasons for assigning disposal of materials to the purchasing/materials management function include the following: (1) They possess knowledge of price trends; (2) contact with salespeople is a good source of information about possible users of the material; (3) familiarity with the company's own needs may suggest possible uses for, and transfer of, the material within the organization; and (4) unless a specific department is established within the firm to handle this function, supply is probably the only logical choice.

In large and highly diversified organizations, there is a great need for the coordination of salvage disposal if the best possible results are to be obtained. Where a corporate supply department is included in the head-office organization structure, even if only in a consulting relationship with the various divisions of the company, available information and records and established channels of communication should help to ensure that salvage materials generated in any part of the company are considered for use in all parts of the company before being offered for sale.

Because the social and financial stakes are high and because of the complexity of laws and regulations, turnkey environmental contracting is a possible option for small- to medium-sized waste generators with needs that are too diverse or too small to be handled directly by treatment, storage, or disposal facilities.

The general conclusion is that, except in the cases of companies with separate salvage or investment recovery departments, management has found the supply department, because

---

[1] P. F. Johnson and M. R. Leenders, *Supply's Organizational Roles and Responsibilities* (Tempe, AZ: CAPS Research, May 2012).

of its knowledge of original suppliers, materials, markets, prices, and possible uses, in a better position than other departments of the company to salvage what can be used and to dispose of what cannot.

Keys to Profitable Disposal

Obviously, the optimum solution would be not to generate materials that need disposal. Although this is not totally possible, every effort should be made, through good planning and taking advantage of technology, to minimize the quantity of material generated.

The disposition of all kinds of obsolete, scrap, and surplus materials always should be handled to reduce the net loss to the lowest possible figure or, if possible, achieve the highest potential gain. The first thought, therefore, should be to balance the net returns possible from each of several methods of disposition available. Thus, excess material frequently can be transferred from one plant to another of the same company. Such a procedure involves little outlay except for packing, handling, and shipping. At other times, by reprocessing or reconditioning, material can be salvaged for use within the plant. Such cases clearly involve a somewhat larger outlay, and there may be some question about whether, once the material has been so treated, its value, either for the purpose originally intended or for some substitute use, is great enough to warrant the expense.

Because the decision whether to undertake the reclamation of any particular lot of material is essentially one of production costs and of the resultant quality, it should be—and commonly is—made by the production or engineering departments instead of by supply or the investment recovery department. The most the supply manager can do is to suggest that this treatment be considered before the material is disposed of in other ways.

Disposal Channels

There are several possible means of material disposal. In general, the options, in order of maximum return to the selling company, are as follows:

1. Use elsewhere within the firm on an "as is" basis. An attempt should be made to use the material "as is," or with modification, for a purpose other than that for which it was purchased: for example, substitution for similar grades and nearby sizes, and shearing or stripping sheet metals to obtain narrower widths. In the case of a multidivision operation, periodically each division should circulate to all other divisions a list of scrap/surplus/obsolete material and equipment; arrangements then may be made for interplant transfer of some of the items.

2. Reclaim for use within the plant. As a result of the materials shortages of the early 1970s, and more recently the sustainability movement, many firms have become interested in the possibilities of recycling materials such as paper, copper, zinc, tin, aluminum cans, and precious metals. For example, can the material be reclaimed or modified for use by welding? Examples include these: Defective and spoiled castings and fabricated metal parts can be reclaimed at little expense; short ends of bar stock and pipe can be welded into working lengths; and worn or broken jigs, fixtures, and machine parts can be built up or patched. Precious metal scrap often is shipped to a precious metal refiner that processes it back into its original form and returns it for use as a raw material, charging a tolling charge for its services. The opportunities for recycling, and thereby reducing the waste

stream, extend beyond municipal recycling systems and include programs that "close the loop" by collecting the material; turning it into cost-competitive, high-quality, recycled content products; and selling it back to the purchaser.

3. Sell to another firm for use on an "as is" basis. Can any other manufacturer use the material either "as is" or with economical modification? It should be noted that sales can often be made directly to other users who may be able to use a disposal item in lieu of a raw material they currently are buying. Or one firm's surplus or obsolete equipment may solve another firm's equipment requirements nicely. A good example of this is the market that has existed in the airline industry for years, where obsolete aircraft for one carrier are bought for use by other carriers. In some cases, and particularly prevalent in public agencies, surplus or obsolete equipment and vehicles are sold at public auction. Some companies permit employees to buy, as part of their employee relations program, used equipment or surplus materials at preset prices. If this is done, adequate controls should be established to ensure that the return to the firm is at a reasonable level and that all interested employees are treated fairly.

4. Return to supplier. Can it be returned to the manufacturer or supplier from whom it was purchased, either for cash or for credit on other later purchases? A great deal of steel scrap is sold by large-quantity purchasers directly back to the mills, which use it as a raw material in the steel production process. Normally, the firm using this disposal avenue must be a large consumer. In the case of surplus (new) inventory items, the original supplier may be willing to allow full credit on returned items.

5. Sell through a broker. Brokers can handle the sale of scrap, surplus, and obsolete equipment and materials. Their role is to bring buyer and seller together, for which they take a commission. Much metal scrap is disposed of through this channel. Brokers also exist to handle the purchase and sale of obsolete, surplus, used, and rebuilt equipment and typically specialize either by industry—for example, food processing—or type of equipment—for example, computers. This medium often is used by the selling organization and may present interesting alternatives for the buyer in the equipment acquisition process. Most used equipment brokers have websites that provide information about equipment availability and pricing.

6. Sell to a local scrap or surplus dealer. All communities of any size will have one or more scrap dealers. The return from sale through this channel likely will be low, for four reasons: (1) There may be only one dealer: a noncompetitive, sole buying source; (2) the dealer assumes the risk of investment, holding, and attempting to find a buyer; (3) the profit margin for assuming this risk may be quite high; and (4) extra movement and handling, which is costly, is involved.

7. Donate, discard, or destroy the material or item. In some instances, a firm may decide to donate used equipment to an educational or charitable organization, taking a tax deduction. A number of nonprofit clearinghouses distribute goods to schools and charities. Because the tax aspects of such contributions are complex, the advice of tax counsel should be obtained as part of the decision process.

Most items can be disposed of profitably by use of imagination, creative thinking, and problem solving. Recent research on the importance of environmental considerations in supply chain management indicates that avoidance of regulatory violations is still the primary focus. Yet many organizations are coming up with creative and cost-effective ways to handle investment recovery challenges. The Investment Recovery Association, an international nonprofit trade association of firms with established investment recovery programs, provides assistance in disposing of recyclable products, capital assets, and surplus materials.

Disposal Procedures

Selling scrap and surplus materials requires that adequate procedures be established that will protect the company from loss due to slipshod methods, dishonest employees, and irregular practices on the part of the purchaser. These procedures must cover a broad range of activities, including segregation and storage, weighing and measuring, delivery, negotiation, supplier selection, and payment.

Contamination of scrap with foreign materials will often significantly reduce its recovery value. If two types of scrap (e.g., steel and copper scrap) are mixed, the return per pound on sale likely will be less than the lowest-priced scrap, because any buyer must go to the expense of separating the scrap before processing. Consequently, scrap should be segregated, prepared, and analyzed systematically during the various stages of the production process in order to protect its value.

Scrap can be segregated by type, alloy, grade, size, and weight and should be done at the point where the scrap is generated. This requires proper planning and organization of segregation activities, which includes providing instructions to employees at collection points. Training programs also can be used to help company employees identify and separate scrap materials. Plants, not the dealers or the processors, should control the collection and classification of scrap materials, and company personnel should be familiar with the grades of scrap produced. Periodic studies should be conducted to evaluate the most effective methods of disposing of scrap in light of changing volumes and different mixes of scrap grades.

Adequate controls should be in place for accurate reporting and payment. All sales should be approved by a department head, and cash sales should be handled through the accounting department and never by the individual whose duty it is to negotiate the sale. All delivery of by-products sold should be accomplished through the issuing of an order form, and a sufficient number of copies should be made to provide a complete record for all departments involved in the transaction. The shipping department should determine the weight and count, and this information should be sent directly to the accounts receivable department.

The department responsible for the performance of this function should maintain a list of reputable dealers in the particular line of material or equipment to be disposed of and should periodically review this list. At frequent intervals, the proper plant official should be instructed to clean up the stock and report on the weights and quantities of the different items or classes of items ready for disposal.

A common procedure is to send out invitations to four or five dealers to inspect the lots and quote their prices FOB factory yard. Such transactions usually are subject to the accepted bidder's check of weights and quantities and are paid for in cash before removal. Not infrequently, acceptable and dependable purchasers with whom satisfactory connections have already been established are relied on as desirable purchasers, and no bids are called for from others. Technology tools are increasingly applied to investment recovery programs. Companies are using the Internet to advertise the sale of surplus and obsolete equipment and materials.

If a firm generates large amounts of scrap materials consistently, the bidders may be asked to bid on the purchase of this scrap over a time period of six months to a year. It is generally advisable to rebid or renegotiate such contracts at least annually to encourage competition. However, when establishing contract duration, plants need to consider the associated transaction costs. Not only are there administrative costs of soliciting bids but other costs need to be taken into account, such as possible production interruptions as equipment provided by the old processor is replaced by the new processor. Plants often negotiate long-term agreements with their processors in order to encourage investment in equipment viewed as beneficial by plant management.

Often the disposal agreement will have an escalator clause in it, tying the price to changes in the overall market, as reported in a specifically designated independent market index, such as AMM.com. The market prices of many types and grades of scrap materials can vary widely over a relatively short time period, which is the reason for the use of escalator clauses.

The contract for sale of scrap items should include price and how it was determined, quantities involved (all or a percentage), time of delivery, FOB point, cancellation privileges, how weights are determined, and payment terms. For reporting purposes, revenues associated with the scrap disposal activities should be credited to separate accounts, as opposed to netting them against a purchase or expense account. The practice of netting scrap revenues against raw material costs may be justified for statement presentation purposes, but such revenue should be itemized on management statements and budgets.

Selection of Disposal Partners

Selection of the appropriate firm to handle waste and scrap removal can be a challenging, yet critical, task. First, most scrap materials can be sold. However, supply managers are used to buying, not selling, materials. Second, hazardous materials must be properly disposed of; failure to do so can result in substantial fines and cleanup costs. This requires an understanding of regulatory issues surrounding residual disposition. Third, disposal methods have implications for the general manufacturing operation. Decisions, such as segregation, impact a plant's processing operations and influence its cost structure. Consequently, traditional supply precepts do not always apply when selecting a firm to handle disposal activities.

In most situations, plants must rely on support from scrap dealers to help manage elements of their disposal activities. As a result of the costs associated with regulatory noncompliance, generators of scrap and waste must be aware of what happens to the material after it leaves the company premises. Consequently, only approved processors, dealers, or brokers should be used, with qualification based on a range of possible criteria: secondary processing and waste treatment capabilities and capacity; size and capacity of truck fleet; ability to provide dependable service; problem-solving capabilities; ability to provide destruction of scrap products in order to avoid entry into the market; and financial stability. Assessing the financial stability of the dealer, broker, or processor often requires obtaining a list of credit references or obtaining a credit report from an organization such as Dun & Bradstreet.

The volume of scrap or waste material has a significant influence on how companies choose to manage their disposal activities. Plants with high volumes often support disposal activities with dedicated staff and employ a greater level of resources in the disposition process. Depending on volume, logistics systems also differ. For example, plants that generate a high volume of a particular grade of scrap may find it cost effective to utilize rail transportation or specialized highway trailers.

Every effort should be made to obtain maximum competition from sources available to buy scrap or surplus material. Unfortunately, the number of potential users and buyers of scrap in a particular area may be small, resulting in noncompetitive disposal situations. Supply should actively attempt to find new buyers and encourage them to compete in terms of price paid and services provided.

Investment recovery involves supplier management issues, which have implications for the overall performance of the firm. Measuring total costs of disposition is useful as a means of identifying a range of opportunities to work with disposal partners with the objective of improving activities. For example, in a cooperative relationship, joint problem-solving efforts can be utilized by the plant and scrap investment buyer as a response to changing issues. Make-or-buy decision criteria can be applied to determine the appropriate mix of activities for the plant; these activities should be reevaluated regularly to adapt to changing situations.

Conclusion

Supply has involvement in a broad range of corporate activities. Receiving, logistics and warehousing, inbound and outbound transportation, production planning, accounts payable, and investment recovery are areas in which supply can play a significant role. The decision whether to give supply direct responsibilities for some or all of these areas should be balanced with the opportunities to reduce costs and improve business processes. Exploring opportunities for supply involvement in some or all of these areas can help to improve integration within the internal supply chain. While supply may not necessarily have direct accountability for all of these activities in every organization, some involvement is likely, making it necessary for the prudent supply professional to be well versed in the opportunities in these areas.

Questions for Review and Discussion

1. Why is responsibility for logistics often given to supply?
2. Why is responsibility for investment recovery often given to supply?
3. What are the advantages and disadvantages for giving responsibility of accounts payable to supply?
4. How can the firm obtain maximum return from disposal of unneeded items?
5. What specific procedures should supply use to dispose of unneeded items?
6. What are the channels used in disposing of items? What are the advantages of each?
7. What is the difference between surplus material, obsolete material, rejects, scrap, waste, and hazardous waste? How do investment recovery and disposal practices differ between these six categories?
8. Where can you achieve cost reductions in disposal and investment recovery activities? What are the major cost drivers?

9. How do environmental concerns affect the disposal of scrap, surplus, and obsolete materials?

10. How can environmental matters be incorporated into supplier selection?

References

The Environmental Protection Agency (EPA). *The Lean and Green Supply Chain: A Practical Guide for Materials Managers and Supply Chain Managers to Reduce Costs and Improve Environmental Performance.* EPA 742-R-99-003, February 2000. www.epa.gov.

The Environmental Protection Agency (EPA). *Enhancing Supply Chain Performance with Environmental Cost Information: Examples from Commonwealth Edison, Andersen Corporation, and Ashland Chemical.* EPA 742-R-99-002, April 2000. www.epa.gov.

Gattiker, T. F., "ISO 14000 at Veris Industries." *Practix.* Tempe, AZ: CAPS Research, July 2009.

Gattiker, T. F.; W. Tate; and C. R. Carter. *Supply Management's Strategic Role in Environmental Practices.* Tempe, AZ: CAPS Research, 2008.

Gobbi, C. "Designing the Reverse Supply Chain: The Impact of the Product Residual Value." *International Journal of Physical Distribution & Logistics Management* 41, no. 8 (2011), pp. 768–796.

Green, K. W.; P. J. Zelbst; J. Meacham; and V. S. Bhadauria. "Green Supply Chain Management Practices: Impact on Performance." *Supply Chain Management* 17, no. 3 (2012), pp. 290–305.

Hall, D. J.; J. R. Huscroft; B. T. Hazen; and J. B. Hanna. "Reverse Logistics Goals, Metrics, and Challenges: Perspectives from Industry." *International Journal of Physical Distribution & Logistics Management* 43, no. 9 (2013), pp. 768–785.

Institute of Scrap Recycling Industries, www.isri.com

Investment Recovery Performance Benchmark Report. Tempe, AZ: CAPS Research, December 2013. www.capsresearch.org.

Turrisi, M.; B. Manfredi; and S. Cannella. "Impact of Reverse Logistics on Supply Chain Performance." *International Journal of Physical Distribution & Logistics Management* 43, no. 7 (2013), pp. 564–585.

Case 16–1

Ross Wood

On Thursday afternoon right after lunch, Ross Wood, vice president of supply management at Dickson Electronics, was visited by Claude Dakin, chief accountant. Claude proposed that accounts payable be moved from accounting to supply.

DICKSON ELECTRONICS

Dickson Electronics, a multibillion international firm, was headquartered in Silicon Valley in California. The firm,

established in 1971, sold a wide range of consumer, industrial, and military products. Major change had taken place at Dickson over the past two years as a new management team tried to improve the firm's financial performance. A number of divisions had been sold and several acquisitions of smaller companies with considerable growth potential had been acquired. The first signs that this major strategic shift was moving the company in the right directions were starting to show, but top management was still far from satisfied with the firm's current performance.

ROSS WOOD

Ross Wood had been second in command in supply management at another California electronics firm. At a school gathering for his daughter, he met Jim Anderson, senior vice president of operations at Dickson Electronics. Jim Anderson indicated that Dickson was in the process of seeking a new head for its centralized supply function. Since in Jim's eyes Ross Wood had all of the qualifications necessary for the job, he offered Ross the position. Since Ross's superior at his current firm was almost the same age as Ross, Ross believed his chances for promotion were limited. Moreover, he was intrigued by the challenge of aligning supply at Dickson to the new corporate strategy. He was also impressed with Jim Anderson's enthusiasm and drive and accepted the offer.

Within three months of Ross' arrival, Dickson's president announced a drive to curtail Dickson's head office headcount and to improve the bottom line significantly. For Ross Wood this translated into two targets: (1) Reduce supply's head office headcount to 200, and (2) deliver savings of $200 million on the corporation's $4.1 billion spend with suppliers. It was two months after these targets were announced that Ross Wood was visited by Dickson's chief accountant, Claude Dakin, with his request that supply accept full responsibility for accounts payable.

Ross Wood had come to the conclusion that the only way in which he could meet the president's directive on headcount was by outsourcing the logistics group in supply. He had started negotiations with several third-party logistics providers and believed that by moving all logistics personnel off his payroll he would be able to just meet the headcount target of 200 by year-end. He also believed that a number of initiatives, including strategic sourcing and going offshore, would allow him to meet his savings target. Therefore, the accounts payable proposal was an unwelcome diversion at this time.

CLAUDE DAKIN'S PROPOSAL

Claude Dakin arrived on a Thursday afternoon right after lunch and was direct:

> I want you to take over responsibility for accounts payable. Now, I know you are in a headcount squeeze and so am I. So, before you say no, hear me out. We've looked hard for efficiency improvements in our department and even brought in some work study specialists to measure productivity. From their work it became very clear that most of the delays and inefficiencies in accounts payable were caused by supply issues: Supplier invoices that do not match purchase orders because of different quantities, prices, or terms are a major problem. And when our accounts payable people try to clear up these matters, your people claim they are too busy, have trouble on the details, and cause multiple further delays. We have checked very carefully and believe that supply-related interference costs us at least 30 percent in productivity. Therefore, we believe that if we moved accounts payable closer to the supply people and have them report to you, significant improvements in communication and cooperation would result. Moreover, by far the largest amount of work in accounts payable relates to supply anyway. I currently have 16 people in this group and we believe this can be reduced to 11 if you take over.

Case 16–2

Raleigh Plastics

On June 8, Richard Kielstra, director of purchasing at Raleigh Plastics in Westland, Michigan, heard that the company had not been awarded a large new contract it had expected from one of its automotive OEM customers. Richard had ordered a substantial shipment of customized plastic resin in anticipation of this contract, and now he wondered how to dispose of the raw material on-hand.

RALEIGH PLASTICS

Raleigh Plastics, an automotive parts manufacturer, had been a supplier in the North American automotive industry for more than four decades. Some of the products manufactured included dash panels, door trim, and seating components for car interiors. The company currently produced more than 50 different parts and employed approximately 150 people.

Raleigh Plastics' mission was, "To produce world-class competitive products that exceed our customers' expectations in quality, cost, and delivery through people, teamwork, and technology."

SUPPLY MANAGEMENT

Raleigh Plastics obtained resins from two major sources: 60 percent came from McFadden Resins from its Farmington Hills, Michigan plant, and the remainder from Saunders Plastics in Knoxville, Kentucky. Both suppliers were leaders in the industry and Richard considered their quality to be among the highest in the industry.

Because of the high demand for plastic resins, delivery schedules varied depending on the type of product requested by Raleigh Plastics. Delivery normally took 10 weeks for standard products and up to 16 weeks for special formulations of resins. Thus, long lead times required extensive inventory planning. Moreover, occasionally raw material had to be ordered prior to confirmation of a customer contract.

The plastic resin suppliers recognized the difficulties with material planning and offered most parts manufacturers a consignment period of 60 to 120 days. The consignment clause meant that Raleigh Plastics only paid for resins it used. Therefore, if a resin had been purchased for a major job prior to the acceptance of a bid, and if that job was awarded to a competitor, the resin could be returned as long as it was unused and had been purchased in the last two to four months. However, consignment agreements did not apply to customized orders.

THE NEW CONTRACT

In July of the previous year, Raleigh Plastics had submitted a bid to manufacture a dash board for a new vehicle going into production the following March. Due to the long raw material lead time, Richard placed an initial order for customized resins in early November. McFadden Resins was selected to provide 200,000 pounds of resin at a cost of $0.90 per pound. After the 16-week waiting period, the 200,000 pounds would be delivered in monthly shipments of 50,000 pounds each.

By March Richard still had not received contract confirmation. The resin began to accumulate in inventory, but he was not concerned because the plant had adequate space. However, on June 8 Richard learned from the company's VP of sales, Walter Merulla, that the contract had been awarded to another supplier. Richard immediately requested cancellation of all remaining deliveries. McFadden Resins agreed to cease all shipments, but by this date Raleigh Plastics had already received 150,000 pounds of customized resin. Inventory had been purchased on credit and the supplier was expecting payment by the end of the month.

THE CURRENT SITUATION

Richard wondered what his best option was with respect to the 150,000 pounds of resin already in inventory. He could see at least two options. First, Raleigh Plastics could return the inventory. McFadden Resins understood the nature of the dilemma and its sales representative had verbally agreed that they could act as the selling agent and try to resell the inventory to another manufacturer. Under this arrangement, Raleigh Plastics would be required to pay a commission of $0.20 per pound and there were no guarantees that the full purchase price of $0.90 could be obtained in the resale market. Even though this would mean a loss for Raleigh Plastics, Richard felt that this option was worth considering.

Richard was also considering keeping the inventory and looking for potential alternative uses. If plastic resins were stored in a cool, dry environment, they could be held for several years. However, Richard understood that most manufacturers would have concerns about the quality of resins that were more than two years old.

Richard understood that there might be an opportunity to use 50,000 pounds of the resin in the next few months on some new business that the company was currently quoting. However, the remaining stock would likely not be completely cleared out for at least another 18 months. Inventory carrying costs at Raleigh Plastics were usually calculated at 2 percent per month at the value of the inventory. There was adequate space to hold the resin in the current facility, but the real concern was potential damage to the inventory. Richard knew that the longer the resin remained in inventory, the greater the probability that the packaging would be damaged, resulting in inventory spoilage. Furthermore, if this alternative was chosen, a payment schedule for the resin would have to be negotiated with the supplier.

Supply Function Evaluation and Trends

Key Questions for the Supply Decision Maker

Should we

- Recognize supply research as a formal activity?
- Develop a consistent, formal system for evaluating supply performance?
- Audit our suppliers' sustainability practices?

How can we

- Measure supply's contribution more effectively?
- Get internal validation for the budgetary impact of supply's performance?
- Make business decisions that are financially superior and environmentally sound?

In a rapidly changing environment, innovation and improvements in productivity can best be managed if we look at what might be possible, develop comprehensive plans, evaluate accomplishments and shortfalls, and report outcomes. Earlier in this text, the discussion primarily focused on identifying the contribution that supply can make to the organization and determining how to make that contribution. Two additional activities must be performed: (1) research to develop and operationalize the plans and metrics, and (2) communication of supply's contribution internally and externally.

The changing demands and increasing expectations of supply have led to a need for supply managers with broader and deeper knowledge and skill sets. Research skills are needed throughout the supply process: first to collect, analyze, and synthesize information that might assist in need recognition and description; next, to identify potential suppliers in light of organizational goals and objectives; then to perform the supplier selection process, manage the supplier relationship throughout its life, and measure the results of these activities.

Metrics also need to be established to capture results as they occur throughout the process. Many of the traditional metrics of purchasing performance focused more on efficiency measures such as price per unit or cost to process a purchase order than on effectiveness measures such as congruence with corporate goals or customer satisfaction. In Chapter 1, supply's contribution was described as strategic, operational, direct, and indirect. Metrics should capture the contribution along each of these dimensions. The challenge is to develop metrics that put supply's contributions in a language that speaks to the audience—internally to senior management and internal business partners and externally to stakeholders such as stockholders, the community, suppliers, and other supply chain members.

This chapter covers supply research, budgets, and performance metrics. It considers the need for supply managers to measure, evaluate, and report on their performance and the requirements senior management places on the supply process for credible results. Chapter 17 also provides an overview of the supply trends and future challenges.

SUPPLY RESEARCH

Supply research is the systematic collection, classification, and analysis of data as the basis for better supply decisions. Figure 17–1 shows some of the data (information) that might be required for effective buying decisions.

The studies conducted in supply research include projects under the major research headings of

1. Purchased materials, products, or services (value analysis).
2. Commodities.
3. Suppliers.
4. Supply processes.

FIGURE 17–1
Ingredients of Effective Buying

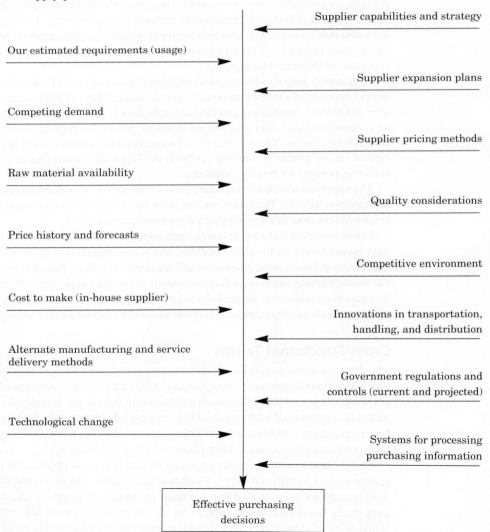

Our estimated requirements (usage)

Competing demand

Raw material availability

Price history and forecasts

Cost to make (in-house supplier)

Alternate manufacturing and service delivery methods

Technological change

Supplier capabilities and strategy

Supplier expansion plans

Supplier pricing methods

Quality considerations

Competitive environment

Innovations in transportation, handling, and distribution

Government regulations and controls (current and projected)

Systems for processing purchasing information

Effective purchasing decisions

Considerable attention has been given to a similar activity in the counterpart function of marketing research. Marketing research generally is well accepted in all medium- to large-sized firms as a necessary ingredient in decision making, and it has produced significant results for those firms that practice marketing research systematically. Supply research, if approached in an organized manner, also has the potential for generating major improvements in supply decision making.

A firm could conduct supply research in one of three ways: (1) full-time research positions, (2) inclusion of research as a part-time responsibility of supply personnel, or (3) cross-functional teams to bring an expanded knowledge base to the research process.

Full-Time or Part-Time Research Positions

As with its counterpart function, marketing research, there are persuasive arguments for the assignment of full-time personnel to perform supply research. These positions typically are titled purchase analyst, cost management specialist, value analyst, or commodity specialist. (See Figure 17–2 for an example of a job description for a supply cost management specialist at Deere and Company.)

A thorough job of collecting and analyzing data requires blocks of time, and in many supply departments the buyers do not have this time. They are fully occupied finding workable solutions to immediate problems. Furthermore, many areas of supply research, such as economic studies and analysis of business processes, require in-depth knowledge of research techniques. These research techniques call for a level of skill not possessed by the typical buyer, primarily because research skill typically is not one of the criteria used in selecting persons for buying positions.

The supply researcher must take a broad view of the overall effects of supply decisions on operating results. The buyer, on the other hand, may be so engrossed in his or her own responsibility area that the big picture goes unrecognized.

In this model of full-time research staff, supply decisions are made by the buyer or business owner based on the data, analysis, and recommendations of the researcher. Conflict may develop between the researcher and the decision maker; thus, the recommendations of the researcher may not receive fair consideration and the value of the efforts will be negated. The part-time researcher model is based on the argument that the buyer is the most familiar with the goods and services acquired and should be responsible for supply research.

Cross-Functional Teams

The division of the supply function into operational and strategic elements, coupled with downsizing and flattening of the organization, has led to an increased use of cross-functional sourcing teams that do the research and planning but do not actually do the buying. This model is somewhat of a compromise between the full-time supply analyst and the part-time buyer-researcher. Such teams have titles such as sourcing team, commodity management team, or value analysis team. (See Chapter 3 for more detail.)

The difficulty with the team approach is that it is hard to pinpoint responsibility for results when it is diffused over a number of individuals. However, the team approach can work satisfactorily, provided that (1) team members are carefully selected to ensure that each really has something to contribute, (2) the team has strong leadership (from a functional point of view, it probably should be someone from the supply area), (3) a specific set

FIGURE 17–2
Deere and
Company Job
Description for
Supply Cost
Management
Specialist

JOHN DEERE

Job Title:	Supply Cost Management Specialist
Department:	Supply Management
Supervises:	None, may facilitate/lead team activities
Job Function:	Enabling the design and procurement processes to obtain the best value from the supply base.

Primary Duties:
1. Develop cost models and tables for direct materials to be used for
   —Evaluating cost competitiveness of product designs.
   —Creating product target costs on a part-by-part basis.
   —Creating supplier target costs to enable fact-based negotiations.
   —Highlighting potential cost-reduction areas.
2. Utilize cost management techniques to give accurate and timely cost evaluations of designs on a part-by-part basis.
3. Support Strategic Sourcing in meeting or exceeding product cost goals for direct material.
4. Support Strategic Sourcing in all aspects of cost-reduction activities including
   —Utilizing cost management techniques to determine potential areas for cost reduction.
   —Tracking, forecasting, and budgeting for cost reduction of Order Fulfillment Process (OFP) cost activities.
   —Facilitating the JD CROP (John Deere Cost-Reduction Opportunities Process) at the unit level.
   —Participating or facilitating the Compare and Share process with Strategic Sourcing and the Value Improvement process.
5. Participate or lead enterprise-level cost management activities such as cost modeling or training.

of objectives and expectations of results is formulated and communicated to each member and the team as a whole, (4) each team member's normal job responsibilities are rearranged to give that person the time and the resources necessary to ensure results, and (5) performance evaluation and reward systems foster team participation and overall team performance. If any of these five conditions is not present, less than optimum outcomes are almost certain.

SUPPLY RESEARCH OPPORTUNITIES

The types of data that bear on a major supply decision are numerous and many different items may be purchased; therefore, the number of possible supply research projects is almost infinite. However, even a company with full-time supply analysts has limited resources and must use some method of deciding which supply research projects should have top priority.

The following is a list of criteria that are used by firms to decide where they will direct their research effort. This is not intended to be in priority order (although the most widely used method is the "top dollar" criterion).

1. *Value of product or service.* Top dollar (current or projected).
2. *Product profitability.* Red dollar (unprofitable end product).
3. *Price/cost characteristics.* Infrequent price changes, frequent or seasonal price fluctuations, end-product cost not competitive, raw materials costs rising at a greater rate than selling price of product.
4. *Availability.* Limited number of suppliers, new suppliers adding to available supply, possibility of international sourcing, possibility of in-house manufacture or outsourcing.
5. *Quality.* Have had quality or specification problem.
6. *Data flows.* Information for decisions often inaccurate, late, or unavailable; cost of data is excessive.

Research projects typically fall into one of four categories: (1) purchased materials, products, or services; (2) commodities; (3) suppliers; and (4) supply processes.

Purchased Materials, Products, or Services

Research is typically conducted on purchased materials, products, or services to ensure that the best value-creating decision is made. These research projects include:

1. *Specification.* Analysis of current specifications compared to the final customers' required performance level to eliminate unneeded attributes or unnecessarily high levels of performance, and to enable competitive sourcing.
2. *Standardization.* Review of how specific products are used and consideration of using one item to fill the needs for which multiple items currently are purchased.
3. *Substitution.* Analysis of the technical and economic ramifications of using a different item than the one presently purchased.
4. *Packaging.* Investigation of processes and materials to determine the optimal method of meeting requirements.
5. *Supplier switching.* Analysis of opportunities to improve value with a different supplier.
6. *Investment recovery.* Analysis of disposal methods (including recycling), channels, and techniques to isolate those that will provide greatest net return to the firm.
7. *Lease or buy.* Collection of data on the advantages and disadvantages of each alternative so that the most attractive decision can be identified.

8. *Make or buy and continue making or outsource.* Comparison of economic and managerial outcomes from each alternative to make an informed choice.

Two techniques are useful when researching purchased materials, products, or services: value analysis and target costing.

Value Analysis

Value analysis is the first supply research method to receive major worldwide attention, publicity, and acceptance. Originally developed by Lawrence D. Miles at General Electric, value analysis (VA) was widely accepted in U.S. industry and in Japan, where it is cited as a cornerstone of Japan's cost-effective manufacturing system. The Society of Japanese Value Engineering created the Miles Award Program to recognize outstanding value analysis/engineering accomplishments in the private and public sectors. Value analysis can be applied to both goods and services.

Value analysis compares the *function* performed by a purchased item with the *cost* in an attempt to find a better-value alternative. The first step is to select a part, material, or service to analyze; next, to form a cross-functional value analysis team (often including a supplier); and finally, to define the function of the item or service in a verb and noun combination. For example, if the can that holds a soft drink is selected for value analysis, its function might be defined as "holds liquid." This approach encourages creative thinking and keeps the team from locking onto the existing solution, an aluminum can, as the only solution. Value analysis is a systematic approach that can be an ongoing part of the supply management process.

The standard value analysis approach is to pose and provide detailed answers to a series of questions about the item currently purchased. Figure 17–3 details this approach and lists standard value analysis questions.

Many discrete goods manufacturers, such as consumer electronics and automotive companies, use value analysis. For example, Toyota uses value analysis with its suppliers to reduce costs in its products and processes. It uses a reverse engineering phase in every project before finalizing product design.[1]

In many instances, a higher-priced item than necessary is purchased because of time pressure or rapidly changing technology and manufacturing methods. The distinction is often made that *value analysis* is done on purchased items used in the ongoing production process and *value engineering* focuses on value improvement opportunities in the design stage. The value analysis process is the same at both stages. Obviously, value engineering to arrive at the best value specification and design that will adequately perform the function is the most efficient way to do the job, but unfortunately this analysis, due to time pressures, often is not done.

Moreover, after a product has been on the market for a while, greater certainty about demand, new technological options, or suppliers may become available; and prices of key materials or components may have changed. Therefore, a careful value analysis after the original design may reveal surprising opportunities for value improvement, even if the original design had been carefully value engineered. Value analysis techniques are equally applicable to services, supply processes, and e-commerce activities.

[1] D. Hannon, "Shorter Is Better for Toyota's Supply Chain," *Purchasing* 137, no. 8 (2008), p. 4.

FIGURE 17–3   The Value of Analysis Approach: Comparison of Function with Cost

I.   Rationale: VA is a systematic and creative approach to improve value without impairing quality.
II. Select a relatively high-cost or high-volume purchased item to value analyze. This item can be a component, material, or service that is believed to cost more than it should.
III. Thoroughly describe how the item is used and what is expected of it—its *function*. Define the function in a verb-noun, two-word combination, such as "holds liquid."
IV. Ask the following questions of the item:
1. Does its use contribute value?
2. Is its cost proportionate to its usefulness?
3. Can basic and secondary functions be separated?
4. Have functional requirements changed over time?
5. Does it need all its features?
6. Is there anything better for the intended use?
7. Are the original specs realistic under today's conditions?
8. Can the item be eliminated?
9. If the item is not standard, can a standard item be used?
10. If it is a standard item, does it completely fit the application or is it a misfit?
11. Does the item have greater capacity than required?
12. Is there a similar item in inventory that could be used?
13. Can the weight be reduced?
14. Have new materials or designs been developed that would alter performance of the product?
15. Are closer tolerances specified than are necessary?
16. Is unnecessary machining performed on the item?
17. Are unnecessary fine finishes specified?
18. Is commercial quality specified?
19. Can the item be made cheaper internally?
20. If being made internally, can the item be purchased for less?
21. Is the item properly classified for shipping purposes?
22. Can cost of packaging be reduced?
23. Are suppliers of the item being asked for suggestions to reduce cost?
24. Do material, reasonable labor, overhead, and profit total its cost?
25. Will another dependable supplier provide it for less?
26. Is anyone buying it for less?
V.   Following the Initial Analysis:
1. Where practical, get samples of the proposed item(s).
2. Select the best possibilities and propose changes.
VI. Follow-up: Were the expected benefits realized?
VII. Outcome: *A thorough study is almost certain to uncover many potential savings!*

Target Costing

Target costing is an approach that starts with the selling price of a final product or service minus the desired operating profit to arrive at a pool of money available for all costs. Responsibility for cost pools is allocated to functions throughout the organization. The supply group further allocates materials and services costs to establish cost targets and assign responsibility to buyers, commodity managers, and sourcing teams. These people develop plans and strategies to achieve the cost targets with suppliers. Effective target costing requires establishing detailed cost breakdowns and performing value analysis to determine how the function of the product or service can be achieved at the targeted cost. Cross-functional teams from supply, engineering, design, sales and marketing, quality, cost analysts, and supplier personnel are often used to work on target costing projects.

Firms that use target costing in the product design process include Honda, Toyota, and Whirlpool. For example, Whirlpool used target costing to address a 30 percent price gap for an aesthetics module on a product. The cross-functional team, which included supply, sales and marketing, engineering, design, production, and quality control, analyzed the module's costs, identified cost drivers, and agreed on an alternative design that met the target cost. The Whirlpool example is a good illustration of the application of value analysis in target costing.[2]

Commodities

The term *commodity* can be used in several ways. In the strictest sense, a commodity is a raw material that is traded on a commodities market, such as flour, steel, or copper. In many organizations, the term is used more broadly to describe a purchase category such as computers, travel, or printed circuit boards. Therefore, commodity studies may be performed on major raw materials as well as manufactured items, such as motors or semiconductors, and services, such as travel.

Typically, commodity research focuses on items that represent a significant percent of annual spend (e.g., A items), but it may be conducted on smaller spend commodities if they are in critically short supply or strategic. This research is designed to predict the short- and long-term future supply environment. It should provide the basis for making sound decisions and present supply and senior management with relatively complete information about future availability and price. This area probably is the most sophisticated in terms of difficulty and skills needed to do a good job.

A comprehensive commodity study should include analyses of these major areas: (1) current and future status of the company as a buyer, (2) production process alternatives, (3) uses of the item, (4) demand, (5) supply, (6) price, and (7) strategy to reduce cost and/or ensure supply. The information resulting from a commodity study should:

1. Provide a basis for making sound procurement decisions.
2. Present supply management and top management with information concerning future supply and price of purchased items.

Figure 17–4 provides a set of guidelines that might be used to make a commodity study.

Some companies do sophisticated commodity research, resulting in a well-documented strategic purchase plan. While a planning horizon of 5 to 10 years is the norm, some firms make a 15-year rolling forecast, updated each year. If a firm makes a 15-year strategic marketing plan, it makes sense to couple this with a strategic supply forecast and plan, for in the long term the acquisition of an adequate supply of critical materials may be the crucial determinant in the organization's success in meeting its market goals. Firms need to make realistic estimates of price trends so that they can plan their strategy of adjusting material

---

[2] P. Teague, "Target Costing Leads to Profits," *Purchasing* 138, no. 10 (2009), pp. 45–47.

FIGURE 17–4 **Commodity Study Guidelines**

The completed commodity study should provide data and/or answers for each of the following categories to the extent required by the particular commodity. Additional items may also be very pertinent.

I. *Current and future status.* Includes a description of the commodity, its current usage and forecast of future requirements, suppliers, price, terms, annual expenditures, mode of transport, and current contracts.

II. *Production or service delivery process.* Includes how the item is made or the service is delivered, the materials used, the supply/price status of these materials, the labor required, the current and future labor situation, alternative production processes, and the possibility of making the item, including costs, time factor, and production or service delivery problems.

III. *Uses of the item.* Includes primary use(s), secondary use(s), possible substitutes, and the economics of substitution.

IV. *Demand.* Includes the firm's current and future requirements, inventory status, sources of forecast information and lead times, and competing demand—current and projected—by industry, by endproduct use, and by individual firm.

V. *Supply.* Includes current producers—location, reliability, quality, labor situation, capacity, distribution channels, and strengths and weaknesses of each supplier; total (aggregate) supply situation, current and projected; and external factors—import issues, government regulations, technological change forecast, and political and ecological trends/problems.

VI. *Price.* Includes economic structure of producing industry, price history, and future forecast, factors determining price, cost to produce and deliver, tariff and import regulations, effects of quality and business cycle changes on price, estimated profit margins of each supplier, price objectives of suppliers, potential rock-bottom price, and price variance among user industries.

VII. *Strategy to reduce cost and/or assure supply.* Includes considering forecasted supply, usage, price, profitability, strengths and weaknesses of suppliers, the company's position in the market, and its plan to lower cost and to assure supply. It also includes consideration of the option to make the item in-house, use a short-term or long-term contract, acquire or develop a producer, find a substitute, import, hedge, perform value-engineering/analysis, and negotiate volume commitments with suppliers.

VIII. *Appendix.* Includes general information such as specifications, quality requirements and methods, freight rates and transportation costs, storage and handling, raw materials reserve; and statistics, for example, price, production, and purchase trends.

inputs to counter this trend. Also, the availability of many commodities is questionable due to dependence on offshore sources whose stability may be doubtful due to international politics and depletion of reserves.

Suppliers

While the first two research areas—purchased materials, products, or services and commodities—were directed primarily at the item being purchased, the third area is directed at the source of the item. The previous two areas were the *what;* this one concerns *from whom.* Obviously, the buyer or sourcing team is better able to select or create best-in-class supply sources and to prepare for and successfully conduct supplier negotiations with more knowledge about present and potential suppliers and their method of operation and market position. Likewise, providing supply managers with access to data in supplier performance measurement systems can provide useful information in future supply decisions.

With greater discipline, consistency, and focus across the organization, the supply group can better capture and communicate the contribution of suppliers and supply to the organization's strategy.

Chapter 12, "Supplier Selection," addresses the issue of supplier evaluation in detail. The main point of that chapter is that each purchase must be assessed according to its value to the organization's final customers and the risk associated with the acquisition. Comparisons between and among suppliers for any given good or service may focus on any number of factors, including supplier competitiveness in terms of price, contract terms and conditions, delivery/supply assurance, quality, replenishment programs, service, and technology. Clearly, effective supplier research for either selection or performance metrics requires alignment of research objectives with organizational strategy to ultimately deliver value to the final customer.

There are 11 specific topic areas in the category of supplier research. Many of these areas were explored in greater detail in Chapter 12.

Analysis of Financial Capacity

A key tool in risk assessment is the investigation of the financial health of current and potential suppliers. This assessment should predict the risk level the buying organization faces based on the probability of the supplier encountering financial problems, identify the potential effects on the buying firm, and enable the buyer to develop risk-minimization strategies. Often, the finance department conducts this analysis, but in some cases it is the responsibility of supply analysts or a cross-functional team. Either way, if the dollar value and risk are high, then the analysis must be thorough and complete. For example, purchasers of computer software and hardware have been surprised suddenly to find that their supplier "has gone bankrupt."

Analysis of Production Facilities

In the quest for lowest total cost, it is important to collect data on the supplier's physical facilities, emphasizing capacities and limitations. Review and analysis of production processes may lead to process improvements and cost savings.

Service Delivery Capabilities

The acquisition of services is an important spend category for most organizations, in areas such as information technology, maintenance, and transportation and logistics. Even suppliers that provide manufactured goods and capital equipment likely have a service component to their customer relationships, such as product delivery or maintenance and repair services. Understanding the service delivery capabilities of key suppliers is as important as reviewing the production capabilities of suppliers that provide manufactured goods, and can be used to identify opportunities to improve processes and reduce costs.

Finding New Supply Sources

It is often worthwhile to search for new suppliers. Research and long-range planning may lead to reverse marketing whereby the buying firm persuades a supplier to develop the ability to meet the buyer's needs now and in the future. Chapter 12, "Supplier Selection," and Chapter 13, "Supplier Evaluation and Relationships," address sourcing and reverse marketing.

Supplier Cost Analysis

Supplier cost analysis (along with value analysis) has become a common research focus, because it produces large and immediate savings. Estimates of supplier costs can be developed for both products and services and should include direct material, direct labor, engineering, tooling, plant/facilities overhead, general and administrative expense, logistics/distribution costs, and profit. Understanding a supplier's cost structure is a powerful tool in negotiations, effective management of supply chain costs, determination of a fair and reasonable price, establishment of target prices, and evaluation of the efficiency of processes. See Chapter 11, "Cost Management," for more details.

Relationship Classification

By forming a partnering arrangement or strategic alliance with a single source, both buyer and seller can focus on joint problem solving, process improvements, and increased profitability. Developing closer relationships with single sources can reduce risks by binding together the futures of the two organizations in a way that encourages cooperation, trust, and commitment to mutual success. Analyzing the supplier's management capabilities and anticipating all contingencies is essential before negotiating a complete contractual agreement. Chapter 13 provides additional information on supplier alliances and partnerships.

Quality Assurance of Purchased Materials

It is useful to develop a system with suppliers to reach agreement on quality standards, arrive at quality yields, determine training needs of supplier production and quality personnel, establish a system for mutual tracking of quality performance, and determine needed corrective action. Quality-related metrics might include parts per million (PPM), A-ranked parts rejections, and slippage in quality or delivery targets.

Supplier Perception Survey

A systematic survey of suppliers' perceptions about the buying firm and its supply process and practices can identify how the buyer–seller relationship could be improved. This information can be used to review and modify the supply organization and/or its policies.

Strategies Used by Suppliers

A better understanding of a key supplier's objectives and the means it is using to achieve these goals, including its sales strategy, allows the buyer to anticipate the supplier's actions. Alignment of strategies between the buyer and its key suppliers will help provide for continued supply at the lowest total costs.

Countertrade

Many countries have countertrade clauses in government contracts requiring local content, usually specified as a percentage or as a fixed-dollar-value amount. This essentially is a barter agreement and some supply analysts are responsible for gathering and analyzing the data that form the basis for such agreements. (See Chapter 14 for a detailed discussion.)

Supply Processes

Adequate knowledge about purchased items and their suppliers is important in attaining maximum value from the purchasing dollar. This knowledge does not, however, ensure that the supply transactions will be handled in the most efficient manner. Efficient supply processes reduce the supply operating expense. Research may be conducted to improve administration of the process, ensure speed and cost-effectiveness by eliminating unnecessary steps, and automate where possible through Internet and intranet applications. Specific topic areas include the requisition to pay flow path and may focus on any or all of the steps in the process. (See Chapter 4 for a detailed discussion about supply processes and technology applications.)

According to quality guru W. Edwards Deming, poor processes, not people, are typically the cause of problems. However, good people are instrumental in transforming a poor process into an excellent one. Therefore, the supply department's hiring, retraining, retaining, and succession planning are important aspects of supply processes.

Assessing Research Results

Supply research can contribute substantially to the ability of the supply function to cope successfully with future materials uncertainties, growing services spend, and the demands for greater supply effectiveness. Where appropriate, supply research should be shared with other functional areas if the maximum benefit to the organization is to be achieved.

SUPPLY PLANNING PROCESS

The actual supply planning process starts with information derived from the annual sales forecast, production/service delivery forecasts, and general economic forecast. The sales forecast will provide a total measure of the requirements of materials, products, and services to be acquired by purchasing; production/service delivery forecasts will provide information on the location at which the materials, products, and services will be required; and the economic forecast will provide information useful in estimating general trends for prices, wages, and other costs.

In most organizations, less than 20 percent of the number of line items purchased account for over 80 percent of the dollars spent (See ABC analysis in Chapter 8). Once high-value purchases have been identified, the broad forecast can be broken down into specific plans. The next step is to make price and supply availability forecasts for each of the major categories or commodities.

The estimates of material and service consumption are broken down into monthly and quarterly time periods. These quantities are checked against inventory control data that take into account lead times and safety stocks and are compared to price trends and availability forecasts to develop a buying plan.

Market conditions must be considered. If the forecasts predict ample supply availability and a possible weakening in prices, a probable buying policy will be to reduce inventories to the lowest level that is economically feasible. If, however, the forecasts predict a short supply and increasing price trend, the buying strategy needs to ensure availability through stock on hand, contractual agreements, or forward buying. If forecasts indicated a trend that will affect the availability and price of component parts and/or services, the conditions expected for the forecasted period in the industries in which the suppliers operate also must be considered.

After the monthly and quarterly quantities and estimated prices are tabulated, and modifications are made as a result of developing a buying plan, individual buyers perform an analysis of the items for which they are responsible. Further modifications in the plan may be made because of changes to the corporate or supply function objectives or target costs.

Any uncertainty, such as in lead times or requirements forecasts, makes planning difficult.

SUPPLY BUDGETS

The supply budgeting process should start with a review of supply goals and objectives, followed by a forecast of action and resource needs to meet the goals, and then the development of a budget. Four separate supply budgets are commonly developed:

Operations purchase budget. The operations budgeting process begins with an estimate of expected operations, based on sales forecasts and plans. Investments in materials and services can be substantial and shortages can lead to expensive stockouts and delays. The primary advantage of the operations budget-planning process is that it identifies cash flow commitments and isolates problems well in advance of their occurrence. Sensitivity analysis can provide management an opportunity to explore and/or develop alternatives. Typically, the operations purchase budget has a planning horizon of one year or less, except in the case of high-dollar, complex, long-production-cycle products or services, such as aircraft or power plants, where a multiyear budget is needed.

MRO budget. The MRO budget covers a purchase plan, typically for a 12-month period, for maintenance, repair, and operating supplies. It can include office supplies in service organizations. The large number of individual line items makes it infeasible to budget for each item; past ratios such as MRO cost adjusted by anticipated changes in inventory and general price levels are used.

Capital budget. The capital expenditure plan often has a multiyear horizon, based on the firm's strategic plan for product lines or services, market share, and new ventures. Decisions can be made on projected capital purchases based on production needs, obsolescence of present equipment, equipment replacement needs, upgrades to hardware and software, and expansion plans. Considerations in capital budgeting include length of supplier lead times, cost of money, anticipated price escalation, and the need for progress payments to suppliers.

Administrative or operating budget. The annual administrative budget, based on anticipated operating workloads, includes all of the expenses incurred in the operation of the supply function. This includes salaries and wages; space costs, including heat and electricity; equipment costs; information technology charges; travel and entertainment expenses; office supplies; educational expenditures for supply personnel; postage and telephone charges; and subscriptions to trade publications. Last fiscal year's budget is compared to actual expenditures to reconcile any substantial differences. Typically, this comparison is done monthly to control operating expenses and detect problem areas promptly. After reviewing the past history, the next fiscal period budget is prepared to make provisions for salary increases, personnel additions or deletions, and estimates of all other expenses as anticipated by the requirements of the supply plan. The final budget is then coordinated with the organization budget.

PERFORMANCE MEASUREMENT SYSTEMS

The supply function, as a major decision area in the allocation of most organizations' resource stream, should be a "major player" in developing overall strategy, executing this strategy, and capturing the results for future decisions. In this text we address three fundamental questions: (1) How can the supply function contribute effectively to organizational objectives and strategy? (2) How can the organizational objectives and strategy properly reflect the contribution and opportunities offered in the supply arena? (3) How can the contribution of supply be captured and communicated? The third question is the focus of this section.

The Value of Supply Metrics

For supply to exert the influence needed to produce results, it needs the respect and support of the CEO. While an increasing number of senior executives recognize that a properly organized supply function, staffed by competent employees, is capable of significant contributions, others remain unconvinced that, if given the opportunity, supply can deliver significant results. To receive recognition as a major contributor to organizational success, supply's contribution must be effectively captured and communicated. It is a major challenge to improve supply performance metrics and evaluation methods and to get validation of supply's results.

The benefits of a careful appraisal of supply performance are many: (1) It focuses attention on the priority areas, making it more likely that objectives will be realized; (2) it provides data for taking corrective action, if needed, to improve performance; (3) by isolating problem areas, it should help to develop better internal relationships; (4) it spotlights training needs of personnel; (5) the possible need for additional resources, for example, personnel or information technology, is documented; (6) it provides information to senior management about supply's contribution; and (7) those people performing at a better-than-normal level can be identified and rewarded, which should improve motivation in the organization.

The Challenges

The old adage, "If you don't measure it, you can't manage it," still applies today. Most managers recognize both the need for performance appraisal and the difficulty in developing meaningful supply metrics and methods of evaluation. Research in organization theory and human behavior has demonstrated that, to attain effective results, there must be a clear definition of the purpose and objectives or goals expected of the function and its employees. A major problem in many organizations has been the lack of clearly defined objectives for the supply department and its personnel. Unless it can be determined what is to be evaluated, the question of how to evaluate has little meaning. Therefore, the first challenge is establishing clear objectives.

The Randall Corporation case at the end of this chapter is an example of the challenges of setting up performance metrics for the supply organization. The CEO of Randall wants a set of 10 metrics: four executive level metrics for the CEO and six functional metrics for the CPO. The question is, What are the right metrics for the organization and for supply?

Setting Objectives

The chief purchasing officer has the responsibility for determining general objectives for the function and the coordination of such objectives with the strategic objectives of the company. An underlying assumption is that the designated metrics support the organizational mission. Identifying industry-accepted performance metrics and linking them to the organizational mission is a critical first step in developing an effective supply performance measurement system. In addition, there must be a quality process for managing improvement—a link to recognition and rewards systems for supply personnel, internal business partners, and suppliers.

Once established, the overall targets are provided to subordinates as general guidelines for decision makers to use to establish the objectives that will govern their activities for some period of time. When properly administered, the individual's objectives act as a motivating force to give direction to work and subsequently a basis for appraising performance. An individual's motivation and satisfaction from accomplishing objectives are driven in part by the degree of responsibility the individual exercises in establishing and implementing objectives.

Two areas of performance measurement are necessary in a world-class supply organization: supplier performance measurement and supply management performance measurement. These are closely related because supply's main focus is capturing the contribution of suppliers to the organization. The following sections address these areas.

Measuring Supplier Performance

Collection and analysis of performance data are the basis for determining how good a job the supplier is doing. This information also allows for more intelligent decisions about sources for rebuys and more useful feedback to current suppliers about areas of improvement. In partnering arrangements or alliances, the performance of the supplier is assessed regularly to reveal cycle time reductions, opportunities for process improvements, cost reduction, and quality and service improvements. Regular performance assessment is a catalyst for continuous improvement. The APC Europe case in Chapter 13 provides an illustration of a company that is using a supplier rating system to monitor and manage supplier performance.

There are many metrics that may be included in a supplier performance measurement system. Some organizations limit metrics to a few critical metrics, while others develop systems that track hundreds. There should be a clear link between data and decisions to avoid expending excessive resources capturing information that is never used by decision makers. Some of the more common metrics are discussed in the following section.

Key Supplier Performance Indicators

Direct measures quantify supplier performance at the time work is completed. Examples are on-time delivery, number of rejects, increase in sales after a marketing campaign, and cycle time to develop a specific product/service/technology in a development stage. Automation of real-time metrics such as on-time delivery measures and careful selection of more time-consuming data collection activities help to reduce the time spent measuring results.

The supplier scorecard may include a summary statement of the supplier's cost, quality, and timeliness performance and a compilation of satisfaction surveys, real-time metrics, variance of invoice amounts to estimates or contract negotiated rates, and other contract-related terms.

Price is one of the most common metrics in supply and supplier performance assessment. There are a number of different ways to measure price performance. These include old price versus new price, lowest acceptable initial bid versus final price, actual versus budget, and supplier quote versus final quote. Another useful means of evaluating the reasonableness of prices actually paid is to compare actual price to an index of market prices. This can provide a good reading on whether the trend of prices paid is better or worse than that being experienced by the overall market.

Supply Management Performance Metrics

Capturing supply management's contribution to the organization is a necessary and challenging task. Traditionally, firms have concentrated on analyzing their own internal trends by comparing their current supply performance with their own past performance to determine improvement. Increasingly, senior supply executives are focusing on developing metrics that capture both the hard-dollar contribution and the "soft" or indirect supply contributions discussed in Chapter 1. Interesting efforts are being made to capture supply's contribution along three dimensions: revenue enhancement, asset management, and cost management. Supply managers also are working with finance and internal business partners to validate supply's contribution.

Each organization has its own unique needs and measures must be tailored to fit the situation. However, there are 12 guidelines managers should follow to establish a measurement system:

1. Metrics need to be designed for use at a point in time.
2. Each organization has specific measurement needs at a given point in time.
3. Measures should address financial results, supplier performance, IT systems, and internal practices and policies.
4. Measures must change as required.
5. Trend analysis often is useful.
6. Measures should not be overdone or underutilized.
7. Measures are only tools.
8. Benchmarking is a source of new ideas and measures.
9. Senior management must see value in the measures used.
10. Measures can show the effectiveness of supply and identify areas needing improvement.
11. The credibility of measures must be ensured.
12. Continuous improvement in supply depends on measurement.

DEVELOPING METRICS

Supply management performance can be measured according to any number of metrics. Three key issues must be addressed: (1) setting targets, (2) establishing effective metrics, and (3) getting internal validation.

Setting Targets

In the planning process, initiatives and targets can be identified for the following fiscal year. For example, cost savings initiatives can be identified and prioritized jointly with internal business partners. In some organizations, these savings are built into budgets and become part of operating plans. During the year, supply personnel track savings, which are validated by finance and internal business partners. The finance manager ensures acceptance of the volumes used and timing of the savings and judges between cost savings and cost avoidance.

One of the key evaluation tools used in most organizations is the budgetary process. If the materials purchase, MRO, capital, and purchasing administrative budgets are carefully prepared, based on realistic assumptions about the future, they do provide a reasonable standard against which actual expenditures can be compared. If significant variances between budget (standard) and actual have occurred, in the absence of documented evidence that the assumptions on which the budget was based have changed, then a judgment can be made that performance was either superior or less than satisfactory, depending on whether the variance was positive or negative.

Standard costs also are used in many organizations to evaluate the supply department's pricing performance. Standard costs should be set based on anticipations of future overall market price movements; to do this with any degree of realism, supply must have a major input in setting such price/cost standards. If the standards are set solely by cost accounting, based almost completely on historical cost performance, then they lose much of their utility as a standard for judging performance. But if realistic standards are set, taking into account overall economic and market trends, then a practical and useful standard for measuring price effectiveness is provided.

Establishing Effective Metrics

Metrics can be grouped into two broad categories, efficiency and effectiveness. Supply executives must determine the key performance indicators for supply in alignment with the key performance indicators for the organization as a whole.

Efficiency Metrics

The traditional approach to measuring supply performance is focused on efficiency, which emphasizes price and departmental operating efficiency. Performance measures include price reductions for materials and services, operating costs, and order processing time. As discussed in Chapter 1, purchasing makes a direct contribution to the bottom line of the firm because of the profit-leverage effect of purchasing. Efficiency or operating metrics attempt to capture how efficient the supply process is. The required information varies by the type of industry but typically includes total dollar volume of purchases, total dollars spent for department operating expenses, and total number of purchase orders issued.

These figures may be used to calculate average figures and percentages to show:

1. Average dollar cost of the purchase orders written as

$$\frac{\text{Dollar cost of operating the department}}{\text{Number of POs issued}}$$

2. Operating costs as a percentage of total dollar volume of purchases.
3. Operating costs as a percentage of total dollar volume of sales.

Comparing the above figures and ratios with similar figures for previous time periods provides some perspective on the efficiency of the supply function. However, these reports are of little use in providing a basis for evaluation of how effectively the supply function is providing the materials, services, and equipment needed at the lowest total cost, considering quality, service, and the needs of the user. Note that the lowest price is not necessarily the lowest total cost.

Effectiveness Metrics

Effectiveness metrics attempt to measure how well something is done. These measures include evaluating direct and indirect contributions to final customer satisfaction, profit, revenue enhancement, or asset management. En-route or interim measures might include the quality of supplier relations or levels of internal business partner satisfaction. The benefits may come from reductions in operating costs or materials costs, enhancements in the performance of others (quality improvements in materials that lead to fewer defects and more satisfied end customers), shorter lead times, faster time-to-market, and/or increased sales due to increased value in the eyes of the end customer.

Operating Reports

Supply operating reports are prepared on a regular basis—monthly, quarterly, semiannually, or annually—and can be classified under the following headings and include

1. Market and economic conditions and price performance.
   a. Price trends and changes for the major materials, services, and commodities purchased. Comparisons with (1) standard costs where such accounting methods are used, (2) quoted market prices, and/or (3) target costs, as determined by cost analysis.[3]
   b. Changes in demand–supply conditions for the major items and services purchased, and the effects of labor strikes or threatened strikes.
   c. Lead time expectations for major items and services.
2. Inventory investment changes.
   a. Dollar investment in inventories, classified by major commodity and materials groups.
   b. Days' or months' supply, and on order, for major commodity and materials groups.
   c. Ratio of inventory dollar investment to sales dollar volume.
   d. Rates of inventory turnover for major items.

[3] One useful means of evaluating the reasonableness of prices actually paid is to compare actual price to an index of market prices. This can provide a good reading on whether the trend of purchasing's prices paid performance is better or worse than that being experienced by the overall market.

3. Purchasing/supply operations and effectiveness.
   a. Cost reductions resulting from supply research and value analysis studies.
   b. Quality rejection rates for major items.
   c. Percentage of on-time deliveries.
   d. Number of out-of-stock situations that caused interruption of scheduled production or service delivery.
   e. Number of change orders issued, classified by cause.
   f. Number of requisitions received and processed.
   g. Number of purchase orders issued.
   h. Employee workload and productivity.
   i. Transportation costs.
4. Operations affecting administration and financial activities.
   a. Comparison of actual departmental operating costs to budget.
   b. Cash discounts earned and cash discounts lost.
   c. Commitments to purchase, classified by types of formal contracts and by purchase orders, aged by expected delivery dates.
   d. Changes in cash discounts allowed by suppliers.

Measures of supplier relations require looking at the relationship from both sides. Measures of supplier performance include the traditional aspects of quality, delivery, cost, and flexibility, but also more qualitative dimensions such as communication and cooperation. The quality of the service provided to the supplier by the buying organization also is measured.

Using end-customer satisfaction as a measure of the effectiveness of supply makes a lot of sense because the actions of supply affect customer satisfaction. In reality, the true impact of supply may be difficult to determine.

Many of the more valuable contributions made by supply and suppliers are difficult to measure. These include attempting to capture supply's contribution to increasing speed to market, asset/resource utilization, increase in cost avoidance, process improvements, improved level of service, revenue generation, and new product/service value engineering.

If supply is to make a strategic contribution to the competitiveness of the organization, it must focus on quality, cost, customer service, and cycle time. To this end, supply must emphasize the creation of a competitive supply base and capture suppliers' contributions to competitive advantage.

Cost Metrics

Cost management is widely recognized as a key performance area for supply. Most people recognize that price paid is only one component of the total cost of ownership. Efforts to develop metrics that effectively capture the total cost impact of a decision or action often fall short. There are four cost categories that might be measured: (1) cost savings, (2) cost reductions, (3) cost avoidance, and (4) process cost savings. Reportable savings might come from discounts, payment terms, renegotiations of prices, deferrals of payments, extended payment terms, standardization, supplier participation, process improvements, alternate material suggestions, change of shipment routings, design/specification changes, and improvements in logistics.

Validating Results

Internal validation of results has become a goal of many senior supply executives. Often, supply is responsible for developing and implementing savings initiatives and capturing the year-over-year savings. However, measurement difficulties lead to understatement and overstatement of supply savings leading to poor decision making and rewarding employees for the wrong behavior. Measurement challenges include (1) systems that don't account for savings, (2) changes in markets, technologies, and volumes, (3) unwillingness to recognize cumulative savings, (4) incomplete definition of supply savings, (5) inability to convert savings into profit, and (6) reluctance to revisit past decisions. Recommendations to overcome measurement and reporting difficulties are to focus on the total cost of ownership, categorize the different types of savings, and hardwire savings to the budget.[4]

Appraising Team Performance

Effective team performance, like effective individual performance, is more likely to occur if specific goals and objectives are established for the team as a whole and if evaluation and reward systems, such as salary increases, promotions, and bonuses, foster participation and performance. Managers in many organizations struggle to develop appraisal and reward systems that foster team participation and output without ignoring individual performance.

Evaluating team performance can be tricky. Three options are possible:

1. Each team member's manager evaluates the individual. However, the manager may be relatively uninvolved in the team and evaluating from a distance. Also, different managers may evaluate similar performance differently. The lack of consistency may result in lessened commitment and lowered morale of the team members.
2. Team members evaluate each other. This ensures that those closest to the team activities perform the evaluations. However, the team members may not be truly objective in evaluating the overall team performance.
3. A joint evaluation or 360-degree process is used. Team members evaluate each other (including the team leader); the team leader evaluates each member; and an external manager evaluates overall team performance.

Supply Performance Benchmarking

Benchmarking is a process of evaluating a company's work methods, processes, service levels, or products and services against meaningful standards to answer the question, How are we doing compared to other firms? Averages and ranges for specific metrics provide data for analysis to allow a company to make better decisions about those changes needed to develop industry best practices and, in turn, superior performance. Industry standards for *overall* firm performance (such as profit, sales, and return on assets) long have been available through published financial reports. But performance numbers for the purchasing/supply function have not been available because of competitive concerns. However, in today's globally competitive business environment, it is essential to monitor an organization's performance relative to its competitors.

Performance benchmarking measures *what* results organizations have achieved in their purchasing/supply activities, and process benchmarking attempts to determine *how* an

[4] P. F. Johnson and M. R. Leenders, "Minding the Supply Savings Gaps," *MIT Sloan Management Review* 51, no. 2 (2011), pp. 25–31.

organization achieves results. To conduct a process benchmarking study, practices used by top-performing organizations are identified and a team visits the top performer in an attempt to identify its best practices. Because no two organizations are identical, direct comparisons are difficult to make. A performance benchmarking study is required to identify the superior performers.

CAPS Research has benchmarking reports available for a wide variety of industries, including aerospace, defense, automotive, chemicals, industrial manufacturing, and financial services. Several of these industries have been benchmarked a number of times to identify performance trends.

The CAPS Research benchmarking data give supply professionals the reference point to evaluate their own organization's performance. As an independent and impartial not-for-profit research organization, CAPS can collect these data from competing firms. CAPS researchers aggregate the data and report the average and range for performance data from the largest 10 to 20 firms in an industry. Individual firms and their specific numbers are never identified.

CAPS has established 20 standard benchmarks to enable cross-industry comparisons:[5]

1. Total spend as a percent of sales/revenue dollars.
2. Percent of total spend controlled/managed by supply management.
3. Supply management employees as a percent of company employees.
4. Percent of supply management employees that are strategic.
5. Percent of companies that reported an increase/decrease in supply management strategic employees.
6. Percent of supply management employees that are operational.
7. Percent of companies that reported an increase/decrease in supply management operational employees.
8. Supply management operating expense as a percent of total spend.
9. Supply management operating expense per supply management employee.
10. Total spend per supply management employee (millions).
11. Managed spend per supply management employee (millions).
12. Percent of total spend via pCards.
13. Annual spend on training per supply management employee.
14. Cost-reduction savings as a percent of managed spend.
15. Cost-avoidance savings as a percent of managed spend.
16. Average purchase order processing cost.
17. Average cycle time (in days) from requisition approval to PO placement for direct goods.
18. Average cycle time (in days) from requisition approval to PO placement for indirect goods and services.
19. Percent of active suppliers that account for 80 percent of total spend.
20. Percent of spend with qualified socioeconomic program suppliers.

The Tanton Foods case provides an illustration of how an organization might use the CAPS benchmarking reports.

[5] www.capsresearch.org, April 2014.

SUPPLY MANAGEMENT TRENDS

The following section reviews the trends facing supply managers for the coming years. As indicated in Chapters 1 and 2, every organization—public-sector and private-sector, large and small, services and manufacturing, international or domestic—is continually scanning the competitive environment and adapting to changes, developments, and opportunities. The prudent supply manager, therefore, is always on the outlook for trends.

While the evidence is not conclusive that all these trends will continue, they are underway now. Some have been with us for a considerable period of time, while others are relatively recent. Each trend, however, represents a challenge and an opportunity for supply.

Emphasis on Total Quality Management and Customer Satisfaction

The emphasis on quality and customer satisfaction is part of a larger trend over the past few decades to improve value. Supply is required to think strategically about its responsibility for, and involvement in, quality management and satisfying the organization's customers by providing better value. It has to "buy into" responsibility for the quality of output of goods and/or services.

This will require a focus on understanding total costs of supply decisions and cost management capabilities. Cost management begins with early supply involvement in product and service design and represents ongoing efforts to analyze cost drivers and target opportunities to reduce total supply chain costs. Such efforts require cross-functional support, supplier involvement, and trained cost management specialists to lead the initiative.

Sustainability

Whether the motivation is a result of government regulations, customer pressures, opportunities to reduce costs, or an incentive to enhance brand image, organizations have embraced sustainability. Increasingly, organizations are paying close attention to the combination of their social, environmental, and financial performance—what has been referred to as the "triple bottom line."[6] This relationship is also sometimes referred to as the "three Ps" of sustainability: planet, people, and profit. Thus, the term *sustainability* is used to include all three pillars of the triple bottom line. This section will focus on two pillars: *environmental sustainability* and *social sustainability*.

Environmental Sustainability

While there are many definitions of environmental sustainability in the literature, we will use the following: "Environmental sustainability is using the earth's resources in such a way to meet the resource needs of the present without compromising the ability of future generations to meet their own resource needs."[7] Examples of environmental sustainability projects include substituting renewable energy for carbon-based energy, reducing greenhouse gases, and eliminating waste anywhere in the supply chain. Environmental

---

[6] J. Elkington, *Cannibals with Forks: The Triple Bottom Line of the 21st Century* (Stoney Creek, CT: New Society Publishers, 1998).

[7] J. L. Hartley, et al., *Environmental Sustainability Across the Extended Value Chain* (Tempe, AZ: CAPS Research Focus Study, 2014).

sustainability not only supports compliance with regulations, improved public image, and brand reputation; but it can also be a source of cost savings, such as reduced energy usage.

Most organizations have been improving their internal environmental performance for years, and the greatest opportunities going forward will be projects that involve external stakeholders, including suppliers. Supply chain-related environmental sustainability projects will permit organizations to tackle difficult internal projects, pursue high-opportunity external projects, and keep up with increasingly stringent regulations. The supply function will play a central role in environmental sustainability in four areas: (1) gathering data and managing suppliers to support compliance with regulations, (2) communicating environmental sustainability expectations to suppliers, (3) measuring suppliers' environmental sustainability performance, (4) identifying and implementing specific supply chain-related projects.[8]

Xerox is an example of a firm that has successfully integrated environmental sustainability within their supply chain. The Xerox product take-back system supports remanufacturing and recycling. The company has a comprehensive process for collecting end-of-life products that permits it to remanufacture and reuse 70–90 percent of machine components by weight without degradation of quality or performance. The Xerox take-back system prevents more than 42,000 metric tons of waste from entering landfills each year.[9]

Social Sustainability

Technology and the 24-hour news cycle provide key stakeholders, customers, and the general public with visibility to what is happening in global supply chains. As a result, firms are being held accountable for the social practices of their suppliers. Concerns include provisions for worker safety, payment of living wages, and child labor. Companies, such as Walmart, have set clear standards for their suppliers that set fundamental expectations related to social conditions in their plants and subcontracting facilities. To ensure compliance, Walmart provides suppliers a detailed supplier manual and conducts regular audits of supplier operations.[10] With the risks of damage to the reputation of companies and their brands, responsible social sourcing will continue to increase in the future.

Global Sourcing

Globalization is not a new trend, but it has been accelerating at a time when the complexities of managing global supply chains are expanding. Until recently, sourcing in so-called "low-cost regions," such as China, was seen as an obvious and necessary step to reduce costs and to maintain competitiveness. However, a growing number of companies are re-examining their global sourcing strategies, in favor of less emphasis on low-cost regions. Caterpillar, General Electric, Apple, Walmart, and Whirlpool are examples of companies that have announced plans to manufacture or source products in the United States that were once produced in Asia.

[8] Ibid.

[9] Xerox *2013 Environment, Health, Safety and Sustainability Report*, www.xerox.com

[10] www.corporate.walmart.com/global-responsibility

The popular term used to describe this change is *reshoring*, but we believe that this description is an oversimplification and inaccurate. An explanation follows.

There are several factors motivating companies to change their global sourcing practices, but the principal issue is total cost of ownership. In the past decade, transportation costs have increased, making it more costly to ship goods from Asia to North America and to Europe. Meanwhile, wages of Chinese workers continue to grow rapidly, at a time when inflation and wage cost increases in North America and Europe have been relatively modest. Other factors are also coming into play. Lower energy costs in the United States and Canada, due to shale gas exploration, have cut the costs of domestic manufacturing. The costs of sourcing in China have also increased due to the appreciation of their currency versus western currencies.

Firms are beginning to understand the cost implications of holding the large amounts of inventory required to support their global supply chains. Lead times of two to three months require huge investments in working capital, not to mention the increased risk of supply disruptions. The long lead times also have the disadvantage of reduced flexibility in responding to changes in customer demand and buying preferences. Organizations, such as Zara and New Balance, are proving that firms can profitably produce close to major markets, and they have demonstrated the competitive benefits of being able to react quickly to customer demand.

Products that will make the most sense to consider for sourcing and manufacturing in North America and Western Europe are high value and expensive to manufacture; are difficult and expensive to transport because they are large and/or heavy; have low labor content; require the use of complex equipment and skilled workers for manufacturing and assembly; and are engineering intensive. A further consideration will be the engineering-manufacturing interface. For some products, ramping up production will be made easier and faster when R&D, new product development, and manufacturing are located in close proximity to facilitate collaboration and innovation.

Changes in global sourcing strategies, however, are not expected to drive a massive resurgence of manufacturing in North America and other developed regions. The range of products that qualify for repatriation from Asia is relatively narrow, based on the criteria described above. Organizations are becoming more sophisticated about where they source products and services, and the days of abundant, high-paying, low-skilled manufacturing jobs in developed countries are not going to return. Rather than a massive shift by North American and European companies in favor of domestic sourcing and manufacturing, these organizations are more likely to focus on supply alternatives from regions close to their major markets that provide a competitive cost structure. Consequently, the real winners may be regions such as Mexico and Eastern Europe, where costs are relatively low, the workforce is skilled, infrastructure is well developed, and the distance to large markets is short.

The development of China as a manufacturing and economic powerhouse reshaped global supply chain management. In many ways China is unique. It had a huge population available to support development of its industrial capacity, a solid infrastructure, and stable political environment. China still has a cost advantage in many areas and its capabilities are difficult to match. There are no other developing low-cost regions on the horizon that will be able to replace China. Countries such as Vietnam may have cheap labor, but they do not have the infrastructure or capacity to compete with China's value proposition. Consequently, firms will continue to find China an attractive option for sourcing and manufacturing. There is also an additional demand on the Chinese economy that needs to be taken into consideration. In the future, an increasing portion of the country's manufacturing output will go to supporting consumption demands of its growing middle class.

Supply managers of the future will need to balance a wider range of competitive and economic factors when making global sourcing decisions. The narrow set of cost factors used in the past will need to be augmented with consideration for a broader range of business issues. Input from other functions, such as sales and marketing to gauge implications of global sourcing decisions on customer satisfaction and market share, will be essential.

Risk Management

Supply risks at many organizations are greater than ever before, and supply chain risk management is a growing concern not only for the chief purchasing officer (CPO) but for every senior executive. Commodity and currency price fluctuations, extended global supply chains, lean operations with low inventories, increased outsourcing, and capacity constraints in the global transportation infrastructure are but some of the sources of risk. Prudent supply managers need to be fully informed and understand how even routine supply decisions jeopardize organizational financial performance and its reputation (see Chapter 2). The Russel Wisselink case in Chapter 9 provides a good illustration of the risks of supply interruptions in a global supply chain context. (Chapter 2 provides detailed coverage of risk management.)

Some supply chain risks, such as natural disasters and commodity price fluctuations, may be impossible to predict. Other risks, such as quality problems, supplier financial issues, and IT interruptions, can be addressed, at least in part, through sound supply management practices. CPOs will continue to search for methods to improve their risk mitigation capabilities in areas such as sourcing, supplier performance measurement, and supplier relationship management. In some cases trade-offs will have to made. For example, dual/multiple sourcing, versus single sourcing, may make it more difficult to achieve price, quality, and delivery requirements on a consistent basis, but provide long-term benefits of assured supply.

Safety and Security

With the increase in global trade, government regulators have become increasingly concerned with supply chain security and safety. For example, the U.S. federal government launched the *National Strategy for Global Supply Chain Security* in 2012. It is an ongoing effort to promote the efficient and secure movement of legitimate goods and to foster a global supply chain system that is resilient to natural and man-made disruptions.[11] Private-sector organizations are also concerned with maintaining public confidence in the products, whether for food or children's toys. Terrorism threats have placed new demands on supply chains for security.

Supply chain security and safety will place increasing demands on supply executives in areas such as supplier selection and supplier management processes, including compliance

---

[11] www.whitehouse.gov/sites/default/files/national_strategy_for_global_supply_chain_security.pdf

audits and material tracking systems. Technology will play a significant role, but it will need to be balanced with sound strategies and management practices.

Supply Processes and Technology

Many organizations have invested heavily in information technology during the past decade. These investments have, up until now, focused mainly on automating supply processes and providing the capabilities to arm decision makers with relevant data. The convergence of technologies will persist in the future, as firms integrate existing information systems (e.g., ERP) with mobile, cloud, and social media technologies (see Chapter 4). This evolution provides the potential to make it easier for employees to access data and create opportunities for collaboration among supply chain stakeholders. Using mobile technology, employees will be able to access information, review purchase orders, and approve contracts while on the go. It will be easier to share information with suppliers and customers in real time, creating opportunities to enhance collaboration with key supply chain partners.

Supply Organizations

A number of trends in supply organizations and leadership will continue. First, there will be more chief purchasing officers without previous supply experience. As organizations continue to move through cycles of rightsizing, downsizing, reorganizing, merging, and divesting, many talented managers are available to move out of their current, now-redundant positions into other managerial functions. Some come to supply because managerial skills and internal credibility are more important than previous supply experience.

Second, teaming will continue to expand and project-based work will become more common. The complexity of many supply and sourcing decisions requires that the analysis and decision making be done by a cross-functional group of key professionals/managers, including a team member from, for example, supply, design engineering, marketing, and operations. Working on cross-functional teams will require a different skill set from traditional purchasing roles, including strong "soft skills" and an understanding of managing cross-cultural relationships when working on global projects. (Chapter 3 reviews supply teams.)

Third, organizations will continue to separate strategic and tactical roles in supply. As processes, practices, and strategies change, the roles in supply become differentiated between strategic and operational (tactical).

Lastly, identifying, attracting, and retaining talent at all levels of the supply organization will continue to be a challenge. This chapter describes the vast range of challenges that supply managers will face in the future. People with the necessary skills and capabilities will be needed to help steer the supply function through what promises to be an interesting period. What should not be ignored are the staffing needs at the operational level of the supply chain. For example, the looming truck driver shortage in North America may create capacity issues in the trucking industry and force organizations to turn to increased use of intermodal transport solutions.

External and Internal Collaboration

Organizations typically have many customers and suppliers and engage daily in cross-enterprise relationships as a normal course of business. For the most part, these exchanges are at an operational level, in the normal course of business. Supply chain collaboration is a *process*, anchored in a strategic relationship between two parties (e.g., supplier and customer), with the objective of achieving significant value that could not be attained independently. Whereas supplier partnerships and alliances, covered in Chapter 13, are relationship-based, collaboration is process-based. Regardless of the nature of the collaborative relationship–internal or external, customer or supplier focused–top management support of collaboration is essential.

Collaboration is labor intensive and requires special mechanisms for communication and sharing of information. As discussed previously in this chapter and in Chapter 4, advances in technology, such as cloud-based computing, have created opportunities to improve the speed and effectiveness of cross-enterprise communication in support of collaborative efforts.

Supply has a unique place in the organization to support and engage in collaboration. Organizations are increasingly relying on supplier collaboration in areas such as cost reduction/avoidance, product/service development, improvements to quality, and development of new technologies. Supplier collaboration requires a governance structure that addresses process issues such as communication flows, personnel assignments, financial obligations, resource requirements, sharing of benefits and intellectual property, and termination.

Long-term buyer–supplier relationships will be a by-product of collaboration, necessitating supplier management approaches that emphasize effective working relationships. However, rather than aligning with a single supply chain, as some academics have suggested, firms must be prepared to operate as part of multiple *supply networks*. Different customer segments will provide distinct opportunities and demands on supply. Companies that may be potential customers in one network could be competitors or suppliers in another. Managing and balancing a diverse set of supplier and customer relationships will be an ongoing challenge.

Supply chain design is a potential source of competitive advantage. Companies need to consider the strategic implications of decisions associated with make or buy and the capabilities of their key suppliers and their suppliers' suppliers. Suppliers network among each other to gain the synergy of their collective design and application expertise, which provides better products and services and results in further reduction in cycle time and cost.

While much of the focus in the supply management literature has been on external collaboration with suppliers and customers, opportunities for internal collaboration often get ignored. Interestingly, collaboration in the internal supply chain can be more difficult. Turf battles between supply and operations, marketing and engineering are common. Decisions for new product design are made without consideration for cost and availability of components. Marketing campaigns are launched without notifying supply of pending changes in customer demand. Production schedules are altered, resulting in expediting of raw materials. Supply, however, can also be the source of grief for its counterparts in other departments. Effective cross-functional relationships can contribute to early supply involvement in key projects.

Metrics and Performance Measurement

As previously discussed in this chapter, greater concern over how to measure the actual contribution of supply to organizational goals and strategies requires the development of new and appropriate measures. Information technology will continue to provide easier access to data to measure supply and supplier performance. The challenge will be to focus on a manageable number of key measures and to resist the temptation to measure everything.

Innovation

Innovation in product and service offerings can be as critical to the success of any organization as innovations in supply processes. Walmart and Toyota rose to the top of their respective industries on the basis of supply chain process innovations. Conceptualizing and implementation represent two parts of the innovation challenge. Conceptualizing innovations requires creativity and thinking in new ways. Implementation requires supplier trust and cooperation and change management skills.

Public Procurement

Governments are playing an increasingly important role in our economies, a trend that most certainly will continue. Often understated is the importance of public procurement in the economy at the municipal, state, provincial, and federal levels of government. Two challenges facing public supply management are competition for talent and achieving value for money spent while maintaining compliance with policies and procedures.

Competing for talent in the marketplace has been a traditional problem for public procurement organizations, which frequently have not paid salary levels that match private-sector firms. However, the potential contribution of supply is no different in public procurement from large private-sector firms. As supply has increased in stature in private-sector firms, opportunities will persist in the future for the same trend in the public sector.

Public procurement policies and procedures can influence the ability for supply to achieving maximum value for money. As budgets in the public sector continue to tighten, public-sector supply organizations will adopt practices from the private sector. The challenge will be to continue to meet objectives of fairness and transparency with stakeholders.

Conclusion

Research and metrics are two components of a successful supply management process. Without adequate research about purchased items and services, commodities, suppliers, and the supply process, it is impossible to make optimal decisions that contribute to organizational success. And, without effective measurement systems, it is impossible to validate the success of research and decision making by supply professionals. Therefore, research and measurement initiatives are well worth the investment of resources.

This is an exciting time to work in supply with several continuing and emerging trends. Some, such as global sourcing, collaboration, and supply technology, have been evolving for several years. Others, such as sustainability and supply chain safety and security, have emerged more recently. Prudent supply executives need to constantly scan for new developments and emerging trends—most certainly new trends will develop in the coming years.

Questions for Review and Discussion

1. How does value analysis differ from value engineering?

2. What are the various subject areas of supply research? Which area do you think would be most productive in (*a*) the short run and (*b*) the long run?

3. In what ways might a firm organize to do supply research? What are the advantages and disadvantages of each? Which would you recommend in a (*a*) small organization, (*b*) a medium-sized organization, and (*c*) a large organization?

4. What questions would be asked in a commodity study? Where would you obtain the information?

5. What is the difference between a supply plan and a supply budget? In which areas should a supply budget be prepared? How would these budgets be established?

6. Why isn't there a standard system for evaluating supply performance that could be used by all types of organizations? How difficult would it be to develop such a standard system?

7. What are the key metrics of supply performance?

8. Are standard costs and budgets useful in the appraisal process? Under what conditions?

9. Why would an organization want to "benchmark" its supply function? How would it do this?

10. What is the difference between performance benchmarking and process benchmarking?

11. What is the triple bottom line? How can supply influence sustainability performance in the organization?

References

Awaysheh, A., and R. D. Klassen. "Supply Chain Structure and Its Impact on Supplier Socially Responsible Practices." *International Journal of Production and Operations Management* 30, no. 12 (2010), pp. 1246–1268.

Carter, P. L.; R. J. Trent; R. M. Monczka, K. J. Petersen; W. J. Markham; E. L. Nichols, and J. L. Hartley. *Collaboration Across the Extended Value Chain*. Tempe, AZ: CAPS Research, 2013.

Fawcett, S. E.; A. M. Fawcett; B. J. Watson; and G. M. Magnan. "Peeking Inside the Black Box: Toward an Understanding of Supply Chain Collaboration Dynamics." *Journal of Supply Chain Management* 48, no. 1, pp. 44–72.

Hora, M., and R. D. Klassen. "Learning From Others' Misfortune: Factors Influencing Knowledge Acquisition to Reduce Operational Risk." *Journal of Operations Management* 31 (2013), pp. 52–61.

Miles, Lawrence D. *Techniques of Value Analysis and Engineering*. 2nd ed. New York: McGraw-Hill, 1972.

Pagell, M.; D. Johnston; A. Veltri; R. D. Klassen; and M. Biehl. "Is Safe Production an Oxymoron? Exploring How Firms Simultaneously Manage Safety and Operational Competitiveness." *Production and Operations Management*, 2014. http://onlinelibrary.wiley.com/doi/10.1111/poms.12100/pdf.

Presutti, W. D, and J. R. Mawhinney. "The Supply Chain–Finance Link." *Supply Chain Management Review* 11, no. 6 (2009), pp. 32–38.

Tate, W. L. "Offshoring and Reshoring: U.S. Insights and Research Challenges." *Journal of Purchasing and Supply Management* 20, no. 1 (2014), pp. 66–68.

Zacharia, Z. G.; N. R. Sanders; and Brian S. Fugate. "Evolving Functional Perspectives Within Supply Chain Management." *Journal of Supply Chain Management* 50, no. 1 (2014), pp. 73–88.

Case 17–1

Randall Corporation

Paul Syrie, senior partner at Newcombe Consulting, was preparing his presentation for the CEO of a large client, Randall Corporation, the following day. Newcombe had been retained by Randall's CEO six months prior to assess the performance of his company's supply organization and to make recommendations that would reduce costs and improve the overall competitive position of the company. It was now Monday, March 23, and the purpose of the meeting on Tuesday morning was to establish appropriate metrics to monitor the performance of Randall's supply function.

THE RANDALL CONSULTING PROJECT

Randall was a Fortune 500 company with annual sales of $33 billion. Its business units competed in the defense, technology, aerospace, and building systems sectors. Randall had a record of consistent profitability over the past decade, but its new CEO, Wesley Riley, had promised to focus on cost control and earnings growth.

Each business unit had a separate supply organization, which was supported by a 50-person corporate supply group. Divisional supply organizations focused on their division's specific needs, so that priorities and resources could be established on a business unit level. Meanwhile, common requirements and corporatewide initiatives were addressed through the corporate purchasing group located at company headquarters in Chicago. Total purchases represented approximately 50 percent of sales. Graham Chambers, the chief procurement officer (CPO), reported to Ronald Muise, executive vice president and chief administrative officer.

Newcombe was retained by Randall's CEO, who believed that the company could be exploiting opportunities in supply. Working with a large team of consultants from Newcombe, Paul and his group found that Randall had too many suppliers and too many people in the supply function, and its costs were too high. The Newcombe team worked with the CPO and created a series of projects to address the problems identified, including changes in business processes and implementation of a new e-procurement system, consolidation and standardization of high-dollar spend categories, and renegotiation of contracts with key suppliers.

SUPPLY METRICS

As a final step in the project, Paul was charged by Wesley Riley with creating a new set of metrics for the supply organization, saying,

> I want four or five key measures reported to me every month so I can tell how well purchasing is doing. You also need to give Chambers a set of metrics so he can keep his eye on the ball. I don't want us slipping back into the same state we were in a year ago. I want to give an incentive for Chambers and his group to hit their targets, so I plan on making these bonusable objectives for Graham and all of his direct reports.

After careful consideration, Paul decided that he would recommend a set of 10 metrics: four executive level metrics for the CEO and six functional metrics for the CPO (see Exhibit 1). Each metric would be reported monthly.

EXHIBIT 1   Proposed Supply Metrics

Executive Level Metrics	Functional Level Metrics
• Number of suppliers representing 80% of spend. • Percentage of total dollar spend on enterprise contracts. • Percentage of total spend through e-business system. • Cost-reduction target.	• Total number of suppliers. • E-business cost per transaction. • Number of transactions per employee in the supply organization. • Percentage of dollar spend through e-auctions. • Percentage of first-time quality acceptance of parts shipped from suppliers. • Health of the supply base.

As Paul examined the metrics, he paused to consider the usefulness of what he had developed. Would Wesley Riley and Graham Chambers find the metrics useful? Were they the "right" measures for Randall? What targets should be set for each? Were there other metrics that should be added to the list? These were all questions that Paul knew he would be asked at the meeting the following day.

Case 17–2
Stewart Corporation

Sara McCormick, vice president and chief purchasing officer at Stewart Corporation, headquartered in New York City, was preparing for the first meeting of the Supplier Sustainability Advisor Council (SSAC). It was February 4th, and Sara was about to begin the process of developing a supplier environmental sustainability scorecard. There were a number of decisions that had to be made in advance of the meeting scheduled for March 11th. Sara felt that the meeting with the council was an important step to get input and buy-in from representatives of the supplier community, and she wanted to create an agenda for the meeting that properly framed the key messages.

STEWART CORPORATION

Founded in 1853 by George W. Stewart, Stewart Corporation (Stewart) was an American multinational consumer goods company that manufactured and distributed personal care products, foods and beverages, and cleaning agents. Profits in the most recent fiscal year were $7.3 billion on revenues of $56 billion. The company sold more than 200 brands in 120 countries and employed 80,000 people.

While Stewart had several large, well-established brands, the company had a culture of innovation. Product innovations came in the form of new product development and enhancements and improvements to established products. It had a target of suppliers providing at least 50 percent of new product innovations each year.

With total purchases of approximately $25 billion, the company had more than 16,000 suppliers for direct and indirect purchases operating in more than 60 countries. The number of strategic suppliers numbered approximately 500.

Each year the purchasing organization conducted Business Performance Assessments (BPAs) with each of its strategic suppliers. The BPA process used a scorecard to evaluate suppliers in areas that included cost, delivery, quality, innovation, and collaboration. Each category used a rating system from 1 to 7, with a rating of 7 representing "exceeds expectations." The BPAs also represented an opportunity for suppliers to provide feedback to Stewart on opportunities to deliver better business results and collaboration. BPA scores were used by the strategic sourcing organization when making supplier selection decisions.

SUSTAINABILITY AT STEWART

Since Stewart was one of the world's largest consumer goods companies, management felt that it had an obligation to be a leader in sustainability. Stewart's sustainability strategy emphasized two principal areas: environmental sustainability and social responsibility. Environmental sustainability focused on using less energy, water, and materials when manufacturing products; requiring fewer resources when they were used by customers; increasing the use of sustainably sourced, renewable materials and renewable energy in products and operations; and identifying ways to eliminate waste at the end of life, so that all manufacturing and consumer waste had value through recycling, reuse, or conversion to energy. Social responsibility focused on providing everyday essentials that helped families who could not afford them or who had been displaced; paying competitive wages; treating employees and employees of suppliers with respect; and supporting hygiene education and everyday healthy behavior to prevent illness.

PREPARING FOR THE SSAC MEETING

The SSAC was a group of 25 strategic suppliers that represented a wide range of industries and regions. While there were several large global suppliers on the council, there was also representation from medium- and small-sized suppliers.

EXHIBIT 1   Supplier Environmental Sustainability Measures

Primary Measures	Secondary Measures
• Greenhouse gas emissions (direct) • Energy usage • Water usage (input and output) • Hazardous waste disposal • Environmental fines and sanctions • Sustainability initiatives related to Stewart products and services	• Volume of waste material recycled, reused, recovered • Renewable energy usage • Indirect greenhouse gas emissions • Transportation fuel efficiency • Environmental certifications and awards

Sara's objective was to build an environmental sustainability scorecard that could be used to track key environmental indicators. She hoped it would meet the needs of Stewart and its suppliers. Getting environmental sustainability information from suppliers that related directly to the creation of Stewart materials and services was the ultimate objective; however, Sara realized that some suppliers may not have the capability to report at that level of detail initially. As an intermediate step, she felt Stewart might have to accept data related to the suppliers' overall sustainability results.

During the meeting on March 11th, Sara hoped to address four main issues. First, was the Stewart supplier environmental sustainability initiative something that the supplier community was prepared to support? Stewart had been measuring the environmental sustainability performance of its operations for several years, and extending it to the broader supply chain seemed to be a logical next step. However, supplier support and buy-in would be essential. Sara needed to be able to articulate at the meeting why suppliers should support the initiative.

Second, working with the Stewart sustainability group, Sara had prepared a draft list of measures to be used in the supplier environmental sustainability scorecard (see Exhibit 1). Was this draft list of supplier sustainability measures appropriate? Stewart purchased a wide range of materials and services globally. Could Sara expect to apply a standard set of environmental measures to suppliers in different industries and regions? Were these the right measures and should the list be modified?

Third, how much time would suppliers need to develop systems and capabilities to report their environmental sustainability performance for Stewart products and services? Sara knew that some suppliers already had systems in place and could provide relevant data easily. However, many suppliers, particularly small- and medium-sized enterprises, were less sophisticated in the area of environmental sustainability and may see the scorecard as an administrative burden.

Lastly, how should the environmental sustainability scorecard be incorporated into the BPA process? Suppliers were understandably anxious about any changes to the BPA process and how it might affect their business relationship with Stewart, including opportunities to win new business. Sara felt that environmental sustainability should eventually be included in the BPAs, but the question was when and how much should it be worth?

Sara wanted to have a successful first meeting of the SSAC on March 11th. She knew questions would be raised in each of these four areas at the meeting, and she would need to develop a position on each as a starting point for dialogue with the supplier community.

Case 17–3

Tanton Foods

Earl Jones, vice president of supply at Tanton Foods, had just received the most recent CAPS Research Purchasing Performance Benchmarks for the U.S. Food Manufacturing Industry. Tanton Foods had not been one of the firms that provided the data for this study.

Tanton Foods' annual sales volume was close to the average sales reported for the sample group and was part of the food manufacturing industry with a wide range of canned, frozen, and packaged consumer goods. Earl Jones carefully read the summary provided in the CAPS report. He knew that some of these benchmarks covered areas in which Tanton Foods had its own performance measures, while others were quite different.

Further explanations of each benchmark and how it was calculated were shown on the following pages of the report. Before worrying about these details, however, Earl was anxious to consider the larger picture first.

Earl Jones wondered of what use the CAPS data might be for his organization. Before requesting one of the ana-lysts in the purchasing research group to determine what Tanton Foods' equivalent benchmark figures would be, Earl Jones wanted to be sure this exercise would be ben-eficial. If Tanton Foods' figures were close to industry average, what would this indicate? Similarly, what if sig-nificant differences existed, either high or low? Earl de-cided he would examine each of the benchmarks closely with these thoughts in mind.

Case Index

Subject Index